HIGHLIGHTS

Financing Start-Ups

How to Raise Money for Emerging Companies

by Robert Brown and Alan S. Gutterman

This revolutionary guide delivers practical strategies for financing companies of all sizes in all stages of development. From primary financing through initial public offering and beyond, *Financing Start-Ups* will tell you how to zero in on the real amount you need; learn how and whom to ask; negotiate so you get what you want; comply with tricky federal and state securities laws; develop an impressive business plan that puts your funding to work; build a long-term financing strategy that keeps you growing; position your company for successive financing stages; take advantage of little-known, alternative sources of financing; and value your business.

2003 Edition

The 2003 Edition includes new and updated information, including the following:

- Description of financing phases — pre-seed, seed, development, first round, and public markets;
- Coverage of Internet securities developments;
- New vignette on selecting the correct bank;
- New chapter on financing R&D through investment partnerships and corporate partnering;
- Detailed description of dot.bombs, the lessons to be learned, and is now the right time to start a business; and
- New agreements, including right of first refusal and co-sale agreement, and amended and restated articles of incorporation.

5/02

For questions concerning this shipment, billing or other customer service matters, call our Customer Service Department at 1-800-234-1660.

For toll-free ordering, please call 1-800-638-8437.

FINANCING START-UPS

How to Raise Money for Emerging Companies

2003 Edition

Robert Brown

Alan S. Gutterman

A Panel Publication

Aspen Publishers, Inc.

A Division of Aspen Publishers, Inc.
A Wolters Kluwer Company
www.panelpublishers.com

Permissions
Panel Publishers
1185 Avenue of the Americas
New York, NY 10036

Printed in the United States of America

ISBN 0-7355-3283-4

1 2 3 4 5 6 7 8 9 0

About Panel Publishers

Panel Publishers—comprising the former Little, Brown and Company's Professional Division, Wiley Law Publications, the Bureau of Business Practice, Summers Press, Harcourt Professional Publishing, and Loislaw—is a leading publisher of authoritative and timely treatises, practice manuals, information services, and journals written by specialists to assist attorneys, financial and tax advisors, and other business professionals. Our mission is to provide practical solution-based how-to information keyed to the latest legislative, judicial, and regulatory developments.

We offer publications in the areas of compensation and benefits, pensions, payroll, employment, civil rights, taxation, estate planning, financial planning, and elder law.

Other Panel products treating tax issues include:

Business Owner's Tax Savings and Financial Deskbook
Choosing the Right Business Entity
Failing and Failed Businesses
Federal Income Taxation of Debt Instruments
Federal and State Taxation of Limited Liability Companies
Federal Tax Course
Federal Tax Course Newsletter
Financial Products, Taxation, Regulation and Design
International Taxation
Limited Liability Companies Guide
Limited Liability and Partnership Answer Book
Limited Liability Partnerships: Formation, Operation, and Taxation
Mergers, Acquistions, and Buyouts
Multistate Corporate Tax Guide
The S Corp: Operation and Planning
The S Corporation Answer Book
S Corporation Taxation Guide
State and Local Tax Answer Book
Structuring Venture Capital
Taxation of Compensation and Benefits
Taxation of the Entertainment Industry

SUBSCRIPTION NOTICE

This Panel product is updated on a periodic basis with supplements to reflect important changes in the subject matter. If you purchased this product directly from Panel, we have already recorded your subscription for the update service.

If, however, you purchased this product from a bookstore and wish to receive future updates and revised or related volumes billed separately with a 30-day examination review, please contact our Customer Service Department at 1-800-234-1660 or send your name, company name (if applicable), address, and the title of the product to:

PANEL PUBLISHERS
A Division of Aspen Publishers, Inc.
7201 McKinney Circle
Frederick, MD 21704

To Keith Dunford,
the Impresario
of Entrepreneurs

ABOUT THE AUTHORS

Robert Brown is a member of Greenebaum Doll & McDonald. He has a Ph.D. from Cambridge University and a Masters degree from Jochi University in Tokyo. During three years of law school, he earned J.D., M.B.A., and Masters degrees from the University of Louisville. Dr. Brown is admitted as an attorney in New York, Washington D.C., California, and Kentucky, and he is qualified as a solicitor in England and Wales, and in Hong Kong. For the past 25 years, he has worked closely with start-up companies as an investment banker and attorney, serving both in-house and as an outside advisor. His previous experience includes assignments in London, New York City, Tokyo, San Francisco, and San Diego. Dr. Brown has taught courses at the law schools of the University of San Francisco and the University of California, Berkeley.

Alan S. Gutterman is an author, consultant, and attorney in private practice in the San Francisco Bay Area. He has over 20 years of experience in representing start-up companies and has recently served as chief operating officer and general counsel of a new media services company in California. He has been a partner in a prominent U.S. law firm in San Francisco and a partner in a Bay Area investment firm. He has a Ph.D. from Cambridge University, a D.B.A. from Golden Gate University, and law and M.B.A. degrees from the University of California, Berkeley. He is a leading author on international and business law issues and is active in state and national bar associations. Dr. Gutterman has taught courses at the law schools of the University of San Francisco and the University of California, Berkeley.

SUMMARY OF CONTENTS

Part V. Case Studies

CONTENTS

PREFACE

Each year thousands of new companies are established. A few will be successful, employ new workers, and provide lenders and investors with returns on their money. Most, however, will not. Often, the critical difference is the ability to raise and manage money to finance start-up and growth.

This book will help you understand what it takes to raise and keep money. Its focus is small business operating in the corporate form, since most lenders and investors will insist on a corporate structure.

In Part I, we describe general finance issues and financing instruments, including equity securities such as common and preferred stock, debt securities, and convertible instruments.

In Part II, we provide an overview of what is the primary regulatory consideration in capital raising: federal and state securities laws. Included in this section are chapters that show how these laws apply to specific financing transactions (private placements, venture capital investment, public offerings, and underwriting arrangements). We also discuss the trading of securities among investors, what it means to be a public company, and liabilities if you get the rules wrong.

In Parts III and IV we turn to the two main types of financings: private and public. In Part III we describe private financing sources:

- **Alternative sources**, such as internal funds, vendor financing, strategic partners, private loans, commercial loans and leases from financial institutions, and government funding programs; and

- **Private offerings**, such as sales to a small group of private or institutional investors and venture capital financings.

In Part III we also discuss the actual process of raising money: looking for funding, valuing the company, writing a business plan, organizing the road show, negotiating the term sheet, conducting due diligence, and closing the deal.

In Part IV, we turn to public offerings, including underwriting, distribution, Internet sales, and trading.

In Part V, we apply the lessons in the previous chapters to two case studies: the first describes how to finance research and development; the second covers what we can learn from dot.bombs.

In the appendices, we include various forms you are likely to need in raising money. We also include important debt and equity funding sources.

Our objective is to provide an overview of the legal and business issues that arise in obtaining and managing funding. Interspersed throughout the book are vignettes from chief executive officers, chief financing officers, and their advisors, describing their personal experiences in raising and maintaining money for emerging companies.

Acknowledgments

James Michener once wrote that the key to an author's success is the editor. Fans of Max Perkins (editor of Fitzgerald, Hemingway, Wolfe, and Jones) will understand what he meant. We have been blessed with two of the best. Jonathan Koschei, as the senior acquisitions editor, and Rosemary DeStefano, as the developmental editor, are the architects of our vision. JoAnn Koppany is the carpenter who sanded out our rough spots, hammered the nails down, and brought the pieces together. We also wish to thank Lauren Humiston for much of the technical data in the CD-ROM and Elaine T. Hackett, a legal assistant, at Greenebaum Doll & McDonald PLLC for double-checking the blueprints.

ABOUT THE DISC

Contents

Document Title	*File Name*	*File Type*
Appendix A: Business Plan	APP-A	RTF
Appendix B: Funding Sources: Venture Capital Funds	APP-B	RTF
Appendix C: SBA Offices	APP-C	PDF
Appendix D: Funding Sources: Banks	APP-D	PDF
Appendix E: Term Sheet	APP-E	RTF
Appendix F: Document/Due Diligence Request/Checklist	APP-F	RTF
Appendix G: Subscription Agreement	APP-G	RTF
Appendix H: Placement Agent Agreement	APP-H	RTF
Appendix I: Private Placement Memorandum	APP-I	RTF
Appendix J: Private Placement Purchase Agreement	APP-J	RTF
Appendix K: Investors' Rights Agreement	APP-K	RTF
Appendix L: Tight of First Refusal and Co-Sale Agreement	APP-L	RTF
Appendix M: Amended and Restated Articles of Incorporation	APP-M	RTF

System Requirements

- IBM PC or compatible computer with CD-ROM drive
- Microsoft® Word 6.0 (or above) for Windows™, Adobe Acrobat Reader 4.0 (or above), WordPerfect® 7.0 (or above) for Windows™, or compatible word processor
- 7 MB available on hard drive (if you wish to place CD contents on your hard disk)

The CD-ROM provided with the 2003 edition of *Financing Start-Ups* contains RTF (Rich Text Format) and Acrobat® PDF (Portable Document Format) files, which correspond to Appendices A–M of the book, including a sample business plan, venture capital funding sources, a list of SBA offices, bank funding sources, sample term sheets, a sample document/due diligence request/checklist, and other sample forms (subscription agreement, placement agent agreement, private placement memorandum, private placement purchase agreement, investors' rights agreement, right of first refusal and co-sale agreement, and amended and restated articles of incorporation).

The list of the Computer Disc Contents is available on your CD-ROM in a file called _Contents.rtf. Open the file _Contents.rtf. To open any listed file, click on the hyperlinked filename. If your word processor doesn't support hyperlinked documents you will need to open each document directly. You can open the contents file and view it on your screen or print a hard copy to use for reference.

Using the Hyperlinked RTF Documents

To use the RTF documents, simply double-click on a filename (in Windows Explorer, My Computer, File Manager, etc.) and your default word processor will then load the document. All modern word processors will automatically import RTF files. You may then edit the document and save it to a location on your hard disk. If you like, you may copy all the document files from this CD-ROM to your hard disk and use them without the CD-ROM inserted in your CD-ROM drive. If you do so, remember to remove the "Read Only" attribute from the files you have copied.

Using the Hyperlinked Acrobat® PDF Documents

To use the PDF documents, simply double-click on a filename (in Windows Explorer, My Computer, File Manager, etc.) and Acrobat Reader® will then load the document. If you like, you may copy all the document files from this CD-ROM to your hard disk and use them without the CD-ROM inserted in your CD-ROM drive. If you do so, remember to remove the "Read Only" attribute from the files you have copied.

If you do not have Adobe Acrobat Reader® installed, and you are running Windows 95 or higher, open the \Acrobat folder on this CD-ROM, and run the file ar50eng.exe (or double click on ar50eng.exe in Windows Explorer or My Computer) to install Acrobat Reader®.

Word Processing Tips

Wherever possible, the text of the documents has been formatted so that you can modify the text without altering the format of the documents.

If you are working within a table, you may find the following tips useful. To maneuver within a table, press TAB to move to the next cell, and SHIFT + TAB to move backward one cell. If you want to move to a tab stop within a cell, press CTRL + TAB. For additional tips on working within tables, consult your word processor's manual. It might be helpful to turn on the invisible table lines in Microsoft Word while modifying the document by selecting Gridlines from the Table menu.

Microsoft Word is equipped with search capabilities to help you locate specific words or phrases within a document. The Find option listed under the Edit menu performs a search in Microsoft Word.

Important: When you are finished using a file you will be asked to save it. If you have modified the file, you will want to save the modified file under a different name rather than the name of the original file. (Your word processing program will prompt you for a file name.) This will enable you to reuse the original file without your modifications.

Print Troubleshooting

If you are having difficulty printing your document, the following suggestions may correct the problem:

- Select Print from the Microsoft Word File menu. Then choose the Printer function.
- Ensure that the correct printer is selected.
- From this window, choose Options.
- In the media box, make sure that the paper size is correct and that the proper paper tray is selected.
- Check your network connections if applicable.
- If you still have trouble printing successfully, it may be because your printer does not recognize the font Times New Roman. At this point, you should change the font of the document to your default font by

selecting the document (CTRL + A) and then choosing Font from the Format menu and highlighting the name of the font you normally use. Changing the font of the document may require additional adjustments to the document format, such as margins, tab stops, and table cell height and width. Select Page Layout from the View menu to view the appearance of the pages before you try to print again.

Software Support

If you experience any difficulties installing or using any of the word processing documents and cannot resolve the problem using the information presented here, call our toll-free software support group hotline at (800) 486-9296 (hours of operation are 8 a.m. to 5:00 p.m., Eastern time, Monday through Friday) or send e-mail to aspentechsupport@libera.com.

PART I • INTRODUCTION

CHAPTER 1 • GENERAL CONSIDERATIONS

CHAPTER 1

§ 1.01 GENERAL ISSUES

Starting a new company is challenging—both scary and thrilling—whether it succeeds or not. If the new business does succeed, the challenges, scares, and thrills just keep growing. In this book, we describe some of the challenges in order to lessen the scares. The thrills remain intact for you to enjoy.

Let's begin by considering where we are going. Table 1.1 below sets out the three main phases businesses go through: concept, development, and commercialization.

Table 1.1

	Concept		Development		Commercialization
Phase	**Investigation**	**Feasibility**	**Development**	**Introduction**	
Stage	(Pre-Seed)	(Seed)	(Development)	(First Round Financing)	(Public Markets)
Duration	2–3 months	2–12 months	3–12 months	Steady state	
Amount ($000)	5	50	200–1,000	2–20,000	
Funds Source	Self	FFF	Angel	Venture capitalist	
Employees	Founder	Founder Interim CFO	Founder Interim team	Founder Team	

The first concept phase is investigation, during which you explore the potential viability of your business concept. During this pre-seed stage, you are likely to spend $5,000 of your own money, and you will probably be working alone. In the second concept phase, the seed stage, you are likely to spend 2 to 12 months (all numbers are incremental from the previous phase) exploring the feasibility of your business in more detail. You can expect to spend $50,000 of your money and whatever you can raise from FFF (friends, family and fools). Hopefully, during this stage you will be able to recruit an interim chief financial officer to help you prepare a business plan and financial projections.

In the first development phase, you are likely to spend another 3 to 12 months and $200,000 to $1,000,000 developing your business as an operating entity. This money is likely to come from angel investors. Since you are creating a full business at this point, you should have an interim management team. You may not yet have all senior management positions filled, but you should have most of them in place. The second development phase is the introduction of your product into the market. During this period, you are likely to spend $2 to $20 million, which you would have raised from venture capitalists in what is called a first round of financing. By this time, you should have a full management team in place that is transitioning operations into those of a full business.

In the last stage, commercialization, the company operates as a complete business, based on raising money from the public capital markets.

With this overview of the evolution of a start-up, let's turn to the focus of this book—its financing.

Although funding for an emerging company can come from different sources, a few generalizations are applicable to all of them. Whatever the source, existing shareholders must consider the economic participation to be given to the funder, the management participation to be given up, the cost of the funding, the duration of the funds, and the security to be provided.

[A] Economic Participation

One of the most difficult decisions in any new financing is the economic participation the funder will receive. For example, an equity investment, particularly in convertible preferred stock, entitles the funder to share in the profits through dividends and any increase in value of the company through appreciated stock. Accordingly, if the company is successful, the funder will receive, and existing shareholders will have to give up, more than would have been necessary in a debt financing.

At the other extreme, the funder may provide a loan, in which the return is limited to the principal amount of the funds advanced plus interest to cover the opportunity cost. Funds obtained from commercial lenders will generally be of this type. Such terms will not usually be appealing to private and institutional investors, who will want to share in appreciated value.

As will be discussed later, there are variations and combinations that can be used to structure an appropriate financing. The use of convertible debt securities (allowing lenders to convert to equity if certain events occur) is one way a funder can hedge its bets.

[B] Management Participation

Of almost equal importance to current shareholders, particularly those involved in day-to-day management, is the effect that the financing will have on overall management and control of the company. As will be discussed later, certain investment instruments are entitled by law to specific voting and management participation rights. By contract, at the time of financing, the parties usually negotiate additional, detailed participation rights.

For instance, most debt instruments will contain limitations on how the company will be managed and will set certain minimum standards. These limitations and standards usually appear in affirmative and negative covenants. Similarly, equity funders will want to describe in detail their rights as shareholders and will insist on some role in management. Most commonly, they will insist on the right to

- Elect certain directors; and
- Vote or approve major actions, such as compensation of management, sale of assets, mergers, or issuance of new securities.

[C] Cost of Funds

Obviously, every funder expects to get its money back, plus something for the use of its money. That *something* depends on the source. As noted above, a bank will usually want a fixed fee: interest. At times, a bank will want its fixed fee plus a bonus, usually an equity kicker in the form of a warrant. An equity investor is better able to absorb the added risk of relying solely on stock appreciation for its return on investment and thus is more interested in the long-term kicker: the appreciation of stock value.

One problem the company must consider is interim cost of money. Many funders will want something for the use of their funds before redemption or repayment. This could be interim payments of interest only (or interest and principal) in the case of debt; or dividends for equity holders, particularly for holders of preferred stock. It is important for the company to consider these interim costs and whether or not it can meet them.

[D] Duration

The durations and terms of fundings vary. For example, equity financing is generally permanent, although there could be an obligation to redeem at some future date. Debt financing, on the other hand, is for a fixed period and must be repaid, although even here the company may have the right to roll over the financing if it meets certain criteria. There are generally three categories of loans:

1. Demand basis—repayment is at any time the lender requests;
2. Short-term basis—for up to one year; and
3. Long-term basis—for over one year.

Managers must select the duration that fits the company's cash flow, including business cycle and needs. It will not be advisable, for instance, to have a loan come due at the low or high point of a business cycle when cash reserves are likely to be thin.

[E] Risk and Security

Every funding type, including a loan, involves a degree of risk. The funder may not receive its anticipated return or, in the worst case, its money back. To guard against such risks, the funder may want some security. If so, management must be aware of the effect that such protection may have on its operations, the interests of existing shareholders and lenders, and its ability to raise money in the future.

Security in commercial lending transactions is a well-known and accepted concept. A bank will invariably seek a security interest in all or a portion of the assets of the company. It wants the ability to force a sale if the borrower defaults. Such a security interest may impair the ability of the company to obtain further funding. Similarly, an equity investor may seek particular security. For example, preferred stock generally carries the right to receive cash or assets equal in value to the amount the preferred stock holder has invested, before any distribution to other equity holders.

CHAPTER 2 • CORPORATE FINANCIAL INSTRUMENTS

Insiders: Toto . . . I Have a Feeling We're Not on Wall Street Anymore

CHAPTER 2

§ 2.01 INTRODUCTION

One advantage of the corporate form is the flexibility it provides owners and managers in structuring financing instruments. The corporation offers a wide variety of economic and voting rights for investors. It permits short-term and long-term financing, both debt and equity. It also allows preferences for distributions of income and assets.

The selection of the appropriate financing depends on a number of factors. The most important are the relative costs (e.g., dividend or interest obligations), dilution of existing owners' economic and voting rights, amount of security to be granted, and temporal characteristics (i.e., short- or long-term) of the security.

The most basic form of financing is common stock, representing ownership of the corporation with the right to share in distributions and appreciation after all debts and obligations to senior equity holders and lenders have been satisfied. At the other end of the spectrum are straight debt securities, which provide the holder with a specified return in the form of an interest obligation and a return of capital at the end of the term. These securities generally have no right to share in any appreciation in the underlying value of the business. In the case of debt securities, distinctions can be made between unsecured debt that is backed only by the good faith and credit of the business, and secured debt that provides lenders with the ability to demand the sale of certain assets of the business in order to ensure payment of amounts owed.

A versatile hybrid form of financing is an equity or debt instrument that allows an investor to change or convert the original security into a different class of equity security or another form of corporate obligation. For example, it may be possible to issue a convertible preferred stock (or debt with option) that provides both a guaranteed return of dividends for as long as the preferred stock is outstanding and the right to convert the preferred stock into common stock to share in any appreciation of the underlying business. The issuance of a convertible security usually allows the corporation to reduce the fixed costs associated with straight senior equity or debt securities, since a convertible security can be sold at a lower interest or dividend rate than a similar security without the conversion right. Depending on the timing and conversion rate, however, actual conversion may significantly dilute the interests of prior shareholders.

§ 2.02 EQUITY SECURITIES

[A] Basic Types of Equity Securities

[1] In General

At common law, and in the absence of any statute or agreement to the contrary, all shares of capital stock enjoy equal rights and privileges. It is now the prevailing practice, however, to divide the capital stock of the corporation into two or more classes with varying rights, preferences, and privileges as to dividends, liquidating distributions, redemption, conversion, and voting rights. While multiple classes of stock can be denominated in a number of different ways, a corporation will generally utilize common and preferred stock as the key elements of its equity capital structure. A third equity security, combining a number of features of both common and preferred stocks, is referred to as a convertible security, although it is often characterized simply as a subtype of preferred stock.

[2] Common Stock

Common stock is the most basic form of equity security and is the type ordinarily utilized in the course of capitalizing the corporation. Common stock has no extraordinary rights or privileges and, in the absence of other classes of stock having senior rights and preferences, represents the entire equity interest in the corporation. Owners of common stock are generally entitled to a pro rata share of any profits of the corporation and its assets upon dissolution. Moreover, unless the shareholders agree to the contrary, each share of common stock is entitled to an equal vote on matters concerning the management of the corporation, such as the right to vote on the election of directors and amend the articles of incorporation.

The typical closely held corporation (company owned by only a few investors—usually founders or family members) will usually issue only a single class of common shares. In some circumstances, two or more classes of common stock, having different rights and privileges, may be created. For example, the shareholders may authorize the creation of a class of common stock with voting power but with no dividend or liquidation rights other than the repayment of its stated par value. On the other hand, it is possible to create a class of common stock with economic rights similar to those generally associated with common stock but without some or all of the voting rights typically provided to holders of common stock. In summary, shareholders for the most part can allocate among themselves the various economic and managerial rights relating to ownership of the corporation.

[3] Preferred Stock

The characteristics of preferred stock are different from those of common stock. Preferred stock is entitled to certain preferences over common stock. The legal basis for preferred stock comes from provisions similar to those contained in the Revised Model Business Corporations Act (RMBCA), allowing the articles of incorporation to authorize one or more classes of shares that

1. Have special, conditional, or limited voting rights, or none at all.
2. Are redeemable or convertible as specified in the articles of incorporation (i) at the option of the corporation, shareholder or another person, or upon the occurrence of a designated event; (ii) for cash, indebtedness, securities, or other property; (iii) in a designated amount, or in an amount determined in accordance with a designated formula or by reference to extrinsic data or events.
3. Entitle the holders to distributions calculated in any manner, including dividends that may be cumulative, noncumulative, or partially cumulative.
4. Have a preference over any other class of shares with respect to distributions, including dividends and distributions on dissolution of the corporation.

Many state statutes empower a corporation to create two or more classes of preferred stock, and the corporation may provide that the rights of one class of preferred stock are superior to those granted to any previously issued class. The RMBCA allows the creation of one or more series of preferred stock, with each series having different preferences, limitations, and rights. As a result, shareholders have a number of different options for drawing distinctions among managerial and economic rights of various investor groups.

The basic form of preferred stock is straight preferred stock. It provides an investor with a fixed and limited rate of return in the form of dividends and with the right to receive on liquidation a preferential amount, usually equal to par value plus accrued dividends, before any distribution to the holders of common stock. The holders of preferred stock frequently do not have any right to share in assets beyond the amount of the preference. As such, straight preferred stock is quite similar to a straight debt instrument.

However, preferred stock is junior to the rights of creditors, including the holders of any debt securities, in any liquidation of the corporation. In addition, preferred stock's right to receive dividends or liquidating distributions is restricted by law, whereas the obligation to repay creditors must be fulfilled even if the corporation has no earnings or profits.

Although it is possible to issue preferred stock having limited voting rights, the holders of preferred stock will always have the right to vote on changes or amendments to the company's articles of incorporation that may have an effect on their preferential rights. In addition, in most cases, the holders of preferred stock will be given the right to vote for the election of directors, particularly if the company is in default on any preferred stock obligations.

A recent innovation is the alphabet or tracking stock. This was popularized by General Motors when buying Ross Perot's EDS; General Motors offered a new GM stock called Series E (for EDS, and thus the alphabet name) to shareholders of EDS. Its return was based not on GM's overall performance but on the performance of EDS within GM. Dividends were paid out of (or tracked) EDS earnings. It was felt that this tracking would offer a higher return, since GM was in a mature industry while EDS was in a high-growth one. Otherwise, holders of the new stock had the same voting and liquidation rights of other GM shareholders. Subsequently, alphabet or tracking stock has been used in a number of other transactions, such as when Carl Icahn persuaded USX (formerly US Steel) to split into two separate divisions: steel and energy. The separate classes of stock tracked each division.

[4] Convertible Securities

The RMBCA permits the issuance of shares that can be converted into another class of securities or that can be converted into cash, indebtedness, securities, or other property of the corporation or another person. Convertible securities can have all of the various rights, preferences, and privileges associated with nonconvertible securities. These include the right to receive a specified amount of dividends, the right to preferential distributions upon liquidation, and the right to vote on certain matters such as the election of directors and fundamental corporate changes.

Convertible preferred stock often has the right to vote on a share-for-share basis with common stock. The number of votes is equal to the number of shares of common stock into which the preferred can be converted. In other cases, the convertible preferred stock, voting separately, will have the right to elect a designated number of directors.

[B] Considerations in Issuing Equity Securities

[1] In General

The terms of equity security offerings depend on many factors. These factors include the stated needs and requirements of the prospective investors and the amount of economic and management control existing shareholders are willing to give up. Most financings require considerable negotiation of the voting, dividend, and participation rights of the new securities; the redeemability of the security; and the privilege of the holders to convert their securities.

[2] Voting Rights

The exact nature of voting rights granted to holders of the new security should be clearly specified in the controlling instrument. This instrument is likely to be the charter documents and any related contractual agreement (e.g., shareholders' agreement or voting agreement). In the absence of any specific provision, voting rights will generally be defined by statutory and case law. If the securities are to have some, but not full, voting rights, any limitations must be clearly expressed and defined.

The negotiation of voting rights generally revolves around whether or not a specific group of security holders will have the right to separately consider and approve certain corporate actions. For example, the holders of a given security may be given the right to vote on the issuance of new securities or on fundamental corporate changes, such as mergers, acquisitions, and dissolution of the corporation. Another area in which voting rights may be important is the election of directors. Holders of a series or class of securities are often given the right to vote separately on the designation of one or more members of the board of directors.

[3] Dividend Rights

The timing and amount of any required dividend payments should be considered. In addition to the rate of dividends (expressed as a percentage of par value), the purchase price or liquidation value of the security, the existence and amount of any dividend preference, and the cumulative or noncumulative nature of the dividend should be described. For example, the security may be given a preference over other classes of stock for payment of dividends. This will restrict the ability of the corporation to make dividend payments to junior securities, such as common stock, before making the required payments to the holders of the new security.

The dividend preference may be *cumulative,* which means that the corporation must make up the amount of any fixed dividend that was not paid in a given year. Alternatively, it may be *noncumulative,* in which case the dividend is payable only if declared by the board of directors.

[4] Participation Rights

A security is said to be a participating instrument if it carries the right to receive dividends or distributions upon liquidation in excess of its fixed preference. For example, a convertible preferred security may have the right to receive payments equal to all dividends paid on the security into which it is convertible. Similarly, a convertible security may be entitled to receive, in addition to any preferential amounts, a share of remaining assets upon liquidation as if such shares had been converted into the junior security.

[5] Redemption

The exact price at which, and the period during which, the shares may be redeemed, and whether at the option of the corporation or of the shareholder, should be set forth in the security instrument. Mandatory redemption rights in favor of investors require the corporation to redeem the outstanding securities at a specified price and at a time or times set in the instrument. This creates a quasi-debt obligation. On the other hand, a right in favor of the corporation to redeem outstanding securities provides the existing shareholders with the ability to refinance the capital structure on more favorable terms in the future.

[6] Convertibility

If the security is convertible, the exact terms of conversion should be described. Among the key factors are the rate of conversion (i.e., the number of shares or units of the new security that will be issued upon conversion of the original security), the effect of any stock splits or stock dividends on the conversion rate, the effect of any recapitalization or issuance of additional securities on the conversion rate, the period during which the conversion rights must be exercised, and the events, if any, that might cause the securities to be automatically converted.

[C] Characteristics of Various Equity Securities

[1] In General

The first issue and sale of equity securities in a new corporation will generally be made to a small group of founders and will usually consist of voting common stock. In many small corporations, the founders may be the only persons who purchase equity securities. Any subsequent capital requirements of such corporations will be satisfied through the issuance of additional common stock or debt securities to the founders or through the retention of earnings for reinvestment in the business. However, the founders may be unable, or unwilling, to contribute additional equity capital at a time when the corporation needs to issue equity securities. In this case, the corporation will need to turn to outside investors, including private or institutional investors and the general public.

Although existing shareholders may be content to issue additional shares of common stock to outside investors, it is more likely that the disparate interests of the two groups will require consideration of alternative forms of equity securities. When an offering is made to outside investors, existing shareholders will be concerned about two things: (1) the effect of the offering on their ability to maintain control of the corporation and (2) the prospective dilution of their interests. Outside investors generally have little interest in monitoring day-to-day operations, but they at least want to ensure that their investment is adequately protected and that their desired financial return is realized. In many cases, however, they will insist on the ability to participate in major decisions.

A wide array of alternatives can be utilized to balance the conflicting concerns and objectives of corporate insiders and prospective investors. For example, while capital stock is generally characterized as either "common" or "preferred," it is possible to create a number of different rights, preferences, and limitations with respect to voting, dividends, liquidation, conversion, participation, redemption, and similar matters. Although the legality of specific terms in an equity security is always a matter of state law, consideration should be given to the following general forms of equity securities.

[2] Voting Common Stock

Common stock is the most basic form of equity security. Absent a provision in the articles to the contrary, holders have full rights to vote on matters affecting the management of the corporation, such as the right to elect directors and approve any major corporate transactions. Common stock holders are also the residual owners of the corporation, entitled to receive all corporate assets remaining after satisfaction of the claims of creditors and holders of senior securities. However, the prospect of potentially unlimited returns is tempered by the fact that the risk of loss associated with an investment in common stock is greater than the risk associated with any other form of equity security. Moreover, holders of common stock are generally not entitled to a return of their investment, or to receive dividends, unless payment is authorized by the directors and permitted by law and the terms of any preferred stock.

[3] Nonvoting Common Stock

The holders of nonvoting common stock have rights identical to those of holders of voting common stock with one exception: they have no right to vote for the election of directors. The right to vote on other corporate matters may also be limited or restricted, although state law will usually require that such holders be allowed to vote on matters affecting their specific rights, preferences, and privileges. Offering nonvoting common stock can alleviate the concerns of existing shareholders about their ability to maintain control of the management of the corporation. However, the stock's lack of voting rights may impair the ability of the corporation to market and sell such securities.

[4] Multiple Classes of Voting Common Stock

Two or more classes of voting common stock can be created with each class having the right to vote, to the exclusion of the other, for its own directors. Other than these separate, parallel voting rights, the economic rights of the classes are identical. By using multiple classes of voting common stock, existing shareholders can retain control over the management of the corporation while permitting new investors to elect one or more representatives to the board of directors and to vote on material matters.

The use of multiple classes of voting common stock can be illustrated by the example of a corporation with a single class of voting common stock held by the founders, who wish to attract additional capital without surrendering management control. If the new investors receive voting common stock, the number of shares issued would likely exceed the number held by the founders, who would lose control. The result would be very different if the corporation issued a new class of voting common stock to the investors with economic rights identical to the old common stock issued to the founders, but with the right to vote only for a minority of the directors.

Differential voting rights may also be used to offset the effect of state law provisions relating to the election of directors. Where cumulative voting exists, minority shareholders may be able to elect one or more representatives to the board of directors without having to create a separate class of securities. If cumulative voting is not permitted, the holders of a majority of the shares will be able to elect all of the directors. In such cases, a separate class of securities must be established to ensure minority representation on the board of directors.

[5] Nonvoting Noncumulative Preferred Stock

If prospective investors prefer a steady stream of income but have little interest, or confidence, in the long-term growth of the corporation, it may be possible to issue a preferred stock instrument that contemplates the payment of a fixed amount of dividends over the term of the instrument. Although the rights of holders of the common stock would be subordinated to those of holders of the preferred stock, the rights of the preferred stock holders would be limited to the amount specified in the instrument. Any growth in excess of the fixed rate would accrue to the benefit of the holders of the common stock. This permits existing shareholders to limit the dilution of their economic interests.

As is the case with nonvoting common stock, holders of nonvoting noncumulative preferred stock generally have no right to elect directors. Such a right, however, may be given in the event of certain defaults by the corporation.

The holders have the right to receive dividends at a fixed rate before any payment of dividends on the common stock. However, the dividend need be paid only if declared by the corporation, and there may be no obligation on the corporation to declare a dividend. Moreover, there is no need to make up in subsequent years the amount of any missed payment. As with any other form of nonparticipating security, upon liquidation of the corporation, holders of nonvoting noncumulative preferred stock would have the right to receive an amount equal to the original purchase price of the securities.

[6] Nonvoting Fully Cumulative Preferred Stock

Like holders of nonvoting noncumulative preferred stock, holders of nonvoting fully cumulative preferred stock would have no voting rights and would have a limited preference upon liquidation of the corporation. However, holders would have the preferential right to receive a fixed amount of dividends *and* the amount of any arrears created by prior failure of the corporation to make dividend payments. In such cases, if the corporation is unable to pay dividends because of lack of earnings, profits, or other legal source of funds, such dividends must be paid as soon as possible. The cumulative dividend requirement may be phased in after a specified period of time, perhaps as a penalty if the corporation fails to reach a specified level of revenues or earnings by a certain date.

A cumulative dividend requirement, or even a requirement that noncumulative dividends must be paid in any year in which the corporation has sufficient earnings or surplus, can severely restrict management. Obviously, one consequence of such a provision will be to make it difficult, if not impossible, for a dividend to be paid to the holders of the common stock. Moreover, the ability of the managers to retain earnings for use in expanding the business will be compromised by a cumulative dividend requirement. In addition, a cumulative dividend requirement is often accompanied by a number of other related provisions designed to protect the holders of the preferred stock. This includes the right to elect a majority of the board of directors in the event dividends are not paid for a specified period of time.

[7] Nonvoting Partially Cumulative Preferred Stock

Fully cumulative dividend provisions can create large potential liabilities for a corporation unable to make the required payments in its early years. In order to alleviate some of the financial pressures, the investors' securities may be structured so that, rather than their having the right to receive all dividend arrears, holders would have a right to receive only a limited amount before any payment of common stock dividends. For example, a limit might be placed on the time period for which the obligation might be carried back, such as three years, or on the portion of the unpaid amounts—perhaps 50%—that must be restored before the payment of common stock dividends.

[8] Adjustable Rate Preferred Stock

In most cases, preferred stock carries the right to receive dividends at a fixed rate over the entire period the stock is outstanding. However, particularly in recent years, many corporations have opted to issue preferred stock providing for the payment of dividends at a rate adjusted periodically. These adjustments are based on interest rate fluctuations. For example, the dividend rate might be set at 1% plus the highest of (a) the 3-month Treasury Bill rate, (b) the 10-year constant maturity rate published by the Federal Reserve Board, or (c) the 20-year constant maturity rate published by the Federal Reserve Board. Such a formula guarantees holders a return in excess of the highest of short-term, intermediate-term, or long-term interest on U.S. obligations.

The method for establishing the rate will depend on the credit rating of the corporation and the requirements of potential investors. The rate will usually be bounded, so that it does not go below a stated minimum or over a stated maximum. A corporation will usually establish the initial rate closer to the upper bound than to the lower bound. By using an adjustable rate instrument, the corporation and investors are able to minimize the risks associated with unanticipated fluctuations in interest rates over the term of the instrument. The disadvantage is that the corporation may be deprived of the advantages of any downward move in interest rates.

[9] Voting Preferred Stock

While preferred stock is generally used to allocate economic returns and risks, it is not unusual for preferred stock holders to participate in management and control through the grant of full or limited voting rights. Depending on the circumstances, holders might vote on a share-for-share basis with the holders of the common stock, or they may have the exclusive right, voting as a separate class, to elect members of the board. State law may also require the consent of a specified percentage of preferred stock holders for amendments to the rights, preferences, and privileges of the preferred stock, as well as for fundamental corporate changes (e.g., mergers).

Voting preferred stock can be issued with any or all of the other economic rights usually granted to ordinary preferred stock, including dividend and liquidation preferences and the right to convert into common stock. In some cases, voting and economic rights of preferred stock holders may be linked. For example, the right to vote on a specified corporate transaction, such as a merger, may arise only if the preferred stock holders are *not* going to receive their liquidation preference or accrued dividends.

[10] Convertible Preferred Stock

In addition to economic and voting rights, preferred shares may be convertible into another class of securities, generally common stock. The rate is established in the preferred stock instrument. The conversion rate and the period during which the conversion can be exercised will be subject to negotiation between the corporation and the holders. In many cases, the corporation will require that the preferred stock be automatically converted into common stock upon the occurrence of certain specified events. This allows the corporation to terminate the preferential rights associated with the preferred stock.

[11] Participating Preferred Stock

As noted, preferred stock gets its name from the preference it takes over common stock for the payment of dividends and distribution of assets at the time of liquidation. After they receive their regular preference, participating preferred stock holders have the right, along with common stock holders, to a share in dividends and liquidating assets. For instance, if $100 is available for dividend distribution with $60 owed to preferred stock holders as their preference, the remaining $40 would be split between common and participating preferred stock holders according to an agreed-upon formula.

The net result is that holders of participating preferred shares do not have to convert their stock in order to share in distributions to common stock holders. This participation feature is more likely to be used when the corporation issues convertible preferred stock.

Although a number of variations are possible to determine the rate of participation by preferred stock holders, the corporation's charter documents generally provide that any assets remaining after satisfaction of the preferential amounts paid to preferred stock holders must be divided among all shareholders in proportion to their holdings of common stock. This includes common stock shares issued on conversion of the preferred stock.

[12] Redeemable Preferred Stock

Preferred stock may give the corporation the right to redeem the shares on a specified date. Similarly, preferred stock may be redeemable at the option of the holders, if the corporation has sufficient funds to lawfully complete the redemption. Redemption of the shares may be mandatory in other instances, thereby obligating the corporation to make appropriate arrangements to set aside or raise the funds.

The redemption price is usually equal to the liquidation preference. The price, timing of the redemption, sinking fund requirements, and other security will be established in the course of negotiations between the corporation and the investors.

Redemption at the corporation's option is advantageous to the corporation but potentially harmful to the holder. The ability of the corporation to redeem outstanding preferred stock allows it to limit or terminate burdens associated with the preferential rights. The holder, however, can be deprived of its stock at the convenience of the corporation.

On the other hand, the right of preferred stock holders to require the corporation to buy back their shares, or "put" the shares to the corporation, may significantly impair the corporation's financial plans. This is particularly the case if the corporation is required to divert working capital into a sinking fund available for the redemption, or if the demand is made at a time when the corporation does not have sufficient funds and may be forced to raise them by an offering under more onerous terms than in the existing instrument.

§ 2.03 DEBT SECURITIES

[A] Introduction

Debt securities do not provide the holder with any residual interest in the value of the corporation. The holder is entitled only to the return of the amount loaned, along with interest for the period the loan remains outstanding. Debt securities are attractive to investors seeking a fixed rate of return. They also appeal to investors who feel uncertain about the residual value of the business and are unwilling to risk an equity position. Assuming repayment burdens can be handled, debt securities can be an attractive method for the company to obtain working capital while retaining the benefits of long-term appreciation for existing equity holders.

[B] Basic Types of Debt Securities

[1] In General

Debt securities tend to be characterized as secured or unsecured. Secured debt instruments are further categorized according to the underlying collateral. In addition, both secured and unsecured debt securities can include a means for converting the instrument into equity, including common stock.

[2] Secured Debt Securities

Secured debt securities, commonly referred to as bonds, are distinguished by the fact that the obligation of the corporation to repay is secured by a security interest in specific property of the corporation. If the corporation defaults on its obligations under the bond, the pledged property is sold pursuant to the security interest. Proceeds will be applied first to pay the principal amount due to bondholders who have a first lien on the pledged property. If the proceeds are insufficient to pay the principal, the bondholders become unsecured creditors for the balance owed them. If the proceeds are more than the amount needed to repay the bondholders, the balance will first be applied to the payment of holders, if any, of debt securities with a junior lien, and any remaining amount will be applied to satisfy the claims of unsecured creditors.

A secured debt instrument permits a corporation with a relatively poor credit rating to access debt financing through the pledge of property as security for repayment of the loan. In addition, interest charges on a secured debt instrument will generally be lower than those on an unsecured debt instrument. On the other hand, the use of a secured debt instrument may impair the ability of the corporation to secure additional debt financing, since a portion of the corporation's assets will no longer be available to satisfy the claims of new lenders.

As with preferred stock, holders of secured debt securities may have different ranks or priorities. Bondholders are considered to be of the same rank if they are secured by the same level of security interest in the pledged property. For example, a security interest may be a first or senior lien, or a junior lien. The rank is set in the debt instrument. A subsequent grant of a higher rank in the same property must be approved by existing creditors. In addition, many loans require the lender's approval for *any* subsequent lien on the same property, even a junior one.

Distinctions may be made among holders of secured debt securities on the basis of the assets serving as collateral. For instance, investors financing a company's acquisition of a particular asset may receive a lien on only that asset.

[3] Unsecured Debt Securities

The preferred position of bondholders is in contrast to that of holders of the most basic form of corporate debt instrument, commonly referred to as a debenture. Debentures are unsecured, and the indebtedness of the corporation evidenced by a debenture is backed solely by the financial condition and creditworthiness of the corporation. Debentures are junior debt securities of the corporation, and debenture holders are unsecured creditors of the corporation. They do not have the additional comfort provided to bondholders by the pledge of a security interest in the corporation's property.

While the rights of debenture holders are senior to those of the holders of equity securities, they are subordinate to the rights of holders of senior or secured debt instruments. They may also be junior to the rights of other creditors. If no secured debt securities have been sold and the property and assets of the corporation have not otherwise been pledged, holders of debentures will share in the proceeds from any sale of corporate assets on the same basis as other creditors. However, if any property has been pledged, the debenture holders will share in the sale proceeds only after the claims of secured creditors have been satisfied.

Since debentures have only a junior claim on the assets of the corporation, they provide the most attractive debt financing alternative for a corporation likely to raise additional capital in the future. Future lenders will be more willing to extend credit to a corporation that has not already pledged its assets. Such lenders, especially if unsecured, want their debt instruments issued on the same priority as those of existing debt holders. By issuing debentures, the corporation will also have the flexibility to issue secured debt instruments in the future—assuming debenture holders have not placed any restrictions on the issuance of senior debt securities.

Since debenture holders do not have the benefit of a security interest to protect their investment in the corporation, they will generally require a higher rate of interest than bondholders. They may also impose restrictions on actions by corporate management, including issuance of senior or equal-rank debt securities that dilute or subordinate their rights. While their junior position is the greatest disadvantage to potential debenture holders, the enhanced ability of the corporation to issue a broader range of debt instruments in the future may actually reduce the company's business risks.

[4] Convertible Debt Securities

Both secured and unsecured debt securities can include the right to convert into some form of equity investment. The conversion terms are specified in the debt instrument. Most convertible debt securities provide that the outstanding principal, as well as any accrued interest, may be converted into an equity security (e.g., common stock) at a specified conversion rate prior to the maturity of the debt instrument. A convertible debt security is similar to convertible preferred stock.

[C] Considerations in Issuing Debt Securities

[1] In General

The key consideration in issuing debt securities is the effect that the stream of required payments will have on the day-to-day activities of the business. This is the same as with equity securities carrying an obligation to pay dividends and/or redeem the shares on a specified date. Where the debt instrument can be converted into equity, the holders of the equity securities must consider the possible dilution of their interests at some future date. Finally, a default under a debt instrument may result in a change in management or the imposition of restrictions on the freedom of managers.

[2] Interest Rate and Payments

Interest may be set at a fixed rate or adjusted while the debt is outstanding. The rate of interest will depend on the creditworthiness of the issuer, the security given to the holders of the instrument, and whether or not the instrument is convertible into an equity security. Interest payments are typically made on a monthly, quarterly, or annual basis. Depending on the anticipated cash flow requirements of the issuer, interest payments may be deferred for some initial period of the loan. In exceptional cases, interest payments may be deferred until the principal is paid.

[3] Repayment of Principal

Repayment of principal is often scheduled in quarterly, semiannual, or annual installments. While it is possible to commence repayment from the date of issuance or from a fixed date after it (e.g., annual principal repayments with the first payment due one year from the date of issuance), the corporation is likely to receive some deferral (e.g., three or four years). In such a case, the corporation would pay interest on a larger outstanding debt balance. At times, the corporation may be able to delay repayment of the entire principal amount until the date of maturity, at which time a single balloon payment is required.

[4] Conversion Rights

Holders of debt instruments may have conversion rights similar to those given to convertible preferred stock holders. In some cases, debt holders receive a straight debt instrument plus warrants exercisable for equity securities. If so, the debt holder may have the right to apply outstanding principal and interest toward the warrants' exercise price.

[5] Optional Prepayment

The issuer of the debt instrument may have the right to prepay the debt, albeit at a premium. Optional prepayment allows the issuer to refinance its obligations when interest rates decline. If the debt instrument could be converted into equity, the prepayment option permits management to extinguish conversion rights that might dilute the interests of existing shareholders.

[6] Subordination

Debt instruments are typically subordinated to bank and other institutional borrowings, whether outstanding at the time the instrument is issued or incurred after the date of issuance. Subordination provisions may prohibit repayment until all obligations of the issuer to senior indebtedness have been fulfilled. As a general matter, some amounts can be paid on the debt instrument so long as no default has occurred on senior indebtedness.

[7] Affirmative and Negative Covenants

Debt financings often involve extensive affirmative and negative covenants and undertakings on the part of the issuer. Many go far beyond those typically included in an equity financing.

[8] Events of Default

A default by the issuer in paying principal or interest may give debt holders certain rights. These usually include the right to accelerate payment of outstanding indebtedness and, in some cases, the right to elect one or more members of the board of directors. Other events of default might include a breach of a representation or warranty, violation of an affirmative or negative covenant, default under any other debt instrument (called a cross default), insolvency, or bankruptcy. Depending on the circumstances, the issuer may be given some period of time to "cure" a default before the debt holders can exercise their rights.

[9] Security

In many cases, investors will purchase unsecured debt instruments, for example, founders and venture capitalists purchasing some form of convertible debt instrument. Institutional investors, however, will usually prefer some type of security interest in material assets of the issuer. The interest may be subordinated to commercial lenders.

[D] Characteristics of Various Debt Securities

[1] In General

Debt securities for financing purposes can take a number of forms. Among the factors that must be considered are the timing of the repayment obligations, whether the company's performance is to be secured by corporate assets or not, and the ability of the holder of the security to convert it into an equity instrument.

[2] Demand Obligations

The simplest debt security is the "demand note"; under its terms the holder has the right to present the note to the issuer for payment at any time. It is payable upon demand. In light of the risks associated with a sudden call for payment, the issuer should bargain for deferring the first date on which a demand can be made.

[3] Unsecured Fixed Term Debentures

An unsecured fixed term debenture requires the issuer to repay the principal amount of the debenture on a fixed date in the future. The performance of the issuer is not secured by any assets. The use of a fixed term will allow the issuer to plan for repayment without fear that the note will be presented for payment earlier than expected.

[4] Secured Fixed Term Debentures

Although debentures, as noted above, are unsecured corporate debt, there is one form of debenture that may be secured: fixed term debentures. They are similar to the unsecured fixed term debentures described above, except for the pledge of corporate assets securing them. Such debentures are usually subordinate to liens for the benefit of commercial lenders.

[5] Real Estate Mortgage Bonds

Real estate mortgage bonds are secured by a security interest in corporate real estate. The pledged property can be limited to a specific parcel of property or can include all the real property owned by the corporation at the time the bonds are issued. In certain cases, the security interest will extend beyond currently owned property to include real property acquired after the bonds are issued. If the value of the pledged real estate increases, in some cases the property may be pledged as security for additional debt securities. The rights of these after-issued securities will probably be subordinate to the originally issued bonds. A disadvantage of a security interest in corporate real estate is that it may prohibit the corporation from issuing unsecured debt instruments.

[6] Equipment Mortgage Bonds and Trust Certificates

Equipment mortgage bonds are secured by an interest in tangible personal property of the corporation, such as furniture and equipment. Equipment mortgage bonds are often used by corporations, such as railroads, that have substantial investments in equipment.

One special form of equipment mortgage bond is the conditional sale bond. Under this arrangement, the equipment securing the bonds is sold to the corporation, but title to the equipment remains with the seller, or with a trustee if the bonds are sold to the public, until the bonds have been repaid. The corporation assumes direct liability on the bonds and makes annual payments sufficient to pay the interest and to amortize the principal. A substantial down payment is made to the seller at the time the bonds are issued so that the face value of the bonds is less than the cost of the equipment.

Another debt financing arrangement involving equipment is equipment trust certificates. In this case, the pledged equipment is sold to a trustee and the trustee leases the equipment to the corporation. The corporation makes a substantial advance payment of rentals to the trustee, which are used as a down payment for the equipment. As with conditional sale bonds, the corporation makes regular rental payments sufficient to pay annual interest and amortization charges. The trustee is primarily liable for payment of the principal and interest due on trust certificates issued to investors. Payment, however, is guaranteed by the corporation.

[7] Collateral Trust Bonds

With collateral trust bonds, payment of principal will be secured by a pledge of stock, bonds, securities, notes, and/or other intangible property owned by the corporation. Even though the collateral is deposited with a trustee, the corporation usually retains the right to receive any dividend and interest payments and to exercise voting rights associated with securities included in the collateral. These rights may revert to the trustee upon any default by the corporation.

The attractiveness of collateral trust bonds depends on the nature of the intangible property securing the obligations. Among the types of property often pledged as collateral are stocks and bonds of subsidiaries, stocks and bonds of unrelated corporations, obligations of the corporation's customers, or any combination of these.

[8] Guaranteed Bonds

With a guaranteed bond, payment of principal—and in some cases interest—is guaranteed by someone other than the issuing corporation. For example, the obligations of a subsidiary corporation may be guaranteed by its parent. A guarantee may be used in connection with any other form of secured or unsecured debt security. Joint guarantee bonds are similar to guarantee bonds, except that two or more persons stand behind the creditworthiness of the issuing corporation.

[9] Convertible Debt Financing Instruments

As noted, holders of convertible debt financing instruments are senior to holders of equity securities, since debt comes before equity. Convertible debt holders expect a fixed return based on interest payments *and* the option to participate in any increase in the overall value of the business by exercising the conversion privilege.

Convertible debt instruments are similar to convertible preferred stock. One key difference is that debt holders wishing to participate in management need to rely on separate voting arrangements; they cannot rely on the rights given in the charter documents to holders of convertible preferred stock.

This type of instrument allows the issuer to reduce the amount of interest payments that would otherwise be required.

Insiders: Toto . . . I Have a Feeling We're Not on Wall Street Anymore

VERAC, INCORPORATED

by Jeff Nash

There is a joke about starting up and financing your own small company. It says, "The really great ones you keep for yourself, the okay ones you share with your friends, and the rest you take public." It's a bad line, because appropriate start-up financing just doesn't work that way, especially in capital-intensive, time-to-market-driven, high-tech-product businesses. But a lot of people start out thinking that it should. Still, if you don't need other people's money to get to market quickly, to give your company stability and working capital, or to build a product, you may be better off not taking it. Bill Bowes, a founding partner of U.S. Venture Partners and one of the first venture investors in Sun Microsystems and many other successful companies, is fond of saying, "More companies have died from overeating than have died from starvation." Put another way, "You can never be too rich or too thin." Here's a self-financed company story that I was privileged to be a part of.

In 1977, I had been working for 18 months at a small, defense technical services think tank in San Diego. As a bright-eyed Ph.D. in engineering with an Army Reserve stint and a few years of weapon and spacecraft engineering at big companies and government behind me, I was still trying to get dry behind my entrepreneurial ears. Every company I had worked for was smaller than the one before it. The company I had most recently joined was great. With offices in La Jolla, California (customers called it "a workingman's Carmel"), we created and studied exotic mathematical descriptions of radars, electronic gear, lasers, submarines, spacecraft, missiles, communications channels, freeway traffic jams, satellite navigation receivers, and a bunch of other amazing stuff for customers that I still can't talk about.

Work was ritually punctuated with daily bodysurfing in the waves that nearly always raged south of Scripps Pier in magazine-cover form, all within jogging distance from the shop. More than one difficult mental problem was solved with the prescription of a lunch-time saltwater dip. Back on the job, armed with surf-soaked sinuses, new ideas, and the pioneering Internet connections we had with DOD and academia around the world, we played competing physical concepts off against each other and studied the performance of many engineering systems that are seeing the light of day only now. Most were labeled classic "duds," and these have been relegated to the status of Classified Artifact forever. There are others that I hope will remain "conceptual" for a very long time.

Three university professors had founded the company in the early 1970s. Like all companies, it evolved to a point in its history where a crisis in growth occurred and a revolution took place to resolve it. During the first crisis period, while I was there, there was a lot of uncertainty and top management made itself scarce. We worker bees were on our own nearly all of the time, directly responsible to customers for output and to our staff for the generation of new business so all could eat. In addition, we had to do the work. I was spending over 60 hours a week at the office writing classified reports and staring at reams of computer printouts of high-energy laser weapon performance and wondering where all that was getting me. Down the hall, with their own agendas and concerns, were two colleagues doing similar things except their specialties were satellites and submarines. The three of us were seeing more of each other on the weekends over the communal coffeepot than we did of our wives . . . or our bosses.

Someone once said, "Nobody works harder than the boss—for very long."

I will always recall a clandestine, bleary-eyed meeting of "The Three" after the company's 1977 annual meeting—my first and last. Much grousing ensued. There were concerns about how much equity participation all of us might be limited to and concerns about our future in a management lineup that was destined to change in ways we could not predict. Everything that could be complained about was. Even the Scripps Pier surf was deemed to lag. Someone finally mumbled the famous Silicon Valley battle cry, "I don't really think we need those guys." Much beer, much techno-chest-pounding, and much general complaining followed, all laced with the tantalizing prospect of wealth beyond the wildest dreams of avarice while the propitious evening decayed into morning.

It's a common story. Successful engineers and marketers decide that in addition to moving products and services, they can earn more by creating businesses—and they attempt to do so. But to be successful, they have to come up with something worth managing, i.e., something profitable. They need a product or service, employees to provide and sell it, and customers to buy it. If you run through this for yourself, remember some basics. Unless you have enough capital to pay for product development, you will be providing a service based on skills your company has. Unless you have enough capital to hire, retain, and motivate employees, you will provide the service yourself (until you make some money or win a contract big enough to hire against). Unless you have enough capital to market and sell your company's services, whether you spend it on airplane rides or advertising campaigns, you will market and sell your service yourself. Now, did I forget to tell you anything you didn't already know about our little situation? Yes, I did.

Between the three of us and our young families, we were seriously broke.

And to make matters worse, one of us decided at the last minute to stay with the Mother Company. Whether he was bought off or just decided that three was one too many, he has never said. Actually, looking back, all may have been for the best. All of us came through the situation very well, including the bosses, one of whom I'm now working with again after 20+ years. As my remaining partner and I were to later discover as we brought additional talent aboard, the degree of difficulty in doing any deal seems to vary as the cube of the number of players. The Three had abruptly become The Two, and we were now equal partners on day one. This duality would be hard enough to deal with normally, but as our business marriage began with an immediate need for cash, the psychology got pretty interesting in a hurry. Both of us looked at our bank accounts and decided (with spousal agreements) to refinance our houses to put up $10,000 apiece—not exactly what Bill Bowes would call a "rich" deal in his venture world. We were a long way from overeating.

Like a lot of small technical service companies, VERAC, Inc., floundered along at first. Our first contract was with the Navy for $15,000. We learned the business ropes, never missed an employee payroll, hired some great talent, and had some fun making money and doing good work for good reasons. The saving grace of our business, as it grew with DOD small-business set-aside contracts in the 1970–80 time frame, was our market. DOD and the security agencies were spending over $170 billion every year in highly regulated procurement of goods and services to bury the Soviets before they buried us if the Cold War ever went hot. Even the greenest rocket scientist knew that you didn't need much of a bucket underneath that kind of spigot to end up with a nice drink. We did our thing. We were green. But VERAC bumbled along.

Until we met Art Biehl.

Biehl is gone now, but anyone who knew him as well as we did will not easily forget him. He remains to me a superbly complex and cantankerously contradictory blend of scientist, engineer, businessman, entrepreneur, yachtsman, pilot, multimillionaire investor, promoter, and practical psychologist. Never shy, frequently blunt, occasionally charming, and always scheming in one capitalistic direction or another, Dr. Arthur T. Biehl was a highly specialized pillar of the nation's military-industrial R&D complex. He had eschewed the halls of both large corporate defense contractors and the Pentagon, in both of which he had served, electing to live by his wits on the fringe of DOD credibility with those of us in small-growing to medium-sized businesses. His contributions to commerce included several of his own companies (notably MBA-Tracor) and essential contributions to the building of many more, including R&D Associates (RDA, now part of Logicon-Northrop), SAIC (privately held +$4 billion), and VERAC (now part of Ball Aerospace +$3 billion).

When a colleague introduced me to him, Biehl was in his early 60s. I first saw him across the room at a racetrack bar, where he sat nestled solo into a booth with his drink. He was wearing a blue yacht club blazer and a thinning, raggedly trimmed gray crew-cut. He studied the room and its patrons with a continuous series of alert, hawklike movements of his head. His eyes took anyone's measure (including mine as I sidestepped an overloaded busboy) in a briefly piercing but mostly incidental glance. As his gaze shifted to scan the room again, I felt his real focus had remained on some invisible, distant shore, and that he was intent on seeing whatever was in his mind, not what surrounded him. I edged through the boisterous race crowd toward his table. That day he was deeply tanned and weathered from days at the helm of an America's Cup racing vessel he had personally designed, built, and sailed to Hawaii. Finally, I slid past a waiter into the booth and introduced myself nervously while I fumbled him a business card, financials, and a company brochure. Before long, he was firing a staccato string of questions at me about our company: customers, technology, growth, markets, employees, incentive programs, billing rates, operational issues, management style, values, personal goals, etc. By the time he finished, I knew I was in the presence of a brilliant artist and I could only hope that VERAC would be his latest canvas.

A few days later we gathered in the "main conference room" of our company's single-story tilt-up concrete facility. With the building being located on the "inactive" Rose Canyon fault line in San Diego, I do recall that the rent was quite low. Why we called it the "main" conference room I do not know. We had only one small conference room, and we used it as library, shipping and receiving facility, storage room, and lunchroom. It was dimly lit and the carpet had a lot of cheap coffee stained into it. Three of us—Art Biehl, Chuck Morefield, and I—were sitting in the room. I was a very energetic 33 (and chomping to get back to my overdue work on the use of high-energy lasers for bomber defense). My business partner, Dr. Charles L. Morefield—a karate black belt, scuba diving instructor, former naval officer, and master of an arcane body of knowledge known as multisensor data fusion—was 38 and an intense bear of a man. He had just presented our financial projections and sat down behind his own characteristic poker face to watch Biehl's reactions. Art sat across our scarred, fake-oak conference table, running his index finger down the offered pages, periodically raising a wild eyebrow with a question, and looking up over his glasses from the paper at one or the other of us. He had an East Coast accent. I'm not sure if it was New York or New Jersey, or New whatever, but it was always delivered with the gravelly modulation of a confirmed Scotch-drinker.

Biehl finally sat up in his chair and cleared his throat with a chuckle that almost growled us to military attention before he spoke. "Looks to me like you boys could use some money. You know that, don't you?"

Did we? Hell, I didn't think it was that bad. We had been through worse and we still had our founding $20,000 in the bank. That was my simpleminded yardstick of business health. How bad could things be if you still had what you started with? Besides, it looked to me that we were finally about to turn the corner—aside from this nagging cash flow thing staring at us, that is.

"We, uh . . . figured we ought to get a bank line pretty soon." Chuck started in on the line of discussion we had been having for weeks with a local banker. He stood up to hand Biehl another few pages to look at. Art froze him in mid-rise with a raised hand.

"No. You need equity here, not debt, and you need it now." Biehl's finger nearly drilled through the balance sheet in front of him. "No bank is going to make a commercial loan to a bankrupt company. No big customer is going to believe in this company. You guys keep on like this and you'll be signing personal loan guarantees until your families are washed up and dried out."

Thus began the first crash course in our long-term study of the Tao of Biehl. We had been gliding narrowly above the dead zone of small start-ups for nearly three years. Biehl thumped us like a rocket-assist on takeoff. The Biehl formula was one he professed at all the service companies he bought into. Make money on every contract. Don't finance the U.S. government with late receivables. Hire only when you have the business in house. Minimize up-front risk funding. Sell stock only to the key players who are going to make something out of the company by tangibly increasing revenues or profits. Don't sell the stock if a player doesn't make the contribution. If the contribution cannot be quantified, it isn't valuable or unique and it doesn't merit additional stock for the individual. If the player leaves, buy the stock back at a current price. Show everyone the value goes up as a function of company performance. Guide yourself with a formula, but don't get hamstrung by it. Tie stock participation to profitable technical service sales. Incentivize sales and key performers with a plan that allows equity "purchase opportunities." Options were unheard of in the early days with Biehl. (For the record, he later relented.) You want stock? Haven't got enough? Here, if you earn it, then you get to buy it. Outside directors join the board? They buy stock, too. Sell services. Sell purchase opportunities. Sell stock! Sell, Sell, Sell. On and on. Biehl's sermons became our mantra and it worked. Much of it was Business 101, but like I said, we were very green. It didn't take long to learn. Like one of Art's slick boats, our company began to run up fast before the strong rising wind of U.S. defense spending.

VERAC grew from under $1 million in revenue to over $22 million in revenue in five years after we adopted and implemented Biehl's systems and methodology. We made 6%–10% after tax every year and finally sold the company (over complaints from Biehl, by the way) in 1987, just before the Berlin Wall came down and the Cold War ended. Interestingly, at the time of the sale, 80% of the company's stock was owned by 20% of our people.

The most important and enduring early business lesson I have carried away from Art Biehl and VERAC is that equity ownership, more than nearly any other management tool available to small business, positively motivates people for the company. If you as a founder can perfectly align the placement of your company's equity with your company's goals, you win and so do all the other equity holders. There is no need to be greedy in this process. If it turns out that 80% of the work is generally done by 20% of the people in your organization, make sure the equity follows that distribution to the right people. The proper programs ensure this.

As a service business founder or a potentially customer-funded product business founder, you may have the tremendous luxury of not needing a lot of outside equity—unless you are intent on huge, immediate growth. Then, you'll want outside money to fund your company. Otherwise, at least think about raising it from the insiders, including but not limited to you. Shareholder-employee insiders are the people who will work side-by-side with founders day and night, holidays and weekends, to grow and improve the place where you all work. Nobody cares more about making the business a success and nobody is better motivated to perform in a business than its owner-operators. Let me summarize.

Make stock available to those individuals whose hard work brings in the revenue and earns the profits your company must have. Then everybody makes more, including you. If people pay for the stock you make available, it has more value to them and you have the capital to grow some more without engaging outside investors.

Dr. J. Robert Beyster, another ardent Biehl admirer, himself Founder and Chairman/CEO of the $4 billion Science Applications International Corporation (SAIC), took a lot of advice from Art while Art was serving as a shareholding consultant to Bob during the early years at SAIC. Bob Beyster molded from, added to, and vitally extended Art's preliminary views into his own special philosophy at SAIC, now America's largest high-tech employee-owned company. The means to success and corporate financial independence as advocated by both men are blueprinted into the mission of a nonprofit foundation founded by Dr. Beyster. The Foundation for Enterprise Development offers a variety of materials on employee-owned companies and the particular benefits and liquidity options (including ESOPS and stock purchase plans) that can be used to keep an employee-owned company going and growing. Their Web address is www.fed.org.

Tell the Foundation that Biehl sent you. Wherever he is now, I'm sure he gets a pre-negotiated piece of the action for doing good. We miss you, Art.

CHAPTER 3 • FINANCING REQUIREMENTS AND SOURCES

CHAPTER 3

§ 3.01 STAGES AND TYPES OF BUSINESS

As outlined in Table 1.1 in Chapter 1, the financing available to a business generally reflects the growth and evolution of the business itself. As a result, financing changes over time:

1. When the business is formed, the founders provide capital in the form of equity and long-term unsecured loans. Capital will also be generated through various forms of internal financing, such as retained earnings and tax savings from depreciation. In many cases, owner financing will be supplemented by secured lines of credit from local banks, usually guaranteed by the owners of the company. In addition, some long-term financing may be available from government programs administered by the federal Small Business Administration and state and local agencies.
2. If the business is successful, additional capital may be raised through private equity and debt placements with wealthy individuals or institutional investors, or perhaps with venture capital firms. These investments may take the form of convertible preferred stock or convertible debt instruments. Additional capital may be available from large commercial lenders. Customers and suppliers may also be willing to enter into arrangements that provide favorable cash flow to the business.
3. After some period of time, the company may be able to sell its securities in the public market. This will provide liquidity for existing investors. It will also be a new source of capital for long-term investments and improvements. The new funds will permit expansion of product lines and research and development. A public company may also gain access to varying types of commercial financing from banks and financial institutions on terms more favorable than those for start-up companies.

The type of financing also depends on the company's line of business. A capital-intensive business may require very little working capital, but it will need long-term debt. In contrast, a retail business will need working capital provided by lines of credit rather than long-term debt.

§ 3.02 FINANCING ALTERNATIVES

The major financing alternatives available to the firm are

- **Alternative sources**, such as internal funds, vendor financing, strategic partners, private loans, commercial loans and leases from financial institutions, and government funding programs;
- **Private offerings**, such as sales to a small group of private or institutional investors and venture capital financings; and
- **Public offerings**, which are generally effected by complying with the securities registration process, or under one of the exemptions from registration.

In Parts III and IV, we will describe these alternatives in more detail.

[A] Alternative Sources

[1] Internal Funds

A company typically resorts to investors, lenders, and other outside sources of capital only after determining that it cannot generate sufficient funds internally. There are several possible internal sources. The first is after-tax earnings from prior operations that are retained in the business rather than distributed to shareholders as dividends. The board of directors generally has the discretion to determine the amount of dividends that can be paid. Its decision is subject to the terms of agreements with corporate shareholders, the restrictions imposed by commercial lenders, and the limitations in the applicable corporations statute. As a general rule, dividend policy must be determined in light of management's goals and objectives for future expansion.

Other internal sources of funds include cash available for use pending payment of future obligations accrued on the company's books and records. For example, federal and state taxes on income generated by the company are not payable until the tax filing date. Such amounts, while accrued as a future liability on the company's financial statements, can be used until the tax payments become due. The company can also increase available cash flow by accelerating depreciation on equipment, since this is a noncash expense that reduces the company's tax liability. The company's ability to take advantage of cash discounts offered by trade creditors for prompt payment may also effectively reduce the company's cost of capital.

[2] Vendor Financing

Another key source is vendor financing. Suppliers may provide discounts based on the amounts purchased over a period of time. If the company is paying its bills on a net 10- or 15-day basis, some vendors may be willing to stretch out their accounts receivable in exchange for future value. If, for instance, the vendor believes the company is growing, it may be willing to trade off delayed payment in the present against larger sales in the future. In some cases, interest on the delayed payment (in cash, stock, options, or warrants) may be necessary. The key, however, is for the company to work with the vendors and be honest with them about what it is doing. They are more likely to be cooperative if the company discusses its financial condition with them in advance. If, after the company has described the situation, the vendors see future gain and trust the company, they may be willing to work with it.

[3] Strategic Partnering

As a company grows and develops, it generally will enter into a variety of business relationships with third parties regarding research and development, product manufacturing, supply of raw materials and semifinished goods, distribution, and service.

Strategic partnering in these relationships has become popular in recent years. Many large corporate investors have begun to develop a good deal of experience in analyzing and valuing technologies of small firms. For small firms, investments by such partners can mean capital for the development of new technologies, as well as a partner who understands how the technology works and the difficulties in bringing products to market. For the investor, an investment allows it to exercise greater management control over the development project and to share in the overall success of the smaller company—a success that results in large part from the investor's agreeing to purchase goods from the small firm.

One of the most popular forms of strategic partnering is a large company with an established line of products and a strong distribution network contracting with a smaller company to purchase and resell goods manufactured by the smaller company. The larger company can do more than gain greater access to the smaller company's technology and provide additional capital that the smaller company can use. It might make an equity investment in the smaller company on terms similar to those in venture capital investment transactions. In some cases, the larger company may receive an option to acquire the smaller company at a later date.

Another popular strategy has been the research and development—or R&D—partnership, which uses capital contributed by outside investors to finance research work of a firm (sponsor), usually one with a previously developed, promising base technology. Under this arrangement,

- The sponsor contributes the base technology to the R&D partnership,
- Investors contribute capital as limited partners,
- The sponsor performs research work for the benefit of the R&D partnership that approximates in value the amount contributed by the limited partners, and
- Investors receive a return on their investment from royalties on the sale of products using the technology developed in the research program.

The sponsor generally has a right to buy out the interests of the limited partners at a price based on an agreed-upon formula.

R&D partnerships enable sponsors to finance development work without using their own funds. The risk that the development work will be unsuccessful is shifted to the investors. For a more detailed description of R&D partnerships, see the case study in Chapter 15.

Investors once sought the tax benefits of being able to deduct the expense of the research work against their ordinary income. In addition, investors often were able to achieve substantial income from the royalties generated by product sales. However, the current "passive income" rules have substantially eroded the benefits of the R&D partnership from a tax perspective. Also, many investors developed concerns about the illiquidity of their partnership interests.

In response to these drawbacks, some sponsors secure financing for development work by contributing the base technology to a new wholly owned subsidiary. Capital is raised by a public offering of "units" that consist of callable shares of common stock of the new subsidiary and warrants to purchase shares of common stock of the sponsor. The sponsor performs the development work on behalf of the subsidiary. It is hoped that the shares of the subsidiary's common stock will appreciate in value upon the successful completion of the development work. A "call" feature allows the sponsor to repurchase the technology from the subsidiary at a fixed price. Investors would still be able to share in the success of the technology, however, through the warrant component of the investment.

[4] Private Loans

The founders of a business, as well as relatives, associates, and other private parties, will frequently extend credit to the company. Such loans may or may not be secured, and they often include the option to convert the amount of the loan into equity at some future date. If such loans remain outstanding when the company secures commercial debt financing, the private lenders will be asked to subordinate to the commercial lenders.

[5] Commercial Loans and Leases

Commercial loan financing, typically from banks and other financial institutions, is an important component of any firm's capital structure. In many cases, the first significant outside funding that a firm receives will come from a commercial bank. The security for such a loan will be the firm's business income and assets, plus guarantees of one or more of the founders. One possible drawback to the use of commercial loan financing is the restrictive nature of covenants that commercial lenders typically impose.

As the firm grows, its commercial lending relationships will become increasingly important. The firm may use a wide selection of lending tools with varying terms and repayment dates ranging from a few months to several years.

Commercial lenders, including banks, finance companies, thrift institutions, and syndicates composed of two or more commercial lenders participating in a loan, are the principal sources of capital for many businesses. Commercial lenders can provide short-term working capital loans, long-term lending, real estate and mortgage lending, inventory and accounts receivable financing, equipment leasing, and other specialized forms of debt financing. In addition, such lenders can be valuable sources of information regarding financial and credit matters in general. (See Appendix D for a list of banks lending to small companies.)

Commercial banks provide a wide variety of forms of credit for businesses on a secured and unsecured basis. Some commercial banks specialize in loans to companies engaged in specific industries.

Even before venture capitalists are interested, commercial bank loans are often available from small, local banks. Large banks, on the other hand, tend to want several years of profitability—something not usually found in a start-up—and loans from them may not be available until after the first round of capitalization by outside investors.

Several Web sites allow small companies to apply for loans, credit cards, and leases. Applications can then be sent to all participating institutions through the same software. For an example, see www.quicken.excite.com/small_business/focus.

Commercial finance companies provide loans to companies that may not be able to secure loans from commercial banks. Commercial finance companies have less strict creditworthiness requirements, provide loans for longer maturities, are usually willing to accept lower quality collateral, and accept higher loan-to-collateral value ratios. In turn, the interest rates charged by them are higher than those charged by commercial banks.

Federally chartered **savings and loan associations** and **savings banks** can invest a portion of their assets in general commercial loans.

Several **leasing companies** have targeted, and are willing to lend to, emerging companies. Initially, borrowers will have to pay a high rate, probably over 20%. As a company matures, the rates decline. The major advantage is that the leases should be off the balance sheet and should not affect future financing.

Debt: How I Learned to Stop Worrying and Love the Debt

TIERNAN COMMUNICATIONS, INC.

by James C. Tiernan

I founded and helped to build a high-tech electronics firm that is now, after 10 years, still in one of its many building stages. There is much that must be learned to survive and prosper for 10 years and still be on the upswing. There are the rules that self-help books give, which are usually easier to write than apply. However, we've learned some very basic things, particularly about financing a company in the modern environment when you are unloved by investors.

I experimented in the first year of the company. The question was, What is most important? What comes first? The choices are people, sales, or capital.

There is a tradition in our area of how to start high-tech companies. We followed this tradition. It is simple: Consult until an opportunity to develop product comes along. This is a very good self-test as well. If founders cannot feed themselves doing consulting, they probably do not have the stature and background needed to start a company. Thus, the initial funding for our company was simply from my consulting income.

I experimented first with seeking capital based on a business plan. I didn't know how to find funders, and those few that might vaguely have been interested, weren't. Thus, no funding. Clearly funding doesn't come first unless you happen to be lucky or are well connected, well known, and well respected. From the vantage point of now, I would say a start-up should not take investors' money right away at any rate. Things are too much up in the air. The shares, on the one side, or the money, on the other side, may be wasted depending on how things break. Too much luck is involved for any start-up business plan to be credible.

Next I tried sales. I got an agreement to provide a major corporation with some video coding units for satellite transmission. It's the business we are in today. This would have been a tremendous leg up, putting us possibly five years ahead on our growth curve. However, in talking with the customer, I said that I had a staff in mind that could do it, but that I would not commit to the customer until I had the staff in pocket. The customer was comfortable with this ethical approach giving me a conditional contract to this effect. In fact, when I presented the situation to the five or six people who had said that they were interested in joining the company, they wobbled and hedged, even with this opportunity in their face. Aha! People come before sales. In fact, in starting a company, people are EVERYTHING. We've followed this lesson religiously ever since.

So, to build the staff for a technology company, I simply started hiring senior technical people who could consult and who had the potential to drive the design of products. The second senior person in a company is the key to success. I was lucky. A competent friend joined me in the consulting role, and he remains now as the head of our research department. A number of other quite senior people either joined the company or associated with us contractually so as to join our consulting teams.

These associates, almost to a person, broke our noncompete clauses and left us. People, individuals, as a rule do not honor contracts. People are important, but they must be employees, not associates. Keep it simple.

So, we got our core cadre. Products were next, because consulting paid the expense of equipment and facilities and of bringing on and training more consultants. Also, we built capability aimed at product design.

Only when a product idea came along that had good market potential, and that confirmed our internal development capability, did we turn to product development. This occurred about five years into the company's growth, when it had 15 or 20 employees. Product development requires capital. We cut back consulting and essentially floated on savings, a residue of consulting, and a year later, on some angel capital. We tried, but were unsuccessful, with venture capitalists, although in retrospect venture capitalists were a viable and reasonable alternative.

We used debt. A company has four sources of "debt": the banks, private lenders, vendors (accounts payable), and customers (advance payments).

Very early on we were using a large bank, which canceled a line of credit at an inconvenient time because "Tokyo now has a higher minimum credit line size." We found that a small bank, which related to us personally, was a much better fit. Our little bank helped us immensely in this period, for which we are forever grateful. At one point, we did default on one loan. Our bank simply worked with us on this problem and got fully paid back with interest and fees a short while later.

With a huge amount of work, we were able to raise a small amount of money through convertible debt with private angels—less than $1 million in total. This turned out to be an excellent investment for the investors. On our side, it was the only kind of investment we seemed to be able to sell to most angel-type investors. If they believe that the company will not go under, and is interesting, they can put in their money and get interest on it while locking in a favorable stock price. Then at the loan term, they can take a look at the progress of the company and decide to convert or simply get their principal back. Of course, it is usually hard for small companies to pay off too heavy a note, but this factor goes into the investor's decision process. Our investors converted. In fact, one investor sued to convert after missing the conversion deadline. This mechanism worked well for us.

Vendors are willing, to a certain extent, based on confidence in the judgment and integrity of the founders, to carry payables to a longer arrear than is normal. It is not an ethical policy to plan to burden vendors in this way. However, in our case we were forced to stretch payables. We had tremendous support from our vendors. This is essentially a mechanism for them to bet on the company with the hope for good future business. Indeed, our vendors have gotten good revenues from us since the early stress period. Their bet paid off for them. Our ability to draw on this form of debt was essential to our success. Of course, the company builds up an obligation to give such vendors first opportunity for future business whenever practical.

Customers who like the products will pay in advance with the tacit understanding that they are helping the company fund the working capital to produce the product. Our company is an innovation engine. Thus, we have a pattern of solving problems that are difficult for our customers to deal with. Such attractive products can command from 30% to 100% up-front payment with the order. This is essentially debt. You have borrowed from the customer and will pay off with product delivery. Most of our major steps forward have been accompanied by a period of strong advance payments on new and exciting products.

With these debt mechanisms, our corporation has sustained an 85%-per-year revenue growth rate, has operated marginally profitably while absorbing the cost of growth, has put over 30% of revenues in research, and has maintained 80% employee and founder ownership.

The negative is that the corporation has been steadily undercapitalized, with all of the limits this places on growth from understaffing to small marketing budgets. Also, the corporation necessarily is highly leveraged when depending on debt to such an extent. When downdrafts come, as they always do, the corporation must fight very hard to maintain focus and a growth posture. This risk-filled environment requires an employee cadre that is comfortable with risk—wealthier senior people, hotshot junior people. One thing that the corporation must maintain under these circumstances is résumé integrity. In other words, the corporation must be a good reference on employees' résumés so that if the corporation sags, employees can move on without career damage. We carefully posture our corporation to have a reputation as a company with the highest caliber employees. We are very successful at this.

Because of the risk of being highly leveraged, it is clear that equity is better than debt. We are always seeking equity to de-leverage and to fund even stronger growth. But, as I discuss here, debt can be used very effectively in a growth company if the equity players won't play. It ain't business school, but if it's what you're forced to do, it can work.

[6] Government Funding

Government loan programs can be a good source of financing for many companies, particularly those qualifying as small businesses. In most cases, the loan terms offered under these government programs are similar to those offered by private commercial lenders. A government loan, however, may be available to a firm that might not otherwise qualify for a commercial loan. If at all possible, managers should acquaint themselves with the resources of the federal and state business development offices in their area. Their local bank can assist in making introductions or referrals.

Particular businesses may qualify for public financing assistance, including long-term loans from the federal Small Business Administration and state and local agencies dedicated to providing support for small business activities. The amount of funding will depend on the size of the business and the amount of financing raised from other sources, as well as the company's line of business.

If the company is exporting products from the United States, the U.S. Export Import Bank (Ex-Im Bank) and some state agencies may be able to provide financing. The company's local bank can arrange the necessary introductions and may be authorized by Ex-Im Bank to provide export financing directly to the company.

[B] Private Offerings

An unregistered or private primary financing transaction is an investment by one or more purchasers under an exemption from the registration requirements of the securities laws. These financing transactions are generally referred to as "private placements" or "exempt" offerings, with offerings made solely or primarily to sophisticated investors such as venture capitalists. These offerings are exempted principally because of the specialized knowledge of the investors, who are deemed not to require the same degree of protection as other investors do. In other words, these investors are expected to take care of themselves.

A private placement may utilize either equity or debt securities. It may consist of a sale to a single investor or a transaction involving, at least in theory, an unlimited number of sophisticated investors meeting certain requirements under the securities laws. A few private placement exemptions are limited in terms of the aggregate amount that can be raised in the transaction. However, an offering made under Section 4(2) of the Securities Act of 1933, or Rule 506 of Regulation D under the Securities Act, may bring in more capital than many public offerings. While private placements are usually associated with the earlier stages of business development, many large firms with public markets for their securities also raise funds through strategic, focused exempt transactions.

Included in the appendices are subscription documents for a private placement of securities. These documents are suitable for almost any type of private placement other than a venture capital financing. The documents include a subscription agreement (Appendix G), containing representations from the issuer and the investors, a description of closing procedures, and investor questionnaires for various types of investors (e.g., individuals, partnerships, and corporations).

Also included in the appendices are the following:

- A placement agent agreement (Appendix H), which can be used when the offering is assisted by an investment banking firm agreeing to use its best efforts to locate suitable investors. The agreement includes a description of the duties and obligations of each of the parties and the compensation to be paid to the placement agent.
- A private placement memorandum (Appendix I) for a private offering of securities. While the content of a private placement memorandum is obviously dependent on the issuer's business, the other sections tend to be quite standardized. This form can be used as a template for various disclosures, including
  — Company and offering summary,
  — Risk factors,
  — Management,
  — Principal shareholders,
  — Description of capital stock,
  — Investor suitability requirements,
  — Plan of placement,
  — Agreements with placement agents, and
  — Subscription procedures.
- A purchase agreement for a private placement transaction (Appendix J). The document assumes that investors are being issued common stock and includes extensive representations and warranties from the issuer regarding its business and the offering procedures.
- A right of first refusal and co-sale agreement, which gives investors the right to purchase shares being offered by founders before they are sold to others and the right to sell their shares along with shares being offered by founders (Appendix L).

- An amended and restated article of incorporation describing the specific rights of new investors (Appendix M).

[C] Public Offerings

It is possible to make what is, in effect, a public offering of securities without completing the formal registration process. Most public primary offerings, however, are broad distributions of securities into the public capital markets—with the assistance of investment bankers who manage the distribution and underwrite the ultimate sale of the securities.

The decision to "go public" is often extremely difficult and requires careful consideration of a number of advantages and disadvantages. In particular, an initial public offering, or IPO, radically changes the manner in which managers of the business approach their duties and establish their operational and financial goals.

For a seasoned company, the main attraction of a public primary offering is the relatively lower cost of capital. The formal disclosure requirements of the federal securities laws have been modified to facilitate registered offerings made by reporting companies—those firms that have already "gone public." It is quite common for such firms to enter the capital markets fairly quickly as market conditions dictate.

§ 3.03 EVALUATING POTENTIAL FINANCING SOURCES

[A] Investment Partners

Firms' capital requirements depend on their underlying business activities. The financing may come from a variety of sources, particularly when a firm is in a technology-based business requiring substantial funding for technology development and product commercialization.

Since investors, such as venture capitalists and corporate partners, become real partners in the success of the firm, they must be chosen carefully. As such, managers should consider the following characteristics when evaluating a potential investment partner:

- *Experience*—The potential investment partner should have experience with the technology and markets in which the firm will conduct its business. In particular, the partner must understand competitive conditions and the amount of capital and lead time that may be required to bring the products to market.

- *Business Plan Development Assistance*—The potential investment partner should be able to assist the firm in developing and executing a coherent business plan. One or more persons within the investment partner's own organization should be able to offer concrete ideas on strategic business planning.
- *Management Participation and Support*—It is important to understand the expectations of the potential partner as to participation in management (i.e., being a part of the board of directors or, in some cases, an officer). In addition, the potential partner should provide support to the firm in locating suppliers or customers.
- *Financial Support*—The investment partner should be able to assist the firm in securing additional financing.

[B] Lenders

Commercial lenders offer a wide variety of financing alternatives. A company may find that, in addition to commercial loans, bankers' acceptance financing, factoring, and leasing provide attractive alternatives for improving its cash flow. Managers need to carefully analyze each of the alternatives and take into account the capital requirements of the business and the philosophy of each potential lender. In many cases, outside investors can recommend, or even make introductions to, lenders.

Commercial loans are available from a variety of banks and other financial institutions. Many lenders can also provide the company with cash management and other useful services. It is important that the company interview different lenders before making a decision. Among the matters that must be considered are the following:

1. *Who will be the loan officers with responsibility for servicing the loans made to the company, and what type of discretion will the loan officers have with respect to renegotiating the loan or granting waivers of conditions in the loan agreement?* If principal decisions must be made at locations other than the office where the loan officer is located, the borrower may be subjected to delays that impair its ability to do business. The overall pattern of decision making at the lender must be examined.
2. *Are there any legal lending limits that may impair the lender's ability to increase its loan as the borrower's requirements increase?* The legal lending limit will vary depending upon the bank's size and whether it is a national or a state bank.

3. *What are the lender's policies in dealing with a borrower that encounters unanticipated financial or operational difficulties during the term of the loan?* While this can be a somewhat delicate subject to raise at the beginning of the relationship, the lender should be able to provide the company with some idea of its prior practices in this regard. The company should also seek input from others who have borrowed from the lender.
4. *What types of information will the lender request from the company over the term of the loan?* The borrower must be sure that the time and effort associated with preparing the information for the lender will not be excessively burdensome.
5. *What types of covenants will the lender require the company to make?* The company may find a particular lender's covenants too restrictive.
6. *Does the lender, as well as the lending officer, have experience in working with firms involved in the same industry or business as the borrower?* This type of experience can be tremendously beneficial, since the lender should understand the borrower's risks and uncertainties. The lender should also appreciate the business cycles that have an effect on the borrower's ability to satisfy its loan obligations.
7. *Will the lender be seeking a participant in the loan?* Loan agreements often permit the lender to assign the loan or grant participations to other institutions. If participants are involved, they may cause difficulties for the borrower when it seeks to renegotiate the terms of the loan or obtain a waiver of a covenant.

Banks: Getting on the Right Bank

MOSAIC TECHNOLOGY PARTNERS LLC

by Jeffrey Rose

While some companies may deal in the lofty world of venture capital and angel investors, the primary source of outside funding for most businesses will usually be the local commercial bank. Many folks believe that all banks are the same. However, that's not necessarily true and you should take heed of several time-tested methods for finding out if a particular bank will be right for you and your business.

Meet the bank personnel who will be personally responsible for your relationship. While the loan application and servicing processing often seems quite sterile and mechanical, your relationship with the bank is certainly quite personal. The bank will have access to sensitive information about your business and will bargain for the leverage to force you to make important decisions regarding the use of funds generated from the business. So, it's important for you to know the account manager that will be responsible for your loan. You should make it clear that you want to meet the manager before the deal is closed to see if the personal chemistry is right and the person actually understands your business model.

Make sure the bank understands your business and the markets that you have targeted for growth and client development. Every business or industry is unique and yours is certainly no exception. When bankers don't understand how a specific business works, they won't be able to appreciate how funds are spent and collected and how the loan can reasonably be serviced without jeopardizing the underlying assets. When interviewing prospective lenders, be sure to ask whether they have made loans to other businesses of similar size. Also, try and find out how familiar they are with the business practices of your prospective clients, since that will impact the timing of collections at your end.

Make sure that the bank is the right size for your business. This is a bit of a trick question since you will want a bank that is large enough to absorb the risks associated with your business and still small enough to provide the required personal relationship. There are a couple of ways to get at this issue. First, check out how the bank breaks out its commercial banking departments. Does it have a small business segment? In many cases, commercial loans under a fixed amount, say $3,000,000, will be handled by a dedicated small business initiative. Second, make sure that the asset base of the bank is big enough to ensure that it will be around for the term of your loan. Third, be sure that the bank is able to "act small" by being available to answer your questions about ratios and covenants. Fourth, ask whether loan requests are processed locally or sent to an off-site location. If the application is not reviewed locally, you'll have no one to turn to with your questions and concerns.

Confirm that the bank is looking for small business customers. Small business is growing exponentially and savvy banks are moving quickly to tap this market and meet their needs. You should be sure that your bank looks at you and your business as an important part of its overall client development strategy. Information published by the bank on its small business initiatives is an important indicator in this area, as are recommendations and testimonials from other local small business owners.

Start with the bank that handles your personal and business checking and savings accounts. Finding the banks that are most appropriate for your business is a difficult task. But, one way to get your feet wet is to approach the bank that you are currently dealing with for your checking and saving account requirements. It should be fairly easy for them to introduce you to a loan officer. But don't let the past influence your decision. If they don't satisfy the conditions listed above, it's time to find a bank that will and move all your business along with it.

PART II • SECURITIES

CHAPTER 4 • REGULATION

CHAPTER 4

§ 4.01 INTRODUCTION

The offer, sale, distribution, and trading of securities are regulated principally by two federal securities laws:

- Securities Act of 1933 (Securities Act), which relates primarily to the initial issuance of securities; and
- Securities Exchange Act of 1934 (Exchange Act), which regulates the trading of securities in the secondary market after initial issuance.

In addition, no offer or sale of securities may be made without complying with

- Requirements imposed by state securities laws, commonly referred to as "blue-sky" laws, in each of the states where the securities are offered; and
- In the case of underwritten offerings made to the public, the guidelines developed and enforced by the National Association of Securities Dealers (NASD), the self-regulatory body of the domestic securities industry.

§ 4.02 FEDERAL SECURITIES LAWS AND REGULATIONS

[A] Introduction

The framework for federal regulation of securities activities is in the Securities Act and the Exchange Act. The Securities Act focuses on disclosures and responsibilities involved in offering and selling securities to the investment community in both private and public offerings. The Exchange Act seeks to prevent fraudulent and manipulative practices in public trading of those securities. It does so by regulating broker-dealers, exchanges, transfer agents, proxies, tender offers, and marketplace disclosures by anyone trading securities.

[B] Securities Act

[1] In General

The Securities Act regulates issuers and their agents who offer and sell securities. Under the Securities Act, offers and sales of securities must be registered with the federal Securities and Exchange Commission (SEC) unless an exemption from registration is available. Disclosures in the registration statement must include all material information regarding the issuer and the terms of the offering. The Securities Act is designed to ensure that the information is given to the investment community before the offering is completed and is not fraudulent.

[2] Registration Requirements

Under Section 5 of the Securities Act (and rules issued under it), it is unlawful to sell, or offer to sell, a security in interstate commerce without registration, unless the security or sale is exempt. Section 5 applies to *all* offers and sales of securities, including

- Original issuance of securities by the issuer,
- Public distribution of previously issued securities by shareholders of the issuer, and
- Transactions in the market between buyers and sellers unrelated to the issuer.

[3] Exemptions from Registration Requirements

Section 3 of the Securities Act (and rules issued under it) exempts from registration certain types of securities, including those by state and federal governments, banks, charitable institutions, and common carriers. Section 3 also contains exemptions for securities issued in certain types of transactions, such as securities offered or sold within a single state and small offerings. Section 4 of the Securities Act exempts securities offered and sold in transactions not involving a public offering; sales and secondary trading transactions not involving an issuer, underwriter, or dealer; and offers and sales to certain investors. For most enterprises, initial capital-raising activities are conducted under one or more of these exemptions. Large companies with securities traded in the public market may also use the exemptions for specific financing transactions.

[4] Registration and Disclosure Procedures

If no exemption is available, before offering the securities for sale, the issuer must file with the SEC a registration statement containing information on the security, the issuer, and the underwriters. To ensure that this information is available to the public, the Securities Act requires that buyers be provided with a prospectus containing the essential information in the registration statement. The SEC has no authority to rule on the merits of an offering, and it lacks resources to conduct an independent review of the facts and statements in the registration statement. However, the SEC can prevent securities from being distributed if the disclosure requirements are not met. It can do so by refusing to approve, or suspending the effectiveness of, the registration statement and giving investors recourse for fraud.

[C] Exchange Act

[1] In General

The basic purposes of the Exchange Act are to regulate securities exchanges and the securities market; to make available to persons who buy and sell securities information relating to the issuers of such securities; to prevent fraud in securities trading and manipulation of markets; and to control the amount of credit that may be used in the securities market.

The Exchange Act primarily concerns the activities of issuers and their affiliates after their securities have been distributed into the public market. The Exchange Act requires the registration of each class of an issuer's publicly traded securities with the SEC. It also requires issuers and their officers, directors, and controlling shareholders to file periodic and other reports with the SEC and securities exchanges. The Exchange Act also regulates the solicitation of proxies concerning registered issuers, as well as tender offers and other specified transactions. Finally, the Exchange Act establishes a number of rules relating to the creation and operation of the securities markets, including requirements for broker-dealers, stock exchanges, clearing agencies, and transfer agents.

[2] Registration and Reporting Requirements

Section 12 of the Exchange Act requires registration of each class of nonexempt equity securities that a publicly held company issues. Registration is required whenever an issuer

- Lists its securities on a national securities exchange (usually at the time the issuer completes a registered public offering under the Securities Act); or
- Has both total assets in excess of $10,000,000 and 500 or more shareholders of any outstanding class of securities.

Once registered, an issuer must file annual and quarterly reports with the SEC containing detailed financial and other information regarding its business. Special reports must be filed with the SEC any time a material event regarding the issuer occurs. In addition, issuers whose securities are registered under the Exchange Act, as well as their controlling persons (for instance, shareholders, directors, and officers), are subject to various rules regarding solicitation of proxies and insider trading.

[3] Market Regulation

Additional provisions of the Exchange Act regulate the trading market, national securities exchanges, and brokers and dealers. For example, registration is mandated for broker-dealers, exchanges, national associations of broker-dealers, electric and gas holding companies, investment companies, investment advisors, and transfer agents. The SEC has the authority to expel or suspend member broker-dealers from exchanges and to revoke or suspend the registrations of over-the-counter broker-dealers for Exchange Act violations. The SEC may also expel or suspend members of registered national securities associations for violations of the Exchange Act. Over-the-counter brokers and dealers must maintain certain records and must, along with exchange members, maintain minimum levels of net capital that can be easily liquidated to meet financial commitments to customers.

[D] Other Federal Securities Laws

[1] Public Utilities Holding Company Act

The Public Utilities Holding Company Act of 1935 was enacted to correct abuses in the financing of electric and gas public utility holding companies. Interstate holding companies engaged through their subsidiaries in the distribution of natural manufactured gas, or involved in the business of electric utilities, are subject to regulation under the statute. They must register with the SEC and are required to file initial and periodic information about the organization, financial structure, and operation of the holding company and subsidiaries.

[2] Investment Company Act

The Investment Company Act of 1940 gives the SEC regulatory authority over publicly owned companies engaged in investing and trading securities (e.g., mutual funds). It also regulates the composition and management of investment companies, their capital structure, and certain aspects of their advisory contracts and investment policies. Under the Investment Company Act, every *investment company,* a term defined in the statute, is required to register with the SEC and disclose its financial condition and investment policies. This provides investors with useful information about its activities. Other provisions prohibit investment companies from altering, without their shareholders' approval, the nature of their business or their investment policies, and require that management contracts—which typically are between the company and its organizers—must be approved by shareholder vote.

[3] Investment Advisors Act

The Investment Advisors Act of 1940 establishes a framework for registration and regulation of persons who engage, for compensation, in advising others on securities transactions. The SEC has the authority to deny, suspend, or revoke the registration of an investment advisor. The SEC also has the power to obtain injunctions for violations of the statute. It can recommend prosecution by the Department of Justice for fraudulent misconduct or willful violation of the law or the rules promulgated under it. No express remedies for private parties are available under the Act.

In general, a person who has $25 million or more in assets under management is required to register with the SEC. A person managing less than $25 million may be required to register under the securities laws of the state or states in which that person does business. There is no requirement for investment advisors to pass any examination or to meet any qualification requirements based on training and/or experience. Investment advisors are required to maintain various books and records. They are also required to disclose the nature of their interest in transactions executed for their clients, and they are prohibited from assigning investment advisory contracts without the consent of their clients.

[4] Trust Indenture Act

The Trust Indenture Act of 1939 applies to the sale of debt securities and interests in interstate commerce. Any security subject to the Trust Indenture Act must be issued under an indenture, absent an exemption. In the case of securities subject to the Trust Indenture Act and required to be registered under the Securities Act, the registration statement cannot become effective unless the security has been issued under an indenture and the trustee is eligible to serve. The indenture is filed with the registration statement along with the trustee's eligibility statement.

§ 4.03 STATE SECURITIES LAWS AND REGULATIONS

[A] Introduction

Section 18 of the Securities Act states that the Act does not preempt the jurisdiction of a securities commission or similar agency that is an instrumentality of any state or territory of the United States. Every state has passed some form of securities law. As a result, participants in a securities offering must also consider regulation of disclosure, fraud, registration, and qualification by state securities laws and regulations. State securities laws are commonly called blue-sky laws.

[B] Uniform Securities Act

[1] In General

The first attempts to regulate securities transactions were initiated at the state level. A uniform sale of securities act was approved by the National Conference of Commissioners on Uniform State Laws (NCCUSL) in 1929 and subsequently adopted by several states. However, the advent of federal legislation rendered that uniform act obsolete and the NCCUSL removed it from the list of approved acts in 1944. A second uniform act, designated the Uniform Securities Act (Uniform Act), was approved by the NCCUSL and the American Bar Association in 1956.

Like the Securities Act, the Uniform Act requires disclosure to the investment community through registration and dissemination of information. The Uniform Act provides for three main types of regulation:

- Requirement that securities offered for sale within the state be registered or qualified with the securities administrator unless exempt;
- Prohibition and prosecution of fraud in the offer and sale of securities; and
- Requirement that local brokers, dealers, and other agents through which the securities are to be sold in the state must be licensed by the state.

In addition, the Uniform Act contains general administrative and enforcement provisions.

Although almost 40 jurisdictions have adopted the Uniform Act in some form, there are numerous variations. Even when the statutes are substantially similar, the broad interpretive authority and discretion of each securities administrator results in regulations and policies that vary greatly from state to state. Moreover, the blue-sky laws of key states such as New York, California, Illinois, Ohio, Texas, and Florida do not follow and are substantially different from the Uniform Act. Therefore, it should not be assumed that a transaction will be exempt from registration in one state simply because it is exempt in other states. It is best to review the laws of each state where an offering will be made.

[2] Types of State Securities Law Regulation

There are several types of state blue-sky law rules:

- Fraud statutes, which do not require qualification or approval of the securities being offered nor licensing of securities dealers, but provide for penalties through injunctive or criminal proceedings to prevent fraud in the offer and sale of securities.
- Licensing statutes, which typically require that securities dealers be licensed within the jurisdiction, but do not otherwise require the qualification of offered securities.
- Registration statutes, which require qualification of securities but do not seek to license securities dealers.
- Licensing and inspection statutes, which are most common, and regulate securities and securities dealers by requiring that the securities be qualified and dealers be licensed.

States that follow the inspection approach present the greatest challenge for prospective issuers. Some of these states, like the SEC, limit their review of the offering documentation verifying that full and adequate disclosure has been provided to potential investors within the state without considering the substance of the offering. Other such states, however, practice "merit review," meaning that the state securities administrator may deny the issuer the right to sell securities within the state if the offering is deemed to be less than "fair, just, and equitable." Full disclosure alone does not satisfy the blue-sky requirements in the merit regulation states, and the administrator maintains a great deal of discretion in the clearance (approval) or denial of proposed offerings. Merit regulation is preempted for offerings under Rule 506.

[3] Registration Requirements

State regulation of securities generally includes a broad requirement that offers and sales be qualified by a filing with the state securities administrator. Registration may be required in specific cases. On the other hand, there are usually a number of exemptions from the registration requirements for certain types of securities and transactions. One of the most frequently used transactional exemptions is for limited and private offerings, although the criteria for such exemptions may differ substantially from their equivalents under the Securities Act. Other exemptions are for transactions otherwise regulated by the SEC, or through disclosures made to the investment community under the rules and regulations of various exchanges.

There are several different forms of state registration under the Uniform Act. Registration by "qualification" entails filing a prospectus and other documents required by the state. Certain high-quality securities traded on a national exchange and securities issued by seasoned issuers may be registered by a simple notification procedure. Most securities for which a registration statement has been filed under the Securities Act may be registered through "coordination." This is accomplished by filing with the state the registration documents required by the Securities Act.

The information required to be included in a registration generally includes the following:

- Description of the issuer, its business and financial condition;
- Brief biographical data and description of the directors, officers, and major shareholders;
- Description of the terms and conditions of the offering and the rights of the security being offered; and
- Description of the use to which the offering proceeds will be put and a summary of the terms of any agreements with brokers or underwriters with respect to the distribution of the securities.

Each state has adopted its own procedures for registration, as well as guidelines describing the conditions that might be imposed for a registration statement to be declared effective.

As noted above, when registration is required, some states extend the scope of their review beyond the disclosure in the application and related offering documents. They may review other issues, including the price of the offered securities, the degree of dilution to new investors, and the voting rights if any attached to the offered securities. In addition, registration often provides the state administrator with the opportunity to review prior transactions of the issuer, including loans to directors, officers, and employees; payments made to promoters; issuances of stock at prices substantially below the price at which the new securities are to be offered; and previously granted options and warrants. Finally, some states will review the expenses associated with the offering, such as amounts to be paid on behalf of selling shareholders and the amount and nature of the compensation paid to any underwriters. Many "merit" states have adopted policy statements by the North American Association of Securities Administrators (NAASA).

[C] Other State Regulations Affecting Securities

In addition to the registration requirements for securities and broker-dealers, many states have adopted rules for investment advisors and investment companies. Some jurisdictions also have laws regulating tender offers and hostile takeovers. Finally, a number of states have special regulations applying to the offering of certain types of securities, such as interests in franchises and real estate limited partnership interests.

[D] Administration

The Uniform Act contemplates the administration of the state securities laws by a person or an agency specified in the individual state's statute. The administrator is authorized under the Uniform Act to make, amend, and rescind such rules, forms, and orders as are necessary to carry out the Uniform Act, including rules and forms governing registration statements, applications, and reports. The Uniform Act also requires the administrator to maintain a register of all applications for registration and registration statements, whether effective, denied, suspended, or revoked. The register must be open for public inspection and contain information from all registration statements, applications, or reports.

§ 4.04 REGULATION OF SECURITIES DEALERS AND PUBLIC MARKETS

[A] National Association of Securities Dealers

The Exchange Act requires all broker-dealers and salespeople to join a national securities association registered with the SEC. To date, the NASD is the only association registered under the statute. The NASD has promulgated the NASD Rules of Fair Practice (NASD Rules). Among other things, NASD Rules prohibit NASD members from using manipulative or deceptive devices to effect a purchase or sale of securities and from making payments to influence market prices. NASD Rules also provide for the regulation of minimum profits and for the fixing of commission rates, allowances, discounts, or other fees to be charged by its members.

The NASD requires all public offerings to be filed for review with its Corporate Finance division in Washington, D.C. In the review, the underwriting arrangement is examined for fairness. The review applies to both underwritten and company-made offerings if the services of a brokerage firm or any of its representatives are used to distribute the securities. The NASD does not review price. The overall underwriting arrangement is analyzed and a yes or a no decision regarding fairness is made and given to the underwriter.

[B] National Securities Exchanges

There are many active, registered national securities exchanges with self-regulatory responsibilities; they include the well-known New York Stock Exchange (NYSE) and American Stock Exchange (AMEX). Pursuant to 15 U.S.C. § 78f(b)(5), each of the registered exchanges must adopt rules

> designed to prevent fraudulent and manipulative acts and practices, to promote just and equitable principles of trade . . . to remove impediments to and perfect the mechanism of a free and open market and a national market system, and, in general, to protect investors and the public interest.

These rules must provide for the disciplining of exchange members, and persons associated with members, in connection with violations of the rules of the exchange, and of the Exchange Act and its rules.

Securities traded on national exchanges must first be listed on the exchange for trading or be authorized for unlisted trading. For a security to be listed on an exchange, the issuer must satisfy the exchange's listing requirements and register the security with both the exchange and the SEC. After the information has been initially provided to the exchange, it must be updated periodically by the filing of current reports, a requirement generally satisfied by providing the exchange with copies of periodic reports that the issuer files with the SEC under the Exchange Act.

National exchanges generally are not concerned with disclosure requirements or with substantive regulation of the companies whose securities are traded by their members. Nevertheless, exchanges generally require listed companies to make timely disclosure of material corporate developments. In addition, several exchanges, including NYSE and AMEX, have rules affecting such substantive corporate matters as voting rights, preemptive rights, audit committees, and shareholder approval of new shares.

[C] Over-the-Counter Securities

[1] In General

Securities not listed on an exchange, as well as some exchange-listed securities, may trade in over-the-counter (OTC) markets. An over-the-counter market for a security is created when a dealer decides to "make a market" for the security by standing ready to purchase or sell the security in a normal trading lot at a quoted ask or bid price. Currently, the over-the-counter markets consist of approximately 1,000 market-makers linked by sophisticated communication systems to other market-makers, their own retail departments, and the retail departments of approximately 3,500 dealers involved in some aspect of the over-the-counter securities business.

[2] Nasdaq System

The largest and most sophisticated market for over-the-counter trading is the NASD's Automated Quotation System (Nasdaq). Only securities registered under the Exchange Act and those of certain insurance companies are eligible for quotation on the Nasdaq stock market. An application for listing must be made to Nasdaq, along with the prescribed application fee and annual fee. Companies must also comply with certain other quantitative and nonquantitative requirements to be eligible for listing. In recent years, Nasdaq has become an increasingly popular method of trading for a substantial number of over-the-counter securities, as well as for securities listed on an exchange.

[3] Over-the-Counter Securities Not Quoted on Nasdaq

Even if not quoted on Nasdaq or traded on an exchange, a security can be traded over-the-counter if it is traded among investors or brokers. Over-the-counter stock can also be listed on pink sheets or on the OTC bulletin board (OTCBB). This over-the-counter market is also subject to regulation by the SEC, and broker-dealer activities in this area are monitored by the NASD. In order to be eligible to be quoted on the OTCBB, issuers must file periodic reports with the SEC, or in the case of banks with the FDIC. One particular concern in the over-the-counter market is erratic and volatile movement of price caused by relatively thin trading volume.

[D] Broker-Dealer Registration and Regulation

Transactions in the various exchanges and over-the-counter markets are executed through and by broker-dealers. As a general rule, broker-dealers must register with the SEC, as well as with the securities administrators in each of the states in which they operate. In turn, registered broker-dealers must also be members of a registered association of securities dealers, which currently means the NASD. Both the SEC and state securities administrators have the authority to deny registration to, or revoke the prior registration of, a broker-dealer on a number of grounds, including willful violations of the securities laws. The SEC and states may also impose other remedial sanctions. The NASD has its own rules and disciplinary procedures.

All broker-dealers engaged in sales activities must be licensed as sales persons or agents under the applicable state blue-sky law and must pass an examination given by the applicable state authority. In addition, if a broker-dealer is employed by a member of the NASD or a national exchange, that broker-dealer must also be registered with the NASD and/or the exchange and pass further examinations administered by the NASD and/or the exchange.

Once broker-dealers have been registered and licensed, they must comply with various rules of practice, including the following:

- General obligation to deal fairly with customers on charges, recommendations, and volume and frequency of trades for the customer's account;

- Duty to comply with detailed reporting and recordkeeping requirements;
- Duty to adhere to SEC regulations on extending credit to customers in trading transactions (i.e., margin trading); and
- Duty to refrain from trading on inside information and otherwise engaging in fraudulent activities with respect to any purchase or sale of securities.

§ 4.05 KEY DEFINITIONS UNDER SECURITIES LAWS

[A] Introduction

The registration requirements of Section 5 of the Securities Act apply to securities that are offered or sold in interstate commerce. Therefore, a transaction that does not involve a *security* or an *offer or sale* can generally be completed without reference to the securities laws. Moreover, even where the transaction does involve the offer or sale of a security, relief from the registration requirements, but not from the antifraud provisions of the securities laws, will be available for *exempt securities* and for secondary transactions by persons other than *underwriters*. Accordingly, it is important to understand the meaning of each of these terms in order to analyze the effect of the securities laws on a particular set of facts.

[B] Statutory and Judicial Definitions of *Security*

[1] Statutory Definitions of *Security*

Section 2(a)(1) of the Securities Act defines *security* as follows:

> The term "security" means any note, stock, treasury stock, bond, debenture, evidence of indebtedness, certificate of interest or participation in any profit-sharing agreement, collateral-trust certificate, preorganization certificate or subscription, transferable share, investment contract, voting-trust certificate, certificate of deposit for a security, fractional undivided interest in oil, gas, or other mineral rights, any put, call, straddle, option, or privilege on any security, certificate of

> deposit, or group or index of securities (including any interest therein or based on the value thereof), or any put, call, straddle, option, or privilege entered into on a national securities exchange relating to foreign currency, or, in general, any interest or instrument commonly known as a "security," or any certificate of interest or participation in, temporary or interim certificate for, receipt for, guarantee of, or warrant or right to subscribe to or purchase, any of the foregoing.

The definition of *security* in the Uniform Act is virtually identical. Accordingly, the interpretation of the term under the federal act might be expected to be similar to the interpretation by states that have adopted the Uniform Act. However, since state securities laws often deviate substantially from the Uniform Act, it is not surprising that the definition of *security* contained in blue-sky laws of some states often varies significantly. The usual effect is to bring additional transactions within the securities laws.

[2] Judicial Interpretations

While the statutory definition of *security* is quite broad, its scope has been expanded through judicial determination that the term is to be liberally construed. Both the federal and Uniform Act definitions of *security* are preceded by the language, "unless the context otherwise requires." As a result, courts have often expressed the view that the substance rather than the form of the transaction will control the question of whether a security exists. They have focused on the economic realities underlying a transaction rather than simply on the name given to the particular item under analysis.

Substance-over-form analysis has generally been used to determine whether a specific transaction constitutes an "investment contract," which is included (but not described) in the definition of *security* under both federal and state securities laws. Although a number of different tests have been formulated to determine whether an investment contract exists, the criterion most commonly employed is whether the arrangement in question involves an investment of money in a common enterprise, with an expectation of profits solely from the efforts of others.

Some courts, however, have extended the concept of an investment contract to include any transaction in which an investor furnishes initial value or risk capital to an enterprise, regardless of whether there is an expectation of profit.

[C] Exempt Securities

[1] In General

Even if it is determined that a transaction involves a security, it must be considered whether the security is exempt from the registration requirements under Section 3(a) or Section 3(b) of the Securities Act, or applicable state securities laws. It is important to remember that while exempt securities need not be registered, offers and sales of them are still subject to the antifraud provisions of the securities law. This often means that substantial information disclosures will still need to be prepared for disclosure to investors.

[2] Section 3(a) of Securities Act

Section 3(a) of the Securities Act lists various securities exempted from the registration requirements of Section 5 of the Securities Act:

1. Securities issued or guaranteed by the federal government, by states or municipalities, or by certain of their public instrumentalities; securities issued or guaranteed by a bank; obligations of the Federal Reserve Bank; common trust fund interests; industrial development bonds paying tax-exempt interest; and interests in certain trust funds issued in connection with a stock bonus, a pension or profit-sharing plan, or an annuity.
2. Notes, drafts, bills of exchange, or banker's acceptances that have a maturity of not more than nine months, if the instrument arises out of a current transaction or the proceeds have been or are to be used for current transactions (i.e., commercial paper).
3. Any securities issued for religious, educational, benevolent, fraternal, charitable, or reformatory purposes, not for pecuniary profit, and no part of the net earnings inures to the benefit of any person, private stockholder, or individual.
4. Certain securities issued by a building and loan association, homestead association, savings and loan association, or similar institution, where substantially all the business is confined to the making of loans to members, or any security issued by a farmers' cooperative.
5. Securities issued by a common or contract carrier if the issuance is subject to the Interstate Commerce Act and is filed and processed with the Interstate Commerce Commission (ICC).
6. Certificates issued by a receiver or trustee in bankruptcy with approval of the court.

7. Insurance or endowment policies or annuity contracts issued by corporations supervised by the insurance commissioner, bank commissioner, or similar agency or officer of any state, territory, or the District of Columbia.

Section 3(a) also contains exemptions for any security

- That is exchanged by the issuer with its existing security holders, where no commission or other remuneration is paid;
- Whose terms have been approved after a fairness hearing before any court or agency of the United States or of any state that is expressly authorized by law to grant such approval; and
- That is part of an issue offered and sold only to residents within the state where the issuer is resident, organized, and doing business.

While these exemptions are technically security-based, their availability really depends on the particular transaction in which the security is issued.

[3] Section 3(b) of Securities Act

Section 3(b) of the Securities Act provides the SEC with the power to exempt additional securities from the registration requirements if small amounts are involved or the scope of the offering is limited. Under this authority, the SEC has promulgated a number of regulations covering certain types of offerings, including the following:

- Regulation A, for securities issued in small offerings where the aggregate offering price does not exceed $5 million and certain other disclosure conditions are satisfied; and
- Rules 504, 505, 506, and 701, which are described in the discussion of certain exempt transactions under Regulation D in Chapter 8 in this book.

[4] Exempt Securities Under State Securities Laws

The Uniform Act exempts certain securities of governmental issuers; securities issued by financial institutions; securities of insurance companies; securities of issuers subject to governmental control regarding the issuance of such securities; securities listed on national securities exchanges; securities of nonprofit issuers; commercial paper arising out of current transactions; and investment contracts for employee stock purchase, savings, pension, profit-sharing, or similar benefit plans.

[D] Offers and Sales

[1] In General

Transactions involving a security are not subject to the securities laws unless there is either an offer or a sale of the security. Accordingly, the second key area of inquiry is the determination of whether there is an exchange or transfer of a security "for value."

[2] Statutory Definitions

Section 2(a)(3) of the Securities Act defines *sales* and *offers* of securities as follows:

> The term "sale" or "sell" shall include every contract of sale or disposition of a security or interest in a security, for value. The term "offer to sell," "offer for sale," or "offer" shall include every attempt or offer to dispose of, or solicitation of an offer to buy, a security or interest in a security, for value. . . . Any security given or delivered with, or as a bonus on account of, any purchase of securities or any other thing, shall be conclusively presumed to constitute a part of the subject of such purchase and to have been offered and sold for value.

Such terms, as well as the term *offer to buy* as used in the registration procedures of Section 5 of the Securities Act, do not include preliminary negotiations or agreements

- Between an issuer (or any person directly or indirectly controlling or controlled by an issuer, or under direct or indirect common control with an issuer) and any underwriter; or
- Among underwriters who are in privity of contract with an issuer (or any person directly or indirectly controlling or controlled by an issuer, or under direct or indirect common control with an issuer).

The Uniform Act defines the terms *sale* and *sell* to include every contract of sale of, contract to sell, or disposition of, a security or interest in a security for value. *Offer* or *offer to sell* includes every attempt or offer to dispose of, or solicitation of an offer to buy, a security or interest in a security for value.

[3] Value Requirement

While the term *value* is not defined in the Securities Act, it apparently was not intended to be distinguished from the term *consideration.* According to the General Counsel of the SEC, value includes not only ordinary forms of consideration such as the transfer of cash or property, but also the waiver or surrender of a right or claim. For example, the consent of holders of outstanding bonds to an extension of the maturity date constitutes *value,* and the delivery of certificates stamped to indicate such extension is a *sale.* Likewise, a loan of money in consideration of the borrower's promise not only to repay the loan at a specific time, but also to give the lender a specified number of shares, was considered to be *value,* with the agreement representing the sale of a security. On the other hand, a bona fide gift of a security does not normally involve an offer or sale.

[E] Underwriters

[1] In General

Section 2(a)(11) of the Securities Act defines *underwriter* to include, among others, any person who

- Purchases a security from an issuer with a view to distribution,
- Offers or sells a security for an issuer in a distribution, and
- Participates in a distribution by an issuer.

Expressly excluded from the definition is any person whose interest is limited to a commission from an underwriter or dealer not in excess of the usual and customary commission. The term *issuer,* within the meaning of the definition of *underwriter,* includes, in addition to an issuer, any control persons of the issuer.

Clearly, the definition in Section 2(a)(11) includes the traditional underwritten offerings in which investment banking firms purchase securities from the issuer and resell them in the open market at a higher price. Because Section 2(a)(11) includes control persons in the definition of *issuer,* as well as *any* person who purchases a security from an issuer or a control person with a view toward selling the security in the public market, underwriter status can attach to persons who are not engaged in the underwriting business. It even picks up persons who might purchase securities from an issuer in one of the private financing transactions commonly used to raise funds for developing enterprises.

If a person is an underwriter of securities, that person's ability to resell securities without registration will be significantly restricted. For instance, Section 4(1) of the Securities Act is the primary exemption for transactions in securities not involving an issuer (i.e., transactions involving outstanding securities). It is not available for any person deemed to be an underwriter. Accordingly, any subsequent resale of such securities must either be registered under the Securities Act or be conducted in a manner that complies with various rules established by the SEC (primarily Rule 144) to ensure that the seller is not an underwriter.

§ 4.06 ROLE OF SECURITIES LAWS IN BASIC BUSINESS TRANSACTIONS

[A] Introduction

While the statutory and judicial definitions of *security* and *offer* and *sale* can seem quite complex to managers and nonsecurities lawyers, it is important to remember that the securities laws can be applied to a number of basic business transactions quite dissimilar from the routine issuance of corporate stock in exchange for cash. In each case, an analysis must be made as to whether a *security* is involved and, if so, whether the transaction involves either an "investment decision" or an exchange for "value."

[B] Corporate Stock, Rights, and Agreements

Conventional financing activities through the issuance of stock, bonds, debentures, warrants, options, or similar rights often involve securities subject to regulation under both federal and state securities laws. Moreover, an agreement to purchase shares in the future, whether for cash or in exchange for property or services, may itself be a security, as are any agreements or subscriptions for stock entered into before incorporation.

[C] Contacts with Prospective Purchasers

The Securities Act expressly provides that "offer to sell," "offer for sale," or "offer," includes every solicitation of an offer to buy. Newspaper advertisements offering securities to the general public are "offers to sell," as are press releases describing an offering now being made or to be made in the future. Also, any preliminary negotiations regarding a future sale of securities may come within the scope of the securities laws, except when the discussions are with prospective underwriters for a contemplated public offering.

[D] Subscription Agreements

Courts have held that the opportunity to subscribe to a future stock issue is an offer to sell the underlying stock. The subscription contract has been found to be a contract to buy or sell securities. In addition, the issuance of a subscription option, under which a party is granted an option to purchase stock, is an offer to sell. Moreover, under most blue-sky laws, a subscription to purchase stock normally involves a sale, whether or not the corporation whose stock is to be issued has been formed at the time of the subscription. Examples of a subscription agreement and related forms are included in Appendices G–K.

[E] Rights to Acquire or Convert Securities in the Future

[1] In General

A corporation or a controlling shareholder will often provide investors and other parties with the right to acquire a security in the future. These rights include warrants and options, which permit the holder to purchase a security at the price and on terms in the warrant or option. In addition, a party may be given the contractual right to subscribe for securities that might be issued in the future. Finally, a security holder may have the right to convert the security into another security, either as a matter of contract or under the terms in the security or articles of incorporation.

[2] Warrants and Options

As a general rule, transferable warrants and options to purchase stock are securities. However, when warrants or options are issued without consideration or in conjunction with the sale of some other security, there is no sale for purposes of the Securities Act unless the warrant or option is immediately exercisable. If it is immediately exercisable, the issuer will be deemed to have made an offer to sell the underlying security. On the other hand, under many blue-sky laws, the warrant or option would be a sale regardless of whether it was exercisable at the time of grant.

[3] Future Conversion and Subscription Rights

Under Section 2(a)(3) of the Securities Act, the issue or transfer of a right to subscribe to, or convert a security into, another security is not an offer or sale if the right cannot be exercised until some future date. However, the issue or transfer of such subscribed or converted security is deemed a sale. The offer or sale of a security that gives the holder a present right to convert into another security is regarded as an offer under the Uniform Act.

[F] Declaration of Stock Dividends

Declaration of a stock dividend is not regarded as a sale under the Securities Act, even where stockholders are offered an alternative of stock or cash dividends, since nothing has been disposed of for value. Where there is an already-declared cash dividend in which the shareholders, through operation of general corporation law, have vested rights and the corporation grants the stockholders the right to waive such vested rights and receive stock dividends instead, the issuance of the securities might constitute a sale.

[G] Fundamental Corporate Changes

[1] In General

The securities laws may apply to a variety of fundamental corporate changes, including alterations in existing shareholder rights, preferences, and privileges by amendment to the charter documents and the exchange of securities in specified statutory mergers, combinations, and reorganizations.

[2] Alterations in Securities Holders' Rights

An exchange of one class of securities for another class of securities of the same issuer involves a sale of a security. Such an exchange, however, is often exempt from the registration provisions under Section 3(a)(9) of the Securities Act. In those cases where no actual exchange occurs, but the various rights, preferences, and privileges of an outstanding class of securities are being modified, there may be a sale if the modification is material. This depends on whether the security holder has been asked to give up something for value and whether or not each security holder had a separate right to approve the proposed modification.

[3] Mergers and Related Transactions

The SEC long took the position that no sale of securities was involved in any statutory merger, consolidation, or reclassification. However, Rule 145 under the Securities Act now expressly provides that an offer, offer to sell, offer for sale, or sale is involved if an agreement or plan for a reclassification, merger, consolidation, or transfer of assets is submitted for the vote or consent of security holders.

[H] Delivery of Promissory Notes

Although both the Securities Act and the Exchange Act define *security* to include "any note," courts have rejected a literal construction of the securities laws and have examined the context of the transaction to determine if a particular note is a security. Historically, a majority of the circuit courts of appeals concluded that when a note was issued in a normal commercial transaction, such as an ordinary, short-term bank loan, it was not a security. However, if a note is issued to a person making an investment, it will normally be considered a security.

[I] Creation of Partnership Interests

Although every partnership interest, including a general partnership interest, is a "certificate of interest or participation in" a plan to share profits, the federal courts have generally applied an investment contract analysis to determine whether a partnership interest is a security. The interest of a general partner who is actively engaged in the management of the partnership business is not a security, nor is the interest of a general partner who does not participate in management but has the right to do so. However, if the general partner is precluded from participating in management, the general partnership interest may be a security. The interest of a limited partner will almost always be a security, because limited partners are by definition not permitted to participate in management and therefore must rely solely on the efforts of others.

[J] Interests in Pension and Employee Benefit Plans

Employee retirement plans that are compulsory and noncontributory are not securities, since there is no actual investment of the employee's money and no expectation of profits from the pension fund. On the other hand, an interest in a voluntary, contributory plan may be a security, because the contributor is investing in a common enterprise with the expectation that profits will be derived from the efforts of others. However, a voluntary, contributory pension plan is not a security if most of the employee's return was dependent on employer contributions rather than investment return on the employee's contributions. Also, an employee's interest in a contributory, mandatory-participation state public employees' plan is not a security if the employee's return is based upon a statutory formula, since the employee has no expectation of any profit on the interest.

[K] Franchises and Distributorships

If a franchisee controls the management of the franchise and offers a product or service to the public, no security is involved. This is the rule even if the franchisor imposes strict standards of operation and provides collateral services to the franchisee. However, a franchise may be a security if the franchisee is not actively involved in managing the franchise or if the franchise fee is risk capital.

[L] Membership Organizations

Memberships in various business cooperatives that provide common services to members, including rebates related to volume purchases, are not usually classified as securities, even if the interest in the cooperative is in the form of stock. The reason is that the member does not receive a return in the form of profits. Also, membership in a private club will not generally be a security if the membership is nontransferable or if it is transferable only at cost and the member has no expectation of receiving a profit from the enterprise.

[M] Pledges of Securities

Generally, the mere pledge of securities does not constitute a sale for purposes of the securities laws, nor does the subsequent release of the securities from collateral upon payment of the obligation. However, when the pledged securities are to be sold upon foreclosure, the transaction will be subject to the registration requirements. Thus, a public foreclosure sale may require registration to the extent that the pledgee is then deemed to be a statutory underwriter.

The Bad News Bears: Dealing with Investors After the Closing, Even When Things Go Bad

ORION CAPITAL

by Dale E. Allison

I have been involved in many start-ups over the past 20 years. While I have made a lot of money for people during that time, I have learned many things about dealing with investors when things are not going well.

Lesson One: You can never walk away. If you have attracted investors, even though you stop being involved in the company's business, the investors will always look to you when things go bad. This applies whether you acted only as a broker attracting the money or were also involved in the management.

I was recently involved in a company that started out quite well. The investors that I attracted were pleased with the early results. Although I had expressed some concern about the CFO's level of expertise, the CEO and founder reassured me that he had sufficient financial background (having been a CFO) to monitor the CFO. Unfortunately, he was wrong.

Long after I ceased my day-to-day involvement with the company, the CFO made a number of decisions that resulted in tremendous losses for the company. When the dust settled, the investors that I brought in lost most of their money.

Soon afterward, the phone calls started. Some of those who lost money started to complain about their losses. A few continue to do so.

Lesson Two: Even if you deal with educated and sophisticated investors, they will still complain if things go bad. Unfortunately, there is no direct relation between the education and sophistication of investors and their acceptance of the ups and downs of investments. In fact, the relation may be inverse.

Educated and sophisticated investors believe they are sufficiently intelligent and sophisticated so that all their investment decisions will be correct. They do not expect any of their investments to lose money.

If one of their investments goes bad, they are more likely to look for other causes, rather than believe they made a mistake in making the investment. For having brought them into the deal, you are a prime target for their finger pointing. In my experience, the investors who are most sophisticated but do not have a close relation with you are the most likely to object.

Lesson Three: Be careful of bringing friends into your deals. They are usually the easiest sources to attract money. Most start-ups begin with money from family and friends. The downside, however, is that if things go bad, these are the people you are most likely to bump into at social events. Such meetings can be quite uncomfortable and embarrassing. Fortunately, their reaction to losses may not be as strong as that of sophisticated investors with no relation to you.

Lesson Four: You will hear about bad news late but often. I usually do not hear from investors that I bring into deals while deals are going well. I will hear from them when deals go bad. This is compounded when the company has not kept investors informed of developments as they begin to go bad and investors suddenly hear bad news.

Recommendations

I have learned a number of lessons from this most recent experience. Let me share them with you:

1. When you withdraw from a company as a founder, send a letter to the investors you brought in advising them of your departure. Let them know you are done with it. Be diplomatic, but let them know you cannot be responsible for the future performance of the company. Review the draft with the company and your attorney, but get the message out there.

The same thing applies if you acted as a broker and will not be involved with the company after the closing. Again be diplomatic and review the wording with the company and your attorney, but thank the investors for the investment, wish them the best, and point out you are not involved in the ongoing management.

The letters probably won't help that much, but if an investor gets nasty, you can pull out the letter and remind him of your warning. At least you will feel better. Nothing is likely to quiet the disappointed investor.

2. The more sophisticated the investor, the more you must point out to them the obvious. Some investments win and some lose. The difference may be beyond your control or the company's control. Consider having them, and possibly all investors, initial the section of the investment offering documents covering these risks.
3. If you do have to bring in money from family and friends, have a heart-to-heart conversation with them before taking their money. Tell them the deal is a risk and they may lose their investment. As with sophisticated investors, point out to them the wording in the offering documents emphasizing this point. Have them initial the section. If you don't have such a document, at least send them a letter pointing out these facts.
4. Keep investors informed of the bad as well as the good. Investors are more likely to be upset if they feel everything is going well and suddenly find out otherwise. It is easier for them to accept the problems when they have been kept informed. The same rule applies to bankers, suppliers, and customers.

This is more difficult when you are no longer involved in the management of the company. At a minimum, if you hear of problems, let the investors you brought in know about them.

CHAPTER 5 • DISCLOSURES

Due Diligence: The Searchers

CHAPTER 5

§ 5.01 INTRODUCTION

One of the cornerstones of the federal securities laws is full disclosure to the investment community of all material facts relevant to the issuer and the offering or transaction. Disclosure is required in each registration statement filed under the Securities Act, as well as in periodic reports filed under the Exchange Act. Even when the transaction is exempt from registration under the Securities Act, antifraud requirements may make it necessary to prepare a disclosure document containing information similar to what is required for registered offerings.

§ 5.02 INTEGRATED DISCLOSURE UNDER FEDERAL SECURITIES LAWS

[A] Overview

In 1982, the SEC adopted a program of integrated disclosure. It was intended to reduce burdens on companies while at the same time ensuring that security holders, investors, and other participants had access to meaningful and timely information for their decisions. The SEC wanted to eliminate the substantial overlap that existed between the information required under the transaction-oriented framework of the Securities Act and the status-oriented framework of the Exchange Act. It did so by standardizing many of the disclosures on the registration forms, periodic reports, and other documents.

The desired standardization of information is accomplished by

- Setting out all nonfinancial disclosure items required in the integrated disclosure system in one place—either Regulation S-K or, in the case of small business issuers, Regulation S-B;
- Setting forth in Regulation S-X substantially all of the accounting statement requirements for documents to be filed under the federal statutes;

- Providing for uniform financial statements; and
- Reducing the burden of potentially duplicative filings by authorizing incorporation by reference of previously filed information.

[B] Forms and Documents Used in the Disclosure System

[1] In General

The forms and documents used in the integrated disclosure system include the following:

- Securities Act registration forms,
- Exchange Act registration forms,
- Exchange Act reporting forms,
- Annual shareholder reports by companies registered under the Exchange Act, and
- Proxy statement materials generally required for shareholder meetings of reporting companies.

[2] Securities Act Registration Forms

The main Securities Act registration forms are as follows:

Form S-1 Form S-1 is the general registration form for primary offerings. Incorporation by reference of information contained in previously filed documents is not permitted.

Form S-2 Form S-2 is available to issuers that have been reporting companies for at least three years *and* have timely filed all reports during the past 12 calendar months. Form S-2 is not available for exchange offers or to issuers that have recently defaulted in their obligations to make dividend payments or sinking fund payments on preferred stock. If available, Form S-2 registration permits extensive incorporation by reference, generally from the issuer's annual report to shareholders. It will be necessary, however, for the issuer to disclose certain information relating to the terms of the specific offering.

Form S-3 This form can be used by issuers meeting registrant requirements for transactions defined in the Transaction Requirements under the Form. The registrant requirements are essentially identical to those applying to Form S-2. An exception is that the period during which the issuer must have been subject to the reporting requirements is reduced from three years to one year. The transaction requirements for primary and secondary offerings for cash will be satisfied if the aggregate market value of the voting stock held by unaffiliated shareholders equals or exceeds $75 million. Form S-3 relies almost exclusively on incorporation by reference to the issuer's Exchange Act reports. It is usually considered the simplest method of registering under the Securities Act.

Form SB-2 Form SB-2 is available to any small business issuer (SBI). An *SBI* is defined as an entity that (1) had revenues of less than $25 million during its last fiscal year, (2) is a domestic or Canadian issuer, (3) is not an investment company, and (4) has an aggregate public float (i.e., the aggregate market value of its outstanding securities held by nonaffiliates) of less than $25 million. Form SB-2 may be used by reporting and nonreporting issuers alike. SBIs may register an unlimited amount of securities on Form SB-2. Form SB-2 may be used for both primary and secondary distributions of a security to be sold for cash.

Other Securities Act Registration Forms In certain instances, issuers may utilize other forms to register securities. For example, Form S-4 is available for the registration of securities issued in business combinations, including mergers and exchange offers for securities of an issuer. Form S-8 can be used to register securities offered to employees under an employee benefit plan. Form SB-1 can be used by certain SBIs to register up to $10 million of securities to be sold for cash. In such a case, the SBI must not have registered more than $10 million in securities offerings, including the transaction being registered, in any continuous 12-month period.

[3] Exchange Act Registration Forms

Form 10 is the basic form for registration under the Exchange Act and calls for extensive disclosure on an item-by-item basis. If the registrant has previously registered its securities under the Securities Act, Form 8-A can be used. That form is fairly simple and relies largely on information included in Securities Act filings. SBIs may register securities under the Exchange Act by filing Form 10-SB, which allows the registrant to choose among three disclosure formats. Two of them track disclosures made in a Regulation A offering. The other sets out items in Regulation S-B that must be addressed.

[4] Exchange Act Reporting Forms

Within 90 days of the end of each fiscal year, reporting companies must file their annual report with the SEC. Form 10-K must be used, which requires extensive disclosures about the financial condition, business, and properties of the issuer. The quarterly report on Form 10-Q must be filed within 45 days after the end of each of the first three fiscal quarters. It includes uncertified financial statements for the quarter and year-to-date presented on a comparative basis with corresponding periods of the prior fiscal year. Finally, current reports regarding material corporate developments must be filed with the SEC on Form 8-K, which enables the investor to receive the information before a 10-K or 10Q would be due. The nature of the event determines when an 8-K would be due (generally 5 business days or 15 calendar days after the event being reported).

SBIs making Regulation S-B disclosures can file on Form 10-KSB (an annual report for SBIs analogous to Form 10-K) and on Form 10-QSB (a quarterly reporting form corresponding to Form 10-Q). For an SBI entitled to use the abbreviated report forms, items under Form 10-KSB and Form 10-QSB are identical to those in Forms 10-K and 10-Q. However, the relevant items in the abbreviated forms are referenced to the simplified requirements of Regulation S-B rather than to Regulation S-K.

[5] Annual Report to Shareholders

Companies with a class of securities registered under the Exchange Act must distribute an annual report prior to annual shareholder meetings at which directors are elected. This annual report must contain standard financial statements and other basic information. Otherwise, it is largely an unstructured document and up to the company to determine what should be disclosed. The SEC has amended the annual-report-to-shareholder requirements for SBIs to permit the use of information prepared within the SBI disclosure system.

[6] Proxy Statement Materials

Companies with a class of equity securities registered under the Exchange Act must also give shareholders proxy statements when soliciting proxies for shareholder meetings. Copies must be filed with the SEC. The content of the proxy statement must comply with the requirements of Schedule 14A adopted by the SEC under Section 14(a) of the Exchange Act. As with the annual-report-to-shareholder requirements, the SEC has amended the proxy rules for SBIs to permit the use of information prepared within the SBI disclosure system.

[7] Disclosures in Nonregistered Transactions

As noted above, an issuer engaged in a financing transaction otherwise exempt from the registration requirements of the Securities Act may still be required to provide disclosure documents to prospective investors. For example, offerings made to nonaccredited investors under certain rules of Regulation D may require delivery of information in accordance with Securities Act registration forms. In such cases, the manner of presentation will vary substantially and no real standard exists because the SEC does not review disclosure documents in exempt transactions. However, it is generally prudent for an issuer to adhere to the disclosure requirements of the integrated system. In particular, a reporting company involved in a private placement can usually satisfy its disclosure obligations by providing copies of its Exchange Act reports, supplemented by additional information on the specific transaction.

[C] Regulation S-K

[1] In General

Regulation S-K sets forth the "Standard Instructions for Filing Forms Under Securities Act of 1933, Securities Exchange Act of 1934, and Energy Policy and Conservation Act of 1975." It is the core of the informational requirements of the integrated disclosure system. The contents of Regulation S-K can be broken down as follows:

- Securities Act standard items covering disclosures about the offering and future obligations;
- Items designed to ensure that the business and properties of the issuer have been fully described, including any material legal proceedings;
- Description of the securities being offered, as well as any other outstanding securities;
- Financial information;
- Information regarding management of the issuer, and significant security holders; and
- Exhibits and other items.

[2] Securities Act Standard Items

Items 501 through 510 of Regulation S-K are common to Securities Act registrations on Forms S-1, S-2, and S-3. These standard items include the following:

- A summary section and a discussion of any risk factors associated with the registrant and/or the offering itself;
- A statement of the anticipated use of proceeds;
- A description of the dilution to the shareholders;
- A brief description of the securities being offered and the methods used to determine the offering price;
- A computation of the ratio of earnings to fixed charges in debt offerings;
- A description of the plan of distribution;
- Information pertaining to any selling security holders;
- Disclosures of any interest in the issuer by named experts and counsel; and
- In certain limited situations, statements relating to indemnification of directors and officers.

[3] Description of Business, Properties, and Legal Proceedings

Items 101 through 103 of Regulation S-K require a full description of the issuer's business, properties, and legal proceedings. As noted below, the description of an issuer's business is extremely broad. It covers products and services, customer base, research and development activities, manufacturing and sales functions, and material competitive factors.

[4] Description of Securities

Under Item 202 of Regulation S-K, each issuer must describe the securities being offered, as well as any other outstanding securities. In addition, Item 201 of Regulation S-K requires the disclosure of information regarding the market for, and dividends on, common equity of the issuer. In the case of a first-time issuer (i.e., an initial public offering), such disclosure is typically limited to a statement that no public market has previously existed for the offered securities. It will also include a description of the issuer's past and expected future policies on dividends.

[5] Financial Information

Items 301 through 304 of Regulation S-K set out the basic requirements for the disclosure of financial information. Issuers must provide standardized financial statements and comparative selected financial information for the last five fiscal years (or the life of the issuer or its predecessors, if less) and any additional fiscal years necessary to keep the information from being misleading. They must allow the reader to compare key financial indicators such as net sales, gross profit, and net income or loss. The required information becomes the basis for the Management's Discussion and Analysis (MD&A) of financial condition and results of operations that must be prepared under Item 303 of Regulation S-K. In addition, the issuer must provide information relating to any change in accountants during the last two fiscal years resulting from a disagreement on accounting and financial disclosure.

[6] Management and Certain Security Holders

Items 401 through 404 of Regulation S-K require certain information about management of the issuer (e.g., its directors and officers), transactions between the issuer and its managers, executive compensation, and information regarding the ownership of management and major security holders.

[7] Exhibits

Item 601 of Regulation S-K lists exhibits that must be filed with the registration statement. These exhibits are available for review by the public, including members of the investment community and competitors. One of the requirements is disclosure of each material contract or agreement relating to the issuer's business or the terms of the offering. The documents disclosed under these requirements supplement the requirements of Item 101 of Regulation S-K.

[8] Miscellaneous Items

Depending on the circumstances, additional disclosures must be included in the registration statement but not in the prospectus. For example, first-time registrants must provide information on all securities issued in nonregistered transactions within the prior three years. All registrants must include information relating to the expenses of the offering. Various disclosures and undertakings will be required if statutes, charter provisions, bylaws, or contracts insure or indemnify officers or directors against liabilities associated with the offering.

[D] Regulation S-X

Regulation S-X sets the form and content requirements of

- Financial statements filed with the SEC under the Securities Act,
- Proxy and information statements filed under Section 14 of the Exchange Act,
- Registration statements filed under Section 12 of the Exchange Act, and
- Annual and quarterly reports filed under the Exchange Act.

Regulation S-X requirements are in addition to, and not instead of, generally accepted accounting principles. They are supplemented by requirements in Regulation S-K, as well as in the SEC's Financial Reporting Releases, Accounting and Auditing Enforcement Releases, and Staff Accounting Bulletins. These releases and bulletins contain SEC opinions and policies on accounting questions, administrative interpretations, and financial statements.

[E] Organization of Disclosure Information

The organization of disclosure items in Regulation S-K is designed to facilitate compliance with each securities form and report. In general, the integrated disclosure system works through the following:

- The basic information package, or BIP, is included in all Securities Act registration forms and many Exchange Act reports;
- In-depth disclosure items relating to the issuer's business, properties, management, and security holders are included in some form in all of the Securities Act registration forms and in Forms 10 and 10-K;
- Securities Act standard items are included;
- Each form and report has its own exhibit requirements; and
- Other disclosures may be required depending upon the filing.

The BIP includes all business and financial information that the SEC considers important to the investment community. Among the items included in the BIP are the following:

- Financial information required by Items 301 through 304 of Regulation S-K, including the MD&A;
- Brief description of the issuer's business and certain information by industry sector;
- Various market and dividend information; and
- For certain issuers, supplementary financial information.

The in-depth disclosures build on the BIP by providing a full description of the issuer's business, properties, and legal proceedings, as well as detailed information regarding management and significant security holders.

[F] Regulation S-B

In 1992, the SEC adopted a series of small business initiatives to facilitate the raising of capital by small businesses and to reduce the costs of compliance with the federal securities laws. One of the most important developments was the creation of a simplified integrated disclosure system for SBIs through the promulgation of new Regulation S-B. This regulation is the counterpart to Regulation S-K. It uses a series of registration forms under the Securities Act, particularly Forms SB-1 and SB-2. The SB forms incorporate the disclosure requirements of Regulation S-B in the same way that the forms used in the general integrated disclosure system incorporate Regulation S-K.

The disclosure standards in Regulation S-B generally follow those of Regulation S-K. These regulations use identical item numbers (e.g., Item 402 under both Regulations S-K and S-B relates to executive compensation). However, there are a limited number of Regulation S-K items, such as Items 301 and 302, that relate to selected and supplemental financial information and that do not appear in Regulation S-B. Moreover, in certain areas, there are differences between the disclosures required by Regulation S-B and the counterpart items in Regulation S-K. These differences include the description of the issuer's business and properties, market and dividend information, description of securities, and the MD&A.

Regulation S-B adopts and continues the significantly less stringent financial reporting requirements of former Form S-18, which was replaced by new Form SB-2. As noted above, Regulation S-B does not include any counterpart to Regulation S-K Items 301 and 302. Instead, Item 310 of Regulation S-B sets out, in narrative form without reference to Regulation S-X, the financial statement requirements that must be satisfied by SBIs. The financial statements of SBIs using Regulation S-B must be prepared in accordance with generally accepted accounting principles. These statements do not, however, have to conform to the requirements of Regulation S-X, except for the accountant's report and independence.

[G] Duty of Full Disclosure

The SEC also requires that disclosure be full and fair. In October 2000, Regulation FD (for "fair disclosure") barring selective disclosure became effective.

§ 5.03 PREPARATION OF REQUIRED NONFINANCIAL DISCLOSURES

[A] Overview

Preparing nonfinancial disclosures in any registration statement or report requires a full understanding of the business activities and corporate structure of an issuer. As a result, a good deal of attention must be paid to the due diligence process of collecting the necessary information. Thereafter, an issuer must prepare a description of its business, the risk factors associated with it, the offering, management compensation, and other disclosure items.

[B] Description of the Issuer's Business

[1] In General

The most important nonfinancial element of disclosure in any of the documents filed within the integrated disclosure system is the detailed description of the issuer's business. Obviously, the issuer must meet the disclosure requirements in the registration and report forms and in Regulations S-K or S-B. The company must communicate to the investment community a clear statement of its business strategy. This statement should include a recognition of the issuer's strategic advantages, the needs of its customer base, and the basis on which other companies compete with the issuer.

[2] Introductory Paragraph

The first paragraph in the business description should briefly describe the activities of the issuer and the major industry segments in which the issuer competes or proposes to compete in the future. Reference should be made to current products and services, delivery methods, and plans for future development and expansion. If possible, reference should be made to the issuer's own particular strategic advantage with respect to the manufacture and distribution of its products. Finally, any significant financial milestones should also be mentioned, such as a material increase in dollar or unit sales.

[3] Industry Overview

It is important to provide the prospective investor with the issuer's own sense of its industry, historical evolution, perceived future trends, and the role the issuer is expected to play. Accordingly, the issuer should provide a general overview of its industry segments and the business, commercial, and social problems that the industry and the issuer are addressing. For example, a health care company might describe the breadth and severity of the particular health problems that its products will address. Also, with respect to each market problem, reference should be made to the various solutions that have been offered by existing products and services.

If necessary, significant industry definitions and classifications should be introduced to the reader at this point. The reader should be given a sense of the industry and its technology, the needs and demands of customers, pricing and costing characteristics, future trends regarding the overall size of the industry, and any changes in the markets and applications for the issuer's products and technology. Finally, even though it may otherwise be covered in the discussion of competition, it is important to describe the basis for competition. This should include the various factors (e.g., cost, manufacturing efficiencies, product reliability, technology, breadth of products, capacity, capital, distribution, or service) that the issuer believes may influence future competition.

[4] Products and Product Strategy

In this section, the issuer should clearly and concisely articulate its strategies regarding development of products and services. In particular, the issuer's disclosures should focus on material aspects of its products and services, including characteristics that distinguish the issuer's products and services, as well as a historical description of the development and introduction of its products and services. Also, reference should be made to the issuer's research and development projects, including how the issuer's products were developed or acquired.

Several different approaches can be used to describe product strategies. For example, one issuer may focus on new technologies, improvement of production efficiencies, cost reductions, quality enhancements, and creation of reliable documentation. This strategy focuses on the production process. Another issuer may focus on extending its existing product lines and developing new distribution channels through joint ventures, reciprocal development agreements, and other strategies. Other strategies might focus on enhancements to existing products, warranties, and service capabilities.

[5] Manufacturing and Production

Depending on its business, manufacturing and production can be important components of an issuer's ability to bring its products to market and fulfill customers' demands. This section should begin with an explanation of the manufacturing process and crucial components. In particular, attention should be paid to the following matters: facilities, testing, production, packaging, raw materials, and government regulations with respect to environmental and quality control matters. Also, research and development relating to manufacturing processes and technologies should be explained, as well as any dependence on vendors or suppliers.

If backlog is important in an issuer's industry and production processes, appropriate disclosures should be made. The amount of the backlog, and any significant customers included in the backlog, should be discussed. Any plans to correct the situation should also be covered. If the backlog may not be representative of actual sales for any succeeding period due to customer changes in delivery schedules or cancellations, disclosure should be made of scheduling and booking practices within the industry. In many cases, the rate of new order bookings varies from month to month. The release of shipping dates and quantities against purchase orders may also fluctuate over time. If they do fluctuate, they should be discussed.

[6] Marketing, Distribution, and Customers

An issuer's ability to identify markets and customers for its products, and to develop distribution channels for introducing those products, is the focus of this section. A typical introductory paragraph would include a listing of markets that the issuer has identified as targets, significant product and service characteristics, delivery manner to projected customers, appropriate uses of the issuer's products, and various applications of the issuer's products. Significant customer relationships should be identified, including all customers accounting for 10% or more of net product sales. Thereafter, reference should be made to the distribution channels, be they direct sales or indirect sales through original equipment manufacturers (OEMs), value-added resellers (VARs), and systems integrators.

Significant sales and distribution agreements should be discussed in detail, including the term of the agreement; any minimum quantity that must be purchased; the number of products purchased to date under the agreement; ordering procedures; any agreement with respect to scheduling; increasing or decreasing the amount of orders; charges for changes in delivery and product mix; and any agreement whereby the distributor could acquire the right to manufacture products. In the event that distributors have significant competition themselves, this should be discussed, as should any factors that might affect the distributor's own customer base or product strategies.

Finally, the issuer's own internal sales and marketing organization should be described, including the number of people in the sales force, the location and coverage of sales offices, trade show and print advertising strategies, service and technical support capabilities, and warranty terms and coverage. If the issuer is planning any significant modification in its marketing strategies, perhaps through the engagement of a third-party marketing partner, it should be discussed in this section.

[7] Competition

Disclosures regarding competition are covered by sections dealing with an issuer's external environment and nonproduct-related resources. Typically, the registrant should discuss the following:

1. The historical development of competition within the industry, including cyclical variations and pricing factors. The discussion should provide the reader with a sense of the environment in which the issuer must develop, produce, and distribute its products or services.
2. The identity of specific competitors, as well as the basis on which they compete with the issuer. Competition may come from specialized firms, as well as from divisions of larger companies.
3. Future competitors and the resources they will bring to the marketplace.
4. The principal elements of competition, including price, performance, product quality, reliability, financial stability, adherence to standards, marketing, distribution, technical resources, production capacity, manufacturing efficiencies, and production yields.
5. How effectively the issuer is able to compete in the above areas and any plan to improve the issuer's performance. Any competitive disadvantage

due to lack of breadth in the issuer's product line or otherwise should also be explained.

6. The nature of significant changes in the competitive environment anticipated in the future, and any plans for remaining competitive. These might include additional plans to lower manufacturing costs, introduce new products, and improve production yields.

The issuer should consider including within the competition discussion appropriate cross-references to risk factors.

[8] Government Regulation

The development, testing, and marketing of an issuer's products may be subject to regulation by a variety of federal, state, local, and foreign agencies. Such agencies (including the Food and Drug Administration and the U.S. Department of Health and Human Services in the case of pharmaceutical and biotechnology companies) regulate product introduction, advertising, manufacturing, labeling, distribution, and recordkeeping activities and practices of industry participants. Typically, before a pharmaceutical and biotech product can be marketed, it must go through a number of stages of preclinical studies and testing. The issuer should describe the stages of premarketing development and identify where each of the issuer's current and developing products stands in the process. An attempt should also be made to describe the issuer's views on how the regulatory process will evolve over time and the effect that any transition might have on the issuer.

[9] Intellectual Property

The competition section should indicate whether patents, trademarks, copyrights, or trade secrets are important in the issuer's industry. If they are, the issuer should discuss its own intellectual property position, including significant patent rights, as well as the relative strengths and weaknesses of competitors. If the issuer has any material licensing arrangements, they should be fully described, including the scope of the licensed rights (i.e., products, territory, and exclusivity) and the financial terms of the license, such as royalty rate and any other payment obligations. The issuer should include not only a description of the license agreement under which it has been granted a license by others, but also any arrangement that permits third parties to use the issuer's technology.

[10] Research and Development

Research and development activities may have been discussed in the context of the issuer's future products. Disclosures under research and development (or future products) should cover the following:

1. The amount, rate, and scope of technological change that has occurred within the industry in the past, and the direction of emerging technology the issuer believes will dominate competition in the future;
2. The issuer's principal research and development activities, and the type of product development efforts undertaken in the past;
3. Research and development activities devoted to improving the issuer's process technology;
4. Research and development activities to enhance existing products and develop new ones; and
5. The amount of research and development expenses, and any independently financed research and development contracts, including partnerships.

[11] Properties and Facilities

As noted above, disclosures regarding an issuer's properties and facilities are specifically required under Regulation S-K. Typical descriptions will include the issuer's principal business and manufacturing facilities, amount of square footage and degree of utilization, and plans for future expansion, and will state whether or not such facilities are properly maintained and adequate for their purposes. Significant lease arrangements should also be included.

[12] Human Resources

The issuer's human resources may have already been discussed in the context of competition, intellectual property, and research and development. Basic disclosure will describe the number of employees. It will also include a breakdown of the number of employees in marketing and sales, research and development, engineering, manufacturing, production and facilities support, and general management (including finance and administration). Any plans for hiring additional personnel in specific areas should be disclosed, particularly as they relate to strategic plans. Significant factors relating to the recruitment and retention of key personnel should also be included.

[C] Risk Factors

[1] In General

A discussion of risk factors is often included in prospectuses used in primary security offerings. Many issuers include risk factors in their Exchange Act reports, although the referenced items will necessarily exclude matters particular to a securities offering (e.g., dilution).

[2] Financial Risks

Typical risks covered under this topic include a new issuer's limited operating history, a prior record of operating losses, and recent adverse trends in sales, earnings, margins, and backlog. In such cases, the prospectus should discuss whether or not the issuer's historical financial results are relevant to its future prospects. Moreover, as discussed below in the context of preparing the MD&A, risks associated with the issuer's future liquidity and ability to meet its debt obligations should also be described. Similar disclosure should be made about the effect of any debt covenants on the issuer's future operations and flexibility. The issuer should also describe its ability to obtain funds necessary to complete required projects.

[3] Product Development Risks

An issuer may not yet have a track record of commercially accepted products and services. Accordingly, an effort should be made to identify any market and/or product development uncertainties, such as the time period and costs required to achieve commercial success. For example, are the needs of the marketplace sufficiently defined to ensure acceptance of the issuer's new products? Alternatively, does the issuer's success depend on its ability to develop or acquire new products in the future? If the issuer has already developed one product, can that product support the issuer until new and additional products are developed?

[4] Technological Risks

Technological uncertainties can affect an issuer's ability to complete its product development efforts on a timely basis. They can also prevent an issuer from

- Achieving and maintaining an advantage based on its research activities, or
- Obtaining legal protection of its technology and intellectual property rights.

Moreover, research can often prove to be very costly, particularly in industries subject to significant government regulations and approvals.

[5] Production and Distribution Risks

A significant risk associated with the distribution of an issuer's products is its reliance on one or more customers. The loss of a major customer may have a material adverse effect on an issuer's financial situation as well as its overall image and perception in the marketplace. Also, as noted above, an issuer may be dependent on one or more key suppliers, licensers, researchers, or distributors. Therefore, consequences of any disruption or termination of those relationships should be addressed. Finally, to the extent that the issuer is involved in foreign distribution activities, any particular risks associated with activities in those markets should be discussed.

[6] Regulatory Risks

Is the issuer subject to regulatory risks that could affect its products, marketing efforts, pricing strategies, service routes or areas, and the timing of product introduction? Antitrust considerations are important where the issuer is expected to be a dominant firm in a definable market area. They may also be important if the issuer wishes to conduct cooperative research and development activities. For issuers in the health care and biotech industries, regulatory approvals necessary to commence testing and distribution are of great importance. As noted above, an effort should be made to explain relevant regulatory procedures in the business section of the prospectus.

[7] Competitive Risks

Competitive uncertainties are of tremendous importance in analyzing the prospectuses. The issuer should candidly assess whether or not it lacks one or more significant production functions or support services to compete effectively in the marketplace. A similar analysis should be made for factors affecting the issuer's ability to realize the expected breadth and volume distribution of its products. Moreover, it is no longer sufficient for the issuer to merely take note of the uncertainties with respect to competition from larger firms. Instead, the issuer should carefully analyze the direction from which competition might come and any plans that it has to establish a countervailing advantage.

[8] Management and Employee Risks

A number of key risks and uncertainties are associated with

- The issuer's dependence on one or more key managers and employees;
- The issuer's ability to recruit and retain qualified employees; and
- The operational experience of current management to lead a growing company in the issuer's industry. This risk factor tends to be included without careful thought about the issuer's own recruiting plans. An attempt should be made to explain the issuer's future plans with regard to available cash and equity compensation for new employees, including the effect of future financing and expansion efforts.

[9] Litigation Risks

For any issuer involved in technology-driven activities, actual or threatened litigation over material elements of its technology portfolio or intellectual property rights can be disastrous. It can severely impair the viability of the proposed offering and significantly deplete the issuer's financial assets. For example, competitors may assert that an issuer infringes on their technology or that the technology arose out of activities of current employees who had previously worked for the competitor.

[10] Environmental Risks

No risk factor section would be complete without an attempt to discern uncertainties that might arise out of general social, political, and economic conditions. This is consistent with the notion that an issuer should conduct an overall scanning of its competitive environment. For example, long-term trends in the nation's health care payment system might have a significant effect on the pricing structure for health care issuers. As another example, political uncertainties in foreign markets might adversely affect an issuer's ability to obtain reliable low-cost labor for its manufacturing activities. If these risks are known, whether or not they have been factored into overall business planning, they should be mentioned in the prospectus.

[D] Management, Certain Transactions, and Compensation

[1] In General

Other important factors that should be described are management, transactions between the issuer and its controlling persons, and the amount and type of executive compensation. This information should be a part of Securities Act registration statements, Exchange Act reports, and annual proxy materials.

[2] Management

Item 401 of Regulation S-K requires information about each executive officer and director of the issuer, including the following:

- Name and age,
- Position(s) held with the issuer,
- Term as an officer and/or director,
- Period of service,
- Description of business experience during the past five years,
- Any arrangement with another person (who must be named) under which such persons have been selected to act as an officer and/or director, and
- Any family relationships among officers and directors.

If the issuer is a nonreporting company, employees who are not executive officers, but are expected to make significant contributions to the business, should be identified. Information must be given about their backgrounds. If any director serves as a director of another reporting company, such service should be disclosed. Finally, information must be provided on legal proceedings relating to officers and/or directors.

[3] Certain Transactions

Item 404 of Regulation S-K requires disclosure of transactions and relationships between the issuer and affiliated persons, including the following:

1. Transactions (or a series of similar transactions) involving $60,000 or more between the issuer and any director, executive officer, director nominee, 5% beneficial owner of any class of voting stock, or any member of the immediate family of any of the foregoing persons.
2. For issuers organized within the last five years and filing a registration statement on Form S-1, disclosure must be made of prior or contemplated transactions between any promoter and the issuer. These disclosures include the nature of the transaction, the name of the promoter, the nature and amount of what was received by the promoter, the consideration received by the issuer, and the method (and by whom selected) used in valuing any asset acquired from the promoter. If transferred assets were acquired by the promoter within two years of their transfer to the issuer, the promoter's cost must be given.
3. Any debt in excess of $60,000 owed to the issuer during the fiscal year by any director, executive officer, director nominee, or any member of the immediate family of any of the foregoing. Disclosure must also be made of similar debt owed to the issuer by corporations, organizations, trusts, and estates in which any director, executive officer, or nominee is an executive officer, partner, beneficial owner of 10% or more of its securities, holder of a substantial beneficial interest, or serves as a trustee or in a similar capacity.

In addition, the issuer must disclose whether any existing or nominated director

1. Has been an executive officer or owner (beneficially or of record) in excess of 10% of a company
   a. To or from which the issuer or its subsidiaries sell or buy property or services above certain thresholds. The standards are receipt (in the case of sales) or the payment (in the case of purchases) in excess of 5% of (i) the registrant's consolidated gross revenues for its last full fiscal year or (ii) the other entity's consolidated gross revenues for its last full fiscal year; or
   b. To which the issuer or its subsidiaries were indebted at the end of the issuer's last full fiscal year in excess of 5% of the issuer's total consolidated assets; or
2. Has been during the last fiscal year a member of (or counsel to) a law firm, or a partner or executive officer of any investment banking firm, that has performed services for the issuer (other than as a participating underwriter in a syndicate in the case of a banking firm); or

3. Is involved in any other relationship substantially similar in nature and scope.

If an affirmative response is given to any of the these items, disclosure must be made of the names of such persons, the identity of the entity with which the relationship existed, the affiliations of such persons, the relationship between the issuer and the entity, and the amount of business done. In the case of relationships with law firms or investment bankers, disclosure of business done is required only if the amount is 5% or more of the firm's consolidated gross revenues for the last fiscal year.

[4] Executive Compensation

Item 402 of Regulation S-K requires a summary compensation table reflecting all compensation paid to the issuer's chief executive officer and the other four most highly compensated executive officers whose annual compensation exceeds $100,000. Disclosure is also required of total compensation paid to all executive officers as a group. Information must be presented in tabular format for each of the following categories: (1) salary, (2) bonus, (3) other annual compensation, (4) restricted stock awards, (5) accrued dividends on restricted stock, (6) long-term incentive payouts, (7) stock options, (8) stock appreciation rights, and (9) other compensation. "Other annual compensation" includes perquisites, annual contributions by the issuer to pension and other retirement plans, annual compensation under deferred compensation plans, and annual premiums on insurance-funded deferred compensation arrangements. "Other compensation" includes compensation that does not fit any of the other categories, such as termination or severance awards (i.e., golden parachutes) in excess of $100,000.

In addition to information in the compensation table, the issuer must deliver a report by the compensation committee of the board of directors indicating the factors relied on in setting the executive compensation. The report should cover the performance criteria used in setting the chief executive's compensation, including profitability, sales growth, return on shareholders' equity, and market share. The report must include a supplemental discussion of general compensation policies for other key executives.

The information in the compensation table and report can be placed in perspective by reference to a line graph comparing the issuer's stock price over the past five years to a broad stock market index, such as the Standard & Poor's 500, and to an industry or peer-group index chosen by the issuer. Issuers must also provide detailed information regarding executive stock options, including estimates of the value of any unexercised stock options or similar rights held by executives.

§ 5.04 PREPARATION OF REQUIRED FINANCIAL DISCLOSURES

[A] Introduction

Securities Act registration forms require substantial financial information on an issuer. For example, when Form S-1 (the basic Securities Act registration form) is used, the issuer must supply the following information:

- Financial statements meeting the requirements of Regulation S-X, as well as any financial information required by Rule 3-05 and Article 11 of Regulation S-X;
- Selected financial data required by Item 301 of Regulation S-K;
- Supplementary financial information required by Item 302 of Regulation S-K;
- MD&A discussion required by Item 303 of Regulation S-K;
- Disagreements with accountants, required by Item 304 of Regulation S-K; and
- Financial statement schedules required by Regulation S-X.

[B] Financial Statement Requirements

[1] In General

Article 3 of Regulation S-X requires that SEC filings contain consolidated balance sheets and consolidated statements of changes in financial position. However, Rule 3-13 provides that the SEC may, upon informal written request by an issuer, permit the omission of one or more required financial statements or the filing of comparable statements in substitution. The SEC may also require the filing of other financial statements in addition to, or instead of, statements required by Regulation S-X.

[2] Balance Sheet Requirements

Specifically, Rule 3-01 requires an issuer to file audited consolidated balance sheets for the two most recent fiscal years. If audited financial statements are not available, an issuer may file (within 45 days of the fiscal year's end) balance sheets (i) through the preceding third fiscal quarter and (ii) for the two preceding fiscal years. Under Rule 3-01(e), filings made more than 134 days after the end of the fiscal year must also include an interim balance sheet for the delayed period. The interim balance sheet may be unaudited and condensed.

[3] Statements of Income and Changes in Financial Position

Rule 3-02 requires that audited consolidated statements of income and changes in financial position be provided for the three preceding fiscal years. As in the case of balance sheets above, interim filings are required but can be unaudited and condensed.

[4] Additional Financial Statement Requirements

In addition to financial statements under Rules 3-01 and 3-02, it may be necessary for an issuer to provide additional financial statements for the following entities:

- Historical financial statements of a predecessor corporation (Rule 3-01);
- Historical financial statements of businesses acquired or to be acquired (Rule 3-05);
- Separate financial statements for unconsolidated subsidiaries, and 50% or less owned affiliates (Rule 3-09); and
- Financial statements of guarantors, and affiliates whose securities collateralize an issue registered or being registered (Rule 3-10).

[C] Management's Discussion and Analysis

Perhaps the most meaningful portion of the prospectus other than the financial statements is the MD&A. It includes a narrative discussion of such things as operations, liquidity, capital resources, and the impact of inflation. The MD&A brings the financial and nonfinancial portions of the registration statement together. According to the SEC,

> The management discussion gives the registrant an unusual opportunity to articulate its objectives and financial policies; to describe where it is headed and how it hopes to get there; and to establish and maintain credibility. Included in the management discussion should be factors about the particular

> business which management is in the best position to know. For each business, there is a limited set of critical variables which presents the pulse of the business.

While the instructions for preparation of the MD&A in Item 303 of Regulation S-K are somewhat self-explanatory, the following items should be considered and adequately explored:

- *Liquidity Analysis*—Liquidity is the ability of its issuer to generate sufficient cash or other working capital to fund its ongoing operations. The issuer should identify any trends, demands, commitments, events, or uncertainties either presently known or reasonably likely to have a material effect on its short-term and long-term liquidity.
- *Fixed Commitments*—Any discussion regarding liquidity should identify and describe known material fixed commitments for capital expenditures.
- *Expansion and Acquisitions*—Liquidity is also relevant to an issuer's ability to implement and complete future plans for debt repayment, capital expansion, acquisition, divestiture, and overall restructuring of credit arrangements and borrowings.
- *Segment Disclosures*—The issuer's financial performance and operations should be discussed in industry segments if appropriate.
- *Revenue and Sales Analysis*—The issuer should provide a narrative discussion of material increases in net sales or revenues, especially if attributable to increases in prices, increases in the volume or amount of goods or services being sold, or introduction of new products or services. Also, reference should be made to the impact of inflation and changing prices on the issuer's financial performance.
- *Key Performance Indicators*—The analysis of revenues and sales should be accompanied by a discussion of key performance indicators for the issuer.
- *Analysis of Period-to-Period Changes*—Material changes in the issuer's financial condition and performance from year to year should be discussed.
- *Extraordinary Events*—The issuer should describe any unusual or infrequent events or transactions and any other items that it feels may not be indicative of future operations. For example, an issuer should discuss the impact of discontinued operations and extraordinary gains and losses if these items may have a material effect on the issuer's reported or future financial condition.

Due Diligence: The Searchers

TRANSTECH INFORMATION MANAGEMENT SYSTEMS, INC.

by Jeff Nash

Ken Olson—founder of several high-tech companies, former Entrepreneur of the Year in San Diego for his role in the success of Proxima Corporation, and a TransTech investor—told me at the end of my involvement as CEO of TransTech that "Not everything that everyone does always works out." What an epitaph he offered. Here's the story.

By the fall of 1993, I was finally minding my own business. At the conclusion of my second company, VISqUS Corporation, our employee-investor team had achieved a moderately profitable venture-financed start-up and sell-off. Hooray! I decided that I needed a break from running with "other people's money" and the nagging responsibility it comes with. Sure, I wanted more independence from boards of directors and investors, but I also wanted to do something that would be exciting, meaningful, and profitable. I wanted to have a lot of fun, do a lot of good, and make a LOT of money at work.

This can be more difficult than it sounds.

While others were building their financial dream castles on foundations of great products in markets for JetSkis, Beanie Babies, GPS receivers, or electronic games, I chose to enter the black hole of a marginal market: specifically, that of general aviation safety software. While the company I founded first produced and sold a product in 1994 and continues to profitably sell that product worldwide, the company is at best a marginal financial success today. The narrow market, which I dearly love and continue to derive great personal pleasure and psychic reward from serving, is just too small for headline-worthy success. In fact, there is a humorous saw that applies:

> Many small fortunes have been made in general aviation—out of large ones.

Fortunately, I did not invite outside investor participation in my aviation safety software company and chose instead to remain a personally financed, Subchapter S company—in effect, a sole proprietorship. I say "fortunately" because few things in business are worse than losing money entrusted to you by friends, associates, and investors. Even if they can afford to lose the money, it's very hard on your own entrepreneurial psyche, and it sure as hell isn't much fun for your erstwhile trusting friends, associates, and investors either. Oftentimes, however, a start-up will require more money than you will want to put up yourself. Personal risk–benefit assessment is frequently a valid reason for such action. In this case, you may turn to a few well-heeled, intrepid types to help seed your early finance round(s). In my experience, you can raise between $200,000 and $300,000 and up to maybe $3 million or more this way. Credibility is the critical factor.

Depending on who you are, how much you are willing to give up, and how people perceive your ideas and relevant track record, this technique of "angel" financing may be a good vehicle for you early on. From the investor's viewpoint, however, angel investing can be a high-risk, high-stakes game that is definitely not for everyone. It's no secret that nine out of every ten new businesses fail every year. All of them take one or more angels or an angel/owner down with them. As a result, nobody is ultimately more skeptical of new business plans than a fallen angel. And there are two kinds of angels: those who have fallen and those who will. It's the nature of the game.

As a high-tech angel investor, even if you know a fair amount about what you're getting into, playing angel to seed rounds is a lot like wildcatting for oil. You are betting on a general field and the track record and/or pitchmanship of the entrepreneur who shows up at your door. If you're the entrepreneur, the roles are reversed. If you don't have the true courage of your convictions and believe 100% in the chances of your own well-digging proposal at the time you ask for another person's check, you're a fraud—not only to others, but to yourself as well. History is a great teacher in this regard, from the formation of General Electric to the Teapot Dome scandal and recent politics as well. Not much about human nature is likely to change, so a healthy dose of caveat emptor still applies to all investment opportunities, particularly in high tech.

Still, judging solely from what they invest in, some angel investors don't seem to mind a little risky action as long as personal integrity is part of the deal. Some investors have more to risk than others. With little time on their hands or minimal technical training in their backgrounds, they often shell out substantial hard-earned dollars into deals along with members of their herd, trusting in the analysis and judgment of the more technically sophisticated and involved investor leaders who they frequently follow. These leaders engage in a form of deductive evaluation, or "due diligence" as it is called, to try to improve everyone's odds.

Figuring out "when to hold and when to fold" is the name of this game. To paraphrase, there's a time to walk away and a time to run. As an investor, when you smell fraud, there is only one piece of advice to follow: Run fast. The rest of the time, walk fast. Don Becker, Ph.D., a former colleague, a brilliant designer of cable modem equipment, and a highly successful consultant to the digital communications industry, has a rule that I try to follow when it comes to angel investing:

> Most ideas are bad.

Which brings us to TransTech Information Management Systems, Inc., and the financing we secured. I had begun to feel constrained by the limits of my aviation safety product, and I became receptive again to the swirl of entrepreneurial activity in the local San Diego high-tech community. I began to mentally thrash about, looking for ways to leverage my experience. Then, out of the blue, as we say in aviation, a former employee working now at Ball Aerospace approached me with an intriguing business plan.

Ball Aerospace ($2–3 billion) had bought VERAC ($20 million and 500 employees), my first company, in 1987. By 1994, some of the VERAC business that Ball had bought was not in line with Ball's plan to be a "pure play" in defense. Ball had determined that it would spin off a business serving the towing and recovery industry. The company had won a municipality-linked contract to develop software to locally manage police-requested towing. Their product worked, and Ball was beginning to earn a modest return on the development effort. Still, the corporate and aerospace management teams decided that the business as a whole was not suited to a defense contractor and that both the contract and the people working it would be better served if they were spun off. One of the employees who would lose his job was a former employee of mine, and he asked me what could be done to start a new company.

I studied the business plan that my former associates at Ball had written, and I was amazed at my former employee's projections. If something looks too good to be true, it generally is. The numbers he showed me were phenomenal. I asked for industry references. I felt

I had to be sure that his idea of a modern, Windows NT client-server based, vertical software application for towing companies was plausibly lucrative before I plunged in and asked others to swim with me. I spoke with knowledgeable and reputable towers (rhymes with "growers")—prospective customers—in Portland, Boston, and San Diego. I went to trade shows. I talked to vendors of current products. It seemed the industry was on the verge of consolidating along predictably corporate lines. There appeared to be a considerable need for a moderately sophisticated software product such as Ball's that would feature a variety of options not offered by any packages then sold or foreseen to be available. If our timing was right, we could sell the integrated vertical application of choice to the towing industry. TransTech would offer business management software, dispatch, accounting, tie-ins to in-vehicle communications, GPS position tracking, mapping, route planning, lot inventory, credit card processing, law-enforcement interfaces, and a world of connectivity to a thin-margin business that would clearly profit from the improved knowledge engineering of its mobile workforce. Or would it?

I introduced my former employee to two private investors and good friends. I had known both of them in separate business contexts for over ten years, and we had analyzed and invested in some deals together in the past. The introduction took the form of a moderated pitch from the Ball "spinees" to the group of "angels" who might invest in their plan. It was an interesting meeting, and I think my former employee and his marketing sidekick really put their best foot forward. Still, neither angel was convinced that the Ball team could carry the plan through without some help. Both of them stared at me. "What are you doing these days, Jeff?"

I rewrote the Ball business plan and negotiated with the spinout team to ascertain what piece of the common stock action I could personally get "pre-money." This created a fair amount of friction early on, but I wasn't going forward without a favorable agreement, and in spite of differences, we were able to agree, patch up differences, and move on. That settled, I switched sides and began negotiating with the angels on behalf of the spinout group concerning what we would all want. These guys are seasoned professionals, and I used all the skill and insight at my command to establish a fair split among the employee group, my fellow cash investors, and Ball Corporation.

Ball recognized that it was contributing technology, a contract, some assets, intellectual property rights, employee loyalty, and goodwill to the new venture. They wanted stock, notes, and interest payments in return. We haggled and gave them what they needed to do the deal. We also had to satisfy a constituency of towers under the contract we were getting from Ball. I met with the community of individuals who made up the group. In spite of everything from last-minute sabotage by certain Ball employees to defection of one of the key software developers, we got the financing. Ball Corporation gave us a contract and took an asset-backed note and preferred stock in return. Several of us, including some towers, a few angels, and several employees, put up the hard cash that was TransTech's seed money in return for preferred stock.

All totaled, in two rounds, we raised over $1.3 million in cash. Ball maintained certain rights to participation in the funding of future rounds. The preferred money received certain premiums that allowed it to get a disproportionately higher return if TransTech failed to deliver according to its revised, less aggressive plan. This was achieved in the form of "participating preferred" or as a "discount upon sale." In either case, it meant the investors were improving their return relative to the common shareholders. I personally played on both sides of this equation, investing in preferred and getting common as an insider, as did most of the employees. Was the split fair? To some extent, the "golden rule" of investing applies: "Whoever has the gold, makes the rules." The fact is that you aren't forced to take anyone's money. As a high-tech entrepreneur, you are in a market for money and if your name is Bill Gates, Andy Grove, Seymour Cray, or something similar, you can probably get the money you need without a lot of "accelerated return mechanisms" being levied on your proposed deal. If you were Jeff Nash trying to do TransTech in 1994, you'd probably have settled for something similar to what we ended up with.

What happened to TransTech? We developed, sold, installed, trained users, and serviced machines for 22 client-server systems with over 120 seats of a product called Transtar. The largest and a few of the smallest towing companies in the country purchased our systems, and Allstate, GEICO, and Signature Group bought IS services from the firm. Revenues exceeded $1 million in our best year.

Our product was very flexible. In software, this means very complex. In spite of the predicted decline in Windows NT hardware prices, our systems were relatively expensive because we needed NT, SQL Server, and some healthy hardware muscle. In a business where margins are thin and DOS applications are widely accepted, this expense was a tough sell for the incremental improvement we offered. Worse, much of the incremental price we were able to charge went to Microsoft and our hardware vendors.

After 30 months in business and 12 months on the market, we had been unable to maintain consistent profitability or raise additional money from angels, venture capitalists, investment bankers, customers, employees, or partners. We cut our cost base to the bone. We also attempted to sell the company when it still looked pretty good, and that was unsuccessful too. We couldn't give it away. By opting for a niche market, we had knowingly violated the second rule ("be in a big market") of successful venture deals. No, Microsoft was not going to compete with us in towing software, and no, Microsoft was not going to buy us either. It was a two-edged sword.

The company was intermittently profitable on a quarterly basis, but ultimately the company was not able to sell its product into the market it sought to serve. The industry required a blend of performance and features including intuitive simplicity that Transtar did not inherently provide. Further, we could not make a decent profit with the degree of rework and customization required to placate each customer before a sale. In short, we never had a product for our market. We failed Marketing 101, and I also failed Due Diligence 101. The company was sold to another software firm that subsequently purchased all three of TransTech's competitors, integrated them under the industry leadership of a former high-ranking law-enforcement executive, and, as of this writing, has yet to show what it can do. TransTech's investors own a greatly diluted share of this new company, and time will tell whether they will get their money back, let alone earn any kind of return. Can I make this sound okay? Sure, but as measured by lost return on investment and alternative cost, no one is less pleased with the outcome than I am.

How do you know when an idea will fall into Olson's euphemistic category of "not working out"? What steps should you follow to ensure that you have sustainable competitive advantage, great market potential, outstanding management, and appropriate financing (at least for a while)?

This is the art of doing deals. There are books, checklists, and rules of thumb that you can follow to improve the odds. Betting on proven performance is one approach, but it isn't necessarily the case that someone who does well at company A in industry Z will do well elsewhere at another time. Again, there are more good people than there are opportunities. If due diligence by itself would accurately reveal losers and winners, there wouldn't be any losers in the venture world. And, since it is an art and not a pure science, there is room for genuine difference of opinion between intelligent, informed investors and managers. Finally, there may be a circumstance similar to that confronting the managers of the Manhattan Project. It may be that the only way to understand how well a concept really works is to pull the trigger and ride. As one angel said to me in commiseration, "You can 'due diligence' any idea to death. You end up with paralysis by analysis and you'll never do anything because time to market is everything." The market doesn't reward that approach very well either.

You have to find the right balance in the presence of imperfect information. That's nothing new. It's management.

CHAPTER 6 • LIABILITIES AND REMEDIES

§ 6.04 Indemnification, Contribution, and Insurance

[A] Introduction

[B] Indemnification

[C] Contribution

[D] Insurance

Advisors: Devil's Advocate

CHAPTER 6

§ 6.01 OVERVIEW

[A] In General

The federal securities laws contain a number of prohibitions relating to the offer and sale of securities. Liabilities exist for violations of these prohibitions under federal and state common and statutory laws. Civil and criminal liabilities may be imposed on primary violators, as well as on persons "in control" of the primary violator. In appropriate cases, indemnification agreements, insurance, and contribution can minimize potential liabilities.

The Private Securities Litigation Reform Act of 1995 made significant procedural changes to existing law, as well as some important substantive changes.

[B] Sources of Liability in Securities Transactions

There are three basic sources of liability for persons involved in the purchase or sale of securities:

- **Federal securities laws**, specifically the Securities and Exchange Acts;
- **Common law** rights of action; and
- **State blue-sky laws**, which take their name from trying to prevent sellers from promising the sky, and which vary in both scope and focus.

Liability typically arises from three general categories of activities:

- Failure to comply with applicable registration requirements,
- Misrepresentation or withholding of material facts by a purchaser or a seller, or
- Use of deceptive or fraudulent practices in the purchase or sale of a security.

The liability provisions overlap. It is often possible to bring concurrent claims under the Securities Act, the Exchange Act, and state and common law based on the same transaction.

[C] Types of Actions and Proceedings

There are five types of actions or proceedings to enforce the securities laws:

- Injunctive actions,
- Private damage actions,
- Suits seeking disgorgement,
- Administrative proceedings, and
- Criminal proceedings.

Determining which actions are available requires knowing who the aggrieved party is, whether a statutory violation is alleged, and whether the relevant statutory provision has been interpreted to authorize the particular type of claim.

As a rule, private parties acting individually or as a class may bring injunctive or private damage actions. The SEC and, under certain blue-sky laws, state authorities may bring injunctive and disgorgement actions. The SEC has the exclusive power to institute administrative proceedings against market professionals, but only the federal Department of Justice or state criminal authorities may bring criminal actions.

[D] Parties to Actions

Actions for violations of the securities laws are usually brought by a purchaser. The antifraud provisions of the Exchange Act and most state securities laws, however, may be invoked by both sellers and purchasers of securities. Liability for securities law violations is joint and several. It will be imposed on the principal violator, aiders and abettors, co-conspirators, principals under traditional agency law, and persons in control of the principal violator.

Accordingly, a plaintiff alleging a false or misleading statement by an issuer of securities will name the issuer, its directors, partners, officers, and dominant shareholders as defendants in addition to the employee or other person principally responsible for the violation. Also, the issuer's attorneys, accountants, and investment bankers will typically find themselves named.

[E] Remedies

In private damage actions, the remedies available to a plaintiff, and the corresponding liabilities imposed on the defendants, depend on a number of factors, including the following:

- Specific cause of action under which the claim is brought;
- Position of the defendant in the series of events that created the liability;
- Point in the transaction at which the action is brought;
- Subsequent transfers of the purchased securities;
- Subsequent appreciation or depreciation in the value of the security; and
- As between defendants, the effect of any agreement among them as to indemnification or contribution.

Regulators may seek and obtain injunctive relief in appropriate cases. In the case of criminal actions, defendants may be subject to fines or imprisonment.

§ 6.02 FEDERAL PRIVATE CAUSES OF ACTION

[A] Overview

In adopting the Securities and Exchange Acts, Congress believed that private actions for damages could play two important roles. They could assure full and accurate disclosures in securities offerings and prevent fraud or manipulation of the securities market. Private causes of action under Section 11 of the Securities Act, entitled Civil Liabilities on Account of False Registration Statement, are limited to false or misleading statements and the omission of material information.

In addition, Section 12(a)(2) of the Securities Act imposes liability for any untruth or omission in a public offering of securities. The section even applies to securities not subject to registration. Section 12(a)(1) of the Securities Act prohibits offers or sales of securities in violation of the registration requirements of the Act. Section 13 of the Securities Act sets forth the statute of limitations for actions under Sections 11 and 12. Under the Exchange Act, Section 10(b) and Rule 10b-5 impose liability for manipulative and deceptive devices in the purchase or sale of any security. Control persons are also liable for violations of the federal securities acts under Section 15 of the Securities Act and Section 20(a) of the Exchange Act.

[B] Section 11 of Securities Act: Misrepresentations in Registration Statements

[1] Overview

Section 11 of the Securities Act is the primary private remedy under the federal securities laws for false or misleading statements, or the omission of material information, in the registration statement. Specifically, Section 11(a) encourages careful preparation of the registration statement and prospectus by providing that

> [i]n case any part of the registration statement, when such part became effective, contained an untrue statement of a material fact or omitted to state a material fact required to be stated therein or necessary to make the statements therein not misleading, any person acquiring such security (unless it is proved that at the time of such acquisition he knows of such untruth or omission) may . . .

sue for damages. Although materiality is an element of an action under Section 11, a plaintiff who purchases shares in an original distribution need not show fraud, deceit, or a causal connection to its loss.

[2] Categories of Potential Defendants

The categories of potential defendants in an action under Section 11 of the Securities Act include the following:

- Every person who signed the registration statement, which will include at least the chief executive officer, chief financial officer, and principal accounting officer of the issuer;
- Every person who was a director of the issuer at the time of the filing, or every person named in the registration statement as about to become a director;
- Every accountant, engineer, appraiser, or person whose profession gives authority to his statement (an "expert"), and who consented to be named as having prepared or certified any report, valuation, or part ("expertise portion") of the registration statement;
- Every underwriter with respect to the security, although participants in the selling group who do not actually make an underwriting commitment are not covered; and

- Every person who controls (through stock ownership, agency, or otherwise) any of the foregoing persons (i.e., controlling shareholders who are not directors or officers of the issuer). No liability arises if the controlling person had no knowledge of or reasonable grounds to know of the action for which liability is alleged.

The above persons are jointly and severally liable. Section 11(f) of the Securities Act, however, allows every person who is not actually guilty of fraudulent misrepresentation, but who makes any liability payment, to recover from those who are actually guilty of such misrepresentation.

[3] Materiality

A "material fact" is a fact that, if it had been correctly stated or disclosed in the document, would have deterred or tended to deter the average prudent investor from purchasing the securities. Rule 405 restates this requirement when it defines the term *material* to mean information relating to "matters to which there is a substantial likelihood that a reasonable investor would attach importance in determining whether to purchase the security registered."

[4] Defenses for Issuers

The issuer is often said to have absolute liability for violations of the securities laws in a primary offering. Thus, the issuer may avoid liability for such a violation only if it can show that one or more of the requisite elements of a cause of action are not present. To avoid liability under Section 11 of the Securities Act, the issuer must be able to show that

- The statements were *not* false or misleading and none of the information required to be included in the registration statement was omitted,
- The false or misleading statement or omission of required information did not pertain to a material matter, or
- The plaintiff knew at the time of purchase that the representations were false or misleading or that required information was not included.

[5] Defenses for Nonissuers

Obviously, defendants other than the issuer in a Section 11 action may avail themselves of the defenses raised by the issuer. Moreover, Sections 11(b) and (c) further limit the liability of potential defendants based, in large part, on their relationship to the alleged violation. Pursuant to Section 11(b), no person is liable who proves

> (1) that before the effective date (of the registration statement). . .
>
> (A) he had resigned from . . . or ceased or refused to act in, every office, capacity, or relationship in which he was described in the registration statement as acting or agreeing to act, and
>
> (B) he had advised the Commission and the issuer in writing that he had taken such action and that he would not be responsible for such part of the registration statement; or
>
> (2) that if such part of the registration statement became effective without his knowledge, upon becoming aware of such fact he forthwith acted and advised the Commission . . . and, in addition, gave reasonable public notice that such . . . registration statement had become effective without his knowledge.

Nonissuer defendants may also rely on the due diligence defense, which turns on whether the defendant is an expert and whether the alleged false or misleading statement is part of the expertise portion of the registration statement. As to the portion that an expert prepared, under Section 11(b)(3)(A), the expert can defend on the grounds that

> (i) he had, after reasonable investigation, reasonable ground to believe and did believe, at the time such part of the registration statement became effective, that the statements therein were true and that there was no omission to state a material fact required to be stated therein or necessary to make the statements therein not misleading, or
>
> (ii) such part of the registration statement did not fairly represent his statement as an expert or was not a fair copy of or extract from his report or valuation as an expert.

Nonexperts' defense depends on whether their statement is in the nonexperts' or experts' portion of the registration. If the statement is in the nonexperts' portion, a defendant must carry the burden of proof and establish that he made a reasonable investigation. He must also show that after the investigation he had reasonable grounds to believe and did believe the statements were true and not misleading. If the statement is in the experts' portion, he must carry the burden of proof that he had no reasonable grounds to believe and did not believe that the statement was untrue or misleading. The standard of care for measuring reasonable investigation and reasonable grounds for a belief is the degree of care that a prudent person would use in the management of his or her own property.

[6] Statute of Limitations

For actions brought under Section 11, the statute of limitations is one year after the discovery of the untrue statement or omission, or one year after such discovery should have been made by the exercise of reasonable diligence. An action cannot be brought more than three years after the security was offered in good faith to the public, although actions calculated to conceal the violation can toll the three-year period. The one-year period cannot be shortened by an offer of rescission.

[7] Damages

The damages recoverable in a Section 11 action can be quite large, although the amounts will depend on the role of the defendant in the transaction. Moreover, Section 11(f) makes it clear that each of the defendants "shall be jointly and severally liable," subject to their ability to obtain contribution from other defendants as referred to above. According to Section 11(e) of the Securities Act,

- Damages may be recovered equal to the difference between (A) the amount paid for the security (subject to the limitation that such amount shall be no greater than the public offering price) and (B)(1) the value of the security as of the time such suit was brought (rather than the value at the time of delivery); or (2) the price at which such security was sold prior to the suit; or (3) the price at which such security was sold after the suit but before judgment if such damages would be less than the damages calculated as if (B)(1) above applied.
- Damages otherwise available under this formula may be reduced to the extent the defendant can show that any depreciation in value of the security is attributable to reasons other than the alleged false statement.
- Underwriters (unless they knowingly received from the issuer additional consideration) are not liable under Section 11(a) for damages in excess of the total price offered to the public. Accordingly, the underwriting agreement is generally written so that the

underwriter's obligations to purchase securities are several rather than joint obligations.

- Reasonable attorneys' fees and expenses are recoverable from a party in a Section 11(a) action if it is determined that the suit or defense of such party is without merit.

[C] Section 12(a)(2) of Securities Act

[1] Basis for Liability

Section 12(a)(2) of the Securities Act imposes liability on any person offering or selling a registered or exempt security who makes an untrue material statement or omits a material fact. Privity is generally required in an action under Section 12(a)(2). The misrepresentation or omission must be caused by the seller of the securities or someone in control of the seller. However, liability for damages may extend to aiders and abettors, co-conspirators, and principals. The plaintiff need not show an intent to defraud. A failure on the part of the seller to exercise reasonable care is sufficient to make the seller liable. In the 1995 decision of Gustafson v. Alloyd Co., the Supreme Court held that Section 12(a)(2) liability is limited to statements made in connection with a public offering that requires the delivery of a prospectus.

[2] Defenses

Defendants may defend against a Section 12(a)(2) action by showing that

- The plaintiff knew the truth of the misrepresented or omitted material fact,
- The misrepresented or omitted fact was not material, or
- The defendant did not know, and through the exercise of reasonable care could not have known, of the misrepresentation or omission of a material fact (i.e., the due diligence standard).

It is important to note that the due diligence standard for Section 12(a)(2) is not identical to that under Section 11 of the Securities Act. Under Section 12(a)(2), sellers distant from the preparation of the offering materials are held to a lower standard of liability than sellers under Section 11 are.

[3] Statute of Limitations

For actions brought under Section 12(a)(2) of the Securities Act, the statute of limitations is the earlier of one year after constructive discovery of the misstatement or omission and three years after the sale occurred.

[4] Damages

Section 12(a)(2) provides that an aggrieved purchaser

> may sue . . . at law . . . to recover the consideration paid for such security with interest thereon, less the amount of any income received thereon upon the tender of such security.

Rescission is the principal remedy for a purchaser who still owns the security. If the purchaser has sold the security, damages will be awarded. Prior to the 1995 Private Securities Litigation Reform Act, damages under Section 12(2) were measured by the difference between the purchase price and the subsequent sale price, increased by interest it would have earned and reduced by income or return of capital actually received. Under new Section 12(b), the defendant in a Section 12(a)(2) action has a "loss causation" defense whereby the defendant can establish that some portion of the value lost resulted from factors unrelated to the misstatement or omission.

[D] Section 12(a)(1) of Securities Act: Violation of Registration Requirements

[1] Basis of Liability

Under Section 12(a)(1) of the Securities Act, a purchaser of a security that does not meet the registration requirements has the right to recover damages identical to those in Section 12(a)(2) actions. A claim may be made by a purchaser only against the seller of unregistered securities that the purchaser alleges should have been registered, although some courts extend liability in egregious cases to participants in the alleged violation. A person may be liable under Section 12(a)(1) irrespective of fault, negligence, or intent. Section 12(a)(1) is very restrictive. A single violation of the registration provisions toward one buyer will create liability to all purchasers.

[2] Defenses

The seller has many defenses for an action under Section 12(a)(1). The seller may show that registration was not required because the offering was not public, the securities were exempt, or the sale was not made by an issuer, underwriter, dealer, or controlling person. Defenses of estoppel, waiver, and release are available, and a control person may avoid liability if it had no ground to believe wrongdoing was involved.

[3] Statute of Limitations

For actions brought under Section 12(a)(1), the statute of limitations is the earlier of one year after the alleged violation of Section 5 and three years after the security is first offered to the public. Neither period is tolled pending discovery of the alleged violation, but the periods do not begin to run until after the last offer, sale, or delivery has occurred.

[4] Damages

As noted above, a plaintiff in a successful suit under Section 12(a)(1) of the Securities Act has a right to recover damages identical to those recoverable in an action under Section 12(a)(2). Accordingly, a plaintiff may sue to rescind the transaction in the event that he still owns the securities. If not, he may sue to recover damages based on the difference between the original purchase price and the subsequent sale price, subject to the adjustments in Section 12(a)(2).

[E] Rule 10b-5: Material Misstatements or Omissions

[1] In General

Sections 11 and 12 of the Securities Act cover a broad range of potential violations. Whether or not the offering is subject to registration, the following antifraud provisions of Rule 10b-5 promulgated under the Exchange Act apply:

> It shall be unlawful for any person, directly or indirectly, by use of any means or instrumentality of interstate commerce, or of the mails or of any facility of any national securities exchange,
>
> (a) To employ any device, scheme or artifice to defraud,

(b) To make any untrue statement of a material fact or to omit to state a material fact necessary in order to make the statements made, in the light of the circumstances under which they were made, not misleading, or

(c) To engage in any act, practice or course of business which operates or would operate as a fraud or deceit upon any person.

The Exchange Act focuses primarily on trading and transactions in existing markets. Rule 10b-5, however, applies to oral or written communications in connection with *any* purchase or sale of securities, whether or not registered under the Securities Act.

One of the most important applications of Rule 10b-5 is its use as a sanction against insider trading. Rule 10b-5 is designed to protect the public and secure fair dealing by promoting full disclosure of information that would be relied on by investors in trading a company's securities. The perceived benefits of disclosure are so great that Rule 10b-5 has been used to prohibit unaffiliated persons from trading a company's securities if they are in possession of material inside information.

[2] Elements of Proof

For an action to be asserted under Rule 10b-5, the prohibited conduct must occur in connection with the purchase or sale of a security. *Purchase* and *sale* have been broadly defined. They include issuance of securities, sale of stock for fictitious consideration, loans against future distribution of shares, dissolution of limited partnership interests, redemption of convertible debentures, and "forced sale" by a minority shareholder in a short-form merger.

As with actions brought under Sections 11 and 12(a)(2) of the Securities Act, Rule 10b-5 applies only to misstatements or omissions of material facts. The test is objective. A fact is material if it is substantially likely that a reasonable investor would consider it important in making an investment decision.

The alleged statement or omission must be a proximate cause of the loss alleged by the plaintiff in a Rule 10b-5 claim. The plaintiff must also be able to show reliance on the misstatements and that they were a substantial factor in inducing action. Reliance may be disproved by showing the plaintiff did not attach any significance to the misrepresented facts, had no knowledge of them, or was aware of the true state of affairs. Individuals do not need to prove individual reliance on misleading statements in the case of publicly-traded securities. Rather, under the "fraud on the market" doctrine, there is a rebuttable presumption that the price resulted from the misrepresentation.

Finally, in order for a Rule 10b-5 action to be successful, a plaintiff must establish that the defendant owed a duty of disclosure to the plaintiff. The plaintiff must also show that the defendant acted with knowledge while engaging in the prohibited conduct. A violation of Rule 10b-5 must

- Be committed with an intent to deceive, manipulate, or defraud; or
- Occur under circumstances that
  — Demonstrate recklessness or highly unreasonable conduct,
  — Involve not merely simple or inexcusable negligence, but
  — An extreme departure from standards of ordinary care, and
  — Present a danger of misleading buyers or sellers, and
  — Were either known to the defendant or so obvious that the defendant must have been aware of them.

Negligence, even when gross, grave, or inexcusable, is insufficient for liability under Rule 10b-5.

[3] Potential Defendants

Besides the principal defendant responsible for the misstatement, omission, or deceptive practice, other employees, corporate officers, directors, partners, dominant shareholders, underwriters, and brokers are often named as secondary defendants in Rule 10b-5 actions. There is no private right of action for aiding and abetting under Section 10, but the SEC can bring actions against aiders and abettors for a violation of Rule 10b-5. An employer may be liable as principal for violations of an employee under traditional agency principles.

When Rule 10b-5 is applied to insider trading, potential liability may extend to "tipees" (beneficiaries of nonpublic information from insiders or market sources), as well as officers, directors, and others with personal knowledge of the relevant information. Receipt of such information creates a duty to disclose it or refrain from trading. However, the duty to disclose runs only to the buyer. Therefore, a tipee is not obliged to disclose information to the market generally before engaging in trading activities.

[4] Statute of Limitations

A Rule 10(b)(5) action must generally be brought within one year after discovery of the facts constituting the violation and no more than three years after the violation.

[5] Remedies

Relief in Rule 10b-5 actions may take a number of forms. Generally speaking, if the plaintiff still owns the securities, the appropriate remedy is rescission and damages. The amount of damages will be the price paid if the plaintiff is a buyer, or the price at which the securities were sold if the plaintiff is a seller. If the plaintiff, as a buyer, subsequently sold the shares, the amount of damages is usually determined by the out-of-pocket measure. This is defined as "the difference between the contract price, or the price paid, and the real or actual value at the date of sale, together with such outlays as are attributable to the defendant's conduct." Recovery may be reduced if the defendant can show that a low sales price resulted from causes other than purported misrepresentations or omissions.

[F] Private Securities Litigation Reform Act

The Private Securities Litigation Reform Act provides a safe harbor for "forward looking statements" if the statements are accompanied by meaningful cautionary language or are immaterial, or plaintiff fails to establish that the person or entity making the statement knew it to be false. The safe harbor does not apply to statements made in a company's financial statements, during a tender offer, or in an IPO.

[G] Other Potential Civil Liabilities Under Federal Securities Law

[1] In General

In addition to civil liabilities under Sections 11 and 12 of the Securities Act and Rule 10b-5 of the Exchange Act, a number of other provisions may be used to impose civil liabilities.

[2] Antifraud Provisions Under Section 17(a) of Securities Act

The general antifraud provision of the Securities Act, Section 17(a), makes it unlawful to employ materially misleading statements, or fraudulent or deceptive devices, in connection with the offer or sale, but not the purchase, of securities. Some courts have recognized a private right of action under Section 17(a). The growing trend, however, is to deny a private right of action and to limit enforcement proceedings to the Department of Justice or the SEC.

[3] Short-Swing Profit Liability Under Exchange Act

Section 16 of the Exchange Act applies to officers and directors of an issuer with securities registered under Section 12 of the Exchange Act. It also applies to persons who beneficially own 10% or more of the securities registered by an issuer under Section 12. Section 16 focuses on persons (insiders) who profit from their access to information about the issuer that is not available to the public. Liability may exist under Section 16 even when the violator was not trading on inside information.

Section 16 relies on a system of required disclosures and prohibited trading activities. Specifically, Section 16(a) requires insiders to report their stockholdings and certain transactions in securities. Section 16(b) imposes liability on insiders of the issuer for profits they derive from short-swing trading (a purchase and sale, or sale and purchase, in any six-month period). Section 16(c) makes it unlawful for insiders to engage in short sales of the issuer's equity securities. The only means for enforcing Section 16(b) liability is an action by the issuer or a derivative action by a shareholder.

[4] Insider Trading Sanctions

Insider trading is trading in securities while in possession of material nonpublic information. As noted, it may constitute a violation of the general antifraud provisions of Section 10(b) of the Exchange Act and Rule 10b-5 thereunder. In addition, in response to abuses of insider status, Congress adopted the Insider Trading Sanctions Act of 1984 (ITSA) to create additional remedies for insider trading. ITSA requires registered broker-dealers and investment advisors to use certain procedures to prevent insider trading.

ITSA was supplemented by the Insider Trading and Securities Fraud Enforcement Act of 1988 (ITSFEA, or Insider Trading Act). Together they create an additional remedy for insider trading violations through a civil penalty "not to exceed three times the profit gained or loss avoided as a result of such unlawful purchase or sale." ITSFEA defines *profit gained* or *loss avoided* as the difference between the sale price (or purchase price) and the value (presumably market price) of the security. The value is determined at a reasonable period of time after the withheld information is publicly disseminated.

ITSFEA does not make purchasing or selling a security while in possession of material nonpublic information unlawful. It applies only when a person violates any provision of the Exchange Act or rules or regulations adopted thereunder "by purchasing or selling a security while in possession of material nonpublic information." The resulting transaction must be through an exchange, broker, or dealer and (except for standardized options) must not involve a public offering. In addition, the Act makes it clear that a penalty can be imposed on a person who violates the Act by communicating material nonpublic information (i.e., by tipping).

Originally, civil penalties for inside trading could be imposed only by the SEC and were payable to the U.S. Treasury. However, ITSFEA created an express private remedy against unlawful trading by insiders for the benefit of persons who traded the same class of securities contemporaneously.

Recently, the SEC approved new rules, 10b5-1 and 10b5-2 under the Exchange Act. The new rules create a presumption that a person who is aware of material nonpublic information has "used that information in trading."

[5] Misrepresentations in Proxy Solicitations

Section 14(a) and Rule 14a-9 of the Exchange Act impose liability for deceptive or inadequate disclosures in proxy solicitations. They are applicable only to issuers with securities registered under the Exchange Act. The purpose of Section 14(a) is to prevent management and others from obtaining proxies through misstatements or deceptions. For an action to be successful under Section 14(a), the misrepresentation must be material. The necessary causation exists if the proxy solicited (not necessarily the particular misrepresentation in the proxy) was essential to accomplishing the transaction. The plaintiff is not required to show reliance by it or any intent to deceive on the part of management.

[6] Misrepresentations in Tender Offers

Section 14(e) of the Exchange Act imposes liability for material misstatements or omissions in tender offers, whether or not the securities are registered. The elements of a violation are identical to those for violation of Rule 10b-5. Money damages are available. Most actions, however, involve efforts by the target company to enjoin the use of communications by the offeror to the target's shareholders by alleging material misstatements or omissions.

[H] "Control Person" Liability

Wherever a person becomes liable under the Securities Act or the Exchange Act, any person who "controls" the violator is also jointly and severally liable. *Control* is the ability to direct the policies of another whether through stock ownership, management, authority, or other means. Persons typically deemed to be in control include directors, officers, and major shareholders of a corporation, as well as general partners of a partnership.

For a control person to be liable, such person must be "in control" at the time the liability accrues. The plaintiff must also show that the control person had at least some level of knowledge. Under the Securities Act, the controlling person is not liable if there was no knowledge of, or reasonable grounds to believe in the existence of, the facts giving rise to the liability. Under the Exchange Act, the controlling person is not liable if it acted in good faith and did not directly or indirectly induce the acts constituting the violation. In addition, a control person may defend against liability by showing that appropriate supervisory procedures existed and were followed.

To the extent that controlling persons are liable for the acts of the persons controlled, such liability is coextensive with that of the controlled person. Thus the measure of damages would be determined in the same manner.

§ 6.03 COMMON LAW AND STATE STATUTORY CAUSES OF ACTION

[A] Introduction

In addition to civil and criminal liabilities under federal law, defendants may be liable under state common law. Nearly every state has regulations

- Imposing civil liability on offerors or sellers who violate the state's laws,
- Granting the securities administrator injunctive and investigatory powers for securities transactions, and
- Imposing criminal penalties on persons who violate the state's securities laws.

[B] COMMON LAW ACTIONS

There are three primary causes of action under common law for securities transactions: breach of warranty, rescission, and misrepresentation. An action for misrepresentation may be brought as a tort action. Actions based on breach of warranty or rescission may be brought as a defense to an action to enforce a contract for sale. Other common law remedies include reformation, specific performance, receivership, constructive trust, and equitable relief.

Common law remedies can be used by a court to fashion a remedy to suit the circumstances. The courts have a fair degree of latitude in structuring appropriate relief. They can consider the type of violation, the fairness of the transaction, the relative degree of knowledge of the parties, and the culpability of the parties. A court may permit the injured party to choose among remedies, provided that the basic elements of the claim have been proven to the court's satisfaction.

[C] Civil Liabilities

[1] In General

The main civil liability provisions of the Uniform Securities Act (Uniform Act) are in Section 410 of the Act. Liability may be imposed for violations of the registration and approval process, as well as for fraud in a particular securities transaction.

[2] Violations of Registration Requirements

To ensure that registration and approval procedures are complied with, Section 410(a)(1) of the Uniform Act imposes liability on any person who

> . . . offers or sells a security in violation of [the sections making it unlawful to transact business as a broker-dealer or agent unless registered; to offer or sell any security unless it is registered or exempt from registration; or to make any representation that registration constitutes approval by the administrator], or of any rule or order under [the section] which requires the affirmative approval of sales literature before it is used, or of any condition imposed under [the sections relating to prospectus delivery requirements in registered offerings; escrow

of securities and impoundment of proceeds in a registered offering; and form of sales contract used in a registered offering].

[3] Violations of Antifraud Provisions

The antifraud provisions of the Uniform Act are set out in Section 410(a)(2), which imposes liability on any person who

> . . . offers or sells a security by means of any untrue statement of a material fact or any omission to state a material fact necessary in order to make the statements made, in the light of the circumstances under which they are made, not misleading (the buyer not knowing of the untruth or omission), and who does not sustain the burden of proof that he did not know, and in the exercise of reasonable care could not have known, of the untruth or omission.

The antifraud provisions of the blue-sky laws are broadly construed, and the term *fraud* has been defined to include all deceitful practices contrary to plain rules of common honesty. However, it has been held that, to be actionable, a fraud action based on a misrepresentation must concern existing or past facts. A promise, prophecy, or opinion of a future event is not sufficient unless the declarant falsely represents his opinion of a future happening.

[4] Potential Defendants

Under Section 410(b) of the Uniform Act, joint and several liability is imposed on anyone who controls a seller; partners, officers, directors, and similar persons; employees materially aiding the sale; and broker-dealers or agents materially aiding the sale. These persons are liable to the same extent as the seller for violations of Section 410(a). Liability will be excused for persons able to sustain the burden of proof that they did not know, and in the exercise of reasonable care could not have known, of the facts for which liability is alleged. All persons found liable will be obligated to contribute funds.

[5] Statute of Limitations

Section 410(e) of the Uniform Act provides that no person may sue under Section 410 more than two years after the contract of sale. In addition, a person may not sue if

- The seller offered in writing, at a time when the buyer owned the security, to refund the consideration paid together with interest, and the buyer failed to accept the offer within 30 days; or
- The seller made such an offer in writing, at a time when the buyer did not own the security, and the buyer rejected the offer in writing within 30 days.

Some states have requirements for rescission offers and require prior approval by the state securities law administrator. In addition, any condition or agreement waiving compliance with the Act is void under Section 410(g).

[6] Damages

Under the Uniform Act, the buyer may sue either at law or in equity to recover the consideration paid for the security. The buyer may also recover interest from the date of payment, costs, and reasonable attorneys' fees, less the amount of any income received on the security or on the tender of such security. If the buyer no longer owns the security, or prefers to affirm the contract, the Uniform Act allows a suit for damages. The measure is the difference between the real value of the stock and the represented value of the stock at the time of the sale.

§ 6.04 INDEMNIFICATION, CONTRIBUTION, AND INSURANCE

[A] Introduction

In many cases, the potential exposure for violations of the securities laws far exceeds any benefits that might be received. Accordingly, the availability and use of indemnification agreements, contribution arrangements, and insurance policies are important factors in allocating responsibility for damages for breaches of the securities laws.

[B] Indemnification

Indemnification gives the indemnified party reimbursement for any loss, damage, or penalty due to the party's position or responsibilities in a given organization or transaction. The availability of indemnification depends on the law of the issuer's incorporating jurisdiction, the articles or certificate of incorporation of the issuer, the bylaws of the issuer, and the terms of any written indemnification agreement between the indemnified party and the issuer. States have adopted indemnification statutes to alleviate the concerns of corporate director candidates. For instance, the Delaware Supreme Court stated that Delaware's statute was intended to encourage capable men to serve as corporate directors, secure in the knowledge that expenses incurred by them in upholding their honesty and integrity as directors will be borne by the corporation they serve. [Hibbert v. Hollywood Park, Inc., 457 A.2d 339 (Del. 1983)]

The position of the SEC is that indemnification for securities actions is against public policy in the Securities Act and is therefore unenforceable. Courts have supported the SEC's position, at least as it relates to officers, directors, and underwriters. In one case [Steinberg v. Pargas, Inc., (1984-5 Transfer Binder) Fed. Sec. L. Rep. (CCH) ¶ 91,979], however, it was held that indemnification of an officer's or director's legal expenses resulting from meritless claims is proper and acceptable. However, the same court stated that the enforceability of indemnification depends on the nature of the alleged violations. It also said that it would be inappropriate to provide indemnification in instances where the behavior constituted knowing or reckless misrepresentation of material facts resulting in a violation of the federal securities laws.

[C] Contribution

While indemnity generally is not available for the majority of violations of the Securities Act, Section 11(f) of the Act provides that defendants

> . . . may recover contribution as in cases of contract from any person who, if sued separately, would have been liable to make the same payment, unless the person who has become liable was, and the other was not, guilty of fraudulent misrepresentation.

Thus, courts have recognized that, unlike indemnification, contribution will not dilute the deterrent impact of securities fraud and as a result have held that potential defendants, particularly underwriters, are entitled to contribution. Contribution is also specifically provided for in Section 18 of the Exchange Act, the counterpart of Section 11 of the Securities Act, which imposes liability for false statements in Exchange Act filings.

Violators of Rule 10b-5 may also seek contribution from others who have participated in the fraud.

[D] Insurance

In addition to the right to contribution, officers and directors may rely on liability insurance covering directors, officers, and their agents. In contrast to indemnification, the SEC does not object to a liability insurance policy. For example, Rule 461(c) of the Securities Act specifically provides the following:

> . . . insurance against liabilities arising under the Act, whether the cost of insurance is borne by the registrant, the insured or some other person, will not be considered a bar to acceleration, unless the registrant is a registered investment company or a business development company and the cost of such insurance is borne by other than an insured officer or director of the registrant.

Insurance policies have become tremendously expensive and are often unavailable to specified classes of issuers. If coverage is obtained, care should be taken to ascertain its scope. For example, a policy may apply to investigations or administrative proceedings, or it may be limited to reimbursement for indemnification payments by the issuer to directors and officers. A policy will most likely contain deductibles, will be a "claims made" policy, may or may not define "loss," and may differ as to whether or not legal fees can be paid prior to adjudication. Also, policies vary as to whether a settlement is considered a loss. State statutes may be of little help, because they tend to remain silent on the issue. Finally, misrepresentations or omissions of material facts in the insurance application may be a bar to recovery from the insurer.

Advisors: Devil's Advocate

CELLULAR PHONE AGENCY

by Paul Markwell

I have been an entrepreneur for the past 20 years. I have started two businesses from ideas, purchased three existing businesses, and participated as a minority shareholder/partner in two others. I have learned many lessons over the years—some more important than others, but all valuable.

I would like to share one of my more costly lessons with you, hoping that I can save someone else the pain of learning this lesson the hard way. About 13 years ago, I was cashing out of my first venture. This was a seven-year adventure into the depths of retail. If you ever want to know what sweat equity, hard work, and minimal profits are all about, start your career in retail. If you survive this industry and still want to work for yourself, you will have acquired the skills to tackle just about any industry left—with perhaps the exception of the restaurant business.

So, after my survival in retail I decided to go into the cellular agency business. I became an agent for one of the regional Bell operating companies and started to market my products and services to the public. After a short period of time, the company was profitable and leading the market in sales. As a result of my early success, I was introduced to a larger competitor in the same business but in a different market. This competitor expressed a desire to purchase my shop and bring it under its corporate entity. Instead of selling out, I decided to merge my operation with it and to invest in several other locations with it as well. As things grew, so did my responsibilities, income, and profits.

After two years, the company that I had put so much time and dedication into was in a position for a merger and a subsequent public offering. Everyone's dream, or so I thought! As these events came to pass, I was excited just to be a part of something so big and successful. We had made the transition from a large privately held company to a small public company.

Over the next two years, the company would be acquired and merged into two more large public companies. After five years of hard work building a dream, we found ourselves no longer the core business of our new owners. It was soon decided that our assets would be sold off and our division closed down.

This is when reality set in. Senior management, including myself, began to review and evaluate our positions and holdings. We all quickly calculated in our heads at what level we would be cashing out. This is when I learned my most expensive lesson. What was that lesson, you ask? How can you avoid the same mistake?

The lesson I learned was fundamental: In the fast pace of growth, early success, and lucrative income, I neglected to get independent professional legal representation and advice that had my interests as the primary concern during each of the mergers, acquisitions, and buyouts. I was now cashing out of a multimillion-dollar communications company for less than 10% of what my partners were netting. It was an expensive lesson that taught me what cash calls, dilution, and preferred stock were all about. But, more important than that, I learned how expensive the lack of good legal representation really is.

I always wondered if I could afford to retain a good law firm. I have since learned that I can't afford *not* to have good legal representation.

PART III • PRIVATE FINANCING

CHAPTER 7 • ALTERNATIVE SOURCES

CHAPTER 7

§ 7.01 INTRODUCTION

In this chapter, alternatives to private financing and public offerings are discussed. The alternatives are internal funds, vendor financing, strategic partners, private lenders, commercial banks, financial institutions, commercial lessors, and government programs.

If properly structured, these alternatives can allow equity owners to leverage their assets and skills and maximize their investment return. However, financing of any type, particularly when provided by independent commercial financiers with no other stake in the business, can prove very risky if the company encounters unforeseen business difficulties.

§ 7.02 INTERNAL FUNDS, VENDOR FINANCING, AND STRATEGIC PARTNERS

In Chapter 3 and in Table 1.1 in Chapter 1, we emphasized that a start-up's first source of funds is its own. Reserves for future taxes can be used until the due date. But, a start-up must be careful. When the due date comes, the start-up must have the cash needed to pay federal or state tax authorities. Similarly, depreciation is a noncash expense that can be used as a source of funds. A start-up should check its depreciation schedule and ask, Is it appropriate for the firm, or could the firm adopt a more accelerated one? If acceleration is possible, the firm can free up more money by reducing taxes.

Vendor financing was also mentioned in Chapter 3. Net 15- or 30-day payment schedules may be lengthened considerably. The start-up may have to pay for the increase, but it is a source of funds. If negotiated properly, vendor financing may be even cheaper than bank financing.

On the flip side, customers may be willing to prepay a portion or all of a purchase price. They may pay a nonrecurring research and development fee that will enable the start-up to develop a product they need. A start-up may even persuade customers to purchase from the start-up all the products they need. If so, a long-term commitment (particularly from a prominent company) may encourage lenders and investors to provide additional financing. Also, a start-up shouldn't overlook the possibility that a prominent customer may want to invest in the start-up. Many customers have sophisticated investment departments looking for such opportunities. (For an example of a research and development strategic alliance case study, see Chapter 15.)

§ 7.03 PRIVATE LOANS

[A] Business Considerations

In many cases, the initial capital for start-ups is provided by private lenders, including founders and their friends and associates. Private debt financing is generally short-term in nature. It may be accompanied by some form of equity investment or the right to purchase equity securities in the future. Depending on the circumstances, the documentation associated with private lending may be minimal. The parties may rely on a simple promissory note containing the principal amount, the interest payment terms, and the due date.

In raising funds from private lenders, founders must be sure that they do not impair the ability of the company to secure future funding. In many cases, the private debt may have to be repaid or subordinated to subsequent venture capital financing. Alternatively, the outstanding indebtedness may be converted into equity on the same terms and conditions given to the new investors. A private lender may request a position on the company's board of directors. Any agreement on this matter should be made subject to future requirements of new investors.

[B] Legal Considerations

[1] Promissory Notes

Private loans are generally evidenced by a promissory note executed by a borrower in favor of a lender. The note contains a promise by the borrower to repay the borrowed funds together with interest at the time or times specified in the note. The note usually does not contain all the agreements between the parties regarding the loan. Instead, the parties may enter into a separate loan agreement, which contains representations and warranties from the borrower to the lender, covenants to be honored by the borrower, and events of default that give the lender the right to accelerate payment of the loan.

So long as the promissory note is retained by the original lender, the borrower will be entitled to all of its rights under the separate loan agreement. However, this will not be the case if the note is a negotiable instrument and is transferred to a third party who is deemed to be a holder in due course. The third party will have the right to enforce the payment terms of the note even though the borrower might have a valid defense against the lender under the loan agreement.

[2] Negotiable Instruments

Article 3 of the Uniform Commercial Code (UCC) is the basic law regarding promissory notes. Section 3-104 provides that the following requirements must be met for a written promissory note to be a negotiable instrument:

1. The note must be signed by the maker (the person obligated to pay the note);
2. It must contain an unconditional promise to pay a sum certain in money and not contain any other promises except as provided for in Article 3;
3. It must be payable on demand or at a definite time; and
4. It must be payable to order or bearer.

If an instrument is negotiable and negotiated to a third party who is deemed to be a holder in due course, the third party has the right to demand payment on the terms specified on the face of the promissory note. Terms of the note supersede any provisions in the original loan agreement allowing the borrower to extend or defer the time of payment. "Negotiation" occurs when all of the lender's rights under the instrument are endorsed to a third party.

By providing that the note is payable to only the named payee and not to "the order of" a named payee "or order," borrowers may ensure that a promissory note is not a negotiable instrument. A note will also not be a negotiable instrument if the promise to pay is "subject to or governed by any other agreement." Such a provision must make it clear that a person reading the note should refer to the other agreement for all the payment terms. Merely including a reference to another agreement will not be sufficient to prevent the note from being negotiable.

[3] Holder in Due Course

Section 3-302 of the UCC provides that for a third party to be considered a holder in due course, the third party must take the instrument

1. For value;
2. In good faith; and
3. Without notice
   — That it is overdue or has been dishonored, or
   — Of any defense against, or claim to, it by another person.

If the instrument is held by a holder in due course, Section 3-305 of the UCC provides that the instrument is held free from the following:

- All claims to the instrument by any person; and
- With few exceptions, all defenses of any party to the instrument that the holder has not dealt with.

§ 7.04 COMMERCIAL LOANS AND LEASES

[A] Introduction

Virtually every start-up ultimately seeks working capital from banks and other financial institutions. Commercial debt financing can be an attractive way for the owners to leverage their investment. The loan terms, however, should not unduly hamper the ability of managers to make decisions.

[B] Types of Loans

[1] Term Loan

A term loan is made for a fixed period, usually from five to ten years. It provides for installment payments of principal on a periodic basis and generally requires interest payments on a monthly basis. A term loan is commonly used for long-term capital needs, such as equipment or fixed asset purchases. The type of asset purchased dictates the timing of principal payments. If the capital improvements financed by the loan have a long life, the loan will frequently have a balloon payment at the end of the term. However, if the useful life of the financed improvements is short, principal payments generally will be amortized over the term of the loan.

[2] Revolving Line of Credit Loan

A revolving line of credit loan is like a credit card. The borrower draws on the available credit when needed. Accordingly, the loan balance fluctuates over the term of the loan. This type of loan is usually used only for short-term working capital rather than capital improvements. Borrowers prefer fixed rates for long-term purchases.

A revolving line of credit is frequently evidenced by a demand note accompanied by an agreement describing the loan terms in more detail. The agreement can be fairly simple, with the borrower able to borrow money merely by requesting it. It can also be complex, with the borrower obligated to present certificates listing the collateral securing the loan (e.g., accounts receivable and/or inventory) each time an advance is requested.

[3] Revolving Credit Loan

A revolving credit loan combines the features of revolving lines of credit and term loans. Revolving credit loans begin as a revolving line of credit for a specified period of time, during which only interest payments are made. However, the borrower is given the option of converting all or part of the loan into a term loan. This type of loan is very advantageous to a borrower that needs a term loan but cannot determine its needs until several years after borrowing the money.

[C] Secured Loans

[1] In General

A borrower may have to secure a term loan, revolving line of credit loan, or revolving credit loan by granting the bank a lien on or security interest in specific assets. A security interest permits the lender to sell the secured assets in the event of default and to apply the proceeds against the debt. In addition, a security interest prevents the borrower from granting security interests to other parties.

The most common types of collateral are accounts receivable, inventory, equipment, and real property. The standard security agreement used by most banks will include not only property owned by the borrower at the time of the loan, but also property of the same type acquired by the borrower at a later date. In effect, the lender is seeking an automatic security interest in any after-acquired property of the borrower.

[2] Accounts Receivable Financing

Many commercial financiers lend money secured by accounts receivable. The maximum amount a borrower may have outstanding at any one time is a fixed percentage, typically from 70% to 85%, of the face amount of eligible receivables. The actual percentage depends on the nature, quality, and terms of the pledged receivables. Troubled accounts, such as habitually delinquent or disputed ones, will be ineligible and not included in the borrowing base. Advances against accounts receivable typically are due on demand or within 90 days. Terms of the credit extension, including interest rate and advance rate, typically are reviewed by the lender annually.

The borrower retains the risk and expense of credit extension and collection. In some cases, a borrower's customers are not aware of the assignment of the accounts and continue to make direct payment to the borrower. However, a lender will often require that a borrower's customers be instructed to make payments directly to a post office box controlled by the lender. In addition, the bank may send verifications in the borrower's name to customers and insist on the right to make periodic unannounced audits and inspections of the borrower's accounts receivable records.

[3] Inventory Financing

Loans may also be made on the basis of the raw material, work-in-process, or finished goods inventory of a business. As with accounts receivable financing, the maximum amount a borrower may borrow is fixed as a percentage of the cost or market value of its eligible inventory. Since inventory is far more difficult to value, and is less liquid, the maximum percentage of inventory value that a lender is willing to advance is generally much lower. For example, a lender may be willing to advance a borrower up to 75% of the face value of its eligible receivables but will limit borrowings against inventory to 50%.

As with accounts receivable financing, inventory financing promissory notes generally mature on demand or within 90 days. A lender may insist on the right to inspect inventory. It will also demand that a borrower maintain appropriate insurance policies covering the inventory and related items. As a general matter, it is difficult to obtain inventory financing without accounts receivable financing.

[4] Equipment Financing

Commercial banks and finance companies often make loans secured by new and used machinery and equipment. Maturities range from one to seven years. The repayment schedule may provide for equal periodic payments, varying payments geared to a borrower's seasonal income, or small monthly payments with a balloon payment at maturity. As noted above, the timing of principal payments, as well as the term of the loan, can be tied to the anticipated useful life of the equipment.

The primary factor used in determining the amount of an equipment loan is the liquidation value of the equipment. The maximum loan amount is generally between 70% and 85% of the appraised liquidation value. In the event of default, a lender usually must repossess and sell the equipment as expeditiously as possible by either public or private sale under the UCC.

[5] Purchase Money Security Interests

As noted above, borrowers must often grant commercial lenders extremely broad security interests covering both the then-owned assets and any after-acquired assets. These assets are used to secure existing indebtedness and any future advances that may be made by the lender to the borrower. The security interests and corresponding rights granted to the first lender make it very difficult for a borrower to obtain loans from others. However, one means of obtaining additional financing is through a purchase money security interest.

A purchase money security interest is a special type of security interest available to a seller of goods or to a person making advances to enable a borrower to acquire goods. If the security is properly perfected, the holder of a purchase money security interest will have priority over the holder of any other security interest in the goods. In order to qualify for a purchase money security interest, the seller must follow strict requirements as to timing and notice, which vary depending on the type of goods involved.

To obtain a purchase money security interest, the parties involved must follow certain steps. Before delivering inventory to the purchaser, the seller (or lender financing the purchase) must give notice to any existing secured party with an after-acquired property financing statement. The seller (or lender) must also file a financing statement covering the inventory before the purchaser receives the goods. For example, if a firm that granted a blanket security interest in all of its assets wishes to purchase new inventory from a supplier who insists on security, the transaction can still be done. Before any inventory is delivered to the firm, the supplier files a financing statement and notifies the holder of the blanket security interest that the inventory is covered by a purchase money security interest.

As to goods other than inventory, there is no requirement of notice to other secured parties. The seller (or lender) will have a prior security interest merely by perfecting its security interest (by filing a financing statement) not later than 10 days after the purchaser receives the goods.

One area of constant litigation is determining when the goods have actually been received by the purchaser. This is particularly difficult when deliveries are made over an extended period of time and formal acceptance of the goods is required following setup and testing.

[6] Mortgage and Trust Deed Lending

A number of commercial lenders may be willing to provide long-term financing secured by a first and, in some cases, second mortgage or trust deed covering a borrower's real property. Common lenders are commercial banks, commercial finance companies, and savings and loan associations. This type of financing may not be available to many businesses, particularly small businesses, since they often lease their facilities rather than purchase the real property.

[7] Combination Loans

It is possible to combine two or more of the above financing methods in a single transaction. For example, if a borrower purchases substantial inventories of raw materials that are converted into finished goods for resale to customers, the appropriate loan arrangement might initially be an inventory loan. It could be replaced by an accounts receivable loan once the work is completed and the goods are sold.

[D] Loan Negotiation

[1] In General

Negotiation of a loan includes a balancing of competing interests. A lender wants to ensure that principal and interest are repaid on time. A borrower's desire is to use the funds without undue interference from the lender. It is best if the parties can approach the loan documents in a manner that is not adversarial.

Borrowers should be forthcoming about their plans and concerns. Failure to make full disclosure will not only result in surprise after the funds are disbursed but may be a breach of the loan agreement. In turn, the lender should fully discuss each of the material terms of the documentation with the borrower. In many cases, however, the size of the transaction may not justify the time necessary to tailor each provision of the lender's standard documentation.

[2] Credit Analysis

One of the first steps in the lending process is an analysis of the borrower's creditworthiness. While each lender has its own procedures, most lenders will do the following:

1. Analyze recent and projected financial statements of the borrower (including balance sheets, income statements, and tax returns),
2. Assess the quality of management,
3. Visit the borrower's physical facilities, and
4. Review the borrower's business plans.

The creditworthiness analysis not only determines whether a borrower qualifies for credit, it is the principal factor determining the interest rate to be paid. Also, information from the investigation is used to structure the terms and conditions of the loan.

[3] Commitment Letters

Assuming the borrower satisfies the lender's creditworthiness criteria, the lender will issue a commitment letter. It is, in effect, a nonbinding statement of the lender's intent to negotiate a loan agreement. The letter will list the basic financial terms proposed by the lender, such as the amount to be borrowed, interest rate, amortization schedule, loan collateral, and principal financial covenants such as debt ratios and working capital requirements. In addition, the letter will include a reference to "other usual and customary terms and conditions." It will clearly provide that no legally binding agreement will exist until the loan agreement is executed.

[E] Basic Terms of the Loan Arrangement

[1] In General

The loan arrangement should specify the following:

- Amount borrowed or, in the case of a revolving line of credit, the maximum amount of the credit line;
- Term of the loan, including the availability of any renewals;
- Interest rate to be charged over the term of the loan;
- Fees and expenses associated with the lender's commitment;

- Consequences of any prepayment of the outstanding loan amount;
- Required security interest and its terms;
- Requirement that any owners provide personal guarantees; and
- Events of default that permit the lender to demand accelerated repayment of the loan.

[2] Amount of the Loan or Credit Line

The maximum amount that a lender is willing to lend a borrower is a function of many considerations. Most important are the overall creditworthiness of the borrower and the degree of risk that the lender is willing to assume. Where uncertainty exists about the borrower's anticipated future cash requirements, a portion of the credit may be available as a term loan. The remaining amount may be drawn down under a revolving line of credit arrangement.

[3] Loan Term and Renewals

There can be little misunderstanding about the duration of the loan when the arrangement is for a fixed term. However, the parties may be confused about the length of time that funds will be available under revolving line of credit loans. As described above, these loans are usually evidenced by a demand promissory note, and the bank may believe that the amounts due under the note can be called at any time. The borrower, on the other hand, may believe a commitment has been made for a definite period of time, and that during that time the line of credit will be available so long as the borrower meets its obligations under the loan agreement. It is important for the parties to ensure that any uncertainties in this area are resolved before loan amounts are advanced.

You should also consider what happens on expiration of the original loan term. The borrower may seek an option to renew the loan on terms to be negotiated at the time the original loan expires. It may be appropriate to include in the loan documents a provision requiring that the bank give advance notice if it decides not to renew the loan. This would provide the borrower with time to work out a lending relationship with a different bank or to obtain funds from other sources.

[4] Interest Rate

There are two basic interest rate options. A fixed rate is determined at the time the loan is made, and it does not vary over the term of the loan. A variable rate is pegged to a standard that may vary over the term of the loan. It is worth asking the lender about other alternatives that may be consistent with the lender's sources of money. For example, on loans with long maturities, the parties may agree on a fixed rate that is adjusted at periodic intervals.

Fluctuations in market rates of interest have increasingly caused lenders to require borrowers to pay variable rather than fixed rates. The most popular variable rates in commercial loan transactions are tied to the following:

1. The prime rate (labeled "base rate" or "reference rate" by some lenders). Most commercial lenders now define prime rate as the rate of interest that a lender identifies or publishes as its prime rate;
2. Rates quoted by New York dealers for certificates of deposit in an amount and for a maturity approximately equal to borrower's loan. Such rates may be adjusted slightly for Federal Deposit Insurance Corporation (FDIC) insurance premiums and reserves;
3. Rates at which funds in an amount and for a maturity approximately equal to borrower's advance are available to a lender in the London Interbank or other foreign markets (adjusted slightly for reserves); and
4. Rates tied to U.S. Treasury bills, certificates, and notes.

[5] Fees and Expenses

A bank loan frequently involves payment by the borrower of one or more fees in addition to payment of the bank's out-of-pocket costs in making the loan. A single fee payable at the outset is normally based on a percentage of the entire loan amount. If the loan amount is subject to fluctuation, there may also be a fee—payable periodically from time to time over the life of the loan—based on the loan amount not yet disbursed. Let's consider both types of fees.

In addition to charging interest, commercial lenders often request that borrowers pay a fee at the outset of a loan transaction. This fee, called a facility fee or loan fee, is often charged in transactions involving substantial credit investigation or documentation requirements. The fee, generally ranging from one-eighth of 1% to 7% of the loan amount, is sometimes assessed instead of a higher interest rate.

Lenders who contractually obligate themselves to lend for a definite period of time often desire a fee for such obligation. The fee, sometimes called a commitment fee, generally ranges from one-quarter to one-half of 1% per annum of the unused portion of the commitment. An alternative may be a requirement that the borrower maintain a certain deposit balance (compensating balance) with the bank. This type of requirement has the same effect as an increase in fees or an increased interest rate.

[6] Prepayment Penalties and Restrictions

Whether or not a borrower has the option to repay all or any portion of the loan at any time is important. Commercial lenders generally fund long-term loans by purchasing long-term funds at fixed rates. The lender then establishes a rate of interest for the loan to the borrower that ensures the lender will receive a specified rate of return over the life of the loan. An early prepayment of the loan can present significant risks for creditors during periods of declining interest rates. As a result, commercial lenders usually include penalties for or prohibitions against prepayment.

[7] Security Interest

Most small business loans from commercial lenders will be secured by borrower's current or future assets. Such security is necessary since the borrower's business is unlikely to generate sufficient cash flow for the lender to be content with the borrower's general creditworthiness. The key issues in this area are the assets to be subject to the security interest and the borrower's ability to further encumber or dispose of such assets during the term of the loan.

In determining the assets to be subject to the security interest, the borrower should consider future borrowing requirements and the purpose of the borrowed funds. For example, if the current loan is being used primarily for working capital and the borrower will need to borrow in the future for capital improvements or equipment, the collateral should not extend beyond assets typically generated by working capital: accounts receivable and inventory. Similarly, if the desired loan is for the replacement of equipment or for capital expansion, only capital assets should be covered by the security interest.

As noted above, a lender will almost always seek a security interest in after-acquired property. Such security will be needed if the collateral covered by the security agreement is inventory and accounts receivable. These types of properties are continually being sold and collected by a borrower. The value of a lender's security interest would rapidly evaporate if future inventory and accounts were not included. However, when the loan involves equipment or capital improvements, an argument can be made that the security interest should apply only to the specific assets purchased with the loan proceeds.

The loan agreement should also address the ability of a borrower to grant other security interests in the collateral or to sell a portion of the collateral. As noted above, it may be necessary for a borrower to grant a purchase money security interest in assets that would otherwise be after-acquired property subject to the security agreement. Particularly where the lender insists on including after-acquired equipment and capital improvements as part of the collateral, the borrower may seek permission to sell or dispose of such assets. In such a case, the borrower may have to satisfy the minimum financial standards in the loan agreement.

[8] Events of Default

An event of default under the loan agreement will entitle the lender to demand repayment or foreclose on its security. Examples of defaults are the borrower's failure to make required payments of principal and interest, its insolvency, breach of a warranty or representation, failure to perform an affirmative covenant, or violation of a negative covenant. Nonpayment of indebtedness to others or default under agreements with other parties (cross default) may be additional events of default.

The borrower should require the lender to give it notice of an event of default and allow it, in appropriate circumstances, to "cure" the condition within a fixed period. Another limitation the borrower should include is a "materiality" threshold (e.g., a default under other agreements constitutes a default under the loan agreement only if the amount involves a specified dollar amount).

[9] Guarantees

In the case of a small business owned by relatively few individuals, a lender will almost certainly insist on personal guarantees from all, or most, of the owners. The need to provide a guarantee by definition increases the potential personal liability of the owners. The lender's ability to obtain a guarantee from individuals with substantial net worth or earnings, however, makes it more likely that the loan application will be approved and/or the interest rate will be lower.

Guarantors generally have very little bargaining power in negotiating the terms of the guarantee, particularly when the guarantors are closely involved in the day-to-day business of the borrower. Especially when the loan is secured by assets of the borrower, the borrower may wish to require the lender to enforce its security interest against the borrower's assets before enforcing the guarantee. Also, the lender's rights under the guarantee might be limited to specific items of the guarantor's property.

[F] Contents of the Loan Documentation

[1] In General

Commercial loan documentation depends on the nature and size of the transaction and the lender's wishes. Almost all transactions will be evidenced by a promissory note. Security documents may include a security agreement, mortgage, commercial trust deed, and UCC financing statement. If the loan is to a corporation, board of director's borrowing resolutions and an incumbency certificate (confirming officers' positions) are usually required. If the loan is to a partnership, a resolution of the partnership is usually required.

A lender will usually require a borrower to execute a loan agreement. The loan agreement can take a variety of forms, from a simple one-page printed document to a long and complex document with several exhibits and attachments. No matter what format is used, the agreement will cover the following items: the general terms of the loan; representations and warranties required of the borrower; affirmative and negative covenants relating to the business after loan proceeds are made available; and conditions to closing, including legal opinions and officers' certificates.

[2] General Terms of the Loan

The general terms of the loan arrangement should have been settled as part of the preliminary negotiations. Once again, these terms include the amount of credit to be made available, the term of the loan, the dates on which principal and/or interest must be paid to the lender, the interest rate to be charged on outstanding principal amounts, commitment fees and related expenses, prepayment provisions, security interests, events of default, and guarantees.

[3] Representations and Warranties

As with any form of financing arrangement, the loan agreement will contain a number of representations and warranties by the borrower. While these representations and warranties tend to be boilerplate, the borrower should always take time to determine whether the statements requested by the lender are necessary to the loan transaction. Otherwise, the borrower would incur an unnecessary expense due to having to investigate, or have counsel investigate, its own activities. In addition, if necessary, the borrower should request modifications to the statements to ensure that they are accurate and that the borrower is not immediately in default.

[4] Covenants

Commercial lenders will seek a number of covenants that allow them to exercise some control over a borrower. Such control is intended to ensure that loan amounts are repaid on a timely basis. Since it is unlikely that lenders (unlike equity investors) will participate in the management of a borrower, covenants tend to be more extensive in debt financing than in equity financing. As with representations and warranties, failure of the borrower to observe a covenant is a default under the loan agreement, and it gives the lender the right to accelerate repayment of the entire loan.

Covenants in loan agreements are both affirmative and negative. Affirmative covenants focus on the obligations of the borrower to provide the lender with information, to maintain insurance on the borrower's assets, and to comply with operating and financial requirements. Negative covenants restrict the ability of the borrower to make material changes in its business or in its accounting procedures, to dispose of or encumber material assets, or to make certain payments or investments.

While affirmative and negative covenants in commercial loan documents are generally extensive, banks tend to focus on two points: their ability to receive financial information from the borrower and the borrower's ability to manage its cash and other assets. The following are typical requests:

1. The borrower must provide the lender with a variety of information, including financial statements, notices of labor disputes, legal proceedings, and changes in any material contracts. Information requirements are further supplemented by the lender's right to inspect the books and assets of the borrower.
2. The borrower must maintain sufficient insurance to protect the value of its assets and is prohibited from selling or disposing of any assets without consent of the lender.
3. The borrower must attend to corporate housekeeping matters, including maintaining proper books and records, paying all taxes when due, and complying with applicable laws and regulations.
4. The borrower is precluded from creating any liens or encumbrances or incurring any additional indebtedness. In some cases, the borrower may be prevented from making any major expenditure on fixed assets, even if an expenditure does not create new indebtedness.

5. Distributions to shareholders, either by redemption or by dividend, may be restricted. In the case of loans made to small closely held businesses, compensation payments (such as salaries and other fringe benefits) to the owner-employees may be restricted.
6. No material changes will be allowed in the borrower's business, including entry into new lines of business, changes in management, changes in ownership, mergers, divestitures, and changes in the borrower's articles of incorporation.
7. The borrower must adhere to specified minimum working capital and financial ratio requirements.

[5] Legal Opinions and Closing Certificates

Commercial lenders will usually require various legal opinions regarding the borrower and the particular transaction, as well as several officers' certificates and copies of documents. Matters generally covered in a legal opinion include proper incorporation of the borrower, corporate good standing, the borrower's corporate power and authority to carry on its business and to enter into the transaction, authorization of the loan arrangement by the borrower, and enforceability of the loan agreement against the borrower.

Officers' certificates delivered in commercial loan deals include an acknowledgment that all representations and warranties in the loan agreement are true and that the borrower complies with the loan covenants as of the closing. Borrowers must provide lenders with certified financial statements, copies of charter documents, and board and shareholder resolutions covering the transaction.

Equipment Leasing: To Lease or Not to Lease

BENEFICIAL CAPITAL LEASING, INC.

by James Bishop

In today's competitive and rapidly changing markets, no one understands better than owners about the need to acquire capital to build their businesses. Many owners are migrating into the world of business and are coming face-to-face with the need to secure financing. They want and need the convenience and flexibility of leasing as a means of providing capital for equipment acquisitions. A quality lease program offers businesses an excellent alternative to conventional financing of their capital equipment.

Flexibility and convenience are two of the major reasons why the popularity of leased equipment is on the rise. Rapid growth in leased equipment is expected to continue throughout the next millennium. Today, nearly 80% of major American companies use leasing as a financial tool, and more and more decision-makers are becoming part of the leasing generation. Leasing puts equipment to work for you without a substantial capital investment, without depleting your traditional bank credit, and with fixed payment schedules.

The following benefits should be carefully considered:

1. Acquire the capital equipment without tying up capital. Traditional financing may require a large down payment in order to receive your equipment; leasing can provide 100% financing. Most lease arrangements require only one or two monthly payments down in order for you to obtain the equipment.
2. Protect your lines of credit at the bank. Lease payments typically have no effect on your credit lines with your bank. You can preserve your borrowing power for future acquisitions and business opportunities.
3. Maintain a competitive edge and have the latest and best capital equipment. Leasing gives you the advantage of having cutting edge technology at a minimal cost.

4. Deploy the latest technology and upgrade your equipment once it has outlived its useful life. The cutting edge technology you are working with today may not remain that way for long. With a lease you have the flexibility of planned obsolescence, with the option of purchasing your equipment at the end of the lease.
5. Assist with soft costs such as delivery and installation. A lease can include everything to get your business up and running.
6. Account for lease payments as operating expense for tax purposes and reduce your tax liability. Applied as a pretax business expense, lease payments come out of pretax dollars.
7. Simplify accounting. Lease payments are typically only a line item in your monthly cost of operation—a minimal bookkeeping effort that frees you from time-consuming depreciation schedules.

In summary, many questions should be addressed when deciding whether to buy or lease your capital equipment, such as

- How long with you be using the asset?
- What is the expected life of the asset?
- Will a greater savings result from leasing or from buying?
- Is there sufficient cash available for a purchase?
- Will avoiding debt-financed purchases improve your balance sheet?

Suggestions

- Own that which appreciates, and lease that which depreciates.
- Maintain liquidity and conserve working capital for income producing investments.

§ 7.05 GOVERNMENT FUNDING

[A] Overview

Financing programs are available to small businesses through federal agencies, as well as from state and local governments. Government financing may be available on terms more attractive than those offered by private sources. Moreover, businesses may find it easier to qualify for government financing than for conventional loans.

The largest source of government financing for small businesses is the federal Small Business Administration (SBA), which provides both regular business loans and special loans available only to certain businesses or under certain circumstances. (See Appendix C for addresses and phone and fax numbers of SBA offices.) In addition, other federal agencies will make financing available to small businesses that satisfy their qualification requirements. Historically, state and local government financing has been provided through the issuance of industrial development bonds. Although the use of these bonds has fluctuated in recent years, governmental agencies at the state and local levels have developed their own programs for providing financial assistance to small businesses.

[B] SBA Commercial Business Loans

[1] In General

The SBA lends either directly or in participation with banks and private lenders. Its loans are designed to provide working capital, finance plant construction, and enable inventory or plant equipment acquisition. SBA financing is available to businesses that fall within the definition of *small business* and that satisfy all of the following criteria:

1. Financing from private commercial sources must not be available;
2. There must be a reasonable assurance that the loan will be repaid; and
3. The loan must be for an appropriate business purpose.

In reviewing loan applications, the SBA gives special consideration to veterans of the armed forces and their survivors or dependents.

[2] Definition of *Small Business*

Applicants for SBA small business loan programs must fall within the definition of *small business,* that is, a business independently owned and operated, not dominant in its field, and which satisfies standards in its industry for number of employees, sales, or receipts. For example, a wholesaling business is considered "small" if the average number of employees in the preceding 12 calendar months did not exceed 100. A retailing business is considered "small" if annual gross sales or receipts are not over $3,500,000 (or up to $13,500,000 in some industries).

[3] Regular Business Loans

The SBA will make regular business loans to small businesses that satisfy certain general credit requirements. These loans are available to finance plant construction or expansion, to acquire inventory or equipment, and to provide working capital. SBA loans are made either directly with government funds or through private participating lenders on a guarantee loan basis. Private lenders include banks, savings and loan associations, mortgage lenders, credit unions, and similar firms subject to either state or federal regulation. (See Appendix D for information on banks that make SBA loans.)

SBA business loans may be approved for up to 25 years, whereas working capital loans are usually limited to 7 years. The SBA requires all available business assets to be pledged. Personal guarantees of the principals in the business are always required. Also, the SBA often requests that applicants obtain hazard insurance on business assets and life insurance on key persons.

In order to qualify for an SBA regular business loan, an applicant must

1. Be of good character;
2. Show ability to operate his or her business successfully;
3. Have enough capital invested so that, with the requested SBA loan, he or she can operate the business on a sound financial basis; and
4. Show that the past earnings record and future prospects of the business are adequate to repay the loan and other fixed debt, if any, out of profits.

As noted, the SBA will consider a loan application only when the requested funds are not available from normal credit sources on reasonable terms. Additionally, the applicant must not be able to raise money by liquidating or borrowing against assets personally owned by the applicant's sole proprietors, partners, or principal shareholders. A principal shareholder is a person owning 20% or more of the outstanding stock. Furthermore, the SBA will not make loans

1. To pay off a loan that is inadequately secured; to make payments or distributions to owners, partners, or shareholders of the applicant; or to replace funds previously used for one of these purposes;
2. For speculation in any kind of property to be held for investment or resale;
3. To nonprofit enterprises, except for certain types of business cooperatives;
4. To newspaper, magazine, or book publishing businesses;
5. If any portion of the gross income of the applicant is derived from gambling, unless legal;
6. To an enterprise engaged primarily in lending or investing;
7. If the loan would encourage a monopoly or be inconsistent with the accepted standards of free competition; or
8. To finance the construction or acquisition of recreational or amusement facilities not open to the public.

For guarantee loans, the SBA may guarantee up to 90% of the loan amount or $500,000, whichever is less. The interest rate is set by the lender within a ceiling rate established by the SBA, although a variable interest rate pegged to the cost of money by the federal government may be used. A guarantee fee of 1% is usually paid by the applicant on approval of the application by the SBA. When the SBA makes a direct loan using its own funds, the amount of the loan normally cannot be in excess of $150,000. The interest rate is determined by the SBA's cost of borrowing from the U.S. Treasury.

[4] Special Business Loans

In addition to regular business loans, the SBA has a wide variety of special business loan and credit programs, including the following:

Economic Opportunity The SBA makes economic opportunity loans to assist firms operated by low-income or socially disadvantaged individuals. An economic opportunity loan may be up to $100,000 and can have a term of up to 15 years.

Disaster Loans SBA loans are available to businesses, homeowners, and nonprofit entities that have suffered substantial uninsured losses in natural catastrophes. The catastrophe must be declared a disaster by the president of the United States, the secretary of agriculture, or the SBA administrator. These loans may be up to $500,000 for businesses and have a maturity of up to 30 years. The interest rate is fixed by Congress. In addition, the SBA can make loans to businesses and agricultural cooperatives situated in a disaster area that have suffered, or are likely to suffer, substantial economic injury as a result of the disaster.

Small Business Energy Loans SBA loans are available to small businesses to manufacture, engineer, distribute, market, install, or service energy devices that will conserve the nation's energy sources. The amount of these loans may not exceed $350,000 as a direct loan or $500,000 as a guaranteed loan. The term of the loan cannot exceed 15 years.

Export Revolving Lines of Credit The SBA can provide revolving lines of credit to small businesses exporting to or seeking to develop foreign markets. Applicants must have been in operation for at least 12 months before filing an application and must not have outstanding debt in excess of $500,000.

State and Local Development Companies The SBA provides assistance to state and local governments interested in attracting new businesses or in expanding existing businesses. It will also make loans to, and guarantee debentures issued by, qualified development companies.

[C] Small Business Investment Companies

Small Business Investment Companies (SBICs) were created pursuant to the Small Business Investment Act of 1958. Although they are private corporations formed under the corporate laws of the state in which they are located, they are licensed and regulated by the SBA. SBICs provide operating capital to "small business concerns," as defined under SBA regulations, through long-term loans and equity investments. In addition, an SBIC can provide management and consulting services for a fee.

SBICs often make equity investments in small businesses, which may take the form of outright stock purchases or a convertible debt instrument. In those cases where SBICs provide loans, the term may extend up to 20 years. The rate of interest may be up to the smaller of 15% per annum or the maximum rate permitted under the law of the state in which the SBIC operates.

SBICs generally obtain a portion of their capital from private investors. Once the initial capital has been obtained, SBICs may borrow operating funds from the SBA or from banks and other private financial institutions through SBA guaranteed loans. As a general rule, SBICs may invest their funds in almost all types of retail, manufacturing, and service industries run by small business concerns under the SBA regulations. Some restrictions on SBIC activities are as follows:

1. Funds may not be provided for relending to another firm or for any purpose contrary to the public interest, such as gambling or encouraging a monopoly;
2. Funds may not be provided for foreign investment, agricultural enterprises, or any business not conducted as a regular or continuous activity;
3. While SBICs may invest in real property enterprises, the aggregate amount of such investments cannot exceed one-third of the SBIC's portfolio; and
4. The total funds loaned to or invested in equity securities of a particular portfolio company may not exceed 20% of the paid-in capital and surplus of the SBIC.

[D] Small Business Innovation Research Program

Under the Small Business Innovation Research Program (SBIRP), federal agencies involved in research must make research awards to small business. Grants must equal 2.5% of each agency's total budget. They are issued in two phases: Phase I awards for up to six months and $100,000, and Phase II awards for up to two years and $750,000. Awards are available for early stage ideas and prototypes.

The program—exceeding $1.1 billion—is larger than any commercial venture fund. It also has a higher applicant acceptance rate. Over 10% of applicants in Phase I are approved. The percentage of Phase II applicants who are approved is even higher—about 45%. However, this number may not be representative since Phase II applicants must have received a Phase I award.

[E] Small Business Technology Transfer

Similar to SBIRP, Small Business Technology Transfer (STTR) is a federal program that funds cooperative research and development work between small businesses and nonprofit research institutions. It was established in 1992 by the Small Business Research and Development Enhancement Act and is funded through money set aside from federal research and development. The program is intended to stimulate technological innovation, strengthen small businesses in meeting federal research and development needs, and increase private sector commercialization of federal research projects.

STTR is a much smaller program than SBIRP. For fiscal year 2000, SBIRP's budget was $1.1 billion, while STTR's budget was only $62.4 million. Many of the agencies participating in SBIRP also participate in STTR, such as Departments of Defense, Energy, Health and Human Services; National Aeronautics and Space Administration; and National Science Foundation. SBIRP, however, does have more participating agencies than STTR.

To be eligible for STTR, you must meet many of the same requirements as for SBIRP. You must be a small business, be independently owned more than 51% by U.S. persons, be for-profit, and have less than 500 employees including affiliates. Separately, research institutions are eligible to participate in STTR.

Like SBIRP, STTR provides two phases of funding. Phase I is good for one year for up to $100,000. Phase II is available for two years for up to $500,000.

[F] Advanced Technology Program

Advanced Technology Program (ATP) provides later-stage funds than SBIRP, and products financed under it must have a clear commercial application. It also provides larger grants—up to $2 million. ATP funding falls into two categories: general and priority.

Competition is fierce. Applicants must prepare a lengthy report and defend it before a board in Washington, D.C.

[G] Cooperative Research and Development Contracts

Companies can work with scientists in federally funded research and development organizations under Cooperative Research and Development Contracts. Projects are negotiated between the company and the R&D organization. Research results can be exclusive or nonexclusive to the parties, depending on the agreement negotiated.

[H] Dual Use Applications Program

This program replaced the Technology Reinvestment Project, better known as TRP, that was shut down several years ago due to political pressure.

Applications under Dual Use Applications Program (DUAP) must be for the development of militarily useful products with commercial applications. Successful applicants will receive grants or be allowed to participate in cost-sharing development. Projects can be for development of new technology or for application of existing technology to new uses.

[I] Manufacturing Extension Partnership

The Manufacturing Extension Partnership (MEP) is federally funded but, like the SBA, administered locally, with about 50 local centers. MEP's focus is to help start-ups adopt modern management and production techniques. It is run by the National Institute of Standards and Technology. Unlike the SBA, the MEP charges a fee for advice and assistance.

[J] Export Assistance

Even the smallest company can receive funding from the U.S. Export-Import Bank (Ex-Im) for exports. Funding by Ex-Im is available in several forms: working-capital guarantees, direct loans and guarantees, export credit insurance, insurance policies for small businesses, short-term single buyer policies, and medium-term insurance.

Ex-Im has authorized certain local banks to commit funds on behalf of Ex-Im. This means a small company can work with its local bank (if approved by Ex-Im) without having to deal with distant authorities in Washington, D.C.

The Department of Commerce is also a valuable resource for small companies looking to export their products. Through the foreign offices it maintains in U.S. embassies, it can help U.S. companies locate overseas customers, distributors, and suppliers.

[K] Other Federal Programs

[1] In General

Financing and finance assistance for small businesses are available through a number of other federal agencies, including the Farm Service Agency (FSA), the Economic Development Administration (EDA), the Bureau of Indian Affairs (BIA), and the Department of Housing and Urban Development (HUD).

[2] Farm Service Agency

The FSA provides loans to farmers and ranchers for a variety of purposes, including operating expenses, acquisition of land and equipment, conservation, housing, and watershed protection.

[3] Economic Development Administration

The EDA has loan funds available for plant acquisition, construction, modernization, and expansion that will create new jobs in areas experiencing unemployment and underemployment.

[4] Bureau of Indian Affairs

The BIA assists businesses owned by members of Indian tribes that are located on or near Indian reservations.

[5] Department of Housing and Urban Development

HUD has several financial aid programs relating to housing and community development. These programs include mortgage guarantees on multifamily and rental housing, and loans and other assistance to property owners for urban renewal and housing.

[L] State and Local Governments

In addition to federal programs, many state and local governments have developed various schemes designed to encourage and financially assist small business enterprises. Historically, industrial development bonds were a good source of financing for businesses. Currently, state and local assistance may take the form of favorable tax rates, direct donations or loans, and the construction of facilities that are then made available for lease to specified businesses.

Existing programs fall into three categories:

1. Those that retain existing businesses and attract new ones,
2. Those that assist more traditional firms adopt modern technology, and
3. Those that assist start-ups.

Recently, assistance to new companies has received a great deal of attention. Many states and municipalities sponsor "incubators" for start-ups: Participants receive a range of advice and assistance—from inexpensive office space to professional services, such as legal and accounting advice. Many states also offer financial support—either directly or by referral to private funding.

Government Support: Right Here in River City—How One City Supports Entrepreneurs

COLLEGE OF BUSINESS AND
PUBLIC ADMINISTRATION
UNIVERSITY OF LOUISVILLE

by Robert L. Taylor, Dean

Governments can be a great source of support for entrepreneurs. Louisville, Kentucky, nicknamed the River City, is an example.

Over the past three decades, Louisville, Kentucky, was transformed from a midwestern manufacturing hub to a service economy. Yet, the historical context of a distribution hub continued to characterize the community. The city was formed as a place where goods were unloaded from barges on the Ohio River because the "Falls of the Ohio" prevented seamless river transport. As the cargo was carried on wagons past the falls and reloaded onto barges, a thriving distribution center emerged. When the railroads converged in Louisville in the early 1900s, this scenario was repeated. And again, when the interstate highway system was developed, Louisville found itself a distribution hub with river, rail, and truck systems serving the needs of America's largest population centers. Convenient transportation attracted large manufacturing firms for farm equipment, automobiles, and appliances. However, the manufacturing activities slowly moved to offshore locations in quest of cheap labor. Yet, distribution remained important.

Then, in the 1990s, UPS created an air hub where most of the transcontinental and international packages converged, were sorted, and loaded on more than 120 planes for delivery the next day. Once again, a transportation hub was the economic engine of the city.

As the 20th century drew to a close, supply chain management and e-commerce defined the business model for the global economy. Essentially, this was a redesign of physical distribution management with information as the hub. Overnight, new ventures were launched that connected producer with consumer through electronic means, reducing the time from when a need for goods and services was identified to when the need was satisfied. UPS adopted the motto, "Moving at the Speed of Business." The only constant was change, and the city embarked on an impressive transformation.

The first step was the development of a regional strategic plan for economic development. Some 120 people from all walks of life met to craft the future of the community. At the same time, city leaders engaged a consultant, Ross Boyle, to assess our strengths and suggest alternatives. With vigor and enthusiasm, public and private sector groups came to consensus. Distribution was still a strength. Information technology was a critical element that needed development, and the university needed strengthening. Most important, the community had to develop a climate that fostered entrepreneurship—in spirit as well as substance.

From the resulting reports, business groups merged with government organizations to create Greater Louisville, Incorporated. This organization brought all of the business attraction and retention initiatives into a single, focused group. To look to the future, the Enterprise Corporation was established as a corporate subsidiary to stimulate and nurture the development of new companies. To meet the rapidly changing technological and economic environments, community leaders knew that an adaptive and responsive organization would best serve the economic development of the community.

Interestingly, the Enterprise Corporation was charged with communicating the philosophy of entrepreneurship as much as it was asked to support the development of emerging businesses. Through publicity, speeches, and the celebration of new ventures, civic and business leaders articulated that Louisville was a great place to start a business. It helped to have some early successes in information technology. A local entrepreneur sponsored a technology "summit," which disclosed that over 100 companies were located along a corridor on the East End of the community. Soon, people were talking about this phenomenon and the city was cited in a popular journal as one of the best medium-sized cities for entrepreneurship. A number of events helped to demonstrate that the community was focused: getting people to "believe" that Louisville was engaged in e-commerce, the selection of UPS as *Forbes* best company in 1999, announcement of a new Small Business Investment Corporation, the top-10 ranking of the University of Louisville College of Business and Pubic Administration by *Success* magazine, and co-locating new venture and small business development centers into a single entity.

By taking inventory of what existed, combining public and private resources for supporting new ventures, and building upon success, Louisville quickly emerged as an "entrepreneurial" city. Once expressed, people within and outside the community recognized the energy and commitment. Thus, this is a real success story of how the spirit of entrepreneurship can change a community.

CHAPTER 8 • PRIVATE OFFERINGS

CHAPTER 8

§ 8.01 INTRODUCTION

[A] The Private Placement Market

Many federal securities regulations concentrate on organized exchanges and over-the-counter markets for publicly traded securities. Nevertheless, a large amount of financing activity takes place in the private placement market. This market is composed of offerings exempt from the registration requirements of the Securities Act.

As a rule, participants in the private placement market are sophisticated and knowledgeable about the business and prospects of issuers. At least in some cases, however, the suitability of the investors is determined only by reference to their place of domicile, not by their ability to make informed investment decisions. Potential investors include relatives of the original promoters, venture capitalists, banks, and other institutional investors. Private placements are generally by issuers who do not have securities traded in a public market. Public companies, however, raise capital in the private market from time to time.

The private placement market is not unregulated. There are detailed requirements that must be satisfied for the original sale to be exempt from registration. In addition, securities purchased in a private placement are restricted. They cannot be resold to the public for some period of time or at all without the filing of a registration statement. Also, in most cases, the availability of the exemption depends on disseminating information about the issuer and the offering to investors. When the offering is pursuant to one of the "safe harbors" established by the SEC, the issuer must provide information that is functionally equivalent to that required in a registration statement. In addition, a private placement transaction will be subject to the antifraud provisions of both federal and state securities laws.

[B] Statutory Framework

In addition to exemptions from registration for specified securities, the Securities Act and SEC rules provide transactional exemptions. These exemptions fall into two principal classes: private offerings and limited offerings. *Private offering* exemptions allow an issuer to make isolated sales to persons, who because of high levels of net worth or involvement with the issuer, are considered knowledgeable and sophisticated investors. It is assumed that they do not need the disclosure protections of the Securities Act. In a *limited offering*, the dollar amount that can be raised is strictly circumscribed. Purchasers in a limited offering must have access to all material information concerning the issuer and the securities being offered. The manner in which the offering may be conducted is also strictly regulated.

The private offering exemptions are in Section 4(2) of the Securities Act and in Rule 506 of Regulation D issued under it. The limited offering exemptions are found in Sections 3(b) and 4(6) of the Securities Act and in Rules 504 and 505 of Regulation D and in Regulation A thereunder. In addition, because of the limited nature of the *transactions* in which they are issued, under Section 3(a) of the Securities Act the following securities are exempt from the registration requirements:

- Single issuer exchanges addressed in Section 3(a)(9),
- Regulated exchanges addressed in Section 3(a)(10), and
- Intrastate offerings addressed in Section 3(a)(11) and Rule 147 issued under it.

[C] General Characteristics of Private Placements

[1] Manner of Offering Requirements

The marketing of private and limited offerings must be strictly limited. The securities may not be offered by any general solicitation or advertising, including an advertisement or article published in a newspaper, magazine, or similar media. Similarly prohibited are seminars and meetings in which participants are solicited.

[2] Disclosure Requirements

Qualified private and limited offerings will be exempt from the formal registration requirements of the Securities Act, such as the need to file detailed information on the issuer and the terms of the offering. An issuer will still be required to distribute material information needed by an investor to make an informed investment decision. For example, nonaccredited investors in a Rule 505 offering must be given information substantially similar to that in a registration statement. Similarly, Regulation A offerings require detailed offering circulars.

[3] Resale Restrictions

Private and limited offering exemptions relate only to specified transactions, not to the securities themselves. Except in a few limited exceptions under Rule 504 and Regulation A, a purchaser may not transfer the securities without registering them or qualifying under an exemption. An example is the Rule 144 "safe harbor" (actions that are unlikely to be challenged) for resale of restricted securities.

[4] Principles of Integration

One important question in structuring a nonregistered transaction is whether the offering will be integrated with another offering. If so, the two offerings are combined and treated as a single transaction under the securities laws. For example, a private placement to a limited group of investors could precede a subsequent public offering. If they are integrated because of proximity in time, the first offering would be considered part of the public offering. Since the private sales were made before the registration statement was filed, the issuer has violated Section 5 of the Securities Act. Similarly, the integration of two Regulation D transactions might result in a single offering exceeding the dollar volume limits or the maximum number of unaccredited investors allowed under Regulation D.

Generally, integration is a question of fact based on factors such as the following:

- Offerings are part of a single plan of financing,
- Offerings have the same consideration,
- Timing of the sales is similar,
- Offerings are for the same class of securities, and
- Offerings were made for the same general purpose.

Rule 502(a) of Regulation D incorporates each of these factors and then creates a safe harbor:

> Offers and sales that are made more than six months before the start of a Regulation D offering or are made more than six months after completion of a Regulation D offering will not be

considered part of that Regulation D offering, so long as during those six month periods there are no offers or sales of securities by or for the issuer that are of the same or a similar class as those offered or sold under Regulation D, other than those offers or sales of securities under an employee benefit plan as defined in Rule 405 under the Act.

§ 8.02 NONPUBLIC OFFERINGS UNDER SECTION 4(2)

[A] Introduction

Section 4(2) of the Securities Act provides that the provisions of Section 5 do not apply to "transactions by an issuer not involving any public offering." The Securities Act does not define *public offering*. However, the exemption has been interpreted to permit an issuer to make isolated sales to persons with access to information about the issuer and the transaction. As noted, it is assumed that purchasers equipped with such information do not need the protection of the Securities Act disclosure requirements. Traditionally, Section 4(2) has been regarded as exempting private placements with institutions and closely related persons. It is not available for offerings of speculative issues to unrelated and uninformed persons.

[B] Standards for Availability of Exemption

[1] In General

The Section 4(2) private placement exemption turns on whether purchasers need the protection of a Securities Act registration. This depends on their ability to fend for themselves and their access to information. Over the years, the SEC and courts have tried to develop guidelines on when the exemption is available. Although each situation is different and requires a thorough analysis of relevant circumstances, the factors generally considered are (a) the number of offerees, (b) the sophistication of the offerees, (c) the size and manner of the offering, and (d) the relationship of the offerees to the issuer.

While each of these factors is considered by the SEC and the courts, the primary focus is on purchasers' access to information about the issuer, purchasers' sophistication, and their ability to understand information they received in making a decision. Factors such as manner and size of the offering are also relevant. Obviously, the intent of purchasers to hold the securities for some period of time and not make a public distribution is fundamental to the exemption.

Section 4(2) can be used by any type of issuer and for the sale of an unlimited amount of securities. However, issuers should be aware of the uncertainties underlying the above factors, as reflected in decisions by the SEC and the courts over the years. Rule 506 of Regulation D was designed to provide a safe harbor for issuers using the Section 4(2) exemption. If Rule 506 is not used, the issuer must carry the burden of proof that it satisfied the Section 4(2) exemption as to each offeree (not just each purchaser).

[2] Access to Information

There is no specific statutory explanation of Section 4(2) offerings. For the exemption to be available, it is generally thought each offeree must have the kind of information that would be disclosed in a registration statement. Information is the cornerstone of the exemption. It is not sufficient that an investor is sophisticated or experienced. Those traits are of no use if the investor does not have personal knowledge of, or access to, appropriate information. The issuer has the burden of showing that offerees have been provided with appropriate information.

[3] Sophistication of Offerees and Purchasers

Offerees and purchasers in an exempt private placement must be "sophisticated." This means that they must have such knowledge and other experience in business and financial matters that they are capable of evaluating the merits and risks of the prospective investment. The knowledge and expertise can be personal or through investment or financial advisors. Sophistication without access to information is not sufficient. Investors can fend for themselves only where there is personal knowledge of or access to the information.

The relevant degree of sophistication and experience is not related to transactions in securities. It is the ability to evaluate the profit potential of an issuer's particular business.

[4] Manner of Offering

The manner of offering is critical. For instance, a general solicitation of investors or a public advertising indicates that the offering has been made to the general public. On the other hand, transactions involving direct negotiation are more likely to be nonpublic. Those effected through a public distribution (underwriters) are more likely to be public.

[5] Number of Offerees

The general counsel to the SEC stated, in an early interpretation of the Securities Act, that the availability of the private offering exemption is not to be determined exclusively by the number of prospective offerees. It is generally believed that the greater the number of offerees, the less likely the offering will be private. The SEC believes that the greater the number of offerees, the more likely that persons relatively unfamiliar with the issuer will become involved in the offering. Similarly, as the number of offerees increases, the uniformity of information provided to potential investors tends to disintegrate.

The general counsel to the SEC also stated that the basis on which offerees are selected is important in determining what constitutes a substantial number of offerees. Thus, an offering to a group selected at random is more likely to be a public offering than an offering to a larger number of persons, all of whom are members of a restricted group.

[6] Investment Intent

The disclosure requirements of the Securities Act are intended to protect the ultimate purchaser. Thus, it is important to know whether the purchasers will hold the securities or act as conduits.

An issuer relying on the private placement exemption must exercise reasonable care to assure that the purchasers have not purchased with a view toward distribution. If they have, they may be "underwriters" within the meaning of Section 2(11) of the Securities Act. Issuers should take the following actions to restrict transfers:

- Make reasonable inquiries to determine whether each purchaser is acquiring the securities for its own account,
- Inform each purchaser in writing that the securities are unregistered and cannot be resold unless they are subsequently registered or an exemption is available,
- Print on each certificate a legend referring to the restriction on transferability, and
- Give stop-transfer orders to the issuer's transfer agent for violations of the transfer restrictions.

[7] Resale Restrictions

Given the need to ensure that the purchasers have the requisite investment intent and are not underwriters, it is essential that an issuer take steps to restrict the resale of the securities. Securities acquired directly or indirectly from an issuer in a nonpublic offering are restricted securities. As such, they can be resold only under certain conditions, including registration or compliance with Rule 144 (SEC's safe harbor for resale of private placement securities) or Rule 144A (as described in Chapter 14).

An issuer should inform a purchaser that a legend will be placed on its certificate and a stop transfer order will be issued to the transfer agent to prevent unauthorized transfers. If an issuer has no contractual obligation to register the securities, it is a deceptive practice to fail to make that fact clear. If an issuer represents that it will register the securities, it must inform the purchaser when and under what circumstances it will do so. An issuer should also advise the purchaser whether the issuer will furnish information needed to make routine sales under Rule 144.

§ 8.03 REGULATION D AND SECTION 4(6)

[A] Overview

[1] Regulation D

Pursuant to Sections 3(b) and 4(2) of the Securities Act, the SEC enacted Regulation D. The Regulation integrates and liberalizes the registration exemptions, unifies federal and state exemptions, and facilitates capital formation. Regulation D is actually a series of eight rules, Rule 501 through Rule 508, organized as follows:

1. Rule 501 defines terms applicable to the three exemptions in Rules 504, 505, and 506, including *aggregate offering price, accredited investor,* and *purchaser representative;*
2. Rule 502 establishes general conditions for each exemption, such as how the offering is made, resale conditions, integration, and disclosure requirements;
3. Rule 503 provides a uniform notice-of-sales form, designated Form D, to be filed with the SEC;

4. Rule 504 permits sales of up to $1,000,000 in securities in a 12-month period, without regard to the number of purchasers;
5. Rule 505 permits an issuer to sell up to $5 million of securities in a 12-month period to a limited number of accredited investors and to 35 or fewer nonaccredited investors;
6. Rule 506 permits sales of an unlimited dollar amount of securities to an unlimited number of accredited investors and not more than 35 unaccredited purchasers;
7. Rule 507 disqualifies an issuer from future use of Regulation D if it fails to file a Form D; and
8. Rule 508 contains a substantial and good faith compliance defense.

[2] Section 4(6)

The Section 4(6) exemption is available for offers by an issuer:

- Solely to one or more accredited investors,
- If the aggregate offering price does not exceed the limit of Section 3(b), and
- If there is no advertising or public solicitation.

Although there are no disclosure requirements for offerings under Section 4(6), the antifraud rules of the federal securities laws apply. The definition of *accredited investors* for purposes of Section 4(6) conforms to Regulation D. Any securities purchased in a Section 4(6) offering are restricted.

[B] Rule 504

Rule 504 provides an exemption from registration for offerings and sales of up to $1,000,000 of securities during any 12-month period. It applies to all issuers other than "blank check companies," reporting companies, or investment companies. The dollar limitation includes securities sold during the applicable 12-month period in violation of the registration provisions. It also includes sales under the Section 3(b) exemption (including Rule 505 and Regulation A offerings). It does not include Rule 506 or Rule 147 offerings. There is no limitation on the number of offerees in an offering under Rule 504. Nor are there specific offeree and purchaser requirements.

Offers and sales under Rule 504 must comply with the terms and conditions in Rules 501 through 503. However, the general limitations on manner of offering and resale in Rule 502(c) and (d) do not apply under

Rule 504. Accordingly, general solicitation and advertising may be used to sell securities under Rule 504. In addition, such securities may be resold freely without registration. This makes Rule 504 a vehicle for a limited value public offering.

No specified disclosure document has to be used for a Rule 504 offering. However, the offering will remain subject to antifraud provisions of federal and state securities laws. In addition, a disclosure document of some type may be required under state blue-sky laws. In any case, consideration should be given to preparing a simple disclosure document. It should include relevant risks to be considered by investors.

[C] Rule 505

[1] In General

Rule 505 exempts offers and sales to no more than 35 nonaccredited investors and an unlimited number of accredited investors where the aggregate offering price does not exceed $5,000,000 over a 12-month period. As with Rule 504, the aggregate offering price includes proceeds from other sales under Section 3(b) of the Securities Act. Rule 505 can be used by any issuer, except investment companies and issuers that have been disqualified because of prior conduct as described in Rule 262 of Regulation A. These exemptions are commonly known as "bad boy" provisions.

In a Rule 505 offering, issuers must disclose certain information to nonaccredited investors. The content depends on whether the issuer is subject to reporting requirements of the Exchange Act, and if not, depends on the aggregate offering amount of the securities involved. General solicitation and advertising cannot be used to sell securities under Rule 505. Securities purchased in a Rule 505 offering are restricted securities and cannot be resold without registration or an exemption.

[2] Offerees and Purchasers

If there is no general solicitation or advertising, a Rule 505 offering can be made to an unlimited number of offerees. Such an offering can involve an unlimited number of accredited purchasers as well as 35 nonaccredited purchasers. Nonaccredited purchasers may have to meet sophistication or suitability requirements under the state laws. In addition, they may have to demonstrate that they are able to bear the risks associated with the investment.

[3] Information Requirements

Under Rule 502(b)(1), if an issuer sells securities under Rule 505 to any nonaccredited investor, it must furnish the purchaser with the information specified in Rule 502(b)(2). A note to Rule 502(b)(1) also suggests that information provided to nonaccredited investors should be given to accredited investors as well, in view of antifraud rules. These information requirements can be somewhat onerous, particularly for issuers not yet subject to the reporting requirements of the Exchange Act.

[4] Resale Restrictions

Securities acquired under Rule 505 have the same status as securities acquired under Section 4(2) of the Securities Act. This means they are restricted securities and may not be resold without registration or an exemption.

[D] Rule 506

[1] Overview

Rule 506 is a private offering exemption under Section 4(2) of the Securities Act. It exempts offers and sales of an unlimited dollar amount of securities to an unlimited number of accredited investors and to no more than 35 nonaccredited purchasers. An issuer must reasonably believe that the nonaccredited investor, either alone or with its representative, has such knowledge and experience in financial and business matters that it is capable of evaluating the investment. In many ways, Rule 506 serves as a safe harbor for the broader Section 4(2) exemption.

General solicitation and advertising cannot be used to sell securities under Rule 506. Securities purchased in a Rule 506 offering are restricted and cannot be resold without registration or an exemption. The disclosure requirements for Rule 505 offerings apply to Rule 506 offerings, and nonaccredited investors must be given the same information as under Rule 505. Where the dollar amount of the offering exceeds $7,500,000, a nonreporting issuer must provide the same kind of information as required in Part I of registration statements.

[2] Eligible Issuers

Any issuer, including an investment company and issuers subject to reporting requirements of the Exchange Act, can use the Rule 506 exemption. Unlike

Rule 505, Rule 506 does not disqualify an offering because of the prior conduct of persons affiliated with an issuer.

[3] Restrictions on Aggregate Offering Price

Since Rule 506 was promulgated under Section 4(2) of the Securities Act, offerings under it are not subject to any restrictions on aggregate offering price. Such restrictions apply to offerings under Rules 504 and 505, since these Rules were issued under Section 3(b) of the Securities Act.

[4] Offerees and Purchasers

Rule 506 permits sales to an unlimited number of accredited investors and to 35 nonaccredited investors. The nonaccredited purchasers of a Rule 506 offering, either alone or with the assistance of a purchaser representative, must have sufficient knowledge and experience in financial and business matters to evaluate the prospective investment. Under Rule 506 the sophistication requirement applies solely to purchasers and not to offerees.

Rule 501(h) defines a *purchaser representative* as any person who satisfies all of the following conditions or whom an issuer reasonably believes satisfies *all* of the following conditions:

1. Is not an affiliate, director, officer, or other employee of the issuer; or beneficial or direct owner of 10% or more of any class of issuer's equity securities; except where the purchaser is
   (i) A relative of the purchaser representative by blood, marriage, or adoption and not more remote than a first cousin;
   (ii) A trust or estate in which the purchaser representative and any persons related to him as specified in (i) above or (iii) below collectively have more than 50% of the beneficial interest (excluding contingent interest), or of which the purchaser representative serves as a trustee, executor, or in any similar capacity; or
   (iii) A corporation or other organization of which the purchaser representative and any persons related to him as specified in (i) or (ii) above collectively are the beneficial owners of more than 50% of the equity securities (excluding directors' qualifying shares) or equity interest;
2. Has such knowledge and experience in financial and business matters that he is capable of evaluating, alone, or together with other purchaser representatives of the purchaser or together with the purchaser, the merits and risks of the prospective investment;

3. Is acknowledged by the purchaser, in writing, during the course of the transaction, to be his purchaser representative in connection with evaluating the merits and risks of the prospective investment; and
4. Discloses to the purchaser in writing a reasonable time prior to the sale of securities to the purchaser any material relationship between himself or his affiliates and the issuer or its affiliates that then exists, that is mutually understood to be contemplated, or that has existed at any time during the previous two years, and any compensation received or to be received as a result of such relationship.

[5] Information Requirements

Rule 502(b)(1) applies to an issuer selling securities to any purchaser who is not an accredited investor. In such cases, the issuer must furnish the information specified in Rule 502(b)(2) to the purchaser within a reasonable time prior to sale. Many issuers, taking into account the antifraud provisions of the federal securities laws, will prepare an offering document in a Rule 506 offering even when all of the purchasers are accredited investors.

[6] Resale Restrictions

Rule 502(d) provides that securities acquired in a transaction under Rule 506 are restricted securities and may not be resold without registration or an exemption.

[E] Accredited Investors and Counted Purchasers

[1] Accredited Investors

The concept of an accredited investor plays an important role in many exemptions under Regulation D and Section 4(6):

1. Purchasers who are accredited investors are not counted for determining the 35-purchaser limitations of Rules 505 and 506.
2. A disclosure document does not have to be delivered to an accredited investor. Accordingly, in an offering made entirely to accredited investors, no disclosure document is required.
3. If written information is furnished to accredited investors but not to nonaccredited investors, the nonaccredited investors must be advised of this fact. On request, they must be furnished the same information.
4. Section 4(6) offerings can be made only to accredited investors.

Rule 501(a) defines an *accredited investor* as any person who falls within specified categories or whom an issuer reasonably believes comes within one of them at the time of sale. Accredited investors are presumed to have sufficient sophistication and experience without an issuer making any subjective judgment. Among the included categories are the following:

Individuals Persons who individually or jointly with their spouse have a net worth of $1 million are accredited investors. Also included are persons who individually have an income in excess of $200,000 (or jointly with their spouse of $300,000) and who have a reasonable expectation of reaching the same income level in the current year.

Affiliates of an Issuer An executive officer, director, or general partner of an issuer (or of an issuer's general partner) is an accredited investor. *Executive officer* is defined broadly to include the president; any vice president in charge of a principal unit, division, or function; and any other officer (including executive officers of a subsidiary) or any other person who performs a policy-making function.

Institutional Investors The accredited investor category includes several types of institutions:

- Banks as defined in Section 3(a)(2) of the Securities Act,
- Savings and loan associations or other institutions as defined in Section 3(a)(5)(A) of the Securities Act whether acting in an individual or a fiduciary capacity,
- Insurance companies as defined in Section 2(13) of Securities Act,
- Investment companies registered under the Investment Company Act of 1940,
- Business development companies as defined in Section 2(a)(48) of the Investment Company Act,
- Small Business Investment Companies licensed by the U.S. Small Business Administration under Section 301(c) or (d) of the Small Business Investment Act of 1958,
- Private business development companies as defined in Section 202(a)(22) of the Investment Advisors Act of 1940, and
- Broker-dealers registered with the SEC under the Exchange Act.

Employee Benefit Plans An employee benefit plan within the meaning of the Employee Retirement Income Security Act (ERISA) is an accredited investor. The investment decision must be made by a plan fiduciary as defined by that Act. The fiduciary must be "a bank, savings and loan association, insurance company, or registered investment adviser," or the plan must have total assets in excess of $5 million. Employee benefit plans established by states, or their political subdivisions, agencies, and instrumentalities, are now accredited investors. A self-directed plan in which investment decisions are made solely by persons who are accredited investors is an accredited investor.

Business Associations Any nonprofit, tax-exempt organization, corporation, partnership, or business trust with total assets of $5 million or more is an accredited investor. The entity must not have been formed for the sole purpose of purchasing securities under Regulation D. In addition, certain nonbusiness trusts will qualify as accredited investors, as will corporations and partnerships in which all the equity owners are accredited investors.

[2] Counting Nonaccredited Purchasers Under Regulation D

Under Rule 501(e)(1), for determining the 35-person limitation, the following are treated with the purchaser as one person under Rules 505 and 506:

- A relative, spouse, or relative of the spouse of a purchaser who has the same principal residence as the purchaser; and
- Trusts, estates, corporations, and other organizations in which the purchaser owns collectively more than 50% of the beneficial (equity) interest.

Rule 501(e)(2) provides that a corporation, partnership, or other entity is counted as one purchaser unless it is organized for the specific purpose of acquiring the securities being offered. If the latter, each beneficial owner of the entity's securities is counted. In analyzing whether an entity should be regarded as organized for the specific purpose of making an investment, the investor must consider a number of factors:

- The existence and nature of prior activities by the entity,
- The structure of the entity (i.e., whether the entity has centralized management and decision making),
- The proposed activities of the entity,
- The relationship between the entity's investment in the offering and the entity's capitalization, and
- The extent to which all equity owners of the entity participate in investments by the entity.

Angel Investors: Angels in the Infield

HSA CORP

by Kent Oyler

If starting a cutting-edge, high-tech telecommunications firm in Kentucky poses a challenge, locating and selecting a locally based venture capital group to guide and back such a venture is an even more formidable task.

High Speed Access Corp (HSA Corp) started its business life with a vision of leapfrogging the big cities by bringing high-speed data services and Internet access to rural Kentucky markets, a process we billed as "rural datafication." In many ways, HSA Corp was a typical Silicon Valley garage start-up—the brainchild of a zealous visionary with a half-completed plan and no money. That visionary, a computer services marketer named David Gibbs, came to me in late 1996 seeking business guidance and a working phone line. Having started several other unrelated businesses and desiring to make a foray into the Internet world, I provided David with a subsistence salary, a corner of my conference room, and some plane tickets. The money came out of my management firm's meager business development budget in return for stock. (I strongly believe there is a growing role for entrepreneurial development firms to serve as farm teams for promising business plans.)

Over a period of several months, after dozens of toner cartridges and more than a little anguish, a business plan and a demonstration site were created. Our product was high-speed Internet access over cable TV systems, and the company was finally incorporated in 1997 as CATV.net, LLC. The service delivered Internet access at about 100 times the speed of dial-up connections. The demonstration site was Maysville, Kentucky (Rosemary Clooney's hometown). The first customer was the misnamed First National Bank, a rough biker bar that hooked up their stool-mounted PC to a coin slot and bookmarked all kinds of interesting Web sites. We also wired the schools and government offices for free and homes for $39.95 per month. Not pretty, but we had actually brought the first privately funded broadband access to rural Kentucky. Money invested was topping $200,000.

By that time it had become evident that there existed a market for broadband in smaller markets. It was also clear that the cost of delivering such access would be much more than my own checkbook could support. That started the search for a venture capital firm to take us to the next level. We purchased a CD-ROM of all the VC firms that might have interest in our type of business. We talked to local CRGs (Certified Rich Guys), or "angels." We worked through a San Jose–based VC marriage maker. We followed up through our accounting firms. In all, we probably talked to 20 potential backers, most of them out of town.

It soon became clear that the foremost criterion for selecting a VC firm must be integrity. They all had money, and most had good contacts, but would they have integrity to do right by the founders and have the stomach to stand by the plan? Throughout our search we kept in contact with a locally based VC firm, Chrysalis Ventures. Chrysalis was formed by Doug Cobb (who had sold out his PC book and magazine publishing company, The Cobb Group) and by David Jones, Jr., whose family had created Humana. We finally approached them asking for (1) corporate guidance, (2) contacts, and (3) funding, in that order. Chrysalis immediately struck us as people of their word. They assigned a partner to work with us, and he thoroughly researched the industry, our business, and us personally. They also wanted to know that they were dealing with people of integrity. They helped us redraft our business plan and lined up four other VC firms to make an initial $2.5 million convertible preferred stock investment. Our first board consisted of three current or ex-Fortune 500 CEOs, which addressed our corporate guidance issues.

In the process of conducting due diligence on CATV.net, Chrysalis looked into our potential competitors and determined that at least one of them was also worthy of their funding. HSA.net was a Denver-based cable Internet service provider at about the same size and stage of development as CATV.net. After a short courtship, Chrysalis funded HSA.net with the same term sheet CATV.net had used. Eventually, we merged our two start-ups to form HSA Corp. Now, some eight months later, we are in the midst of a $50 million second-round financing involving world-class strategic investors, and we have gained entry into some of the leading telecommunications and computer firms in the country.

Most of HSA Corp's success, and certainly our success in attracting investment, is attributable to work done by our local VC firm. I am now a firm believer that VC firms should be not silent investors but close partners with their portfolio companies. This isn't the easiest arrangement for a CEO, because such a VC firm will be a very involved board member and partner, but start-ups can and must learn and benefit from this guidance and control. We feel fortunate to have located a helpful partner that we can see from our window and can have access to at almost any time. Perhaps the Internet industry won't supplant bourbon distilling and horse racing in Kentucky, but now we know that it is possible to start and prosper as a VC-backed high-tech firm in the Bluegrass State.

[F] Information Requirements

[1] In General

As previously noted, nonaccredited investors purchasing securities in a Rule 505 or 506 offering must be supplied with certain information prior to the purchase. What information is required depends on whether the issuer is a reporting company, and if not, depends on the aggregate size of the offering.

[2] Disclosures by Nonreporting Issuers

The disclosure required from issuers not subject to the reporting requirements of the Exchange Act depends on the size of the offering. For offerings over $7,500,000 (which can only be done pursuant to Rule 506), issuers should expect to have to provide Form S-1-type disclosure. For offerings over $2,000,000 but not above $7,500,000, issuers may choose between the extensive disclosures on Form S-1 and, if available to the issuer, new Form SB-2. For offerings up to $2,000,000, in addition to these two alternatives an issuer can provide the information required in a Regulation A offering.

[3] Disclosures by Reporting Issuers

A reporting company would ordinarily furnish its annual report for the most recent fiscal year, information contained in its most recent proxy statement, and any interim reports (i.e., Forms 10-Q, Form 8-K, or equivalents in the SB series) recently filed. In addition, a copy of the most recent Form 10-K or Form 10-KSB must be furnished if an investor requests it in writing.

As an alternative, an issuer may furnish the most recent among its Form 10-K or Form 10-KSB; registration statement on Form S-1, Form S-11, or Form SB-2; or registration statement under the Exchange Act. A reporting company must also furnish a brief description of the securities being offered, the intended use of proceeds from the offering, and any material changes not reflected in the documents furnished.

[4] Timing of Disclosures

There is no prescribed time (except in the course of the offer and a reasonable time before the sale) at which the required disclosure document must be delivered under Rule 505 or 506. Accordingly, an issuer may use a summary document at the outset of the offering, but a disclosure document meeting the requirements of Regulation D must be delivered within a reasonable time prior to sale.

[5] Additional Inquiries and Information

Within a reasonable time before a purchase by a nonaccredited investor, an issuer must furnish a brief description of any written information provided to an accredited investor. At a reasonable time before any purchase, an issuer must offer a purchaser an opportunity to ask questions and receive answers on the offering and to verify the accuracy of information previously supplied.

[G] Other Requirements and Conditions of Regulation D

[1] Limitations on Manner of Offering

Except for Rule 504 offerings, unregistered securities may not be offered or sold by any form of general solicitation or general advertising, including any advertisement or article published in a newspaper, magazine, or similar media and any seminar or meeting in which participants are solicited. While there are no restrictions on the payment of commissions or other remuneration for offerings under Regulation D, state securities laws may impose such restrictions.

[2] Resale Restrictions

Securities issued pursuant to Rule 504 are not subject to any restrictions on resale. Shares sold under Rule 505 or Rule 506 are restricted securities. As such, they can be resold only if registered or pursuant to an applicable exception. Rule 502(d) calls for an issuer to exercise reasonable care to ensure that purchasers are not underwriters within the meaning of Section 2(11) of the Securities Act. The Rule goes on to state that reasonable care may be demonstrated by

1. Reasonable inquiry to determine if a purchaser is acquiring the securities for itself or other persons;
2. Written disclosure to each purchaser prior to sale that the securities have not been registered under the Securities Act and, therefore, cannot be resold unless registered under the Securities Act or unless an exemption is available; and

3. Placement of a legend on the certificate, or other document that evidences the securities, stating that the securities have not been registered under the Securities Act and setting forth or referring to the restrictions on transferability.

[3] Form D Filing Requirements

Issuers relying on any of the exemptions under Regulation D are required to file five copies of a Form D with the SEC no later than 15 days after the first sale of securities pursuant to the exemption. One copy of the Form D must be signed by a duly authorized person on behalf of the issuer. If reliance is placed on Rule 505, the issuer must undertake to furnish to the SEC, on request, a copy of the disclosure document to be furnished to nonaccredited investors. Once the initial filing has been made, no further filings are required. Amendments, however, may be necessary to correct information that is inaccurate at the time of the original filing or that becomes inaccurate in a continuing offering.

Although issuers relying on Regulation D routinely file a Form D, the filing is not a condition to the availability of the exemption. However, under Rule 507, if an issuer fails to timely file Form D, the SEC can obtain an order from a court of competent jurisdiction directing a filing. Once such an order is issued, the issuer is disqualified from relying on Regulation D in future transactions. The disqualification can be waived if the issuer can show good cause that the exemption should not be denied.

[4] Rule 508 and Insignificant Failures to Comply

The Regulation D exemption originally required compliance with all terms and conditions of Rules 501 through 503 and of the specific Rule (504, 505, or 506) on which reliance was being made. Regulation D was amended to add new Rule 508, which is an attempt to provide comfort to issuers that insignificant deviations from a term, condition, or requirement of Regulation D will not cause the exemption to be lost.

Rule 508 provides that failure to comply with a condition or requirement will not result in a loss of the exemption if

- Such condition or requirement was not directly intended to protect the complaining party,
- Failure to comply was "insignificant to the offering as a whole," and

- A good faith and reasonable attempt was made to comply.

Failure to comply with the following, however, "shall be deemed to be significant to the offering as a whole":

- Dollar limitations of Rules 504 and 505;
- Number of purchaser limitations of Rule 505 and 506;
- Limitations, to the extent applicable, on general solicitations or general advertising; and
- An action brought by the SEC.

§ 8.04 OTHER EXEMPT TRANSACTIONS UNDER FEDERAL SECURITIES LAW

[A] Introduction

While Section 4(2) and Regulation D are the most common exemptions from registration, there are several other possibilities:

- Intrastate offering exemption, which can be used when offers and sales are confined to the state in which the issuer has been incorporated and conducts its primary business activities;
- Regulation A exemption, which involves the preparation of a detailed disclosure document that must be reviewed by the SEC prior to the commencement of sales;
- Exemptions for voluntary exchanges with existing shareholders and for transactions that have been approved by specified governmental bodies;
- Regulation S exemption for offshore offerings; and
- Rule 701 exemption for employee benefits.

[B] Intrastate Offering Exemption

[1] In General

Under Section 3(a)(11) of the Securities Act, an intrastate offering is exempt from registration. It is defined as a security offered and sold only to residents within the state or territory where (a) if the issuer is a person, the person is residing and doing business, or (b) if the issuer is a corporation, it is incorporated and doing business. The exemption applies only to local financings by local industries carried out by local investments. It is based on the assumption that intrastate transactions are adequately policed by state regulation. The exemption, if available, is an exemption from the registration requirements only and not from the antifraud provisions of the federal securities laws.

[2] General Requirements of Section 3(a)(11)

Section 3(a)(11) offerings generally must satisfy fairly strict conditions, including the following:

1. Offers and sales must be limited to the state in which (a) the issuer is organized, (b) the issuer has conducted a substantial amount of its operations, and (c) the proceeds of the offering are to be used.
2. All offerees and purchasers must be resident in the state, which has been interpreted to mean that they must be domiciled in the state.
3. Procedures must be implemented to ensure that no resale is made to persons outside the state for at least one year following completion of the offering.

There is no limit on the amount of funds that may be raised in a Section 3(a)(11) offering. Nor is there any requirement regarding the information to be supplied to offerees and purchasers. An issuer need not make any filings with the SEC. The state blue-sky law requirements, however, must be satisfied.

[3] Rule 147

The SEC adopted Rule 147 as an interpretative regulation clarifying the Section 3(a)(11) exemption for intrastate offerings. Rule 147 attempts to give objective content to pivotal concepts such as "resident" and "doing business." It also clarifies the requirement that the securities actually come to rest within the state in which the offering occurs. Rule 147 is not exclusive. Reliance may still be placed on the exact statutory language of Section 3(a)(11), as interpreted by the SEC and the courts. Given that prior interpretations of Section 3(a)(11) have been largely restrictive, it is generally prudent to rely on Rule 147.

[C] Regulation A Offerings

[1] In General

Regulation A provides an exemption from registration requirements of the Securities Act for public offers and sales of securities up to $5,000,000 during any 12-month period. An issuer must comply with certain requirements, including the filing of a notification (analogous to a registration statement) and an offering circular (resembling a prospectus). The number of offerees or purchasers in a Regulation A offering is unlimited. Purchasers need not meet any criteria with regard to wealth, residence, or investment sophistication. Nor are restrictions imposed on commissions or other remuneration for sales. Moreover, the securities issued in a Regulation A offering are not restricted and may be freely resold.

Regulation A is an exemption from the registration requirements. Detailed disclosure conditions, as well as the need for a filing with and review by the SEC, actually make Regulation A a simplified registration procedure for small public offerings. Requirements as to information to be included in an offering circular are generally less stringent than in a registration statement. Nevertheless, preparation of the notification and offering circular can be expensive and time-consuming. Also, the need for SEC review can create uncertainties on when the offering can begin and the date proceeds will be available.

[2] Issuer Requirements

Regulation A is generally available for issues by a corporation, association, or trust incorporated or organized under the laws of the United States, Canada, or a state or province of either. The issuer must also have its principal business operations in the United States or in Canada. Regulation A also can be applied to securities issued by an individual who is a resident of, and has principal business operations in, any state or province of the United States or Canada. It is not available if the issuer, or any underwriters or related persons, within specified periods, have been convicted of securities violations, have been subject to SEC disciplinary proceedings, or were parties to certain other proceedings.

[3] Regulation A Procedures

Regulation A procedures mimic the procedures for filing and processing registration statements, with minor exceptions. The document filed under Regulation A is an offering statement in contrast to a registration statement. There is one form for the offering statement (Form 1-A) rather than the several forms on which registration statements can be filed. The disclosure counterparts to a preliminary prospectus and definitive prospectus are a preliminary offering circular and a final offering circular.

An offering statement has to be qualified before a security offered in reliance on the Regulation A exemption can be sold. Qualification is accomplished by filing the offering statement with the SEC office in the region where the issuer's principal operations are conducted. In theory, an offering statement is qualified on the 20th calendar day after filing. As a practical matter, effectiveness of the offering statement will be delayed until the SEC has reviewed the statement, given its comments to the issuer, and approved amendments to the offering statement made in response to the comments. The effectiveness of the offering statement can be deferred by a delaying notation on the facing page. The SEC has the power to enter a suspension order to ensure that the offering does not commence until the SEC completes its review.

The issuer may use preliminary offering circulars to obtain indications of interest while the SEC reviews the offering statement. Technically, each amendment to the offering statement commences the 20-day period again. However, once the SEC staff has finished its review and is prepared to allow the offering statement to become effective, the delaying notation is removed. The director of the Division of Corporate Finance and Regional Administrators then accelerates the process by declaring the offering statement effective without the expiration of any current 20-day period.

Regulation A contains various requirements for delivery of the offering circular prior to sales. They are similar to the requirements for delivery of a prospectus in a registered offering. The issuer is also required to update any offering circular that becomes false or misleading during an offering. In the case of continuous offerings, the offering statement must be requalified 12 months after the date of initial qualification. At that time, it must be revised to include, among other things, updated financial information.

[4] "Test-the-Waters" Documents

Amendments to Regulation A permit companies to "test the waters" before filing an offering statement under Regulation A. This rule allows a company without an established market for its securities to communicate factual information about itself and its business to prospective investors. It can then assess investors' interest in the company, before incurring any legal, accounting, and other costs in preparing a Regulation A offering document.

Rule 254 describes how the test-the-waters procedure works:

- Issuers are permitted to publish or deliver to prospective investors a written document or make scripted radio or television broadcasts to determine whether there is any interest in a contemplated securities offering;
- The written document or script must (a) state that no money or other consideration is being solicited, and if sent in, will not be accepted; (b) state that no sales of, or commitment to purchase, the securities are possible until an offering circular is delivered; (c) state that if a prospective investor indicates an interest in the offering, doing so will not create any obligation or commitment; and (d) identify the chief executive officer of the issuer and its business and products;
- On or before the first use of the written document or the script, the issuer must submit a copy to the SEC's regional office where the issuer's principal business operations are conducted or proposed; and
- Once the document or script has been submitted to the SEC, the issuer may commence oral communications with investors and make broadcasts. However, sales may not be made until 20 calendar days following the last publication or delivery of the document or broadcast. This assumes that the other requirements of Regulation A have been fulfilled. Also, once the issuer has filed its Regulation A offering circular, it must cease any further use of the test-the-waters materials.

The SEC has revised Rule 254 to make it clear that a written test-the-waters document complying with Regulation A is not a prospectus. While the use of such a document amounts to an exemption from prohibitions on general solicitation, information in the documents and oral communications will be subject to the antifraud provisions of the federal securities laws. This may dictate that, as a precaution, securities counsel must still be heavily involved in the preparation of the materials.

The test-the-waters procedures were adopted over intense criticism by state securities regulators. They were concerned that the lack of definitive disclosure requirements virtually eliminated federal oversight of the offer process. Since the test-the-waters materials will likely be an offer under the laws of most states, issuers must be certain they do not violate state securities rules.

[5] Preparation of the Offering Statement

Form 1-A contains the requirements for the notification, offering circular, and exhibits under Regulation A. The notification provides information necessary for the SEC staff to determine whether Regulation A is available. The notification must disclose the predecessors, affiliates, directors, officers, promoters, and principal security holders of the issuer, the underwriter, and persons affiliated with the underwriter. It must also describe any prior disqualification under Regulation A and, if there is any prior disqualification, why a waiver is sought. The notification is also designed to disclose the extent to which prior sales of unregistered securities reduced the availability of Regulation A.

Three choices are available for the narrative disclosure portion of the offering circular. First, if the issuer is a corporation, it may use Model A, a replication of the Form U-7 registration form adopted by the North American Securities Administrators Association, Inc. (NASAA) as a model registration form for small corporate offerings. Second, corporate or other issuers may furnish the information specified in Model B, which is based on disclosures previously required by Regulation A. It is similar to disclosures under the now-obsolete Form S-18. Third, corporate or other issuers may furnish information (except for financial statements) required by Part I of Form SB-2, the new registration form for SBICs.

The financial statement requirements are the same under all three models. Typically, an issuer is required to furnish a balance sheet as of a date within 90 days prior to the filing of the offering statement (or such longer time as the SEC may permit, within certain parameters). It must also file statements of income, cash flows, and stockholder equity. These statements must cover each of the two fiscal years preceding the date of the most recent balance sheet being filed (or for the period of the issuer's existence, if shorter). An issuer may file unaudited financial statements unless it has already prepared audited ones.

Part III of Form 1-A specifies the exhibits to be filed. These exhibits include consents of experts and a consent of each named underwriter. Generally, the exhibits required in a Regulation A filing are not substantially different from those required in a registered offering. They include all material contracts other than those entered into in the regular course of business. Form 1-A also requires an opinion of counsel as to the legality of the securities being offered. A copy of the test-the-waters materials also must be attached.

[6] Liability for Fraud

Section 11 of the Securities Act applies to false or misleading statements in a registration statement. It does not apply to filings pursuant to Regulation A. Section 12(2) of the Securities Act and Rule 10b-5 under the Exchange Act, however, do apply to false or misleading statements in the offering circular or under a Regulation A offering.

[D] Voluntary Exchanges with an Issuer's Own Security Holders

An exchange of one security for another is a sale under the securities laws. Hence, an exchange offer by one corporation to the shareholders of another corporation is subject to the registration requirements of the Securities Act. However, Section 3(a)(9) of the Securities Act provides an exemption from the registration provisions for

> . . . [a]ny security exchanged by issuer with its existing security holders exclusively where no commission or other remuneration is paid or given directly or indirectly for soliciting such exchange.

The Section 3(a)(9) exemption allows an issuer to restructure its capital structure. For example, if an issuer had a class of preferred stock outstanding, it could offer to exchange such shares for a new class of stock. It cannot pay any commission for such exchange. This does not preclude the corporation from paying cash to the shareholder as a term of the exchange offer. Except in limited circumstances, the security holders cannot be asked to pay anything for the exchange.

The offering must be exclusively with the issuer's security holders. This raises a question of integration when an issuer is offering the same security more or less simultaneously to others.

[E] Judicially or Administratively Approved Reorganizations

Section 3(a)(10) of the Securities Act exempts from registration any securities issued in exchange for other securities if the issuance has been approved by a court or appropriate administrative body. In order for the exemption to apply, the administrative or judicial approval must be after a hearing at which all persons to whom the issue is proposed have the right to appear.

As a rule, resales of securities acquired under the exemption must be registered under the Securities Act or resold pursuant to Rule 144. However, the SEC has indicated that stock acquired in a merger in which the fairness has been passed on by a state agency is exempt under Section 3(a)(10). In such a case, the stock received by shareholders is not restricted stock under Rule 144.

The Section 3(a)(10) exemption is a relatively narrow one, because not all approved reorganizations are covered. First, there must be express statutory authority for the approval by a state or federal governmental authority. Second, there must be a formal hearing and approval after the fairness of the exchange is considered. Finally, the exemption is not available if the terms of the exchange are finalized before the governmental hearing is held.

[F] Regulation S: Offshore Offerings

Under Regulation S, "offers and sales that occur outside the United States" are not subject to the registration requirements of Section 5 of the Securities Act (Rules 901 and following). Under Rule 903, an offer or sale is deemed to occur outside the United States if it is in an offshore transaction made without any directed sales efforts in the United States. Certain procedural safeguards, which depend on the type of issuer, must be satisfied. An "offshore transaction" is an offer made to a person not in the United States at the time the buy order is originated. U.S. citizens resident abroad, and U.S. citizens who go abroad to buy non–U.S. securities, may purchase securities under Regulation S.

Regulation S contains several requirements applicable to U.S. issuers not yet subject to the Exchange Act reporting requirements. These requirements include

- Legends on the offering documents,
- Contractual undertakings by participants in the distribution to comply with the requirements of Regulation S,
- Specified confirmation notices to securities professionals,
- A restricted period of 40 days during which offers and sales to or for the account of persons in the United States may not be made,
- A one-year lock-up for equity securities along with stop-transfer restrictions, and
- Certifications by purchasers that they are not U.S. persons and are not purchasing for the account of U.S. persons.

Moreover, the offering must be completed without direct sales efforts in the United States. *Direct sales efforts* includes advertising in publications with a general circulation in the United States.

Rule 904 contains the resale exemption under Regulation S. Rule 904 permits secondary distributions without registration in offshore transactions. It can be used for resale of securities purchased both within and outside the United States in private placement transactions.

Accordingly, Regulation S can be used by a nonreporting company to make what amounts to an initial public offering of its securities to overseas investors. It will, of course, be subject to any foreign securities requirements.

[G] Rule 701: Compensatory Benefit Plans

Rule 701 exempts offers and sales of securities pursuant to certain compensatory benefit plans and contracts relating to compensation. Issuers must not be subject to Exchange Act reporting requirements, nor be an investment company. Issuers are still subject to the disclosure and antifraud rules, as well as state laws. Only registration under the Securities Act is exempt. Stock issued under Rule 701 is restricted, and any resales must comply with the registration requirements.

The purpose of the offer and sale is relevant. If the issuance is designed to raise capital, rather than reward employees, registration is required.

To qualify for exemption under Rule 701, the issuance must be pursuant to

1. A written compensation benefit plan established by the issuer (or an affiliate) for employees, officers, directors, general partners, trustees, consultants, and advisors. In the case of consultants and advisors, they must have provided bona fide services that are not in connection with the benefit plan; or
2. A written contract relating to the compensation of one of the above classes of individuals.

A compensation benefit plan includes any purchase, savings, option, bonus, stock appreciation, profit-sharing, thrift, incentive, pension, or other plan.

The amount of securities that may be sold under Rule 701 in one year may not exceed the greatest of

1. $1 million,
2. 15% of the issuer's total assets, or
3. 15% of the outstanding securities in the class.

§ 8.05 LIMITED OFFERINGS UNDER STATE BLUE-SKY LAWS

[A] In General

Even though an offering may be exempt from registration under the federal securities laws, an issuer must still determine if it is subject to the blue-sky laws of any state in which the securities will be offered. A number of states have exemptions for private offerings similar to Section 4(2) of the Securities Act. As a rule, the limited offering exemptions under the state blue-sky laws bear little resemblance to federal exemptions.

Section 402(b)(9) of the Uniform Securities Act (Uniform Act) exempts offers made to not more than a specified number of persons within the state during a 12-month period. All purchasers must acquire the securities for investment, and no commissions can be paid. The maximum number of permitted offerees varies between 10 and 25. The state administrator generally has the ability to modify the number of offerees or allow the payment of commissions. An issuer must file an application for such modification with the state administrator. The application must contain information similar to that required for qualifying the transaction.

The Uniform Act also contains an exemption in Section 402(b)(8) for offers and sales to institutional investors. Commissions are permitted under this exemption. Such offers and sales need not be counted for purposes of any exemption under Section 402(b)(9) of the Uniform Act.

[B] Uniform Limited Offering Exemption

The NASAA has adopted a Uniform Limited Offering Exemption (ULOE). The ULOE is contained in a "Uniform Rule." Despite its name, states can and did modify the rule when adopting it. The Uniform Rule is an exemption for offers and sales that comply with Rules 501–503, 505, and 506 of Regulation D. It contains a number of limitations beyond those in the federal rules:

1. No commission or other remuneration (direct or indirect) or finder's fee can be paid to any person for soliciting a prospective purchaser unless the person is registered in the state.
2. Bad boy disqualifications are expanded to address whether the issuer has any currently effective stop-orders for nonregistration in any state within the past five years; has been convicted within the past five

years for any felony involving fraud, deceit, forgery, embezzlement, or larceny; is subject to a state securities administrative order or judgment within the past five years; or is subject to a restraining order for making a false filing with any state. The state administrator can, on showing of good cause, waive any ground for disqualification by finding it is not necessary.

3. An issuer must file a Form D. The state has the option to require that the form be filed prior to receipt of any consideration or subscription agreement. The state can require an issuer to (a) pay a filing fee in connection with the filing of Form D, (b) file a consent to service of process, and (c) furnish disclosure documents.
4. As to nonaccredited investors, an issuer must have reasonable grounds to believe and after making reasonable inquiry shall believe *one or the other* of the following conditions: (a) the investment is suitable for the purchaser based on the purchaser's other security holdings, financial situation, and needs; or (b) the purchaser, either alone or with a purchaser representative, has such knowledge and experience in financial and business matters to be capable of evaluating the merits and risks of the prospective investment. A purchaser is presumed to satisfy the first requirement if the investment does not exceed 10% of its net worth.

By incorporating the requirements of Regulation D, the ULOE effectively adopts the Regulation's conditions regarding number and type of purchasers, aggregate size of offering, and information that must be disclosed to purchasers within the state. However, the ULOE allows the administrator to waive conditions of the offering and increase the number of permitted purchasers. The person claiming the exemption has the burden of proof under the ULOE.

[C] Form U-7: Small Corporate Offerings Registration Form

NASAA Form U-7, titled "Small Corporate Offerings Registration Form," was originally adopted for securities offered on the federal level under Rule 504. Form U-7 serves as both a registration statement and a disclosure document. According to its instructions, the form is designed for use by "companies, the attorneys and accountants for which are not necessarily specialists in securities regulation." Form U-7 is far from a do-it-yourself form, as is clear from the assumption that an attorney and accountant will be involved. Nor does the form call for only a bare-bones disclosure. In fact, the information required is quite extensive and rivals Form S-1. Form U-7 has been adopted by a number of states. It may be available for use in Rule 504 or Regulation A offerings.

Disclosures required by Form U-7 are to be presented in a question and answer, fill-in-the-blank format. That is, the form contains 50 questions with lines to be filled in after each question. An issuer's officers should be able to complete the first draft of the form themselves. Required disclosures cover such things as risk factors; business and properties; offering price factors; use of proceeds; plan of distribution; capitalization; description of securities; dividends, distributions, and redemptions; officers and key personnel; directors; principal stockholders; management relationships, transactions, and remuneration; litigation; and federal tax matters.

Breaking Away: Getting Founders to Let Go

ORION CAPITAL

by Dale E. Allison

Getting the founder to let go is a difficult problem for start-up companies.

Individuals with strong personalities establish start-ups. Founders would not have otherwise fought such tremendous odds to establish a company. It takes a strong belief in yourself. You must believe that you can make a success of a company doing something no one else has done.

Founders make the company a success in part because of this strong personality. It is this same personality that makes it difficult for founders to delegate when the company becomes too big for them to single-handedly manage. At some point, they must begin to delegate if the company is to expand. For many companies, $1 million in sales and 50 employees is a critical point when delegation becomes a critical issue.

Having recently worked with a brilliant founder and having persuaded him to let loose the reins of power, I can make a few observations.

First, if the company is to be a success, a founder must bring in professional managers that he can rely on. This will cost him some shares or options, and thus some ownership. It will also cost him some control. He will no longer be able to dictate or determine all decisions. And having brought in professionals, he will be bumping up against other individuals with strong wills. He must learn to work with others, probably for the first time in the company's history.

Second, having brought in professionals, he must rely on them. There is too much for him to control or at least control well.

Third, there are a number of lessons that must be understood if you want to persuade a founder to delegate.

- When being hired, get a description of what you are being hired to do and your authority levels. Put them in your contract. When a dispute arises, you may be able to persuade the founder by referring to the agreement.

- Sit down with the founder on an informal basis (rather than standing in front of his desk in what might be perceived as a threatening stance).
- Don't fight the battle by yourself. Have your discussion with another professional manager along with you so that the founder will not dismiss your issues as personal and just your whim.
- Don't expect this to be a single conversation. Expect a long series of conversations to build on.
- Be patient. In many ways, this is an emotional decision for the founder. The company is his child, and he has worked hard to bring it to life and help it grow. He will not want to turn it over to strangers.
- Take a strategic view. Identify with the founder where the company wants to be in one year and what it will take to achieve that goal.
- Then, agree on specific delegations to achieve the strategic goal and how they will be achieved as a result of the delegation. Start small. Agree on specific delegations.
- Act quickly once you have the delegation. Don't wait for the next morning. Delegation remorse can set in quickly, particularly when the founder goes home and wonders why he agreed to what he did.
- When the specific goals are met, having proved yourself, go back again, point out the success, and seek further delegations.
- Be prepared to walk away if you do not receive the delegation you believe is necessary for your job. Without the appropriate delegation, you are more likely to fail and the company is less likely to be successful. Leave before the collapse.

Fourth, founders are more likely to accept such delegation in areas where they lack expertise. An engineer, for instance, is more likely to delegate financial issues to a CFO and less likely to delegate technology issues to a CIO.

Similarly, certain personalities are more likely to delegate. The best examples are individuals who are able to discuss problems and look at all sides of issues before deciding. Those with prior start-up experience who have undergone similar delegations are more likely to delegate the next time around. Individuals who are less likely to delegate are those who have become emotionally attached to their company and who tend to be hotheaded or emotional. When interviewing, it is a good idea to get a sense of the founder's personality and his willingness to delegate. Try a trial balloon such as getting him into a debate and observe his style.

CHAPTER 9 • BUSINESS PLANS

§ 9.17 Why Are There So Many Typos and Mistakes?

§ 9.18 Don't You Have More Recent Numbers?

§ 9.19 I Don't Think This Business Is Relevant for Me.

§ 9.20 Good Business Plan. I Like It.

§ 9.21 Good Business Plan. I Also Liked It Last Time.

Business Plans: The Myth and the Reality

CHAPTER 9

Over the years, we have reviewed hundreds of business plans. In that time, we have learned many lessons and have tried to teach them to other entrepreneurs. In the sections below, we list some of the more important comments we have heard from readers and reviewers of plans. Make certain your plan anticipates or answers them.

§ 9.01 WHAT IS YOUR COMPETITIVE ADVANTAGE?

Out of the billions of people on this planet, what makes you think you can accomplish your business goals? Right now there are probably several other businesspeople in Seattle, San Jose, New York, London, New Delhi, and other places sitting around thinking about your business concept. Don't kid yourself into thinking you are the only one. Given that fact, how are you and only you going to make the business plan a success? How are you going to prevent hundreds of other businesses from springing up and replicating your business plan?

Translation: We have a good friend, Charles Buddeke, who is an entrepreneur in residence at the University of Louisville (one of the top business schools in the nation for entrepreneurs) and spends a good part of his day reviewing business plans. We call this question the Buddeke Principle, since it is always his first question. It is probably in the top three for most other entrepreneurs. Therefore, carefully describe your patents, copyrights, trademarks, intellectual property, exclusive agreements, and anything else that will prevent others from entering the market, competing with you, and taking your business away.

§ 9.02 I'M NOT INTERESTED IN A $100 MILLION MARKET.

Translation: Most major investors are looking for major market opportunities. This usually means a $1 billion market. If yours is much smaller, you will have to focus on local funding sources that are willing to put up smaller amounts of money.

§ 9.03 DO YOU REALLY THINK YOU CAN GET AN 80% MARKET SHARE IN THREE YEARS?

I know you will have a patent and will be the only one able to make this product, but does that mean that 80% of the market will buy it?

Translation: While major investors are looking for large markets, they do not expect you to achieve a major share. On the contrary, too large a market share too quickly will seem unrealistic and encourage them to question other aspects of your business plan. Start with a small share, maybe 1% to 5% in the first year, growing at a reasonable rate over five years. What that rate is will depend on your product.

Consider Quicken. It may have more than 50% of the market for computerized checking account systems, but it competes with people who still balance their checkbooks manually. Therefore, its true market share is much smaller.

§ 9.04 HOW ARE YOU GOING TO PRODUCE THE PRODUCT, BRING IT TO MARKET, AND MANAGE THE COMPANY?

Translation: Don't forget the three Ms: manufacturing, management, and marketing. Don't spend all your time in the plan describing your product or service. It is only one component of your total business. Manufacturing or producing it, managing the business, and marketing it are just as important. A great product or service alone is not enough. You have to get it to market at a profit. That is where the three Ms come into play.

§ 9.05 WHEN WILL YOU MAKE A PROFIT?

Translation: Investors are less interested in your sales growth than in your profit margins. Increasing sales can be expensive to achieve. New salespeople must be hired. New advertising campaigns may be required. New distributors may be needed. It may even be necessary to open new plants to meet demand. All these things cost money. Will you have to borrow or raise more money to support this growth? Or will you be able to make a profit as you increase sales? If that is the case, describe how you will do it and how much you will make. Remember that sales do not provide a cushion that protects investors' money. Profits do.

§ 9.06 HOW REALISTIC ARE THESE NUMBERS?

Translation: This is the kiss of death. If your numbers are unrealistic or not convincing, an investor is unlikely to believe you or the rest of your plan. Therefore, make the numbers as convincing as possible. Use the Tolstoy approach. He once wrote that a battle description involving thousands of deaths is not as dramatic as a description of one person's death.

In your case, this means that you should not start with aggregate annual sales. Break apart your sales. Start with one product and show its cost, sales price, and profit margin. Give details on the costs. Then show how many units you will sell in the first month, then the next, and onward up to a year. Make sure you show trends, seasons, and cycles. One thousand units in month 1 should not be repeated over and over in the first year, with 2,000 repeated each month in the second year. That sounds suspicious.

However, do not just plug in numbers and allow for some adjustments up and down during the year, with gradual growth from year to year. Do your homework and research. Explain how the changes will occur and show the reasons why.

§ 9.07 HOW MUCH MONEY DO YOU NEED?

Translation: Having gotten their interest, ask for investors' money. Don't let them walk away from your business plan without telling them what you want: how much and when. The numbers should be tied back to the financial projections, showing when cash will be needed. If the projections show a $1 million shortfall, that is what you should be asking for—not $100,000 or $10 million.

§ 9.08 WHAT DO I GET FOR MY MONEY?

Translation: Don't forget to let the investors know what they will get for their money. Will it be preferred stock, Class B common stocks, or convertible debt?

There is a contrary view that investors will tell you what they want and are willing to take. Our preference, however, is to put on the table about what you want. Set the parameters. Occasionally an investor may ignore your proposal, but most investors will not. In addition, a carefully thought out investment strategy indicates that you have done your research and are a knowledgeable businessperson.

§ 9.09 WHAT DO YOU NEED MY MONEY FOR?

Translation: Be sure to describe how you will use the invested funds. Investors will not want to see it being used to pay off early investors who are taking their money out of the company. There will also be some hesitation if a large percentage of it is being used to pay off third-party debts. Investors want their money to stay in the company and be used for constructive purposes. Product development, new production facilities, and the establishment of a sales network are favored uses.

Be as specific as possible. The more detailed you are, the more confident investors will be that the money will be spent effectively. You don't need to specify down to the dollar, but down to the $10,000 or certainly the $100,000 for a $1 million fund raising is expected.

§ 9.10 YOU DESCRIBED THE GOOD, BUT WHERE ARE THE BAD AND THE UGLY?

Translation: Not every aspect of your business is likely to be the Land of Oz. If there are problems, face them, describe them, and explain how you learned from them or will overcome them. If there are competitors, tell the investors how you are better and will beat them. Do not be caught by an investor having to ask you about a problem you skipped over. The investor probably will not bother to ask but will toss your plan aside for not being reliable or honest.

§ 9.11 FLIP, FLIP, FLIP.

Translation: Don't make readers have to flip pages to get to the heart of your business plan. They won't do it. Include an executive summary. Since most potential investors will not get beyond the summary, make certain the summary is catchy and effective. A good one increases the chance that your investors will read the rest of the plan. A bad summary decreases that chance.

As we will see in a later chapter, the summary is not a mini-business plan. It is designed to get investors to meet with you in person. As such, it is a marketing tool—even more so than the rest of your plan. Use it to sell your idea or concept.

Most advisors will tell you to write the executive summary last. That makes sense. Since you will learn a great deal from the discipline of writing a business plan, save the summary until you have learned the lessons and then write it. Having learned the lessons, you are in a better position to describe what you have learned about the business.

§ 9.12 WHO ARE YOU?

How do we get in contact with you? Where are you located?

Translation: Maybe once a month we see a business plan that does not have a return address, telephone number, facsimile number, or e-mail address. Don't make it hard for the readers to reach you if your plan is appealing. Let them know where to reach you and give them lots of options.

Even worse, several times a year we see a business plan without a company name on it. We can only shake our heads at such plans—just before tossing them in the trash can.

§ 9.13 GREAT RÉSUMÉ, BUT WHAT DO YOU BRING TO THE TABLE?

Translation: Your résumé in the management section should not be a listing of your education and previous jobs. It should focus on your prior experiences and how they relate to the proposed business. The same rule applies to the rest of your team.

Don't be afraid to list your failures. Some investors will invest only in companies whose founders have previously failed. They want managers who know that everything they touch will *not* turn into gold and realize that they must work to make the business a success. They also prefer managers who have had to deal with adversity, have learned that they can cope, and will not panic at the first downturn.

§ 9.14 I KNOW YOU ARE SMART, BUT WHAT ARE YOU TALKING ABOUT?

In your business plan you have dropped so many terms, acronyms, and jargon that I can tell you understand the business. But I can't. Tell me what are you really going to do in a few simple sentences that even I can understand.

Translation: This is another lesson we learned from Buddeke. If he weren't so busy reading other plans and teaching us, he would be writing this book. As he points out, the initial reviewers of most business plans will be individuals new to the industry or recent MBA graduates just starting out in a venture capital firm. Give them a break. They are unlikely to have any knowledge about your business. Write it so that they can read it easily, relate to it, and understand it. One way to do that is to make your point and move on to the next one in a clear and logical manner.

§ 9.15 WHAT IS THE POINT?

Translation: You have the readers' attention for only a short period. Initially, you have to catch them in the first minute. At any time afterward, you can lose them if you drift for up to a minute of reading time. Get to each of the points you want to make as quickly as possible. Don't lose the reader's attention.

§ 9.16 ZZZZZZZZZZZZZZZZZZ.

Translation: The business plan is a marketing tool. Make it interesting and even exciting. If your business is such a great deal, show some enthusiasm and let it come through in the plan. Get the reader excited about your business. You probably have some passion about your product or service, so let that come through.

§ 9.17 WHY ARE THERE SO MANY TYPOS AND MISTAKES?

Translation: Come on, now. You are asking people to trust you with their money because you are a thorough businessperson who will manage the business and their money carefully. How can you expect them to believe that if the plan is filled with typing mistakes or grammatical errors? Run spell and grammar checks, but don't stop there. Read it over and over. Then have someone else read it.

§ 9.18 DON'T YOU HAVE MORE RECENT NUMBERS?

Translation: Update the plan at least annually. Quarterly would be better. Don't be caught in the embarrassing situation of handing out business plans that are out of date. We often see business plans referring to last year as being in the future, for instance, a 2001 business plan describing expected 2000 sales.

§ 9.19 I DON'T THINK THIS BUSINESS IS RELEVANT FOR ME.

Translation: Be prepared to customize the plan. Don't keep sending the same one to every investor. Take a paragraph to show how the business relates to the individual investor. Describe any strategic opportunities or relationships to the investor's existing interests. The plan is not carved in stone but stored on a hard drive. It can and should be changed for the individual situation.

§ 9.20 GOOD BUSINESS PLAN. I LIKE IT.

After reading a first draft of this chapter, Buddeke sent us an e-mail message reminding us of this point. Many times you walk out of an investors' meeting glowing from praise about your plan. After several meetings with different investors, all of whom have complimented you on the plan, you begin to feel pretty confident that you have a good one.

Translation: Listen to investors' actions, not their words. If you have received lots of praise and no money, there is probably something wrong with your plan. Take it back for peer review and try to figure out why the investors are not biting. Once you figure it out, change the plan to address their concerns.

§ 9.21 GOOD BUSINESS PLAN. I ALSO LIKED IT LAST TIME.

As a venture capitalist, I see thousands of business plans every year. As a result, I can recognize business plans prepared from off-the-shelf software programs, including which program was used.

Translation: You are trying to convince the reader that your business and plan are unique and that there is nothing like them in the world. That is the reason the reader should invest in you. You do not want the reader to realize that you used a standard software program.

It will be more work, but don't buy a business plan software program. Write the plan yourself. Read books and articles, but when it comes time to draft the plan, the writing, style, and design have to be yours.

By the way, if you feel compelled to use such software, be sure to delete instructions such as "Insert a Description of Your Company's Competitive Advantages." Periodically, we see business plans that have been prepared with such software but in which the writer has not been thorough enough to reread the plan and look for such obvious mistakes.

Business Plans: The Myth and the Reality

COLLEGE OF BUSINESS AND PUBLIC ADMINISTRATION
UNIVERSITY OF LOUISVILLE

by Bruce H. Kemelgor, Ph.D.

Having worked with hundreds of start-up firms and with our award-winning M.B.A. student business plan teams both domestically and internationally, I've discovered that conventional thinking about business plans is flawed. The primary reason for writing a business plan *is not* to raise money, but rather to flesh out ideas and to look for weak spots and vulnerabilities. A source of capital (investor, banker, or venture capitalist) will want to carefully examine your business plan, of course, but the primary issue is, does this concept seize an opportunity with the necessary drive and skills of its people? Here are my top ten keys to a successful business plan:

1. Use writing of the Business Plan as an opportunity to create the discipline needed to capture an opportunity. The dream, the idea, has to be grounded in reality.
2. Clarify one's goals and confront both positives and negatives when writing a Business Plan. You develop a clearer understanding of your purpose and the strengths and weaknesses of the concept.
3. Stress implementation. Describe how key objectives will be attained. It is critical for operational success that various details regarding *how* things will be accomplished are stated.
4. Make the Plan workable by distilling your goals to one-page action summaries for each section of the Plan. "Plan your work and work your Plan." This isn't how you write the Plan, but rather how you make the Plan, once developed, work for you.
5. Recognize, and include as part of the management team, professionals that you will need to retain such as an accountant, a lawyer, and a marketing expert. If your firm is going to be a small start-up, these professionals may be contracted for service. If yours will be a larger enterprise, then plan for the inclusion of

people with these talents and abilities. *Create a management team that has complementary skills to get the job done.*

6. Schedule regular meetings with your management team to discuss *only* the Plan and nothing else. Set keys goals for each core business area. Develop brief strategy statements for the next three-month period. Then go back and fill in the financial figures. Whether yours is a small- or medium-sized enterprise or simply a concept on paper, this is a sound approach to generating realistic financial projections based on agreed-upon goals.
7. Discipline yourself to maintain balanced attention to all areas. Don't focus only on the financials or marketing. Seize opportunities to continuously improve by stressing the strengths of all areas and commitments to overcome weaknesses.
8. Plan for contingencies—both positive and negative. Your plan should reflect anticipation for the unexpected; for example, what if a new competitor enters the market? By engaging in some contingency planning, your ability to be proactive and undertake planned action is far better than having to react and put out fires.
9. Review your Plan *each month* to maintain progress control. Being action-oriented people, entrepreneurs like to be doing things and not necessarily sitting and thinking. Yet statistics support the success rate of those who engaged in periodic review of their Plan. It's a working document, not simply meant to be placed on a shelf to gather dust. Creativity, energy, and drive keep a business on track to succeed.
10. Update your Plan every six months—that way you extend the Plan for another year. As previously mentioned, this is a working document. It helps guide your decisions and reasoning as to why you are doing certain things. It keeps you focused on your mission and goals. It's your map on the road to success.

CHAPTER 10 • VENTURE CAPITAL

Venture Capitalists: Show Me the Money

CHAPTER 10

§ 10.01 INTRODUCTION

Companies usually obtain most, if not all, of the funding to establish and develop their business from private placement transactions. These fundings are based on exemptions from Securities Act registration requirements. Private placement investments may be made by individuals, institutional investors, or other business entities. One distinct type of private placement is by professional venture capitalists.

The first step is to find a venture capitalist, and Appendix B is a list of most of the leading venture capital funds in the United States, alphabetically and by specialization. A company should not simply send the venture capital funds information about itself, however, because they receive thousands of inquiries a year. A company should have someone, such as a banker or an attorney, introduce the company to the venture capitalist. Local investors also may be helpful referrals. A recent development is the venture capital fair, where investors and start-ups come together. A company can contact its local chamber of commerce, bank, or attorney for the location of a nearby fair. It may also be possible to locate an investor over the Internet. (For more information, see Chapter 13 and Gutterman, Brown, and Stanislaw, *2001 The Professional's Guide to Doing Business on the Internet,* published by Aspen.)

Issues raised during a venture capital financing are similar to those in any private placement; however, some characteristics of venture capital financing must be distinguished. First, the venture capitalist is attracted to investments in relatively unproven, high-risk enterprises. As a result, the investment must yield a significantly greater return than in lower-risk cases. Second, venture capitalists will be much more involved in the management and operation of the company after investment. They will, for instance, become members of the board of directors.

Although a venture capital investor may be an individual, most such investors are organized as limited partnerships. The limited partners of these investment funds are institutional investors, large corporations, and wealthy individuals who have contributed cash. Their money is invested and managed by general partners with experience in working with small, emerging high-risk ventures. The funds are invested in a number of "portfolio companies." While general partners contribute only a nominal amount (e.g., 1%) of total capital, profits are usually allocated 20% to general partners and 80% to limited partners. This provides general partners with a substantial incentive to maximize investment return.

Since not every venture capital investor is the same, management of the company seeking funding should conduct its own investigation of potential investors. Management should consider whether the investor has the requisite skill, experience, and business connections to provide assistance to the company. Management should conduct reference and background checks on the fund and the general partner who will be responsible for relations with the company. The company should also contact managers and founders of other companies that have received investment capital from the fund. Finally, given the close relationship that typically exists between management and venture capital investors, it is important for managers to determine whether a basis exists for cordial and respectful relations. Managers should get to know potential investors and ask themselves whether they like the investors and whether they could get along with them—in good times and bad.

§ 10.02 NEGOTIATING A VENTURE CAPITAL INVESTMENT

[A] Introduction

Negotiating and documenting the terms and conditions of the capital investment often set the tone for the long-term relationship between management and investors. Parties must be able to anticipate, and appreciate, the continuously evolving needs and requirements of the company. They must be able to draft documentation that provides management with sufficient flexibility. At the same time, documents must protect the legitimate interests of investors. Although a number of documents used in the venture capital area have become standardized, it is important that special concerns be reflected in the agreements.

The first step in documenting the transaction is preparation of a *business plan,* or private placement memorandum. It describes the company's business and the proposed financing terms, at least from the company's perspective. Once serious investors have been located, a *term sheet,* or commitment letter, will be prepared that summarizes principal financial and other terms of investment. Thereafter, investors will conduct a detailed investigation, or *due diligence,* of the company, including its business activities and organizational structure. If, following investigation, investors remain interested, the parties will negotiate the *investment agreement.* That agreement contains detailed terms of the investment and ancillary agreements, including voting agreements, employment and proprietary information agreements, and employee stock option or purchase agreements.

[B] Preparation of a Business Plan

The business plan often takes the form of a formal offering circular or prospectus. We discussed this topic in more detail in Chapter 9. The business plan is the key disclosure document in the venture capital financing process. An example is included in this book as Appendix A. As a rule, venture capitalists use the business plan to understand the strategic strengths and weaknesses of the issuer, including key products and services the issuer offers, needs of its customers, risks posed by competitors, and overall risks.

There is no established format for a business plan. However, it should include most, if not all, information in a disclosure document prepared for the federal integrated disclosure system. At a minimum, the document should describe the following:

- Assets, resources, products, and skills of the issuer;
- Needs of the marketplace;
- Strategies the issuer intends to use regarding products, services, positioning, pricing, distribution, and manufacturing;
- Anticipated responses and strategies of actual and potential competitors; and
- Possible future changes concerning technology, customer needs, governmental regulation, or social values.

The business plan is not prepared with the same degree of formality as a securities disclosure document. Nevertheless, care must be taken to ensure that it does not contain any material misstatements. It should also be reviewed to be certain it does not omit to state anything material. Either mistake could cause a company to be found liable under antifraud provisions of federal securities laws.

Information in the business plan is generally confidential and proprietary. That confidentiality should be maintained. Recipients should be screened and individually approved by management. A legend should be included on the plan stating that it is "Proprietary and Confidential," and prospective investors should sign a confidentiality agreement before receiving a copy of it.

[C] Negotiation of a Term Sheet or Commitment Letter

If an investor and issuer determine that an investment is desirable, they will draft a preliminary agreement. This preliminary understanding can take a variety of forms, from a cursory, informal letter to a more formal and detailed memorandum. In most cases, the term sheet or commitment letter will reflect the parties' understanding on the following:

- Value of the business;
- Allocation of ownership between existing shareholders and investors;
- Key financial and legal terms of the transaction; and
- In some cases, enforceable obligations of the parties—for example, that the company will pay the investors' expenses if a transaction does not close, or that the company is prohibited from negotiating with other parties pending completion of the proposed transaction.

While the length and content of the term sheet or commitment letter may vary depending on the style of the investor, it should address the following:

1. Amount to be invested, type of security to be issued, and relative percentage of ownership of investors and other shareholders following financing;
2. Rights, preferences, and privileges of investors, including dividend rights, liquidation preferences, redemption provisions, conversion rights, antidilution protection, registration rights, special voting rights, and board positions;
3. Representations, warranties, and covenants to be made by the company and founders;
4. Right of investors to participate in future company financings;
5. Terms of any employee stock purchase or option agreements and plans, employment agreements, and confidentiality agreements; and
6. Agreement, if any, of the company to pay all or a portion of legal fees and expenses of the investors with respect to the financing.

Included in Appendix E are two examples of term sheets typically used by venture capitalists in preferred stock financings.

In addition to establishing parameters for the proposed transaction, a term sheet can educate management about the expectations and requirements of investors. Also, the term sheet gets a number of potentially sensitive issues "out on the table" before a good deal of time and effort has been expended.

[D] Due Diligence and Corporate Housekeeping

[1] In General

Once preliminary negotiations have been completed, investors will investigate the company's business and affairs. Referred to as a due diligence investigation, this exercise allows investors and their counsel to independently verify information that has been provided to them about the company. At the same time, the company, as well as investors, will focus on a number of "corporate housekeeping" items. These items are required as a result of material changes in control and ownership triggered by the venture capital financing. Satisfactory completion of the due diligence investigation and corporate housekeeping is a condition to closing the financing.

[2] Due Diligence

There is no standard set of procedures for conducting a due diligence investigation in a venture capital financing. The amount of effort will depend on the particular company and the style of the investors. It also will depend on the size of the proposed investment—both in a dollar amount and as a percentage of the investor's portfolio.

The due diligence process usually begins with a venture capitalist sending a company a lengthy list of documents that it wants. The list is likely to take a company many days to complete. An example is included in this book as Appendix F. The following are among the items commonly covered:

1. Corporate structure, including articles of incorporation, bylaws, minutes books, stock records, and shareholder agreements;
2. Prior financing documents, including stock purchase agreements, loan agreements, and security agreements;
3. Material agreements;
4. Agreements relating to purchase of the company's securities, such as warrants, options, rights of first refusal, subscriptions, preemptive rights, and registration rights;
5. Intellectual property rights, including patents, copyrights, trademarks, and trade secrets, as well as procedures followed to perfect and protect such rights;
6. Pending, threatened, or anticipated litigation and claims involving the company and key employees;

7. Employment agreements or arrangements involving key employees, as well as any agreements that key employees had with prior employers (e.g., employment agreements, noncompetition agreements, or confidentiality agreements);
8. Audited and unaudited financial statements, including footnotes, for the entire period of the company's existence;
9. Current and past relationships with banks, creditors, suppliers, competitors, and trade associations;
10. Material communications with key company officials and marketing and operating personnel regarding the company's business;
11. The company's property, plant, and equipment; and
12. Government permits, as well as governmental regulations applicable to the company (including any environmental regulation).

Document review will be supplemented by interviews with key company officials, accountants, suppliers, customers, and others having useful information about the company. All information that investors and their counsel receive regarding the company, particularly data and trade-secret information, should be subject to a confidentiality agreement.

[3] Corporate Housekeeping

The due diligence investigation allows a company and its investors to identify and take care of corporate housekeeping matters. The term *corporate housekeeping* refers to internal and external changes involving the company and its key stakeholders (e.g., directors, officers, and shareholders) that must be made for the financing. Some of the changes are necessary to prepare the company for its altered state after the financing. Others reflect requests that new investors have presented in the term sheet. Among the areas of concern are operational structure of the company, amendments to charter documents, contractual agreements among shareholders, minutes books, stock records, prior investment agreements, restrictions in third-party contracts, and intellectual property rights.

Operational Structure For a business enterprise that ultimately will seek a public offering (as is the case with most venture-backed investments) the preferred structure is a single corporation, possibly with one or more distinct operational subsidiaries. Accordingly, if an enterprise has been run as a partnership, a limited liability company, or a trust, it should be reestablished as a corporation. At this time, a state with greater protections for management, such as Delaware, may be chosen. Similarly, if the business has been run in combination with one or more affiliated entities ("brother–sister" corporations), it may be necessary to reorganize the overall legal structure by a series of mergers, consolidations, or reincorporations.

Charter Documents At the time of any significant financing transaction, a company's charter documents (its articles of incorporation and bylaws) should be reviewed for compliance with applicable law. This is also a good time to ascertain whether amendments are necessary to remove provisions that will be inappropriate after the financing. Provisions also could be added that might be more difficult to adopt when the company has a large number of shareholders. A number of matters must be considered:

- Elimination of preemptive rights or rights of first refusal if permitted by law;
- Increase in authorized capital stock to an amount significantly in excess of the amount being sold in the offering. This increase should cover outstanding options, warrants, convertible securities, future offerings, and other contingencies;
- Removal of close corporation provisions (which allow closely held corporations to streamline management, such as dispensing with board meetings) and other restrictions on structure, duration, or purpose of the company;
- Amendment of articles of incorporation and bylaws relating to the election, composition, size, and protection of the board of directors. Desirability of cumulative voting procedures should be considered. Also, permitted size of the board of directors should be increased to accommodate the addition of outside directors;
- If the company's state of incorporation does not provide sufficient corporate flexibility, this is the time to change. It will be easier now, with fewer shareholders, to incorporate a new company in another state or to change the state of incorporation by merging an existing company into a newly formed corporation.

Contractual Agreements among Shareholders Rights of shareholders in charter documents may have been supplemented by contractual agreements among key shareholders. These agreements should be reviewed, amended, and, in some cases, terminated prior to investment. For example, an agreement may govern how shareholders elect representatives to an issuer's board of directors. It may also establish special voting requirements relating to certain corporate actions. These provisions may be unacceptable to a new investor group. Investors will also object to any right of first refusal regarding new financings granted to prior investors. Such provisions may need to be renegotiated.

Prior Investment Agreements The terms of any investment agreement with prior investors should be carefully reviewed. For example, the prior investment agreement may contain a number of financial and nonfinancial covenants and restrictions that need to be reconsidered in light of new financing. A company should seek a uniform set of covenants for all investors rather than two or more sets of obligations that may overlap or, in the worst case, be in conflict.

Employee Contracts and Arrangements A company's human resources are a key corporate asset. Consideration must be given to employee benefit plans and to agreements with key employees concerning noncompetition, nondisclosure, and protection of technical information. A review should also be made of internal procedures for hiring, promotion, protection of confidential information, noncompetition, and termination. This review includes an inspection of offer-of-employment letters, nondisclosure or confidentiality agreements, and employee handbooks and manuals.

Restrictions in Third-Party Contracts Terms and content of a company's principal contracts with third parties should be examined closely. Such contracts include loan agreements, leasing arrangements, supply contracts, distribution agreements, and labor agreements. It is important to determine if they contain any material restrictions on the company's business or its ability to consummate the proposed financing. For example, a loan agreement may require that proceeds received from any financing be used only for specified purposes. Similarly, a company's ability to issue dividend-bearing securities may be restricted by covenants in a credit agreement prohibiting dividends.

[E] Valuation and Pricing

[1] In General

If the venture capital investment involves an equity instrument or a debt instrument convertible into equity, the parties must agree on the "value" of the business to determine what portion of equity ownership will be allocated to new investors. Once the value is determined, the price of the instrument, stated on a per-unit basis, can be derived.

The amount of equity ownership that must be given to new investors is a function of many factors. The major ones are the stage of a company's development, the perceived risks associated with attaining objective levels of financial success, and the return on investment that investors require. A company should not underestimate this last factor, since it provides management with an indication as to how and when investors will seek future liquidity.

[2] Size of Investment

From a company's perspective, the size of the financing should be sufficient to allow it to achieve its next major operational milestone without raising additional funds. Management should have conservatively estimated such capital requirements when preparing the business plan. In most cases, the requested amount should be increased to cover unforeseen problems, because in the future it may be difficult to raise emergency funds quickly and cost-effectively.

[3] Pricing of Investment

The pricing of the investment depends on the company's valuation agreed to by the parties. Valuation, in turn, depends on several internal factors, including the company's business plan and financial position, as well as a variety of external factors. The following are among the items that might be considered:

1. Total amount of financing and resultant future dilution;
2. Pricing of comparable investments; this requires an analysis of actual and potential competitors, both private and public. To a lesser extent, the price paid by earlier-round investors is considered;
3. Attractiveness of competing investment opportunities, as well as the need for the investor to retain capital to fund existing portfolio companies;
4. Risks associated with the company—evaluated by analyzing the business history of the company, the industry it operates in, and the skills and experience of management;
5. Historical and projected earnings and profits of the company, the need to retain income for future investment, and the ability to make dividend payments;

6. Restrictions on the transferability of securities and the ability of holders to vote or become involved in management of the company;
7. Book value, assets, and overall financing condition of the company (Book value is rarely a good method for valuing a business engaged in developing new products and with little manufacturing capability or inventory.); and
8. How long an investor must wait before it can liquidate its investment in a public offering.

The most common valuation methods are discounted cash flow (based on the present value of a future stream of profits to be generated by the company) or a multiplier of the last 12 months of sales. In some cases, the multiplier may be applied to the next (or rolling) 12 months. The multiplier chosen is based on multipliers applied to investments or acquisitions of similar companies.

For instance, if a competitor with annual sales of $10 million was purchased for $30 million, the multiplier is three. If a similar company seeking funding has $1 million in sales, it can be assumed the value is roughly $3 million. This value is then calculated on a per-share basis. In the above case, assuming it has 1 million shares means a value of $3 per share.

The number of shares to be sold can then be calculated. In the above case, if a company is trying to raise $300,000, at $3 per share, it will have to give up 100,000 shares, or 10%.

§ 10.03 TERMS OF INVESTMENT INSTRUMENT

[A] Selecting the Investment Instrument

Some of the more important factors in selecting the appropriate investment instrument are

- Objectives of investors,
- Level of maturity of the company,
- Degree of risk associated with the company's business plan,
- Current and future capital requirements of the company,
- Relative interests of other shareholders,
- Amount of control that investors wish to have over management,

- Need for liquidity, and
- Terms of outstanding agreements with prior investors or lenders.

Venture capital financings sometimes involve the use of common stock, convertible debt, nonconvertible preferred stock, and debt coupled with warrants. (The warrants entitle the holder to receive common stock.) By far, the most popular investment instrument for venture capitalists dealing with early stage companies is convertible preferred stock. The preferences associated with convertible preferred stock allow the company to continue selling common stock to others, such as employees, on different terms. Convertible preferred stock also allows investors to participate in any upside growth in the company while establishing a preference on liquidation if the venture is not successful. Finally, convertible preferred stock can be given protective rights customized for the investor, including antidilution protection and separate voting rights on specified transactions.

Included as Appendix K is an investors' rights agreement for use in a private placement. The form describes various rights typically granted to outside investors for registration of their shares, information, and opportunities to participate in future financings.

[B] Terms of Convertible Preferred Stock

[1] In General

The principal terms of convertible preferred stock that usually appear in term sheets or commitment letters are (a) dividend rights (cumulative or noncumulative, with or without participation), (b) liquidation preference, (c) voting rights, (d) conversion (right to convert and mandatory conversion) and antidilution protections, and (e) redemption provisions (optional and mandatory).

[2] Dividend Rights

In most cases, preferred stock has a preference over common stock for dividends. Other preferred stock dividend provisions may simply state that preferred stock is entitled to dividends on the same basis as common stock. If a dividend preference is given, it will be on either a noncumulative or a cumulative basis. *Cumulative* means that any dividend not paid when scheduled because of a lack of funds will be paid when the funds become available. In the case of noncumulative dividends, any that are skipped are not made up.

[3] Liquidation Preference

Preferred stock is generally given a priority claim over common stock by being given a fixed dollar amount on liquidation. The liquidation preference typically equals the original purchase price of the preferred stock, plus any accrued but unpaid dividends. In many cases, the articles of incorporation will provide that mergers and similar transactions will be deemed to be a liquidation. This ensures that preferred stock holders will at least have the right to receive their original investment back upon such a transaction occurring.

In many cases, holders of preferred stock upon liquidation will be better off converting their shares into common stock and sharing in distributions made to all holders of common stock. If preferred stock is "participating," holders will be entitled to receive their liquidation preference, plus the amount they would have received if they had converted their stock into common stock. Participating preferred stock can substantially dilute the economic interest of common stock holders. As a compromise, participation can occur after common stock receives some fixed amount or can be limited to a specified level of return.

[4] Voting Rights

Holders of convertible preferred stock typically vote along with holders of common stock. Preferred stock is entitled to one vote for each share of common stock into which it can convert. In addition, holders of preferred stock may be given the right to vote as a separate class on major issues, such as issuance of new senior securities; mergers; acquisitions; and amendments to the rights, preferences, and privileges of preferred stock.

Preferred stock may be given a class vote in the election of directors. For example, the parties may provide in the articles of incorporation that holders of preferred stock have the right to designate two out of five directors, with the remaining directors elected by holders of common stock. In other cases, holders of preferred and common stock, voting separately, will elect an equal number of directors. Any remaining director or directors will be elected by preferred stock and common stock holders voting together. Sometimes, preferred stock will be given extraordinary voting rights to designate a majority of directors if a material event occurs, such as failure to pay dividends, make mandatory redemptions, or default in financial and other covenants.

When directors are elected by class voting, investors and certain common stock holders may sign a voting or shareholder agreement covering how they will vote for directors. If there is more than one new investor, the new investors may agree among themselves in a similar agreement how they will vote for directors.

[5] Conversion Provisions

By definition, convertible preferred stock can be exchanged for common stock. Convertible preferred stock is generally automatically converted into common stock if certain events occur.

One of the most common triggers for automatic conversion of preferred stock is an underwritten public offering of the company's common stock. Frequently, for the automatic conversion provision to apply, a minimum per-share price and minimum total amount must be reached. The minimum per-share price may be three to five times the equivalent common stock price paid by the investors. The minimum aggregate offering price is intended to ensure that the public market is large enough for investors to convert and liquidate their common stock.

Automatic conversion may also occur if the company attains certain performance goals and objectives, such as closing a private placement financing in excess of a certain minimum dollar amount or achieving specified revenue or net sales. In addition, conversion may be triggered by vote of a certain percentage of holders of preferred stock (e.g., $66^2/_3\%$). This permits a recapitalization of the corporation without an amendment of the articles of incorporation.

Typically, the conversion ratio is established initially on a one-to-one basis (one preferred for one common). The conversion ratio for preferred stock is adjusted for stock splits, stock dividends, and consolidations. This ensures that preferred stock holders' rights are protected. Preferred stock also includes an antidilution mechanism that kicks in if common stock is issued at a price lower than the equivalent common stock price paid by the investors. In such a case, antidilution adjusts the conversion price downward. Accordingly, a downward adjustment in conversion price will increase the number of shares issued to the protected investors on conversion.

The most common antidilution provision uses a "weighted average." The conversion price is based on the number of shares outstanding before and after new issuance and on the price per share paid for new securities. The adjustment is weighted for the number of new shares issued. Thus, if a few shares are issued at a bargain price, it will have little effect on the conversion ratio. A somewhat drastic alternative is "ratchet-down" antidilution protection, which reduces the conversion price to the most recent lower price at which new common stock equivalents were issued, regardless of how many shares were issued. In this case, just one share issued at a lower price would cause the conversion ratio to be reduced to that level. Thresholds, such as issuances of over $100,000 of common stock, can moderate the ratchet.

Not all new issuances of securities trigger antidilution provisions. One of the most common exceptions is issuance of up to a fixed number of shares to employees and consultants under stock purchase and option plans. Other exceptions include securities issued to suppliers, distributors, customers, lenders, and other strategic partners. Finally, the board of directors may be given power to waive antidilution provisions in certain instances.

[6] Redemption

Some, but certainly not all, convertible preferred stock includes redemption provisions. There are two types of redemption provisions:

1. Optional redemption provides the company with the right to repurchase or redeem preferred stock at the purchase price plus a redemption premium; and
2. Mandatory redemption imposes an absolute obligation on the company to repurchase preferred stock at dates, and on terms, specified in the articles of incorporation.

In addition, there are situations where investors can force the company to redeem shares at their option. This right is in effect a "put" and is little different from a mandatory redemption.

Optional redemption allows the company to force conversion of preferred stock into common stock. By forcing conversion, the company can eliminate any special rights to dividends, liquidation, and voting held by preferred stock. Investors are generally reluctant to agree to such provisions. On the other hand, the company may be able to obtain their agreement on this issue if it agrees to defer exercise of the option for a specified number of years.

§ 10.04 INVESTMENT AGREEMENT

[A] Introduction

The central legal document in venture capital financing is the investment agreement. It is often called a stock purchase agreement in the case of an equity investment and a note purchase agreement in the case of a debt investment. The agreement is a detailed record of the understanding between the company and investors. It is also a means for the company to disclose all historical, business, and financial information that may be relevant to the transaction. Depending on the circumstances, the investment agreement can describe ongoing covenants and agreements that apply after the financing is completed.

[B] Description of Transaction

The investment agreement should begin with a description of the transaction, including securities to be sold; number of shares to be purchased; price per share; and time, date, and location of the initial closing. As a rule, if more than one investor is participating in the financing, all of the investors will execute a single investment agreement rather than a separate agreement for each investor.

Two variations in closing procedures are worth noting. First, the basic investment agreement may permit the company to raise additional funds, but only on the same terms. Second, the company and investors may agree that funding will be provided in two or more installments (or tranches) over fixed periods of time. The later infusions may be conditioned on there being no material adverse change to the company and possibly on the company attaining particular financial or operational objectives. Any form of staged investment provides an incentive for management to adhere to the original business plan and budgetary projections.

[C] Company Representations and Warranties

[1] Introduction

The investment agreement will contain extensive representations by and warranties on behalf of the company. Accompanying it will be detailed exhibits and schedules. The representations and warranties achieve two purposes: they create liability of the company for breach, and they force the company to disclose all material information. By the time the company has prepared representations, warranties, and related schedules, investors should have received the information they need to evaluate the investment.

Such representations and warranties have become standardized, although they vary somewhat depending on the company's stage of development. For example, representations of a start-up company focus on the right of the founders to invent, produce, and distribute products described in the company's business plan. A schedule of exceptions is used to point out any facts or circumstances unique to the company.

[2] Basic Representations and Warranties

Basic representations and warranties in the investment agreement are as follows:

- The company and its subsidiaries are duly incorporated, validly existing, in good standing in their respective jurisdictions of incorporation, and qualified to do business in each jurisdiction where they conduct business or own property;
- The company has the authority to enter into the investment agreement and sell the offered securities to investors;
- All consents or approvals from the board of directors, shareholders, and any third parties that may be required for execution of the investment agreement and sale of securities have been obtained;
- The company has the authorized capital stock set forth in the investment agreement, and the shares to be sold in the offering will be validly issued, fully paid, nonassessable, and free of any liens or encumbrances;
- Execution and performance of the investment agreement and sale of offered securities will not violate any contract, law, or rule to which the company is subject;
- Financial statements provided to investors are accurate and have been prepared in conformity with generally accepted accounting principles, and there have been no casualty losses, undisclosed liabilities, or adverse changes in the company's business since the date of the latest financial statements provided to investors; and
- There are no untrue statements or omissions of material facts in the investment agreement or in any business plan or disclosure document distributed to investors.

[3] Additional Company Representations and Warranties

In addition to requesting basic representations and warranties, investors may ask the company for other representations that focus on matters of particular importance to them in light of the company's business and future plans. Such areas of concern may include

- The absence of any material litigation,
- The company's good and marketable title to its material assets,

- The absence of any violation or default under any material agreements,
- The company's right to use its intellectual property free from conflicting ownership claims and without infringing on the rights of third parties,
- The payment of all taxes and liabilities, and
- The maintenance of adequate insurance coverage.

[4] Founders' Representations and Warranties

In some cases, one or more of a company's founders will provide their own representations and warranties. If a company is quite small and its affairs are clearly managed by the founders, the founders may be asked to warrant that representations made by the company are true and correct. In addition, a founder may be required to represent that he or she is free to perform anticipated services for the company and that there is no conflict with a previous employment agreement. Similarly, a founder may be asked to represent that he or she has assigned to the company all the rights in any technology or business ideas described in the company's business plan.

[D] Investors' Representations and Warranties

Each investor will make a limited representation regarding its authority to enter into the financing transaction. In addition, the company should make certain that purchasers of securities are purchasing for themselves and not for resale, since such resale would necessitate Securities Act filings. To do so, it should obtain assurances that each investor is purchasing securities for its own account. The company also wants representations that investors are aware the securities have not been registered under the Securities Act and cannot be resold until registered or exempt. These representations will be supplemented by transfer restrictions and a legend on the share certificate.

[E] Company Agreements and Covenants

[1] Introduction

Investors will typically require the company to sign a series of management agreements. These agreements (or covenants) generally fall into two broad categories: (1) affirmative covenants that impose duties and obligations on future activities of the issuer and (2) negative covenants that prohibit the issuer from taking certain future actions. A common affirmative covenant is the obligation of the company to provide investors with certain financial information. Standard negative covenants prohibit the company from entering into specified transactions, such as a merger or an acquisition, or from amending charter documents without the venture capitalists' approval.

The scope and nature of the covenants vary with each investor and investment instrument. For example, if investors will control the issuer's board of directors, covenants will not be very burdensome. Investors will rely on their control of the board to manage the issuer's continued operations. On other hand, if equity investors will not control the board, the covenants will be more extensive. If the investment is a debt instrument and investors will not participate directly in management, covenants will be even more extensive.

These agreements and covenants by the company may be in the investment agreement, in separate agreements with each investor, or in the articles of incorporation. As a rule, covenants will remain in effect for as long as a specified amount of the funding is outstanding. Most covenants will terminate on completion of the company's initial public offering or on conversion of preferred securities into common stock.

[2] Information Rights

A company will usually agree to provide investors with certain financial and operating information, such as annual and quarterly balance sheets and income statements. This information must be prepared in accordance with generally accepted accounting principles applied on a consistent basis. In addition, major investors (defined by the amount of their investment, such as $500,000 or more) may be given supplemental rights. They may be entitled to monthly reports of sales, production, shipments, profits, cash balances, receivables, payables, and backlog; budgets and projections; statements filed with the SEC or other agencies; and notice of significant lawsuits or other legal proceedings. In some cases, financial statements must be accompanied by a certificate from the company's chief executive or financial officer. Its auditors may also have to provide a letter stating the company has complied with the financial covenants in the investment agreement.

[3] Management Participation

One of the principal differences between a venture capital investment and other investments is the desire of venture capitalists to actively participate in management. At a minimum this means a seat on the board of directors. The degree of participation depends on the circumstances. For example, investors may be content to elect a minority of board members. In other cases, investors may insist on a majority. Another common arrangement is to provide that the investor group and the company's founders have equal representation on the board. There may be an added option of allowing the venture capitalist directors to appoint additional independent board members.

There are a number of pros and cons to be considered by management regarding the amount of control to be given to the investor group. Investor participation provides a good way for investors to be apprised of corporate activities. Venture capitalists generally have a wealth of experience working with other emerging companies, and they can share such experience with the board. On the other hand, management may believe that investor control of the board will impair management's ability to make key strategic decisions.

[4] Registration Rights

Most venture capital investments are made under a registration exemption. They tend to be nonpublic offerings under Section 4(2) of the Securities Act or one of the exemptions under Regulation D. In either case, the securities acquired by an investor are restricted securities. They can be resold only in accordance with Rule 144 or as part of a registered offering. This limits the investor's liquidity. Therefore, investors put a good deal of importance on their registration rights, that is, their right to have the securities registered by the issuer.

Registration rights fall into two general categories. Under a "demand" registration right, an investor can require a company to file a registration statement. Such a registration is an expensive, time-consuming process and exposes management to potential liabilities under federal and state securities laws. A demand right, therefore, can be quite onerous for a company. The other type of registration right—a "piggyback" right—allows an investor to include its securities in any registration statement a company files for some other purpose. Piggyback rights are far less burdensome for a company.

Although demand registration rights are rarely exercised, their existence gives the holder significant leverage in dealing with management. For that reason, investors usually insist on demand registration rights.

A company has several ways to restrict demand registration rights. Among the most common are the timing of demands, the minimum size of a demand registration, and the number of demands that can be made.

Since in piggyback registrations, investors "piggyback" on an existing registration statement, a company's incremental expenses and administrative burdens are minimal. As a rule, very few limitations will be imposed on the investors' ability to request a piggyback registration. In some cases, a company may be excused from including an investor's securities in an IPO registration statement if underwriters believe such an inclusion would have an adverse impact on the offering's marketability. After the initial public offering, investors are usually guaranteed a minimum participation.

[5] Participation in Subsequent Financings

Investors may be given the right to participate in future company financings. This allows them to maintain or increase their ownership interest in the company. Participation rights may take the form of a right of first refusal to purchase all securities offered by the company in the future. Alternatively, investors may be given the right to purchase pro rata shares of future offerings. This allows them to maintain their ownership percentage. A third alternative is simply the right to discuss financing opportunities with the company before it begins negotiations with third parties.

Participation rights may be limited to *major investors,* defined as investors who own a certain minimum amount of a company's securities. In addition, the offer and issuance of certain securities may be excluded from participation rights. These include securities issued on conversion of outstanding securities or exercise of outstanding options or warrants, securities issued in acquisitions or other strategic transactions, and securities issued under employee benefit or compensation plans. Participation rights may also be limited to equity securities. This preserves a company's ability to issue debt securities as appropriate. Participation rights generally expire on completion of a company's initial public offering. An investor's right may terminate earlier if it is not exercised in one or more financings.

[6] Affirmative and Negative Covenants

A company's obligation to provide investors with information, registration rights, access to management, and participation in subsequent financings are examples of affirmative covenants. While these are the major ones, many agreements contain additional affirmative covenants, such as the company's obligations to

1. Maintain insurance covering such risks as required by law, as well as such additional insurance as is customary for companies engaged in the same or similar business;
2. Use proceeds of the offering for working capital or for such other purposes as specified in the investment agreement;
3. Pay all taxes, assessments, and governmental charges on the company and its subsidiaries, or against their respective properties, before penalties accrue, unless such taxes are contested in good faith and by appropriate proceedings;
4. Pay all lawful claims (whether for labor, materials, supplies, services, or anything else) that might become a lien on properties of the

company, unless the validity or amount is contested in good faith and by appropriate proceedings;

5. Maintain its corporate existence in good standing, keep its properties in good repair, and carry on—by itself or through its subsidiaries—the business described in its business plan;
6. Promptly give investors written notice of (a) any material casualty to any property, any other force majeure, or any investigation or proceeding involving the company, the result of which might have a material adverse effect on the company's financial condition or business; (b) any action, proceeding, or claim, of which the company may have notice, that may be commenced or asserted against the company unless such action, proceeding, or claim involves payment of a fixed sum of money less than a specified amount or is fully covered by insurance; or (c) occurrence or claimed occurrence of an event of default under any agreement to which it is a party, or any event that, with notice or lapse of time or both, would constitute an event of default under any agreement;
7. Furnish to the investor copies of all instruments creating indebtedness, security interests, or liens, and all consent letters, waivers, or modifications to any such instruments;
8. Maintain in full force all rights to use patents, processes, licenses, trademarks, trade names, or copyrights owned or possessed by it and deemed by the company to be useful in its business, and take all necessary steps to protect proprietary developments made in the future, including causing key employees to sign confidentiality and proprietary rights agreements;
9. Comply with all applicable laws and regulations relating to the conduct of its business, and ownership and use of its properties or assets; and
10. Maintain in full force and effect insurance on the lives of specified officers and employees of the company for a fixed term, with the proceeds made payable to investors.

Negative covenants generally limit or restrict management's ability to take certain actions without the consent of investors. They are often the subject of long and extensive negotiations. Investors will demand the right to vote on matters that have a fundamental impact on their investment, such as acquisitions, mergers, and issuance of new securities that dilute their interest or control. Additional negative covenants that may be discussed are any actions by the company:

1. To create, incur, assume, or suffer to exist any indebtedness. There may be exceptions for indebtedness to banks and other financial

institutions, indebtedness under common commercial financing arrangements, and indebtedness not exceeding a specified amount;

2. To create, incur, assume, or suffer to exist any lien on any of its property, assets, or revenues, whether currently owned or acquired after closing, except for minor liens similar to those described in the company's representation and warranty;
3. To agree to, or assume, guarantee, endorse, or otherwise in any way become responsible or liable, directly or indirectly, for obligations of any person;
4. To enter into any merger, consolidation, or amalgamation; liquidate, wind up, or dissolve itself (or suffer any liquidation or dissolution); or convey, sell, lease, transfer, or otherwise dispose of, in one transaction or a series of related transactions, all or a substantial part of its business or assets;
5. To declare any dividends (other than dividends payable solely in stock of the company);
6. To make any payment on account of, or set apart assets for a sinking or analogous fund for, purchase, redemption, retirement, or other acquisition of any shares of the company;
7. To permit the ratio of current assets to current liabilities, or tangible net worth to be less than a specified amount;
8. To make, or commit to make, any advance, loan, extension of credit, or capital contribution to any party; to purchase any stocks, bonds, notes, debentures, or other securities, or all or substantially all of the business or assets of any party; or to make any investment in any party;
9. To enter into any transaction directly or indirectly for the benefit of an affiliate, except in the ordinary course of and pursuant to reasonable requirements of its business, and on fair and reasonable terms not less favorable to the company than would be obtained in a comparable arm's-length transaction with a nonaffiliate;
10. To authorize or issue any additional shares except as specifically approved in the investment agreement;
11. To amend the articles of incorporation or bylaws in a manner that adversely affects investors; and
12. To enter into any employment agreement or other personal service contract with officers or key employees that extends beyond a specified term or that provides for annual compensation in excess of a specified amount, or to approve any acceleration or termination of vesting schedules applicable to stock held by officers, directors, and employees.

Defaults under affirmative and negative covenants can have a number of consequences. In debt financings, a default may allow an investor to accelerate the debt, declaring the entire principal and all accrued interest immediately due and payable. Alternatively, an event of default in an equity or debt financing may create a right for an investor to designate a majority of the board of directors. These "vote switch" provisions, which are included in the articles of incorporation, require that a special meeting of shareholders be convened to elect representatives of the investors to a majority of the board positions. In most cases, the right to elect a majority of the board continues until the default is cured.

§ 10.05 ANCILLARY AGREEMENTS

[A] Introduction

In addition to the investment agreement, a number of other agreements may be entered into at the time of the financing. For example, investors may enter into shareholders' agreements with the company and other major shareholders concerning voting rights and other matters.

[B] Shareholders' Agreement

One common agreement requested by investors covers transfer and voting of equity securities held by major shareholders. The purpose is to provide investors with guarantees on continued participation of management and the composition of the board of directors. The following are among the issues that might be covered in this type of agreement:

1. Management shareholders grant the company and/or investors a right of first refusal on sales of their securities to third parties. This protects investors from unwanted changes in ownership. There will be exceptions for transfers of shares by gift to family members or as collateral in a bona fide loan. The transferee or pledgee must agree in writing to be bound by the agreement. Investors usually will *not* agree to provide a corresponding right to management shareholders as to their shares.
2. The company and/or investors may be given the option to purchase securities of any management shareholder at fair market value upon the occurrence of certain events, such as death, personal bankruptcy, or attachment of shares by legal process as in a divorce.

Detailed procedures, usually appraisals by disinterested persons, are provided to assure a fair valuation.

3. Management shareholders must provide investors with a right to participate in sales of their shares to third parties. These rights are referred to as "co-sale" or "take-along" rights. They are designed to prevent management shareholders from bailing out on investors by selling their interests to third parties. A sale to a third-party subject to a co-sale arrangement must first survive any right of first refusal described above.
4. Founders and investors will vote their shares for election of directors in a specified manner.

Shareholders' agreements will usually terminate on the earlier of a public offering by the company or a fixed date. The validity and legality of these provisions may be restricted by state law.

[C] Employee Stock Purchase Arrangements

Many employees may want to purchase company shares. Some purchases will occur at the same time that the investor contributes its money. Other employees may want to purchase later.

Investors recognize the advantage of allowing employees to purchase at the same time as their investment. It confirms the employees' commitment to the company and underscores their belief that the company's future is positive. Investors also recognize that to attract and maintain employees in the future, it may be necessary to allow them to purchase shares or receive options. A pool of shares will be set aside for these purposes. The size of this pool will generally range from 5% to 20% of fully diluted equity. Shares in the pool will be exempt from any negative covenants, antidilution provisions, or right of first refusal.

The pool has an impact on pricing. For example, assume the current value of a company's business, prior to financing, is $2 million, and investors are willing to contribute an additional $2 million. One-half of postfinancing ownership is likely to be given to investors and one-half to founders and other key employee-owners. Each is to receive 100,000 shares, for a total of 200,000. Any shares set aside for purchase by employees will dilute the investors' interests. If 10% of outstanding shares (i.e., 20,000) are reserved for the employee pool, investors will have 100,000 of 220,000 or slightly more than 45%. It would be better for investors to request an amount equal to (a) one-half of existing shares plus (b) one-half of any set aside shares. This will keep investors' ownership at one-half. Otherwise, they should adjust their purchase price.

The next question is how to establish the procedure for issuing shares to employees. Such shares may be issued in a number of different ways:

- Stock purchase plans provide for the sale of shares to employees, generally at a reduced price;
- Incentive stock options allow employees to purchase shares at a later date (usually at the time of an IPO) at a price equal to the fair market value when the option was granted; and
- Nonstatutory stock options may be granted in higher amounts and at lower prices than those of incentive stock options. When such stock options are exercised, however, tax treatment is less favorable.

Employee stock arrangements may be either immediate purchases or option grants that allow the employee to defer purchase and payment until a later date (often five to ten years out) when the employee exercises the option.

Shares issued to employees often are subject to vesting restrictions, which require an employee to remain with the company for a specified period of time before the employee becomes entitled to all the securities. For example, under a five-year vesting scheme, the agreement may provide that no stock vests for the first year of the purchaser's employment; but at the end of that year, 20% vests. The remaining 80% vests over the next four years, in equal monthly or quarterly amounts. As a result, each employee must remain with the company for at least one year before getting any benefit from "sweat equity." Vested stock may be subject to a repurchase option in favor of the company at a price equal to the amount originally paid by the purchaser. Unvested options lapse if the employee quits before vesting. In addition, shares issued to employees may be subject to a right of first refusal in favor of the company.

[D] Other Employee Agreements

Other agreements that may be required at the time of a venture capital investment include employment and noncompete agreements with the founders and other key management employees. Proprietary information and assignment of inventions agreements from most, if not all, of the company's employees will also be required.

Employment and noncompetition agreements set out the terms of the employment relationship between the employee and the company, including duties, compensation, fringe benefits, and restrictions on engaging in competing activities during and after employment. Proprietary information and assignment of inventions agreements are designed to protect the company's trade secrets and ensure that the company has the right to own and use any intellectual property rights arising out of an employee's activities on behalf of the company.

§ 10.06 CLOSING CONDITIONS

[A] Introduction

Completion of purchase and sale of securities will occur at a closing. Many venture capital investments will close simultaneously with the execution and delivery of the investment agreement. There is no need for conditions covering the time between the execution of the agreement and the closing. Nevertheless, most investment agreements will contain "conditions precedent to closing" for both investors and the company. The conditions serve as a valuable checklist for ensuring that corporate formalities have been observed, all material business conditions have been satisfied (e.g., completion of a loan agreement satisfactory to investors), all ancillary agreements have been executed, and all required legal opinions and certifications have been delivered.

[B] Investors' Closing Conditions

[1] In General

In the venture capital investment process, the closing conditions for investors typically include delivery of a satisfactory legal opinion by counsel for the company; execution of any required ancillary agreements; appropriate amendments to the company's charter documents; election of investor representatives to the board of directors; delivery of certificates by senior management, including a certification regarding truth and accuracy of representations and warranties in the investment agreement; and satisfaction of explicit closing conditions. In addition, the company will usually agree to deliver such other documents as may reasonably be requested by the investors or their counsel, including copies of the company's minutes books and share records.

[2] Legal Opinion of Company Counsel

One of the most important conditions of the investors' obligation to close the transaction under the investment agreement is receipt by investors of an appropriate opinion from the company's counsel. If selling shareholders are involved, an opinion of their counsel will also be required. In rare instances, investors will also receive a relatively brief opinion from their own counsel on certain basic matters specifically relating to the transaction.

The opinion of a company's counsel usually covers most, if not all, of the following items: legal existence of the company and its material subsidiaries; capitalization of the company; power and authority of the company to enter into the investment agreement; authorization and approval of the investment agreement by the board of directors, shareholders, regulators, and other parties; absence of any material conflict between the terms of the investment agreement and any contract, law, or rule to which the company is subject; absence of any material litigation; legal status of securities to be issued to investors; the company's compliance with all laws, contracts, and licensing requirements to which it may be subject; and enforceability of the investment agreement against the company.

[3] Officers' Certificates and Related Documents

Investors will require, in addition to an opinion letter from the company's counsel, certificates executed by senior officers of the company, as well as certificates from regulatory bodies and various other documents, relating to the offering. The most important certificate is the officers' certificate executed by the company's chief executive officer and secretary. It confirms that all representations and warranties in the investment agreement are accurate as of the closing, that all conditions to closing have been satisfied, that there have been no material changes in the business of the company, that charter documents have not been amended, and that board and shareholder resolutions approving sale of securities have not been rescinded. Governmental certificates will include copies of the company's articles of incorporation and confirmation that the company remains in legal good standing.

[C] Company's Closing Conditions

The obligation of the company to consummate transactions specified in the investment agreement will also be subject to conditions. These normally include continued accuracy of investors' representations and warranties as of the closing date, compliance with applicable federal and state securities law requirements, and tender of a specified minimum amount of funds by the investor group. In some cases, a company may insist that investor funds be immediately available for company use, either by wire transfer or by delivery of certified check.

Venture Capitalists: Show Me the Money

FLEMMING, LESSARD & SHIELDS, LLC

by Gary L. Shields, CFA

As an investment banker, I see roughly one thousand investment opportunities each year. In reviewing them, I ask myself five questions. Only a few applicants have the correct answers.

1. How big could the opportunity be?
   What is the opportunity?
   How big is the market?
   What is the business model?
   What is the sustainable "unfair" competitive advantage?
   How big can the company become?
   What percentage of market penetration is required for the projections?
   How much will I own?

2. What happens if something goes wrong?
   What if the projections aren't met?
   How much more money could I be required to invest?
   How can the burn rate be controlled?
   What is the structure of the investment?
   Will I control enough voting power/board positions to influence my investment?
   Is there a "liquid" market for the company?

3. What is the exit strategy?
   What is the time horizon of the investment?
   Can the company realistically carry out an IPO?
   Are there obvious strategic buyers?

4. Who will be my partners in the deal?
   How much money does the entrepreneur have in the deal?
   Are there other venture capitalists?
   Are there strategic investors?
   What are the relationships with the banks?
   Who are the advisors to the company? Attorneys? Accountants?

5. How good is the management?
   Is there a management team in place?
   Does the team have experience in building successful companies?
   Can the management team build this company?
   Are there unrealistic founder issues?
   What is the marketing strength of the organization?
   Where are the management holes and how can we fill them?
   How easy will it be to change management members if necessary?

PART IV • PUBLIC FINANCING

CHAPTER 11 • PUBLIC OFFERINGS

CHAPTER 11

§ 11.01 INTRODUCTION

The registration process for the offer and sale of securities is time consuming and must be done carefully. This is true both of a primary offering of newly issued securities and of a secondary offering in which outstanding shares are registered for resale. The registration statement covering such sales must be prepared carefully. All the regulatory hurdles raised by the SEC, state blue-sky authorities, and the NASD in the case of an underwritten offering, must be surmounted.

In some cases, preparation of the registration statement only means incorporating by reference information previously disclosed under the federal securities laws. Particularly when the filing is for an initial public offering (IPO), the registration statement will contain full narrative disclosures and detailed financial information. When a registrant has not previously registered securities under the Securities Act, the SEC will review the disclosures thoroughly and probably have comments.

In this chapter, emphasis is placed on the decisions that must be made, and the procedures that should be followed, in registering securities for the first time under the Securities Act. Chapter 14 will cover resales.

§ 11.02 CONSIDERATIONS IN SELECTING PUBLIC FINANCING MECHANISM

[A] Alternatives to Public Securities Offerings

The question of whether a registered public offering is an appropriate financing depends on the goals and objectives of the issuer and its owners and managers. In most cases, attracting additional capital is the primary objective. This means one or more economic factors must be considered:

- Amount of funds required and expected use of proceeds;
- Potential capital providers (i.e., banks, individuals, institutions, the public);

- Price, and its relationship to tangible measures such as book or market value;
- Timing;
- Offering method—possible use of an investment bank; and
- Risks associated with successfully completing the offering.

If the issuer is seeking additional financing to expand operations or repay debt, it can raise capital in many ways outside the public market. There is a well-developed private placement market. The company could also use strategic partnerships, such as technology funding arrangements; research and development partnerships; or licensing and marketing agreements. Any of these alternatives might be attractive when a public offering is inappropriate for internal or external reasons.

On the other hand, if the issuer's prime objective is to enable existing shareholders to liquidate their investment, then a public offering is probably the best vehicle. Another option is to find a party willing to acquire the firm (or shares of owners wishing to exit).

[B] Advantages of Public Company Status

The following are among the advantages of being a public company:

- *Prestige*—Creating a public market for an issuer's securities provides the issuer with a competitive advantage derived from greater visibility, credibility, respect, and prestige within the issuer's industry and community.
- *Increased Operational Flexibility*—An issuer whose stock is traded publicly will find it easier to make acquisitions. The ability to offer both cash and marketable securities in future acquisitions may enable the issuer to vigorously pursue additional lines of business.
- *Liquidity for Current Shareholders*—The initial public offering creates a trading market for existing securities. It provides a source of liquidity to current shareholders.
- *Attraction of Key Employees*—A public market for an issuer's securities substantially increases the value of the securities. This becomes an advantage in recruiting and retaining key employees.

[C] Disadvantages of Public Company Status

There are many regulatory considerations related to becoming and maintaining a public company. Being public will result in drastic change in the way the issuer and its managers conduct business. For all the advantages of a public offering, there are a number of significant potential disadvantages, including

- *Fiduciary Obligations*—Management, directors, and controlling shareholders will owe fiduciary duties to their new outside shareholders. Officers, directors, and 10% shareholders will be subject to the short-swing profit limitations of Exchange Act Section 16(b). They must also be aware of civil and criminal liability for trading in securities on the basis of undisclosed material information.
- *Loss of Managerial Control and Discretion*—At the public offering, outside directors and new management will be added to the firm. This will dilute the control previously enjoyed by existing managers.
- *Investment Community Scrutiny*—Once the company is public, management's judgment will be increasingly subject to analysis and evaluation by the investment community. To maintain share price, management may unwisely focus on short-term profitability at the expense of the company's long-term viability.
- *Disclosure*—The disclosure requirements imposed on a public company may result in the publication of sensitive information regarding management compensation and significant transactions. Such disclosure may significantly impact preexisting salaries, fringe benefits, and other arrangements between the issuer and insiders.
- *Financial and Other Costs of Administrative Compliance*—Assuming the offering is completed, the issuer will be exposed to significantly greater administrative burdens due to SEC reporting requirements. The most obvious is preparation of audited financial statements. Management must also develop and maintain new relationships with public shareholders, regulatory staff, and the investment community. Other costs include transfer agent services, increased legal and accounting services, shareholder meetings, public relations, and administration fees.

§ 11.03 REGULATORY FRAMEWORK

[A] Overview

Each of the states, as well as the regulatory and certification body of the securities and investment banking industry in the United States, has an interest in the offer and sale of securities. However, it is the federal Securities Act, and the registration process established by it, that is most important to persons raising capital through a public offering. Section 5 of the Securities Act prohibits offers and sales of securities without registration unless an appropriate exemption is available. If registration is required, a registration statement containing the required disclosures must be filed with the SEC before any *offer* can legally be made. The SEC must declare the registration statement effective before any *sale* can legally be consummated.

The Securities Act's extensive disclosure requirements require the issuer to give prospective investors a wide range of historical and prospective information regarding its business, operations, and finances. Where an active trading market for the issuer's securities has not existed prior to the offering, the information in the registration statement will be the basis for all subsequent disclosures.

[B] Section 5 of Securities Act

Section 5(c) of the Securities Act regulates activities of a prospective *issuer*, which is defined in Section 2(4) of the Securities Act as any person who issues or proposes to issue a security before the filing of a registration statement. An issuer *is* permitted to engage in preliminary negotiations with a prospective underwriter. No other activities can occur during this prefiling period that might constitute an "offer to sell." Accordingly, no potential purchasers can be contacted; no written materials that might be an illegal prospectus can be circulated to the investment community; and press releases, press conferences, publicity campaigns, and the like should be avoided if they would stimulate or condition the market for the offering.

Offering activities may begin in earnest once the registration statement has been filed with the SEC. Section 5(b)(1) of the Securities Act applies to this waiting when the issuer awaits comments from the SEC. It permits oral offers and offers through a prospectus that complies with Section 10 of the Securities Act. (The prospectus is included as an integral part of the registration statement.) However, no additional *written* sales materials—so-called free-writing—may be used until after the registration statement has been declared effective by the SEC. Even then, the written materials must be preceded or accompanied by a final prospectus that meets the requirements of Section 10(a) of the Securities Act.

The disclosure requirements of Section 5 are implemented by the integrated disclosure system, particularly Regulations C, S-K, S-B, and S-X. They cover the procedural guidelines for preparing Securities Act registration statements and the applicable registration form. Moreover, the broad requirements in Sections 11, 12, and 17 of the Securities Act and Rule 10b-5 under the Exchange Act must be considered. They require that *all material* information be included in the prospectus, whether or not specifically requested by the registration form.

[C] State Securities Laws

In 1996, Congress adopted the National Securities Market Improvement Act of 1996 (NSMIA). NSMIA preempted state securities laws with respect to "federal covered securities" (e.g., securities listed or authorized for listing on the New York Stock Exchange, the American Stock Exchange, or the NASDAQ National Market System). If the securities offered are not "federal covered securities," issuers will need to comply with the blue sky laws of each state in which the securities are offered.

In each state in which securities that are not "federal covered securities" will be offered, blue-sky administrators will also receive copies of the materials filed with the SEC. This is part of the process of qualifying the securities in such states. Some states will, like the SEC, carefully review all of an issuer's disclosures in the offering materials. Most states, however, will focus on certain key issues concerning pricing, underwriters' compensation, and the issuer's structure. For example, blue-sky administrators in such states will scrutinize the following:

- Percentage of the issuer's capital contributed by founders and promoters (i.e., promoters' equity investment),
- Prices at which outstanding securities have been previously issued to insiders and how they compare to the public offering price (i.e., promotional shares),
- Loans and other relationships between insiders and the issuer,
- Selling expenses related to the offering,
- Public offering price,
- Dilution to be sustained by existing shareholders, and
- Other issues relating to the issuer's charter and bylaws.

[D] NASD Review and Regulation

While the NASD will receive copies of the registration statement, it will typically limit its review to the underwriting arrangement, especially underwriter's compensation. Compensation can take a number of different forms, including customary underwriters' commission or discount, expense allowances, warrants, equity incentives, and rights to manage the issuer's future offerings. Also, the NASD will examine the terms of any directed distribution to friends of the issuer or preferred customers of the underwriters.

§ 11.04 PREOFFERING CONSIDERATIONS

[A] Introduction

As the public offering process begins, the issuer and underwriters turn their attention to a variety of matters. Most important, the issuer and its counsel must organize the vast amounts of information necessary to prepare the registration statement and conduct due diligence. In addition, certain corporate housekeeping issues should be addressed. The issuer's organizational and capital structure should be reviewed and, if necessary, amended. Finally, an organizational meeting should be held for all parties to discuss the terms and timing of the offering, restrictions on communications during the offering, selling shareholders, and exchange listings.

[B] Due Diligence and Corporate Housekeeping

[1] Due Diligence Investigation

In any securities offering, a due diligence investigation must be undertaken to collect information regarding the issuer and its officers, directors, and shareholders. The purpose is to facilitate preparation of the registration statement. The due diligence investigation is particularly important for IPOs. The issuer and its control persons and underwriters may be exposed under the Securities Act to significant liabilities for false or misleading statements in the registration statement. As a rule, the investigation is a cooperative process among the issuer, the underwriters, and their respective legal counsels.

[2] Corporate Housekeeping

Depending on the prior financing history of the issuer, certain corporate housekeeping issues may need attention. Even where an issuer has previously received venture capital financing or institutional funding, potential IPO candidates must generally consider certain corporate issues: amendment of existing rights of preferred shareholders, number and pricing of options granted to employees, amendments to articles of incorporation and bylaws to incorporate antitakeover and other provisions suitable to a public company, and the effect of registration rights granted to shareholders in previous financings.

[C] Organizational Meeting and Offering Timetable

[1] Organizational Meeting

One of the first steps in launching the public offering is convening an initial organizational or "all-hands" meeting for participants in the offering process. Such a meeting will include management of the issuer, representatives of the managing underwriter, legal counsel for the issuer and the managing underwriter, and the issuer's independent public accountants. At this meeting, a tentative timetable for the offering will be set and responsibilities will be assigned. Issues likely to be discussed are the structure of the offering, disclosure matters, and registration period activities.

A typical agenda for an organizational meeting will address a number of possible items, depending on the time available and the degree of preparation to date. Special note will be taken of the following points:

- Timing of the offering, anticipated size and offering price, and participation of selling shareholders;
- Schedule for the remaining drafting and due diligence sessions, and responsibilities of participants for different provisions of the registration statement;
- Prefiling modifications to the issuer's capital structure and other corporate arrangements necessary to properly price the offering and eliminate blue-sky concerns;
- Substantive disclosure items to be addressed in the registration statement, including litigation, insider transactions, potential acquisitions, new products, and competition;
- Dates of financial statements to be included in the registration statement;
- Off-balance-sheet financing and recent acquisitions for which audited financial statements must be prepared; and
- Desirability of reincorporating in a jurisdiction that provides officers and directors with the greatest amount of personal protection from liability to shareholders.

[2] Offering Timetable

The managing underwriter and its counsel will prepare a timetable and list of responsibilities for all parties at the organizational meeting. (A simplified example appears in Chapter 12.) This document includes a schedule for the basic steps in the registration process. It fixes key deadlines, which turn on assumptions by the issuer and the managing underwriter about the proper timing of the offering. It also assigns responsibilities for particular tasks and requisite coordination. Experience has shown that listing each of the important items is far more important than settling on an exact timetable, since it is often difficult to predict each of the items with absolute certainty.

The following are among the important milestones that should be established:

- Availability of the initial draft of the registration statement, including required financial information;
- Schedule of due diligence meetings with officers and the issuer's key employees;
- Board and shareholder actions regarding housekeeping matters and approval of the offering;
- Filing of the registration statement with the SEC and other regulators, and anticipated period of review;
- Schedule of postfiling marketing activities, including road show presentations;
- Preparation and filing of material amendments to the registration statement to address comments from the SEC and other regulators;
- Effectiveness of the registration statement, execution of the underwriting agreement, and commencement of the sale of offered securities; and
- Closing of the sale and purchase of offered securities.

[D] Restrictions on Issuer Communications During Registration

[1] Introduction

Sections 5(b) and (c) of the Securities Act restrict communications before the registration statement becomes effective. These rules apply throughout the period that a security is "in registration." This period begins when the issuer reaches an understanding with the managing underwriter on the offering and ends when dealers are no longer required to deliver prospectuses pursuant to Section 4(3) of the Securities Act.

[2] Prefiling Communications

Under Section 5(c) of the Securities Act, no offer or sale of a security can be made before the registration statement is filed with the SEC. Accordingly, the basic problem is to determine what activities might constitute an offer to sell. Section 2(3) of the Securities Act defines *offer to sell* to "include every attempt or offer to dispose of, or solicitation of an offer to buy, a security or interest in a security, for value." Further guidance comes from interpretations of the SEC and the courts, which make it clear that press releases, press conferences, and publicity campaigns can constitute offers to sell, since they stimulate or prepare the market for the offering.

One important exception to this general prohibition on communications is contained in Rule 135 under the Securities Act. It provides that an offer to sell does not include a notice by an issuer that it will make a public offering. The notice must state that the offering will be made only by a prospectus. It must contain certain information, such as the name of the issuer; the title, amount, and basic terms of the offering; the amount of the offering, if any, to be made; the anticipated time of the offering; and a brief statement of the manner and purpose of the offering. Underwriters cannot be named.

[3] Waiting Period Communications

After the registration statement has been filed, Section 5(b) of the Securities Act permits issuers, underwriters, and broker-dealers to conduct preliminary marketing activities. They can make oral offers. They can also use a prospectus complying with Section 10 of the Securities Act. Notices, circulars, advertisements, letters, and other communications containing the Rule 134 statements are also permitted.

Rule 134 makes possible "tombstone" advertisements that appear regularly in the *Wall Street Journal* and other financial publications. They simply identify the issuer, security being offered, price, and persons from whom a prospectus can be obtained. No other materials containing an offer for sale can be used during the waiting period. The key concern is whether any other "writing," such as advertising or publicity, might be a nonstatutory prospectus, violating Section 5(b) of the Securities Act.

[4] Regulation of Corporate Communications

In spite of the restrictions in Section 5(c) of the Securities Act, it is not necessary for an issuer to discontinue the public disclosure of factual information in reports and advertisements. Such disclosures may be made in the normal course of business. When an issuer's securities are in registration, however, activities such as speeches by corporate officials, product advertising, and distribution of brochures will be closely scrutinized for inappropriate disclosures. Authorities will consider the nature of the publication, the extent of distribution, the time lag between publication and filing the registration statement, and any relation of the issuer to the publisher.

Management and counsel should meet regularly during the offering period to discuss public relations and advertising activities. Any uncertainties in the minds of management should be referred to the underwriters and their counsel for consideration. General guidelines covering most, if not all, of the following items should be circulated and reviewed in detail at the organizational meeting:

- A review should be made of any existing or proposed advertising content, and any that could be deemed an effort to sell securities rather than products should be omitted. An issuer may continue to advertise products and services under existing advertising campaigns, but no significant increases can be made in the coverage or frequency of such efforts. Any decision to commence a new advertising campaign should probably be deferred unless the parties are satisfied it will not broaden the issuer's publicity significantly or condition the market for the issuer's securities.
- An issuer may issue standard product releases directed toward the trade and technical press regarding important developments. Issuers should also continue to release standard factual information regarding business and financial developments (i.e., receipt of a contract, strike settlements, plant openings, or similar events of interest). Publication of new events raises questions as to whether material amendments should be made to the registration statement. Accordingly, many issuers are counseled to avoid starting negotiations for, or entering into, a major transaction.
- Nonpublic companies typically have limited communications with the investment community. This should continue during the waiting

period. An issuer should, therefore, discourage interviews that might result in articles or press coverage prior to the offering.

- Appearances by an issuer at industry forums organized by investment banking firms, trade groups, and analysts should be reviewed on a case-by-case basis. Presentations should be reviewed by counsel to ensure that the presentation does not result in selective disclosure of information not available in the preliminary prospectus. Written materials that might be interpreted as a prospectus should be avoided. Also, responses in question and answer sessions should be carefully considered to avoid predictions, forecasts, projections, and estimates of sales and earnings.
- Road show presentations taking place during the waiting period should not include catalogues, brochures, or articles that might be considered improper prospectuses.

One company official should be given responsibility for responding to all press inquiries during the offering period. Responses should be made only after counsel has been consulted. Any unsolicited inquiries the issuer receives from third parties, employees, and current shareholders regarding the offering should be referred to the managing underwriter.

[E] Selling Shareholders

Management will usually ask shareholders if they wish to participate in the offering. In most cases, those allowed to participate are shareholders with the right to have securities registered in a public offering. Such a right may be subject to a variety of restrictions. As noted, one common restriction flows from the managing underwriter's ability to limit or exclude selling shareholders if necessary for the offering's success. If shares owned by existing shareholders, known as "secondary shares," are included, the issuer may be required under its agreement with them to pay their registration and other selling costs, other than underwriting discounts.

Once the selling shareholder group is identified, each seller must sign a custody agreement and related documents. By signing, the sellers become parties to the underwriting agreement and agree to be bound by the terms of the offering. While practice varies on whether the custody agreement must be executed before the registration statement is filed, the agreements will be in place before the statement becomes effective. When the selling shareholder group includes venture capital investors, they will often take an active interest in selecting the managing underwriter and pricing the offering.

[F] Exchange and Nasdaq Listings

[1] In General

Both the issuer and the managing underwriter want the issuer's securities listed on an appropriate exchange or listing system immediately following the public offering. They therefore apply to be listed on the appropriate exchange or trading system at the same time the registration statement is filed. Requirements for listing must be satisfied by the time trading begins.

[2] Exchange Listing

An issuer may wish to list its securities on a national or regional securities exchange. Listing on these exchanges, including the New York Stock Exchange and the American Stock Exchange, may provide an issuer with the following:

- Enhanced prestige with investors, customers, and suppliers (many technology companies choose to list on Nasdaq because it has an image as a cutting edge high-tech market);
- Increased ability to attract and hold employees by offering options for shares in a registered company—shares that can be readily sold;
- Ability to use own listed shares to fund acquisitions;
- A higher and more readily ascertainable value for the security;
- The issuer's increased ability to have its press releases and quotations widely disseminated by the news media;
- Advantages under state law (i.e., for NYSE-listed securities, the absence of statutory appraisal rights);
- Existence of trading specialists who will make a more orderly market for the issuer's securities, thereby minimizing price volatility; and
- Closer spreads between bid and offered quotations than in the over-the-counter market.

Issuers whose securities are traded on one of the major exchanges (i.e., NYSE or AMEX) must abide by certain policies with respect to corporate governance:

- Eliminate material transactions between the issuer and its management or major shareholders;

- Not list a common stock without voting rights or with unduly restricted voting rights;
- Require quorums at shareholder meetings sufficiently high to ensure representation of minority voting interests;
- Require shareholder votes on matters not previously required under state law;
- Require an audit committee that facilitates substantial participation by outside directors;
- Control future issuances of shares through supplemental listing applications; and
- Promptly disclose material information.

[3] Nasdaq Listing

Due to restrictive practices of NYSE and AMEX, and recent significant improvements in the management of the over-the-counter market by Nasdaq, many issuers now seek a trading symbol on Nasdaq National Market System (NMS). To qualify, an issuer must meet certain standards concerning the size and effect of its offering. If the issuer qualified, it may receive an immediate designation from Nasdaq NMS.

An NASD condition to NMS designation is that the securities must be registered under the Exchange Act. If advised by the NASD that the securities can be NMS-designated, an issuer must file a registration statement with the SEC on Form 8-A. This can be completed easily by "wrapping" the prospectus around the Form 8-A application. Registration under the Exchange Act becomes automatically effective on the later of filing the Form 8-A or at the same time that the Securities Act registration statement becomes effective.

[4] Financial Manual Listings

Issuers that do not qualify for listing on NMS or on the first tier of one of the major exchanges may want to obtain listings in a widely distributed financial manual. The leading ones are Moody's *Industrial Manual* and Standard & Poor's *Register of Corporations, Directors and Executives.* Being included in such publications will help the issuer develop a strong market in which secondary trading can occur. This may not be necessary in states that allow secondary trading after a fixed number of days. Such states may, nevertheless, require a notification filing of such trading.

§ 11.05 PREPARING AND FILING THE REGISTRATION STATEMENT

[A] Overview

After preoffering matters have been discussed and considered, the parties turn to the drafting of the registration statement and prospectus. The prospectus is the part of the registration statement that contains substantive disclosures regarding the issuer, the securities being offered, and the method of their distribution. The prospectus will be the main written marketing tool for the offering. The balance of the registration statement contains undertakings, signatures, consents, and exhibits that are filed with the SEC and available for public inspection. They are not distributed to potential investors.

In some cases, registration statements may consist primarily of material incorporated by reference from previous filings.

In the course of preparing a registration statement, the parties generally consult the following:

- Instructions accompanying the relevant registration statement form;
- General rules and regulations under the Securities Act, particularly Regulations S-K, S-B, S-X, and S-T;
- Releases issued by the SEC giving its official positions and interpretations of the rules and regulations; and
- Views of the SEC staff in staff interpretive and no-action letters.

In addition, prospectuses and Exchange Act reports of companies in similar fields can be an invaluable source of information regarding the activities of competitors. They will also indicate the type of disclosure deemed material in the industry.

[B] Content of the Registration Statement

[1] In General

The required content of the registration statement is described in the instructions that accompany it. For example, Form S-1 refers to 17 different items that must be included in the prospectus, or outside the prospectus but as a part of the registration statement. While each of the items has a title, such as "Information with Respect to the Registrant," the required disclosures can be understood only by reference to one or more items in

Regulation S-K. Thus, Item 9 of Form S-1 is titled "Description of Securities to Be Registered." An issuer can respond by furnishing information required by Item 202 of Regulation S-K ("Description of Registrant's Securities").

Disclosures in the registration statement are part of the integrated disclosure system of the federal securities laws described earlier. Specific requirements are listed on an item-by-item basis in the appropriate form. The effect is to require inclusion of the basic information package, in-depth disclosures, and the Securities Act standard items, as described earlier. In addition, the registration statement may need to include other disclosures, such as the "market overhang," the issuer's proposed plan of operations, and recent sales of unregistered securities. Disclosure depends on a number of factors, including any previous registration(s) of securities by the issuer.

[2] Content of SBI Registration Forms

As noted earlier, SBI Securities Act registration forms—Form SB-1 for transitional SBIs and Form SB-2—differ from traditional Securities Act registration forms. There are similarities to old Form S-18, a simplified registration for small offerings. That form was canceled when SBI forms were adopted.

The narrative and financial information required in a Form SB-1 prospectus can be provided in two ways. First, an issuer may furnish the information required by Model B, Part II of Form 1-A (the form used for Regulation A offerings). In that case, the issuer must also provide information on the offering, significant parties, relationships between the issuer and experts named in the registration statement, legal proceedings, accounting relationships, and indemnification. Second, as an alternative, corporate issuers may furnish the information required by Model A of Form 1-A, plus the above information. In either case, issuers must furnish the financial information required by Item 310 of Regulation S-B. Nonprospectus disclosures on Form SB-1 are similar to those in any registration statement and must refer to Regulation S-B.

Form SB-2 requires 28 items of information, which are similar to those appearing in Form S-18. The substantive scope of disclosures in Form SB-2 is similar to the requirements of a Form S-1 registration statement. For example, the registration statement must include a description of the issuer's business, its securities and properties, legal proceedings, amount of ownership by management and principal shareholders, and information equivalent to that required under Regulation S-B for all prospectuses. Form SB-2 does not require financial data or supplemental financial information, and disclosures relating to an issuer's business and executive compensation are simplified.

[C] Organization of the Registration Statement

[1] In General

The registration statement consists of a facing page, prospectus (Part I of the Form), Part II information (e.g., schedules to financial statements), appropriate undertakings, signature page, and exhibits, including consents of named experts.

[2] The Facing Page

The contents of the facing page are established by the applicable form. The page will include the name and address of the registrant, state of incorporation, IRS employer identification number, primary standard industrial classification code number, name and address of agent for service of process and a table permitting calculation of the registration fee.

[3] The Prospectus

The prospectus and registration statement are actually two separate documents. In truth, the registration forms are divided into two parts: information required in the prospectus and information required in the registration but not in the prospectus. Duplication between the prospectus and Part I of the registration statement is avoided by permitting the narrative prospectus to serve as Part I.

[4] Part II of the Registration Statement

Part II of the registration statement contains information required to be in the statement but not in the prospectus. Forms S-1, S-2, S-3, S-4, and S-8 all require identical disclosures about indemnification of officers and directors, exhibits specified by Item 601 of Regulation S-K, and undertakings required by item 512 of Regulation S-K. Forms S-1, S-2, and S-3 must include information on distribution expenses as required by Item 511 of Regulation S-K. In addition, Form S-1 must include information on unregistered securities sold during the past three years (Item 701 of Regulation S-K).

[5] Signature Page

The signature page will contain signatures called for by Section 6(a) of the Securities Act, including those of the principal executive officer or officers, chief financial officer, comptroller or principal accounting officer, and majority of the board of directors or persons performing similar functions. Signatures can be by power of attorney. If they are, the power of attorney must be filed as an exhibit. When filed electronically, the signature is indicated by "/s/".

[6] Consents of Experts

Experts named in the registration statement as having prepared or certified any part of the registration statement, or a report or valuation in the registration, are liable under Section 11 of the Securities Act. To prevent unauthorized use of their names, Section 7 of the Securities Act requires that their written consents be filed as part of the registration statement. Consents must be dated.

[7] Exhibits

When filing a registration statement under the Securities Act, a registrant must also file certain exhibits. The specific requirements are listed in Item 601 of Regulation S-K and depend on the registration statement used.

For an IPO using Form S-1, the exhibits will be numerous. They include the issuer's charter documents, voting control and management documents, material contracts, loan agreements, and employee benefit plans. Once an issuer has registered under the Securities Act or the Exchange Act, exhibits for subsequent filings can incorporate previously filed documents by reference.

[D] Drafting the Prospectus and Registration Statement

The initial draft of the registration statement is typically compiled by representatives of the issuer, its counsel, and public accountants. The issuer usually drafts the business disclosures, while counsel and accountants handle sections within their own areas of expertise. The parts concerning the underwriting and distribution will be prepared by underwriters. The timetable and list of responsibilities distributed at the organizational meeting usually covers document drafting responsibilities.

The initial draft of the registration statement will be reviewed and redrafted, both separately and at "all-hands" drafting sessions attended by representatives of the issuer, the managing underwriter, their legal counsel, and the issuer's accountants. At some stage, the registration statement will be turned over to a financial printer. Final prefiling changes to the document will be made at the printer's office or electronically. Thereafter, the registration statement will be packaged for filing.

[E] Filing Procedures

[1] General Considerations

Once the registration statement has been completed, the parties must turn to the mechanics of getting it on file with the SEC, the NASD, and blue-sky administrators in states where the securities will be offered. During the days leading up to the filing, several things should be kept in mind:

- Review the NASD's Corporate Financing Interpretation, applicable stock exchange requirements and procedures established by appropriate state administrators.
- Filing fees should be calculated well in advance of the expected filing, and the appropriate wire transfer instructions should be ready for submission with the filing. The issuer will transfer funds covering all blue-sky filing fees to the underwriter's counsel, which will forward its own wire transfer to each state.
- Officers and directors must review the final draft of the registration statement. The officers' and directors' questionnaire distributed early in the process should be recirculated and revised, if necessary. Any modifications should be reflected in the registration statement. Due diligence questions must be raised and disposed of at this point. Counsel should be certain that appropriate substantiating material has been received to back up the information in the registration.
- Corporate resolutions authorizing filing of the registration statement and related transactions should be adopted. Care should also be taken to ensure that all housekeeping actions have been completed and any third-party consents (i.e., registration rights waivers) have been obtained.
- Even though filing will be made electronically, at least one original must be executed and kept on file in issuer's office. Therefore, signatures will need to be collected from a majority of the directors and from the principal executive, financial, and accounting officers of the issuer. These signatures should be collected at the meeting of the board. In some cases, due to geographical constraints, they may need to be collected in advance.

[2] SEC Filing Procedures

The issuer must file the registration statement electronically with the appropriate office of the SEC, usually in Washington, D.C. A wire transfer covering the appropriate fee should be made prior to filing. The fee is based on the number of shares being registered and the anticipated offering price. The transmittal letter should briefly describe the purpose of the filing, the proposed time schedule for the offering, and any special disclosure or accounting issues the issuer wishes to bring to the SEC's attention.

[3] Requesting Confidential Treatment

The description of the issuer and its business in the prospectus will usually emphasize the issuer's unique assets and strategies. In some cases, an issuer will be reluctant to disclose information that it feels would be damaging if disclosed to the public and to competitors. If this is the case, the issuer will need to limit its disclosures and, if necessary, request confidential treatment.

The procedures for seeking protection of information are covered by Rule 406 of Regulation C. Under Rule 406, an issuer should omit the confidential portion from the filing, indicating in the appropriate space that the confidential portion has been filed separately with the SEC. It should also file an application requesting confidentiality, along with a copy of the confidential portion clearly marked "confidential treatment requested." The application should state the reasons for the request and a justification of the time period for which confidential treatment is sought. It should also explain why disclosure is not necessary to protect investors.

Most requests for confidential treatment relate to material contracts with customers, suppliers, or research and development partners. The SEC will not entertain requests for blanket declarations of confidentiality covering an entire agreement. Accordingly, great care must be taken to alert the SEC to specific items that the issuer believes should not be disclosed. Typically, confidentiality requests concern pricing terms, quantity terms, penalty provisions, description of current or proposed research efforts, and names of others who are parties to the contract or are involved in the research.

[4] Blue-Sky Filing Procedures

Public offerings of "federal covered securities" do not require any blue-sky filings. A public offering of securities other than "federal covered securities" will require clearance from the blue-sky administrator in each state where the securities are to be offered. Since offers through a preliminary prospectus cannot occur until the appropriate state application has been filed, state filings will quickly follow the SEC filing. Blue-sky filings are usually made by counsel for the underwriters. Associated fees and expenses, however, are borne by the issuer.

A preliminary blue-sky memorandum is prepared by the underwriter's counsel and sent to the issuer, underwriters, selling group, and broker-dealers in the states where the securities are being qualified. The memorandum will cover timing of offers and sales, circulation of preliminary prospectuses, broker-dealer requirements, sales and promotional activities, and institutions that may purchase under an exemption.

Before filing with the SEC, the managing underwriter will select states where it will offer and sell the securities and will determine the number of shares to be qualified or registered in each state. Thereafter, attention turns to preparing the state filing packages. Although generalizations should be avoided, and each state's filing requirements should be closely reviewed, some common features exist. The initial filing package will usually include notarized signatures; filing fees; a copy of the SEC registration statement; copies of sales and advertising literature to be used in the offering; copies of current charter documents; copies of selling, purchase, and underwriting contracts; and a consent to service of process.

[5] NASD Filing Procedures

At the time of the SEC filing (at least 15 business days before the anticipated offering), the managing underwriter should file the registration statement with the NASD. It should also file any underwriting agreement, agreement among underwriters, dealer agreement, agency agreement, purchase agreement, letter of intent, consulting agreement, warrant agreement, escrow agreement, and other document describing the underwriting or issuance. The underwriter should also file any information or document that is material to the offering and that may have a bearing on the NASD's review. The NASD also requires payment of a filing fee by wire transfer based on the gross amount of the offering.

§ 11.06 WAITING PERIOD ACTIVITIES

[A] Overview

Filing the registration statement and related materials with regulators marks the beginning of the waiting period. During this period, underwriters engage in preliminary marketing activities. At the same time, the SEC, blue-sky administrators, and the NASD are conducting their reviews of the disclosure materials and terms of the proposed offering.

[B] Marketing Activities

[1] In General

After the registration statement is filed with the SEC, it is permissible to print and distribute preliminary prospectuses. Typically in the case of an IPO, the preliminary prospectus will not be printed until initial comments from the SEC are received. After the financial printer is asked to prepare a number of preliminary prospectuses, the underwriters will distribute the printed preliminary prospectuses within their own distribution networks. They will also contact investment bankers who might join the underwriting group.

As mentioned previously, marketing activities during the waiting period are strictly limited under Section 5 of the Securities Act. The principal marketing tool during this period is the preliminary prospectus, sometimes referred to as the "red herring." It is the prospectus portion of the registration statement as filed and will be substantially similar to the final prospectus. The preliminary prospectus will be supplemented by Rule 134 communications, telephone and other oral conversations, and informational meetings with investors.

[2] Underwriting Syndicate

Immediately following the regulatory filings, the managing underwriter will invite firms to be members of the underwriting group. The invitation typically includes copies of the registration statement, drafts of the agreement among underwriters (the AAU) and underwriting agreement, the preliminary blue-sky memorandum, a power of attorney, and the underwriter's questionnaire. For good-sized offerings by attractive issuers, the invitation goes to every firm from which the managing underwriter would expect to receive a similar invitation. The invitation will be consistent with the bracketing system prevalent in the industry. Regional brokerage firms are often added to the list if requested by the issuer or if there is local buying support.

[3] Solicitations of Interest and Road Show

As the underwriting syndicate takes form during the waiting period, the underwriters will circulate the preliminary prospectus among their retail and institutional clients for indications of interest.

In addition, a series of road show presentations will educate prospective institutional investors about the issuer and the offering. Frequently conducted at luncheons and receptions, these meetings include management presentations followed by question-and-answer periods. In addition to group presentations, one-on-one meetings for institutional investors are often arranged. Investor meetings should be as close as possible to the anticipated receipt of SEC comments so that interest in the offering can quickly be converted into sales once the registration statement is effective.

It may be possible to conduct some of the road show by video or over the Internet. (For more explanation of this trend, see Gutterman, Brown, and Stanislaw, *2001 The Professional's Guide to Doing Business on the Internet,* published by Apen Publishers.)

[C] SEC Review

[1] SEC Review Procedures

A registration statement is automatically effective 20 days after it is filed with the SEC, unless the issuer includes a "delaying amendment" as is customary. The "delaying amendment" prevents the registration statement from becoming effective until the issuer has responded to SEC comments, at which time the SEC "accelerates" the effectiveness of the registration statements. At least one amendment in response to SEC comments should be expected in any IPO.

The SEC's Division of Corporation Finance performs the detailed analysis, examination, and review of registration statements. When appropriate, its chief counsel and chief accountant issue opinions interpreting the Securities Act and its rules and regulations. Five major operating sections, referred to as "branches," have been organized within the SEC along industry lines. This enables reviewers to develop expertise in specific industries. The divisions function through assistant directors, supervising administrators, branch chiefs, attorneys, examiners, analysts, accountants, engineers, and other experts.

SEC review of a registration statement will be by a team consisting of an examiner, a staff accountant responsible for the financial information, and a branch chief (or assistant branch chief) coordinating the review. For all practical purposes, there are two types of review: none and full. When no review is appropriate, the SEC staff will inform the issuer by letter and indicate that it will consider an acceleration request. When full review is required (generally when the issuer has not previously filed a registration statement), the SEC will formally advise the issuer of its opinion in a comment or deficiency letter.

A full review will require 30 to 40 days from the original filing. Anticipating SEC concerns and making appropriate disclosures in the initial filing will mitigate the need for substantial revisions when the SEC completes its review. Typically issuers in an IPO wait to receive comments before printing prospectuses. The prospectus will need to be revised and recirculated if the SEC identifies significant deficiencies.

[2] Comment Letter and Response

On completing the initial review, the examiner will give the SEC's comments to the appropriate branch chief, who will then send a comment letter to the issuer and its counsel. The issuer should revise the registration statement promptly to address SEC concerns, so that the SEC is not required to initiate a formal stop-order proceeding. In some cases, the SEC examiner may assist the revision process by giving comments to the issuer and its counsel by telephone and sending the formal comment letter later.

After receiving the comment letter, counsel for the issuer and counsel for the underwriters will discuss the SEC comments. They will consider which ones are appropriate and which ones they may reject. The rejections can be conveyed in a telephone conversation with the examiner or in an explanatory letter accompanying the amended registration statement. The reason for not making a requested change should be explained in detail. Also, participants should consider whether any modifications are necessary in light of developments during the waiting period.

[3] Material Amendments to Registration Statement

After the SEC comments have been analyzed by the issuer and its advisors, an amendment to the registration statement is prepared and filed with the SEC. It will be accompanied by a transmittal letter listing each SEC comment in numerical order, describing the issuer's response, and identifying the page of the prospectus where additional language has been inserted. Courtesy copies of the amendment and transmittal letter are usually sent to the branch chief, examiner, and accounting examiner immediately after filing. This will facilitate a rapid final review of the amended registration statement. At this time, conforming amendments will also be made to filings with the NASD and the blue-sky administrators.

If substantial changes are made to the filing after a preliminary prospectus is distributed, a revised preliminary prospectus must be distributed to underwriting and selling group members under Rule 15c2-8 of the Exchange Act. If the amendment reflects material changes that will be important to investors who have already indicated an interest, the revised preliminary prospectus must be sent to them at least 48 hours before any sales confirmations.

The managing underwriter is responsible for ensuring that filings are made. If the managing underwriter is notified by the SEC that an arrangement in the registration statement is unfair or unreasonable but does not obtain the issuer's consent to modify it as requested, the managing underwriter must notify the underwriting and selling group members of that fact.

[4] Acceleration Requests

Once the SEC has reviewed all changes and has no further comments, the issuer and the managing underwriter must determine the date that the offering will commence. At that time, the issuer and underwriters file an "acceleration request," and the SEC then accelerates the effective time of the registration statement.

[D] Blue-Sky Review Procedures

[1] Introduction

As noted earlier, in 1996, Congress adopted the National Securities Market Improvement Act of 1996 (NSMIA). NSMIA preempted state securities laws with respect to "federal covered securities" (e.g., securities listed or authorized for listing on the New York Stock Exchange, the American Stock Exchange, or the NASDAQ National Market System). If the securities offered are not "federal covered securities," issuers will need to comply with the blue sky laws of each state in which the securities are offered.

Although marketing efforts may occur during the waiting period in each state where the managing underwriter wants to sell the securities, other than "federal covered securities," sales cannot occur until the review by blue-sky administrators is finished. Counsel may be involved in negotiations with several blue-sky administrators during the waiting period. As the effective date approaches, a decision must be made whether to offer in states with unresolved issues.

Blue-sky regulatory approaches can be divided into two categories: states that (like the SEC) limit their review of the offering documentation to ensuring that full and adequate disclosure has been provided to potential investors (and that allow effectiveness in their state concurrent with SEC effectiveness), and states that practice merit review. Under the latter approach, state securities administrators can deny the registration if the offering is deemed to be less than "fair, just, and equitable." Most states follow NASAA (North American Securities Administrators Association) guidelines, which adopt the limited review approach.

[2] Merit Review

The SEC's and disclosure states' procedures are aimed at full and fair disclosure of all material facts. They leave it to the marketplace to determine the quality of the offered securities. Merit review states, on the other hand, conduct an in-depth review of the filed materials and can halt or restrict the sale of securities if they are dissatisfied with the structure of the offering, including the offering price; amount of underwriter's compensation; and prior operations, performance, and organization of the issuer.

"Cheap stock" or "promotional shares" have long been a subject of intense concern to blue-sky administrators. While the definition may differ from state to state, these terms generally refer to equity securities issued before the offering and for consideration substantially lower than the proposed public offering price. Typically, the number of cheap shares cannot exceed a given percentage of shares outstanding after completion of the offering. Exceptions can be made for cheap stock placed in escrow or subject to an agreement that restricts the holder from selling for a specified period of time after the offering. Both exceptions prevent excessive dilution of public shareholders' interests.

Blue-sky administrators will also be concerned if the proposed offering price is much greater that in previous private sales. They will also review proposed offerings with excessive price/earnings multiples (e.g., higher than 20 or 25 to 1) and dilution of the interests of shareholders higher than 33.3%. Several states object if an issuer has a negative net worth, has not made profits, or is not expected to produce profits within a reasonable period of time.

More than a few states regulate the offering of securities with no voting rights; loans to an issuer's officers, directors, and employees; issuance of excessive amounts of options and warrants; use of supermajority provisions to avoid hostile takeovers; the amount of cash paid into an issuer by promoters; and the payment of selling shareholders' offering expenses.

[E] NASD Review Procedures

The NASD reviews filings to see if the underwriting arrangements, terms, and conditions are fair and reasonable. Specifically, the NASD focuses on the type and amount of an underwriter's compensation and how the securities will be distributed.

The NASD review typically parallels the SEC's initial review of the registration statement and usually takes about four to five weeks. The NASD issues four types of comment letters: (1) defer review, which means that there is not enough information to begin the requisite review; (2) defer opinion, which means that more information is required on a limited number of supplemental issues; (3) no objection letter, which indicates that compensation is reasonable; and (4) an unreasonable letter, which means that disciplinary proceedings will be instituted if the offering proceeds on the terms disclosed.

§ 11.07 COMPLETING REGISTRATION AND SELLING THE SHARES

[A] "Going Effective" and Pricing the Offering

After filing any material amendment to the registration statement, the issuer and its advisors must await confirmation from the SEC that it has no further comments. After the SEC has indicated that it has no further comments or after all comments have been addressed, an issuer will request (with the managing underwriter joining in the request) that the SEC accelerate the effective date of the registration statement. The next steps are for the offering to be priced, the underwriting syndicate to be finalized, and the underwriting agreement to be executed.

The last step is for all the price and syndicate information to be put into a pricing amendment, filed with the SEC before the securities markets open on the morning the offering commences. On receipt of the pricing amendment, the SEC will declare the registration statement effective. Trading of the offered securities can then commence upon the market opening.

Rule 430A provides an alternative to the pricing amendment mechanism. Such an amendment is not required if the prospectus is in a registration statement that has been declared effective.

Whether or not Rule 430A is used, by the time the material amendment has been filed, the managing underwriter will have had several conversations with the syndication department of each firm participating in the underwriting group. It should have a good idea of the number of shares each participant wishes to underwrite or to retain for sale through its brokers. That information should give the managing underwriter a fairly good sense of the best price for the offering.

On the day before the effective date of the registration statement, the issuer and the managing underwriter will conduct a pricing meeting to determine the offering price and underwriting commission. The managing underwriter will then notify the participants of their respective final underwriting obligations and the number of shares to be retained by them for sale. If no objection from any underwriter is received within a specified period of time, the managing underwriter will execute the AAU and the underwriting agreement on behalf of all firms participating in the underwriting group. In doing so, it will rely on powers of attorney granted to it by members.

Any omitted information (such as final price and commission) must be filed with the SEC in a final prospectus. Under Rule 424(b), it must be submitted within two days of a pricing determination or the first use of the prospectus. In no event can it be filed later than five business days after the effective date.

[B] Closing the Transaction

On receipt of the order of effectiveness from the SEC and clearances from the NASD and blue-sky administrators, the public offering begins. The closing, however, will not he held for several days. Usually, it is held within three days of the offering commencing, although it could be later if there are problems with distributing the securities. The delay allows underwriters time to collect funds from their customers.

At the closing, underwriters pay the amount collected (less underwriting commission) to the issuer and any selling shareholders. In exchange, underwriters receive securities, certifications, opinions, and other documents specified in the underwriting agreement.

Road Show: Road Warriors

DAEDALUS VENTURES, LLC

by Douglas A. Vetter

Outside the investment community, the "road show" is little known. Once you have done one, you will never forget it.

When a company decides to raise money, it has to get its story out to as many potential investors as possible. They are scattered around the country and, in some cases, around the world.

Unfortunately, your window of opportunity is very narrow. You have to visit as many of those potential investors as possible between the time that securities laws finally allow you to start marketing your company and the day the shares go on sale. This window may not be much more than 10 to 15 days.

The first lesson that this gives rise to is that the road show is a grueling effort. During this period, you will not see your family. You will spend every night in a different city. You will probably visit two to three cities a day, some of them more than once in the same day. You will see the insides of hotels, taxis, and conference rooms. And you will do it from six in the morning until well past midnight.

The second lesson is that you will be making maybe 100 presentations during this time, and each one has to be good. To make them good, you will be coached, groomed, molded, and practiced—over and over again. You may think you are a good presenter now, but you probably aren't. None of us are. We can all be better. Experts will be brought in to make you better.

The third lesson is a combination of "ex's"—exhaustion and exhilaration. By the time it is over, the blur of events will lead to exhaustion. If it is successful and your company's securities are sold out, it also leaves you with a great sense of exhilaration.

The fourth lesson is that how well you do in the road show determines your stock's initial price. Since your red-herring (pre-offering) document only specifies a price range, your ability to achieve the upper end (or even exceed the range) is dependent on how well you do in the road show.

All in all, for the thrill, excitement, and sense of achievement, I can't wait for the next one.

CHAPTER 12 • UNDERWRITING AND DISTRIBUTION

CHAPTER 12

§ 12.01 OVERVIEW

[A] Outline of the Underwriting and Distribution Process

[1] Underwriting Group

Securities offered in a public offering are actually sold by the issuer and selling shareholders to a group of investment bankers called the underwriting group. The sale is pursuant to an underwriting or purchase agreement among the issuer, selling shareholders, and members of the underwriting group. This purchase agreement, or underwriting agreement, is signed immediately before the offering. The shares are sold to the underwriting group at a discount (i.e., the underwriters' commission) from the public offering resale price. Members of the underwriting group bear the risk of any failure to resell the securities.

[2] Selling Group

The underwriters may sell the shares allocated to them in the underwriting agreement directly or may utilize other broker-dealers as distributors. This means the underwriters' ability to profit from the offering and minimize their potential risks depends not only on themselves but also on the selected dealers not acting as underwriters. Together, these two groups make up the selling group, which is responsible for actually selling and distributing the offered securities.

When broker-dealers are used, the underwriter grants a portion of the underwriting discount to the broker-dealer as compensation for its distribution services. The underwriting group will enter into a selected dealer agreement (SDA) at the start of the offering, authorizing the broker-dealers to sell the securities. Under the SDA, the dealers will buy the securities from the underwriting group at a discount (but not the full underwriter's discount). In turn, these dealers may resell the securities to the public at the public offering price or to other broker-dealers at a stipulated discount from the public offering price.

[3] Managing Underwriter

The interests of the underwriters and the selling group are protected by the managing underwriter. This underwriter is the investment banking firm selected by the issuer and selling shareholders to conduct the offering on behalf of the sellers. It also assists in preparing the registration statement, forming the underwriting and selling groups, and marketing and distributing the securities. The managing underwriter is granted a great deal of discretion by its investment banking colleagues in the agreement among underwriters (AAU). This agreement is entered into by the members of the underwriting group immediately before the execution of the underwriting agreement.

The reputation and record of the managing underwriter are important considerations in the success of an offering. Therefore, issuers seek out investment banking firms with a proven record of successfully managing offerings in comparable industries. Successful investment banking firms can pique the interest of institutional investors. In many cases, two or more managers will be chosen for the offering, particularly if they can bring separate customer bases to the distribution network.

[B] Negotiation Process

[1] In General

Negotiations among the issuer, selling shareholders, and potential underwriters generally commence well in advance of the filing of the registration statement. In some cases, the parties may choose to draft and execute a detailed letter of intent. This letter will cover the proposed offering terms, underwriter's compensation, allocation of offering expenses, and the scope of corporate housekeeping actions required prior to the offering. The formal underwriting agreement will not be executed until immediately before the offering.

[2] Letter of Intent

Although execution of the underwriting agreement may be deferred, in some cases the preliminary understandings among the issuer, its controlling shareholders, and prospective underwriters will be memorialized in a letter of intent. If there is a letter of intent, it will be signed before beginning the difficult process of preparing the registration statement and conducting due diligence. The scope and content of the letter of intent vary substantially. At a minimum, it will cover the basic financial terms of the offering, including underwriters' compensation, duties and responsibilities of participants in preparing the registration statement, and representations and covenants by the issuer concerning its business and related activities.

[3] Underwriting Agreement

The formal agreement regarding the offering is the underwriting agreement. An initial draft of the underwriting agreement will be prepared by counsel for the managing underwriter. A draft must be included as an exhibit to the registration statement. However, the agreement will not be signed until immediately before the offering. The SEC and other regulatory bodies must first complete their review of the registration statement. In addition, the underwriters will want to test the market before signing the agreement.

The underwriting agreement is essentially a stock purchase agreement. It sets forth the basic relationship among the issuer, selling shareholders, and underwriting group. The content of the agreement is fairly standard, including the terms and conditions of sale, representations and warranties, closing conditions, and indemnification. In some cases, the language in the agreement depends on the style and custom of the particular managing underwriter.

The managing underwriter and the issuer generally agree on the price and other terms of the offering immediately after the market closes on the day before the offering is to be made. The next morning, the managing underwriter (on behalf of the entire underwriting group), the issuer, and any selling shareholders execute the underwriting agreement. The agreement becomes effective at a specified time (e.g., noon) on the first full business day after the registration statement becomes effective.

[C] Investment Bankers in the Private Placement Process

Although the balance of this chapter is devoted to the underwriting terms in a public offering, it is common for an investment banker to be involved in the private placement of securities. Typically, the banker will act as a finder or intermediary in locating suitable investors and in negotiating the terms of the transaction. An investment banking firm involved in a private placement is entitled to compensation, which is usually set as a percentage of the proceeds of the offering. The underwriter may also receive one or more other forms of compensation (discussed later in this chapter). Investment banking firms will not actually underwrite a private placement, nor will they give any guarantees that the offering will be completed. Generally, the NASD has little interest in investment banking compensation paid in private financings. Many states, however, restrict the payment of commissions and limit the total amount of selling expenses.

An example of the time required for a public offering is shown on the following page.

§ 12.02 BASIC FINANCIAL TERMS OF AN OFFERING

[A] In General

The basic terms of the offering include the type of securities offered (e.g., common stock, debt securities, or a combination of equity securities and warrants); the size and price of the offering; the type of underwriters' engagement (e.g., firm commitment or best efforts); and the overall expenses that are associated with the offering, excluding underwriters' compensation.

Typical Public Offering Time Schedule

Day	*Activity*
1	All Hands Meeting to Organize Offering
25	Review Officers and Directors Questionnaires
40	Distribute First Draft of Registration Statement
45	All Hands Meeting to Revise Registration Statement
50	Distribute Revised Draft of Registration Statement
55	All Hands Meeting to Revise Registration Statement for SEC Filing
60	File Registration Statement with SEC
61	Mail Red Herrings to Proposed Underwriters
65	Road Show Begins
100	Receive SEC Comment Letter
114	All-Hands Meeting to Revise Registration Statement to Reflect SEC Comments
115	Effective Date
120	Closing

[B] Types of Securities Offered

The choice of security depends on a number of factors concerning both the issuer and the market conditions at the time of the offering. The offered securities will usually be common stock. The offering, however, may consist of preferred stock, a unit consisting of common stock and warrants to purchase common stock, or a unit consisting of common stock and convertible debentures. If more than one type of security is offered, the issuer should consider a separate trading market for each security (such as OTC for one and Pacific Stock Exchange for another) and whether registration rights will be granted to all types.

[C] Size and Price of an Offering

The size and price of the offering are functions not only of the proceeds that the issuer wishes to realize but also of the marketplace's assessment of the issuer's value. Accordingly, the issuer and the managing underwriter first determine the amount to be raised in the offering. That amount should bear a direct relationship to the use of the proceeds stated in the prospectus. The issuer's management and existing shareholders should also decide what degree of dilution they are willing to accept. Finally, the offering should be large enough to ensure that enough shares are available to support after-market activity in the securities.

For example, if the issuer has 5,000,000 shares of common stock outstanding before the offering and is looking to raise $20,000,000, the number of shares to be issued depends on the perceived "value" of the issuer before and after the offering. If the managing underwriter believes the issuer's value, based on values of comparable issuers, is $50,000,000 (or $10 per share) before the offering, then presumably the infusion of an additional $20,000,000 will make the immediate postoffering valuation $70,000,000. (Some upward allowance may be necessary to take into account the present value of any future expansion opportunities made possible by the financing. A downward adjustment might be made if a significant number of additional shares might be sold into the market under Rule 144, thereby depressing demand for the securities.) In this situation, the offering will consist of 2,000,000 shares of common stock offered at a price per share of $10 (for a total of $20 million).

Blue-sky administrators reviewing public offerings of securities other than "federal covered securities" are concerned with any great discrepancy between the public offering price and the price previously paid by existing shareholders. They want to ensure that the respective amounts of capital supplied by old shareholders and new investors bear a reasonable relationship to their respective risks. Many states have adopted guidelines on the maximum permissible offering price for securities. The guidelines are based on a maximum price/earnings ratio. They also place limitations on dilution of new public shareholders in public offerings of "federal covered securities" (e.g., securities listed or authorized for listing on the New York Stock Exchange, the American Stock Exchange, or the NASDAQ National Market System are not subject to review by blue-sky administrators.

[D] Type of Underwriters' Engagement

The underwriters' engagement may be on either a firm commitment or a best-efforts basis. In a firm commitment, the underwriters are contractually bound to purchase the offered securities. In contrast, a best-efforts underwriting involves the same marketing efforts, but the underwriters have no commitment to ultimately purchase the securities themselves if purchasers cannot be found. Conceptually, the differences between a firm commitment and a best-efforts underwriting are significant:

- In a firm commitment underwriting, members of the underwriting group purchase securities from an issuer as principals. Once the underwriting agreement is signed, members of the group are at risk for the purchase price if they are unable to redistribute the securities. In a best-efforts underwriting, the underwriter acts as an agent for the issuer and is never at risk, other than for offering expenses.
- In a firm commitment underwriting, the managing underwriter typically forms an underwriting group to share the underwriting risk. Since there is no risk (other than offering expenses) in a best-efforts underwriting, there will usually not be an underwriting group. The underwriter, however, may use other brokers and dealers to assist in the distribution.
- In a firm commitment underwriting, members of the underwriting group must be concerned about the SEC's net capital rules applicable to underwriters. Their underwriting commitment will be considered a liability and deducted from the underwriter's market value, which cannot fall below a level set by the SEC. There is no comparable capital adjustment in a best-efforts underwriting.

In practice, however, the differences between the two types of offerings are less significant. In a firm commitment, the underwriting agreement is not signed until there is reasonable certainty that the issue has been presold and the managing underwriter will not be stuck with it. This means that in a bad market, if an issue is not presold, the underwriting agreement will not be executed, the offering will be aborted, and each of the parties will bear its own expenses (unless, of course, some other arrangement is provided for in the letter of intent). Thus, under those circumstances, the issuer may be worse off than if an underwriter had been acting on a best-efforts basis.

Two variations of a best-efforts underwriting are an all-or-none underwriting and a minimum-maximum underwriting. In an all-or-none underwriting, the closing is conditioned on the sale of all the securities being offered. If they are not sold during a specified period of time, the offering will terminate and none of the tendered subscriptions will be accepted. In a minimum-maximum underwriting, a specified minimum number of securities must be subscribed for (committed to be purchased) before any securities are sold. If the amount is not reached, the offering terminates and none of the tendered subscriptions will be accepted. Once subscriptions for the minimum amount of securities are received, an initial closing will be held, the subscription amounts will be released to the issuer, and the underwriters will sell up to the maximum number.

[E] Expenses of an Offering

Both the letter of intent and the underwriting agreement will be very specific about the allocation of offering expenses among the issuer, any selling shareholders, and the underwriters. Typically, the issuer will bear all costs and expenses for the issuance, offer, and delivery of the securities, including the following:

- Expenses and fees for the filing of the registration statement and any filing with the NASD;
- Costs and counsel fees for qualifying under blue-sky laws;
- Fees and disbursements of the issuer's counsel and accountants;
- Travel and other expenses incurred by the issuer's officers and personnel in making presentations to institutional investors and to prospective members of underwriting and selling group during the road show; and
- Costs for preparing and printing the registration statement, the underwriting documents, prospectuses, and preliminary prospectuses.

The managing underwriter will pay all fees and expenses of its own counsel (other than counsel fees relating to blue-sky filings). It will also pay advertising, mailing, telephone, travel, clerical, and other office costs incurred by it or its sales personnel. However, in some instances, the issuer will reimburse the managing underwriter for such costs.

§ 12.03 UNDERWRITERS' COMPENSATION

[A] Overview

The most hotly negotiated—and most heavily regulated—aspect of the agreements among the issuer, selling shareholders, and the managing underwriter concerns the compensation to be paid to the underwriting group. The following are among the key elements of the underwriters' compensation:

- Underwriters' discount or commission;
- Underwriters' expense allowance;
- Securities to be issued to the underwriters in the offering;
- Registration rights;
- Advisory and consulting arrangements;
- Right of first refusal for future offerings by the issuer; and
- Noncompensatory rights, such as the right to designate a representative to the issuer's board of directors.

[B] NASD Regulation of Underwriters' Compensation

[1] In General

The NASD, using guidelines in its Corporate Financing Interpretation, will "make a determination as to the fairness and reasonableness of the underwriting and other arrangements in connection with or related to the distribution and the terms and conditions related thereto."

[2] Elements of Underwriters' Compensation

The Corporate Financing Interpretation divides the review of underwriter compensation into arrangement and compensation factors. Arrangements include restrictions on securities received by the underwriters or their affiliates for services during the offering, issuer-directed securities programs, over-allotment options, and sales incentives. Compensation, on the other hand, includes the following items:

- Gross amount of underwriters' commission or discount;
- Total expenses, whether accountable or nonaccountable, payable by the issuer to, or on behalf of, the managing underwriter for expenses that the managing underwriter normally fronts;
- Underwriters' counsel's fees and expenses;
- Finder's fees and financial consulting and advisory fees; and
- Other items of value accruing to underwriters and related persons, such as stock, options, warrants, and other securities, received in connection with the offering.

Expenses normally borne by the issuer, such as printing costs, registration fees, blue-sky fees, and accountant's fees, are excluded from compensation even if paid through the underwriter.

[3] Fairness and Reasonableness of Compensation

Once underwriters' compensation (generally expressed as a percentage of gross proceeds) has been determined, it is analyzed in light of several factors to determine fairness and reasonableness. The following are among the factors to be considered under the Corporate Financing Interpretation:

- Size of offering;
- Type of commitment by underwriter (i.e., firm, best-efforts minimum-maximum, or best-efforts all-or-none);
- Type of securities offered;
- Restrictions on, and amount of, stock, warrants, options, or convertible securities received by the underwriter in connection with the offering;
- Nature and amount of overall compensation;
- Underwriter's relationship to the issuer and its affiliates; and
- Whether arm's-length bargaining exists or there is a conflict of interest.

The determination of permissible underwriter's compensation is a function of a number of unpublished administrative practices by the NASD. As a general matter, many practitioners believe that the NASD will impose an overall limit of 15% of the offering's gross proceeds for a best-efforts offering and 18% for a firm commitment offering. The entire amount may be a commission if no other elements of compensation are used. If other elements are present, commissions generally will be limited to 10% of gross proceeds, with the balance being allocated among the other items of compensation. These amounts represent a somewhat conservative consensus. Some commentators believe that the maximum limit may approach 20% of gross proceeds.

[C] Blue-Sky Regulation of Underwriters' Compensation

The NASAA adopted a Statement of Policy Regarding Selling Expenses and Selling Security Holders (NASAA Expense Policy) that is used by blue-sky administrators. According to the policy, an offer may be disallowed if selling expenses (including underwriter's compensation) exceed specified percentages of gross proceeds.

The NASAA Expense Policy covers all expenses of an issuer in connection with an offering, specifically

- Commissions;
- Nonaccountable fees or expenses;
- Warrants, valued at 20% of the public offering price;
- Future registration rights, at the issuer's expense, of the underwriter's options, warrants, or shares, valued at 1% of the public offering price;
- Right of first refusal, valued at 1% of the public offering price;
- Solicitation fees, valued at the lower of actual cost or 1% of the public offering price if payable within one year of the offering; and
- Consulting, financial advisory agreements, or other types of agreements or fees valued at actual cost.

Most states have adopted policies on the maximum permissible level of expenses for an offering. The rules, however, are hardly uniform from state to state. For example, some states regulate the maximum amount of underwriters' compensation, as well as the overall level of expenses of the offering. Other states leave the regulation of underwriters' compensation to the NASD, which provides that selling expenses (exclusive of underwriters' commissions) must be limited to a specified percentage of gross proceeds. Finally, a few states set a very specific percentage limit, such as 15%, that will vary only in relation to the type of underwriting and the type of securities being offered.

[D] Underwriters' Discount or Commission

The principal cash element of underwriters' compensation is the discount or commission (spread) between the price at which the issuer sells the securities to the underwriter and the public offering price. The amount of the underwriting discount depends on a number of factors. The most important are the degree of risk associated with the proposed offering and the competition among underwriters to serve as managers. For instance, the discount will be higher for an IPO than for subsequent offerings.

[E] Underwriters' Expense Allowance

The second major element of underwriters' compensation is the expense allowance. This is usually expressed as a percentage of gross proceeds of the offering. In certain instances, the expense allowance can run as high as 3% to $3^1/_2$% of gross proceeds of the offering. Under the Corporate Financing Interpretation, it is permissible for the expense allowance to be made on either an accountable or a nonaccountable basis. The accountable expense allowance, however, cannot include underwriters' overhead, salaries, or other ongoing expenses.

A managing underwriter may request an advance against its expense allowance to defray out-of-pocket costs before the distribution. These include legal fees, traveling expenses, postage costs, due diligence expenses, and road show meetings. Advances may be paid in installments. A common approach is as follows:

- A portion is paid on execution of the letter of intent;
- The next portion is paid on filing of the registration statement with the SEC (or, if paid earlier than that, within a specified period following execution of the letter); and
- The final installment is paid on or before the effective date of the registration statement (or, if paid earlier than that, a specified number of days after execution of the letter).

[F] Securities Received in Connection with an Offering

[1] In General

In addition to cash compensation, underwriter compensation can include equity interests in the issuer, including warrants, options, convertible securities, and cheap stock. Since underwriters can realize significant appreciation on such securities, their acquisition as compensation will be closely examined by the SEC.

[2] Recipients

The Corporate Financing Interpretation covers warrants, options, convertible securities, and cheap stock acquired by the underwriter and broker-dealers, as well as persons related to, or associated with, them. For purposes of the Corporate Financing Interpretation, the terms *underwriter* and *related persons* are broadly defined and include

> . . . underwriters, underwriter's counsel, financial consultants and advisers, finders, members of the selling and distribution group, and any and all other persons associated with or related to any of the aforementioned persons.

These individuals are frequently referred to as the compensated group.

[3] Timing of Securities Issuances

The Corporate Financing Interpretation focuses on transactions during the 12-month period before the filing of the registration statement. Typically, purchases made by members of the compensated group within six months of the filing will be part of the offering package and will be considered to have been acquired in the offering. Purchases during the 6- to 12-month period will be analyzed in light of a number of factors. These include price, timing, number of shares purchased in relation to size of the offering, presence or absence of arm's-length bargaining, and business and investment risks associated with earlier purchases. In a few cases, the NASD may scrutinize purchases made more than a year prior to the filing, particularly if there is any possibility of a lack of arm's-length bargaining or a conflict of interest.

[4] Limitations on Amounts of Securities

Not only are securities included in the computation of overall compensation to underwriters, they are also subject to their own ceilings and limitations. For instance, warrants, options, convertible securities, and cheap stock acquired by members of the compensated group cannot, in the aggregate, exceed 10% of the total number of shares being offered in a best-efforts underwriting.

[5] Transfer Restrictions

For one year from the effective date of the registration, members of the compensated group must hold warrants, options, convertible securities, and cheap stock they acquired in the offering. However, the NASD may require a longer restrictive period if the spread is deemed high, the number of shares obtained is substantial, or the holder has a degree of involvement in the issuer's business deemed undesirable by the NASD. During the one-year period, a managing underwriter may assign the shares to its officers and partners or to an underwriting or selling group firm. The assignees, however, would still be bound by the transfer restrictions.

[6] Valuation

Cheap stock compensation is the difference between the stock's cost and the proposed public offering price. Other relevant factors may be considered. In the case of securities with a bona fide independent market, however, the compensation will be the difference between the cost of the stock and the market price on the date of purchase. If there is a binding obligation to hold the stock for a substantial period of time, the value will usually be adjusted downward.

The value of option and warrant shares is based on their number and terms, their acquisition cost, the lowest exercise price, the date they become exercisable or transferable, and other relevant factors. A lesser value will be assigned if the exercise price is above the public offering price or if the restriction on exercise or transfer extends for a lengthy period. Assuming no public market exists for the options or warrants, they usually will be valued at 20% of the public offering price of the shares they represent.

[7] Registration Rights

Warrants, options, and other securities received by underwriters for the offering, including securities issuable on exercise of warrants or options, will typically be subject to transfer restrictions. The most significant restriction is that they must be registered for resale under the Securities Act. Accordingly, an underwriter will bargain for the right to have such securities registered for resale. These registration rights are treated as part of the overall compensation package.

As noted, registration rights of underwriter's warrants have developed over a period of years and tend to be quite complex. They tend to include both demand and piggyback registration rights. The duration of the registration rights will depend on the circumstances. For securities covered by Rule 144, an argument can be made that the rights should terminate when such shares are freely tradable under Rule 144 without volume restrictions. As for warrants and securities issuable on their exercise, the rights will usually run for seven years from the date the warrants were issued. This takes into account the maximum exercise period of the warrants (i.e., five years) and the subsequent Rule 144 two-year holding period for the underlying securities.

[G] Advisory and Consulting Arrangements

The managing underwriter may provide a full range of investment banking services to the issuer before the public offering. It may act as a financial advisor in private offerings, provide representatives to serve as directors or officers of the issuer, engage in consulting arrangements, and, in some cases, provide capital. Such services raise the issue of whether the managing underwriter is being paid compensation within 12 months of the public offering. If the underwriter is paid for such services, the compensation should be included in the calculation of the maximum permissible compensation.

The managing underwriter may require the issuer to enter into a consulting agreement for the postoffering period. In such an agreement, the issuer retains the managing underwriter or a member of its staff as a consultant for a period of years following the completion of the offering. The agreement fixes the compensation for such services. Such arrangements provide a continuing income stream for the managing underwriter. They also keep the underwriter closely associated with the issuer—to further assure the issuer's success as well as the underwriter's participation in future offerings. The NASD may deem compensation derived from such arrangements to be underwriting compensation, especially if the underwriter is not required to perform any specific services.

[H] Right of First Refusal

Another common component of the underwriters' arrangement is a right of first refusal to serve as the issuer's investment banker for future offerings. The duration of this provision varies widely, with some underwriters seeking such protection for as little as two years and others up to five. The provision may differ widely in scope. Some underwriters receive only the right to underwrite subsequent public offerings of the issuer's securities, while others also insist on receiving a similar right regarding subsequent private placements and even mergers. The grant of a right of first refusal is compensation to the managing underwriter. The amount depends on the duration and breadth of the right.

§ 12.04 UNDERWRITING AGREEMENT

[A] Overview

As noted above, the underwriting agreement is the definitive statement of the relationship among the issuer, selling shareholders, and underwriting group. The agreement begins with a statement of the offering's key economic terms:

- Security being offered,
- Type of offering (i.e., primary, secondary, or combination),
- Size and price of offering,
- Amount of underwriters' commission,
- Existence and amount of any over-allotment option, and
- Whether the underwriters' engagement is a firm commitment or a best-efforts.

The remaining contents of the underwriting agreement are similar to a stock purchase agreement and can be divided into the following:

- Representations and warranties of the issuer and the selling shareholders;
- Closing matters, such as procedures for delivery of share certificates, legal opinions, comfort letters, and officers' certificates;
- Agreements and covenants of each of the parties;
- Conditions to underwriters' obligation to purchase securities;
- Indemnification and contribution;
- Default; and
- Effectiveness and termination of the underwriting agreement.

[B] Basic Obligations of the Issuer

The issuer's basic obligations are to sell the offered securities, file and maintain the registration statement, and make available to members of the underwriting and selling groups a sufficient number of prospectuses for marketing. Specifically, the issuer will commit to the following in the underwriting agreement:

- To issue and sell shares to the underwriting group;

- To use its best efforts to cause a registration statement to be declared effective by the SEC, and to notify the underwriting group of such effectiveness;
- To notify the underwriting group of any SEC stop order, special qualification of the stock in any jurisdiction, or initiation of proceedings for any of the foregoing;
- To amend or supplement the prospectus to keep it current for as long as required by the Securities Act; and
- To deliver signed copies of the registration statement (with amendments), and to furnish the underwriting group with preliminary and final prospectuses in the requested quantities.

[C] Sellers' Representations and Warranties

[1] In General

Detailed representations and warranties in the underwriting agreement will be required from the issuer and selling shareholders. In some cases, they may be required from the owners of substantial blocks of stock, for instance, a founder owning a majority of the outstanding shares. The representations and warranties are a basis for allocating risks among the parties and, in the event of problems, for the underwriter's terminating their obligations. They remain effective regardless of any investigation by the underwriter, payment for the shares, or termination of the underwriting agreement. They also serve as a guide in the due diligence process and on matters to be covered by the legal opinions of counsel for the issuer and underwriter.

[2] Issuer's Representations and Warranties

Representations and warranties are an important part of any stock purchase transaction. Given the potential liabilities for underwriters, it is not surprising that the underwriting agreement will contain a broad range of representations and warranties regarding the issuer, offering, and registration disclosures. At a minimum, the underwriters will require that the underwriting agreement contain a representation that

- A registration statement covering the offered securities has been filed with the SEC according to the Securities Act;
- The SEC has not issued any stop orders or orders suspending the use of the preliminary prospectus, nor are there any proceedings in any jurisdiction that would suspend the use of the preliminary prospectus;

- The registration statement (and each amendment or supplement) complies with the requirements of the Securities Act and the rules and regulations under it;
- There are no untrue statements or omissions of material facts in the registration statement or the prospectus;
- The issuer and its subsidiaries, if any, are duly incorporated, validly existing, and in good standing in their respective jurisdictions of incorporation and are qualified to do business in each jurisdiction where they conduct business or own property;
- The issuer has the authority to enter into the underwriting agreement and sell the offered securities to the underwriting group; and all consents or approvals from the board of directors, shareholders, and third parties required for the execution of the underwriting agreement and the sale of the offered securities have been obtained;
- The issuer has the authorized capital stock set forth in the prospectus;
- The shares to be sold in the offering will be validly issued, fully paid, nonassessable, and free of any liens or encumbrances, and will conform to their description in the registration statement;
- Execution and performance of the underwriting agreement and the sale of the offered securities will not violate any contract, law, or rule to which the issuer is subject; and
- The issuer has not engaged in any conduct that could be deemed to constitute stabilization or manipulation of the securities' price.

In addition to such standard representations and warranties, the managing underwriter will usually request from the issuer a variety of additional representations that cover most, if not all, of the matters generally covered by securities investment agreements. Representations and warranties in first drafts of the underwriting agreement are unlimited. The issuer must correct any circumstance that would make the representations untrue and modify the language whenever possible to limit its own risks.

[3] Selling Shareholders' Representations and Warranties

Selling shareholders may be required to make many of the representations and warranties made by the issuer. The desire for such representations and warranties, as well as their scope, depends on several factors. The most important are the closeness of the selling shareholder and issuer and the relative size of the selling shareholder's participation in the offering. In some cases, selling shareholders may simply make a general representation that they reviewed the representations in the underwriting agreement and the registration statement. They will then confirm that neither document is false or misleading, or fails to disclose any material fact, information, or condition regarding the issuer or its business as far as is known to the selling shareholder.

Regardless of whether or not the selling shareholders back the issuer's general representations and warranties, certain representations and warranties are typically required of the selling shareholders regarding their own sale of securities. They will be asked to give assurances that the custody agreement (i.e., the agreement for transfer of shares to the underwriters, typically through a power of attorney) has been executed and delivered, that the share certificates have been placed in escrow as required by the custody agreement, that they have authority to enter into the custody agreement, that they have obtained all consents necessary for performance of their obligations, and that they have good and marketable title to their shares being sold.

[D] Covenants and Further Agreements of the Issuer

[1] In General

The underwriting agreement will include a number of covenants and agreements by the issuer. These concern offering and postclosing matters. The key issues are restrictions on shareholders selling the issuer's shares during and immediately following the primary distribution and the filing of reports on the issuer's activities.

[2] Future Shareholder Sales (Lock-Up Agreements)

The underwriting agreement, as well as any letter of intent used in the transaction, will almost always require officers, directors, and principal shareholders of an issuer to sign a "lock-up" agreement. Under such an agreement, during a specified period following the offering (e.g., 90 to 180 days), shareholders agree not to sell, assign, or transfer any of the issuer's shares without the prior written consent of the managing underwriter. The specifics, such as the period of the restriction and any exceptions, are matters for negotiation. Many shareholders, however, may already have agreed to such restrictions in the agreements they signed at the time of their original investment in the issuer.

[3] Postoffering Period Covenants

A number of covenants in the underwriting agreement continue to bind the issuer even after the registration statement becomes effective and the offered securities are sold to the underwriting group. Typically, they relate to the issuer's use of proceeds raised in the offering, delivery of specified financial reports to the issuer's shareholders and the managing underwriter, and after-market stabilization. To summarize, in these covenants the issuer agrees

- To provide a 12-month earnings statement to security holders in accordance with Section 11(a) of the Securities Act;
- To apply net proceeds from the offering as described in the prospectus;
- To deliver annual and quarterly reports to shareholders, whether or not required under the Exchange Act, within a specified period after the applicable accounting period;
- To provide members of the underwriting group with copies of all reports furnished to shareholders and with copies of all information, documents, and reports filed with the SEC for a specified period (generally five years after the offering); and
- To not take any action that could be deemed stabilization or manipulation of the price of the stock.

[E] Conditions to Underwriters' Obligations

[1] In General

The obligations and commitments of the underwriting members under the underwriting agreement are generally limited to the purchase of the offered securities from the issuer and the selling shareholders. The purchase will occur at a closing described in the underwriting agreement. The obligations of all parties will be subject to the fulfillment or waiver of various conditions included in the agreement.

[2] Closing Procedures

The underwriting agreement will specify the time, date, and place of the closing and the payment method. It will also cover postponing the closing in the event of a default by any member of the underwriting group or due to other contingencies. The underwriting agreement will provide for the closing to occur a specified number of business days (usually five) after the registration statement becomes effective and the offering commences. A preclosing will be held in the offices of counsel for the managing underwriter the day before the closing. At that time, all documents will be signed and held in escrow pending the actual closing at the opening of business on the following day.

Payment is generally made by certified check, payable in clearinghouse funds. Share certificates are typically made available to the underwriters for review a specified number of days (generally two) before the closing to ensure that the certificates are registered in such names and denominations as may have been requested by the underwriters.

The underwriting group's obligation to purchase the securities will depend on, among other things, the following:

- The registration statement having become effective,
- No stop orders having been issued prior to the closing,
- No proceedings for issuing a stop order having been started or threatened by the SEC, and
- Underwriters not having discovered any untrue statements or omissions of material facts in the registration statement.

In addition, the underwriters will use the closing conditions as a way to satisfy their due diligence investigation. They will require the issuer, issuer's counsel, and issuer's independent public accountant to review and confirm the accuracy of certain information contained in the prospectus. They may also require that they be shown such opinions, certificates, comfort letters, and other documents as they reasonably request, all in a form reasonably satisfactory to them and their counsel.

[3] Legal Opinion of the Issuer's Counsel

One of the most important conditions to the underwriters' obligation to close the transaction under the underwriting agreement is receipt of an opinion from the issuer's counsel. This opinion will cover matters usually covered in an investment transaction opinion. In addition, it will address other issues particular to the sale of securities in a registered offering, including the following:

- The description of the offered securities in the prospectus is true and accurate and complies in all material respects with the requirements of the Securities Act and rules and regulations thereunder;
- The registration statement has become effective under the Securities Act and no stop orders are pending or threatened;
- The registration statement and prospectus comply in all material respects with the requirements of the Securities Act and rules and regulations thereunder;

- Counsel has no knowledge of any contract, document, lease, or legal proceeding required to be described in the registration statement or prospectus, or to be filed as an exhibit, that has not been described or filed; and
- Counsel has no reason to believe the registration statement or prospectus contains any untrue statement or omits any material facts. (This is called the Rule 10b-5 opinion.)

[4] Legal Opinion of the Selling Shareholders' Counsel

If the offering includes a secondary offering by existing shareholders, counsel for selling shareholders (who may be the same as counsel for the issuer) will usually be asked to render the following opinions:

- The custody agreement (i.e., the agreement for transfer of shares to the underwriters) and the underwriting agreement have been duly authorized, executed, and delivered by or on behalf of each selling shareholder;
- Each selling shareholder has authority to enter into the custody and underwriting agreements and to sell its shares under the underwriting agreement;
- Execution, delivery, and performance by selling shareholders of the custody and underwriting agreements will not violate any contract, law, or rule by which they are bound; and
- Members of the underwriting group will acquire good, valid, and marketable title to the shares free and clear of liens.

These matters—particularly the opinion on title to shares acquired by members of the underwriting group and standards of materiality or knowledge—are often subject to negotiation. Some of the opinions may be difficult to render if counsel is not familiar with the personal business affairs of the selling shareholders. In those cases, counsel will require, and will rely exclusively upon, certificates from each selling shareholder.

[5] "Cold Comfort" Letters

The underwriting agreement will require the issuer's independent accountants to deliver two "cold comfort" letters to the underwriting members. The first is delivered on execution of the underwriting agreement. The second, which is a bring-down letter stating there have been no changes to information in the first letter, is delivered at the closing. Some underwriters also request a letter at the time the registration statement is originally filed.

The underwriting agreement will specify the cutoff date relating to statements in each letter (e.g., five business days before the date of the letter).

Comfort letters are not required under the Securities Act and are not filed with the SEC. Instead, they are contract terms in the underwriting agreement. The comfort letter requires the accountants to thoroughly review substantially all financial information included or incorporated in the registration statement. A comfort letter will generally cover the following subjects:

- Independence of the accountants;
- Compliance of the audited financial statements included in the registration statement (or incorporated by reference) with accounting requirements of the Securities Act;
- Changes in financial statement items subsequent to the date and period of the latest financial statements included in the registration statement;
- Unaudited financial statements, condensed financial statements (capsule information), or pro forma financial information included in the registration statement; and
- Tables, statistics, and other financial information included in the registration statement.

[6] Officers' Certificates and Related Documents

In addition to opinion and comfort letters from professionals involved in the preparation of the registration statement, the managing underwriter will require certificates from the issuer's senior officers. It will also require certificates from regulatory bodies, as well as other documents concerning the offering. The items to be delivered are described in the underwriting agreement and tend to be similar to those required in any investment transaction. For example, each of the issuer's chief executive and financial officers will deliver a certificate that

- No stop order suspending the effectiveness of the registration statement has been issued, and no proceedings for that purpose have been taken or, to the issuer's knowledge, are contemplated by the SEC;
- There has been no change in the capital stock as described in the prospectus, nor any increase in long-term debt from that in the prospectus;
- There has been no material adverse change, financial or otherwise, in the condition or results of the issuer's (and its subsidiaries') operations, taken as a whole, from that in the prospectus;

- The issuer and its subsidiaries have no material liabilities or obligations, direct or contingent—other than those reflected in the prospectus—that are not in the ordinary course of business;
- Representations and warranties of the issuer in the underwriting agreement are true and correct; and
- The issuer has performed or complied with all applicable agreements contained in the underwriting agreement.

[7] Other Closing Documents

In addition to each of the above opinions, certificates, and documents, the underwriting agreement contemplates the delivery of other items at the closing, including the following:

- Copies of correspondence between the SEC and the issuer (or its counsel) regarding the registration statement and offering.
- The letter from the issuer instructing the transfer agent to issue shares in the names and denominations requested by the underwriting members.
- Certificates representing the issuer's common stock registered in the names and denominations specified by the underwriters. These names are usually "street names," which means that the broker holds the certificate in its name (and not its customer's) for ease of transfer. The securities themselves are inspected, packaged, and delivered to the underwriters. Delivery should be verified before transfer of funds from the underwriters to the issuer and selling shareholders.
- The transfer agent's certificate confirming its due appointment and authorization to act as transfer agent and registrar for the securities being issued; the due issuance and registration of the securities; and the authority of the employees, transfer agent, and registrar to countersign the certificates.
- The order of effectiveness of the registration statement from the SEC.
- A check from the managing underwriter payable to the issuer for the proceeds from the sale of the stock. Payment—usually a certified or official bank check payable in New York clearinghouse funds—is delivered to the issuer and selling shareholders in a lump sum by the managing underwriter. Among the underwriters, the AAU gives the managing underwriter the right to specify the form, time, and place of payment from the members of the selling group to the managing underwriter.

- A declaration by counsel for the issuer, dated on the closing date, concerning telephone confirmation from the SEC that no stop order was issued against the offering.
- Cross-receipts by the managing underwriter acknowledging receipt of the issuer's stock certificates and by the issuer acknowledging receipt of the check from the managing underwriter.

[F] Indemnification

The underwriting agreement will provide for cross-indemnification between the issuer (and selling shareholders) and members of the underwriting group. The cross-indemnification will be for

- Any losses, claims, damages, and liabilities;
- Suffered or incurred by the indemnified party;
- Arising out of, or based on, alleged or actual misstatements or omissions attributable to the indemnifying party; and
- Contained in any preliminary prospectus, registration statement, prospectus, or any amendment or supplement to them.

Indemnity agreements typically extend to persons controlling the issuer, to officers and directors of the issuer who signed the registration statement, and to any underwriter within the meaning of the Securities Act.

The indemnification provisions do not vary significantly from transaction to transaction. They cover a variety of procedural matters, such as selection of counsel, payment of legal fees and expenses, ability of the indemnifying party to participate in the defense of an action, and how claims can be settled. The SEC's position that indemnification provisions are unenforceable as against public policy has driven participants toward contribution agreements, which are permitted under Section 11 of the Securities Act.

[G] Termination of Underwriting Agreement

Prior to becoming effective, the underwriting agreement may be terminated by any party on written notice. After the agreement becomes effective, underwriters can refuse to close if the issuer or selling shareholders have not met any conditions to the underwriters' obligation to purchase the securities. Underwriters will also be able to terminate the agreement on the occurrence of other events, including the fabled "market-out." This clause permits underwriters to terminate the offering on the occurrence of certain events in the securities market. Over the years, these provisions have been substantially narrowed. Currently, market-out agreements are limited to extraordinary events, such as war, natural disasters affecting the trading markets, and cessation of trading in the markets for reasons unrelated to the issuer.

CHAPTER 13 • INTERNET SALES

[A] U.S. Government and Regulations

[1] U.S. Government Web Sites

[2] U.S. Statutes, Codes, Rules, and Regulations Online

[3] Courts and Decisions

[B] U.S. Securities Organizations

[1] U.S. Exchanges and Securities Organizations

[2] Initial Public Offerings, Direct Public Offerings, and Bulletin Boards

[3] Road Show Sites

[4] Electronic Communications Networks (ECNs)

[5] Day-Trading Sites

[C] International Securities Organizations

[1] International Market Regulators

[2] International Exchanges

[D] Information Services

[1] Business and Investor News Sites

[2] Corporations and Securities Law Information Sites

CHAPTER 13

§ 13.01 OVERVIEW

Start-up companies selling securities on the Internet has become a hot topic over the past few years. There are many stories of successful fundraising efforts. For now, the reality is that the successful cases are but a small portion of the overall efforts. In large part, this is because the e-securities market is still evolving and not firmly established. The rules are in place, the Internet structure is ready, and many start-ups are looking for funds on the Internet. The investors, however, are slowly coming to the Internet stock market.

This is changing with more investors investing in companies through the Internet. This evolution will continue as more large companies offer securities on the Internet. For example, Salomon Brothers created an Internet site for an initial offering of new Class B stock by Berkshire Hathaway. Although purchasers still had to purchase through an underwriter, the mere display of the offering on a Web site was progress. The public offering of Yahoo! common stock went another step. The offering materials could be read on the site and downloaded. Similarly, Mobil Oil Corporation's Web site included a prospectus for its Stock Purchase and Dividend Reinvestment Plan and an enrollment form that prospective investors could print and mail directly to Mobil's stock transfer agent. Again, purchases had to be through the underwriter or another broker-dealer.

The first company to sell securities on the Internet was Spring Street Brewing Co., a microbrewer of Belgian beer. In March 1996, it raised $1.6 million from more than 3,500 investors. Others soon followed. Real Goods Trading Corp., an alternative energy products company, raised $1.8 million in 1997. Zap Power Systems, a producer of solar-powered bicycles, raised more than $2 million in the same year.

A related development is the growth of Internet stock exchanges, called electronic communications networks (ECNs). ECNs allow investors to buy and sell directly between one another without paying fees to broker-dealers. It also enables investors to look for the best price rather than buying through a market maker who may be trying to support the price. ECNs are particularly popular with day traders, private individuals who trade for their own account over the Internet. A few of them offer longer trading hours than Nasdaq and the physical stock exchanges. Some of the most widely used ECNs are Reuters' Instinet with

70% market share, Island, and Archipelago. A listing of Web sites for ECNs appears in at the end of this chapter.

With all these rapid developments, it is important to understand the rules and how money can be raised on the Internet.

§ 13.02 ADVANTAGE OF INTERNET SECURITIES

The Internet is in some ways a wonderful way to sell securities. It also has several disadvantages.

[A] Advantages

The Internet is particularly beneficial for small offerings of stock:

- *Cost*—The expense is considerably less than traditional offerings. This is appealing for a small company with little or no money to cover the cost of an offering. Since there are no printing and distribution costs, total expenses can start as low as $10,000.
- *Avoids Intermediaries*—Small offerings are usually of little interest to underwriters (the people who market the stock), so a company is not really losing much by directing the sale itself.
- *Earlier to Market*—Stock markets prefer issuers that have late-stage products and several years of sales and profits. The trouble is that a start-up needs money now, not in three years. E-commerce offerings avoid this wait.
- *Speed*—Once the papers are filed and any waiting period has passed (as discussed later), a button can be hit to distribute the offering materials electronically.
- *Exposure*—Thousands, if not millions, of potential purchasers can be reached rather than the comparatively small number who usually receive mailings.

[B] Disadvantages

All is not digitally correct in the Internet world. There are several disadvantages to selling securities on the Internet:

- *Lack of Due Diligence*—Without an established underwriter, there is no outside party to vouch for a company's stock. Potential investors may be wary of situations where no third party has conducted due diligence and confirmed the statements in an issuer's offering materials. A company is left to tout itself. For this reason, many issuers have limited their marketing to customers or people with similar interests.

- *Fraud Potential*—Not having an underwriter or third party to confirm offering materials means that the Internet sale of securities poses many fraud risks.
- *Limited Liquidity*—Since the market is very narrow, investors may find it difficult to resell their stock. Many may not buy for this reason.
- *Perception*—At least for now, many people do not have favorable opinions of companies that raise money on the Internet. This will change over time, but that is the present reality.

§ 13.03 REGULATORY FRAMEWORK

Federal and state securities laws apply to all securities sales, including those offered over the Internet. This also includes audiotapes, videotapes, facsimiles, CD-ROM, e-mail, electronic bulletin boards, Internet Web sites, local area networks (LAN), and online services.

[A] Adapting Securities Laws to Internet Securities Sales

Securities agencies, however, have been trying to adapt their standard rules to Internet securities sales. Some of the initiatives over the last few years include

- Interpretive guidance from the U.S. Securities Exchange Commission (SEC) to corporate issuers, mutual funds, and other market participants regarding use of the Internet and other electronic media to provide information (e.g., prospectuses, shareholder reports, and proxy statements) to investors;
- Interpretive guidance from the SEC to intermediaries (e.g., broker-dealers and investment advisers) regarding use of the Internet and other electronic media to provide investment services and related information to investors;
- Interpretive guidance from the SEC to issuers and broker-dealers regarding creation and operation of online trading systems;

- Establishment of the Electronic Data Gathering, Analysis, and Retrieval (EDGAR) system to facilitate electronic filing of documents under the federal securities laws and Internet access to such filings; and
- Development of enforcement procedures focused on detection and prosecution of fraudulent securities offering activities on the Internet.

[B] Types of Internet Offerings

Start-up companies can rely on many of the securities exemptions discussed in Chapter 8 when offering securities over the Internet. The most frequently applicable exemptions are as follows:

- Regulation A (Reg. A) allows offerings of up to $5 million over a 12-month period. No minimum stock price is required.
- Rule 504 of Regulation D permits companies not already registered with the SEC to sell up to $1 million of nonrestricted securities over 12 months.
- Small Corporate Offering Registration (SCOR), also known as Uniform Limited Offering Registration (ULOR) in some states, allows a small company to raise up to $1 million. Minimum stock price is $5.

These exemptions are available at the federal level; however, they may not all be available on a state-by-state basis.

If a company and its offering fit into one of these categories, it can make a Direct Public Offering (DPO) or Internet Initial Public Offering (IIPO) without registering the securities.

[C] Direct Public Offering and Internet Initial Public Offering

DPOs and IIPOs are of particular value to small companies. Companies must be careful, however, to meet applicable regulatory requirements.

[1] Reports

If a company offers securities through DPOs or IIPOs under an exemption from registration, it must still file a report with a federal or state agency. The form the company uses depends on the exemption that covers it.

Form 1-A for Reg. A Offerings A company must include most of the documents that would be filed with a regular securities registration. This includes a detailed business plan and financial statements. Financial statements do not have to be audited unless the company is already audited.

Form U-7 for SCOR Offerings SCOR filings consist of a 30-page questionnaire. The requested information is considerably less than that required for an initial public offering. Audited financial statements are required.

[2] Disclaimers and Legends

The North American Securities Administrators Association (NASAA) recently developed a resolution exempting Internet offers from state registration in states where sales are not made. To apply, offering materials, tombstones, and prospectuses must contain a legend specified by the NASAA that states, "no offers or sales are being made to residents of a state unless it is one of the states listed in which it is effective."

[3] Qualifications for Issuers

There are several limitations on who can issue exempt securities. Reg. A issuers, for instance, cannot be public, oil and gas, or investment companies. Please refer to Chapter 8 for more information on these qualifications.

[4] Qualifications for Purchasers

There are no limitations on who can purchase under Reg. A.

Since SCOR filings are made at the state level, purchasers must be residents of the state where the offering was filed. To protect itself, a company should implement many of the protections discussed below under foreign offerings.

[5] Application of Other Rules

Reg. A is a federal exemption. State filings may still be required for companies trying to issue securities under this rule.

SCOR has been adopted by nearly all states. Some states require that a minimum amount be raised under an offering before any money can be distributed to the issuer. Before that threshold is reached, all money raised must be held in an escrow account. If the threshold is not reached, the money must be returned.

[6] Timing

Merely filing a report with the appropriate federal and state securities agencies is not enough. The regulatory authorities must have time to review the filings and make comments. This is called the waiting or quiet period as discussed in Chapter 11. Oral offers can be made, but no written sales literature or other materials can be used to solicit investors. This includes Internet postings.

The SEC feels that establishing a Web site just before or during this period may be "jumping the gun," if there is no other purpose for the site than to promote the stock. Similarly, linking the company's site to an analyst's report on the company during or before the waiting period is prohibited. It is better to create the site well in advance and to offer a wide range of information. Obviously, the offering materials cannot be posted on the Web site until the waiting period is over.

[D] Registering Internet Offerings

As noted, one of the problems with selling securities on the Internet without an underwriter is that resale is difficult. Most broker-dealers will not handle securities unless they are registered with the SEC under the Securities Exchange Act. Because such registration is not required until there are 500 shareholders and at least $10 million in assets, small companies are not covered.

One thing that can be done to help resales (and thus sales) is to voluntarily register. The above limits are mandatory—not minimum—thresholds. If a company registers, it will have to agree to make more reports, but this will make its securities more attractive to investors.

To register with Nasdaq, a company must have

- 500 shareholders,
- $10 million in assets,
- Two market makers,
- Minimum bid price, and
- Public float (shares owned by public) of certain minimum number and value.

These are mandatory and would exclude most small companies.

[E] Road Shows

Whether or not shares are sold on the Internet, it can still be used for road shows.

To build interest in the stock during the waiting period, the underwriter, if engaged, and the issuer will visit a number of broker-dealers scattered around the United States. These visits are designed to line up broker-dealers to support the stock. In these presentations, the company's business, the market, and the intended use of the money are explained, and any questions are answered.

Before March 1997, this could only be done in a grueling process of visiting each potential broker-dealer. Since that date, the SEC allows video roadshow presentations to registered broker-dealers who have received a copy of a preliminary prospectus in advance of the broadcast. The SEC extended the rule to Internet broadcasts as long as

- Attendees are registered broker-dealers,
- Passwords and encryption are used to limit access to authorized persons, and
- Attendees receive a preliminary prospectus in advance of the broadcast.

Examples of Web sites containing information for road shows are listed at the end of this chapter.

[F] Internet Distribution of Prospectus

After the necessary report is filed with federal and state securities agencies, and any applicable waiting period has passed, an offering document or prospectus can be distributed to potential investors. In October 1995, the SEC announced that electronic delivery of a prospectus constituted "good delivery." This allows a company to post its offering documents on the Internet by opening its Web site or hyperlinking a new page containing offering information to its existing site. Simply posting on the Internet, however, is not enough. Potential investors receiving information regarding the offering by some means other than the company's Web site must be given a notice advising them of the posting. The SEC also requires Internet recipients be given access to the same degree of information as recipients by mail.

The number of printed copies of the offering materials can be reduced by requiring potential investors visiting the company's Web site to accept only electronic delivery. If a company prefers the option of making printed copies available, however, there are a few printers that will print a prospectus only as requested. This saves a company from printing several thousand in advance without knowing its needs.

Unfortunately, printed copies of offering materials cannot be completely eliminated. Hard copies may be needed for

- Investors who change their mind after agreeing to electronic delivery and request a hard copy before the electronic delivery is sent;
- After-market purchasers (purchasers from initial investors); and
- Investors unable to receive e-copies because of computer lack, incompatibility, or failure.

[G] Stock Chat and Cybersmear

Chat rooms, message and bulletin boards, online newsletters, and Web sites are important avenues for start-up companies to get recognition. Many companies raising money get on a bulletin board where buyers and sellers post offers and contact numbers. Some even set up their own bulletin board for their securities. These are called Issuer Bulletin Boards. A few companies have developed chat rooms where investors can inquire about the company and try to sell their shares.

Use of these methods, however, raises two issues. To what extent can an issuer use them to promote its stock, and how can it address derogatory statements about it that appear on a board or in a room?

[1] Self-Promotion

The SEC is willing to accept Issuer Bulletin Boards as long as the information is kept up to date. It has even allowed boards that provide a forum for information about prospective buyers and sellers but do not actually process transactions or accept funds. The parties contact each other to conclude any transaction. Similarly, chat rooms will not draw the SEC's ire as long as they comply with the same requirements.

The SEC, however, is paying particular attention to issuers promoting their stock over the Internet by fraud or manipulation. Some of the activities that have attracted the SEC's enforcement action include commentators who have

- Lied about their company's prospects,
- Lied about their independence from the issuers, and
- Failed to adequately disclose compensation received from the issuer for making comments.

[2] Cybersmear

Many companies have discovered derogatory comments about themselves on the Internet. The result has often been quick drops in stock price. Examples have proliferated in the past few years:

- One company found a false obituary about one of its key employees had been posted on the Internet.
- Another company prepared scripts for nine of its employees to carry on a derogatory chat room "dialogue" about a competitor.
- Kentucky Fried Chicken (KFC) was the victim of a hoax that alleged its chickens were cyberchickens developed by a U.S. university. Both KFC and the university were deluged by questions.

Prompt attention to cybersmear is important to minimize stock impact. There are several courses of action that can be taken.

- *Defamation*—A company's reputation is protected under the common law tort of defamation. This includes corporate reputations. To bring an action under this tort, a company must show a false published statement was defamatory to it and was made by someone acting with actual malice (if a public official or figure is involved) or negligence (in other cases). There are a number of pending cases involving claims by companies whose stock dropped as a result of Internet messages.
- *Maintain an Updated Web Site*—KFC responded to the cybersmear about it by devoting a Web page to information about its chickens. Similarly, a company can provide shareholders and potential investors with access to correct information. It can also correct misinformation. Real-time access to human operators should be available from the Web site on a full time basis (24/7).
- *Correspondence and Press Releases*—A company should periodically issue press releases and send letters to shareholders to accustom them to receiving news from the company so that they will come to the company for news rather than going to others. When negative news is published about a company on the Internet, the company can then send out a correction and it will not be perceived as running scared or overreacting. If there is bad news, better that it comes from the company with its explanation rather than from someone else who may put the worst interpretation on it.
- *Monitor Chat Rooms and Bulletin Boards*—A company should watch for news about itself. If it sees incorrect information, the company

should respond quickly with accurate information and provide the name of someone who can be contacted for more information.

- *Ask the Internet Service Provider (ISP) to Remove*—A company should inform the ISP of the incorrect information and ask that it be removed.

A company can sue the person posting the defamation or derogatory statement. The ISP on whose site it appears is not liable under the Communications Decency Act. To uncover the identity of the defamer, a company will have to serve a subpoena on the ISP to get the users' e-mail address and then obtain a court order to derive the author's real name from its e-mail address.

[H] Internet Enforcement of Securities Laws

Illegal activities described in previous chapters do not change character simply by being conducted on the Internet. If they were illegal off the Net, they are illegal on the Net.

The SEC is devoting considerable resources to cracking down on Internet manipulations of stock. The SEC is focusing on surveillance, litigation, and education. It has created a Web Site (http://www.sec.gov), an electronic database of periodic reports by companies (EDGAR), SEC releases describing enforcement proceedings, and investor alerts. Many divisions of the SEC are actively involved in Internet securities issues. The Division of Corporation Finance analyzes Internet securities offerings to make certain they comply with SEC registration and disclosure requirements. The Division of Market Regulation monitors the impact of the Internet on services offered to investors by broker-dealers, such as online brokerage and daytrading firms, and is developing additional rules in this area. The Office of Compliance Inspections and Examinations uses the examination process to regulate online brokerages and daytrading firms. The Office of the General Counsel has developed rules covering online fraud and the application of federal privacy laws to online investigations. The Office of International Affairs works with the SEC's enforcement staff and with foreign authorities to obtain information on persons based in the United States. The Office of Investor Education and Assistance tries to increase investor awareness of and knowledge about Internet trading and fraud.

Two of the most important SEC offices involved in Internet securities are the Office of Internet Enforcement (OIE) and the CyberForce. The OIE was created in July 1998 within the Division of Enforcement. Initially, it acted as a coordinator of the SEC's Internet program and as a liaison with federal, state, and local agencies. Since the spring of 1999, its staff has grown from 3 to 20, including 16 lawyers. The OIE conducts surveillance and identifies new areas for monitoring; analyses complaints received in the online Enforcement Complaint Center (ECC), as described below; formulates investigative procedures; conducts law enforcement training for SEC staff and outside agencies; engages in technology-related projects; ensures staff compliance with federal privacy statutes; conducts Internet-related investigations; and acts as a resource on Internet matters for the SEC. It has a state-of-the-art lab and maintains its own internal SEC Intranet Web site on Internet securities issues.

The CyberForce has more than 200 lawyers, accountants, and investigators conducting regular Internet surveillance. It also undertakes special projects, such as "Surf Days," as described below. Formed in 1996, the CyberForce participates in coordinated surveillance projects with other federal agencies.

The Enforcement Complaint Center (ECC) offers an online mailbox, referred to internally as C.H.A.R.T. (Complaint, Handling, Assignment, Response, and Tracking), through which investors can inform the agency electronically of potential securities law violations. The ECC averages 300 to 400 investor complaints a day. Recently, the SEC spent $2 million to upgrade the C.H.A.R.T. system. C.H.A.R.T. modernized the SEC's electronic complaint process by enabling SEC lawyers to process, track, and assign complaints while assembling a comprehensive, searchable complaint database.

The SEC's two favorite Internet securities enforcement techniques are Surf Days and its Internet Search Engine. The OIE coordinates quarterly Surf Days, with the goal of locating potential frauds in key program areas, such as market manipulation, fictitious investment schemes, momentum trading, suspicious stock offerings, false statements, and unregistered entities. On a designated Surf Day, CyberForce members surf the Web in a focused manner, targeting, for example, message boards, Web sites, or violation types. They forward their results to OIE, where the material is reviewed for possible violations.

Science Applications International Corporation (SAIC) designed the SEC's Internet Search Engine. Using search words and phrases, the search engine identifies relevant signs and newsgroup postings in the Internet's public areas. The engine uses a battery of search terms and algorithms to target suspicious conduct. After searching the Internet, the engine filters out irrelevant materials, ranking the information by pertinence or likelihood of violation. OIE staff can access the search engine's database in pursuit of investigations.

The National Association of Securities Dealers (NASD) is also concerned about Internet securities activities. It has a Web page called Internet Guide for Registered Representatives (http://www/nasdr.com/4040.htm), which is designed to educate representatives about what they can and cannot do on the Internet. The site includes information on enforcement proceedings. The NASD is also launching Netwatch, an automatic compliance screening software. It will monitor chat rooms and bulletin boards looking for key words that may indicate violations of securities laws and report apparent violations to the appropriate authorities.

The North American Securities Administrators Association (NASAA) has also focused on this area. It has opened an e-mail address (cyberfraud@nasaa.org), where investors can file complaints about apparent Internet fraud.

The SEC has recommended that online broker-dealers offering investment chat rooms regulate the comments. A few have responded. E*Trade's chat room has moderators who monitor comments and postings. It also requests participants to include their names and addresses in advance and to sign a contract in which they agree not to manipulate stocks.

The SEC also requested ISPs to control securities discussions in their chat rooms and bulletin boards. The Motley Fool, an online service provider that operates investment bulletin boards, has adopted policies similar to E*Trade's. It has moderators who screen its message boards for securities law violators and question anyone appearing to push or hype a stock.

Most other online service providers have declined to do so. Yahoo! allows its users to chat about anything they want, including small company stocks. It does not regularly monitor comments. AOL limits itself to warning users to abide by securities laws and to be careful of stock advice and comments on the Internet.

[I] Application of U.S. Securities Laws to Foreign Securities Offerings

Traditionally, if the offering was purely offshore, U.S. rules did not apply. The difficulty is that Web sites do not stay offshore. They can be accessed by anyone. The SEC recently resolved this problem by distinguishing between passive and active offerings. If the Web site simply sits there and no communication is sent to U.S. investors about the site and any offering it contains, then U.S. securities laws do not apply. If, however, a letter or e-mail message is sent to U.S. investors advising them of the site, then U.S. rules apply.

To reduce the likelihood that U.S. securities laws will apply, offshore offerings through Web sites should

- Not send messages to recipients that might be in the United States;
- Contain a prominent disclaimer on the Web site that
  - — No offer or sale is intended to take place in the United States,
  - — No offer is directed to the United States,
  - — No sale will be made in the United States;
- Present a screen listing places where the offering is qualified (The user must confirm that it resides in a qualified jurisdiction by clicking on one of the listed places.);
- Require investors to provide address and telephone information to confirm that they are not in the United States;
- Not contain any statements indicating an offering is advantageous to U.S. persons, such as a representation that the investment can be used to reduce U.S. taxes; and
- Not be promoted through other sites aimed at U.S. persons.

If a company simultaneously has an offshore offering and an offering in the United States, it must segregate the two. The U.S. offering cannot refer to the offshore offering, and participants in the offshore offering must not be allowed to participate in the onshore one.

§ 13.04 LOCATING INVESTORS

It is not enough to put offering materials on a Web site and hope investors find the site. It is important to publicize it. A good Web site designer can help. There are also many Web sites devoted to Internet offerings—a company should be on one or more of them (see list at the end of this chapter).

WR Hambrecht + Co. is particularly interesting. On its site (http://www.OpenIPO.com), a company can post the number of shares it wants to sell or the amount of money it wants to raise. Investors submit bids online for how much they want to buy at what price. The firm's software then conducts a reverse auction, accepting the highest bid price, and working down in bid price until all shares have been sold or the money raised. The lowest price reached in order to sell all shares is the final price for everyone. Hambrecht charges 3% for the service.

§ 13.05 INTERNET SECURITIES SITES

[A] U.S. Government and Regulations

[1] U.S. Government Web Sites

Bureau of National Affairs	http://www.bna.com
The Congressional Record	http://www.access.gpo.gov/su_docs/aces/aces150.html
Fed World	http://www.fedworld.gov
Library of Congress	http://www.loc.gov
Office of the Solicitor General	http://www.usdoj.gov/osg
Securities and Exchange Commission	http://www.sec.gov
Thomas Legislative	http://thomas.loc.gov/System home/thomas.html
U.S. Business Advisor	http://www.business.gov
U.S. Department of Justice	http://www.usdoj.gov
U.S. House of Representatives	http://www.house.gov
U.S. Senate	http://www.senate.gov
White House	http://www.whitehouse.gov

[2] U.S. Statutes, Codes, Rules, and Regulations Online

Code of Federal Regulations	http://www.access.gpo.gov/nara/cfr/cfr-table-search.html

Federal Register	http://www.access.gpo.gov/su_docs/aces/aces140.html
Federal Rules of Civil Procedure	http:/www.law.cornell.edu/rules/frcp/overview.htm
Federal Rules of Evidence	http://www.law.cornell.edu/rules/fre/overview.html
The Securities Act of 1933	http://www.law.uc.edu/CCL/33Act/index.html
Rules Under 1933 Act	http://www.law.uc.edu/CCL/33ActRls/index.html
Regulation A	http://www.law.uc.edu/CCL/33ActRls/regA.html
Regulation D	http://www.law.uc.edu/CCL/33ActRls/regD.html
Rule 504	http://www.law.uc.edu/CCL/33ActRls/rule504.html
Rule 505	http://www.law.uc.edu/CCL/33ActRls/rule505.html
Rule 506	http://www.law.uc.edu/CCL/33ActRls/ru1e506.html
Forms Under the 1933 Act	http://www.law.uc.edu/CCL/33forms/index.html
The Securities Exchange Act of 1934	http://www.law.uc.edu/CCL/34Act/index.html
Rules Under 1934 Act	http://www.law.uc.edu/CCIL/34ActRls/index.html
Forms Under 1934 Act	http://www.law.uc.edu/CCL/34forms/index.html

Uniform Commercial Code	http:/www.law.cornell.edu/ucc/ucc.table.html
U.S. Code	http://www.law.cornell.edu/uscode
U.S. Constitution	http://www.law.cornell.edu/constitution/constitution.overview.html
U.S. Tax Code	http://www.fourmilab.ch/ustax/ustax.html

[3] Courts and Decisions

Supreme Court	http:/www.supremecourtus.gov/
U.S. Court of Appeals—First Circuit	http://www.law.emory.edu/1circuit
U.S. Court of Appeals—Second Circuit	http://www.tourolaw.edu/2ndcircuit/
U.S. Court of Appeals—Third Circuit	http://vls.law.vill.edu/Locator/3/index.htm
U.S. Court of Appeals—Fourth Circuit	http://www.law.emory.edu/4circuit
U.S. Court of Appeals—Fifth Circuit	http://www.law.utexas.edu/us5th/us5th.htm
U.S. Court of Appeals—Sixth Circuit	http://www.law.emory.edu/6circuit
U.S. Court of Appeals—Seventh Circuit	http://www.kentlaw.edu/7circuit
U.S. Court of Appeals—Ninth Circuit	http://www.ce9.uscourts.gov/web/newopinions.nsf/Opinions+by+date?OpenView&Start=1&Count=100&Expand=1.1

U.S. Court of Appeals—Eleventh Circuit	http://www.law.emory.edu/11circuit/

[B] U.S. Securities Organizations

[1] U.S. Exchanges and Securities Organizations

American Stock Exchange	http://www.amex.com
Boston Stock Exchange	http://www.bostonstock.com
Chicago Board Options	http://www.cboe.comExchange
Chicago Stock Exchange	http://www.chicagostockex.com
NASD Regulation Inc.	http://www.nasdr.com
NASD Inc.	http://www.nasd.com
NASDAQ Stock Market	http://www.nasdaq.com
Pacific Exchange	http://www.pacificex.com
Philadelphia Stock Exchange	http://www.phlx.com

[2] Initial Public Offerings, Direct Public Offerings, and Bulletin Boards

Activate.net of CMGI, Inc.	http://www.Activate.net
Angel Capital Electronic Network	http://www.ace-net.org
Billington's Stocks Investing Newsletter Point	http://www.ipos.com
Bay Street Direct Toronto	http://www.baystreetdirect.com

Business Partners Unlimited	http://www.Businesspartners.net
The Dinner Club	http://www.Thedinnerclub.com
Direct Stock Market	http://www.dsm.com
eSignal.com	http://www.esignal.com
FairShare	http://www.Fairshare.com
Garage.com	http://www.Garage.com
Hoover's Online	http://www.hoovers.com http://www.ipocentral.com
Internet Capital Group	http://www.Internetcapital.com
InvestorGuide	http://www.investorguide.com
Invest Quest	http://www.investquest.com
Ipo.com	http://www.ipo.com
Netstock Direct	http://www.netstockdirect.com
NVST.com Private Equity Network	http://www.Nvst.com
Securities Web	http://www.securitiesweb.com
Venture Associates	http://www.venturea.com
VentureCapital.com	http://www.Vcapital.com
Vfinance.com	http://www.vfinance.com
Virtual Wall Street, Inc.	http://www.virtualwallstreet.com
WebFinance	http://www.webfinance.com
Wit Capital	http://www.witcapital.com
W.R. Hambrecht + Co, LLC	http://www.OpenIPO.com

[3] Road Show Sites

iBean Broadcasting	http://www.ibeam.com
Netroadshow	http://www.netroadshow.com
NextVenue	http://www.nextvenue.com

[4] Electronic Communications Networks (ECNs)

Archipelago	http://www.tradearca.com
Attain Trading System	http://www.attain.com
Bloomberg Tradebook	http://www.bloomberg.com
Instinet	http://www.instinet.com
Island	http://www.island.com
NexTrade	http://www.nextrade1.com
RediBook	http://www.redi.com
Terra Nova Trading	http://www.terranovatrading.com

[5] Day-Trading Sites

Day Traders Network	http://www.daytrades.com
RML Trading	http://www.rmltrading.com

[C] International Securities Organizations

[1] International Market Regulators

Financial Services Authority	http://www.fsa.gov.uk
Futures Industry Association	http://www.fiafii.org
International Federation of Stock Exchanges (FIBV)	http://wwwfibv.com

International Organization of Securities Commissions	http://www.iosco.org
Investment Management Regulatory Organisation (IMRO)	http://www.fsa.gov.uk/imro
North American Securities Administrators Association	http://www.nasaa.org
Securities and Futures Authority (SFA)	http://www.sfa.org.uk

[2] International Exchanges

Amsterdam Exchanges	http://www.aex.nl
Athens Stock Exchange	http://www.ase.gr
Australian Stock Exchange	http://www.asx.com.au
EASD	http://www.easd.com
EASDAQ	http://www.easdaq.be/easdaq.asp
Frankfurt Stock Exchange	http://www.exchange.de/fwb/fwb.html
Hong Kong Stock Exchange	http://www.hkex.com.hk
Italian Stock Exchange	http://www.borsaitalia.it
Korea Stock Exchange	http://www.kse.or.kr
LA SBF—Bourse de Paris	http://www.bourse-de-paris.fr/
London International Financial Futures and Options Exchange (LIFFE)	http://www.liffe.com
London Stock Exchange	http://www.londonstockexchange.com

Montreal Exchange	http://www.me.org
Nagoya Stock Exchange	http://www.nse.or.jp/index-e.htm
Osaka Securities Exchange	http://www.ose.or.jp/e/main_f/html
Securities and Exchange Board of India	http://www.sebi.com
Singapore Stock Exchange	http://www.ses.com.sg
Swiss Exchange	http://www.swx.ch
Taiwan Stock Exchange	http://www.tse.com.tw/docs1/index.html
Tokyo Stock Exchange	http://www.tse.or.jp
Warsaw Stock Exchange	http://www.wse.com.pl

[D] Information Services

[1] Business and Investor News Sites

Bloomberg	http://www.bloomberg.com/welcome.html
Business Today	http://www.businesstoday.com
C/Net	http://www.cnet.com
CBS Marketwatch	http://www.cbsmarketwatch.com/news/
CEO Express	http://www.ceoexpress.com
Individual Investor	http://www.individualinvestor.com
Newsweek	http://www.newsweek.com

Red Herring	http://www.redherring.com
Smart Money	http://www.smartmoney.com
The Industry Standard	http://www.thestandard.net
The New York Times	http://www.nytimes.com
U.S. News and World Report	http://www.usnews.com
Wired	http://www.wired.com/news

[2] Corporations and Securities Law Information Sites

American Corporate Counsel Associates	http://www.acca.com
Corporate Financials Online	http://www.cfonews.com
Cybersecurities Law	http://www.cybersecurities law.com
EDGAR Database of Corporate Information	http://www.sec.gov/ edgar.shtml
Hoovers On Line	http://www.hoovers.com
Securities Class Action Clearing House	http://securities.stanford.edu
Securities Law Homepage	http://www.seclaw.corn
Uniform Business and Financial Laws Locator	http://www.law.cornell.edu/ uniform/vol7.html

CHAPTER 14 • TRADING

CHAPTER 14

§ 14.01 OVERVIEW

A start-up company's work is not finished when its securities are sold. The final stage of the financing process occurs next. Similarly, regulatory attention turns to the resale of the securities and protecting investors not involved in the original distribution.

As a rule, resale transactions, referred to as secondary trading, can be made without registration. However, there are certain situations where secondary trading can occur only if the securities have been registered. Additionally, they can be sold if the seller is not an underwriter of the securities.

Secondary transactions will be subject to the integrated disclosure system's formal requirements in two cases: (1) if the issuer has completed a registered primary offering of its securities or (2) if the issuer has become subject to the reporting provisions of the Exchange Act. In either case, the transactions will be subject to annual and periodic reporting.

Public-company status can be quite burdensome to a company. The advantage, however, is access to public capital markets.

§ 14.02 TRADING MARKETS

Most of the regulatory activity under the federal securities laws focuses on trading in organized markets, including the national stock exchanges and the over-the-counter markets. These trading markets involve previously issued securities bought and sold on a routine basis. There is no requirement for special selling efforts such as when a large block of shares is sold by the issuer or a major shareholder. Regulatory oversight applies to all sales. The oversight also covers broker-dealers.

Trading procedures depend on whether the securities are traded on a national stock exchange or in the over-the-counter market. Where a security has been listed for trading on a national stock exchange, a specialist will be assigned to establish and maintain an orderly trading market for the security. The specialist, who is subject to regulation by the exchange and the SEC, matches buy and sell orders and attempts to maintain some liquidity in the security. This could be by purchasing shares for his or her own account. The specialist is subject to minimum capital requirements established by the exchanges and the SEC.

Nasdaq allows market-makers to submit their quotations for specified securities electronically. The quotations are then made available to all subscribing broker-dealers on computer monitors. To effect a trade, the executing broker-dealer first queries the system for the best available quotation in the security. Armed with this information, the broker-dealer immediately contacts the appropriate market-maker to complete the purchase or sale of the required number of shares.

Some actively traded over-the-counter securities are not quoted on Nasdaq, either because they are not eligible for quotation or because no market-maker has elected to register them for quotation. For such securities, quotations are likely to appear in the privately published National Daily Quotation Sheets, often referred to as the "pink sheets" (quotations for equity securities are on pink sheets, while quotations for debt securities appear on yellow sheets). Market-makers who subscribe to the National Daily Quotation Service pay to have their quotations reflected in the pink sheets. The pink sheets are disseminated, albeit on a somewhat delayed basis, to other dealers, who use them to determine the market in a quoted security. In order to effect a trade, a broker-dealer contacts the market-maker with the apparent best market in the security. The broker-dealer then executes the customer's order.

§ 14.03 LEGAL FRAMEWORK FOR SECONDARY TRADING ACTIVITIES

[A] Overview

[1] In General

As a rule, secondary trading activities do not need to register under Section 5 of the Securities Act. There are two notable exceptions. First, securities originally issued in an exempt or nonregistered transaction may not be resold to the public unless purchasers are sufficiently informed about the issuer's condition. Second, the sale of a large block of securities by persons in control of the issuer may be restricted. The position of the seller in such control cases is similar to that of an issuer.

[2] Statutory Framework

Secondary trading transactions are addressed by the Securities Act. The general rule under Section 5 is that registration is not required for "transactions by any person other than an issuer, underwriter or dealer." Additionally, most dealer transactions are exempted under Section 4(3). (The dealer exception, however, does not exist during the period that a public distribution is occurring.) Accordingly, the availability of an exemption for a nonissuer turns on whether or not the issuer or an underwriter is involved.

Section 2(11) expands *issuer* to include "affiliates":

> As used in this paragraph [that is, for purpose of defining an *underwriter*] the term "issuer" shall include, in addition to an issuer, any person directly or indirectly controlling or controlled by the issuer, or any person under direct or indirect common control with the issuer.

Section 2(11) of the Securities Act defines an *underwriter* as follows:

> The term "underwriter" means any person who has purchased from an issuer with a view to, or offers or sells for an issuer in connection with, the distribution of any security, or participates or has a direct or indirect participation in any such undertaking. . . .

The net effect of these expanded definitions in Section 2(11) is

1. A person purchasing shares from an issuer with the intention to distribute (generally a resale to the public) would be an underwriter, and the sale would not be exempt under Section 4(1). Therefore, persons purchasing from an issuer in an exempt transaction are at risk of being statutory underwriters in any future resale.
2. If an issuer's affiliate makes a distribution of *any* issuer shares, including shares purchased in the open market, it may not be able to rely on the Section 4(1) exemption. Anyone purchasing shares from the affiliate may be an underwriter if the shares are purchased for distribution.
3. Anyone purchasing shares in the trading market from someone other than an affiliate are free to resell such shares without registration.

Persons involved in secondary transactions must be careful to avoid becoming underwriters. If they do become underwriters, their sales may violate the registration requirements. If shares are purchased from an issuer in an exempt transaction, the buyer should demonstrate that the shares are being purchased for investment, not for distribution. To reduce risks in this area, the SEC adopted Rule 144 as a safe harbor. It can be relied on for public resale of securities in circumstances that might otherwise run afoul of Section 4(1).

[B] Rule 144 Transactions

[1] In General

Rule 144 is a safe harbor for the sale of restricted securities, as well as for the sale of restricted and nonrestricted securities by an affiliate (controlling person). Restricted securities in both cases are acquired directly or indirectly from an issuer or an affiliate in a nonpublic offering.

[2] Definition of *Affiliate*

Rule 144 defines an *affiliate* of the issuer as "a person that directly, or indirectly through one or more intermediaries, controls, or is controlled by, or is under common control with, such issuer." The SEC staff has determined that the following individuals are affiliates: (1) an officer or director of the issuer, (2) a person owning more than 10% of the issuer's common stock, (3) a person whose spouse is an officer or director of the issuer, and (4) a corporation with an officer or director serving as a director of the issuer.

[3] Current Public Information Requirement

As a rule, Rule 144 can be used only when there is adequate public information available about the issuer. The test can be satisfied in two ways. The issuer can be current with its periodic reporting requirements under the Exchange Act. Alternatively, the current information requirements can be satisfied by proof that what is called "Rule 15c2-11 information" has been made publicly available.

[4] Holding Period Requirement

When relying on Rule 144 for the resale of restricted securities, with certain exeptions there is a one-year (formerly two-year) minimum holding period. The period is calculated from the date of acquisition from the issuer (or affiliate) to the date of resale. The period does not begin until the full purchase price or other consideration has been paid. There are detailed rules applicable to the holding period of donees, trusts, and estates that permit the holding period of the donor, settler, or decedent to be used. The holding period condition does not apply to shares acquired in the open market by an affiliate.

[5] Limitations on Amount of Securities Sold

The amount of shares sold over-the-counter pursuant to Rule 144 by any person during a three-month period cannot exceed 1% of the outstanding class of securities. For listed securities and over-the-counter securities traded through Nasdaq, the limitation is the greater of that 1% amount or the average weekly trading volume during the current four-week period. In determining these limitations, detailed attribution and aggregation rules must be considered.

[6] Manner of Sale Requirements

Other than in transactions pursuant to Rule 144(k) as described below, Rule 144 securities can be sold in two ways: to a market-maker, or in an *unsolicited* agency transaction with the broker acting as agent for the seller and receiving only a customary brokerage commission. If the shares offered by the seller exceed 500 shares or $10,000 in aggregate sales price, a Form 144, describing the transaction and how it is exempt, must be filed with the SEC. If the security is listed on an exchange, it must also be filed with the appropriate exchange.

[7] Removal of Certain Conditions for Shares Held by Nonaffiliates for Long Periods

Rule 144(k) applies to persons who have not been affiliated with the issuer for at least 90 days and who held the issuer's securities for two years (determined in the same manner as the one-year holding period). They can sell such securities in unrestricted quantities without regard to the type of transaction, commissions, or discounts paid, and without filing a Form 144. In addition, information on the issuer need not be available to the purchaser. A Rule 144(k) seller may simultaneously sell restricted securities, although the seller must comply with the volume limitations for restricted securities. Rule 144(k) sales, however, are not aggregated with restricted securities sales in calculating volume limitations.

[C] Rule 144A: Resales by Qualified Institutional Buyers

[1] In General

Rule 144A exempts from registration nonissuers that reoffer and resell unregistered securities to offerees and purchasers that are (or that the seller reasonably believes to be) qualified institutional buyers. Rule 144A is intended to facilitate the development of an orderly and liquid market among large institutional investors for private placement transactions. A related development was the NASD's creation of the Private Offering, Resale and Trading through Automated Linkages system (PORTAL), which provides a computerized, screen-based quotation, trading, settlement, and clearing system for securities sold in reliance on Rule 144A.

[2] Qualified Institutional Buyers

A *qualified institutional buyer* is typically defined as

- In purchasing the unregistered securities, the buyer is acting for its own account or for the accounts of other qualified institutional buyers (Account Requirement); and
- The buyer, in the aggregate, owns and invests at least $100 million in securities, excluding securities of its affiliates (Securities Held Requirement).

Entities that may be qualified institutional buyers include insurance companies, registered investment companies, employee benefit plans (private or governmental), registered investment advisors, corporations, partnerships, and business trusts. In addition to satisfying the Account Requirement and the Securities Held Requirement, a bank or savings and loan institution must also have a net worth of at least $25 million.

[3] Excluded Securities

The Rule 144A exemption does *not* apply to securities that are the same class as securities already listed on a registered national securities exchange or quoted in Nasdaq. Eligibility is determined at the time the Rule 144 security is issued. Therefore, eligibility is not affected if a class of securities not publicly traded or quoted at the time of issuance later becomes so. In addition, securities convertible into publicly traded securities are treated as part of the same class as the traded securities. Warrants exercisable for publicly traded securities are treated in the same manner.

[4] Information Requirements

If the issuer of the securities is a reporting company under the Exchange Act, there are no information requirements under Rule 144A. If the issuer is not a reporting company, however, the seller must have the right to obtain information from the issuer. In addition, the prospective purchaser must receive that information from the issuer, the seller, or a person acting for either of them at or prior to the sale. The information that must be made available includes

- A brief statement of the issuer's business, products, and services within 12 months of the resale; and
- Specified financial information (e.g., balance sheet and profit and loss statements).

[5] Resales of Rule 144A Securities

Securities purchased by a qualified institutional investor under Rule 144A are restricted securities and can be resold only in reliance on Rule 144 or Rule 144A.

[D] Section 4 (1 1/2) Exemption

The purchaser of securities in an exempt transaction may wish to subsequently sell the securities and rely on either a registration statement or Rule 144. Ordinarily, in such a case, the person would risk being an underwriter. The sale could be used as evidence that the securities were originally acquired for resale and not for investment. Underwriter status, however, applies only if the shares were acquired with a view to distribution. This typically means a public offering. If the subsequent sale is a private placement, the sale will be exempt under Section 4(1) on the theory that an underwriter was not involved.

These secondary private placements have been referred to as Section 4 (1 1/2) transactions. The claimed exemption falls under Section 4(1), but the criteria utilized are more akin to those for issuances under Section 4(2) for issuers. In any case, securities sold in such transactions are deemed restricted securities for purposes of Rule 144, with the sale starting a new holding period. The purchaser cannot rely on the seller's holding period.

[E] Registered Secondary Transactions

One way to ensure that secondary distributions comply with the registration requirements is to register them. However, only the issuer can file a registration statement, even for secondary sales. Accordingly, persons acquiring shares in an exempt transaction, such as a private placement under Section 4(2), must turn to the issuer and demand that it register such shares. If the issuer does register the shares, a number of Securities Act registration forms, including Form S-1 and Form S-3, can be used for resales. Form S-3 essentially consists of incorporating certain Exchange Act filings by reference.

[F] Secondary Trading Under State Securities Laws

In contrast to the exemption for trading included in Section 4(1) of the Securities Act, Section 301 of the Uniform Securities Act subjects *all* sales of *nonexempt* securities, including trading transactions, to the registration provisions. Securities listed on the principal stock exchanges are exempt. In most jurisdictions, an exemption is also available for issuers about which information is published in a recognized securities manual (primarily Moody's or Standard & Poor's). Many jurisdictions also have exemptions broad enough to cover the typical trading in isolated nonissuer transactions. State blue-sky laws permit the administrator, on appropriate grounds, to revoke the exemption for any particular security.

§ 14.04 PUBLIC COMPANY STATUS

[A] Overview

Issuers can become subject to the ongoing disclosure requirements of the Exchange Act as a result of

1. Registration of an offering pursuant to the Securities Act, or

2. Registration of a class of securities under Section 12 of the Exchange Act.

In either case, the issuer must file the following reports with the SEC:

- Form 10-K (or the counterpart for SBIs), an annual report, which must be filed within 90 days after the end of each fiscal year;
- Form 10-Q (or the counterpart for SBIs), a quarterly report, which must be filed within 45 days after the end of the first three quarters each fiscal year; and
- Form 8-K, for significant events (such as changes of control and acquisitions), which must be filed within 15 days of the first event or within 10 days after the end of the month in which a material event occurs.

(Note the SEC has proposed changing these timeframes.)

In addition, issuers subject to continuous disclosure requirements must comply with the following Exchange Act provisions:

- Rules on the solicitation of proxies, including the requirement that an annual report be prepared and distributed to shareholders;
- Rules regulating tender offers for registered securities; and
- "Going private" rules for transactions that deregister an issuer's securities under the Exchange Act, or that cause an issuer's securities to be delisted by an exchange or over-the-counter market.

In addition, short-swing profit rules impose liability on insiders of the registrant for profits they realize in trading the registrant's securities.

[B] Disclosure Obligations Under the Exchange Act

[1] In General

Issuers subject to disclosure obligations under the Exchange Act must file an annual report on Form 10-K, quarterly reports on Form 10-Q, and, if required, reports of special events on Form 8-K. SBIs have the option of complying with the Exchange Act reporting obligations by using special report forms adopted by the SEC. Those forms incorporate the simplified form of disclosure under Regulation S-B. In addition, issuers subject to the proxy rules must prepare and distribute an annual report to their shareholders.

[2] Form 10-K

Part I of Form 10-K consists of Item 101 (description of business), Item 102 (properties), and Item 103 (legal proceedings), as well as information on any matter submitted to a vote of security holders during the fourth quarter of the fiscal year. Information on other major developments in the company needs to cover only those events that occurred since the last fiscal year.

Part II of Form 10-K includes the basic information package (BIP). Part III of Form 10-K consists of Item 401 (officers and directors), Item 402 (management remuneration and transactions), and Item 403 (security holders of management and 5% beneficial owners). Part IV of Form 10-K consists of schedules to the financial statements and separate (as distinguished from consolidated) financial statements of the registrant, a list of financial documents and exhibits, and a statement as to whether any reports on Form 8-K were filed during the last quarter of the fiscal year. The exhibits include articles of incorporation, bylaws, and all material contracts. If any of these documents have been previously filed with the SEC, they may be incorporated by reference.

A registrant may incorporate by reference annual report information into Parts I and II of Form 10-K. Since the annual report includes only a portion of the information called for by Item 101 (description of business), however, it may not include all required information. A registrant may also incorporate by reference into Part III information from the proxy statement for its annual meeting if the proxy statement is filed with the SEC within 120 days of the end of the fiscal year. If the proxy statement is not filed within this period, the Part III information must be filed in Form 10-K within 120 days of the end of the fiscal year.

[3] Quarterly Reports on Form 10-Q

Form 10-Q requires a balance sheet and statements showing profit and loss, and source and application of funds. Profit and loss statements must be for the latest year and quarter and be compared to the prior year and the equivalent quarter of the previous year. Balance sheet information must be as of the end of the quarter and on a comparative basis for the equivalent quarter of the previous year. The statement of source and application of funds must be on a year-to-date basis for the current and prior year. The statements do not have to be audited, but they must be reviewed by an independent public accountant prior to filing. Form 10-Q must be prepared in accordance with Accounting Principles Board Opinion No. 28 relating to a change in accounting principles.

The Form 10-Q must also include an MD&A document covering material changes from the end of the latest fiscal year to the date of the 10-Q balance sheet. The MD&A should also discuss material changes in results of operations between the most recent quarter and the comparable quarter in the prior year, and between year-to-date and the comparable date of the prior year.

Part II of Form 10-Q must include information on the following events during the quarter:

- Legal proceedings initiated (and material developments) (item 1);
- Modifications in and limitations on the rights of registered security holders (item 2);
- Changes in collateral securing registered securities (item 3);
- Material default in the payment of principal, interest, or sinking fund installments not cured within 30 days (item 4);
- Increases in outstanding securities (including debt securities) exceeding 5% of the outstanding securities, and any exemption relied on (item 5);
- Decreases in outstanding securities exceeding 5% of the class (item 6); and
- Results of any matter submitted to a vote of shareholders (including election of directors) (item 7). An uncontested election of directors does not have to be reported if proxies were solicited. Similarly, procedural matters, and selection or approval of auditors, do not have to be reported.

[4] Form 8-K

Form 8-K must be filed if one of the following occurs:

- Changes in control of the registrant (item 1);
- Acquisition or disposition of a significant amount of assets not in the ordinary course of business (item 2);
- Appointment of a receiver and issuance of material orders in a bankruptcy or reorganization proceeding (item 3);
- Resignation or dismissal of the certifying accountant (with information about any disagreement), and a confirming letter from the accountant to the SEC (item 4); and
- Resignation of a director over a disagreement about the registrant's operations, if the director requests that the matter be disclosed (item 6)

The registrant may also include, at its option, information on any other matter it believes is of material importance to security holders (item 5).

Form 8-K must be filed within 15 calendar days of the event reported in the case of items 1 to 3 and 5 business days in the case of items 4 and 6.

Other material events (optional item 5) can be reported at any time. Registrants are encouraged, however, to file promptly after occurrence of the event. They must consider accuracy and currency of information in any Securities Act registration statement, such as Form S-3, that incorporates by reference Form 8-K reports.

A Form 8-K can also be filed as a means of complying with a company's obligation under Regulation F-D (which bans selective disclosure of material information).

[5] Exchange Act Reporting by SBIs

SBIs that want to meet their Exchange Act reporting obligations by using Regulation S-B disclosures can make their filings on Form 10-KSB. It is an annual report for SBIs analogous to Form 10-K. They can also use Form 10-QSB, a quarterly reporting form corresponding to Form 10-Q. Relevant items in Forms 10-KSB and 10-QSB are covered by the simplified requirements of Regulation S-B rather than Regulation S-K. The SEC has also adopted corresponding simplifications to the proxy rules and requirements for annual reports to shareholders.

[6] Annual Report to Shareholders

An annual report must be sent to shareholders before or with the proxy statement for the annual election of directors. Seven copies must be filed with the SEC concurrently. The annual report includes the BIP, certain segmental and geographic financial information, limited narrative information relating to the company's principal products and services, and a brief description of the company's business during the most recent fiscal year. The annual report must also include the name and principal occupation or employment of every director and executive officer, as well as the name of and principal business where each is employed.

The annual report may include any other information the issuer wishes (e.g., a letter from the registrant's chief executive officer). The annual report may be in any form, provided that the required information is included. For instance, annual reports often include bar charts, graphs, and pictures. All of the structured portions of the annual report other than the financial statements may be included in an appendix or a separate section. If they are, readers must be directed to such presentation. For their annual report, some issuers use Form 10-K (typically without Part III included in the proxy statement) and a letter from the chief executive officer inside an attractive cover.

[C] Regulation of Corporate Governance

[1] In General

The federal securities laws, particularly the Exchange Act, have a significant impact on corporate governance of issuers with registered securities. Among the most important areas are procedures for soliciting proxies, tender offers for registered issuers, and "going private" transactions. Issuers with securities listed on national securities exchanges or in the over-the-counter market, particularly Nasdaq, must also consider corporate governance rules imposed by those markets.

[2] Proxy Solicitation Procedures

Section 14(a) of the Exchange Act makes it illegal to solicit proxies in violation of SEC rules and regulations. Under Section 14(a), the SEC has adopted extensive regulations controlling the solicitation of shareholders' proxies for election of directors, approval of compensation plans, extraordinary corporate actions (e.g., mergers, consolidations, and acquisitions), and shareholder proposals. In particular, if a proxy solicitation (or similar consent) is directed to more than 10 persons, a proxy statement and form complying with the proxy rules must be filed and used. With some exceptions, the proxy statement must be filed as preliminary proxy material with the SEC at least 10 days prior to the actual mailing.

[3] Tender Offer Regulation

A tender offer is an attempt to acquire a substantial portion of the outstanding stock of a company. It is done by an offer to purchase at a fixed price all shares, up to a specified number, tendered by shareholders within a specified period. The price is usually at a premium above the market price. Since a successful tender offer can result in a change in control of the target company, such offers are subject to extensive rules in Regulations 14D and 14E. Regulation 14D rules, all of which begin with a 14d prefix, apply to tender offers for equity securities registered under the Exchange Act. Regulation 14D also covers equity securities of certain insurance companies. Regulation 14E rules, all of which begin with a 14e prefix, are applicable to *all* tender offers.

A person making a tender offer (called the bidder) must file with the SEC as soon as practicable a tender offer statement on Schedule TO. The Tender

Offer Statement must identify the bidder; the source of the bidder's funds; the bidder's purpose (including future plans) in making the tender offer; any securities of the target company previously acquired by the bidder; and, if the bidder is not a natural person, appropriate financial statements on the bidder's financial condition.

Rule 14e-1(a) requires tender offers to remain open for at least 20 business days. If the bidder changes its offer, the open period cannot expire until at least the 10th day after the change. The changes triggering this 10-day period are an increase or a decrease in percentage of securities being sought, consideration offered, or dealer's soliciting fee.

In the case of a tender offer covered by Schedule TO, any person depositing securities may withdraw them at any time before the tender offer expires. If more shares are tendered than were requested in the tender offer, and are more than the bidder is willing to purchase, the bidder must purchase on a pro rata basis. The bidder is also required to disclose the extent to which it presently intends to purchase overtendered shares.

The tender offer rules are supplemented by the Williams Act. Under that Act, anyone acquiring a substantial block of equity securities must notify the SEC and the subject company about the acquisition and must disclose, among other things, its ultimate intentions regarding control of the company. The Williams Act applies to any person or group that

- Acquires 2% or more of the outstanding shares in a class registered under the Exchange Act; and
- As a result of that acquisition, becomes the owner of 5% or more of the outstanding shares.

Once this threshold is met, the person or group must file a Schedule 13D with the SEC (with a copy to the company) within 10 days.

[4] Rule 13e-3: "Going Private" Rules

The "going private" rules apply to the purchase of (or tender offer for) the equity securities of a reporting company by the issuer or one of its affiliates. The result must be that the issuer will no longer be subject to Exchange Act registration requirements. The going private rules also apply to a merger of a reporting company with, or the sale of all of the corporate assets of the company to, an unregistered affiliate. Rule 13e-3 was adopted to ensure full and fair disclosure to the public shareholders. The purpose of such disclosure is to reduce the potential for self-dealing and misuse of inside information.

The going private rules require any issuer or affiliate engaged in a going private transaction covered by such rules to file with the SEC a transaction statement on Schedule 13E-3. In addition, if the transaction requires the consent of shareholders and the security is registered under the Exchange Act, either a proxy statement or an information statement must be filed with the SEC. Similarly, if a tender offer by the issuer is involved, the issuer must file a Schedule 13E-4 issuer tender offer statement. If an affiliate makes a tender offer for an equity security registered under the Exchange Act, a Schedule TO must be filed.

PART V • CASE STUDIES

CHAPTER 15 • FINANCING RESEARCH AND DEVELOPMENT: INVESTMENT PARTNERSHIPS AND CORPORATE PARTNERING

CHAPTER 15

§ 15.01 INTRODUCTION

This chapter builds on the discussion in Chapters 3 and 7 of research and development financing alternatives. For many emerging technology-based firms, the most difficult task in developing new products is obtaining the large amounts of financing needed to complete the development work, obtain all required regulatory approvals, and commence commercial exploitation of the products and underlying technology. Many firms obtain the needed funding by issuing additional amounts of equity securities, either in private placement transactions to one or more venture capitalists or institutional investors or through public offerings to the broader investment community. However, firms are always searching for new ways to finance research and development without incurring substantial dilution to the equity interests of the founding shareholders, either by obtaining funding tied to the success of a specified technology or by locating investors willing to pay a premium for their equity interest based on the attractiveness of the firm as a potential business partner.

Research and development partnerships have proven to be one reliable method for securing funding for development work without the need to issue additional equity securities, at least at the time the development funds are secured. These partnerships are based on the combination of the firm's technology and research skills, on the one hand, and financing provided by investors, on the other. If the development work succeeds, the investors receive a return based on the commercial performance of the products created during the development period, although they may also have a right to receive some equity in the firm at a later date. Due to recent changes in the tax laws, research and development partnerships have lost a good deal of their former attractiveness, although new investment instruments have been created based on similar principles.

Corporate partnering relationships are another alternative for technology-based firms seeking additional financing. As mentioned below, corporate partnering can refer to a number of arrangements; however, the focus in this chapter is on transactions in which a large, established firm makes a strategic equity investment in a smaller firm with a promising technology base. The larger firm willingly pays a premium for its equity interest because it will most likely also negotiate one or more separate deals with the smaller firm for contract research work and/or the right to distribute the smaller firm's products when the development work is completed.

In this chapter, we apply many of the explanations and lessons from earlier chapters to these two alternatives. We draw particularly on Chapter 2, but rather than requiring that the reader refer to that chapter, we simply incorporate and apply its basic concepts here.

§ 15.02 RESEARCH AND DEVELOPMENT PARTNERSHIPS

[A] Overview

Research and development partnerships have been used for a number of years by new and emerging companies to finance the development of their core technologies, as well as by large and mature companies to raise significant amounts for development of new technologies, applications, and products. While the initial research and development partnerships were structured, at least in part, to allow investors to take advantage of favorable tax treatment, a number of recent tax law changes have diminished the appeal of research and development partnerships as tax shelter. However, the vehicle continues to survive as an alternative form of capital for technology-driven companies.

Although research and development partnerships can take a number of different forms, the basic structural form, which has been used for a number of years, is that of a limited partnership in which a sponsor corporation seeking additional capital for development of its new technology acts as the general partner and contributes the rights to such technology to the limited partnership. The capital for the development of the technology comes from limited partner investors, who contribute sufficient cash to fund the development effort. The sponsor corporation conducts the research work on behalf of the limited partnership, and the expenditures of the limited partnership are allocated to the investors as losses for tax purposes. When, and if, products are developed out of the research effort, the sponsor corporation assumes responsibility for sale activities and the investors have the opportunity to recoup their initial capital through royalties or similar payments based on the commercial use of the technology.

The general partner of a limited partnership has full authority to manage the affairs of the limited partnership and is subject to unlimited liability for debts and obligations incurred by the limited partnership.

Limited partners have no rights to participate in the management and control of the business of the limited partnership; however, they are also not liable for any of the debts or obligations of the limited partnership in excess of the amount of capital they contributed to the partnership. For tax purposes, profits and losses from the limited partnership are "passed-through" to each of the general and limited partners in the proportions provided for in the limited partnership agreement. As a general rule, the partners are free to allocate profits and losses in any manner they decide, even if the allocations are disproportionate to the capital contributed to the partnership, provided the allocations have "substantial economic effect" under Section 704(b) of the Internal Revenue Code of 1986, as amended (IRC). (Allocations made under a partnership agreement will have "substantial economic effect" if the capital accounts of the partners are actually increased by the amount of any profits allocated to them for tax purposes and are actually decreased by the amount of any losses allocated to them for tax purposes. These capital accounts will be used in partnership accounting to determine how the assets of the partnership will actually be distributed on liquidation of the partnership, after taking into account any adjustments that might be required to allocate any unrealized profits or losses attributable to any change in the value of the partnership's assets. The capital accounts are generally not allowed to become "negative," and the partners will be required to restore any negative amount in their capital accounts prior to liquidation.)

The ability to deduct the tax losses from the research and development activities generated a significant economic incentive for investors to participate in research and development limited partnerships, even in the face of material risks that the research efforts would be unsuccessful. However, with the adoption of the passive activity loss rules included in IRC Section 469, which restricted the ability of noncorporate investors to use losses from research and development limited partnerships to offset income from other income-producing activities, the continued utility of the research and development limited partnership as a financing vehicle began to depend more and more on the quality of the sponsoring corporation and the underlying commercial potential of the technology. (A corporate investor can still take advantage of deductions for losses incurred by a research and development limited partnership in which the corporation invests, provided the corporate investor is not required to report its income on a consolidated basis for tax purposes with the sponsoring corporation.)

In recent years, many major investment banking firms have organized public and private limited partnerships for the purpose of investing as research and development limited partnerships. Such a fund might raise $50 million to $150 million to be used in investing in a number of research and development deals, with each specific investment running from $2 million to $10 million. An affiliate of the investment banking firm generally serves as the general partner of these "blind pool" investment partnerships and takes responsibility for negotiating the terms of each transaction with the sponsoring corporation. For their trouble, the investment banking firms receive a "carried interest" in any profits that may be received from the investments made by the limited partnership.

[B] Royalty/Warrants Structure

[1] In General

The "royalty/warrants" structure anticipates that the investors will receive a return on their investment through the payment of royalties from the use, license, or sale of products developed during the research effort. In most cases, this return would be "capped" at a specified amount negotiated at the outset of the transaction with the sponsoring corporation. In addition, the investors would have the opportunity to participate in the overall success of the sponsor, including any products not part of the research project, by exercising warrants to purchase shares of the sponsoring corporation's common stock issued at the commencement of the transaction.

[2] Formation of Limited Partnership

The relationship between the sponsoring corporation and the investors begins with the formation of a limited partnership. In most situations, the sponsor corporation or an affiliate acts as the general partner of the limited partnership and receives its interest in the limited partnership in exchange for an exclusive royalty-free license that allows the limited partnership to use existing technology owned by the sponsor corporation in designing, developing, manufacturing, and marketing products that fall within the proposed scope of the partnership's activities. In turn, the sponsoring corporation will receive a small fee from the limited partnership or a royalty-free cross-license to use any technology developed during the limited partnership's research program for applications that fall outside the proposed scope of the limited partnership's activities. As limited partners, the investors will contribute an amount of cash sufficient to provide funding for the proposed research work.

In recent years, sponsor corporations have been able to rely on existing limited partnerships organized by investment bankers as financial partners in the development of new products. The general partners of these "blind pool" investment funds seek out attractive technological opportunities and invest capital in a number of different transactions, much like a venture capital fund. When relationships with these investment partnerships are formed, no new limited partnership is formed, and the sponsor corporation does not need to act in a general partner capacity. Instead, the sponsor corporation will license the subject technology to the investment partnership for the purpose of further development for the account of the investment partnership.

[3] Research Agreement

Once the limited partnership has been formed, it will enter into a research agreement with the sponsoring corporation pursuant to which the sponsoring corporation performs the work necessary to develop the technology previously licensed by it to the limited partnership. Depending on the circumstances, the term of the development work can extend anywhere from one to three years. The sponsoring corporation will be obligated to use its best efforts to complete the development work on a timely basis; however, no guarantees are made that the development process will be successfully completed. The limited partnership will own the technology developed during the research program, subject to the license granted to the sponsoring corporation for applications that fall outside the scope of the partnership's activities.

The sponsoring corporation will receive a research fee from the limited partnership for the work conducted under the research program. The amount of the fee, which is intended to cover the direct and indirect costs and, in some cases, to provide a slight profit for the sponsoring corporation, is agreed on in advance and paid to the sponsoring corporation in installments over the term of the research work. In return for the research fee, the sponsoring corporation will agree to a number of restrictions on its activities. For example, the research fee cannot be used for any other purpose than the research work. In addition, during the research project, the sponsoring corporation will be prohibited from working on any products that might compete with those being developed for the limited partnership. Moreover, if the sponsoring corporation develops any competitive products following the research project, it will be required to pay royalties to the limited partnership based on revenues derived from such products.

The research fee paid to the sponsoring corporation will depend on the amount of funds required to complete the project and the aggregate amount of capital investors are willing to invest in the limited partnership. The amount of the offering must be sufficiently large to cover not only the estimated costs of the research project, which may be somewhat uncertain at the time the limited partnership is formed, but also certain other expenses, including the limited partnership's capital contribution to the joint venture that may be formed following the research program, the investment banking fees and legal expenses associated with the offering of the limited partnership interests, and a reserve that will remain available to cover the operating expenses of the limited partnership itself.

The research fees will cover only specified expenses of the research program, and the sponsoring corporation will be prohibited from using the research fees to acquire any facilities or capital equipment. Instead, the sponsoring corporation will commit itself to obtain such facilities and capital equipment from its own funds, either by direct purchase or by lease or other financing arrangements. However, a portion of the research fees may be used to cover any normal depreciation of facilities or capital equipment resulting from their use in the research program.

The research agreement will specify that the inventions and technical information arising out of the research program will be owned by the limited partnership. The sponsoring corporation will be obligated to make periodic reports to the limited partnership as to the progress of the research work and to take such actions as may be necessary to perfect and maintain any intellectual property rights (e.g., filing and prosecuting patent applications) that may arise from the research program. The sponsoring corporation will also be required to maintain insurance to cover any liabilities to third parties that may arise out of the conduct of the research program.

[4] Joint Venture Arrangement

After the development work has been completed, the sponsor corporation has the option to enter into a joint venture with the limited partnership to commercialize the newly developed products. The use of a joint venture assures that the limited partnership will be deemed to be engaged in a trade or business so that the research and experimental expenditures can be deducted under IRC Section 174. The joint venture option first becomes exercisable at the time that the initial products are ready for manufacturing and will lapse if the sponsoring corporation does not exercise the option within a specified period of time.

The joint venture option became popular in the mid–1980s. Prior to that time, rather than using the joint venture option, the sponsoring corporation was usually granted an option to acquire the technology in the event that the development work was successful. For tax reasons, the option could not be exercised until at least one year following completion of the research work; however, to permit the sponsoring corporation to begin manufacturing and marketing activities prior to the date the acquisition option became exercisable, it was granted the option to acquire from the limited partnership a non-exclusive license of the technology for that interim period. (Delaying the exercise date of the acquisition option for at least one year establishes a 12-month holding period for long-term capital gain on the sale of the developed technology by the limited partnership and helps to demonstrate that the limited partnership is engaged in a trade or business so that the research and development expenditures can be properly deducted under IRC Section 174. A nonexclusive license to the sponsoring corporation can be used during the interim period so as to prevent the transfer to the sponsoring corporation from being characterized as a sale or exchange prior to the running of the long-term capital gains period.)

The sponsoring corporation is also granted an option to purchase the partnership's interest in the joint venture if the joint venture option is exercised. The purchase option generally becomes exercisable on the later of (1) the last day of the first calendar month in which the sum of any joint venture profits allocated to the partnership, computed on a cumulative basis, exceeds the sum of the joint venture losses allocated to the partnership, computed on a cumulative basis, by a predetermined amount, and (2) a fixed date at least 12 months after the joint venture begins. The purchase option will expire on the earlier of (a) notice by the sponsoring corporation to the partnership that it will not exercise the purchase option, (b) 90 days after the purchase option first becomes exercisable, or (c) a fixed date, usually three to five years, after the joint venture begins if the purchase option has not yet become exercisable.

If the sponsoring corporation decides to exercise the joint venture option, the partnership will contribute the rights to the technology developed during the research program. In turn, the sponsoring corporation will commit to contribute, through capital contributions or loans, a sufficient amount of cash to permit the joint venture to commercialize the products developed under the research agreement. The sponsoring corporation will also agree to manufacture and distribute the products on a cost-only basis for the benefit of the joint venture.

The joint venture will be established under the terms of a joint venture agreement between the sponsoring corporation and the limited partnership. The joint venture agreement will specify that separate capital accounts will be maintained for each of the joint venturers and that profits and losses from the joint venture activities will be allocated between the joint venturers on a predetermined basis. As a general rule, the percentage of joint venture profits allocated to the partnership will decrease as the aggregate level of profits grows. While the sponsoring corporation will have responsibility for the management and conduct of the day-to-day business of the joint venture, the overall management and control of the business affairs of the joint venture will be exercised by a management committee that includes representatives from each joint venturer as well as independent members jointly selected by both parties.

Unless the sponsoring corporation exercises its option to purchase the partnership's interest in the joint venture, the joint venture will continue until the occurrence of one of the following events: (1) the election of the partnership to terminate the joint venture after lapse of the purchase option; (2) the election of the sponsoring corporation to terminate the joint venture at any time after 12 months following the lapse of the purchase option; (3) the election of the partnership if it becomes aware that the sponsoring corporation is unable to fulfill its commitments with respect to providing the resources for the commercialization of the products; or (4) the mutual agreement of the joint venturers.

[5] Purchase of Limited Partnership's Joint Venture Interest

If the sponsoring corporation exercises the purchase option, it will become obligated to purchase the joint venture interest of the limited partnership by making royalty payments based on the amount of revenues received by the sponsoring corporation and its affiliates from the license, sale, or other disposition of the joint venture's products or technology. As a general rule, the terms of the royalty arrangement are as follows:

1. The limited partnership will be entitled to receive a guaranteed minimum amount of royalty payments, without regard to the amount of revenues that may be actually received by the sponsoring corporation. In turn, the total amount of royalties to be paid by the sponsoring corporation will be "capped," so that the final purchase price will not exceed a specified amount.
2. While royalties will generally be paid on a periodic basis as revenues from the technology are received by the sponsoring corporation, the limited partnership may often receive a lump-sum cash down payment at the time the purchase option is exercised. The down payment amount may or may not be offset against any additional amounts that the limited partnership may be obligated to pay as royalties in the future.
3. The royalty percentage (i.e., the percentage of revenues to be paid to the limited partnership) usually declines as the cumulative amount of royalties increases. For example, the royalty percentage on the first $500,000 of revenues may be 5% and the royalty percentage on any amount over $500,000 may decline to 3%.

4. The limited partnership will be granted a security interest in the technology and the related receivables to secure performance of the royalty obligations by the sponsoring corporation.
5. The sponsoring corporation may be given the right to prepay its future royalty obligations by making a lump-sum payment to the limited partnership equal to an amount determined by application of a predetermined formula. In many cases, one or both of the parties will be given the right to require that the prepayment amount be paid in freely-tradeable shares of common stock of the sponsoring corporation.

[6] Warrants to Purchase Sponsoring Corporation's Stock

In addition to the anticipated return from the development project, limited partners may participate in the overall growth of the sponsoring corporation by exercising warrants for the purchase of shares of the sponsoring corporation's common stock that will be issued to the limited partnership at the commencement of the entire relationship. While the warrants will usually be held by the limited partnership, they may, at the sole discretion of the general partner, be distributed in whole or in part to the limited partners. The warrants will become exercisable, usually in two or more blocks, without regard to the success of the development work and will usually become fully exercisable on the occurrence of certain events, such as a merger or acquisition of the sponsoring corporation or the sale of substantially all of its assets. (Failure to keep the conditions of the exercisability of the warrants completely independent of the success or failure of the development project may subject the sponsoring corporation to adverse financial accounting treatment, as well as create adverse tax consequences for the limited partners. As to the sponsoring corporation, the difference between the value at the date of exercise of the stock purchased and the exercise price would be charged to the purchase price of the technology and amortized over the technology's useful life. With respect to the limited partnership, a similar charge would be made to the purchase price, thereby resulting in additional income to the limited partners. See *Simmons Precision Products, Inc.,* 75 T.C. 103, (1980).)

The warrants will have an exercise price that reflects a premium over the market value of the common stock at the time they are issued and may provide a "net exercise" right pursuant to which the warrant holders can exercise the warrant, without any cash payment, for that number of shares equal in value to the excess of the aggregate fair market value (on the date of exercise) of the shares for which the warrant is exercised over the aggregate exercise price payable for such shares. The sponsoring corporation will generally grant warrant holders a right to have the shares registered for immediate resale under federal securities laws.

[7] General Terms of Business Relationship

Although the formation of the limited partnership, the development arrangement, the formation of the joint venture, the exercise of the purchase option, and the purchase and exercise of the warrants are all discrete transactions, the entire relationship will usually be documented in the context of an omnibus agreement that sets forth the respective rights, obligations, covenants, and warranties of each of the sponsoring corporation and the limited partnership. This agreement, which is entered into at the time the limited partnership is formed, includes a number of representations and warranties from both parties, obligates the corporation to provide various types of financial and business information to the limited partners on a periodic basis, calls for delivery of various certificates and legal opinions, and, finally, incorporates all of the terms of the ancillary agreements covering the transactions referred to above.

Common representations and warranties made by a sponsoring corporation in this situation include (1) that it has authority to enter into and perform the various agreements with the limited partnership; (2) that it has sufficient right and title to the base technology necessary for development of the technology; (3) that it has obtained all the governmental approvals necessary to conduct its business and carry out the research and development project with the limited partnership; and (4) that it is not in violation of its articles of incorporation or bylaws or any material agreements with a third party or any statute or regulation applicable to the sponsoring corporation or its assets. For its part, the limited partnership and the general partner, which often is the sponsoring corporation itself, will make representations as to their authority to perform each of their obligations under the agreements with the sponsoring corporation and the absence of any conflict between those obligations and the terms of any existing material contract or regulation to which the limited partnership or the general partner may be subject.

[C] Equity Structure

[1] In General

The equity research and development limited partnership structure attempts to provide investors with the tax benefits of the partnership form during the development stage coupled with the ability to take their share of profits from commercialization of the technology in the form of capital gains after the partnership is converted into a corporation when the development work has been completed. The first stage of the equity model involves formation of a limited partnership to perform the research and development work on the new technology. Limited partners can use the losses incurred during the development stage to offset other income from nonpartnership sources, subject to the limitations on passive activity losses that apply to noncorporate investors. Once the technology has been developed and commercial activities begin, the business is incorporated; any future profits will be taxed at the corporate level, and the investors will be permitted to take out their share of profits at capital gains rate when they ultimately liquidate their investment.

[2] Formation of Limited Partnership

The equity structure begins with the formation of a limited partnership. While the founders of the fledgling business may be the general partners of the limited partnership, it is more common to use a corporate general partner to provide insulation from unlimited liability and to permit the founders to recruit new employees by offering them equity interests in the corporation. In either case, the contribution of the general partner(s) consists of the technology to be developed. The limited partners will contribute a sufficient amount of cash to complete the development project. Although the limited partners would not have any right to participate in the management of the limited partnership, a representative of the investor group may sit on the board of directors of the general partner corporation.

To provide the investors with the tax benefits from the losses generated by the limited partnership during the research effort, the limited partnership agreement will allocate almost all, generally 99%, of the losses to the limited partners until they have been allocated aggregate losses equal to the total amount of capital originally contributed by them to the limited partnership. Thereafter, any further losses would be allocated to the general partner, which would be liable to third parties for such amounts. Once the limited partnership achieves profitability, all of those profits would be allocated to the limited partners until they have received profit allocations equal to the losses that may have previously been allocated to them. After the losses have been restored, further profits are allocated to all of the partners in accordance with their original capital accounts.

Unlike the royalty/warrants structure, an equity partnership structure does not include a separate research agreement. Instead, the research work is conducted by the limited partnership itself and the resultant technology is owned by the limited partnership itself. (By having the research conducted directly by the limited partnership, rather than by the sponsoring company pursuant to a separate research agreement, the parties can avoid the need to account for any subsequent "roll-up" of the partnership into a corporation as a purchase for financial accounting purposes, which would result in an adverse effect on future earnings of the new corporation once commercialization activities have begun. See FASB Technical Bulletin 84-1.) As the limited partnership uses the contributed funds on the work, the losses are allocated to the limited partners in the manner set out in the partnership agreement. Once the development work has been completed, the limited partnership will continue in existence to begin sales and marketing activities with respect to products developed during the research period, thereby assuring that the limited partners will be able to avail themselves of the deductions relating to the research expenses incurred during the development period. (Continued operation of the limited partnership after the research work is required to satisfy the trade or business requirement of IRC Section 174, which concerns the deductibility of research expenses. Tax-exempt limited partners may have unrelated business income from the commercialization activities of the partnership. In some cases, allowing them to invest directly in the sponsoring corporation or through a wholly-owned corporate subsidiary can mitigate the adverse effects of the unrelated business income to such investors.)

[3] Conversion of Limited Partnership to Corporate Form

Once the limited partners have been assured of their ability to deduct the development expenses and the sales activities of the limited partnership begin to produce net profits, consideration will be given to effecting a tax-free conversion of the business from a limited partnership to a corporation. The method used for this conversion, generally referred to as a "roll-up," depends on the aggregate interest of the limited partners in the limited partnership. If the limited partners own 80% or more of the adjusted capital accounts of the limited partnership prior to the roll-up, they should be able to transfer all of their limited partnership interests to the sponsor corporation in exchange for shares of the corporation's stock without recognizing any gain on the transaction. However, if the 80% test cannot be satisfied, all of the shares of the sponsor corporation, as well as all of the limited partnership interests, must be simultaneously exchanged for shares of a new corporation in order for tax-free treatment to be available for the conversion. (In those cases where the investors are all corporations, and the investments are made by wholly-owned subsidiaries formed solely for the purpose of participating in the partnership, the roll-up can be effected tax-free by merging each of the corporate limited partners into the sponsoring corporation.)

Whatever method is used to effect the roll-up, the intent is that the relative interests of all of the partners, general and limited, in the business be the same after the transaction as they were before the conversion occurred. Accordingly, the exchange ratios will be determined on the basis of the relative balances in the capital accounts of each of the partners. In cases where the limited partnership is rolled-up into the sponsoring corporation, the transaction will be deemed to be a liquidation for partnership accounting purposes, and the capital accounts will be adjusted to reflect the value of the assets of the limited partnership at the time of the roll-up. Assuming that the roll-up qualifies for tax-free treatment, the limited partners will carry over their basis in their partnership interests to the stock received in the exchange, and for holding period purposes they will be deemed to have held such shares since the date that they acquired their partnership interests.

Although it is almost always contemplated that the limited partnership will eventually be converted into the corporate form once the business becomes profitable, care must be taken that the partnership entity is recognized for tax purposes so that each of the limited partners can avail itself of the tax benefits from the allocation of losses. As a general rule, this means that a firm agreement to convert the limited partnership to a corporation should be avoided. Instead, disclosures regarding the corporation in the offering documents should be limited to a description of the potential benefits of incorporation; the books of the enterprise should be carefully maintained in accordance with the principles of partnership accounting; and the roll-up should not occur until a formal offer of exchange is made to each of the limited partners. If, for some reason, the partnership form is disregarded, limited partners will be deemed to have purchased corporate stock as of the date of their original investment and would not be entitled to the tax benefits from the losses during the development effort.

[4] Management and Operation of Successor Corporation

On completion of the roll-up, the resultant corporation generally takes on the form of any other technology-driven firm. If, as is often the case, the limited partners receive preferred stock in exchange for their limited partnership interests, it will be possible for the corporation to issue common stock to employees at lower prices. Also, the corporation may be able to raise more capital in subsequent financings by issuing another series of the preferred stock with rights, preferences, and privileges that differ from those granted to the original investors in the research and development limited partnership. Ultimately, the objective of the corporate manager is to be able to take the corporation public, at which point the stock issued to the limited partners could be sold in the public market.

[D] Joint Venture Structure

Another structure used for research and development activity is a joint venture between the sponsoring corporation and a limited partnership consisting of all of the investors. In contrast to the royalty/warrants structure, where the joint venture is formed after the completion of the development work, this structure establishes the joint venture at the same time that the investment partnership is formed. The terms of the joint venture will be described in a formal joint venture agreement covering the contributions of the respective parties, the conduct of the research activities, and such other matters relating to the management of the venture as may be appropriate.

The sponsoring corporation will contribute an existing active trade or business, such as manufacturing operations, to the joint venture to ensure that the joint venture is engaged in a trade or business from the outset. The investment partnership will not only supply funds for the development work, which may either be carried out by the sponsoring corporation under separate contract or by the joint venture itself, but may also provide funds for the further commercialization of the resultant products, since these non-research costs can be deducted under IRC Section 162. As is the case with the royalty/warrants structure, the corporation will have the option to purchase the limited partnership's interest in the joint venture once the development work is completed.

[E] A New Alternative: "SWORDs"

R&D partnerships became much less attractive with the changes in the tax laws that prevented the limited partners from deducting the partnership's losses against their ordinary income. Moreover, many limited partners were frustrated at the illiquidity associated with their partnership interests, since generally no market existed into which limited partners could sell their interests and convert their investment into cash. As a result, firms in search of funds for development work have devised a new structure, referred to as a "SWORD," which provides the required "off balance sheet" funding, while addressing the liquidity requirements of the investors.

When a SWORD is used, the sponsoring corporation establishes a new subsidiary for the purpose of conducting the research work. The sponsoring corporation grants an exclusive license to the new subsidiary to use the base technology for development work, and the sponsoring corporation contracts with the new subsidiary to perform the development work. The research funding is obtained through a public offering of units consisting of both a share of stock in the new subsidiary and a warrant to purchase share(s) of stock in the sponsoring corporation. The sponsoring corporation will have the option to "call," or repurchase, the shares of stock in the new subsidiary at a specified premium over the original purchase price; however, the investors may still continue to participate in the success of the research work by exercising the warrants.

At some point following the public offering, the components in the original unit will be separated, and a public market will exist for both the shares of the new subsidiary and for the warrants to purchase the sponsoring corporation's shares. As a result, each of the investors has the flexibility to convert their interests into cash, although there are no tax advantages to the investors unless the entire investment proves to be worthless. For its part, the sponsoring corporation can earn contract research revenues in the same way as an R&D partnership, retain the right to recover title to the technology, and place the risk of failure of the development work on the investors. However, SWORDs do create a significant potential legal liability to the sponsoring corporation in light of the conflict of interest between it and the subsidiary, as well as the strong possibility that the research and development work will not be successful.

§ 15.03 CORPORATE PARTNERING RELATIONSHIPS

[A] Overview

Corporate partnering relationships can involve one or more types of ongoing arrangements between a large firm with relatively mature functional capabilities in areas like product development, manufacturing or distribution (the "senior partner") and a small, entrepreneurial technology firm lacking the capital and production and marketing skills to bring its products to market (the "junior partner"). Some of the basic corporate partnering relationships can be described as follows:

- Senior partner makes an equity investment in the junior partner on terms typically associated with any venture capital-type investment. Senior partner receives the right to designate one or more representatives on the junior partner's board of directors and junior partner makes various covenants regarding the operation of its business activities.
- Senior partner engages the junior partner to conduct a contractual research and development project. The junior partner is paid a research

fee and, perhaps, a royalty based on specified use of the technology developed during the research project, which will be owned by the senior partner.

- Senior partner agrees to act as an OEM or distributor with respect to one or more products developed by the junior partner.
- Senior partner provides funding to junior partner for development of new products using base technology owned by junior partner. Senior partner would agree to buy new products from junior partner at a multiple of the junior partner's cost of manufacturing, and junior partner would pay royalties to the senior partner on any product sales made to third parties.
- Senior partner makes an equity investment in junior partner on the terms described above and also agrees to provide additional funding for the junior partner to conduct research and development work on one or more specified technologies. The senior partner would have a right to participate in the management of the research project and to license the resultant technology for use in various areas and applications.
- Senior partner provides funding for the junior partner to conduct research and development work on a new product. The results of the research project would be owned by the junior partner; however, senior partner would be entitled to purchase rights to the product for a front-end payment and future royalties based on product sales.
- Senior partner makes an equity investment in junior partner on the terms described above, agrees to fund research and development work of the junior partner and/or purchase products from the junior partner, and receives an option to purchase the junior partner in the future at a price based on a specified formula.

The most complex, and potentially long-lasting, types of corporate partnering relationships involve some form of equity investment by the senior partner in the junior partner. An equity investment provides the junior partner with needed capital to use in developing new technology and products and in building its own manufacturing and distribution functions. For the senior partner, an equity investment allows it to gain fuller access to some of the new technologies being developed by the junior partner. Moreover, the senior partner would be able to share in successes the junior partner achieved outside the specific areas in which the parties might otherwise contract for research work or marketing and distribution.

Equity investments by corporate partners have now become an alternative to traditional venture capital financing, although the terms of the investment tend to be similar to those that have been negotiated with venture capitalists.

Many senior partners, lacking a history of making and managing investments in new high technology companies, may require a greater degree of control over the affairs of the junior partner than would be the case with venture capital investors. The junior partner, however, would benefit from having a major investor that understands its underlying technology and the steps necessary to address and capture new market opportunities. Also, finding the right corporate partner can mean instant credibility for the "start-up" venture.

When an equity investment corporate partnership is being considered, the parties must first select the appropriate form of investment instrument. Since, as a general rule, the investor will require the same form of convertible preferred stock that venture capitalists have come to favor, the next step in the process will be to negotiate the terms of this security, including any dividend rights, liquidation preferences, voting rights, conversion features, and use of any redemption provisions. The parties must then set out the various agreements and covenants of the junior partner with regard to the operation of its business following the date that the investment is consummated. Finally, the parties must give appropriate attention to the terms of any separate agreements that might cover a separate technology-based relationship, such as any contract research work that the junior partner might be called on to perform for the senior partner.

[B] Selecting the Investment Instrument

[1] In General

Selecting the appropriate investment instrument for use in completing the financing will depend on a number of factors, including the objectives of the senior partner, the maturity of the junior partner, and the degree of risk associated with the execution of its business plan, the current and future capital requirements of the junior partner, the relative interests of the other shareholders of the junior partner, the amount of control that the senior partner wishes to have over the management of the junior partner's affairs, the need for liquidity, and the terms of any outstanding agreements with any prior investors or lenders. The most common choices for use in an investment are as follows:

- Common Stock
- Convertible Preferred Stock
- Convertible Debt
- Nonconvertible Preferred Stock or Debt coupled with Common Stock or Common Stock Purchase Warrants

[2] Common Stock

While common stock is the simplest form of investment instrument, it is rarely used in connection with a venture capital or corporate partnering investment, at least when the financing occurs at the early stages of the company's development. Investors cannot have any dividend or liquidation preferences. Moreover, the sale of common stock to investors will establish a market value for that type of stock that must be applied to stock sales or option grants made to employees, thereby greatly increasing the cost of equity ownership to this group.

[3] Convertible Preferred Stock

Convertible preferred stock is by far the most popular investment instrument for venture capitalists and other outside investors at the early stages of the company's development. The preferences associated with the convertible preferred stock allow the company to continue to sell common stock at "cheap" prices to employees without the adverse income tax consequences that might result if the investors decided to purchase common stock. Also, convertible preferred stock allows the investors to participate in any "upside" growth in the company while establishing a preference on liquidation in the event that the venture is not successful. Finally, the convertible preferred stock can be given a number of other protective rights, including antidilution protection and the right to a separate vote on specified transactions.

[4] Convertible Debt Securities

Convertible debt securities may be appealing to certain investors, particularly large corporate investors with some desire for a fixed rate of return while the company is maturing, albeit at a lower rate than might otherwise be available due to the conversion feature. Debt securities would be senior to convertible preferred stock with respect to repayment on liquidation, and the right to receive interest payments would not be limited by corporate laws that might restrict the payment of dividends. However, holders of convertible debt securities would have no direct right to control the company and would need to rely on voting agreements and various covenants in the investment agreement.

Convertible debt securities have a number of drawbacks from management's perspective. First, it appears as debt on the company balance sheet and, absent a subordination agreement, may limit the ability of the company to obtain credit from lenders, suppliers, and other creditors.

Second, convertible debt usually does require the company to make some periodic payments of interest, which must be made regardless of whether the company is profitable. In contrast, dividends on convertible preferred stock need only be paid out of earnings. Finally, since holders of convertible debt will not have any direct voting rights, they may insist on a variety of covenants and the right to accelerate the indebtedness in the event of any defaults.

[5] Nonconvertible Equity or Debt Securities

Companies interested in venture capital financing rarely use nonconvertible equity or debt securities. Nonconvertible instruments are unattractive to companies because they will usually have to be retired, either by redemption, in the case of an equity security, or by repayment, in the case of a debt security. From the investor's perspective, a fixed and limited return is generally not very appealing, regardless of how safe it might be. Instead, the investor will opt for an investment instrument that provides it with an opportunity to participate in the significant increases in value often realized by technology-driven companies.

Nonconvertible securities are sometimes issued along with warrants, which allow the investor to purchase common stock or some other type of equity instrument at an established price at some time in the future. Investors often like this option, since they are able to delay the decision to commit funds to a junior equity instrument while retaining some of the security offered by using a nonconvertible preferred stock or debt instrument. However, the use of warrants may give rise to an "original issue discount" on the related senior security, resulting in adverse tax consequences to the investor, and the investor's holding period on the common stock or other securities issuable on exercise of the warrants for federal securities law and tax purposes does not begin until the warrants are exercised.

[C] Terms of Convertible Preferred Stock

[1] In General

As noted above, convertible preferred stock is the most commonly used investment instrument in early stage venture capital financings and in corporate partnering arrangements. The principal terms of convertible preferred stock, which will usually be agreed on in the term sheet or commitment letter, are (1) dividend rights (cumulative or noncumulative and with or without participation), (2) the liquidation preference, (3) voting rights,

(4) conversion provisions (right to convert and mandatory conversion) and antidilution protections, and (5) redemption provisions (optional and mandatory).

[2] Dividends

In most cases, preferred stock is given some form of preference over the common stock with respect to the payment of dividends, although some preferred stock dividend provisions will simply state that the preferred stock will be entitled to receive dividends on the same basis as the common stock as if the preferred stock had been converted into common stock at the time the dividend is to be paid. If a dividend preference is given, it will be on either a noncumulative or a cumulative basis.

When a noncumulative dividend provision is used, there is no absolute commitment on behalf of the company to make any dividend payments to the holders of the preferred stock. Instead, holders of preferred stock will only be entitled to receive dividends if, when, and as declared by the board of directors. Accordingly, even if there are funds legally available to make a dividend payment, if the board decides not to make a distribution and retains the funds for use in the business the dividend is lost to the holders of the preferred stock.

In contrast, cumulative dividends that are not paid will continue to accrue over time and will be payable whenever funds are available or when declared by the board of directors. The amount of accumulated dividends is generally added to the amount that must be paid to the holders of the preferred stock on liquidation of the corporation or redemption of the preferred stock, although in some cases the amount of any accumulated dividends payable at the time of liquidation is subordinated to payment of liquidation preferences on any series of preferred stock that is not entitled to cumulative dividends. Sometimes the dividend provisions may be noncumulative at the time of issuance but become cumulative after some date in the future, which date is usually set by reference to certain financial and operational milestones.

[3] Liquidation Preference

Holders of preferred stock are generally given a priority claim over the holders of common stock to receive a fixed dollar amount on liquidation of the corporation before any distribution is made with respect to the common stock. The preferential amount on liquidation typically equals the original purchase price of the preferred stock plus any accrued but unpaid dividends. In many cases, the articles of incorporation will provide that mergers and similar transactions will be deemed to be "liquidations," thereby insuring that the preferred stock holders will at least have the right to receive their original investment back on the occurrence of such a transaction.

In many cases, holders of preferred stock will be better off on liquidation by converting their shares into common stock and sharing in the distributions made to all holders of common stock. If the preferred stock is "participating," holders thereof will be entitled to receive not only their liquidation preference but also the amount to which they would have been entitled had they elected to convert the preferred stock into common stock. A participating preferred stock can substantially dilute the economic interest of the common stock holders. As a compromise, the participation of the preferred stock can be subordinated to payment of some fixed amount to the holders of the common stock or can be limited to a specified level of return.

[4] Voting Rights

Convertible preferred stock typically votes along with the common stock on all matters and is entitled to one vote for each share of common stock into which the preferred stock is permitted to convert at the time of the vote. In addition, holders of the preferred stock may be given the right to vote as a separate class on certain corporation transactions, including the issuance of new senior securities, mergers and acquisitions, and amendments to the rights, preferences, and privileges of the preferred stock.

The preferred stock may be given a class vote with respect to the election of directors. For example, the parties may provide in the articles of incorporation that the preferred stock will have the right to designate two out of the five directors and that the remaining directors will be designated by the holders of the common stock voting as a separate class. In other cases, the holders of the preferred stock and common stock, voting as separate classes, will be entitled to designate an equal number of directors; the remaining director or directors will be elected by the preferred stock and common stock voting together. Sometimes, the preferred stock will be given extraordinary voting rights to designate a majority of the directors on the occurrence of an event specified in the articles of incorporation, such as failure to pay dividends or to make mandatory redemptions or any default by the company in the performance of financial or other covenants.

[5] Conversion Provisions

By definition, convertible preferred stock can be converted into shares of common stock at the discretion of the holder. Also, convertible preferred stock is generally automatically converted into common stock on the occurrence of certain events, such as the completion of a firmly underwritten initial public offering of the common stock of sufficient size to merit eliminating the preferences of the preferred stock. Typically, the conversion ratio for the preferred stock is initially established at one share of common stock for each share of preferred stock; however, the conversion ratio is subject to adjustment over time to account for future dilutive events, such as the issuance of new securities at a price lower than the preferred stock purchase price.

Automatic conversion of the preferred stock is usually required on the closing of a firmly underwritten public offering of the company's common stock at a per share price and for an aggregate offering price in excess of stipulated levels. The per share price generally depends on the timing of the investment and may be set at anywhere from three to five times the common stock equivalent price paid by the investor. The aggregate offering price condition is intended to insure that the public market for the common stock is sufficiently large to provide liquidity for the shares of common stock received by the investors on conversion.

Automatic conversion may also occur on the company's attainment of certain performance goals and objectives, including the closing of a private placement financing in excess of a certain minimum dollar amount or the achievement of specified revenue or net sales standards. In addition, conversion may be triggered by the vote of a certain percentage of the holders of the preferred stock (e.g., 66 $^{2}/_{3}$%), thereby permitting a recapitalization of the corporation without the need for an amendment of the articles of incorporation. Moreover, allowing a majority, but less than all, of the holders of the preferred stock to effect a conversion of all of the preferred stock provides a means for insuring that a small number of preferred stock holders are not able to continue to use the special voting rights granted to the class to disrupt the affairs of the corporation.

The conversion ratio for the preferred stock is always adjusted for stock splits, stock dividends and consolidations to insure that the economic interests of the holders of the preferred stock remain unchanged following such events. However, more importantly, preferred stock provisions often include some type of antidilution mechanism, which applies to certain issuances of common stock or common stock equivalents (e.g., other classes of preferred stock with conversion features), at prices lower than the common stock equivalent price paid by the investors. These antidilution provisions make downward adjustments in the conversion price of the preferred stock, which is originally established as the price per share paid for the preferred stock, thereby increasing the number of shares issuable on conversion.

[6] Redemption

Some, but certainly not all, convertible preferred stock includes redemption provisions. There are two general types of redemption provisions: "optional" redemption, which provides the company with the right to repurchase or redeem the preferred stock at its purchase price plus a redemption premium, and "mandatory" redemption, which imposes an absolute obligation on the company to repurchase the preferred stock at the dates and on the terms specified in the articles of incorporation. In addition, in some situations the investors will be given the right to force the company to redeem the shares at the option of the investors. This right, which, in effect, is a "put," is little different from the mandatory redemption provision when the investors are given the right to waive or defer redemption.

Optional redemption provisions provide the company with a method for forcing the investor to convert the preferred stock into common stock if the investor wants to retain its interest in the growth of the company. By forcing conversion, the company is able to eliminate the special rights associated with the preferred stock with respect to dividends, liquidation, and voting. Realizing the leverage that optional redemption rights can provide the company, investors are generally reluctant to agree to such provisions. On the other hand, the company may be able to obtain agreement on this issue if it agrees to defer the exercisability of the option for a specified period of years.

Mandatory redemption provisions generally call for the repurchase of the preferred stock in installments commencing on a specified date in the future (e.g., five years). The obligation to redeem the preferred stock is always subject to availability of a sufficient amount of funds to legally complete the redemption. If the funds are not available, the obligation carries over to the next scheduled redemption date. In some cases, the company will be required to establish a "sinking fund" into which funds are deposited prior to the scheduled redemption date to secure the performance of the company's obligations on the redemption date.

[D] Agreements and Covenants of the Junior Partner

[1] In General

The senior partner will typically require that the junior partner enter into a series of agreements and covenants regarding the management of the junior partner's affairs. These agreements and covenants generally fall into two broad categories: affirmative covenants, which impose duties and obligations on the future activities of junior partner, and negative covenants, which prohibit the junior partner from taking certain future actions. For example, one common affirmative covenant is the obligation of the junior partner to provide the senior partner with financial information. Standard negative covenants would prohibit the junior partner from entering into various specified transactions, such as a merger or an acquisition, or from amending the charter documents, without first obtaining the consent of the senior partner.

The scope and nature of the required covenants varies with every investor and the nature of the investment instrument. For example, if the investors will control the issuer's board of directors following the closing of the transaction, the covenants, if any, will generally not be very burdensome, since the investors will rely on their control of the board to manage the issuer's continued operations. On the other hand, if the investors will not control the board following closing, the required covenants will necessarily be more extensive. Since the senior partner will not usually insist on control of the board of directors at the time of the initial investment, it is fairly common to see a fair number of covenants in a corporate partnering investment transaction.

[2] Information Rights

The junior partner will almost always agree to provide the senior partner with certain financial and operating information, including annual and quarterly balance sheets and income statements prepared in accordance with generally accepted accounting principles applied on a consistent basis. In addition, the senior partner may be given supplemental rights to receive monthly reports of sales, production, shipments, profits, cash balances, receivables and payables, and backlog, as well as budgets and projections. In some cases, the financial statements must be accompanied by a certificate from the company's chief executive or financial officer and, in the case of audited financial statements, its auditors, to the effect that the junior partner is in compliance with all provisions of the investment agreement.

[3] Management Participation

The senior partner in a corporate partnering investment transaction will usually be interested in having some means for participating in the management of the junior partner by having one or more representatives on the junior partner's board of directors. The degree of participation will vary depending on the particular circumstances. For example, the senior partner may be content to elect a minority of the members of the board. In other cases, the senior partner may insist on the right to name a majority of the directors. Another common scheme is to provide that both the senior partner and the junior partner's founders and managers will have equal representation on the board, perhaps with the added option of allowing the designated directors to appoint additional independent board members.

There are a number of pros and cons to be considered by management with respect to the degree of control that will be given to the senior partner. Certainly, senior partner participation on the board provides a good method for insuring that the senior partner is kept apprised of corporate activities and for building a strong consensus on appropriate business strategies. Also, the senior partner's representatives may be able to provide assistance in recruiting independent members of the board of the directors who can bring additional expertise or business relationships to the junior partner. Finally, if the parties are involved in one of the various forms of functional relationships, such as a manufacturing or distribution arrangement, the senior partner representative can help ease any difficulties that junior partner personnel might be having with their counterparts at the senior partner.

On the other hand, management, as well as any other outside investors, may have grave concerns about significant amounts of senior partner participation on the board of directors. An issue of some importance is the effect that senior partner involvement will have on the ability of management and the other investors to make key strategic decisions, including entertaining relationships with actual or potential competitors of the senior partner. In the event that the junior partner also has representatives of any traditional venture capitalists on the board, consideration must be given as to how the disparate objectives of the senior partner and the venture capitalists might be reconciled in monitoring the performance of the founders and managers.

The procedures for senior partner representation on the board will vary depending on the form of instrument used in the transaction and on the voting rights otherwise available to the senior partner under applicable law. If the investment takes the form of common stock or debt, a separate voting agreement will be used between the senior partner and each of the principal non-investor shareholders of the company. When the senior partner is purchasing preferred stock, the articles of incorporation may provide for class voting and allocate to the preferred stock the right to designate a specified number of directors.

If the senior partner does not wish to have a representative serve on the board of directors, or management or the other outside investors are unwilling to have such a representative, provision might be made to give the senior partner the right to designate a person to attend board meetings as a nonvoting "observer" and to receive notice of meetings and any written materials distributed to the directors. Any information that might be made available to an observer must be maintained in confidence, and the observer may be asked to leave the meetings during any discussions regarding the relationship with the senior partner.

[4] Registration Rights

The sale of securities to the senior partner is generally concluded pursuant to an exemption from the registration provisions of the federal securities laws, either under the statutory exemption set forth in §4(2) of the Securities Act of 1933 (as described in Chapter 4) for transactions by an issuer not involving a public offering or pursuant to the exemption provided by Regulation D (as described in Chapter 8). In either case, the securities acquired by the senior partner are "restricted securities" that can only be sold in accordance with Rule 144 or as part of an offering in which the securities are registered under the Securities Act. Since Rule 144 may limit the ability of the senior partner to gain liquidity as to the securities purchased, particularly when it holds a significant shareholder position in the junior partner, a good deal of attention will be attached to negotiating "registration rights": the right of the senior partner to have the securities registered for public resale under the Securities Act.

Registration rights fall into two general categories. A "demand" registration right allows the senior partner to require that the junior partner file a registration statement that covers the securities that the senior partner wishes to have resold into the public market. Since registration can be an expensive and time-consuming process that exposes management to potential liabilities under federal and state securities laws, the exercise of a demand registration right can be quite onerous for the junior partner. The other type of registration right, referred to as "piggyback rights," would simply allow the senior partner to include securities in a registration statement that the junior partner has already decided to file for a primary offering or some other purpose. The exercise of piggyback rights is perceived as being far less burdensome for the junior partner than a demand registration.

The parties will generally negotiate a number of issues relating to registration rights. One area of intense discussion is the number of demand registrations and any restrictions that might be imposed on the senior partner's ability to exercise such rights. For example, the exercisability of the demand registration may be delayed for some period of time, perhaps until after the date that the junior partner makes its initial public offering. The expenses of including securities in any registration must be allocated and, in most cases, the junior partner will be obligated to pay for the expense of registering the senior partner's securities, except for any commissions or legal fees of the senior partner in excess of an amount that the junior partner agrees to pay.

[5] Right to Participate in Subsequent Financings

The senior partner will usually be given the right to participate in future junior partner financings, thereby allowing the senior partner to maintain or increase its ownership interest in the junior partner. The participation rights may either take the form of a right of first refusal to purchase all of the securities offered by the junior partner for financing purposes in the future; preemptive rights, which will allow the senior partner to maintain its pro rata ownership percentage after the financing has been completed; or a right to discuss financing opportunities with the company before negotiations commence with any third parties.

The senior partner may be asked to integrate its rights as to future financing with those already granted to venture capitalists and other outside investors. Moreover, certain issuances will be excluded from the participation rights, including (1) any securities issuable on conversion of any outstanding securities; (2) any securities sold in a public offering; (3) any securities issued in connection with acquisitions or similar transactions; or (4) any securities (or related options) issued to any employees, officers, directors, consultants, or other persons performing services for the junior partner, including distributors, sales representatives, and suppliers. The participation rights generally will expire on the junior partner's initial public offering. However, the right may expire earlier in some cases; for example, the right to participate may terminate if it is not exercised as to a subsequent financing.

[6] Covenants Regarding Conduct of Business Activities

The obligations of the junior partner as to providing the senior partner with information, allowing the senior partner to participate in management of the business, registration rights and participation in subsequent financings are examples of "affirmative" covenants and agreements that extend beyond the closing of the transaction. While each of the foregoing areas are perceived as being of the greatest import to the senior partner, many times the investment agreement will include a number of other agreements and covenants regarding the conduct of the junior partner's business activities after the financing. These agreements are referred to as "affirmative" and "negative" covenants and serve as guidelines for the conduct of the junior partner's business activities after the initial investment has been completed. The covenants will remain effective until the earlier of the junior partner's initial public offering or the date that the senior partner's equity interest in the junior partner falls below a specified percentage.

The scope and content of the affirmative covenants will vary depending on the activities of the junior partner, the particular concerns of the senior partner, and the degree to which the senior partner will be allowed to participate in the management of the junior partner. Among the most commonly discussed and included obligations are the following: maintenance of insurance coverage, use of proceeds for purposes specified in the investment agreement, payment of taxes and other lawful claims, preservation of corporate existence and properties, conduct of business in the manner set out in the investment agreement, compliance with applicable laws and regulations, and protection of intellectual property rights. The junior partner will also be obligated to provide the senior partner with copies of certain information relating to litigation or disputes that might have a material effect on the junior partner.

Negative covenants generally limit or restrict management's ability to take certain actions without obtaining the consent of the senior partner and, as such, often become the subject of long and extensive negotiations. The senior partner will usually insist on a vote with respect to matters that will fundamentally impact its investment in the junior partner, such as acquisitions and mergers and the issuance of new securities that would dilute its interest in, and control over, the junior partner. Moreover, it is common to see restrictions on the following matters: creation of indebtedness or any lien on the junior partner's property, liquidation or sale of all the assets of the junior partner, declaration of dividends, any loans by the junior partner, transactions with directors or officers of the junior partner, and amendment of the articles of incorporation or bylaws. In debt financings, various financial covenants, such as minimum net worth requirements, may also be used from time to time.

Failure of the junior partner to comply with a covenant can have a number of consequences. Obviously, in the case of a debt financing, an event of default may trigger the ability of the senior partner to declare the outstanding indebtedness due and payable. Alternatively, an event of default in either equity or debt financing may create a right for the senior partner to designate a majority of the members of the board of directors. These "vote switch" provisions, which are often included in the articles of incorporation, require a special meeting of the shareholders be held to elect representatives of the senior partner to a majority of the positions on the board of directors. In most cases, the right to elect a majority of the board continues only for so long as the default has not been cured.

[7] Ancillary Agreements

In addition to the investment agreement, a number of other agreements may be entered into at the time of the investment, such as the following:

- Management shareholders will grant the company and/or the senior partner a right of first refusal with respect to proposed sales of company securities to a third party, thereby protecting the senior partner from any unwanted changes in the ownership of the junior partner.
- The company and/or the investors may be given the option to purchase the securities of any management shareholder at fair market value on the occurrence of certain events, such as death, personal bankruptcy, or attachment of shares by legal process, as in the divorce context. "Key man" life insurance might be purchased on the lives of the founders and key managers.
- Management shareholders will be required to provide the senior partner with the right to participate in sales that such shareholders may be permitted to make to third parties. These rights are generally referred to as "co-sale" or "tag-along" rights and are designed to prevent management shareholders from "bailing out" on the senior party by selling their interest to a third party without giving the senior party the benefit of any increase in value from the sale.
- Employees and officers who receive shares of common stock of the company, or options to purchase shares of common stock, will be required to agree to "vesting" provisions that allow the company to buy the shares back from the shareholder if the shareholder's employment expires prior to a specified date. The shares would be repurchasable at the shareholder's cost, rather than at their fair market value at the time of the purchase.
- The founders and other key management employees would be required to enter into employment and noncompetition agreements. The employment agreements often will contain various limitations on the salaries to be paid to the officers during the early stages of any development work that might be conducted for the benefit of the senior partner.
- All employees would be required to execute assignment of inventions and confidentiality agreements. The founders would also be required to assign to the junior partner all of their rights in technology related to the business of the junior partner that may have been developed prior to the formation of the junior partner.

[E] Equity Investment and Funding for Research and Development

While many equity investments by senior partners are not encumbered by any requirement that the funds be used for work on a specific project, one typical variation on this basic structure is for the senior partner to supplement the equity investment with additional funding to be devoted to the development of new technology of special interest to the senior partner. The senior partner would have certain rights to use the new technology deriving from the development work, and the junior partner would benefit from a close working relationship with the senior partner on a particular product or application.

Funding for the development work could be provided in a variety of different ways. For example, the senior partner could either loan funds to the junior partner or enter into a license agreement covering the resultant technology and pay the junior partner a technology licensing fee that approximates the amount of additional funds needed to complete the research work. Alternatively, the senior partner might simply enter into a basic research and development agreement with the junior partner pursuant to which the junior partner performs "fee-for-service" research for the senior partner.

As a general rule, the junior partner will own the rights to the technology developed during the research program. However, the senior partner will either have a license covering the technology or the option to enter into a license when the development work has been completed. In those cases where the research work has been financed pursuant to a basic research and development contract, the senior partner will usually own the rights to the technology but may grant the junior partner a license to use the technology in any areas that fall outside the senior partner's field of interest. If the senior partner has loaned funds to the junior partner as a means for funding the research work, the loan can usually be repaid out of any royalties that might be due to the junior partner under a subsequent license agreement with the senior partner.

Funded development work necessarily requires a good deal of cooperation and communication between the parties. By using a cross-licensing arrangement, both parties will have the right to use technology developed and owned by the other in the specified field of interest. Moreover, the parties will usually provide one another with technical assistance and training and exchange any new technical information that may be of interest. The junior partner may have concerns about the degree of control that may be exercised by the senior partner over the research program; however, it may well be able to tolerate any temporary loss of autonomy if it is able to use the senior partner to accelerate the maturation of its technical capabilities and bring new products to market on a timely basis.

[F] Senior Partner Option to Acquire Junior Partner

In many cases, the senior partner may make an investment in the junior partner as a first step in the ultimate acquisition of the junior partner. In this type of transaction, the senior partner will be given an option to purchase the interests of the existing shareholders of the junior partner at a price based on a predetermined formula. (The option price can be determined in any number of different ways. For example, one method that might be used is to multiply the junior partner's pre-tax earnings per share by the senior partner's pre-tax earnings multiple and subtract from that amount any contingent liabilities of the junior partner that may not yet have been charged against the junior partner's earnings prior to the option exercise.) Assuming that the purchase of the shares held by the existing shareholders will be sufficient to provide the senior partner with control of the junior partner, the shares held by any other shareholders at the time that the option is exercised may be left outstanding or such shareholders may be given the right to "put" their shares to the senior partner on the same terms as the shares subject to the option. The senior partner will insist on restricting any new issuances of shares to control the aggregate acquisition price. The senior partner, however, may permit a certain number of shares to be issued to future key employees, provided that such employees agree to make their shares subject to the senior partner's purchase option.

A purchase option may be an attractive means for the junior partner shareholders to obtain value for their interests. Also, an option of this sort provides the senior partner with a degree of flexibility in gaining control over "cutting-edge" technologies. However, there are drawbacks for both parties. From the viewpoint of the senior partner, the senior partner must take a charge against its earnings equal to the amount by which the purchase price exceeds the book value of the stock. For its part, the junior partner may be unable to take advantage of other business opportunities due to its lack of independence and may lose some of its entrepreneurial drive due its dependence on the senior partner.

CHAPTER 16 • DOT.BOMB LESSONS

CHAPTER 16

The 21st century started not with a bang, but with a bust. Spectacular dot.coms became spectacle dot.bombs. Many companies that started as dramatic successes were equally dramatic failures. A popular game became watching Web sites such as the Dead Dot-Com List of *www.hoovers.com* or its even lengthier Dot-Com Layoff List. Books such as John Cassidy's *Dot.com: The Greatest Story Ever Sold* replaced articles on 20 and 30 year-old employees becoming millionaires and retiring. College students shifted their thinking from retiring at 30 after working for a few years at a dot.com to retiring after working for 30 years.

With any economic defining moment, there are lessons to be observed and learned. In this chapter, we describe dot.bomb lessons and what they mean to anyone starting a company in the post–dot.com era.

§ 16.01 GENERAL LESSONS

Dot.bombs provide eight key lessons.

[A] What Goes Up . . .

The dot.bombs collapse is not a new phenomenon. It is as old as human nature. Charles Mackay in *Extraordinary Popular Delusions and The Madness of Crowds* describes similar events. One reason his book is so fascinating is that it was published in 1852. It describes many great bubbles and busts throughout economic history, such as the Mississippi Scheme undertaken by John Law in 1719, the South-Sea Bubble of 1720, and the Tulipmania that overtook the Dutch in 1634–1636. Unfortunately, we need not look that far back to find prominent examples. Share prices in the United States rose dramatically beginning in 1921. By 1932 they had dropped dramatically—back to where they had started. Similarly, Japan saw a rapid increase in stock prices beginning in 1981. By 1992, they were back to their starting point.

What made the collapse of dot.bombs so dramatic was not that they fell so far, but that they ran up so high in value. Priceline's worth went from zero to a market capitalization above that of the entire American airline industry before dropping to less than the price of two Boeing 747s.

The problem was not its return in worth to the value of a few airplanes, but its having ever been valued at more.

The underlying cause for the run-up in value of dot.coms was similar to that of other bursting bubbles. Dramatic events led to early rational enthusiasm that gave way to irrational exuberance. This is an important lesson for any new business. While it is tempting to get swept up in the moment, keep your company's business in perspective. Is your ramping up (hiring new employees, renting new space, leasing new equipment, buying new machinery) logical and sustainable? Or are you ramping up for a vision of glory that will disappear within a year or so, leaving you with too many debts to pay for those ramp-up assets and no choice but to accept bankruptcy?

[B] Stick to Basic Business Principles

A solid business adheres to basic principles. The most fundamental is that businesses grow by profits and that profits result from revenues that exceed expenses. This is the most effective way of financing growth, since it is based on solid business principles. The president and founder of one surviving start-up, Jim Carroll of Buzzbeepring.com, credits his stick-to-the-basics approach for keeping his company alive. "We kind of ran it like you should run a start-up business. We were conservative up front and made sure we had customers before spending a bunch of money."

On the other hand, according to one dot.bomb casualty quoted in the article "Crash and Learn" in the June 2001 *ABA Journal,* her company failed because it was not prudent or attuned to business fundamentals. Her company's approach was typical of many. Most dot.bombs financed their operations with inflows of cash from investors. When investors grew tired of financing them or the market changed and investor cash was no longer available, their operating funds ceased to exist. Consider the table below.

Table 16.1.
Control Your Cash Flow

	January	February	March	April
Cash balance	$1,000,000	750,000	500,000	250,000
Profits	0	0	0	0
Start-up expenses	250,000	250,000	250,000	250,000
Balance	750,000	500,000	250,000	Oops

This table describes a company's burn rate, or how quickly it uses money raised. In the upper left box, we see the start-up has a hefty bank balance of $1,000,000. We can imagine the celebrations, toasting, and high-fives that went around when the funding closed. In the first month, the new company started ordering all those supplies that had been needed but had gone unpurchased for a year or more. In addition, a few extras were ordered—maybe a few plants, some newer desks, better computers. They were expensive, but after years of struggling, the staff deserved them. Over the next several months, the focus was the same: ordering new equipment and finishing development of the product. By April, however, management suddenly realized that they were still several months away from finishing the product, but they were out of cash.

This same scenario played out at many dot.bombs. They spent money as needed to develop their final product, without considering interim products that could have produced sales that might have carried them until the final product was available. Consider what would have happened over the same period if the start-up had released interim products. Table 16.2 describes this scenario.

Table 16.2.
Controlling Cash Flow

	January	February	March	April
Cash balance	$1,000,000	750,000	550,000	450,000
Profits	0	50,000	150,000	200,000
Start-up expenses	250,000	250,000	250,000	250,000
Balance	750,000	550,000	450,000	400,000

In this simplified model, the company creates sales that start in the second month and continue to build. By the fourth month, the company is almost at a self-sustaining break-even point.

[C] Avoid Debt and Unrelated Investors

By staying focused on sales and profits, you can minimize the need to borrow money or take funds from investors. At the least, debt means you will have to make interest payments. If you don't, the lender can foreclose, putting you out of business. Unrelated investors, such as venture capitalists, will push you to grow quickly and often lose sight of realistic goals. They may be more interested in getting you big than in making you strong.

Here's an example. In 1998, one of the authors moved from California to Kentucky, where he continued to work with start-up companies. Many of his new clients in Kentucky complained about the lack of the cheap and ready financing available in California. While many of his new clients thought of pulling up stakes and moving their headquarters to California, most did not. The ones that did, borrowed heavily or raised a great deal of money. They did not stay focused on sales, and when the debt and equity funding dried up, they had to close their doors. The ones that stayed in Kentucky did not raise a lot of money, stayed focused on product development and sales, and are still in existence.

Consider another dot.bomb with which the authors were involved. This company spent nearly one year trying to raise investor money. During this time, the CEO spent 100% of his time and the CFO spent 50% of his time trying to raise money. Other issues, including product development, did not receive senior management attention. As a result, by the time the money was raised, the company had missed the market, and its product was behind those of new competitors.

[D] Look for Alternative Sources of Funds

If you still need money to grow before sales can carry you, consider alternative sources. First, look back at Table 1.1 in Chapter 1. Do not seek outside money until you are in the development stage. Prior to that time, you should be using your own money or that of FFF (family, friends, and those, inappropriately, called fools). Second, as described in Chapter 7, consider government grants and assistance, equipment leasing, vendor financing, customer prepayments, and strategic partners.

[E] Control Cash Flow

Money is hard to raise, so don't let it out of your hands easily. Manage it carefully and hold on to it with tight fists. Look back at the description following Table 16.1. You do not need plants in your offices. You do not need new furniture. And most importantly, the founder does not need a big draw for a new car to replace the junker she has been driving for 10 years. In the start-ups we have worked with, an almost direct relation exists between expenditures on such items and failure. They indicate that management is not careful with money and may well run out of funds before the firm becomes self-sustaining.

Steve Gerbsman, founder of Internet Recovery Group, in Kentfield, California, operates as a crisis CEO and is often brought in to deal with dot.coms in danger of slipping into dot.bombs. According to Gerbsman, the companies he deals with all have the same symptoms. They lack financial and business controls, and they spend money injudiciously. Most operate with the attitude "life's a party," and they do not show any discipline in managing money. For many of them, he believes, simple business planning could have made the difference between survival and failure.

The importance of controlled cash flow is illustrated in Table 16.3.

Table 16.3.
Controlled Cash Flow

	January	February	March	April
Cash balance	$1,000,000	750,000	550,000	450,000
Profits	0	50,000	150,000	200,000
Start-up expenses	250,000	250,000	250,000	200,000
Balance	750,000	550,000	450,000	450,000

In this scenario, the company achieves breakeven in the fourth month simply by controlling expenses. At this rate, the firm can continue indefinitely, independent of the need to raise more cash from investors or lenders.

[F] Raise Enough to Carry You Through the Next Stage

Table 16.3 underscores another point. Raise enough money to carry you through breakeven. Do not get seduced by small amounts that keep you going on a hand-to-mouth basis. Look for enough to get you though your next product stage. Otherwise, you will spend too much time raising money and not enough on product development, as in the example described above.

Another reason for raising enough money is that if you run out in the middle of a product development stage, the next investors will know you are desperate and in need of their money if you are to finish your product. Their ownership demands will increase accordingly. While the first $1 million to start a product development may have cost you 10% of your company, the next $500,000 to finish the development could cost you 20%.

[G] Build and Hold on to Your Management Team

Your company is based on the people in it. Certainly, the technology is important, but many dot.bombs had great technology. What distinguishes the successful ones from the rest is the quality of managers in all key positions. Good managers, for instance, can take average technology and reposition it into the right technology for the right market. Average managers can mismanage even great technology.

Many dot.bombs failed to recruit managers for its major positions, or, when they did, failed to hold on to them. One reason for this is covered by the next lesson.

[H] Founders Must Let Go

Many companies failed to develop or retain successful management teams because founders were never willing to let go and turn over management functions to others. They treated the company as their child and could not, even when necessary, relinquish its care to outsiders. The threshold at which founders can no longer manage all aspects of a business often comes at $10 million in sales or 100 employees. This is usually too much company for one person to manage. Without delegation and capable managers with authority to address key issues, companies become strangled from lack of or slow decision-making.

§ 16.02 SPECIFIC LESSONS

According to Tolstoy in *Anna Karenina,* happy families are all alike, but every unhappy family is unhappy in its own way. This is not necessarily true with start-ups. Many of them make the same mistakes—some make them over and over. In the previous pages, we described some common themes underlying many start-up failures. In this section, we describe specific financial and legal mistakes.

[A] Financial Fiascoes

The most common financial mistakes made by start-ups, both those that fail and those that succeed, are the following:

[1] Creating Cheap Stock

When selling stock, a company must sell it at fair market value. Any amount below that price is income to the recipient. Consider this example. If the fair market value of stock is $3, but the company offers its new stock at $1, the difference of $2 is income to the buyer: The buyer receives $2 of value without paying for it. This becomes an issue not only for the Internal Revenue Service, but for the Securities Exchange Commission, which looks for cheap stock issued to insiders, such as founders and officers, just before a public offering.

[2] Blowing the Section 83(b) Election

If a purchaser of stock does not immediately receive complete ownership but must wait for a period of time to acquire full, unrestricted ownership, then it has acquired restricted stock. An example is an officer who receives 100 shares as a signing bonus, but the company retains the right to take back the stock if she leaves within one year. Such restricted stock is treated as income when the recipient acquires full ownership (in the above example, at the one-year mark). The income attributable to the employee is the value of the stock on the vesting date. Assume in this example that the value of the stock is $1 on the date of hire but $3 after one year. The employee will pay taxes on $3 of income per share, rather than $1. To reduce the tax consequences, the Internal Revenue Service allows the employee to treat the stock as earned on the date of grant, but she must pay taxes on the value as of that date ($1 in the above example). This is the Section 83(b) election. While it increases the employee's tax burden in the year of the grant, it reduces the overall taxes that the taxpayer would have paid if she paid when vesting occurs.

Of course, over the long term, the tax burden is equal. The difference is that the immediate taxes are lower at a time when there is no market for the stock and the shares cannot be sold to pay for taxes. In this example, the employee exercising the Section 83(b) election must pay taxes on $1; if the stock is later sold at $10, the employee must pay taxes on an additional $9, for a total of $10. The employee not exercising the Section 83(b) election pays taxes on $3 and then on the difference of $7 when the stock is sold for a total of $10. The difference is that the first employee pays $1 in cash out of her pocket, but $9 out of proceeds of the sale. The second employee pays $3 out of her pocket, but $7 out of sale proceeds.

The problem is that the Section 83(b) election must be made within 30 days of receipt of the stock. Many employees do not discuss with their advisors their receipt of stock until the end of the tax year, at which point it is too late.

[3] Selling Securities to Unaccredited Investors

In Chapter 8, we discussed the limitations on selling securities. There we noted that companies can sell shares to an unlimited number of accredited investors, but that federal and state limitations restrict how many investors can be unaccredited investors. (If you read "accredited" as "wealthy" and "unaccredited" as "everyone else" this makes sense. The federal and state securities agencies are more concerned with protecting everyone else; they expect accredited investors to fend for themselves.)

Too many early-stage start-ups, however, raise money from family, friends, and others (FFFs, as described in Chapter 1). They are more concerned with getting the money they need to survive than with the consequences.

The problem occurs when it is time to make a public offering, and the start-up finds that it has already used up its permissible unaccredited investors. This is important since the amount raised from a specific investor is unimportant. For instance, $1,000 accepted from an early unaccredited investor means one less $100,000 investment can be accepted from another investor later on. Even worse, if the company has exceeded its permissible number of unaccredited investors, it must refund the money raised. For a start-up short on cash, this can be a virtual impossibility.

[4] Not Adopting Proper Stock Option Plans

Stock option plans are wonderful creations for increasing employee retention. Under a typical plan, an employee, on joining a company, receives a stock option grant that entitles her to 1,000 shares, for example, with vesting over four years beginning on the first year and quarterly thereafter. This means that, on the first anniversary, the employee is entitled to purchase 250 shares and, each quarter thereafter, she can purchase one-quarter of 250 shares. By the end of four years, she is entitled to purchase all 1,000 shares. The purchase price of the stock option is set as of the day of the grant (for instance, $1) rather than as the value on the date of the exercise on the first year (for instance, $2); or the value by the fourth year (for instance, $5).

Even better, the employee is not required to purchase the stock at the time of vesting; she can wait for up to 10 years to make the purchase. It is hoped that by this time the company will have gone public and that the employee can simultaneously purchase and sell the shares without having to pay anything out of pocket. The employee then pays taxes at the lower capital gains rate on her profits, which are equal to the difference between the purchase and sales prices.

There is strong incentive for employees to remain with their companies until their options have vested and they can exercise them. If they leave before, options that have not vested are lost. To keep employees around, most companies grant annual bonuses in stock options, which restart the four-year cycle.

This scenario presents start-ups with two common problems. First, some companies do not recognize the value of stock option plans as a means of retaining employees, and they consequently suffer high turnover rates. In many cases, they may lack knowledge of the advantages of option plans. In other cases, the firm's founders may be selfish, not wanting to share the wealth. In either case, the consequences are sufficiently adverse that most venture capitalists insist on employee stock option plans before they will invest.

Second, some companies issue stock options to employees under employment agreements without adopting stock option plans that qualify for favorable tax treatment. This means that employees, thinking they had qualified stock options entitling them to capital gain treatment, as described above, find they have nonqualified plans and must pay taxes on ordinary income. This can create significant employee dissatisfaction and defection.

[B] Legal Lapses

Following are the most common legal mistakes made by start-ups, whether failed or successful.

[1] Not Maintaining Proper Records

Most entrepreneurs are fascinated by the future and growth. Most inventors are intrigued by developing technology. Few of them have much interest in legal matters or put much weight on them. The results can be major problems. Each of the authors has had clients come to him to get their corporate records in order, only to find that they have been selling shares that were not authorized. As a result, clients have had to go through formal revocation offers entitling the shareholders to unwind their investments. A few have missed stock market windows for new offerings while waiting for the revocation periods to expire.

Other clients have such disorganized records that it is virtually impossible to identify the investors and what they own. In one case, a founder-client of one of the authors had to form a new company because he could not determine who the shareholders in the old one were.

[2] Employment Mistakes

Under most state laws, employees own anything they develop—even while working during company hours using company equipment for company purposes. The same would apply to outside contractors. An exception to this general rule is employees and outside contractors covered by written agreements under which ownership to the technology is granted to the company. Unfortunately, many start-ups are very busy in their early years and never draft employment or subcontractor agreements. Others do not want to pay legal fees to have them drafted. As a result, they do not own their technology, and they must undertake major negotiations with employees and suppliers to obtain ownership.

Another common problem occurs when companies hire employees subject to noncompete restrictions. For instance, an employee of Company A has an employment agreement that prevents her from working for a competitor, which would include Company B. That employee then assumes a key position in Company B. Assuming the noncompete rules are reasonable under applicable law, Company A can sue to prevent the employee from working for Company B, leaving Company B with a major hole to fill.

On the flip side, many companies forget to put noncompete and confidentiality provisions in their employment contracts. While the noncompete prevents the employee from working for a competitor, the confidentiality provision requires her to keep all information obtained during her employment in confidence and not use it, whether working for a competitor or not. Without such protections, companies lose a chance to limit defections of employees and technology.

A related problem occurs when an employee is hired to work on a key technology and records are not developed to show that she is not using technology brought from her former employer. Often this can be addressed simply by having the employee keep proper records detailing her work. In other cases, the problem cannot be solved, since it will be difficult to show that the employee developed a technology after she started work that was not based on what she had done at her previous employer.

[3] Failing to Register a Name

Many start-ups fail to register their intellectual property. This often starts from the beginning. While most will establish their company and formally register their name in the state of organization, many will not register the name in other states where they expect to do business. For instance, if you decide to establish your company in Delaware (the traditional state for registering businesses other than in the state in which the founders are located) or in Nevada (the current "in" state for registration), but are located in Illinois, then you should also qualify to do business in Illinois. If you are going to be servicing a major customer in New York, you should also qualify there. In addition to state-level registration, many states require city registrations if you will have an office.

Similar, you should select your Internet domain name, and the domain name should match your corporate name. You will not want to spend a significant amount of money registering a particular name in each state, only to find the domain name is not available.

A third name registration that should be coordinated with state and domain name filings is your trade name registration. When selecting a name, make certain that you can register your proposed name with the U.S. Patent and Trademark Office.

Unfortunately, few companies check all three registrations (state, domain, and trade name) before selecting a name. As a result, costly filings must be made at a later date or names on which considerable brand building has been spent must be abandoned.

[4] Failing to Protect Technology

Several common mistakes arise under this category. One of the most frequent is failing to protect intellectual property. We noted that employees and outside contractors should be covered by agreements stating that the company owns the technology. Similarly, access to important technology should not be easily available within the company, but should be restricted. Too many companies leave important documents out where other employees or outsiders can see them. A good example is notes left on chalkboards after meetings.

In addition, as technology is developed, someone within the company should be responsible for checking to see if it can be patented. If it can be, filings should be made. Unfortunately, many companies are hesitant about spending time on patent filings, arguing that they are only 3 to 12 months ahead of the competition and that their best protection is to stay ahead of competitors rather than filing patents on technology that will soon be out of date. This approach ignores one of the key questions asked by investors: "How many patents do you have?" Saying you are ahead of the competition and will stay that way is unlikely to get you money. Saying you have 10 patents is more likely to get you something.

§ 16.03 YOU CAN STILL START A NEW COMPANY WHEN ECONOMIC TIMES ARE SLOW

The worst of times may be the best of times. While most of us assume that businesses are started during times of growth, a majority of the 30 companies in the Dow Jones industrials, for instance, were started during recessions. There are several reasons for this contra-cyclical trend.

When the economy is growing, workers are busy meeting customer demands and do not have as much time to think about their own plans. When the economy slows, people have more time to contemplate their own visions. Due to layoffs, some people have even more time to devote to their own projects. A few (particularly older managers with valuable experience) simply cannot find other jobs and are forced to start their own businesses. For instance, it has been estimated that 25% of mangers over the age of 40 started their own companies in the late 1980s and early 1990s. Even those not laid off begin to worry whether they will be in the next round and start to develop plans.

Additionally, those that decide to start new companies in slow times find qualified people available, due to RIFs (reductions in force). Salaries also tend to be less expensive during these periods, making it easier for start-ups to recruit without busting their budgets. Other items are also cheaper during economic slow-downs. Office space, furniture, and equipment are less expensive, no longer demanding a premium. Some items can even be picked up at fire-sale or bargain prices.

Funding may not be a problem during slow economic times. While many investors hold on to their money during such times, others see it as the best time to make smart investments at low prices. In addition, companies looking for money may encounter less competition from other companies seeking the same money, improving their chances of obtaining financing.

The result of these factors is that start-ups continue to form during slow economic times. This observation was confirmed by a May 2001 article in *Inc.* magazine, in which entrepreneurs were asked, "Is now a good time to start a company?" Even though they were interviewed at the peak of the dot.bomb crisis, the vast majority agreed that it was a good time. Cliff Numark, president and CEO of San Diego Regional Technology Alliance in San Diego, stated it was "an ideal time to start a business." Andrew Zacharakis, who teaches entrepreneurship at Babson College, points out that, although it seems counterintuitive, "I'd start a business now."

Many writers, investors, and business advisors believe that the next wave of companies being founded in today's slow economic times will be stronger and more successful than were those founded in times of cheap and ready money. They argue that many founders will be from dot.bombs and that they will have learned their lessons. According to Vivek Wadhwa, chief executive officer of Relativity Technologies, in Cary, North Carolina, many entrepreneurs are picking themselves up from their failed companies and launching new ones with the benefit of lessons learned.

Additionally, strong indicators show that the U.S. economy is improving. According to a monthly survey by Chicago outplacement firm Challenger, Gray and Christmas, dot.com job cuts fell to just under

3,000 in September 2001. This is the lowest level since July 2000, the month generally considered the start of dot.com job cutting. The peak appears to have been April 2001, when 17,500 jobs were cut.

In summary, the next generation of start-ups can learn from the mistakes of the dot.bombs. And, now is a good time to start showing that the lessons have been learned.

APPENDICES

APPENDIX A • BUSINESS PLAN

Appendix A is an example of a business plan. For confidentiality purposes, names, tables, figures, inserts, and exhibits are not included.

EXECUTIVE SUMMARY

The following summary is qualified in its entirety by the detailed information and projections appearing elsewhere in this Business Plan.

The Company

Overview

ABC, or the Company, was formed in March 1969. ABC's primary business objective is to become a leading system integrator. In the years since the Company was founded, it has been able to establish a distinguished reputation for the quality of its services to a prestigious list of clients in the finance, information systems, and industry sectors. In 1988, ABC was certified as a "Registered System Integrator." In the future, ABC intends to expand both horizontally and vertically through strategic alliances, internal research and development, and acquisitions.

Current Business Activities

ABC's main business activities are:

System Integration. System integration (SI) is a solution providing business which integrates all the other major business activities of the customer. Since 1989, the ratio of system integration turnover in relation to ABC's overall business has been getting larger. In 1991, ABC completed several large-scale system integration contracts. ABC's substantial experience with system integration has enhanced the Company's credibility with existing and potential clients.

System Development. System development concentrating on the design and production of software systems has been a big part of ABC's business.

System development is a more technical oriented business in which the clients have developed their own solutions and look to the developer, such as ABC, to assist with the process of implementation.

Facility Management. In 1974, ABC began providing total facility management services in the area of banking and retail. However, since the early 1980s, ABC has shifted its business to system development and integration. Facility management is a kind of outsourcing business in which the customers use ABC's personnel and hardware facilities for their operations. In most cases, facility management services will be provided following the development of a system for the customer.

Product Development. Product development is a product-based business in which ABC distributes the products it has developed or licensed from other developers. Most of ABC's products were originally made for in-house use and then packaged for sale. These products have included project management systems, cost accounting systems, and quality control systems.

Consulting Services. ABC has growing experience in the area of system consulting, which is a solution-providing business. All application system engineers are in charge of consultations with customers to define their requirements. The consulting business is getting larger as the Company's system integration services expand.

Vending Activities. The Company occasionally supplies computer hardware and associated items, including software products, manufactured by other companies. This portion of ABC's business is relatively small, less than 10%; however, it may increase as the Company continues to become more involved with system integration.

Business Strategy and New Products

ABC's strategic planning for the next few years will be based upon the assumption that legacy software methodology will be a diminishing factor in the market and that the future requirements of the Company's client base will lie with the implementation of prefabricated software into the client's procedures in order to provide them with their own unique business solutions. Since ABC's business is extremely client-oriented, ABC's mission will be to develop and acquire software products which ABC believes will meet the requirements of its customer base and as to which ABC can approach those clients with appropriate solutions.

In order for ABC to execute its strategic plan, it must establish core expertise in both technology and application. The core expertise in the technological area will be pursued not only through internal research and development, but also through the acquisition of suitable strategic products from outside parties which ABC believes can be easily adapted to the requirements of its client base in the market. The Company completed its initial efforts with respect to arrangements with third parties by entering into arrangements with two European companies, DEF and GHI. DEF, which is based in the United Kingdom, is a large-scale system integrator with operations mainly in Europe. It is a large system integrator, and its stock is listed. GHI, established in 1981, developed and distributes a financial product, and its stock is listed.

ABC will be granted the exclusive distribution rights to DEF's software products, which are the two main banking products in DEF's product line. ABC will also be granted the exclusive distribution rights to GHI's innovative product, which is an executive information system based on accounting and procurement.

While the strategic partnerships with DEF and GHI will be important sources of revenue over the next few years, ABC will be continuing to look for other strategic partnering opportunities that will allow it to acquire a larger share in the market. Partnerships of this type will include close cooperation in basic research and development, cross-border joint projects, and licensing arrangements. ABC may either build a relationship with foreign partners through software products, expertise transfer, joint marketing, and new investment or assist established foreign companies in their efforts to localize their products. In addition, ABC hopes to build on its relationship with DEF and move into other market opportunities, such as in the public service and energy areas.

Financing Strategy

ABC anticipates that the execution of its strategic plans relating to the new product rights to be acquired from DEF and GHI will require a capital infusion of approximately $________. ABC hopes to raise the required capital through an equity or debt financing aimed solely or primarily to investors on terms to be negotiated. In order for ABC to be able to achieve its projected results of operations and market the new products on a timely basis, the required financing should be obtained no later than ________.

Selected Historical Financial Information

The following table presents certain selected historical financial information of the Company.

Net Sales
Cost of Sales
Ordinary Income
Extraordinary Loss
Net Income before Taxes

Current Assets
Fixed Assets
Current Liabilities
Long-term Liabilities
Shareholders' Equity
Retained Earnings

Selected Financial Projections

The following table presents certain selected financial projections regarding the Company's future operations. All financial projections contained herein should be read in conjunction with, and is subject to, the detailed assumptions included at "Projected Financial Performance—Pro Forma Financial Information Assumptions."

Net Sales
Cost of Sales
Ordinary Income
Extraordinary Loss
Net Income before Taxes

Current Assets
Fixed Assets
Current Liabilities
Long-term Liabilities
Shareholders' Equity
Retained Earnings

Certain Factors

The information contained in this business plan should be read in light of the various factors set out in "Certain Factors."

Further Information

All the information included herein has been prepared exclusively by ABC and it takes sole responsibility therefor. Further information regarding the Company, its products, and any other matters referred to herein can be obtained from __________, who can be reached at the principal executive offices of ABC at __________.

BUSINESS

ABC, or the Company, was formed in March 1969. ABC's primary business objective is to become a leading system integrator. In the years since the Company was founded, it has been able to establish a distinguished reputation for the quality of its services to a prestigious list of clients in the finance, information systems, and industry sectors. In 1988, ABC was certified as a "Registered System Integrator." In the future, ABC intends to expand both horizontally and vertically through strategic alliances, internal research and development, and acquisitions.

ABC's main business activities are:

System Integration. System integration (SI) is a solution providing business which integrates all the other major business activities of the customer. Since 1989, the ratio of system integration turnover in relation to ABC's overall business has been getting larger. In 1991, ABC completed several large-scale system integration contracts. ABC's substantial experience with system integration has enhanced the Company's credibility with existing and potential clients.

System Development. System development concentrating on the design and production of software systems has been a big part of ABC's business. System development is a more technical oriented business in which the clients have developed their own solutions and look to the developer, such as ABC, to assist with the process of implementation.

Facility Management. In 1974, ABC began providing total facility management services in the area of banking and retail. However, since the early 1980s, ABC has shifted its business to system development and integration. Facility management is a kind of outsourcing business in which the customers use ABC's personnel and hardware facilities for their operations. In most cases, facility management services will be provided following the development of a system for the customer.

Product Development. Product development is a product-based business in which ABC distributes the products it has developed or licensed from other developers. Most of ABC's products were originally made for in-house use and then packaged for sale. These products have included project management systems, cost accounting systems, and quality control systems.

Consulting Services. ABC has growing experience in the area of system consulting, which is a solution-providing business. All application system engineers are in charge of consultations with customers to define their requirements. The consulting business is getting larger as the Company's system integration services expand.

Vending Activities. The Company occasionally supplies computer hardware and associated items, including software products, manufactured by other companies. This portion of ABC's business is relatively small, less than 10%; however, it may increase as the Company continues to become more involved with system integration.

See "ABC's Business Activities" for a detailed description of each of the Company's main business activities.

ABC currently is a privately held company with no special affiliation or relationship with any computer manufacturer. The Company's head office is currently located at __________. ABC also has branch offices in __________ and in __________. The Company currently has two operating subsidiaries: __________, which is wholly owned by ABC, and __________, which is 94%-owned by ABC.

Overview of the Software Market

The story of the software market is linked, in large part, to the economy as a whole. During the many years of economic growth, many enterprises made large investments in their computer technology for their information processing and office automation. These companies considered those investments as assets and utilized them for their corporate expansion. The software industry, including ABC, enjoyed this rapid growth in the market (___% on an annual basis), and a number of large software firms were able to complete an initial public offering. However, the recent economic conditions have not only made it impossible for many firms, such as ABC, to undertake an initial public offering, it has also resulted in several other important changes in the competitive environment.

First, many of ABC's existing and potential clients, particularly in the financial area, became reluctant to make any further investments in computer technology, including development of new software products and applications. Since, historically, ABC derived almost half of its revenues from that sector of the economy, it became quite difficult for ABC and other companies in the software industry to pursue long-term planning and marketing efforts.

Second, along with the market conditions, there came a technological innovation, namely an era of smaller computers. Until the beginning of the 1980s, the software market was focused upon main frame computer applications. Large main framers developed computer systems that could be used in both the business application and process control engineering area, and FORTRAN, ALGOL, and COBOL were the main languages. Since then, however, the market has shifted sharply toward UNIX- and LAN-based processing networks. While until a few years ago there was a heavy mix of these two business environments, it is anticipated that the UNIX/LAN-oriented concept will achieve market dominance by ______.

Finally, it became apparent that software innovation was to play an important factor in the future of the industry. In the past, the software was bespoke-type products, and there were few application package software except operating systems and development tools. Application software had to be customized to the need of the client. However, ABC perceives that the role of computers in businesses has changed significantly in the past few years. Computer systems have long been used for automation and speedup of daily processes. During that period, partial effectiveness has been realized without changing the whole social and corporate structure. Recently, however, the strategic trend has turned to redesigning the total process and structure of the business, a movement which has been accelerated by a new technology wave. ABC anticipates that the role of the computer will be the subject of serious reevaluation and that the software requirements among the business community will change substantially to include products which have the function of global business processing with multilanguage, multicurrency, and network capability and which can be integrated into the client's business procedures in order to provide a solution for the client's specific needs.

The chart above shows the typical structure of the information technology industry. In the early 1970s, a number of firms, including the Company, were heavily involved in facility management services, which exclusively covered data entry, data processing, machine time leasing, and the operation of computers. Since the early 1980s, firms began to shift their main business from facility management to the area of system development due to larger profitability. Recently, the structure of the industry has changed once again to focus on the areas of system integration, which integrates a number of subcontractors into a single team with strong leadership, and outsourcing, which is quite similar to facility management.

The interest in system integration stems from the fact that as the paradigm of the corporate competitive condition shifts to "time base" and "borderless," information technology (IT) will play much more important roles in all industries. For example, the focus at many companies is shifting from hierarchies to teams, from vertical, departmental organizations to horizontal, process-oriented ones. In order to realize the best solution, companies are looking at integrated application solutions which allow for common customer, logistical, and financial information to be shared across the emerging matrix organization.

Structural changes have been accompanied by shifts in the economic environment. As industry enters an increasingly global economy with various close relationships, increasing numbers of companies expect worldwide functionality and product support. Above all, support for multiple languages, currency, local taxes, payment types, localized documentation, and service staff are increasingly expected. There is increasing macroeconomic concern that huge investments in IT have failed to significantly increase "white collar productivity." The recent, significant reductions in middle management personnel at large corporations has further heightened the need for employees to be substantially more productive. Most companies are looking for software which will improve the managerial productivity as well as the ability to process transactions. This has become part of the basis for ABC's future strategic plans.

The software industry is populated with a large number of small- and medium-sized companies, many of them privately held. It is typically a fragmented industry. There are no market leaders with the power to shape industry events, and no firm has a significant market share and can strongly influence the industry outcome. The main reasons the industry has been fragmented are that it has low entry barriers, that production is job shop, and that no firms have been able to develop the skills and resources to command a significant market share. Leadership and competitive advantage in the software industry are generally a function of technological innovation, which occurs when a firm develops or obtains advanced technology or otherwise establishes a de facto standard.

Potential software purchasers have long preferred to develop and maintain a stable and familiar relationship with a single supplier, and clients generally will not change suppliers as frequently as firms might do in the United States and Europe. However, in the area of new prefabricated software, clients may well be willing to evaluate products offered by a new supplier if that supplier has been able to attain credibility with respect to its products and services.

ABC believes that the changing marketing conditions, particularly those which mandate companies to focus on practices which make them more competitive, have created strong investment opportunities in the software industry. In the past, businesses have streamlined processes while implementing new applications. More recently, the focus is shifting toward new strategies of reengineering business processes in line with the reshaped organizations and customer focus, and then selecting the software which best supports the new processes. Deregulation will be a trigger to reshape the social structure in every field, such as banking, retail, medical, manufacturing, and other market sectors, and will lead to the reengineering of the social systems. As the nation becomes even more closely related with other markets, business systems will drastically change toward the end of this century and early next century. ABC believes that computer software will be an important factor in the rapid transformation of the economic infrastructure.

According to industry sources, 54% of the software products sold are made in the United States, 45% of the software products sold are made in Japan, and the remaining 1% of the software products sold are made in Europe. Most of the United States–made software products are operation system (i.e., MS-DOS, Windows, UNIX) and language software (COBOL, C). Most Japanese-made products are Japanese word processing software and the application system specified to the domestic business process. Oracle, with 41%, was the leading UNIX-based database firm in 1993, although Informix, Unify, and Sybase also enjoyed significant shares of the market.

Estimates of the future growth of the software market have been tempered by recent economic events. In 1992, a survey and analysis forecast that the annual market growth rate for the software development market, including system integration, would be ___% for the period from 1990 to 2001, a rate which was similar to that experienced in the previous decade. However, in light of the economic conditions which have prevailed since 1992, the estimated rate of growth has been decreased substantially, and ABC is now projecting that the software development market will grow at a rate of between 5% and 10% over the remainder of the decade. It can be expected that the government will attempt to stimulate the entire economy, as well as certain industry sectors, through the use of various monetary and fiscal measures, as well as through large-scale public projects in the computer technology area.

ABC has chosen to base its estimates regarding its own future growth rate on conservative macroeconomic growth and its own historical experiences. During the period from 1982 to 1992, ABC's own annual growth rate was approximately ___%. ABC does not believe that inflation will be a serious factor over the next few years and, in fact, anticipates that salaries, rents and commodity prices will either remain flat or decrease over that period. Also, some deregulation policies will be useful in the reduction of the general pricing level. See "Projected Financial Performance—Pro Forma Financial Information Assumptions."

Historical Development of the Company

ABC was formed in 1969. Since that time through 1992, ABC has kept a steady growth in its turnover, income, and the number of employees. During the ten-year period from 1982 to 1992, its turnover grew from $_____ million to $_____ million, its net income from $_____ million to $_____ million, and its employees from _____ to _____. Unfortunately, in the last two years, ABC has had a difficult experience under the serious situation of the economic environment. However, as noted below, ABC has devised a new strategic plan which it believes will lead to increased profitability and faster growth over the rest of the decade. See "ABC's Strategic Business Plan."

Major events in the Company's history are as follows:

[Insert Description]

ABC's Strategic Business Plan

ABC has traditionally pursued a job shop–style production strategy which has largely focused upon the creation of special varieties of software application products which could be sold to clients at premium prices. However, ABC also pursued strategies of cost leadership and standardization by modularizing products and composing them into final products. Low cost position has given ABC a defense against rivalry from competitors and high margins which can be reinvested in new technologies and facilities. Cost leadership has required pursuit of cost reductions from experience, tight cost, and overhead control.

While some large system integrators may be able to attain relatively large market shares in the software industry, ABC believes that the historically fragmented structure of the industry will not change so dramatically in the future. While ABC will continue to follow its strategies of cost leadership and standardization, its primary strategic focus in the future will now emphasize specialization by product segment and customer type, as well as research and development and other acquisition of products which have advanced technological capabilities. ABC anticipates that a strategy of "technology advantage" will allow it to meet the changing needs of the business market, which will be involved in the process of "Business Process Reengineering" and "Deregulation."

ABC's changing business strategy will also entail changes with regard to its relationships with outside parties. In those cases where a project consisted primarily of system development and facility management, the Company did not require any outside suppliers of software or hardware products. The only significant requirement in order to complete those projects was the internal programming manpower. However, in order for the Company to be able to pursue its objectives in the system integration area, it will be necessary for it to acquire access to a variety of new suppliers and distributors. As described in the chart below, in any given system integration project, ABC, which will serve as the prime contractor, will coordinate all the various suppliers of hardware, software, network, and information and will provide the new products to clients through any possible distribution networks.

Outsourcing, which is another important trend in the software industry, requires a large investment in facilities, including computer hardware, land, buildings, and software. The level of investment required differentiates the outsourcing process from the facility management projects which ABC and others undertook in the 1970s. ABC remains interested in becoming involved in the outsourcing area, given its skills and experience with facility management; however, it is unlikely that ABC will make the investment required to enter that area in a significant fashion until the end of the decade.

ABC's strategic planning for the next few years will be based upon the assumption that legacy software methodology will be a diminishing factor and that the future requirements of the Company's client base will lie with the implementation of prefabricated software into the client's procedures in order to provide them with their own unique business solutions. Since ABC's business is extremely client-oriented, ABC's mission will be to develop and acquire software products that will meet the requirements of its customer base.

In order for ABC to executive its strategic plan, it must establish core expertise in both technology and application. The core expertise in the technological area will be pursued not only through internal research and development, but also through the acquisition of suitable strategic products from outside parties which ABC believes can be easily adapted to the requirements of its client base in the market. In accordance with this aspect of its strategic plan, ABC has been involved in a search for strategic partners since the summer of 1993. While ABC was looking for partners that would provide the Company with strong support and technical assistance, ABC was also looking for one or more products which could be adapted and released to the market on a timely basis. Without limiting to the local market, ABC made a broad search for complimentary firms in Europe. Recently, the Company completed its initial efforts by entering into arrangements with two European companies, DEF and GHI. See "New Products."

DEF, which is based in the United Kingdom, is a large-scale system integrator with operations mainly in Europe. It is one of the largest system integrators in the world, and its stock is listed. DEF has about ____ employees and its annual turnover and income after taxes and dividends for the year ended 1993 were $_____ million and $_____ million, respectively. Three-quarters of the turnover was from system integration activities and the remainder was from facility management and product development. See Exhibit A for further information regarding DEF, its products, and its technology.

DEF-Asia is owned by DEF and is in charge of distributing DEF's banking network products in the Asian market. DEF-Asia, which has about ____ employees, is headquartered in Singapore and also has offices in Malaysia and other countries in Southeast Asia. ABC is planning to start the business with DEF-Asia's Singapore office for the exclusive local distribution of the financial products and for joint R&D. In the future, ABC will expand the partnership with DEF's headquarters in Europe.

GHI, established in 1981, developed and distributes a financial product called GHI Product. GHI sales began in 1983, sales of an integrated version of GHI Product commenced in 1984, and GHI released GHI Product in 1993 for open platform. GHI Product is designed for reengineering of the enterprise, not only for the accounting. Its sales record is over _____. GHI stock has been listed. As of January 1993, GHI had ____ employees. GHI's annual turnover in 1992 was $_____ million, and its income before taxes in that year was $_____ million.

In 1989, GHI entered into a joint marketing agreement with U.S. Co., which was followed by a capital alliance in 1990. In 1994, GHI entered into a distribution agreement with U.S. Co. for the distribution of GHI Product in that market. GHI's turnover can be divided as follows: products (28%), maintenance (28%), and training, technical support, and consultancy (44%). As to markets, the turnover can be divided as follows: manufacturing (34%), public services (17%), finance (21%), service (13%), and wholesale and retail (15%). See Exhibit B for further information regarding GHI, its products, and its technology. See Exhibit C for further information regarding U.S. Co.

ABC will be the exclusive local distributor of GHI Product and also will be participating in the development and distribution of the product throughout the total Asian market. It is anticipated that ABC and GHI will be heavily involved in the exchange of the technical information required for adaptation of GHI's products, and the cooperation between the parties has already begun.

While the strategic partnerships with DEF and GHI will be important sources of revenue over the next few years, ABC will be continuing to look for other strategic partnering opportunities that will allow it to acquire a larger share in the market. Partnerships of this type will include close cooperation in basic research and development, cross-border joint projects, and licensing arrangements. ABC may either build a relationship with foreign partners through software products, expertise transfer, joint marketing, and new investment or assist established foreign companies in their efforts to localize their products.

In addition, ABC hopes to build on its relationship with DEF and move into other market opportunities. For example, it is believed that there may be significant opportunities for new development efforts in the public service and energy areas. ABC has several excellent clients in these fields. They are operating well even in the current situation because they are practically government-owned companies. Although they have a big demand for the computer systems, ABC is rather weak in the fields of material logistics and power station systems. ABC will ultimately be requesting that DEF transfer its technical expertise in these areas to the Company. In the public sector, ABC has started the consulting services for a large-scale document management system for a government organization with database facilities. This project is called ABC Program, which is focused on the next generation specialties. In this project, ABC considers DEF Product, which is DEF's product, as a document analyzer. ABC expects a good synergy with DEF on this project.

Although much of ABC's future business strategy is based upon entry into new areas with different types of products, it does not believe there should be a strict separation between the "old" and "new" businesses. ABC prefers to emphasize that its strategic plan focuses upon using its substantial expertise and experience to assist customers in finding new solutions for their existing business problems. Accordingly, ABC's ultimate goals have not changed, but rather they have moved to different levels of functionality. However, all of ABC's experience in the past will serve as a solid base for the future product and process changes and innovation at the Company.

ABC's Business Activities

ABC's business activities can be characterized as system integration, system development, facility management, product development, consulting services, and vending activities. These business activities have generally developed independently without being associated with each other, primarily since the Company has not heretofore been that active in providing its customers with total-solution services. However, in recent years, the Company has become more involved in system integration activities, which call upon it to provide total solutions. As such, these activities have become more closely aligned.

System Integration

System integration (SI) is the ultimate goal of ABC's business. SI encompasses all other business activities of ABC and makes full utilization of its historical assets. Basically, the SI process starts with consulting services, followed by software development with software/hardware products vending, and sometimes is followed by facility management services. Several typical SI projects which the Company has been involved with are described below.

Securities Co. In 1990, ABC completed a system integration project for Securities Co., which enables end investors to trade many financial products from their own terminal computers in their home. The requirement by Securities was designing the total system covering hardware selection, network consultancy, user interface design, test data, and programming. Using a mainframe computer, ABC chose terminals as the end-users interface through telephone network. Just after completion of the version, new terminal machines specially designed for Securities were developed by another company. The duration of the project was over one year and the required man-months labor cost was 300.

Shipping Company. In 1991, ABC got a SI contract from Shipping Company. The major function of the target system was financial control for office automation. Their requirements were to implement the total management system for all processes with an online network between the head office and all branch offices. The jobs of ABC were technical consulting, definition of system requirements, program design and writing, hardware selection, and system maintenance. The total contracted amount was $_____ million for system implementation and $_____ million per year for system maintenance. The duration of the project was over two years and the required man-months labor cost was 900.

Banking. Another big SI order in 1991 was from Banking Ltd, which is one of ABC's oldest clients. The major requirement was complete conversion of the "investment trust" system from the conventional batch operation to an online real-time type of system. The jobs of ABC were technical consultation, definition of system requirement, program design and writing, hardware selection, and system maintenance. The total contracted amount was $_____ for system implementation. The duration of the project was over two years and 6 months and the required man-months labor cost was 1,100.

Manufacturer. One of the more recent cases of a big SI order was in 1992 from Manufacturer. This project involved total integration of Manufacturer's financial accounting system. Manufacturer's requirement was online operated accounting processes which enabled them to communicate between the head office and all branches through EDI, to summarize the consolidated charts, to generate flexible reports to the government, and to use all data for management forecasting. These functions are exactly what one of the Company's new products can realize. See "New Products." The jobs of ABC included technical consultation, definition of system requirement, program design and writing, hardware selection, and system maintenance. The total contracted amount was $_____ million for system implementation and the duration of the project was over one year and 7 months. The required man-months labor cost was 1,100.

ABC's prior experiences with SI are relevant to its ability to exploit its proposed new products, since both emphasize solution-oriented activities. The new projects with the licensed products will be much more oriented to business consulting rather than to information technology. The licensed products can facilitate ABC's consulting services. Once the consulting phase is completed, all subsequent system implementation work will be done by ABC's experienced system engineers.

System Development

System development is defined as all phases of requirement classification, software design, programming, testing, and software maintenance, with the specific requirements of the client determining the scope of the project. There are some differences in the process between mainframe computers and smaller computers such as UNIX workstations and PCs; however, the basic processes are generally identical. The licensed products can skip some phases or reduce the labor-oriented portions of the work. ABC has traditionally acted as a software factory creating software on a custom basis particularly for banks, insurance companies, and retailers.

ABC has system development experience in areas such as:

[Insert Description]

Projects involving information systems pertain to all computer-based information technology which allows a firm to utilize data quickly and efficiently. Management systems and accounting systems are both application-oriented concepts, with accounting systems being more functionally specified. Projects relating to management systems include accounting, logistics, production, financial, and all other management functional systems. Network systems are technological design projects in which more than one computer device at separate locations are connected together through wire. Information and network systems projects are designed to enhance the speed and accuracy of the transaction process, regardless of the size of the system, and clients also seek security, capacity, and expandability. As to management and accounting systems, application viewpoint, user interface, and flexibility are the first priorities for clients.

Some of ABC's current system development projects are as follows:

[Insert Description]

ABC's system development expertise can be categorized as UNIX-based and mainframe projects. In the mainframe system development, the best solutions sometimes are given by computer manufacturers because all the peripherals should be their own brands. On the other hand, because a UNIX system has an open environment, which means that the system is not dependent upon a particular brand, the end users can choose the best combination of server computers, network, databases, and peripherals, as well as the third-party software required to provide them with the best solution. For UNIX systems, a wide variety of software development tools have been prepared and they allow for higher productivity in system development.

ABC's experience and skills with respect to system development will be very useful in exploiting the capabilities of the new products. In the system development phases of the new SI projects, the licensed products will be quite advantageous due to the excellent technical functionality, thereby increasing the rate of productivity of the development phase by as much as 70% over conventional methods. In addition, the sophisticated base of technology available with the new products will assist ABC in training its younger engineers, which will have the effect of producing even greater productivity in the future.

UNIX-Based System Development Projects

ABC has completed a variety of system development projects with UNIX-based systems. There are some unique aspects of UNIX-based systems that are worth noting. The first feature of a UNIX system is that it supports network computing for the purpose of distributing the workloads of each application. Integrated multiple UNIX systems can obtain better cost-performance in their application systems than those on mainframe computers. The second feature of a UNIX system is that it has the functionality to provide excellent man–machine interfaces. The most intensive requirement for UNIX system development will be a wider range of knowledge in network and various kinds of other systems.

Decision Support Systems (Movie Film Production Firm). The system collects all real-time information about the title of film, number of audience, and revenue, and it reports the summary to the management. The management uses the data for analysis of cost performance in public relations, profit and loss for each product, and so on. They are going to make quicker and more realistic budgets and projections and are constructing an overall network which covers the whole country with a client-server model on the platform of UNIX workstations. They are targeting the paperless office automation and online data entry through connecting with their existing accounting system on their mainframe computer.

Asset and Liability Management System (Pension Fund). Due to the decrease of the domestic interest rate, the total yield for pension funds has been reduced. This trend has led to the new entry of trust banks and investment advisory firms into the pension fund market, which was historically dominated by life insurance firms. In order to maintain their positions, insurance companies are planning to construct excellent simulation systems for more effective investment methods. With all data simulated on the UNIX workstations with the client-server model, PCs, client machines, will display the result. This project will be performed together with the client and ABC by the methodology of "scrap and build" using some prototype.

Bond Dealing Support System. With the trend to deregulation in the finance field, Treasury Bonds were listed. In this opportunity, ABC developed a bond dealing support system with 50 workstations on their network for a leading commercial bank. Through the online connection, the system acquires real-time trading information and simultaneously displays the chart graphically on the workstations for quicker analysis.

After completion of the first phase, the client was interested in developing a similar system for use in the areas of foreign exchange and commodity dealing. ABC expanded the information source to Reuters and Telerate and replaced all workstations in order to increase the number of the devices. In addition to the increase, ABC enhanced the function of the displays to realize multiwindows. Several additional functions have been added to the system for paperless routines and risk management. The client is now integrating all products and functions into the total system covering the foreign exchange and money market control. With the expected deregulation of entry into the securities business, the client is preparing the system for its subsidiaries.

Expert System for Stock Positioning. Trust banks have a profit center that invests the funds in a variety of stocks. Their problem is that the yields are heavily dependent on the ability of individual analysts and traders. The goal in this project is to summarize the experiences of excellent performers in order to construct a quantitative knowledge base. It will be very difficult to develop this expert system, since it must take into account knowledge, environment, individuals' inspiration, and so on. ABC anticipates many trials and errors by the "scrap and build" method and discussions with the end users. The target machine is workstations.

Mainframe Computer Projects

ABC's most conventional type of project is the implementation of the business application system with mainframe computers. For example, with Gas Co., ABC designed their accounting systems and implemented them. The main function was purchase order processing for procurement and raw material forecasting. ABC kept in touch with the client through a maintenance agreement for upgrading the existing system and for better design of future technology. ABC's team consisted of one system designer, three application system engineers, and five to ten programmers.

A list of some of the mainframe computer projects undertaken by ABC in the finance area in the past is as follows:

[Insert Description]

A list of some of the mainframe computer projects undertaken by ABC in the process control area in the past is as follows:

[Insert Description]

While there certainly is a strong movement toward UNIX-based systems, there are still many mainframe applications that are difficult to offload. These applications typically have large I/O and transaction processing requirements. Airline reservation and banking systems, for example, must be able to handle huge numbers of concurrent transactions applied to a single and complex database. The mainframe remains the logical place to centralize access to information, because it's specifically designed to do so. Mainframes have been the only platform to support the number of disk devices required for large database applications. Traditional mainframe systems continue to be the platform of choice for these systems.

Facility Management

Facility management is a kind of outsourcing business in which the clients use ABC's staff and hardware facilities for all of their operations. It would be ideal if ABC could have an computer operation building for all services to clients; however, the investment required in order to build such a facility is too large for the Company to undertake in the near future. In usual cases, facility management services follow the phase of system development. There are some cases where clients have no computer operators or technicians, and they depend on ABC for everything. ABC believes that this presents a good opportunity, since during the facility management process ABC stands very close to the clients and has opportunities for getting further orders from them.

Although, for the time being, facility management is a relatively minor business of ABC, the Company has been involved in a couple of projects in this area. For example, for a chain restaurant group, ABC covers all phases of information technology services from system design to operational management. The first phase was system design followed by software development and programming. With ABC's expertise in the field of merchandise control and managerial accounting, ABC implemented a total management information system on personal computers. All management information is transferred to the PC located in ABC's technical site by file transfer. ABC's operators analyze the data and produce management reports. In addition to facility management, ABC has a contract of software maintenance services with them for system upgrading.

In addition, ABC is currently engaged in a project for a book distributor. After completing all system development phases, ABC received a facility management contract covering the collection of all book circulation data and customer information, uploading them to databases, printing management summaries, and producing mailing labels for direct marketing. The computer facilities for the work were originally located at the Company's facilities, but have now been transferred to a subsidiary of ABC. See "Human Resources and Organizational Structure."

Another example of a facility management engagement is a contract for Group, which runs facilities for wedding ceremonies and receptions. The client wished to control the schedule, staff assignment and costs, product sales, and entertainment management. All data was stored in the mainframe computer located in ABC's head office through VAN network. After six years of operation, the client renewed all of its system on smaller computers and educated its own staff. Today, ABC does not have facility management activity with Group.

Product Development

Since ABC's main focus has historically been in the area of developing bespoke software, the Company has not had a formal strategic plan for the development of its own software products. However, ABC has had experience with product development in relation to its internal project management systems. As described below in "Research and Development," the Company has previously designed and implemented an excellent project management and cost-control system only for internal use. Cost leadership was the only key factor in the labor-intensive style of ABC's historical business, and ABC's competitors often adopted the same strategy. As such, they were very interested in ABC's internal management system and requested that ABC sell the system to them. Since it seemed very risky for ABC to sell its system to its competitors, it was decided that the Company would sell only an old version of the product to them. The Company sold ten sets of the system and is not aware that the sales have resulted in any adverse effect on ABC's competitive position in the industry.

In the future, ABC does not expect to engage extensively in product development activities. Instead, it will concentrate on acquiring new products from third parties through the licensing and strategic partnering strategies described elsewhere, such as the acquisition of the rights to distribute certain products from DEF and GHI.

Consulting Services

Consulting for computer-based systems is very important to developing sales. Once the consultancy services are successfully completed, new orders of system development or system integration always follow. The latest example is a project for the Information Center of Science and Technology (ICST), which is an affiliate institute of the government. A chief consultant with senior engineers in ABC worked over two years for ICST in the investigation of market, database and network designing, scheduling, and projections. ICST's demand is the implementation of an intellectual database of science and technology and the interface with the Internet. With a long experience in database design and quick study of the Internet, ABC made a successful presentation and acquired a big order for implementation work of software development. The Company believes that consulting services will be a critical factor for ABC's future business, since the availability of consulting services is a key factor in the completion of system integration projects.

Vending Activities

The Company occasionally supplies computer hardware and associated items, including software products, manufactured by other companies. This portion of ABC's business is relatively small, less than 10%. It might be possible that ABC will become a distributor of hardware in the future if it enters into a strategic partnership with hardware manufacturers and vendors as part of the expansion of its systems integration activities; however, ABC has no definite plans in that area as of this time.

New Products

GHI Product

GHI Product, which was developed by GHI and will be licensed to the Company on the terms described below, is an executive information system based on accounting and procurement. GHI Product can be used for reengineering of the business process and the Company anticipates that it can be successfully marketed to medium- or large-sized enterprises (especially manufacturers and retailers). The General Ledger is the core module for GHI Product and has various other products and applications, including Sales Ledger, Purchase Ledger, Fixed Assets Management, Inventory Control, Purchase Order Control, and Project Management. The products can be combined in accordance with the specific requirements of each customer.

The key technical elements of GHI Product are T and what is referred to as M technology. T is an automatic program generator for business application software. Business application software generally requires at least 700 lines of source code. In addition to writing the source code, a good deal of work is required for "debugging," which means changing logical errors or mistyped codes. In the case of conventional software development, most of the program logic for business applications is covered by several general module structures, such as data inquiry, data editing, and sorting and merging. T prepares about 20 types of skeleton programs and many functional modules. The best combination of skeleton programs and modules will easily generate the target business application programs. Accordingly, T dynamically reduces the volume of work associated with the development process. New processes can easily be produced as new program modules, which are listed in a repository and used for generating other application programs. In summary, the Company believes that T will give it over 70% higher productivity in programming and wider applicability to new business areas.

The basic concept of M technology is the separation of the application programs from the user's technology platforms. M is a software layer which sits between the application modules (such as General Ledger and Purchase Ledger) and the user's specific combination of hardware, relational database, and operating system. M differs from the software structure in the previous generation of technology, which was typically seen in mainframe computers, in that it allows the applications to adopt the characteristics of any of the desktop metaphors which are currently employed. The Company believes that M will allow GHI Product to be the truly open product that is necessary for use in the emerging environment of open systems. See Exhibits B and D for further information regarding GHI, its products, and its technology.

Acquisition of the rights to use the GHI Product technology was important to ABC for a variety of reasons, such as the following:

- In the market, there has never been an integrated software package like GHI Product. To date, all users have produced their internal system using a step-by-step approach by patchwork and have had an interface problem among all functions. Integrated software has long been in demand in order to provide a solution to these problems.
- ABC has over 20 years of experience in many business areas, such as finance and factory automation. It believes that GHI Product will allow the Company to move quickly into new business areas and that the core application software will expand its opportunities with existing and new clients.
- Acquisition of GHI Product allows the Company to make the best use of its current technicians. T and M technology are generally written in COBOL, which is the language that is most familiar to the largest group of ABC technicians.
- Since T and M technology are the leading tools for software development, their acquisition will allow the Company to pursue its strategic plan of reducing the labor costs associated with development.
- GHI Product–UNIX version runs on the databases of Oracle, Sybase, Ingres, and Informix. Collectively, these databases hold approximately 80% of the total market of UNIX databases.

GHI has had more than 120 installations of GHI Product, mainly in Europe. GHI Product has been licensed to U.S. Co., which develops and markets accounting applications software. See Exhibit C for further information regarding U.S. Co. The decision to license GHI Product to the Company is part of GHI's own global strategic plan and indicates the confidence that GHI has in ABC's ability to assist it in recovering the costs of financial and technical investment which GHI has made in the new product. Two examples of the application of GHI Product are as follows:

University. Previously, the University's accounting and information systems were run by the city council. In order to achieve true independent corporate status, they began a partnership with GHI. The University looked for four modules: General Ledger, Purchase Ledger, Purchase Order Processing, and Commitment Accounting. Sales Ledger was also considered as a future requirement. According to the staff at the University, competing products were developed based on old technology and lacked the required real-time integration. GHI demonstrated a clear technological vision that would enable the University to make a long-term commitment to its GHI product.

The University's chosen environment for the new system is IBM's UNIX-based RISC System/6000 machine which uses Oracle's relational database and is accessed across a network based on the University's corporate-wide Windows strategy. The planned live date for the General Ledger, Purchase Ledger, and Sales Ledger modules is ____, with Commitment Accounting and Purchase Order Processing implementations to be completed by autumn ____. GHI's multidimensional reporting module will be used to meet the enhanced information needs being generated across the campus.

Inter-Airline Settlement. In adverse trading conditions, sound business practices provide a bulkhead against the pressures of escalating costs and reduced cash flow. The airline industry has suffered but survived in recent years by rigorously adhering to corporate financial strategy, which is the cornerstone of sound business practice. As a result, and against a background of ever fiercer competition and higher operational costs, airlines have maintained standards of performance which are the envy of many other businesses. However, even the most efficient business has room for improvement. A prime objective of any company under pressure is to achieve and maintain healthy cash flow, and for airlines a critical component of the cash flow equation is inter-airline settlement.

Inter-airline settlement is a task which makes formidable demands on accounting staff time, with disproportionate results in terms of revenue, especially where large volumes of traffic are involved. Transaction information for each customer or creditor airline must be recorded and stored against eventual documentation, including business categories (i.e., passenger or cargo), currency type, currency rate, and currency zone.

GHI Product has developed an industry specialized functional product like Inter-Airline Settlement, which is a specialty in airline companies. Inter-Airline Settlement (IAS) is a comprehensive system that allows airlines to handle inter-airline billing and settlement of both IATA (International Air Transport Association) Clearing House and Bilateral accounts. Integrated with Accounts Receivable and Credit Management System, GHI Product provides total debt and cash management solutions for airlines keen to maximize cash flow and achieve fast reconciliation of inter-airline accounts.

The system, which was jointly developed by GHI with Airways, has been closely scrutinized and acknowledged by IATA as meeting its needs for inter-airline transactions. Close cooperation allowed GHI to analyze the critical operating procedures and regulations with which airlines are organized and governed in this difficult area of operation. GHI Product has a market for airline companies such as _______ and some other airline firms.

License Terms

The Company expects to enter into a definitive license agreement with GHI in ______ with respect to distribution of GHI Product by the Company. ABC will be granted exclusive rights to sell and support GHI Product, across all developed platforms. In addition, subject to the terms of any other agreements GHI has or may have, ABC will have the right to supply GHI Product, on a nonexclusive basis, to customers in other countries.

ABC will, upon execution of the license agreement, pay GHI $______ in cash on deferred terms to be agreed upon and will also provide GHI an equity stake in ABC equal in value to $______, with the actual amount of shares to be determined on the basis of the valuation of ABC made by its outside investors in the proposed financing. In addition, ABC will pay royalties to GHI equal to 45% of the software license revenues obtained by ABC with respect to GHI Product and 50% of the maintenance revenues obtained by ABC with respect to GHI Product. Exact payment terms are to be negotiated by the parties.

ABC will agree to pay GHI minimum annual royalties during the term of the agreement. In ABC's fiscal year ending March 31, _____, the minimum annual royalty payment amount will be $______. In ABC's fiscal year ending March 31, _____, the minimum annual royalty payment amount will be $______ . For all of ABC's fiscal years ending after March 31, _____, the minimum annual royalty payment amount will be $______ increased by an appropriate index of price increases applicable to the industry. If ABC fails to achieve the minimum royalty figure in any year and pays GHI the difference between the figure which was actually achieved and the target figure, then in the following year the target figure for that year will be reduced to the actual figure achieved in the previous year plus the increase in the index.

ABC will agree to pay for the language translation of GHI Product (software plus documentation and help test), which is expected to cost about $______. Also, the parties will agree to cooperate in the rewriting of P to make it applicable to the market. It is anticipated that this process will take about 1,200 man-days, with GHI contributing 1,000 man-days and ABC 200 man-days, and the estimated time for completion of the process is 12 months. ABC's involvement will be largely in testing the finished product so that ABC staff can gain training in the technology and use of GHI Product.

GHI will provide start-up support to ABC up to March 31, _____, as follows: (1) 100 man-days free of charge except for expenses, (2) a further 100 man-days at $_______/man-day plus expenses, and (3) further requirements at $_______/man-day plus expenses.

The license will continue for as long as ABC is committed to the project and as long as the minimum royalty payment obligations to GHI are satisfied.

Market Size

The Company estimates that the total market size for GHI Product will be approximately _____ companies for which the estimated total sales amount will be $_______. See "Projected Financial Performance—Pro Forma Financial Information Assumptions." Within this general market, ABC anticipates that the largest initial interest in GHI Product will be in the manufacturing sector. For example, ABC contacted a cosmetics firm that has its production and logistics center in Asia. This company has an urgent need for a core accounting system with the function of multilanguage, multicurrency, and network solution. They are very interested in GHI Product and are waiting for the ABC version.

The Company has also had discussions with a chemical firm which wants to establish a UNIX technology as a core platform and is interested in T. Other companies have indicated to ABC that they are looking for an integrated software which covers a wide variety of basic business functions, such as accounting, logistics, marketing, and manufacturing. In most cases, these companies, due to currency appreciation and rising labor costs, will be shifting their production centers to Asian countries, thereby creating an important requirement for flexible computer network systems of the type which can be serviced by GHI Product.

The Company projects that the average revenue from a single system will be approximately $_______, 50% of which will come from the product and the remaining 50% from the software development and customization work. Development costs for a single system are assumed to be approximately $______, and royalties to GHI will be 45% of the product revenue. The Company estimates that development and customization of the GHI Product system will require approximately six months for each project. ABC forecasts the number of installations for GHI Product as follows:

Year 1	__
Year 2	__
Year 3	__
Year 4	__
Year 5	__
Total	__

GHI has accepted these figures as a sensible and achievable basis for determining minimum royalty obligations under the licensing agreement. See "Projected Financial Performance—Pro Forma Financial Information Assumptions."

Marketing Activities

The marketing strategy for GHI Product will be the following three ways:

1. Development of the customized application (T will greatly reduce the manpower).
2. Provide T to the clients who are demanding base technology and dominate their application plan (T is a kind of a case tool).
3. Charge the maintenance fee and keep communication with the clients.

ABC began making presentations to potential clients for GHI Product in October _____ and expects to make between 20 and 30 presentations to its existing and potential clients before the end of the year. The Company already has a prospective client that wishes to order GHI Product, and ABC anticipates that this initial project will begin in April _____.

DEF Products

Cost and Pack are the two main banking products in DEF's product line and supply two of the areas of functionality needed by banks in managing their businesses. DEF believes that banking software can be divided into three main areas of functionality, namely back office systems, wholesale banking systems, and retail banking systems. Cost, which is an ATM-POS ("Point of Sale") switching system, satisfies the needs of the banks with respect to their retail operations, and Pack is used in the wholesale area. However, DEF has gone beyond the narrow confines of an individual software product to develop a "Customer Product Management System" called Page, which is designed to provide the banks with an integrated approach to serving their customers' needs.

The basic concept of Page, which is not a packaged product itself, is that three databases must be created in order to administer bank operations, namely a product database, a customer database, and a bank organization structure database. Each of the individual functional operations within a bank must be integrated with, and interact with, these three databases in order to permit a bank to quickly bring new products and services to its customers. DEF has been able to deal with 1,000 separate computerized banking processes and integrate these into a Page framework for one of their principal banking customers. The Page concept has been recently sold to an Asian customer, as DEF has won a $_____ million contract to reorganize the customer's systems by scrapping all of its existing IT systems and replacing them with a large IBM software package.

DEF and ABC both believe that banks will find this approach to be quite appealing. Banks already have made substantial investments in particular functional software programs. In some cases, the banks will wish to keep these functions unchanged, and in other cases the banks may wish to buy new packages. However, above the functional levels, the banks will probably wish to have higher-level integration available through Page. DEF and ABC also think that there is much more potential for ABC in adopting an approach similar to Page because replacing a bespoke system at a bank customer with a standard product will only add a small amount of value to the customer and will be only worth a relatively small amount of revenue and profit to ABC whereas persuading one of the banks to adopt a higher level of integration like Page could generate substantial income for ABC. Both companies have a higher level of interest in system integration of this kind than in discrete product sales.

Pack

Pack is an application software program covering the function of credit card management. Pack is recognized as the leading integrated card management system in the world, with over ___ installations worldwide processing transactions on more than ___ million cards. Pack comprises five modules: Cardholder and Merchant Processing, On-line Collections, On-line Authorizations, Memo Tickler System, and Acquisition and Scoring System. These modules can operate in a stand-alone manner or can combine to provide a full management system. Pack can be implemented on-site or in a service bureau. A full description of the Pack management system and each of aforementioned modules appears in Exhibit A.

While, as described below, Cost will have a number of immediate applications in the market, Pack must be enhanced before it can be released to banks and credit card firms. While Pack covers all the basic processes of credit card management, all of the major banks and credit card companies already have their own capabilities in this area. However, ABC believes that banks and credit card companies would be interested in a new and enhanced version of the product which can be used for strategic purposes, in addition to financial settlement. Such a product would include the ability to create a customer database, an interface to the customers' management information systems, smart card possibilities, and a multimedia base. DEF has already begun to enhance the product in other areas to provide smart card functions, and ABC will join the development process in order to introduce a new version of Pack into the financial sector. Also, while Pack will have a limited market in the banking area, ABC believes that it will be accepted by many retailers who are about to enter the credit card business.

Cost

Cost is a nonstop network switching system with the function of authorization. Cost has high reliability and can be used for various communications protocols, including front-end switching between any ATMs, POS terminals and CATs (Credit Authorization Terminals), and banking systems. Cost currently focuses on communications with Visa and Mastercard but will also be applicable to multiple protocol handling. Cost components are structured with functionally separated modules, such as communication, terminal controls (for ATM and POS), and business process applications. Each module consists of more fragmented parts, and replacement of the parts will easily generate a new functional module. In this way, Cost can be applied to various kinds of communication protocols and terminal devices. It can also be easily expanded with additional parts. With regard to the message protocol, Cost uses the international standard (ISO8583) for intermodule interfaces and is to be distributed as a worldwide message interface product.

Acquisition of the rights to use the Cost technology was important to ABC for a variety of reasons, such as the following:

- Cost has a high capability for interfacing with other application software because all application processes are modularized in it. Cost will be applicable to all computer systems which have the function of remote communication.
- Historically, electronic mail has been developed uniquely in each respective enterprise. For this reason, the standardization of EDI (Electronic Data Interchange) communication has not been achieved rapidly. However, the use of EDI has begun to increase substantially. For example, it is forecast that retailers will come to use EDI in order to automate their ordering process. It is anticipated that Cost technology will be very useful in this area. In addition, the shift toward the use of offshore production facilities will heighten the use of EDI, given the need for quicker data exchange among a firm's functional centers. According to the Company's research, many companies arc planning to use EDI within the corporate group and for procurement.
- Currently in the linking system for the banking networks, one network is connected to another network through its host computers (shown as (1) below), but it is reported that de-regulation will drive the direct connection (shown as (2) below). Cost will have a market chance in this move of the banking deregulation.
- The market will be demanding the network switching system. ABC's research shows that all credit card firms want a much larger number of ATMs for their wider services and that many commercial banks want to rent their own ATMs for outsiders and charge commission fees for them.
- More than one set of Cost can be installed in one entity because larger companies have many gateways to common networks at their separate sites.

License Terms

While ABC is still in the process of negotiating the definitive terms of the distribution agreement with DEF, it is anticipated that (1) ABC will have the rights to distribute Cost and Pack, which will be licensed to ABC; (2) ABC's distribution rights with respect to the products will be exclusive; (3) ABC will pay a royalty to DEF which is to be determined, although ABC has projected a royalty rate of ____% for Cost and ____% for Pack; and (4) ABC would have the right to sublicense the products to any subdistributors. The target date for signing the agreement is January _____, and discussions to finalize the terms of the arrangement will be held in December _____. In parallel with the discussions of product distribution, the parties will begin joint research and development work relating to the products in November ____, and the work to be provided by ABC should be considered a substantial investment which will be taken into consideration in determining the amount of any royalty payments. See "Research and Development."

Market Size

There are two separate markets for the Pack product: the financial sector market and the nonfinancial sector market. ABC believes that government agencies have approved financial institutions to issue credit cards. These financial institutions can be categorized as banks, credit companies, insurance firms, agriculture and fishery financing institutions, and securities firms. In each case, prospective clients, as well as their system infrastructures, would be under strict government controls. See "Projected Financial Performance—Pro Forma Financial Information Assumptions."

In addition to possible clients in the financial sector, the Company believes there will be card-issuing business applications among entities which have direct and indirect consumers in any of their marketing network. In determining the total nonfinancial market for Pack, ABC used the same methodology by which it arrived at an estimated market for GHI Product. Since clients in the nonfinancial sector would not be authorized card-issuing entities, it can be expected that there will be various types of card processing applications. In summary, ABC believes that the total market for Pack will be at least ____ companies for which the sales amount will be $____. See "Projected Financial Performance—Pro Forma Financial Information Assumptions."

The Company believes that Cost is a synergetic product with Pack; therefore, a portion of the market for Cost will be essentially the same as the total projected market for Pack. In addition, ABC believes that another potential market for this product will be nonfinancial institutions with a demand for EDI. While it is difficult to determine the total number of companies that might be interested in EDI network technology, ABC believes that it is reasonable to take the same approach referred to above as to the size of the market for GHI Product. Accordingly, ABC believes that the total market size for Cost will be at least ____ companies for which the sales amount would be approximately $____.

Market Surveys

ABC has contacted more than 100 organizations which either currently deal with credit card systems or which will be possible customers for Cost and Pack.

Large Department Store. ABC contacted an affiliate of one of the largest department stores. The store already had a huge card management system on the mainframe computer with over ten million cardholders. The problem in the existing system is that they are suffering from high operating cost. The store indicated that some other card issuers want to shift their facility and operation to outer sources; however, their card system is too big to sell to other organizations as a packaged product. They implied that some of their rivals would be replanning the design of card management systems. Additionally, they forecast that when the financial market was deregulated, all banking networks would be reorganized and nonstop switching systems like Cost would be best-sellers then.

Hotels. Top-ranked hotels are demanding an excellent card management system for their strategic marketing in addition to financial settlement. Many high-ranked hotels are now experiencing a hard time in their corporate management. Most of their computer facilities are placed for their hotel operation rather than for marketing. Some hotels have mainframe computers, but most of the others have medium-sized computers. They advised us that their sales strategy should be to provide a total consulting service of marketing to them and to convert the products for smaller computers.

Life Insurance Companies. All leading life insurance companies issue their own house card for customer services. Their problem is that their own cards are not effectively utilized by the clients. In addition to credit for insurance premiums, they want to provide total services through the cards, for example, claim management including automated suggestions.

Local Community Membership Groups. Local community membership groups often issue their own credit cards. For example, one group contacted by the Company has issued over 40,000 cards. Some are credit-card-type and others are non-credit-card-type house cards. They are planning various kinds of events in which their cardholders use the cards. The main purpose of such events will be the renewal of the customer information database for the group's future marketing strategies. They want any proposal for card business because they are not card management experts. There are many other such local groups all over the country, and they are connected together through network. The group ABC contacted is in the substantial position in the networked group, and there may be millions of cardholders in all the groups.

Retail Stores. Although most of large retailers have already had their own card management system, many medium-sized retail stores are still at the entry level. Powerful customer information databases would be the most important factor for the card management products to prevail. Also, small retailers or chain stores might have an interest in a product which could be used on PCs, since the movement to small-sized computers will be unavoidable. In addition, retailers of all sizes may have an interest in enhancements to their card management system to improve direct marketing opportunities to card holders.

Computer Suppliers. Hardware suppliers may be interested in providing total credit card systems to customers. If this is so, the Company may be able to forge alliances with the computer suppliers to write proposals for solutions in the total application systems. Computer suppliers would be primarily interested in quick response to maintenance calls, upgrades, troubleshooting, and operational instruction.

Development and Sales Plans

ABC has concluded that the market for Cost and Pack would be quite different from those of Europe.

- ABC believes that many potential customers are looking for a product which will allow for total system integration of credit card and banking strategies. As this is different than the current products, ABC must gain a greater understanding of the detailed technical information of each module of Cost and Pack. This will require a transfer of technical expertise to ABC through an exchange of technical personnel.
- Customers may be interested in purchasing not only the whole product, but also the individual modules of them. Pricing should be a function of the data volume and system scale. In addition, it will be important to produce new modules for demand, such as a powerful database for customer information.
- Customers are interested in the response time and throughput of online network interfaces.
- Customers are concerned about the possibility of the interface with proprietary networks. The kinds of services or data that would be offered to clients is an important matter, too.
- The portability to UNIX environment should be considered. Given the anticipated movement to smaller machines, it will be important that the products be rewritten for smaller computers, such as IBM AS400 workstations and PCs, for the large and uncultivated market. Also, the function for local area network should be considered.

- Customers will be concerned about the continuous involvement of the original supplier for maintenance, upgrades, troubleshooting, and operational instruction. Accordingly, provision should be made for ongoing access to DEF personnel.

Localization of the products will require (1) translation language in screen display, report, and operation manual, (2) making the network protocol modules, and (3) making modules for proprietary business customs. At the beginning, ABC will organize into two groups for marketing and technical works, both of which will be directly controlled by top management of the Company. Both marketing and technical staff need to travel to Singapore and to the United Kingdom to master how to apply the products to clients' solutions. After the localization work, the two groups are integrated into a single team, which means that sales engineers will be supporting both sales and technical matters. ABC is preparing to reorganize the internal structure at the beginning of April ____, and is ready to increase the staff. See "Research and Development."

The Company estimates that development and customization of Pack will require approximately six months for each project. ABC projects that the average revenue from a single system will be approximately $_____: 50% of which will come from the product and the remaining 50% from the software development and customization work. Development costs for a single system are assumed to be approximately $_____, and royalties to DEF will be 60% of the product revenue.

ABC has already begun to contract the Economic Journal for promotion of the current version of Pack for use on the IBM mainframe and IBM AS400. ABC cannot begin selling the product until enhancement work has been completed. ABC forecasts the number of installations for Pack as follows:

Year 1	—
Year 2	—
Year 3	—
Year 4	—
Year 5	—
Total	—

The Company estimates that development and customization of the Cost network system will require approximately five months for each project. ABC projects that the average revenue from a single system will be approximately _____: 66% of which will come from the product and the remaining 34% from the software development and customization work. Development costs for a single system are assumed to be approximately $____, and royalties to DEF will be 60% of the product revenue.

Sales promotion of Cost will begin in January ____; however, the Company has already begun to contact the Economic Journal for pre-promotion. ABC anticipates that the first project which will be ordered by one of its prospective clients will begin in April. ABC forecasts the number of installations for Cost as follows:

Year 1	__
Year 2	__
Year 3	__
Year 4	__
Year 5	__
Total	__

See Exhibit E for a description of the timetable for the development and commercialization of the new products.

Customers and Marketing

Customers

One of the significant strategic advantages which ABC holds is its strong relationships with a broad base of customers in a variety of industries. For example, in the finance area, ABC has successfully completed projects with mainframe computers, various types of UNIX-based platforms, and process control, and it has worked with a number of leading banks. In addition, ABC has worked on projects for securities firms, insurance firms, and credit card companies, and the Company is now engaged in projects which involve integration between the banking system and retailers. In the process control field, ABC has worked on several projects in the telecommunications area. The Company anticipates that its work in the financing and telecommunications areas will produce a good synergy to cope with new technologies, such as LAN remote control of 24-hour nonstop operations and logistics control.

Customer Base

ABC's customer base for the last three fiscal years was as follows: ______. The customer base in each year can be further broken down as follows:

[Insert Description]

Segment information for those three fiscal years was as follows:

[Insert Description]

ABC's client list includes the following:

[Insert Description]

Among ABC's current customers, there are approximately __ financial institutions, including credit card companies, and __ global operating corporations with remote network systems. The Company believes that these customers will be potential clients for the new products. This is because regardless of the scale of the financial institutions, they must follow the general direction of globalization and deregulation. From a technical viewpoint, these companies will be forced to participate in the global banking network beyond the internal and domestic networks. This means that, operationally, banks must adapt to the standards of BIS (Bank of International Settlement) and National Bank Standard's chart of accounts. ABC has already made a number of presentations to its existing clients in the financial area and has gotten a strong response and interest in the new products for the above reasons. See "New Products."

Terms of Customer Contracts

As a general matter, ABC customary contracts with its customers cover obligations, inspection, guarantees, payments, intellectual property rights, nondisclosure, termination, duration, nontransferability, and dispute resolution. All specific design elements and contents of the software are part of the sale order documentation and are incorporated into the general contractual agreement. There are two basic types of sales orders. The first type calls for the completion of specific products in accordance with the particular requirements of the customer. The actual sale of the product by ABC is conditioned upon inspection and acceptance of the final product by the customer. The second type of sales order covers consultancy services under which ABC system engineers will provide on-site assistance to customers with respect to a wide variety of matters. See "ABC's Business Activities." These consulting services are charged at hourly rates as well as by setting a specific base rate per month.

Historically, ABC's pricing for software development was based largely on the number of labor hours, which was calculated in man-hours.

Accordingly, the price for ABC's products has always been heavily dependent on labor cost and expenses. As ABC changes its general marketing strategies to emphasize technology-intensive products rather than labor-intensive products, it can be expected that ABC's pricing reflects the value to the customer from ABC's higher productivity, the technology embodied in ABC's products, and the expertise provided by ABC's consultants. See "ABC's Strategic Business Plan."

The sales orders for ABC's new products will include both product and consultancy services and will be divided into two general categories. The first category would itself be broken down into two phases. The first phase will include the work required to adapt the basic software to the requirements of the customer, a process of developing business solutions that is similar to system integration. In this case, the clients are willing to pay a premium to ABC for its business consulting services and will not be as concerned regarding pricing of the specific products. The second phase will cover the technical support necessary for the customer to operate the products in their own environments, including maintenance, upgrading, and troubleshooting. In the second category, contracts will simply cover products, in which case the client will not be as concerned regarding consulting services.

Marketing

The Company has sales offices in ______. Salespersons in each office are marketing its territory and get the first contact to prospective clients. Consultants follow the clients' demand and give them presentation of system proposals. Service system engineers keep in contact with the clients after the Company has completed the projects and hear the new demands of the customers. See "Human Resources and Organizational Structure."

Marketing personnel can be broken down as follows:

[Insert Description]

Revenues among the various sales offices over the past four years are broken down as follows:

[Insert Description]

ABC's sales process begins with presales by sales persons. The head office and branches have several sales persons for the first contact to the possible clients. Consultants follow the first contact and make interviews/presentations to them. All terms and conditions of the agreement with clients are discussed by sales persons and consultants. All the projects take at least several months to be completed, and ABC has an opportunity to take other orders during that period, thereby allowing the Company to simultaneously perform multiple projects with a single client. For the continuous business with the existing clients, ABC's service system engineers are in charge of the maintenance phase of each projects and remain informed about the new demands or requirements of the clients. Branch offices have the same policy of sales and marketing regardless of their smaller size. In some cases, salespersons and consultants from the head office help the branches' sales promotion because the head office outnumbers the branches in sales personnel and consulting capability. Even though research and development activities are conducted only in the head office, all technology and business consulting expertise are transferred to and from the branches.

Human Resources and Organizational Structure

As of _______, the Company had a total of _____ employees, of which _____ were technical employees and _____ were nontechnical employees. ABC's human resources pool can be broken down as follows:

[Insert Description]

The government policy has a long-term education plan for system engineers to enhance the future national technology base. As part of that plan, the government has developed a certificate program. The certificate is not a type of license; however, it is a kind of diploma which shows the standard of technical levels for individual engineers. Among the _____ technical employees of the Company as of _______, _____ have been certified.

While most of ABC's engineers are relatively young, with an average of _____ years, _____ of them are senior system engineers or analysts with over ten years of experience. Three system auditors are dedicated to quality control. ABC has a quality first recruitment policy and invests heavily in staff training. The Company believes that its unique combination of commitment, specialist skills, and experience has been essential to the successful completion of its various projects for its clients.

Description of Current Business Organization

The current business organization for the Company's existing businesses is as follows:

[Insert Description]

The activities of the various organizational groups within the Company can be briefly summarized as follows:

Business Development Group. ABC has a separate group of strategists who make an overall corporate design. The strategists drive the overall marketing and technology of the Company toward the ideal direction. This group has primary responsibility for the Company's global partnership strategies (e.g., DEF and GHI), brand-new advanced technology (ICST project), and ISO9000 consulting services (see below). _______ currently belongs to this group and is in charge of the global partnership strategy. He will be moving to the new business unit described below.

Administrative Department. ABC has a rather small administrative organization. Administrative personnel at ABC's head office handle all of the Company's financial, legal, and secretarial functions.

Information System Department. All engineers in this department are specialized in mainframe technology. Regardless of the global trend to downsizing and open architecture, ABC considers that mainframe business will keep a stable position for large-scale computing. With long years of experience in mainframe technology, ABC has a steady growth projection for this cluster. New technological trends, however, can also be seen in mainframe technology. The new role of mainframe computers is the network server to global networks. Therefore, there will be a need for frequent exchanges of technology with the Advanced Technology Department.

Advanced Technology Department. As all staff in this department face the most advanced technology, they play an important role as a profit center and a research and development center. UNIX will be the base technology for the time being and this department is in charge of UNIX technology. At the same time, the future technology base, namely personal computers, is being followed by some of the staff in this department. Another characteristic of this department is that the duration of a single project is rather short and flexible.

District Representative (Branches). Branch offices are mainly to allow ABC to provide quick services in remote geographic areas. See "Customers and Marketing."

Subsidiaries

ABC has two active material subsidiary companies: System and Services. System was organized in ______ and is headquartered in ______. System, which is wholly owned by the Company, currently has ____ employees. The president of System is ______, who is a director of ABC. Services was organized in ______ and is headquartered in ______. Services, which is ____% owned by ABC, currently has ____ employees. Mr. ______ also serves as the president of Services.

System was established to meet the special demands of local clients and to assist in recruitment. The company started with the computer operation activity and afterwards entered the software development business of CAI (computer aided instruction) application products. System has a branch office, which was recently expanded in order to make an infrastructure of outsourcing business, which ABC believes will be a potential market in future. System's main businesses are in the facility management area, including monitoring services, computer operation services, and hardware maintenance services. The turnover in ______was $______, and forecasted turnover for ____ is $____.

Services was formed for the purpose of marketing for specific cluster, government-related projects. Some of the projects of this company are essentially duplicative of those undertaken by System; however, the main objective of this joint venture is to target the government projects by acquiring the status of the registered contractor. Services' main business is in the area of facility management, including monitoring service, 24-hour nonstop operating computers, computer operation services, error checking services for optical fiber screens, and local area network maintenance services. The turnover in ______ was $______ with net income of $____, and forecasted turnover in ______ is $______ with net income of $____.

Organization of New Business Unit

In connection with the development and exploitation of its new products, the Company will be forming a new business unit which will be structured as follows:

[Insert Description]

The new business unit for the new project has already started as a project steering team and will be formally organized as a new department. The manager of the department will report directly to ABC's president. The department consists of three functional teams operating in the areas of strategic planning, marketing, and technology and will be operated by ______ as director.

Strategic Planning Team. The strategic planning team is in charge of the overall strategy in this project, including the communication between the Company and DEF and GHI, financial issues in the project, human resources, subdistributors, market-technology interfaces, and management. Currently, ______ has all responsibility for the functions of the team. At the start of the department in ______, another _____ people will join the team.

Marketing Team. The marketing team is in charge of public relations, presales, product demonstration and presentation, business consulting, help desk, and all other services to clients. Currently, ______ and ______ have responsibility for the functions of the team. At the start of the department in ______, another _____ people will join the team.

Technology Team. The technology team is in charge of all technical matters in the project, including product localization, translation, technical training and consulting, and overall technical services to clients. Currently, ______ has all responsibility for the functions of this team. At the start of the department in ______, another _____ people will join the team.

Customer Solution Teams. Customer solution teams will be organized every time new orders come in from clients. As more fully discussed in "ABC's Business Activities," a typical project for respective clients requires _____ consultants and application engineers. The core teams (strategy team, marketing team, and technology team) will select the required staff from the other departments and flexibly organize the team. A team leader will also be selected among the staff from other departments. The solution teams will be disbanded after the project is completed. The core teams will provide all required assistance to the customer solution team during the project. It is anticipated that the composition of the customer solution teams will be rotated in order to build a broad range of expertise among the Company's personnel.

Future Human Resource Requirements

In accordance with the Company's expansion program, it is anticipated that additional personnel will be required in the near future. ABC currently has an ongoing recruiting policy which is designed to maintain current levels of employment, but in the case of unexpected changes, it is possible that additional skills will be obtained through professional recruiters and the acquisition of other software development companies. In any case, the Company believes that it will be able to easily recruit excellent system engineers from outside sources in order to meet the requirements of the new products, thereby substantially increasing its production capacity. Since the requirements of ABC's existing businesses are similar to those for the new products, the Company believes that the new personnel can be used for expansion across all of its existing and proposed businesses.

Employee Benefits

The Company maintains an Employees Shareholders Group, which is open to all ABC employees except board members. The Employees Shareholders Group currently holds _____% of the outstanding shares of ABC and provides an incentive to the employee-shareholders to enhance the performance of the Company and an opportunity for them to be able to participate in the management of the Company. ABC also offers the following personal benefits to employees: (1) training center and (2) membership.

Research and Development

In the past, ABC's internal research and development work generally was limited to the development of project management systems, cost accounting systems, and quality control systems for in-house use, although the Company has made limited sales of such products in special circumstances. See "ABC's Business Activities." The internal research and development process for the project management system was made in a practical way. The system design arose out of discussions among management and personnel from various other sections, such as the accounting section, business development group, technology departments, and branches. The purpose of the new system was the integration of the individual processes that had previously been independently used by each section and for corporate strategic use. After the design, all development work was done by the technical staff with job rotation. The entire system development process was exactly the same as in any of the Company's ordinary projects for its clients.

Development Work for New Products

Each of the new products will require further development, which will be undertaken in accordance with the schedule attached hereto as Exhibit E. ABC has already begun the localization work required for GHI Product and anticipates that the work will be completed by ______. ABC hopes to install all hardware and operating software in connection with GHI Product by ______ or as soon as financing for the project is received.

With regard to the development work for Cost, five system engineers from ABC will be working with DEF from ______ to ______. The main purpose of the joint development work is to convert Cost into the UNIX platform, since ABC expects that the product will work for both Tandem and UNIX workstations. In parallel with the joint development work, ABC will proceed with the translation and localization work and complete that phase of the project by ______.

The development plans with respect to Pack have not yet been finalized. ABC has noted two requirements as to the use of Pack. First, while it is true that the current functions will be accepted by newcomers to the credit card market, additional functions, such as "smart card handling," will need to be added in order for the product to be attractive to larger financial institutions. Second, it will be necessary to develop a downsized version of Pack which can be operated on the UNIX platform. This process will probably be completed as part of a joint development project similar to that which is to be undertaken for Cost.

Other Research and Development Projects

ABC has also been involved in several other research and development projects, including the following:

Project Tools. In order to participate in the Project, ABC acquired a set of development tools of Project in parallel with mastering the technology of Project. Project technology inclusively covers all software development phases from upstream to downstream. It enables a new methodology of software designing in the most risky phase, which is the definition of requirements. The main feature is that system engineers can easily define the requirements of the system without any application knowledge and give higher productivity in the most labor-intensive phases of the software. ABC is acquiring a distributor's license from the original developer. ABC has had several clients which might benefit from the Project technology, one of which is a contract for train technology. Project has contributed $______ to ABC's revenue over the last two years and remains in process.

UNIX Software. In addition to the UNIX workstations with local area network, ABC requires more specific software for wider services to its clients, such as e-mail systems and network control systems. The new environment is being utilized for new projects. For example, the Information Center of Science and Technology (ICST) project with network and database technology is one of the largest-scale and longest-term works. ABC will gain revenue with this UNIX-based system environment.

Optical Fiber Screen System. For maintenance service of optical fiber screens, ABC needed a set of software for maintenance. Data Communications is the client of this maintenance project. ABC is expanding its market in this segment.

Production

System Development and Production Process

In most cases, new systems are produced by project teams consisting of 3–40 staff. During the first stage, one or two consultants work 4–8 weeks with clients in order to classify and define their system requirements. Sales persons participate in the discussion with the clients about the contractual issues, such as product size, period, project team organization, pricing, and payment terms. The second stage involves software design and programming. In mainframe projects, the total system is divided into several modules of functions and each module is implemented by a smaller group. In small computer projects, the work is done by a single team. This stage involves a variety of tests, all of which can be quite time-consuming. Among the tests conducted are module relation tests, system tests, and total operation tests, and all test data should cover every possible case. These tests take several trials and errors with feedback method and therefore takes much more labor than any other phase. After the various total operation tests have been completed, the new system is installed on a target computer, and the finished product must be adjusted to the client's operation and must be inspected and approved by the client. Once the inspection is finished, ABC recognizes the product as sold. Maintenance is usually provided under a separate contract and includes a free-of-charge guarantee with respect to specified performance characteristics. See "Service" below.

Project Management and Support

ABC has developed an in-house project management system to monitor the system development and product process described above. The system includes quality control, schedule control, operational management, staff allocation control, and cost control. The main functions of the system are:

- Standardization of process, documents, and technology

- Optimization of staff allocation
- Forecasting
- Profit and cost control

The system is being operated on the in-house Local Area Network (LAN) and interfaces with the two branch offices through telecommunications network. This system has now been packaged for sale.

The Project Management System defines all project phases, work levels, work items, and the products from all of the work items.

The phases are specifically defined as follows:

[Insert Description]

Quality Control

With respect to quality control, ABC is now preparing for certification of ISO9000. ISO9000 is the standard for software quality guarantee and is similar in function to the guarantees provided for tangible products. While this certification is not yet covered by government regulation, it is anticipated that in several years the government will be requiring every software company to obtain the certificate. In fact, ISO9000 consulting services may well become a new potential market, and ABC is considering entering one or more strategic alliances with accounting and/or consulting firms in order to get into this new business.

Service

One of ABC's strategic advantages is the service capacity which it makes available to its customers. There are basically two separate types of service projects: the implementation of products and consultancy services. In the former type of project, there is at least six months of guaranteed "warranty-type" maintenance provided free-of-charge to clients. As a general rule, service and maintenance charges outside of the warranty are approximately 15% of the product price. In the latter type of project, all of ABC's jobs are consultancy services and there are no obligations regarding the completed work. In this case, the services are usually charged at an hourly rate.

Backlog

ABC has no raw materials and finished goods inventory for its software development projects, instead it has work-in-process inventory.

Work-in-process inventory is valued by reference to the amount of staff salaries and outsourcing expenses associated with the project, and generally does not exceed 80% of the estimated sales revenues from the project. In addition, ABC has from time to time some computer software/hardware inventory, which is valued at cost, and is usually held for a short period of time.

The beginning balance of back orders this year, including work-in-process inventory, was $______ which was _____% lower than that of the previous year. However, the amount of new orders in the first four months of this year was _____% larger than that in _____. These new orders will lead to larger sales revenue in the latter half of this year and early next year. The Company believes this trend shows that the market decline has stopped.

Future Order Forecast

It is forecast that the total sales revenue in _____ will be $______. Among that amount, $_____ has already been finished or is in process. The remaining amount ($______) will be gained from future new orders.

The forecast figure of new orders from ______ to ______ will be $______. It can be concluded that new orders will be at a higher pace than in _____ because of the market recovery.

Competition

In the major sectors in which ABC operates, competitors include medium-sized software companies which do not have any affiliation with computer manufacturers or major computer users, including ______. Based on _____ revenues, ABC was ranked _____ by turnover. The industry remains very fragmented and may actually include several hundred competitors in nominal numbers.

The key competitive factors appear to include pricing, service structure, and the ability to use the products on a wide variety of hardware/software platforms. Also, while companies compete on cost leadership and quality, in most cases, customer loyalty to a supplier is quite high and customers generally seek to have stable and familiar relations with a single supplier. ABC believes that, compared to possible competitors, it has an advantage because it already has a substantial production and service capacity, a prestigious list of clients, geographical accessibility to the area, and accumulated expertise of software technology. ABC also has effectively competed through cost reduction, as shown by its high level of profitability per engineer.

ABC's strategic plans for the future include seeking competitive advantages with respect to the development and/or acquisition of new "leading-edge" technological products, such as GHI Product. In this area, the competition can be seen as other firms with an established reputation with mainframes which are now seeking to address the open systems market. The Company believes that successful products should be multirelational database, multidesktop environment open systems products. In order for ABC to seize a competitive advantage from development of these products, it must be able to introduce the products to the market on a timely basis, because competitors may be able to move quickly with their own development efforts, particularly if they are able to effectively use software produced by third parties as building blocks to accelerate their development efforts.

ABC also expects to be able to enhance its competitiveness through modifications in its pricing policies. As ABC changes its general marketing strategies to emphasize technology-intensive products rather than labor-intensive products, it can be expected that ABC's pricing will no longer be based solely upon labor costs, but rather will begin to reflect the value to the customer from ABC's higher productivity, the technology embodied in ABC's products, and the expertise provided by ABC's consultants. In fact, it is anticipated that ABC will actually be able to reduce its labor costs and related expenses with respect to its new software development work, and that such savings can be passed along to its customers.

Intellectual Property Rights

Since ABC's conventional business was mainly in the area of bespoke software development, it owns no patents, copyrights, or trademarks with respect to the systems developed for its clients, all of whom retain the intellectual property rights associated therewith. While ABC obviously retains the expertise relating to such projects, it is restricted under the terms of its various confidentiality agreements with its clients from freely using the expertise on other projects. ABC does have trademark rights with respect to its company logo mark.

GHI has all copyrights and trademarks for GHI Product and protects all their intellectual property rights with patents, copyrights, and trademarks. All written software programs are copyrighted by GHI, and the name of GHI Product and the GHI logo mark are registered trademarks. All technology expertise, such as M and T, are protected with patents. Under the license agreement, GHI will offer ABC the rights to use all their copyrighted software with their trademarks.

DEF has all copyrights and trademarks for Cost and Pack. DEF protects all their intellectual property with patents, copyrights, and trademarks. All written software programs are copyrighted by DEF, and the names of Cost and Pack and DEF's logo mark are registered trademarks. All the technology expertise embodied in Page is protected by patent rights. DEF will offer ABC the rights to use all their copyrighted software with their trademarks.

Physical Facilities

ABC owns all of its real properties and does not have any lease contracts relating to its facilities. ABC believes that there will be adequate space for corporate expansion of up to an additional ___ personnel in its existing facilities.

HISTORICAL FINANCIAL INFORMATION

[Insert "Annual Financial Statements _______"]

[Insert "Interim Financial Statements for _______ Fiscal Year"]

Management's Discussion and Analysis of Historical Financial Information

Operational Breakdown

ABC breaks its operation down into two segments: software development and product sales.

Results of Operations

For the twelve months ended _______, ABC's revenues from software development and sales totaled $_______. Because of the market, the revenue was reduced _____%.

Operating expenses consist of cost of sales, including labor cost, outsourcing cost, depreciation and raw materials, and selling and administrative expenses. Labor costs amounted to $_______, and outsourcing costs amounted to $_______. ABC performed a radical restructuring by layoffs, office moves, and so on in order to reduce expenses.

Depreciation of fixed assets during the year ended ______, amounted to $______.

Interest expense for the period amounted to $______. By reducing the bank loans, the Company cut the interest payment by _____%.

Extraordinary losses occurred in the way of restructuring as follows:

- Losses on property sold and disposed: When ABC moved out of the old offices, many office supplies were disposed of. This is not an ordinary operation.
- Reserve for doubtful accounts receivable: The total amount of doubtful receivables in this period was $______ and a half of the amount was amortized in this period.
- Other extraordinary loss: When ABC moved out of the old offices, it paid the rent for a few months to repair them. This is not an ordinary operation.

Because ABC had a negative figure of income before taxes, the Company was exempt from all income taxes. It only paid the operational tax (expense).

Having experienced economic difficulties in a whole industry, ABC resulted in the net loss for the year ended ______. In the year, ABC was involved in restructuring activities, such as layoffs, office move, and disposal of doubtful receivables. As a result, ABC was forced to write off the extraordinary loss which amounted to $______. After cutting those negative factors, ABC will recover its net income in the year ended ______, along with the market recovery. As more fully described in "Business-Backlog," the pace of new orders has increased since ______.

Seasonality

The chart shows the recent four years' average of ABC's seasonal volatility of sales revenues:

[Insert Description]

Owing to the clients' budget schedule, monthly revenue peaks were in ______. Because the scale of each project is getting larger, the volatility will be bigger. The ratio of annual sales revenue has been _____% in the first half and _____% in the second half for the recent four years. In _____, therefore, the revenue in the first half will be $______ and in the second half $______. Annual revenue will be $______.

Liquidity and Capital Resources

ABC expects to meet its cash requirements primarily from cash provided from operations and the net proceeds of the proposed offering. The Company also expects its capital requirements to increase substantially as a result of its expansion program. ABC believes that it will have access to sufficient funds from commercial banks to cover its working capital needs.

PROJECTED FINANCIAL PERFORMANCE

Projected Financial Information

The following projected financial information should be read in conjunction with, and is subject to, the detailed assumptions following the projections.

[Insert Description]

Pro Forma Financial Information Assumptions

1. The projected financial information with respect to ABC presented above has been prepared by the management of the Company based on the most recent information coming to their attention regarding the business activities of ABC, overall trends in the economy and software markets, and the rights which the Company anticipates acquiring from DEF and GHI. It represents management's best estimate of the possible results of operations for the Company given each of the following assumptions. However, ABC cannot provide any assurance that these estimates of operations can actually be realized. See also "Certain Factors."
2. The pro forma financial information is based on certain assumptions regarding macroeconomic conditions during the periods covered by the information. The data on such macroeconomic conditions was derived from published forecast and on further analysis made by _______. Based on the foregoing, it is assumed that Gross Domestic Product ("GDP") will recover during the periods covered by the information but will remain flat in relation to prior periods _______. It is assumed that the rate of inflation, the capital investment ratio, and the government bond interest rate will all remain

stable during the periods. The following chart sets out certain historical information and ABC's future projections as to macroeconomic conditions:

[Insert Description]

Historical information is based on data published by the government. As to projections relating to future macroeconomic conditions, see "Business—Overview of the Software Market."

3. It has been assumed that the Company's annual growth rate will be at least 5% per annum during the periods covered by the pro forma financial information without any expansion into the new business areas. ABC believes that this rate of growth, which is below the projected annual growth rate for the entire industry during the periods, is reasonable and consistent with the Company's own annual rate of growth of 5% during the period from _______ to _______. See "Business—Overview of the Software Market."
4. The pro forma financial information is based on a total market size for the GHI Product system of $_______ and approximately _______ companies. In arriving at this estimate of the market size, the Company made a variety of assumptions, the most significant of which are as follows:
   - The total investment in a GHI Product system would be $_______, with _______ devoted to hardware and _______ to software.
   - Potential customers will spend 0.1% of their total revenue to invest in the development and upgrading of their management information systems. The basis for this assumption is as follows:

     [Insert Description]

   - The total market for the GHI Product system can be clustered into three groups based on total revenues, with the computation of estimated total revenues based on the assumption that the amount of earnings expressed as a percentage of total revenues will be approximately 2.5%, which was the percentage in fiscal year _____ as published by the government and referred to above.
   - The clustering of the groups in the chart was based on methodology which has been used by a major research institute to estimate the market size for an accounting support software product. The rate referred to in the chart is the percentage of firms within the specific cluster which ABC anticipates would be likely purchasers for the product and is also based upon the aforementioned methodology,

although the rate has been adjusted upward to reflect GHI Product's UNIX base and wider range of applications.

- The average revenue of a single project will be $______: _____% on the product and the rest for software development and customization work.

5. The pro forma financial information is based on a total market size for Pack of $______ and approximately _____ companies. In arriving at this estimate of the market size, the Company made a variety of assumptions, the most significant of which are as follows:
   - The total investment in Pack would be $______, with ______ devoted to hardware and ______ to software.
   - ABC believes that possible clients in the financial sector are as follows, based on available information:

[Insert Description]

   - The rate referred to in the chart is the percentage of firms within the specific group which ABC anticipates would be likely purchasers for the product which is based on the experiences of analysts which ABC believes to be reliable.
   - Potential customers in the nonfinancial sector will spend 0.1% of their total revenue to invest in the development and upgrading of their management information systems.
   - The total nonfinancial sector market for Pack can be clustered into three groups based on total revenues, with the computation of estimated total revenues based on the assumption that the amount of earnings expressed as a percentage of total revenues will be approximately 2.5%, which was the percentage in fiscal year _____ as published by the government.
   - See Assumption (4) regarding GHI Product for an explanation of the structure and meaning of the chart.
   - The average revenue of a single project will be $______: _____% on the product and the rest for software development and customization work.

6. The pro forma financial information is based on a total market size for Cost of $______ and approximately _____ companies. In arriving at this estimate of the market size, the Company made a variety of assumptions, the most significant of which are as follows:
   - The total investment in Cost would be $______, with ______ devoted to hardware and ______ to software.

- All possible clients for Pack would also be possible clients for Cost. In addition, a separate market for Cost is assumed to exist among nonfinancial entities with a demand for Electronic Data Interchange ("EDI"). The size of this market was approximated in the same manner that the potential market for GHI Product was determined (i.e., potential customers will spend 0.1% of their total revenue to invest in the development and upgrading of their MIS, and the total revenues for potential customers computed on the assumption that the amount of earnings expressed as a percentage of total revenues will be approximately 2.5%).
- The rate referred to in the chart has been defined as the percentage of the investment amount to their information system divided by their estimated total revenues. The rate depends upon the level the product will be targeted to each market cluster.
- The average revenue of a single project will be $_______: _____% on the product and the rest for software development and customization work.

7. The Company has assumed that for the development and customization work associated with the GHI Product system, 18 man-months of manpower should be needed per installation during six months, as follows:

[Insert Description]

Development of the GHI Product system, which is focused on the UNIX-workstation platform, will require the use of UNIX-base system engineers. It is believed that the project will require 1.5 (men/month) application engineers for UNIX per month. Since ABC currently has _____ UNIX-based system engineers, it estimates that the maximum number of GHI Product system projects which it can handle simultaneously in a single month will be _____.

Development costs for a single GHI Product system were estimated to be approximately $_______ (18 man-months of manpower times $_______).

8. The Company has assumed that for the development work associated with the Cost network system, 10 man-months of manpower should be needed per installation during five months, as follows:

[Insert Description]

Development of the Cost network system will require the use of network system engineers, since the product is not a kind of application software. It is believed that the project will require one network engineer per month. Since ABC currently has ____ network system engineers, it estimates that the maximum number of Cost network system projects which it can handle simultaneously in a single month will be ____.

Development costs for a single Cost system were estimated to be approximately $____ (10 man-months of manpower times $____).

9. The Company has assumed that for the development work associated with the Pack project, 24 man-months of manpower should be needed per installation during six months, as follows:

[Insert Description]

Development of the Pack project will require the use of both application and network system engineers, since the product is an application software with network capabilities. It is believed that the project will require one network and one application (UNIX-based) engineer per month. Since ABC currently has ____ network system engineers, it estimates that the maximum number of Pack projects which it can handle simultaneously in a single month will be ____.

Development costs for a single Pack project were estimated to be approximately $____ (24 man-months of manpower times $_____).

10. As Cost and Pack are complimentary projects, the Company assumes that there may be situations where both products are installed for one client at the same time. When this occurs, the development work schedule would be as follows:

[Insert Description]

Simultaneous development of Cost and Pack projects for the same client impose the same manpower requirements and constraints as described above with respect to projects that are solely Pack.

11. ABC's projections for installations of new products over the period are as follows:

[Insert Description]

In arriving at this estimate of projected installations, the Company made a variety of assumptions, the most significant of which are as follows:

[Insert Description]

12. License fees for the GHI Product, Cost, and Pack products are assumed to be 45%, 60%, and 60%, respectively, of product revenues.
13. All maintenance charges are assumed to be 15% of the product price and are accumulated on the following years. Manpower for the maintenance work is assumed to be only one man-month per five sets of the respective products.
14. In Table 2 (Long-Term Cash Flow), it is assumed that the initial investment amount will be $______ and will be paid in the first year. Income and expenses are calculated on the basis of the number of product sets installed (see Table 4). See "Use of Proceeds."
15. The amounts for depreciation and amortization of the initial investment amount in Table 3 (Periodical Income Statement) are deferred for five years in accordance with accounting practices as follows:

[Insert Description]

16. In Table 3 (Periodical Income Statement), the amount for manpower is the total of manpower for development and maintenance in Table 2 (Long-Term Cash Flow) and the amount for "Other" is the total of management and miscellaneous in Table 2.
17. In Table 4 (Sales Forecast), the initial release dates for the new products will be as follows:

GHI Product:

Cost:

Pack:

18. In Table 5 (Long-Term Profit Plan without New Project), it is assumed that the sales revenues from ABC's existing business will grow at 5% per annum, that expenses will grow 3–6% per annum, and that overhead (other than staff payroll) will remain at the same level. It is also assumed that the reduction of the borrowing by $______ every year will decrease the interest expense by $______ each year.

USE OF PROCEEDS

The proceeds from the offering will be used to fund the research and development and operating expenses associated with the adaptation of the new products to, and the marketing of the new products in, the market. The use of proceeds can be further broken down as follows:

[Insert Description]

The Company's capital strategy is that research and development projects of the type required in order for it to implement its new strategic business plans should be covered by either internal funding sources or equity financing. It is unlikely that funding will be available from commercial banks, which are generally only used for working capital, or from venture capitalists, who are typically risk-averse investors. If the proceeds of the proposed offering are not sufficient, ABC anticipates further equity offerings in order to maintain the development time frame for the new projects.

As far as future financing requirements are concerned, the Company does not have any plans for future offerings prior to the year 2000, when ABC is targeting an initial public offering of its shares. However, prior to that time, ABC may be willing to consider another private equity or debt offering in order to take advantage of opportunities in the computer technology area, although ABC does not currently have a specific project in mind. Otherwise, ABC expects to meet its cash requirements primarily from cash that is provided from operations and the net proceeds of the offering.

CERTAIN FACTORS

In assessing the Company's future prospects and its ability to achieve the strategic and financial objectives and forecasts set out herein, the following factors should be considered.

Financial Risks. ABC's ability to rapidly develop its new business opportunities will depend on the availability of working capital. A shortage of working capital may occur due to delays in completion of the financing. The failure to have sufficient working capital will make it difficult for ABC to handle all new orders on a timely basis, which may result in a loss of valuable business opportunities. Also, large-scale system integration projects can pose financial risks, since the system integrator is the prime contractor and therefore takes on most of the financial risks associated with completion of the project. In order to avoid some of the financial risks associated with its business plan, ABC has based its projections on conservative estimates of cash flow. See "Projected Financial Performance."

Product Development Risks. In order to begin distribution of the new licensed products, ABC must be able to complete the ABC version of the products and learn how to customize them to meet the needs of its customers. ABC's ability to develop the products will depend on the availability of full assistance from the licensors. See "Research and Development." The Company's agreements with both licensors call for substantial amounts of technical and marketing assistance from DEF and GHI. See "Business—New Products."

Technological Risks. The Company believes that technological developments may present the biggest risks for its new business strategies. ABC's new business will be focused on UNIX-based technology; however, if UNIX is replaced by other platforms, ABC will be forced to make additional investments in order to allow it to follow the new technology. ABC's technological forecast is that UNIX platforms will keep a dominant position for at least the next five years, followed by PC-based platforms, such as Windows and OS/2. The Company believes that each of the new products can be easily converted to the PC environment. With regard to the technical capabilities of the GHI Product technology and potential risks which might be associated therewith, see Exhibit D.

Customer Budgeting Risks. The budgeting plans of potential customers is one of the most significant risk factors for the Company. Many customers view system development as a form of long-term investment. As most of ABC's business has been system development, changes in the customer's budgeting decisions materially impact ABC's sales volume, seasonality, and pricing strategy. See "Business—Overview of the Software Market."

Market Risks. While the Company believes that there are significant potential markets for each of the new products, it has been suggested that certain markets may not be as large, or expand as fast, as ABC anticipates. For example, as noted in "Business—New Products," certain areas of the credit card system market are already quite developed and it may be that ABC will be unable to develop a new version of Pack that is innovative enough for adaptation by larger financial institutions.

Regulatory Risks. Cost and Pack will be marketed to potential clients in the banking and financial industries, each of which is subject to some form of government regulation. It is anticipated that each of those industries will be deregulated in the future, and the Company expects its opportunities to increase in relation to the degree of deregulation. While the Company believes that deregulation will occur in the near future, it cannot fully predict the timing and effect of such changes. There might be some possibilities that the deregulation will be quickened or postponed for some period because of the political problems.

Competitive Risks. The target market for the new products is believed to be quite large and will necessarily attract a number of new competitors, especially big firms with the ability to make the large investment required to attain the technological resources and skills necessary to compete in the area. ABC believes that even if competitors are able to make the required financial investment, it will still have a competitive advantage due to its experience with regard to technology and application software.

ADDITIONAL INFORMATION

Management

Directors and Executive Officers

[Insert Description]

All directors mentioned above except auditors are executive officers of the Company.

Significant Employees

[Insert Description]

Capitalization

Indebtedness (as of ______)

[Insert Description]

Shareholders (as of ______)

[Insert Description]

Description of Capital Stock

As of ______, ______ shares of the Company's common stock were outstanding. All outstanding shares have a par value of $______, and a minimum unit in order for a shareholder to have voting rights is ______ shares.

The Board of Directors has the power to determine the type of shares to be issued, the fees to be charged for changes in ownership of shares, the terms of any repurchase of fragmented shares (i.e., shares which are not sufficient to constitute a "unit" of 1,000 shares), and any other stock transactions.

The Board of Directors must convene an annual general meeting of shareholders each year within three months from the annual closing date. Each share is entitled to one vote on all matters submitted to a vote of the Company's shareholders at all meetings of shareholders, except for the fragmented shares. Shareholders are entitled to attend and vote at meetings either in person or by legal proxy. The proxies must be signed by the shareholder and deposited at the legal address of the Company, or other such place as specified in the notice of the meeting in order to notice attendance at the meeting.

The shareholders have various other rights under Commercial law, provided that they own a sufficient number of the outstanding shares. Among such rights are the right to propose topics at shareholders' meetings, the right to convene a general meeting, the right to fire directors and auditors, the right to inspect or copy the financial statements of the Company, the right to terminate new stock issuances, and the right to nominate inspectors of the meeting.

Dividend Policy

Dividend distributions with respect to ordinary shares of common stock may be proposed to the Company's shareholders by the Board of Directors and may be paid following approval by the shareholders at a general meeting. Dividends are paid to the shareholders who are listed in the shareholders' list at the date of every annual closing date. Dividends based on the interim income may be paid. Shareholders will lose the right to withdraw cash for dividends after three years from the starting date of the payment of dividends.

ABC has paid the following dividends per share for the last two years:

Year 1 ____
Year 2 ____

ABC had long had a "corporate expansion first" strategy. In this strategy, the most important concern is reserving enough funds from operating revenues to fund investment in new projects. Accordingly, the amount of dividends paid by ABC have been quite small in recent years. As ABC continues to restructure itself and prepares to take on additional investors, the new criteria for management will be return on equity, dividend yield, dividend rate and payout ratio. ABC anticipates that beginning with ____, the target annual dividend rate will be 20% or more of par value.

TABLE OF EXHIBITS

APPENDICES B, C, AND D ARE NOW ON THE CD-ROM ONLY

APPENDIX E • TERM SHEETS

Dear Start-Up Company,

The following represents the terms on which we are willing to invest in your business.

Partners ("Investor") will lead a transaction in which Investor and its Investor Group ("Investor Group") will purchase a total of $x million face amount of newly issued Convertible Preferred Stock ("Preferred Stock") of Start-Up Company ("Start-Up" or "Company"). The Convertible Preferred Stock will be convertible into x% of the outstanding fully diluted common shares at the time of issuance, including any shares allocated or to be allocated to option pools during the life of the investment. The Preferred Stock will have an accruing dividend of x% per annum, which may be deferred and will be paid upon initial public offering ("IPO"), sale, merger, or liquidation of the Company, or upon redemption of the Preferred Stock. In the event of any liquidation, sale, or winding up of the Company, the holders of the Preferred Stock shall be entitled to receive, in preference to the holders of Common Stock, an amount equal to the purchase price plus the greater of (1) any accrued but unpaid dividends or (2) the pro rata share of any remaining proceeds, treating the Preferred Stock on an as-if converted basis. The Preferred Stock will be subject to redemption at the holder's option in years 6, 7, and 8 at the greater of fair market value or cost. In the event of an IPO in which over $x million in new capital is raised and the offering price is at least three times the conversion price of the Preferred Stock, the Preferred Stock will automatically convert to Common Stock.

Investor understands the current fully diluted capitalization of the Company to be x common share equivalents, including x employee shares and options which have been granted or are planned to be granted. Based on that number, Investor will purchase Preferred Stock convertible into x common shares at an initial conversion price of $x per share. This price will be adjusted for splits, stock dividends, etc., and will have standard weighted-average antidilution protection.

The proceeds of the financing will be used for general working capital purposes.

Investor will have the right to appoint a member to the Board of Directors. Direct travel costs incurred by Investor's appointed Board members for the purpose of attending the Board meetings and conducting other company business will be borne by the Company.

The compensation for the members of the management team will be at a reasonable level (industry standard), and if in dispute, will be referred to a committee of the Board of Directors, composed of one management team member, Investor Group's representative, and a third-party director.

Investor Group will have a demand registration right and consecutive piggyback registration rights. All sales of stock will be pro rata in proportion to ownership, subject to underwriter's limitations.

Company will pay all expenses in connection with the demand and piggyback offerings.

Securities shall have voting rights as if converted to Common Stock and will vote as a class on major corporate transactions (merger, dissolution, sale of assets, etc.).

Investor Group will have preemptive rights to maintain its pro rata equity ownership in future private equity financings throughout the life of the investment.

Investor Group will have a right of first refusal and side-by-side selling rights on the sale of stock by management and major shareholders. The side-by-side selling rights will provide that Investor Group will receive their pro rata share in any sale by a management shareholder.

Monthly financial information will be provided to Investor Group within 30 days of the end of each month. An annual budget will be provided to Investor Group prior to each fiscal year-end. Annual audit by an accounting firm of national recognition selected by the Board of Directors will be provided within 90 days of year-end.

Company will make its best efforts to maintain life insurance, with proceeds payable to Company, in the amount of $x million on the lives of the senior management team (x).

Company will neither pay dividends on Preferred or Common Stock, nor repurchase Common Stock, nor repay shareholder loans so long as the Preferred Stock is outstanding. A majority in interest of preferred shareholders may waive these provisions.

The reasonable due diligence expenses, legal fees, and closing costs of Investor Group (not to exceed $x) will be paid out of the proceeds of the financing.

Company and the principal shareholders will grant Investor Group representations and warranties which are standard in an agreement of this kind. In particular, all of the officers of the Company will be asked to certify the accuracy of the financial statements prior to closing.

Subject to the completion of final due diligence, the closing of this transaction will be on or before x.

Closing is conditioned upon satisfactory agreements being reached with the company's lenders.

Upon acceptance of this Term Sheet, Investor Group will commit substantial resources to a due diligence review of Company and the preparation of legal documents relating to this transaction. In consideration of such commitment by Investor Group, Company agrees that, during the period between acceptance of this Term Sheet and the closing date specified above, it will not enter into or continue any discussions with any third party, either agent or principal, concerning a possible investment, initial public offering, merger, acquisition, or other financial accommodation.

Company agrees to provide Investor Group with the information necessary to complete a final due diligence review satisfactory to Investor Group. Investor Group and Company agree that they will use their best efforts to negotiate in good faith the terms of definitive documentation incorporating the provisions of this Term Sheet, and Company agrees that it will make its personnel and business records available to Investor Group and its representatives during normal business hours.

If these terms are acceptable, please sign and return one original to Investor.

Sincerely,

____

Investor

Accepted and agreed:

____

Company

THE.COM, INC.

Summary of Terms for Proposed Private Placement of Series A Preferred Stock with The Placement Agent, Inc.

Issuer:	The.com, Inc. (the "Company")
Amount of Investment:	$5,000,000
Number and Type of Security:	Shares of Series A Convertible Preferred Stock ("Preferred") representing approximately 20% of the shares and options outstanding, after the issuance of the Preferred and the conversion of shares of the Company's Subordinated Convertible Demand Notes ("Notes") from investors.
Use of Proceeds:	The proceeds from the sale of the Preferred will be used for general corporate purposes.
Rights, Preferences, Privileges and Restrictions of the Preferred:	
Dividend Provisions:	The same dividend per share will be paid on the Preferred as is paid on the Common (with the Preferred being treated as equivalent to the number of shares of Common into which it is convertible). The Company's Board of Directors currently anticipates no dividends.
Liquidation Preference:	In the event of the liquidation or winding up of the Company, the holders of Preferred will be entitled to receive in preference to the holders of Common an amount equal to 2x original purchase price for the Preferred plus any dividends declared on the Preferred but not paid. Thereafter, the remaining assets of the Company will be distributed ratably to the holders

	of Common Stock and the Preferred (on an as converted basis). A consolidation or merger of the Company, or sale of all or substantially all of its assets, which results in a change of control of the Company will be deemed to be a liquidation or winding up for purposes of the liquidation preference.
Conversion:	Each holder of Preferred will have the right to convert the Preferred, at the option of the holder at any time, into shares of Common. The total number of shares of Common into which the Preferred may be converted initially will be determined by dividing the original purchase price for the Preferred by the conversion price. The initial conversion price will be the original purchase price for the Preferred, plus any dividends declared on the Preferred but not paid. The conversion rate of the Preferred will be proportionately adjusted following any stock split, reverse stock split, stock dividend or similar event.
Mandatory Conversion:	All Preferred will automatically convert, at the then applicable conversion rate, into Common (i) upon the conversion of at least a majority of the total number of shares of Preferred originally issued, or (ii) on the closing of an underwritten public offering with net proceeds to the Company of at least $15 million at a per share public offering price of at least two times the conversion price then in effect with respect to the Preferred.
Voting Rights:	Except with respect to the election of directors and certain protective provisions discussed below, the holders of Preferred will have the right to that number of votes equal to the number of shares of Common issuable upon conversion of the Preferred. The holders of Common will be entitled to one vote per share. All matters submitted to a vote of the holders

	of Preferred and Common will be decided by a simple majority vote, with the Preferred and Common voting together as a single class.
Antidilution Provisions:	The conversion price of the Series A Preferred will be subject to adjustment in accordance with a full ratchet anti-dilution formula in the event the Company issues certain equity Securities at a purchase price less than the then-effective Series A Conversion Price, subject to the following carve outs: (i) the issuance of common stock to employees, consultants, officers or directors of the Company pursuant to stock purchase or stock option plans approved by the Board (including options granted prior to this Financing), (ii) shares issued in connection with acquisition transactions, (iii) shares issued to financial institutions or lessors in connection with commercial credit arrangements, equipment financings or similar transactions approved by the Board, or (iv) shares issued upon conversion of the Preferred.
Protective Provisions:	Consent of the holders of at least a majority of the Preferred will be required, before the Company: (i) Authorizes or issues any capital stock that is senior or *pari passu* to the Preferred as to dividends, redemption or liquidation; (ii) Effects a change of control of the Company, including merger, consolidation, sale of assets, liquidation or reorganization of the Company; (iii) Increases the size of the Board of Directors; (iv) Hires or terminates the CEO, CFO or COO; (v) Increases the number of option shares reserved for issuance to employees, consultants and vendors of the Company;

	(vi) Alters the rights and preferences of the Preferred;
	(vii) Increases the number of authorized shares of Preferred; or
	(viii) Pays cash dividends or any other distribution on the Common Stock.
Information Rights:	So long as any of the Preferred is outstanding, the Company will deliver to each Investor who owns at least 100,000 shares of Preferred audited annual financial statements, unaudited quarterly and monthly financial statements, annual budgets and other information reasonably requested by the Investors.
Registration Rights:	
Demand Rights:	If, at any time after the Company's initial public offering (but not within six months of the effective date of a registration), holders of 40% of the Preferred request that the Company file a registration statement covering at least 20% of the Common issued or issuable upon conversion of the Preferred (or any lesser percentage if the anticipated aggregate offering price would exceed $10,000,000), the Company will use its best efforts to cause such shares to be registered. The Company will not be obligated to effect more than two registrations under these demand right provisions.
"Piggy-Back" Registrations:	The Investors will be entitled to unlimited "piggy-back" registration rights on registrations of the Company, subject to the right of the Company and its underwriters to reduce in view of market conditions the number of shares of the Investors proposed to be registered in the offering.

Registration Expenses:	The registration expenses (exclusive of underwriting discounts and commissions) of all of the registrations described above will be borne by the Company.
Transfer of Rights:	The registration rights may be transferred to a transferee that acquires at least 20% of the total number of shares of Preferred originally issued. Transfer of registration rights to a partner, member or shareholder of any Investor will be without restriction as to minimum shareholding.
Other Provisions:	Other provisions will include cross-indemnification, the Company's ability to delay the filing of a demand registration for a period of not more than 90 days in certain circumstances, the agreement by the Investors (if requested by the underwriters in a public offering) not to sell any unregistered Common they hold for a period of 180 days following the effective date of the registration statement for the Company's initial public offering and for 90 days following the effective date of the registration statement for any other offering, the period of time in which the registration statement will be kept effective, underwriting arrangements and the like.
Joint Venture Rights:	Preferred holder will have a right of first refusal to participate as a joint venture partner with the Company when and if the Company establishes a joint venture or launching of the Company's products or services with a joint venture partner.
Board Representation:	Preferred holder will have the right to appoint one member of the Board of Directors. The members of the Board at closing of the Preferred shall be ________________, ________________ and a person designated by a majority of Preferred. The Company will

	pay 50% of the Board member's travel costs for attendance at Board and committee meetings.
Preemptive Right for Purchase of New Securities:	So long as any of the Preferred is outstanding, if the Company proposes to offer any equity securities for the purpose of financing its business (other than Reserved Employee Shares, shares issued in the acquisition of another company, shares issued in connection with debt or lease financings or strategic investments in the Company, or shares offered to the public pursuant to an underwritten public offering), the Company will first offer a portion of such shares to the Investors so as to enable them to maintain their percentage interest in the Company.
Employee Option Vesting:	Options granted to employees shall be pursuant to a vesting schedule acceptable to Preferred.
Founders Vesting:	Founders' shares shall be subject to the Company's right of repurchase at nominal value, pro-rated over a four-year period, in the event a Founder terminates employment for any reason.
Right of First Refusal and Co-Sale:	Preferred has the right to participate on a pro rata basis in transfers of stock for value by founders and a right of first refusal on such transfers, subordinate to any Company right of first refusal (except for transfers by founders for no or nominal consideration for estate planning purposes).
Noncompetition, Nondisclosure and Assignment of Inventions:	All employees and consultants shall enter into Company's standard form noncompetition, inventions and proprietary information agreements.

Expenses:	Company and Preferred will each bear their own legal and other expenses with respect to the transaction.

Agreed and accepted this ____ day of ______, ___,

By: The.com, Inc.	By: The Placement Agent, Inc.
______________________________	______________________________
Name:__________________________	Name:__________________________
Title:__________________________	Title:__________________________

APPENDIX F • DOCUMENT/DUE DILIGENCE REQUEST/CHECKLIST

In connection with the proposed investment by Investor in the Company, please answer the following questions in writing or be prepared to answer them in a due diligence meeting. Also, where appropriate, please forward the items listed below to Investor so that we may complete our due diligence. All information will be held in complete confidence.

1. Corporate Records

   A. Charter documents or Articles of Incorporation as amended to date.
   B. By-laws as amended to date.
   C. Stockbook and copies of outstanding stock certificates.
   D. Minutes of meetings of the Board of Directors (and all written actions in lieu of meetings), all committees thereof, and related materials.
   E. A list of jurisdictions in which the Company and any of its subsidiaries are qualified to do business as a foreign corporation.
   F. Copies of all existing contractual provisions, preemptive rights, options, warrants, rights, calls, commitments, conversion plans, or other agreements providing for the issuance of any class of stock.
   G. A list of shareholders, indicating number of shares held.
   H. A list of option holders, indicating number of options held.
   I. Copies of standard option and option plan documentation.
   J. A list of all subsidiaries, identifying the name, jurisdiction of incorporation, and ownership of same.
   K. Copies of any material agreements relating to these subsidiaries.
   L. A list of all corporate obligations to purchase or subscribe, advance or loan monies to, or make any investment in any other corporation, joint venture, partnership, or other entity. Copies of any agreements related thereto.
   M. Copies of any agreements or letters prohibiting or restricting the sale of stock or securities.

N. A description of the history of the Company from founding to the present date.

2. References

A. References on all of the officer-level members of the management team (minimum 6, ideal 15 per individual). References should be business relationships, e.g., prior managers, coworkers, supervisors.
B. Customer or end-user references (minimum 10, ideal 20).
C. Reseller, Distributor, or Value-Added Dealer references (all relationships that sell for the Company).
D. Industry references, industry experts, people who are familiar with the marketplace, etc.
E. Bank references.
F. Accountant references.
G. Legal references.
H. Supplier references.

3. Financial Statements

A. Annual financial statements (P&L, Balance Sheet, Cash Flow) since inception.
B. Quarterly and/or monthly financial statements for the past two years.
C. Any audited or reviewed statements and the name and telephone number of the audit partner and senior accountant who worked on the account.
D. Management letters, if any, that have been prepared by auditors.
E. A schedule of all fixed assets.
F. An aging of accounts receivable (AR) by account and categorized as current, 30, 60, 90, 120, written-off.
G. The last three years of AR loss experience, and the Company's policy on reserving for AR losses.
H. A detailed, line item–by–line item breakdown of the income statement for the last 12 months, preferably in comparison to the latest 12-month operating plan.
I. Financial operating plan. Projections with all assumptions.
J. Historical AR and inventory turn data.
K. History of prior financings or financial sources.

4. Accounting Practices and Policies

   A. Revenue recognition policy. Sales return policy.
   B. Policy on accruals for vacations, audit expenses, AR reserves, inventory reserves, other reserves.
   C. Policy on inventory valuation.
   D. Credit policy.
   E. Capitalization of any expenses, particularly development of software (FASB Statement No. 86).
   F. A description of any other deferred revenue or expenses or accrued revenues or expenses.

5. Product/Service

   A. A description of all products or services offered by the Company.
   B. A description of the product/market fit. Where is this product used?
   C. Copies of all product literature, marketing materials, and advertisements.
   D. Product/service price list.
   E. A list of introduction dates of different products, if applicable.
   F. Product cost data, or gross margins by product.
   G. Detailed breakdown of revenue by product or service for the past three years.

6. New Products/Services

   A. Description of new products or services the Company is developing.
   B. Intended introduction dates of these products?

7. Market Data/Market Share Data

   A. Description of total available market for the Company's product(s)/service(s).
   B. Rate at which this market is estimated to be growing. Who is the source of these estimates, and is written estimate data available?
   C. Description of trends that are driving growth.
   D. Description of other trends in the marketplace.
   E. Projection of the Company's market share and relative market share.

F. Names of industry analysts/experts who can independently verify this data.

8. Revenue/Customers/Accounts

A. A description of how the products are marketed or how the service is provided. Does the Company price off of the price list? Are discounts given? How often are prices negotiated? Is work ever bid for? If prices are negotiated, who has the authority to negotiate on behalf of the Company?

B. A list of the 10 largest customers since inception, indicating dollar volume.

C. A complete list of all customers, with annual volume indicated.

D. A list of all independent distributors and copies of all distribution agreements.

E. Backlog, if appropriate.

F. A copy of the Company's standard credit policy.

G. Copies of any agreements or contracts that govern the relationship with customers.

H. Number of new customers acquired in each of the last three years.

I. Number of customers lost in each of the last three years.

J. Any service agreements with the customer base.

K. A complete description of the data that the Company has on its customer base.

L. Copies of any registration data or customer surveys.

9. Competitors

A. A list of all known competitors of the Company, and any likely future competitors.

B. Additional information on competitors' product/service positioning.

C. Basis of competition in the industry.

D. Reasons why the Company will outperform the competition.

10. Property, Plant, and Equipment

A. Summary description of all real estate owned or leased by the Company.

B. Liens and encumbrances on all real estate owned.

C. Options or agreements on or for any real property.

D. Copies of all leases and subleases pertaining to real estate.

E. Copies of any policies of title insurance relating to such real estate.

F. A complete schedule of all property, plant, and equipment.

G. A schedule of all leases related to property, plant, and equipment.

H. An explanation of the Company's depreciation policy.

11. Contracts and Commitments

A. A summary description and copy of all OEM agreements, reseller contracts, general contracts, other agreements, or other commitments that are material to the business.

B. A copy of any deferred sales contracts or agreements to provide services in the future.

C. Any verbal or oral material commitments that have been made by the officers of the Company.

D. A list of all suppliers to the Company together with copies of any purchasing agreements.

12. Agency

A. Copies of any agreements with sales agents, distributors, resellers, or individuals who have provided services to the Company within the past three years. Any agreements where the Company has been an agent, distributor, or reseller for another firm or product.

13. Inventory

A. Schedule of inventory type, stage, amount, condition, and location as of a recent date. Is any of the inventory on consignment? Is the inventory pledged as collateral for any obligation? Does the Company receive price protection or obsolescence protection on the inventory?

B. What has the Company's returned goods experience been for the past three years?

C. A description of inventory practices, including the following:

(i) Costing methods.

(ii) Frequency and timing of costing methods.

(iii) Standards for obsolescence.
(iv) Frequency of physical inventory.
(v) Other inventory practices.

14. Warranties

A. Copies of standard sales forms, sales acknowledgment forms, warranties, and/or the terms of sale.
B. A description of any damages paid to any third party since inception that resulted from an alleged breach of warranty or alleged product problem or defect.

15. Officers

A. Résumés of all officers of the Company.
B. Home addresses and Social Security numbers for all officers of the Company.
C. Employment agreements and contracts and/or offer letters for all officer-level employees.
D. Details of any oral promises, agreements, commitments, or pledges to compensate any employee or officer in any way in the future, including promises of stock or ownership in the Company.
E. Documentation for any loans or borrowings by any officer from the Company.
F. Schedule of all material transactions between the Company's officers, or any entity in which an officer has an economic interest, and the Company.
G. Have any of the officers ever been involved in a personal or corporate bankruptcy or been charged with, or convicted of, any type of fraud or a felony? Have any of the officers ever been charged or convicted of possession of an illegal substance, substance abuse, or operating a motor vehicle while intoxicated?
H. Are any of the officers seriously ill? Has any officer been seriously ill in the last 10 years? Have any of the officers been diagnosed to have any disease or condition that may affect their work performance during the next 10 years?
I. Do any of the officers have significant personal debt obligations apart from debt associated with education, primary housing, automobiles, or standard credit card debt? If so, describe.

16. Employees and Organization

A. An organization chart showing all reporting relationships.

B. A schedule of all employees showing latest 12-months' salaries, commissions, and bonuses.

C. Officer-level employee job descriptions.

D. A complete list of all employees who have ever left the Company or have been fired. Provide current phone numbers.

E. A description and copies of all existing contracts of employment, collective bargaining agreements, incentive plans, bonus arrangements, and other compensation agreements between the Company and its officers, directors, and employees.

F. A description of any labor disputes or work stoppages since inception, indicating the disposition thereof.

G. A copy of form of nondisclosure agreement obtained from employees.

H. A copy of form of noncompete agreement obtained from employees.

I. A copy of form of assignment of inventions agreement obtained from employees.

J. A schedule listing each employee and indicating whether a signed copy of each of the above agreements is on file for each employee.

K. A description of all pension, employee retirement, bonus, or profit sharing plans that the Company offers.

L. Copies of all employee handbooks or policies and procedures manuals.

M. A description of the nature and extent of medical and dental care benefits.

N. Copies of any employee–union agreements.

O. A list of all employment-related lawsuits that have been filed or threatened in the last five years.

P. Has the Company been charged by any government agency with any employment-related violation? If so, what?

17. Intellectual Property

A. A list of each of the software programs or products of the Company, a description of the functions and features of each, and a chronology of their respective developments. Indicate authorship or ownership of each software product and related technology. If ownership resides with a third party, explain the royalty arrangement and the provisions for buyout, if any. Also discuss the arrangements regarding product enhancements and upgrades.

B. All records and documentation maintained by the Company documenting the development, authorship, or ownership of the software programs and related technology. A list of all public domain materials incorporated in the software programs. A list of all third-party materials incorporated into the software programs.

C. A list of all agreements with third parties, whether now in effect or terminated, for the design, development, programming, enhancement, or maintenance of the software programs. To the extent third parties have designed, developed, programmed, enhanced, or maintained such software programs without having executed any agreement, a list of all such third parties and a description of the work performed and the period during which such work was performed by such party.

D. A description of all policies followed by the Company to protect the copyright and trade-secret rights in its software programs and related technology—including any legends used, how they are used, and whether they are uniformly used—and the manner in which the software is physically protected (regardless of the media on which it is stored).

E. A description of the instances in which source code relating to the software programs of the Company has been disclosed to persons outside the organization of the Company, and any agreements involving disclosure of source code relating to the software programs (e.g., source code escrow agreements).

F. A list of all licenses, franchises, royalty agreements, marketing agreements, distributorships, sales representative agreements, or similar commitments or arrangements relating to the software programs or related technology granted to third parties by the Company or by any third party to the Company.

G. Agreements, options, or other commitments giving anyone rights to acquire any right, title, or interest in the software programs or related technology of the Company.

H. A list of all trademarks and trade names owned or used in the business of the Company, showing the registration number, date of registration, registrant, and a copy of the certification of registration, if any. Samples of any recent or current advertisements or promotional literature relating to the software programs.

I. A list of all patents used in the business of, or owned by, the Company.

J. Copyright registrations (if any) issued or pending relating to the software programs.

18. Litigation

A. A description and copies of any outstanding order, injunction, decree, or judgment of any court or any other administrative or regulatory body or any arbitration tribunal binding upon the Company or any of its property.

B. A description and current status of all actions, suits, investigations, or proceedings by or before any court, arbitration tribunal, or administrative or regulatory body to which the Company is a party.

C. A description and status of any threatened or possible suits based upon the best knowledge of the Company and its officers.

D. Auditors' inquiry letters to attorneys retained by the Company concerning litigation and attorneys' responses thereto since inception.

E. A chronological history of all suits, actions, or threatened actions which have led to settlements either in or out of court, with a description of each dispute and its resolution.

19. Insurance

A. A schedule of all insurance presently carried by the Company, indicating the carriers, risks insured against, amounts of self-insurance or coinsurance, persons or entities or properties insured, and amount of insurance.

B. A description of any pending claims.

20. Regulatory Compliance

A. A list of all regulatory permits and licenses possessed by the Company or by any subsidiary, and the date of expiration of each.

B. A description of any known noncompliance with any zoning or building codes, environmental laws or regulations, or occupational safety laws or regulations, and what action the Company has taken or is taking with respect thereto.

C. All reports to, correspondence with, and notices from national, federal, state, and local regulatory and enforcement agencies (including FTC, OSHA, EEOC, EPA, NLRB, Justice, and their counterparts).

21. Financing Agreements

A. All agreements, memoranda, and offering materials pursuant to which any person has purchased or has the right to purchase securities of the Company.
B. A list and copies of all mortgages, indentures, loan agreements, credit facilities, capitalized leases, letter of credit reimbursement agreements, bank loans, or other indebtedness to which the Company is a party.
C. All correspondence with lending institutions concerning defaults, requests for waivers, extensions, modifications, collateral, and other matters in connection with the loan agreements identified above.
D. A list and copies of all agreements pursuant to which the Company or a subsidiary has guaranteed or provided a surety or letter of credit for the obligations of any person or entity.
E. Recent calculations indicating compliance with the financial covenants contained in the financing agreements and guarantees referred to above, if any.

22. Taxes

A. Notice of whether the Company or any subsidiary is or has been included in a consolidated group for tax purposes with any other person or entity, naming such person or entity.
B. Copies of the national, federal, and state income tax returns for each of the past three years.
C. Notice of current status of any national, federal, or state tax audits.
D. A description of any tax issue raised by an examination of the national, federal, or state income tax returns either by a taxing authority or by your outside auditor.

23. Bank Accounts

A. A list of all bank accounts and safe deposit boxes maintained by the Company and the names of all persons who are authorized to draw thereon or who have access thereto.
B. A list of all credit cards and who is authorized to use them.

24. Other

A. Copies of any management or consultants' reports prepared for the Company or any subsidiary since inception with respect to its business or products.

B. Any available descriptive material relating to the present or proposed products of the Company or any subsidiary, including background material in periodicals or reports regarding the industry, competitive and related products, press releases, etc., since the Company's inception.

C. Any other document or information that, in your judgment, is significant to the Company or its business.

As an officer of Company, I hereby certify that I have provided the information requested above or truthfully answered the question presented above; or that where appropriate I have stated that such information is not available. To the best of my knowledge all of the answers presented above are complete, accurate, and not misleading.

By: ______________________________

Title: ______________________________

Date: ______________________________

APPENDIX G • SUBSCRIPTION AGREEMENT

THE.COM, INC.

PRIVATE PLACEMENT

150 Units

Each Unit consists of 10,000 shares of Series C Convertible Preferred Stock and
A Warrant to purchase 500 shares of Common Stock

Minimum Offering: 10 Units

Maximum Offering: 100 Units

Purchase Price: $100,000 per Unit

Minimum Investment: $100,000 (one Unit)

SUBSCRIPTION DOCUMENTS

---

* Page number references within this document refer to the original agreement and have not been altered for publication of *Financing Start-Ups.*

INSTRUCTIONS FOR INVESTORS

To subscribe for Units, each prospective investor must complete an investor questionnaire and furnish the information requested on and sign the omnibus signature page relating to the investor questionnaire, Subscription Agreement and the Restated Investor Rights Agreement (such documents being the "Subscription Documents"), as follows:

1. Complete the information requested on the signature page in accordance with your investor status:

• Individual investors must complete the Individual Investor Questionnaire and Omnibus Signature Page (Note: If an individual is investing jointly with another individual or spouse, such other individual or spouse must complete a separate Individual Investor Questionnaire.)	blue sheets
• Trust investors must complete the Trust Questionnaire and Omnibus Signature Page	pink sheets
• Partnership investors must complete the Partnership Questionnaire and Omnibus Signature Page	yellow sheets
• Corporate investors must complete the Corporate Questionnaire and Omnibus Signature Page	green sheets
• Retirement Plan investors must complete the Retirement Plan Questionnaire and Omnibus Signature Page	gold sheets

In all cases, the completed documents must be executed by an individual authorized to bind the investor.

2. Return the completed documents to Madison Securities, Inc. (the "Placement Agent") at the following address:

The Placement Agent, Inc.
Attn:

This Offering is conditioned upon the receipt and acceptance of subscriptions for the purchase of at least 10 Units, and the receipt of the full purchase price therefor, on or before the 90th day after the date of this Confidential Private Placement Memorandum (the "Offering Memorandum"), unless such date is extended for up to an additional 60 days at the option of the Company and the Placement Agent without notice to subscribers (the "Offering Termination Date"). The Company has the right, in its sole discretion, to accept or reject any subscription in whole or in part. Purchase price payments will be delivered to ___________ Bank (the "Escrow Agent") for deposit in an interest-bearing account by noon of the next business day following their receipt. If subscriptions for at least 10 Units have not been received and accepted, and the full purchase price therefor has not been received, on or before the Offering Termination Date, the Offering will be terminated and all funds will be returned promptly to subscribers without any interest thereon, and without charge or deduction.

If a subscriber has relied upon an investor representative in connection with evaluating the purchase of Units, such subscriber must have the investor representative complete an Investor Representative Questionnaire, which is available upon request from the Company.

No person is authorized to receive the Subscription Documents unless preceded or accompanied by a copy of this Offering Memorandum. Reproduction or circulation of the Subscription Documents, in whole or in part, is prohibited.

UNITS ARE BEING OFFERED FOR SALE ONLY TO "ACCREDITED INVESTORS" AS THAT TERM IS DEFINED IN RULE 501 UNDER THE SECURITIES ACT OF 1933, AS AMENDED. IN ORDER FOR THE COMPANY TO MAKE A DETERMINATION AS TO A SUBSCRIBER'S STATUS AS AN ACCREDITED INVESTOR, EACH SUBSCRIBER IS REQUIRED TO MAKE CERTAIN REPRESENTATIONS AND WARRANTIES AND TO COMPLETE CERTAIN INFORMATION, ALL OF WHICH IS CONTAINED IN THE PROSPECTIVE INVESTOR QUESTIONNAIRE.

BY EXECUTING THE SIGNATURE PAGE INCLUDED HEREIN, EACH SUBSCRIBER ACKNOWLEDGES AND AGREES AS FOLLOWS:

IN MAKING AN INVESTMENT DECISION, SUBSCRIBERS MUST RELY ON THEIR OWN EXAMINATION OF THE ENTITY ISSUING THE SECURITIES AND THE TERMS OF THE OFFERING, INCLUDING THE MERITS AND RISKS INVOLVED. THESE SECURITIES HAVE NOT BEEN RECOMMENDED OR APPROVED BY ANY FEDERAL OR STATE SECURITIES COMMISSION OR REGULATORY AUTHORITY. FURTHERMORE,

THE FOREGOING AUTHORITIES HAVE NOT CONFIRMED THE ACCURACY OR DETERMINED THE ADEQUACY OF THIS DOCUMENT, THE SUBSCRIPTION DOCUMENTS, OR THE OFFERING MEMORANDUM AND ANY REPRESENTATION TO THE CONTRARY IS A CRIMINAL OFFENSE. THESE SECURITIES ARE SUBJECT TO RESTRICTIONS ON TRANSFERABILITY AND RESALE AND MAY NOT BE TRANSFERRED OR RESOLD EXCEPT AS PERMITTED UNDER THE SECURITIES ACT OF 1933, AS AMENDED, AND APPLICABLE STATE SECURITIES LAWS PURSUANT TO REGISTRATION OR EXEMPTION THEREFROM. INVESTORS AGREE THAT THEY ARE ACQUIRING THE UNITS FOR INVESTMENT AND NOT WITH A VIEW TOWARD RESALE OR DISTRIBUTION AND THAT THEY ARE AWARE THAT NO TRADING MARKET FOR THE UNITS, OR THE SECURITIES COMPRISING THE UNITS, IS LIKELY TO EXIST AT ANY TIME. SUBSCRIBERS SHOULD BE AWARE THAT THEY WILL BE REQUIRED TO BEAR THE FINANCIAL RISKS OF THIS INVESTMENT FOR AN INDEFINITE PERIOD OF TIME, THE COMPANY HAS LIMITED FINANCIAL AND OPERATING HISTORY AND THAT THE UNITS ARE SPECULATIVE INVESTMENTS THAT INVOLVE A HIGH DEGREE OF RISK OF LOSS BY INVESTORS OF THEIR ENTIRE INVESTMENT. SUBSCRIBERS AGREE THEY HAVE NOT BEEN INDUCED TO INVEST BY ANY FORM OF GENERAL SOLICITATION OR GENERAL ADVERTISING.

SUBSCRIPTION AGREEMENT

The.com, Inc.

Gentlemen:

1. Purchase and Sale. The.com, Inc., a _______ corporation (the "Company"), has offered for sale, and the undersigned purchaser (the "Purchaser") hereby tenders this subscription and applies for the purchase of, the number of units (the "Units") set forth on the accompanying Omnibus Signature Page (the "Signature Page") contained in the Company's Confidential Private Placement Memorandum dated as of _____, __, 2000 (as amended from time to time, the "Offering Memorandum") at the purchase price per Unit equal to One Hundred Thousand Dollars ($100,000) (the "Offering"). The Offering is conditioned upon the Company's receipt and acceptance of subscriptions for a minimum of 10 Units (the "Minimum Offering Amount") and the Company's receipt of the full purchase price therefor. Each Unit consists of 10,000 shares of the Company's Series C Convertible Preferred Stock, par value $.01 per share

(the "Preferred Stock"), and a warrant (the "Warrant") to purchase 500 shares of the Company's common stock, par value $.01 per share (the "Common Stock"). Purchaser must subscribe for a minimum of one Unit (i.e., $100,000), which requirement may be waived in the Company's sole discretion. Together with this Subscription Agreement, the Purchaser is delivering to the Company the full aggregate amount of the purchase price for the Units (the "Purchase Price") subscribed for. This subscription may be rejected by the Company in its sole discretion in whole or in part. Upon the closing of the sale of the Units subscribed for hereunder, the Purchaser shall become a party to the Company's Restated Investor Rights Agreement, dated as of [______ ___, _______] (the "Investor Rights Agreement"), which is attached as Exhibit D to the Offering Memorandum. THE SIGNATURE OF THE UNDERSIGNED ON THE OMNIBUS SIGNATURE PAGE CONSTITUTES THE EXECUTION OF THIS SUBSCRIPTION AGREEMENT AND, SUBJECT TO THE CLOSING OF THE SALE OF THE UNITS SUBSCRIBED FOR HEREUNDER, THE INVESTOR RIGHTS AGREEMENT.

2. Amount and Method of Payment. Payment of the Purchase Price required to purchase the number of Units subscribed for hereunder is being made by check payable to "________ Bank as Escrow Agent for The.com, Inc." or wire transfer in the amount of $100,000 for each Unit subscribed for, which represents payment in full for each Unit. If payment is to be made by wire transfer, the Purchaser shall contact the Placement Agent to obtain appropriate wire transfer instructions. If a subscription is rejected in whole or in part or if the Offering is terminated for any reason, the Purchaser's subscription shall be void and all funds received from the Purchaser shall be returned as soon as practicable to the Purchaser without any interest thereon, and without charge or deduction.

3. Representations and Warranties of the Company. The Company represents and warrants to the Purchaser that:

(a) The Company is a corporation duly organized, validly existing and in good standing under the laws of its jurisdiction of incorporation, and has the corporate power and the authority to carry on its business as conducted or proposed to be conducted by it and to hold title to its property, which business and property is described in the Offering Memorandum. The Company has the corporate power and authority to execute and deliver this Subscription Agreement and to perform its obligations hereunder and is duly qualified to transact business and is in good standing in each jurisdiction in which the conduct of its business or its ownership or leasing of property requires such qualification, except to the extent that the failure to be so qualified or be in good standing would not have a material adverse effect on the Company and its subsidiaries, taken as a whole.

(b) Each subsidiary of the Company has been duly incorporated, is validly existing as a corporation in good standing under the laws of the jurisdiction of its incorporation, has the corporate power and authority to own its property and to conduct its business as described in the Offering Memorandum and, except as described in the Offering Memorandum, is duly qualified to transact business and is in good standing in each jurisdiction in which the conduct of its business or its ownership or leasing of property requires such qualification, except to the extent that the failure to be so qualified or be in good standing would not have a material adverse effect on the Company and its subsidiaries, taken as whole; and all of the issued shares of capital stock of each subsidiary of the Company have been duly and validly authorized and issued, are fully paid and nonassessable and are owned by the Company, free and clear of all liens, encumbrances, equities or claims.

(c) The shares of capital stock of the Company outstanding on the date hereof have been duly authorized, validly issued, fully paid and non-assessable, and the authorized capital stock of the Company conforms as to legal matters to the description thereof contained in the Offering Memorandum.

(d) The Units and the securities comprising the Units have been duly authorized and, when delivered to and paid for by the Purchaser in accordance with the terms of this Subscription Agreement will be validly issued, fully paid and non-assessable, and none of such securities will be subject to any preemptive or similar rights.

(e) The shares of Common Stock issuable upon conversion of the Preferred Stock (the "Conversion Shares") and the shares of Common Stock issuable upon exercise of the Warrants (the "Exercise Shares") have been duly authorized and reserved and, when issued upon conversion of the Preferred Stock and upon exercise of the Warrants, in accordance with the respective terms of such securities, will be validly issued, fully paid and non-assessable, and the issuance of the Conversion Shares and the Exercise Shares will not be subject to any preemptive or similar rights.

(f) The Offering Memorandum does not include any untrue statement of a material fact or omit to state a material fact necessary in order to make the statements therein, in light of the circumstances under which they were made, not misleading.

(g) Except as disclosed in the Offering Memorandum, there are no actions, suits, proceedings or investigations pending or, to the best of the Company's knowledge, threatened against or affecting the Company or any of its subsidiaries (i) that could prevent or interfere with or adversely affect the execution and delivery by the Company of this Subscription Agreement, the Investor Rights Agreement or the performance by the Company of its obligations hereunder or thereunder or the offering, issuance and sale of the Units, or (ii) that, individually or in the aggregate, would have a material adverse effect on the value of the assets or the operation of the business of the Company and its subsidiaries, taken as a whole.

(h) All requisite authorizations, approvals or orders from any court, governmental or regulatory official or body necessary to permit the Company to conduct its business as described in the Offering Memorandum have been obtained. No consent, authorization, approval or order of, or qualification with, any court or any governmental or regulatory official or body is required for the consummation by the Company of the transactions contemplated by this Subscription Agreement or the Investor Rights Agreement, except such as may be required by the federal securities laws to perfect any exemption from registration or by the securities or Blue Sky laws of the various states in connection with the offer and sale of the Units and by federal or by state securities laws with respect to the Company's obligations under the Investor Rights Agreement.

(i) This Subscription Agreement has been duly and validly authorized, executed and delivered by the Company and constitutes the valid and binding agreement of the Company, enforceable in accordance with its terms, except that such enforcement may be subject to the effect of any applicable bankruptcy, insolvency, reorganization, moratorium, fraudulent conveyance and other similar laws relating to or affecting creditors' rights generally and general principles of equity (regardless of whether such enforcement is considered in a proceeding in equity or at law).

(j) The Investor Rights Agreement has been duly authorized, executed and delivered by the Company and constitutes a valid and binding agreement of the Company, enforceable in accordance with its terms, except that such enforcement may be subject to applicable bankruptcy, insolvency, reorganization, moratorium, fraudulent conveyance and other similar laws relating to or affecting creditors' rights generally and general principles of equity (regardless of whether such enforcement is considered in a proceeding in equity or at law) and except as rights to indemnification and contribution under the Investor Rights Agreement may be limited under applicable law.

(k) The Company's execution and delivery of this Subscription Agreement, the Investor Rights Agreement, the fulfillment of the terms set forth herein or therein and the consummation of the transactions contemplated herein or therein do not and will not conflict with or constitute a breach or violation of, or default under (i) the Company's articles of incorporation or by-laws, (ii) any material agreement, indenture or instrument by which the Company or any of its subsidiaries is bound (except to the extent such conflict, breach, violation or default would not have a material adverse effect on the value of the assets or the operation of the business of the Company and its subsidiaries, taken as a whole), or (iii) any law, administrative regulation or court decree (except to the extent such conflict, breach, violation or default would not have a material adverse effect on the value of the assets or the operation of the business of the Company and its subsidiaries, taken as a whole).

(l) All sales of securities made by the Company at any time since its inception were issued pursuant to valid exemptions under applicable federal and state securities laws, and except for compensation paid to The Placement Agent, Inc. (the "Placement Agent"), no commissions were paid and no advertising or other general solicitation was made in connection with any of such sales.

(m) The proceeds of the sale of the Units will be utilized substantially in the manner set forth in the Offering Memorandum, and the proposed business of the Company will conform in all material respects to the description thereof contained in the Offering Memorandum.

(n) The Company represents and warrants that the financial statements of the Company contained in the Offering Memorandum have been prepared in accordance with generally accepted accounting principles consistently applied throughout the periods covered thereby, and present fairly the financial position of the Company as of the date indicated. In the opinion of management, all adjustments (consisting only of normal recurring adjustments) have been made which are considered necessary for a fair presentation of such information for the periods presented. Except for the transactions contemplated by the Offering Memorandum, there has been no material adverse change in the condition (financial or otherwise) of the Company and its subsidiaries, taken as a whole, from that set forth in the Offering Memorandum.

(o) The Company is not and, after giving effect to the offering and sale of the Units and the application of the proceeds thereof as described in the Offering Memorandum, will not be an "investment company" or a company "controlled" by an "investment company" within the meaning of the Investment Company Act of 1940, as amended.

(p) Neither the Company nor any of its affiliates has received or is entitled to receive, directly or indirectly, any compensation or other benefit in connection with the Offering including, but not limited to, any commission or similar fee, except as described in the Offering Memorandum.

(q) The Company has not paid or awarded, and will not pay or award, directly or indirectly, any commission or other compensation to any person engaged to render investment advice to a potential purchaser of the Units as an inducement to advise the purchase of the Units, except as such commissions or other compensation may be paid or awarded to the Placement Agent in accordance with this Subscription Agreement in connection with the sale of the Units as described in the Offering Memorandum.

(r) Any written or oral information provided to the Purchaser by authorized representatives of the Company other than the Placement Agent does not contain any untrue statement of a material fact or, when taken together with the information set forth in the Offering Memorandum, omit to state a material fact required to be stated therein or necessary to make the statements therein, in light of the circumstances under which they were made, not misleading.

(s) Other than the Placement Agent, the Company has not contracted with any person to act as a finder or investment adviser in connection with the transactions described herein.

4. Representations and Warranties of Purchaser. In order to induce the Company to accept this subscription, the Purchaser hereby represents and warrants to, and covenants with, the Company as follows:

(a) (i) The undersigned understands that the Units, the securities comprising the Units, the Conversion Shares and the Exercise Shares have not been registered under the Securities Act of 1933, as amended (the "1933 Act"), or the securities laws of any state, by reason of their contemplated issuance in transactions exempt from the prospectus and delivery requirements of the Act, and that the reliance on such exemption from registration is predicated in part on these representations and warranties of the Purchaser. The Purchaser acknowledges that pursuant to Section 7 hereof a restrictive legend consistent with the foregoing has been or will be placed on the certificates for the shares of Preferred Stock, the Conversion Shares and the Exercise Shares. The Purchaser understands that neither the Securities and Exchange Commission ("SEC") nor any state securities commission has approved the Units, the securities comprising the Units, the Conversion Shares or the Exercise Shares or passed upon or endorsed the merits of the investment or reviewed or confirmed the accuracy or determined the adequacy of any information furnished to the Purchaser in connection with the Offering.

(ii) The Purchaser is acquiring the Units and the securities comprising the Units solely for the account of the Purchaser, for investment purposes only, and not with the present intention of reselling or distributing the Units or the securities comprising the Units, or any arrangement or understanding with any other person regarding the distribution of Units or the securities comprising the Units. The Purchaser further agrees not to transfer the Units or the securities comprising the Units in violation of the 1933 Act or any applicable state securities law. The Purchaser confirms that no one other than the Purchaser has any beneficial interest in the Units or the securities comprising the Units;

(iii) The Units, the securities comprising the Units, the Conversion Shares and the Exercise Shares are and will be "restricted securities," as said term is defined in Rule 144 promulgated under the 1933 Act, and the undersigned understands that such securities may not be sold or otherwise disposed of without registration under the 1933 Act or an exemption therefrom, and that in the absence of an effective registration statement covering such securities or an available exemption from registration under the 1933 Act, such securities must be held indefinitely;

(iv) The Purchaser agrees that it will not sell or otherwise dispose of any of the Units, the securities comprising the Units, the Conversion Shares and the Exercise Shares unless such sale or other disposition (x) has been registered under the 1933 Act or is exempt from registration under the 1933 Act and (y) has been registered or qualified or is exempt from registration or qualification under the applicable state securities laws. The Purchaser may not sell, transfer, or otherwise dispose of the Units, the securities comprising the Units, the Conversion Shares and the Exercise Shares except in compliance with the applicable rules of the SEC;

(v) The Purchaser is an "accredited investor," as such term is defined in Rule 501(a) of Regulation D promulgated under the Act; and

(vi) The Purchaser is not an officer, director or "affiliate" (as that term is defined in Rule 405 promulgated under the Act) of the Company.

(b) (i) The Purchaser has received and carefully reviewed the Offering Memorandum;

(ii) The Purchaser has had a reasonable opportunity to ask questions of and receive answers from the Company concerning the Company and the Offering and to verify the accuracy of any representation or information set forth in the Offering Memorandum, and all such questions, if any, have been answered to the full satisfaction of the Purchaser;

(iii) The Purchaser has received from the Company, and has reviewed, such information that the Purchaser considers necessary or appropriate to evaluate the risks and merits of an investment in the Units, including without limitation, the Offering Memorandum. The Purchaser acknowledges that the information set forth under the heading of "Risk Factors" in the Offering Memorandum is specifically incorporated herein by reference and forms an integral part of this Subscription Agreement;

(iv) The Purchaser has such knowledge and expertise in financial and business matters that the Purchaser is capable of evaluating the merits and risks involved in an investment in the Units and acknowledges that an investment in the Units entails a number of very significant risks and funds should only be invested if the Purchaser is able to withstand the total loss of his investment;

(v) Except as set forth in this Subscription Agreement, no representations or warranties have been made to the Purchaser by the Company or any agent, employee or affiliate of the Company (including the Placement Agent). The Purchaser has relied solely on the representations, warranties, covenants and agreements of the Company in this Subscription Agreement and on the Purchaser's examination and independent investigation in making its decision to acquire the Units;

(vi) The Purchaser understands that the Units are being offered and sold expressly conditioned upon the satisfaction of specific exemptions from the registration requirements of the federal and state securities laws and that the Company is relying upon the truth and accuracy of the representations, warranties, agreements, acknowledgments and understandings of the Purchaser set forth herein and in the related investor questionnaire in order to determine the applicability of such exemptions and the suitability of the Purchaser to acquire the Units, and the Purchaser acknowledges that it is solely the Purchaser's responsibility to satisfy itself as to the full observance by this Offering and the sale of the Units to Purchaser of the laws of any jurisdiction outside the United States and Purchaser has done so;

(vii) If an individual, the Purchaser is over 21 years old and is legally competent to execute this Subscription Agreement; if an entity, the Purchaser is duly authorized to invest in the Units, and the individual signing this Subscription Agreement has been duly authorized by the Purchaser to do so;

(viii) The Purchaser has full power and authority to execute and deliver this Subscription Agreement and to perform the Purchaser's obligations hereunder, and this Subscription Agreement is a legally binding obligation of the Purchaser enforceable against Purchaser in accordance with its terms; and

(ix) The Purchaser has not incurred any obligation for any finder's, or broker's agent's fees or commission in connection with the transactions contemplated hereby.

(c) All the information which the undersigned has furnished to the Company, or which is set forth herein, is correct and complete as of the date of this Subscription Agreement, and if there should be any material change in such information, the Purchaser will immediately furnish such revised or corrected information to the Company. Unless the Company receives written notice from the Purchaser furnishing such revised or corrected information, the Company shall be entitled to assume that the information furnished is accurate in all respects on (i) the date on which subscriptions for at least 10 Units have been received and accepted, and full payment of the purchase price therefor has been received, and (ii) on the dates of subsequent closings of the sales of Units by the Company.

5. Binding Effect. The Purchaser understands that this subscription is not binding upon the Company until the Company accepts it, which acceptance is at the sole discretion of the Company and is to be evidenced by the Company's execution of the Signature Page where indicated. This Subscription Agreement shall be null and void if the Company does not accept it as aforesaid. Upon acceptance by the Company and receipt of the Purchase Price, the Company will promptly issue (but in any event within five business days of such sale) to the Purchaser a certificate for the full number of shares of Preferred Stock purchased and a Warrant representing the right to purchase the full number of shares of Common Stock.

6. Acceptance in Part. The Purchaser understands that the Company may, in its sole discretion, reject this subscription in whole or in part and reduce this subscription by any amount and to any extent.

7. Legends. To the extent applicable, each certificate representing the Preferred Stock, the Conversion Shares and the Exercise Shares shall be endorsed with the legend substantially in the form set forth below:

> THE SHARES REPRESENTED HEREBY HAVE NOT BEEN REGISTERED UNDER THE SECURITIES ACT OF 1933, AS AMENDED (THE "ACT"), OR ANY STATE SECURITIES LAW AND MAY NOT BE SOLD, TRANSFERRED, ASSIGNED, PLEDGED, OR HYPOTHECATED EXCEPT AS PERMITTED UNDER THE ACT AND THE APPLICABLE STATE SECURITIES LAWS, PURSUANT TO REGISTRATION OR EXEMPTION THEREFROM. THE ISSUER OF THESE SECURITIES MAY REQUIRE AN OPINION OF COUNSEL REASONABLY SATISFACTORY TO THE ISSUER TO

THE EFFECT THAT ANY PROPOSED SALE, TRANSFER, ASSIGNMENT, PLEDGE, OR HYPOTHECATION IS IN COMPLIANCE WITH THE ACT AND ANY APPLICABLE STATE SECURITIES LAWS.

8. Indemnification on Purchase of Units.

(a) The Purchaser agrees to indemnify the Company and hold it harmless from and against any and all losses, damages, liabilities, costs and expenses (including, but not limited to, any and all expenses reasonably incurred in investigating or defending against any litigation commenced or threatened or any claim whatsoever) which it may sustain or incur in connection with the breach by the Purchaser of any representation, warranty, or covenant made by it herein or in the investor questionnaire.

(b) The Company agrees to indemnify the Purchaser and hold it harmless from and against any and all losses, damages, liabilities, costs and expenses (including, but not limited to, any and all expenses reasonably incurred in investigating or defending against any litigation commenced or threatened or any claim whatsoever) which it may sustain or incur in connection with the breach by the Company of any representation, warranty or covenant made by it herein.

9. Confidentiality. The Purchaser acknowledges and agrees that all information relating to the Company and this subscription, including, but not limited to, the information contained in the Offering Memorandum, shall be kept confidential by the Purchaser, except as otherwise required by law or made public other than by or through the undersigned.

10. Nontransferability. Neither this Subscription Agreement nor any of the rights of the Purchaser hereunder may be transferred or assigned by the Purchaser.

11. Amendment; Entire Agreement; Governing Law. This Subscription Agreement (i) may only be modified by a written instrument executed by the Purchaser and the Company, (ii) together with the Investor Questionnaire, Omnibus Signature Page, and Investor Rights Agreement sets forth the entire agreement of the Purchaser and the Company with respect to the subject matter hereof and supersedes all prior agreements and understandings between or among the parties with respect to the subject matter hereof, (iii) shall be governed by the laws of the State of __________ applicable to contracts made and to be wholly performed therein, and (iv) shall

inure to the benefit of, and be binding upon, the Company and the Purchaser and their respective heirs, legal representatives, successors and assigns.

12. Notices. All notices, requests, demands, claims and other communications hereunder shall be in writing and shall be delivered by certified or registered mail (first class postage pre-paid), guaranteed overnight delivery, or facsimile transmission if such transmission is confirmed by delivery by certified or registered mail (first class postage pre-paid) or guaranteed overnight delivery, to the following address and facsimile numbers (or to such other addresses or facsimile numbers which such party shall subsequently designate in writing to the other party): (a) If to the Company: The.com, Inc., ____________Attention: ________; facsimile: (___) ___-____; and (b) If to the Purchaser: to the address set forth on the investor questionnaire of such Purchaser; with a copy to: The Placement Agent, Inc., ____________, Attention: ____________, facsimile: (___) ___-____.

13. Pronouns. Unless the context otherwise requires, all personal pronouns used in this Subscription Agreement, whether in the masculine, feminine or neuter gender, shall include all other genders.

14. Survival of the Warranties. The warranties, representations, and covenants of the Company and the Purchaser contained in or made pursuant to this Agreement shall survive the execution and delivery of this Agreement and the closing of the sale of the Units subscribed for hereunder.

15. Counterparts. This Agreement may be executed in two or more counterparts, each of which shall be deemed an original, but all of which together shall constitute one and the same instrument.

THIS SUBSCRIPTION AGREEMENT AND, SUBJECT TO THE CLOSING OF THE SALE OF THE UNITS SUBSCRIBED FOR HEREUNDER, THE INVESTOR RIGHTS AGREEMENT WILL BE DEEMED TO HAVE BEEN EXECUTED FOR ALL PURPOSES WHEN THE PURCHASER SIGNS THE OMNIBUS SIGNATURE PAGE PROVIDED HEREWITH.

THE INDIVIDUAL INVESTOR OMNIBUS SIGNATURE PAGE IS CONTAINED ON PAGES E-16 AND E-17.

THE TRUST INVESTOR OMNIBUS SIGNATURE PAGE IS CONTAINED ON PAGES E-24 AND E-25.

THE PARTNERSHIP INVESTOR OMNIBUS SIGNATURE PAGE IS CONTAINED ON PAGES E-32 AND E-33.

THE CORPORATE INVESTOR OMNIBUS SIGNATURE PAGE IS CONTAINED ON PAGES E-41 AND E-42.

THE RETIREMENT PLAN INVESTOR OMNIBUS SIGNATURE PAGE IS CONTAINED ON PAGES E-49 AND E-50.

IMPORTANT:
Please Complete

Investor Name:________________________

Account No.:________________________

Offering Memorandum No.____________
(from the cover of the Offering Memorandum)

ALLOCATED ❑
WAIT LIST ❑

INDIVIDUAL INVESTOR QUESTIONNAIRE

The.com, Inc.

The.com, Inc.

The information in this Questionnaire is being furnished in order to determine whether the undersigned's subscription to purchase the Units of The.com, Inc., (the "Company") may be accepted. The Company will not offer or sell Units to any investor who has not completed a Questionnaire.

ALL INFORMATION CONTAINED IN THIS QUESTIONNAIRE WILL BE TREATED CONFIDENTIALLY.

IF YOU ARE PURCHASING UNITS WITH YOUR SPOUSE, OR, IF YOU ARE MARRIED AND LIVE IN A COMMUNITY PROPERTY STATE, BOTH YOU AND YOUR SPOUSE MUST SIGN THE OMNIBUS SIGNATURE PAGE (PAGES E-16 and E-17).

IF YOU ARE PURCHASING UNITS WITH ANOTHER PERSON NOT YOUR SPOUSE, YOU MUST EACH FILL OUT A SEPARATE QUESTIONNAIRE. Please make a photocopy of pages E-12 through E-15 and return both completed Questionnaires to the Company in the same envelope.

THIS INVESTOR QUESTIONNAIRE WILL BE DEEMED TO HAVE BEEN EXECUTED FOR ALL PURPOSES WHEN THE INVESTOR SIGNS THE OMNIBUS SIGNATURE PAGE ANNEXED HERETO.

I. *PLEASE INDICATE DESIRED TYPE OF OWNERSHIP OF UNITS:*

❑ Individual

❑ Joint Tenants (rights of survivorship)

❑ Tenants in Common (no rights to survivorship)

II. *PLEASE CHECK ONE OF THE FOLLOWING:*

I live in a community property state.

❑ Yes

❑ No

III. *PLEASE CHECK ANY OF STATEMENTS 1-3 BELOW THAT APPLY TO YOU:*

❑ 1. I have an individual net worth or joint net worth[1] with my spouse in excess of $1,000,000.

❑ 2. I have had an individual income* in excess of $200,000 in each of the two most recently completed years and I reasonably expect an individual income in excess of $200,000 in the current year.

❑ 3. My spouse and I have had a joint income* in excess of $300,000 in each of the two most recently completed years and we reasonably expect a joint income in excess of $300,000 in the current year.

---

* For purposes of this Questionnaire, the term "net worth" means the excess of total assets over total liabilities <u>exclusive</u> of home, home furnishings and automobiles. In determining income, an investor should add to his or her adjusted gross income as reflected on his or her most recent federal income tax return any amounts attributable to tax-exempt income received, losses claimed as a limited partner in any limited partnership, deductions claimed for depletion, contributions to IRA or Keogh retirement plans, alimony payments and any amount by which income from long-term capital gains has been reduced in arriving at adjusted gross income.

IV. OTHER CERTIFICATIONS.

By signing the Omnibus Signature Page, I certify the following (or, if I am purchasing Units with my spouse as co-owner, each of us certifies the following):

(a) that I am at least 21 years of age; and

(b) that the name, home address and social security number or taxpayer identification number as set forth in this Questionnaire are true, correct and complete; and

(c) that one of the following is true and correct (check one):

Purchaser	Spouse, if Co-Owner	
❑	❑	I am a United Sates citizen or resident of the United States for United States federal income tax purposes.
❑	❑	I am neither a United States citizen nor a resident of the United States for United States federal income tax purposes.

ALL PROSPECTIVE INVESTORS MUST MAKE THE FOLLOWING CERTIFICATIONS:

The undersigned's total proposed investment in the Units:

does <u>not</u> represent more than:

❑ 10% of the undersigned's net worth.
❑ 15% of the undersigned's net worth.
❑ 20% of the undersigned's net worth.
❑ 25% of the undersigned's net worth.
❑ 50% of the undersigned's net worth.

❑ **does** represent more than 50% of the undersigned's net worth.

V. *GENERAL INFORMATION.*

(a) PERSONAL INFORMATION.

Investor:

Name: ______________________________

Social Security or Taxpayer Identification Number: ______________

Residence Address: ______________________________
(Number and Street)

____
(City) (State) (Zip Code)

Resident Telephone Number: ______________________________
(Area Code) (Number)

Name of Business: ______________ Title: ______________

Business Address: ______________________________
(Number and Street)

____
(City) (State) (Zip Code)

Business Telephone Number: ______________________________
(Area Code) (Number)

I prefer to have correspondence sent to: ❑ Residence ❑ Business

NASD Affiliation or Association, if any: ______________

If none, check here ❑

Spouse, if Co-Owner:

Name: ______________________________

Social Security or Taxpayer Identification Number: ______________

Residence Address: ______________________________
(Number and Street)

____
(City) (State) (Zip Code)

Residence Telephone Number
(if different from Purchaser's): ______________________________
(Area Code) (Number)

Business Address
(if different from Purchaser's): ______________________________
(Number and Street)

____
(City) (State) (Zip Code)

Business Telephone Number
(if different from Purchaser's): ______________________________
(Area Code) (Number)

I prefer to have correspondence sent to: ❑ Residence ❑ Business

NASD Affiliation or Association, if any: ______________________________

If none, check here ❑

VI. SIGNATURE.

The Individual Investor Omnibus Signature Page is contained on Pages E-16 and E-17.

OMNIBUS SIGNATURE PAGE

INDIVIDUAL INVESTOR

The.com, Inc.

Ladies and Gentlemen:

The undersigned subscriber for Units hereby submits to you this Omnibus Signature Page which constitutes the signature page for (a) the attached Investor Questionnaire, (b) the attached Subscription Agreement and (c) the Company's Restated Investor Rights Agreement. The undersigned represents and agrees that THE EXECUTION OF THIS OMNIBUS SIGNATURE PAGE CONSTITUTES THE EXECUTION OF EACH OF THE FOREGOING DOCUMENTS and, in addition, acknowledges, certifies, represents and agrees with you as follows:

1. **Investor Questionnaire**. The information provided in the Investor Questionnaire is complete and accurate as of the date hereof and may be relied upon by you, and the undersigned will notify you immediately of any material change in any of such information which may occur prior to the acceptance of the undersigned's subscription and will promptly send you written confirmation thereof.

2. **Subscription Information** (to be completed by subscriber).

Number of Units Subscribed for: ________________

Aggregate purchase price (number of Units x $100,000): $__________

Name(s) in which Units are to be registered:

____

____

Form of joint ownership (if applicable). (If one of these boxes is checked, subscriber and co-subscriber must both sign all documents):

Tenants-by-Entirety ❑ Joint Tenants ❑

Tenants-in-Common ❑

If the Units hereby subscribed for are to be owned by more than one person in any manner, the undersigned understands and agrees that all of the co-subscribers in such Units must sign this Omnibus Signature Page and complete an Investor Questionnaire in order for this subscription to be accepted.

IN WITNESS WHEREOF, the undersigned represent(s), under penalty of perjury, that the foregoing statements are true and correct and that he or she has (they have) executed the Investor Questionnaire, the Subscription Agreement, the Restated Investor Rights Agreement (subject in the case of the Restated Investor Rights Agreement to the closing of the sale of the Units subscribed for hereunder) and this Omnibus Signature Page this __________ day of ______________________________, ________.
Month Year

______________________________ ______________________________
Please Print Name of Subscriber Signature of Subscriber

______________________________ ______________________________
Please Print Name of Co-Subscriber Signature of Subscriber

AUTHORIZATION TO TRANSFER FUNDS FROM CUSTOMER ACCOUNT TO ESCROW AGENT

The undersigned authorize(s) The Placement Agent, Inc. to debit Account #________________ at The Placement Agent, Inc. and to transfer the amount of the aggregate purchase price for the Units subscribed for to ________ Bank as Escrow Agent.

____
Signature of Subscriber

____
Signature of Subscriber

THE UNITS AND THE SECURITIES COMPRISING THE UNITS HAVE NOT BEEN REGISTERED UNDER THE SECURITIES ACT OF 1933, AS AMENDED (THE "ACT"), OR ANY STATE SECURITIES LAW AND MAY NOT BE SOLD, TRANSFERRED, ASSIGNED, PLEDGED, OR HYPOTHECATED EXCEPT AS PERMITTED UNDER THE ACT AND THE APPLICABLE STATE SECURITIES LAWS PURSUANT TO REGISTRATION OR EXEMPTION THEREFROM. THE ISSUER OF THESE SECURITIES MAY REQUIRE AN OPINION OF COUNSEL REASONABLY SATISFACTORY TO THE ISSUER TO THE EFFECT THAT ANY PROPOSED SALE, TRANSFER, ASSIGNMENT, PLEDGE OR HYPOTHECATION IS IN COMPLIANCE WITH THE ACT AND ANY APPLICABLE STATE SECURITIES LAWS.

TO BE COMPLETED AND SIGNED BY REGISTERED REPRESENTATIVE

I hereby represent on recommending the purchase of Units in the Company that I, the Registered Representative:

1. have reasonable grounds to believe, on the basis of information obtained from the subscriber and any other information known by me, that the subscriber is an "accredited investor" as such term is defined in Rule 501(a) of Regulation D promulgated under the Act; and

2. have, prior to execution of the written Subscription Agreement, informed the subscriber of all pertinent facts relating to the liquidity and marketability of the Units during the term of the investment.

I further represent that I am registered to offer and sell securities of the type offered in this Offering in the state in which this Offering is made.

____

Registered Representative Signature　　　　　　Date

____

Print Name of Registered Representative

____

Broker-Dealer Firm Name

____

Street Address

____

City & State　　　　　　Zip Code

NOT TO BE COMPLETED BY SUBSCRIBER

PAYMENT OF PURCHASE PRICE, OMNIBUS SIGNATURE PAGE AND INVESTOR QUESTIONNAIRE RECEIVED AND SUBSCRIPTION ACCEPTED ON ________________, _____.
Month and Day Year

THE.COM, INC.

By: ______________________________

Its: ______________________________

IMPORTANT:
Please Complete

Investor Name:____________________________

Account No.:__________________________

Offering Memorandum No.____________
(from the cover of the Offering Memorandum)

ALLOCATED ☐
WAIT LIST ☐

TRUST QUESTIONNAIRE

The.com, Inc.

The.com, Inc.

The information in this Questionnaire is being furnished in order to determine whether the undersigned TRUST's subscription to purchase the Units of The.com, Inc., (the "Company") may be accepted. The Company will not offer or sell Units to any investor who has not completed a Questionnaire.

ALL INFORMATION CONTAINED IN THIS QUESTIONNAIRE WILL BE TREATED CONFIDENTIALLY.

THIS INVESTOR QUESTIONNAIRE WILL BE DEEMED TO HAVE BEEN EXECUTED FOR ALL PURPOSES WHEN THE INVESTOR SIGNS THE OMNIBUS SIGNATURE PAGE ANNEXED HERETO.

I. PLEASE CHECK STATEMENTS 1 AND 2 BELOW, AS APPLICABLE:

❏ 1. (a) the TRUST has total assets in excess of $5,000,000; **and**

(b) the TRUST was not formed for the specific purpose of acquiring the Units; **and**

(c) the purchase by the TRUST is directed by a person who has such knowledge and experience in financial and business matters that he/she is capable of evaluating the merits and risks of an investment in the Units and of making an informed investment decision.

❏ 2. The grantor of the TRUST may revoke the TRUST at any time; the grantor retains sole investment control over the assets of the TRUST, **and**

(a) the grantor is a natural person whose individual net worth* or joint net worth with the grantor's spouse exceeds $1,000,000; or

(b) the grantor is a natural person who had an individual income* in excess of $200,000 in each of the two most recently completed years and who reasonably expects an individual income in excess of $200,000 in the current year; or

(c) the grantor is a natural person who, together with his or her spouse, has had a joint income* in excess of $300,000 in each of the two most recently completed years and who reasonably expects a joint income in excess of $300,000 in the current year.

IF YOU CHECKED STATEMENT 2 IN SECTION I AND DID NOT CHECK STATEMENT 1, THE GRANTOR MUST PROVIDE A COMPLETED INDIVIDUAL INVESTOR QUESTIONNAIRE FOR EACH GRANTOR.

---

* For purposes of this Questionnaire, the term "net worth" means the excess of total assets over total liabilities exclusive of home, home furnishings and automobiles. In determining income, an investor should add to his or her adjusted gross income as reflected on his or her most recent federal income tax return any amounts attributable to tax-exempt income received, losses claimed as a limited partner in any limited partnership, deductions claimed for depletion, contributions to IRA or Keogh retirement plans, alimony payments and any amount by which income from long-term capital gains has been reduced in arriving at adjusted gross income.

II. OTHER CERTIFICATIONS.

By signing the Omnibus Signature Page, the undersigned certifies the following:

(a) that the TRUST's purchase of the Units is within the investment powers and authority of the TRUST (as set forth in the declaration of trust or other governing instrument) and that all necessary consents, approvals and authorizations for such purchase have been obtained and that each person who signs the Omnibus Signature Page has all requisite power and authority as trustee to execute this Questionnaire on behalf of the TRUST; and

(b) that the TRUST has not been established in connection with either (i) an employee benefit plan (as defined in Section 3(3) of ERISA), whether or not subject to the provisions of Title I of ERISA, or (ii) a plan described in Section 4975(e)(i) of the Internal Revenue Code; and

(c) that the TRUST's name, address of principal office, place of formation and taxpayer identification number as set forth in this Questionnaire are true, correct and complete; and

(d) that one of the following is true and correct (check one):

- ❑ the TRUST is an estate or trust whose income from sources outside of the United States is includable in its gross income for United States federal tax purposes regardless of its connection with a trade or business carried on in the United States; or
- ❑ the TRUST is an estate or trust whose income from sources outside the United States is not includable in its gross income for United States federal income tax purposes regardless of its connection with a trade or business carried on in the United States.

ALL PROSPECTIVE INVESTORS MUST MAKE THE FOLLOWING CERTIFICATION:

The undersigned's total proposed investment in the Units:

does **<u>not</u>** represent more than:

- ❑ 10% of the undersigned's net worth.
- ❑ 15% of the undersigned's net worth.
- ❑ 20% of the undersigned's net worth.

- ☐ 25% of the undersigned's net worth.
- ☐ 50% of the undersigned's net worth.

☐ **does** represent more than 50% of the undersigned's net worth.

III. GENERAL INFORMATION.

(a) PROSPECTIVE INVESTOR (THE TRUST):

Name: ______________________________

Address: ______________________________
(Number and Street)

____
(City) (State) (Zip Code)

Address for Correspondence (if different): ______________________________
(Number and Street)

Telephone Number: ______________________________
(Area Code) (Number)

State in which Formed: ______________________________

Date of Formation: ______________________________

Taxpayer Identification Number: ______________________________

Principal Activity of Trust: ______________________________

(b) TRUSTEES WHO ARE EXECUTING THIS QUESTIONNAIRE ON BEHALF OF THE TRUST:

Name(s) of Trustee(s): ______________________________

NASD Affiliation or Association of Trustee(s),
if any: ______________________________

If none, check here ☐

IV. SIGNATURE.

The Trust Investor Omnibus Signature Page is contained on Pages E-24 and E-25.

OMNIBUS SIGNATURE PAGE

TRUST INVESTOR

The.com, Inc.

Ladies and Gentlemen:

The undersigned subscriber for Units hereby submits to you this Omnibus Signature Page which constitutes the signature page for (a) the attached Investor Questionnaire, (b) the attached Subscription Agreement and (c) the Company's Restated Investor Rights Agreement. The undersigned represents and agrees that THE EXECUTION OF THIS SIGNATURE PAGE CONSTITUTES THE EXECUTION OF EACH OF THE FOREGOING DOCUMENTS and, in addition, acknowledges, certifies, represents and agrees with you as follows:

1. **Investor Questionnaire**. The information provided in the Investor Questionnaire is complete and accurate as of the date hereof and may be relied upon by you, and the undersigned will notify you immediately of any material change in any of such information which may occur prior to the acceptance of the undersigned's subscription and will promptly send you written confirmation thereof.

2. **Subscription Information** (to be completed by subscriber).

Number of Units Subscribed for: ________________

Aggregate purchase price (number of Units x $100,000): $________

Name(s) in which Units are to be registered:

____

____

3. **Investment Authorization**. The undersigned trust has all requisite authority to acquire the Units hereby subscribed for and to enter into

the Subscription Agreement and the Restated Investor Rights Agreement, and further, the undersigned trustee of the subscribing entity has been duly authorized by all requisite action on the part of such entity to execute this Omnibus Signature Page on its behalf.

IN WITNESS WHEREOF, the undersigned represent(s), under penalty of perjury, that the foregoing statements are true and correct and that he or she has (they have) executed the Investor Questionnaire, the Subscription Agreement, the Restated Investor Rights Agreement (subject in the case of the Restated Investor Rights Agreement to the closing of the sale of the Units subscribed for hereunder) and this Omnibus Signature Page this ___________ day of ____________________________, ________.
Month Year

For Individual Trustee(s):	For Corporate Trustee:
____________________________	____________________________
Name of Trust	Name of Trust
By: ________________________	By: ________________________
Signature, as Trustee	Name of Corporate Trustee
____________________________	By: ________________________
Print Name	Signature of Authorized Officer
By: ________________________	____________________________
Signature of Co-Trustee (If required by Trust Instrument)	Print Name and Title
____________________________	
Print Name	

AUTHORIZATION TO TRANSFER FUNDS FROM CUSTOMER ACCOUNT TO ESCROW AGENT

The undersigned authorize(s) The Placement Agent, Inc. to debit Account #________________ at The Placement Agent, Inc. and to transfer the amount of the aggregate purchase price for the Units subscribed for to __________ Bank as Escrow Agent.

For Individual Trustee(s):	For Corporate Trustee:
____________________________	____________________________
Name of Trust	Name of Trust

By: ______________________
Signature, as Trustee

____
Print Name

By: ______________________
Signature of Co-Trustee
(If required by Trust Instrument)

____
Print Name

By: ______________________
Name of Corporate Trustee

By: ______________________
Signature of Authorized Officer

____
Print Name and Title

THE UNITS AND THE SECURITIES COMPRISING THE UNITS HAVE NOT BEEN REGISTERED UNDER THE SECURITIES ACT OF 1933, AS AMENDED (THE "ACT"), OR ANY STATE SECURITIES LAW AND MAY NOT BE SOLD, TRANSFERRED, ASSIGNED, PLEDGED, OR HYPOTHECATED EXCEPT AS PERMITTED UNDER THE ACT AND THE APPLICABLE STATE SECURITIES LAWS PURSUANT TO REGISTRATION OR EXEMPTION THEREFROM. THE ISSUER OF THESE SECURITIES MAY REQUIRE AN OPINION OF COUNSEL REASONABLY SATISFACTORY TO THE ISSUER TO THE EFFECT THAT ANY PROPOSED SALE, TRANSFER, ASSIGNMENT, PLEDGE OR HYPOTHECATION IS IN COMPLIANCE WITH THE ACT AND ANY APPLICABLE STATE SECURITIES LAWS.

TO BE COMPLETED AND SIGNED BY REGISTERED REPRESENTATIVE

I hereby represent on recommending the purchase of Units in the Company that I, the Registered Representative:

1. have reasonable grounds to believe, on the basis of information obtained from the subscriber and any other information known by me, that the subscriber is an "accredited investor" as such term is defined in Rule 501(a) of Regulation D promulgated under the Act; and

2. have, prior to execution of the written Subscription Agreement, informed the subscriber of all pertinent facts relating to the liquidity and marketability of the Units during the term of the investment.

I further represent that I am registered to offer and sell securities of the type offered in this Offering in the state in which this Offering is made.

Registered Representative Signature Date

Print Name of Registered Representative

Broker-Dealer Firm Name

Street Address

City & State Zip Code

NOT TO BE COMPLETED BY SUBSCRIBER

PAYMENT OF PURCHASE PRICE, OMNIBUS SIGNATURE PAGE AND INVESTOR QUESTIONNAIRE RECEIVED AND SUBSCRIPTION ACCEPTED ON ______________________, _____.
Month and Day Year

THE.COM, INC.

By: ______________________________

Its: ______________________________

IMPORTANT:
Please Complete

Investor Name:________________________

Account No.:________________________

Offering Memorandum No.______________
(from the cover of the Offering Memorandum)

ALLOCATED ❑
WAIT LIST ❑

PARTNERSHIP QUESTIONNAIRE

The.com, Inc.

The.com, Inc.

The information in this Questionnaire is being furnished in order to determine whether the undersigned PARTNERSHIP's subscription to purchase the Units of The.com, Inc. (the "Company") may be accepted. The Company will not offer or sell Units to any investor who has not completed a Questionnaire.

ALL INFORMATION CONTAINED IN THIS QUESTIONNAIRE WILL BE TREATED CONFIDENTIALLY.

THIS INVESTOR QUESTIONNAIRE WILL BE DEEMED TO HAVE BEEN EXECUTED FOR ALL PURPOSES WHEN THE INVESTOR SIGNS THE OMNIBUS SIGNATURE PAGE ANNEXED HERETO.

I. *PLEASE CHECK STATEMENTS 1 AND 2 BELOW, AS APPLICABLE:*

❏ 1. Each of the partners of the undersigned PARTNERSHIP is able to certify that such partner meets at east one of the following conditions:

(a) The partner is a natural person whose individual net worth* or joint net worth with his or her spouse exceeds $1,000,000.

(b) The partner is a natural person whose individual income* was in excess of $200,000 in each of the two most recently completed years and who reasonably expects an individual income in excess of $200,000 in the current year.

(c) The partner is a natural person who, together with his or her spouse, has had a joint income* in excess of $300,000 in each of the two most recently completed years and who reasonably expects a joint income in excess of $300,000 in the current year.

(d) The partner is an entity in which all of the equity owners satisfy (a), (b) or (c) above.

❏ 2. The undersigned PARTNERSHIP: (i) was not formed for the specific purpose of acquiring the Units; **and** (ii) has total assets in excess of $5,000,000.

IF YOU CHECKED STATEMENT 1 IN SECTION I AND DID NOT CHECK STATEMENT 2, YOU MUST PROVIDE A LETTER SIGNED BY A GENERAL PARTNER OF THE UNDERSIGNED PARTNERSHIP LISTING THE NAME OF EACH PARTNER (WHETHER A GENERAL OR LIMITED PARTNER) AND THE REASON (UNDER STATEMENT 1) SUCH PARTNER QUALIFIES AS AN ACCREDITED INVESTOR (ON THE BASIS OF NET WORTH, INDIVIDUAL INCOME OR JOINT INCOME), OR EACH PARTNER MUST PROVIDE A COMPLETED INDIVIDUAL INVESTOR QUESTIONNAIRE.

---

* For purposes of this Questionnaire, the term "net worth" means the excess of total assets over total liabilities exclusive of home, home furnishings and automobiles. In determining income, an investor should add to his or her adjusted gross income as reflected on his or her most recent federal income tax return any amounts attributable to tax-exempt income received, losses claimed as a limited partner in any limited partnership, deductions claimed for depletion, contributions to IRA or Keogh retirement plans, alimony payments and any amount by which income from long-term capital gains has been reduced in arriving at adjusted gross income.

II. *OTHER CERTIFICATIONS.*

By signing the Omnibus Signature Page, the undersigned certifies the following:

(a) that the purchase by the PARTNERSHIP is directed by a person who has such knowledge and experience in financial and business matters that he/she is capable of evaluating the merits and risks of an investment in the Units and of making an informed investment decision; and

(b) that the PARTNERSHIP's name, address of principal office, place of formation and taxpayer identification number as set forth in this Questionnaire are true, correct and complete; and

(c) that the assets of the PARTNERSHIP do not constitute "plan assets" within the meaning of ERISA and regulation § 2510.3-101 promulgated thereunder; and

(d) that one of the following is true and correct (check one):

❑ the PARTNERSHIP is a partnership formed in or under the laws of the United States or any political subdivision thereof; or

❑ the PARTNERSHIP is not a partnership formed in or under the laws of the United States or any political subdivision thereof.

ALL PROSPECTIVE INVESTORS MUST MAKE THE FOLLOWING CERTIFICATION:

The undersigned's total proposed investment in the Units:

does **not** represent more than:

❑ 10% of the undersigned's net worth.
❑ 15% of the undersigned's net worth.
❑ 20% of the undersigned's net worth.
❑ 25% of the undersigned's net worth.
❑ 50% of the undersigned's net worth.

❑ **does** represent more than 50% of the undersigned's net worth.

III. GENERAL INFORMATION.

(a) PROSPECTIVE INVESTOR (THE PARTNERSHIP):

Name: ______________________________

Address: ______________________________
(Number and Street)

____
(City) (State) (Zip Code)

Address for Correspondence
(if different): ______________________________
(Number and Street)

____
(City) (State) (Zip Code)

Telephone Number: ______________________________
(Area Code) (Number)

State in which Formed: ______________________________

Date of Formation: ______________________________

Taxpayer Identification Number: ______________________________

NASD Affiliation or Association of Trustee(s), if any: ______

If none, check here ❑

Number of Partners: ______________________________

Principle Activity of Partnership: ______________________________

(b) INDIVIDUAL WHO IS EXECUTING THIS QUESTIONNAIRE ON BEHALF OF THE PARTNERSHIP

Name: ______________________________

Position or Title: ______________________________

IV. SIGNATURE.

The Partnership Investor Omnibus Signature Page is contained on Pages E-32 and E-33.

OMNIBUS SIGNATURE PAGE

PARTNERSHIP INVESTOR

The.com, Inc.

Ladies and Gentlemen:

The undersigned subscriber for Units hereby submits to you this Omnibus Signature Page which constitutes the signature page for (a) the attached Investor Questionnaire, (b) the attached Subscription Agreement and (c) the Company's Restated Investor Rights Agreement. The undersigned represents and agrees that THE EXECUTION OF THIS SIGNATURE PAGE CONSTITUTES THE EXECUTION OF EACH OF THE FOREGOING DOCUMENTS and, in addition, acknowledges, certifies, represents and agrees with you as follows:

1. **Investor Questionnaire**. The information provided in the Investor Questionnaire is complete and accurate as of the date hereof and may be relied upon by you, and the undersigned will notify you immediately of any material change in any of such information that may occur prior to the acceptance of the undersigned's subscription and will promptly send you written confirmation thereof.

2. **Subscription Information** (to be completed by subscriber).

Number of Units Subscribed for: ________________

Aggregate purchase price (number of Units x $100,000): $__________

Name(s) in which Units are to be registered:

____

____

3. **Investment Authorization**. The undersigned partnership has all requisite authority to acquire the Units hereby subscribed for and to enter

into the Subscription Agreement and the Restated Investor Rights Agreement, and further, the undersigned officer or partner of the subscribing entity has been duly authorized by all requisite action on the part of such entity to execute this Omnibus Signature Page on its behalf.

IN WITNESS WHEREOF, the undersigned represent(s), under penalty of perjury, that the foregoing statements are true and correct and that he or she has (they have) executed the Investor Questionnaire, the Subscription Agreement, the Restated Investor Rights Agreement (subject in the case of the Restated Investor Rights Agreement to the closing of the sale of the Units subscribed for hereunder) and this Omnibus Signature Page this __________ day of ______________________________, ________.
Month Year

____
Name of Partnership

By: ____________________________
Signature of Authorized Person

____
Print Name and Title

AUTHORIZATION TO TRANSFER FUNDS FROM CUSTOMER ACCOUNT TO ESCROW AGENT

The undersigned authorize(s) The Placement Agent, Inc. to debit Account #________________ at The Placement Agent, Inc. and to transfer the amount of the aggregate purchase price for the Units subscribed for to ________ Bank as Escrow Agent.

____
Name of Partnership

By: ____________________________
Signature of Authorized Person

____
Print Name and Title

THE UNITS AND THE SECURITIES COMPRISING THE UNITS HAVE NOT BEEN REGISTERED UNDER THE SECURITIES ACT OF 1933, AS AMENDED (THE "ACT"), OR ANY STATE SECURITIES LAW AND

MAY NOT BE SOLD, TRANSFERRED, ASSIGNED, PLEDGED, OR HYPOTHECATED EXCEPT AS PERMITTED UNDER THE ACT AND THE APPLICABLE STATE SECURITIES LAWS PURSUANT TO REGISTRATION OR EXEMPTION THEREFROM. THE ISSUER OF THESE SECURITIES MAY REQUIRE AN OPINION OF COUNSEL REASONABLY SATISFACTORY TO THE ISSUER TO THE EFFECT THAT ANY PROPOSED SALE, TRANSFER, ASSIGNMENT, PLEDGE OR HYPOTHECATION IS IN COMPLIANCE WITH THE ACT AND ANY APPLICABLE STATE SECURITIES LAWS.

TO BE COMPLETED AND SIGNED BY REGISTERED REPRESENTATIVE

I hereby represent on recommending the purchase of Units in the Company that I, the Registered Representative:

1. have reasonable grounds to believe, on the basis of information obtained from the subscriber and any other information known by me, that the subscriber is an "accredited investor" as such term is defined in Rule 501(a) of Regulation D promulgated under the Act; and

2. have, prior to execution of the written Subscription Agreement, informed the subscriber of all pertinent facts relating to the liquidity and marketability of the Units during the term of the investment.

I further represent that I am registered to offer and sell securities of the type offered in this Offering in the state in which this Offering is made.

____

Registered Representative Signature Date

____

Print Name of Registered Representative

____

Broker-Dealer Firm Name

____

Street Address

____

City & State Zip Code

NOT TO BE COMPLETED BY SUBSCRIBER

PAYMENT OF PURCHASE PRICE, OMNIBUS SIGNATURE PAGE AND INVESTOR QUESTIONNAIRE RECEIVED AND SUBSCRIPTION ACCEPTED ON ____________________, ________.
Month and Day Year

THE.COM, INC.

By: ______________________________

Its: ______________________________

IMPORTANT:
Please Complete

Investor Name:______________________

Account No.:______________________

Offering Memorandum No.____________
(from the cover of the Offering Memorandum)

ALLOCATED ❑
WAIT LIST ❑

CORPORATION QUESTIONNAIRE

The.com, Inc.

The.com, Inc.

The information contained in this Questionnaire is being furnished in order to determine whether the undersigned CORPORATION's subscription to purchase the Units of The.com, Inc. (the "Company") may be accepted. The Company will not offer or sell Units to any investor who has not completed a Questionnaire.

ALL INFORMATION CONTAINED IN THIS QUESTIONNAIRE WILL BE TREATED CONFIDENTIALLY.

THIS INVESTOR QUESTIONNAIRE WILL BE DEEMED TO HAVE BEEN EXECUTED FOR ALL PURPOSES WHEN THE INVESTOR SIGNS THE OMNIBUS SIGNATURE PAGE ANNEXED HERETO.

I. PLEASE CHECK STATEMENTS 1, 2 AND 3 BELOW, AS APPLICABLE:

❑ 1. Each of the shareholders of the undersigned CORPORATION is able to certify that such shareholders meets at least one of the following conditions:

(a) The shareholder is a natural person whose individual net worth* or joint net worth with his or her spouse exceeds $1,000,000.

(b) The shareholder is a natural person whose individual income* was in excess of $200,000 in each of the two most recently completed years and who reasonably expects an individual income in excess of $200,000 in the current year.

(c) The shareholder is a natural person who, together with his or her spouse, has had a joint income* in excess of $300,000 in each of the two most recently completed years and who reasonably expects a joint income in excess of $300,000 in the current year.

(d) The shareholder is an entity in which all of the equity owners satisfy (a), (b) or (c) above.

❑ 2. The undersigned CORPORATION: (i) was not formed for the specific purpose of acquiring the Units; **and** (ii) has total assets in excess of $5,000,000.

❑ 3. The CORPORATION is one of the following:

(a) A "bank as" defined in Section 3(a)(2) of the Securities Act of 1933, whether acting in its individual or fiduciary capacity.

(b) A broker or dealer registered pursuant to Section 15 of the Securities Exchange Act of 1934.

---

* For purposes of this Questionnaire, the term "net worth" means the excess of total assets over total liabilities exclusive of home, home furnishings and automobiles. In determining income, an investor should add to his or her adjusted gross income as reflected on his or her most recent federal income tax return any amounts attributable to tax-exempt income received, losses claimed as a limited partner in any limited partnership, deductions claimed for depletion, contributions to IRA or Keogh retirement plans, alimony payments and any amount by which income from long-term capital gains has been reduced in arriving at adjusted gross income.

(c) An "insurance company" as defined in Section 2(13) of the Securities Act of 1933;

(d) An investment company registered under the Investment Company Act of 1940 or a "business development company" as defined in Section 2(a)(48) of such act.

(e) A Small Business Investment Company licensed by the U.S. Small Business Administration under Section 301(c) or (d) of the Small Business Investment Act of 1958.

(f) A plan established and maintained by a state, its political subdivisions, or any agency or instrumentality of a state or its political subdivisions, for the benefit of its employees, if such plan has total assets in excess of $5,000,000.

(g) A private "business development company" as defined in Section 202(a)(22) of the Investment Advisers Act of 1940.

IF YOU CHECKED STATEMENT 1 IN SECTION I AND DID NOT CHECK STATEMENT 2, YOU MUST PROVIDE A LETTER SIGNED BY AN OFFICER OF THE UNDERSIGNED CORPORATION LISTING THE NAME OF EACH SHAREHOLDER AND THE REASON (UNDER STATEMENT 1) WHY SUCH SHAREHOLDER QUALIFIES AS AN ACCREDITED INVESTOR (ON THE BASIS OF NET WORTH, INDIVIDUAL INCOME OR JOINT INCOME), OR EACH SHAREHOLDER MUST PROVIDE A COMPLETED INDIVIDUAL INVESTOR QUESTIONNAIRE.

II. OTHER CERTIFICATIONS.

By signing the Omnibus Signature Page, the undersigned certifies the following:

(a) that the CORPORATION's purchase of the Units will be solely for the CORPORATION's own account and not for the account of any other person; and

(b) that the purchase by the CORPORATION is directed by a person who has such knowledge and experience in financial and business matters that he/she is capable of evaluating the merits and risks of an investment in the Units and of making an informed investment decision; and

(c) that the CORPORATION's name, address of principal office, place of formation and taxpayer identification number as set forth in this Questionnaire are true, correct and complete; and

(d) that the assets of the CORPORATION do not constitute "plan assets" within the meaning of ERISA and regulation § 2510.3-101 promulgated thereunder; and

(e) that one of the following is true and correct (check one):

❏ (i) the CORPORATION is a corporation organized in or under the laws of the United States or any political subdivision thereof; or

❏ (ii) the CORPORATION is a corporation which is neither created nor organized in or under the United States or any political subdivision thereof, but which has made an election under either Section 897(i) or 897(k) of the United States Internal Revenue Code of 1986, as amended, to be treated as a domestic corporation for certain purposes of United States federal income taxation. (A COPY OF THE INTERNAL REVENUE SERVICE ACKNOWLEDGMENT OF THE UNDER-SIGNED'S ELECTION MUST BE ATTACHED TO THIS SUBSCRIPTION AGREEMENT IF THIS PROVISION IS APPLICABLE); or

❏ (iii) neither (i) nor (ii) above is true.

ALL PROSPECTIVE INVESTORS MUST MAKE THE FOLLOWING CERTIFICATION:

The undersigned's total proposed investment in the Units:

does **not** represent more than:

❏ 10% of the undersigned's net worth.

❏ 15% of the undersigned's net worth.

❏ 20% of the undersigned's net worth.

❏ 25% of the undersigned's net worth.

❏ 50% of the undersigned's net worth.

❏ **does** represent more than 50% of the undersigned's net worth.

III. GENERAL INFORMATION.

(a) PROSPECTIVE INVESTOR (THE CORPORATION):

Name: ______________________________

Principal Place of Business: ______________________________
(Number and Street)

____
(City) (State) (Zip Code)

Address for Correspondence (if different): ______________________________
(Number and Street)

____
(City) (State) (Zip Code)

Telephone Number: ______________________________
(Area Code) (Number)

State of Incorporation: ______________________________

Date of Formation: ______________________________

Taxpayer Identification Number: ______________________________

NASD Affiliation or Association of Trustee(s), if any: ______________

If none, check here ❑

Number of Shareholders: ______________________________

Principal Activity of Corporation: ______________________________

(b) INDIVIDUAL WHO IS EXECUTING THIS QUESTIONNAIRE ON BEHALF OF THE CORPORATION:

Name: ______________________________

Position or Title: ______________________________

IV. SIGNATURE.

The Corporate Investor Omnibus Signature Page is contained on Pages E-41 and E-42.

OMNIBUS SIGNATURE PAGE

CORPORATE INVESTOR

The.com, Inc.

Ladies and Gentlemen:

The undersigned subscriber for Units hereby submits to you this Omnibus Signature Page which constitutes the signature page for (a) the attached Investor Questionnaire, (b) the attached Subscription Agreement and (c) the Company's Restated Investor Rights Agreement. The undersigned represents and agrees that THE EXECUTION OF THIS SIGNATURE PAGE CONSTITUTES THE EXECUTION OF EACH OF THE FOREGOING DOCUMENTS and, in addition, acknowledges, certifies, represents and agrees with you as follows:

1. **Investor Questionnaire**. The information provided in the Investor Questionnaire is complete and accurate as of the date hereof and may be relied upon by you, and the undersigned will notify you immediately of any material change in any of such information that may occur prior to the acceptance of the undersigned's subscription and will promptly send you written confirmation thereof.

2. **Subscription Information** (to be completed by subscriber).

Number of Units Subscribed for: ________________

Aggregate purchase price (number of Units x $100,000): $__________

Name(s) in which Units are to be registered:

____

____

3. **Investment Authorization**. The undersigned corporation has all requisite authority to acquire the Units hereby subscribed for and to enter into the Subscription Agreement and the Restated Investor Rights Agreement, and further, the undersigned officer or partner of the subscribing entity has been duly authorized by all requisite action on the part of such entity to execute this Omnibus Signature Page on its behalf.

IN WITNESS WHEREOF, the undersigned represent(s), under penalty of perjury, that the foregoing statements are true and correct and that it executed the Investor Questionnaire, the Subscription Agreement, the Restated Investor Rights Agreement (subject in the case of the Restated Investor Rights Agreement to the closing of the sale of the Units subscribed for hereunder) and this Omnibus Signature Page to be duly executed and authorized on its behalf this ______ day of ______________________________, ________.

Month Year

____

Name of Corporation

By: ______________________________

Signature of Authorized Person

____

Print Name and Title

AUTHORIZATION TO TRANSFER FUNDS FROM CUSTOMER ACCOUNT TO ESCROW AGENT

The undersigned authorize(s) The Placement Agent, Inc. to debit Account #_______________ at The Placement Agent, Inc. and to transfer the amount of the aggregate purchase price for the Units subscribed for to _________ Bank as Escrow Agent.

____

Name of Purchaser

By: ______________________________

Signature of Authorized Person

____

Print Name and Title

THE UNITS AND THE SECURITIES COMPRISING THE UNITS HAVE NOT BEEN REGISTERED UNDER THE SECURITIES ACT OF 1933, AS AMENDED (THE "ACT"), OR ANY STATE SECURITIES LAW AND MAY NOT BE SOLD, TRANSFERRED, ASSIGNED, PLEDGED, OR HYPOTHECATED EXCEPT AS PERMITTED UNDER THE ACT AND THE APPLICABLE STATE SECURITIES LAWS PURSUANT TO REGISTRATION OR EXEMPTION THEREFROM. THE ISSUER OF THESE SECURITIES MAY REQUIRE AN OPINION OF COUNSEL REASONABLY SATISFACTORY TO THE ISSUER TO THE EFFECT THAT ANY PROPOSED SALE, TRANSFER, ASSIGNMENT, PLEDGE OR HYPOTHECATION IS IN COMPLIANCE WITH THE ACT AND ANY APPLICABLE STATE SECURITIES LAWS.

TO BE COMPLETED AND SIGNED BY REGISTERED REPRESENTATIVE

I hereby represent on recommending the purchase of Units in the Company that I, the Registered Representative:

1. have reasonable grounds to believe, on the basis of information obtained from the subscriber and any other information known by me, that the subscriber is an "accredited investor" as such term is defined in Rule 501(a) of Regulation D promulgated under the Act; and

2. have, prior to execution of the written Subscription Agreement, informed the subscriber of all pertinent facts relating to the liquidity and marketability of the Units during the term of the investment.

I further represent that I am registered to offer and sell securities of the type offered in this Offering in the state in which this Offering is made.

____

Registered Representative Signature   Date

____

Print Name of Registered Representative

____

Broker-Dealer Firm Name

____

Street Address

____

City & State   Zip Code

NOT BE COMPLETED BY SUBSCRIBER

PAYMENT OF PURCHASE PRICE, OMNIBUS SIGNATURE PAGE AND INVESTOR QUESTIONNAIRE RECEIVED AND SUBSCRIPTION ACCEPTED ON ______________________, __________.
Month and Day Year

THE.COM, INC.

By: ______________________________

Its: ______________________________

IMPORTANT:
Please Complete

Investor Name:________________________

Account No.:_______________________

Offering Memorandum No.____________
(from the cover of the Offering Memorandum)

ALLOCATED ❑
WAIT LIST ❑

RETIREMENT PLAN QUESTIONNAIRE

The.com, Inc.

The.com, Inc.

The information in this Questionnaire is being furnished in order to determine whether the undersigned RETIREMENT PLAN's subscription to purchase the Units of The.com, Inc. (the "Company") may be accepted. The Company will not offer or sell Units to any investor who has not completed a Questionnaire.

ALL INFORMATION CONTAINED IN THIS QUESTIONNAIRE WILL BE TREATED CONFIDENTIALLY.

THIS INVESTOR QUESTIONNAIRE WILL BE DEEMED TO HAVE BEEN EXECUTED FOR ALL PURPOSES WHEN THE INVESTOR SIGNS THE OMNIBUS SIGNATURE PAGE ANNEXED HERETO.

I. PLEASE CHECK ANY OF THE FOLLOWING STATEMENTS, AS APPLICABLE:

❑ 1. The undersigned RETIREMENT PLAN certifies that it is an employee benefit plan within the meaning of the Employee Retirement Income Security Act of 1974 ("ERISA"); **and**:

❑ (a) the investment decisions are made by a plan fiduciary as defined in Section 3(21) of ERISA that (i) is either a bank, insurance company or registered investment advisor, or (ii) is a savings and loan association;

❑ (b) The undersigned RETIREMENT PLAN has total assets in excess of $5,000,000; or

❑ (c) The undersigned RETIREMENT PLAN is self-directed, with investment decisions made solely by persons each of whom satisfies at least one of the following conditions:

(i) such person's individual net worth* or joint net worth with his or her spouse exceeds $1,000,000; or

(ii) such person had an individual income* in excess of $200,000 in each of the two most recently completed years and who reasonably expects an individual income in excess of $200,000 in the current year; or

(iii) such person, together with his or her spouse, has had a joint income* in excess of $300,000 in each of the two most recently completed years and who reasonably expects a joint income in excess of $300,000 in the current year.

❑ 2. The undersigned RETIREMENT PLAN certifies that it is an employee benefit plan, Keogh plan or Individual Retirement Account in which each participant satisfies at least one of the following conditions:

❑ (a) such person's individual net worth* or joint net worth with his or her spouse exceeds $1,000,000; or

❑ (b) such person had an individual income* in excess of $200,000 in each of the two most recently completed

* For purposes of this Questionnaire, the term "net worth" means the excess of total assets over total liabilities <u>exclusive</u> of home, home furnishings and automobiles. In determining income, an investor should add to his or her adjusted gross income as reflected on his or her most recent federal income tax return any amounts attributable to tax-exempt income received, losses claimed as a limited partner in any limited partnership, deductions claimed for depletion, contributions to IRA or Keogh retirement plans, alimony payments and any amount by which income from long-term capital gains has been reduced in arriving at adjusted gross income.

years and who reasonably expects an individual income in excess of $200,000 in the current year; or

❏ (c) such person, together with his or her spouse, has had a joint income* in excess of $300,000 in each of the two most recently completed years and who reasonably expects a joint income in excess of $300,000 in the current year.

IF YOU CHECKED STATEMENT 1(c) or STATEMENT 2 AND NOT STATEMENT 1(a) OR STATEMENT 1(b), YOU MUST PROVIDE A LETTER SIGNED BY A PERSON DULY AUTHORIZED BY THE RETIREMENT PLAN LISTING, AS APPLICABLE, (I) THE NAMES OF THE PERSONS (OR ENTITIES) MAKING THE INVESTMENT DECISION OR (II) THE NAMES OF ALL THE PARTICIPANTS IN THE PLAN AND THE REASON (UNDER STATEMENT 1(c) OR STATEMENT 2) THAT SUCH PERSON (OR ENTITY) QUALIFIES AS AN ACCREDITED INVESTOR (ON THE BASIS OF NET WORTH, INDIVIDUAL INCOME OR JOINT INCOME OR OTHERWISE), OR EACH SUCH PERSON (OR ENTITY) MUST COMPLETE THE APPROPRIATE QUESTIONNAIRE (*i.e.*, FOR AN INDIVIDUAL, TRUST, PARTNERSHIP OR CORPORATION).

II. OTHER CERTIFICATIONS.

By signing the Omnibus Signature Page, the undersigned certifies the following:

(a) that the RETIREMENT PLAN's purchase of the Units will be solely for the RETIREMENT PLAN's own account and not for the account of any person or entity; and

(b) that the RETIREMENT PLAN's governing documents duly authorize the type of investment contemplated herein, and the undersigned is authorized and empowered to make such investment on behalf of the RETIREMENT PLAN; and

(c) that the purchase by the RETIREMENT PLAN is directed by a person who has such knowledge and experience in financial and

* For purposes of this Questionnaire, the term "net worth" means the excess of total assets over total liabilities <u>exclusive</u> of home, home furnishings and automobiles. In determining income, an investor should add to his or her adjusted gross income as reflected on his or her most recent federal income tax return any amounts attributable to tax-exempt income received, losses claimed as a limited partner in any limited partnership, deductions claimed for depletion, contributions to IRA or Keogh retirement plans, alimony payments and any amount by which income from long-term capital gains has been reduced in arriving at adjusted gross income.

business matters that he/she is capable of evaluating the merits and risks of an investment in the Units and of making an informed investment decision; and

(d) that one of the following is true and correct (check one):

❑ the RETIREMENT PLAN is a retirement plan whose income from sources outside of the United States is includable in its gross income for United States federal tax purposes regardless of its connection with a trade or business carried on in the United States; or

❑ the RETIREMENT PLAN is a retirement plan whose income from sources outside the United States is not includable in its gross income for United States federal income tax purposes regardless of its connection with a trade or business carried on in the United States.

ALL PROSPECTIVE INVESTORS MUST MAKE THE FOLLOWING CERTIFICATION:

The undersigned's total proposed investment in the Units:

does <u>**not**</u> represent more than:

❑ 10% of the undersigned's net worth.
❑ 15% of the undersigned's net worth.
❑ 20% of the undersigned's net worth.
❑ 25% of the undersigned's net worth.
❑ 50% of the undersigned's net worth.

❑ **does** represent more than 50% of the undersigned's net worth.

III. GENERAL INFORMATION.

(a) PROSPECTIVE INVESTOR (THE RETIREMENT PLAN):

Name: ____

Address: ____
(Number and Street)

____
(City) (State) (Zip Code)

Address for Correspondence
(if different): ______________________________
(Number and Street)

Telephone Number: ______________________________
(Area Code) (Number)

State in which Formed: ______________________________

Date of Formation: ______________________________

Taxpayer Identification Number: ______________________________

(b) INDIVIDUAL WHO IS EXECUTING THIS QUESTIONNAIRE ON BEHALF OF THE RETIREMENT PLAN:

Name: ______________________________

Position or Title: ______________________________

SIGNATURE.

The Retirement Plan Investor Omnibus Signature Page is contained in Pages E-49 and E-50.

OMNIBUS SIGNATURE PAGE

RETIREMENT PLAN INVESTOR

The.com, Inc.

Ladies and Gentlemen:

The undersigned subscriber for Units hereby submits to you this Omnibus Signature Page which constitutes the signature page for the (a) the attached Investor Questionnaire, (b) the attached Subscription Agreement and (c) the Company's Restated Investor Rights Agreement. The undersigned represents and agrees that THE EXECUTION OF THIS SIGNATURE PAGE CONSTITUTES THE EXECUTION OF EACH OF THE FOREGOING DOCUMENTS, and in addition acknowledges, certifies, represents and agrees with you as follows:

1. **Investor Questionnaire**. The information provided in the Investor Questionnaire is complete and accurate as of the date hereof and may be relied upon by you, and the undersigned will notify you immediately of any material change in any of such information that may occur prior to the acceptance of the undersigned's subscription and will promptly send you written confirmation thereof.

2. **Subscription Information** (to be completed by subscriber).

Number of Units Subscribed for: ____________________

Aggregate purchase price (number of Units x $100,000):
$______________

Name(s) in which Units are to be registered:

____

____

3. **Investment Authorization**. The undersigned trust has all requisite authority to acquire the Units hereby subscribed for and to enter into the Subscription Agreement and the Restated Investor Rights Agreement, and further, the undersigned signatory of the subscribing entity has been duly authorized by all requisite action on the part of such entity to execute this Omnibus Signature Page on its behalf.

IN WITNESS WHEREOF, the undersigned represent(s), under penalty of perjury, that the foregoing statements are true and correct and that he or she has (they have) executed the Investor Questionnaire, the Subscription Agreement, the Restated Investor Rights Agreement (subject in the case of the Restated Investor Rights Agreement to the closing of the sale of the Units subscribed for hereunder) and this Omnibus Signature Page this __________ day of

___________________, ________.
Month Year

____
Name of Retirement Plan

By: ___________________________
Signature of Authorized Individual

____
Print Name and Title

AUTHORIZATION TO TRANSFER FUNDS FROM CUSTOMER ACCOUNT TO ESCROW AGENT

The undersigned authorize(s) The Placement Agent, Inc. to debit Account #________________ at The Placement Agent, Inc. and to transfer the amount of the aggregate purchase price for the Units subscribed for to _______ Bank as Escrow Agent.

____
Name of Retirement Plan

By: ___________________________
Signature of Authorized Individual

____
Print Name and Title

THE UNITS AND THE SECURITIES COMPRISING THE UNITS HAVE NOT BEEN REGISTERED UNDER THE SECURITIES ACT OF 1933, AS AMENDED (THE "ACT"), OR ANY STATE SECURITIES LAW AND MAY NOT BE SOLD, TRANSFERRED, ASSIGNED, PLEDGED, OR HYPOTHECATED EXCEPT AS PERMITTED UNDER THE ACT AND THE APPLICABLE STATE SECURITIES LAWS PURSUANT TO REGISTRATION OR EXEMPTION THEREFROM. THE ISSUER OF THESE SECURITIES MAY REQUIRE AN OPINION OF COUNSEL REASONABLY SATISFACTORY TO THE ISSUER TO THE EFFECT THAT ANY PROPOSED SALE, TRANSFER, ASSIGNMENT, PLEDGE OR HYPOTHECATION IS IN COMPLIANCE WITH THE ACT AND ANY APPLICABLE STATE SECURITIES LAWS.

TO BE COMPLETED AND SIGNED BY REGISTERED REPRESENTATIVE

I hereby represent on recommending the purchase of Units in the Company that I, the Registered Representative:

1. have reasonable grounds to believe, on the basis of information obtained from the subscriber and any other information known by me, that the subscriber is an "accredited investor" as such term is defined in Regulation D of the Rules and Regulations promulgated under the Act; and

2. have, prior to execution of the written Subscription Agreement, informed the subscriber of all pertinent facts relating to the liquidity and marketability of the Units during the term of the investment.

I further represent that I am registered to offer and sell securities of the type offered in this Offering in the state in which this Offering is made.

____

Registered Representative Signature Date

____

Print Name of Registered Representative

____

Broker-Dealer Firm Name

____

Street Address

____

City & State Zip Code

NOT TO BE COMPLETED BY SUBSCRIBER

PAYMENT OF PURCHASE PRICE, INVESTOR QUESTIONNAIRE AND OMNIBUS SIGNATURE PAGE RECEIVED AND SUBSCRIPTION ACCEPTED ON ____________________, _______.
Month and Day Year

THE.COM, INC.

By: ______________________________

Its: ______________________________

APPENDIX H • PLACEMENT AGENT AGREEMENT

THE.COM, INC.

100 UNITS EACH CONSISTING OF 10,000 SHARES OF SERIES C CONVERTIBLE PREFERRED STOCK AND A WARRANT TO PURCHASE 1,000 SHARES OF COMMON STOCK

PLACEMENT AGENT AGREEMENT

THE PLACEMENT AGENT AGREEMENT (the "Agreement") is entered into as of the date set forth on the signature page hereof by and between The.com, Inc., a ______ corporation (the "**Company**"), and The Placement Agent, Inc., a ______ corporation (the "**Placement Agent**").

The Company proposes to offer and sell to "accredited investors" (the "**Investors**") as such term is defined in Regulation D promulgated under the Securities Act of 1933, as amended (the "**Act**") upon the terms and subject to the conditions set forth in the accompanying form of subscription agreement (the "**Subscription Agreement**") attached as an exhibit to the Placement Memorandum (as defined below), a minimum of 10 Units and a maximum of 100 Units (the "**Units**") for a purchase price of $100,000 per Unit, aggregating respectively $1,000,000 and $10,000,000 (the "**Offering**"). The Company may sell up to 50 additional Units if the offering is oversubscribed. Each Unit consists of (i) 10,000 shares of the Company's Series C Convertible Preferred Stock, par value $.01 per share (the "**Preferred Stock**") and (ii) a warrant (each a "**Warrant**") to purchase 500 shares of the Company's common stock, par value $.01 per share (the "**Common Stock**"), at an exercise price of $10.00 per share. If the maximum number of Units is sold, the Company will issue an aggregate of 1,000,000 shares of Preferred Stock (the "**Preferred Shares**") and Warrants to purchase an aggregate of 50,000 shares of Common Stock (the "**Exercise Shares**"). The Preferred Shares and the Warrants are herein referred to as the "**Securities.**" An investor must purchase a minimum of one (1) Unit (*i.e.*, $100,000); provided, however, that the Company in its sole discretion may waive this requirement. All Units are offered subject to the right of the Company to reject any subscription for Units in whole or in part and subject to certain other conditions.

The Company has determined to use the services of the Placement Agent as its exclusive agent to solicit subscriptions for the Units on a "best efforts" basis through the earlier of (a) _____ __, 2000, or (b) the sale of all Units offered, which period can be extended by the Company and the Placement Agent in their discretion for an additional 60 days without notice to investors (the "**Offering Period**"). The Placement Agent hereby agrees to act in such capacity and to use its best efforts to find purchasers for the Units in accordance with the terms and conditions of this Agreement.

Accompanying this Agreement is a copy of the Company's Confidential Private Placement Memorandum (the "**Placement Memorandum**"), the subscription documents attached as an exhibit thereto (the "**Subscription Documents**") and prepared for use in conjunction with the offer and sale of the Units and the Company's Restated Investor Rights Agreement (the "**Rights Agreement**") attached as an exhibit to the Placement Memorandum. Investors who subscribe for the Units (the "**Subscribers**") will be required to complete the Subscription Documents and execute the Subscription Agreement and the Rights Agreement. Such Placement Memorandum together with the Subscription Documents and the Rights Agreement are herein called the "**Offering Materials**," except that if the Confidential Private Placement Memorandum shall be supplemented or amended as herein provided, the term "Placement Memorandum" shall refer, from and after the date the supplement or amendment has been delivered to the Placement Agent, to the Confidential Private Placement Memorandum and the exhibits thereto as so amended or supplemented.

1. Representations and Warranties of the Company. The Company hereby confirms for the benefit of the Placement Agent the representations and warranties made by it to the Subscribers in Section 3 of the Subscription Agreement as if such representations and warranties were fully set forth herein, and hereby further represents and warrants to the Placement Agent that:

(a) The Company has the corporate power and authority to execute and deliver this Agreement, to perform its obligations hereunder, and to consummate the transactions contemplated by this Agreement.

(b) No consent, authorization, approval or order of, or qualification with, any court or any governmental or regulatory official or body is required for the consummation by the Company of the transactions contemplated by this Agreement, except such as may be required by the

Federal securities laws to perfect any exemption from registration or by the securities or Blue Sky laws of the various states in connection with the offer and sale of the Units and by Federal or by state securities laws with respect to the Company's obligations under the Rights Agreement.

(c) This Agreement has been duly and validly authorized, executed and delivered by the Company and constitutes the valid and binding agreement of the Company, enforceable in accordance with its terms, except that (i) such enforcement may be subject to the effect of any applicable bankruptcy, insolvency, reorganization, moratorium, fraudulent conveyance and other similar laws relating to or affecting creditors' rights generally and general principals of equity (regardless of whether such enforcement is considered in a proceeding in equity or at law) and (ii) the indemnification provisions of this Agreement may be held to violate public policy (under either federal or state law) in the context of the offer or sale of securities.

(d) The Company's execution and delivery of this Agreement, the fulfillment of the terms set forth herein and the consummation of the transactions contemplated herein will not conflict with or constitute a breach or violation of, or default under (i) the Company's articles of incorporation or by-laws, (ii) any material agreement, indenture or instrument by which the Company or any of its subsidiaries is bound (except to the extent such conflict, breach, violation or default would not have a material adverse effect on the value of the assets or the operation of the business of the Company and its subsidiaries, taken as a whole), or (iii) any law, administrative regulation or court decree (except to the extent such conflict, breach, violation or default would not have a material adverse effect on the value of the assets or the operation of the business of the Company and its subsidiaries, taken as a whole).

(e) None of the Company, any of its directors, officers, or beneficial owners of 10% or more of any class of its equity securities, or any of their respective affiliates (or any other person serving in a similar capacity):

(i) has been convicted within ten years prior to the date hereof of any crime or offense involving the purchase or sale of any security, involving the making of a false statement with the Securities and Exchange Commission (the "**Commission**"), or arising out of such person's conduct as an underwriter, broker, dealer, municipal securities dealer or investment adviser;

(ii) is subject to any order, judgment or decree of any court of competent jurisdiction temporarily or preliminarily enjoining or restraining, or is subject to any order, judgment, or decree of any court of competent jurisdiction, entered within five years prior to the date hereof, permanently enjoining or restraining such person from engaging in or continuing any conduct or practice in connection with the purchase or sale of any security, involving the making of a false filing with the Commission or arising out of the conduct of the business of an underwriter, broker, dealer, municipal securities dealer or investment adviser;

(iii) is subject to an order of the Commission entered pursuant to section 15(b), 15B(a), or 15B(c) of the Securities Exchange Act of 1934, as amended ("**Exchange Act**"), or is subject to an order of the Commission entered pursuant to section 203(e) or (f) of the Investment Advisers Act of 1940, as amended;

(iv) is suspended or expelled from membership in, or suspended or barred from association with a member of, an exchange registered as a national securities exchange pursuant to section 6 of the Exchange Act, an association registered as a national securities association under section 15A of the Exchange Act, or a Canadian securities exchange or association for any act or omission constituting conduct inconsistent with just and equitable principles of trade;

(v) is subject to a United States Postal Service false representation order entered within five years prior to the date hereof; or is subject to a restraining order or preliminary injunction entered under section 3007 of title 39, United States Code, with respect to any conduct alleged to constitute postal fraud;

(vi) has been or has been named as an underwriter of any securities covered by any registration statement which is the subject of any pending proceeding or examination under section 8 of the Act, or is the subject of any refusal order or stop order entered thereunder within five years prior to the date hereof;

(vii) has taken or failed to take any other act or is subject to any other order or proceeding that would make unavailable any limited offering exemption from registration or qualification requirements of the federal or state securities laws;

(viii) has filed a registration statement that is the subject of a currently effective stop order entered pursuant to any state's securities law within five years prior to the date hereof;

(ix) has been convicted within five years prior to the date hereof of any felony or misdemeanor in connection with the offer, purchase or sale of any security or any felony involving fraud or deceit, including but not limited to forgery, embezzlement, obtaining money under false pretenses, larceny or conspiracy to defraud;

(x) is currently subject to any state administrative enforcement order or judgment entered by that state's securities administrator within five years prior to the date hereof or is subject to any state's administrative enforcement order or judgment in which fraud or deceit, including but not limited to making untrue statements of material facts and omitting to state material facts, was found and the order or judgment was entered within five years prior to the date hereof;

(xi) is subject to any state's administrative enforcement order or judgment that prohibits, denies or revokes the use of any exemption from registration in connection with the offer, purchase or sale of securities; or

(xii) is currently subject to any order, judgment or decree of any court of competent jurisdiction temporarily or preliminarily restraining or enjoining, or is subject to any order, judgment or decree of any court of competent jurisdiction permanently restraining or enjoining, such party from engaging in or continuing any conduct or practice in connection with the purchase or sale of any security or involving the making of any false filing with the state entered within five years prior to the date hereof.

(f) Other than the Placement Agent, the Company has not contracted with any person to act as a finder or investment adviser in connection with the transactions described herein and the Company agrees to indemnify the Placement Agent with respect to any claim for such a finder's fee in connection with the Offering. No director or shareholder of the Company is a member of a broker-dealer registered with the National Association of Securities Dealers, Inc. (the "**NASD**") or an employee or associated member of a broker-dealer registered with the NASD.

2. **Representations and Warranties of the Placement Agent.** The Placement Agent hereby represents, warrants and agrees with the Company that:

(a) The Placement Agent is a corporation duly organized, validly existing and in good standing under the laws of the State of ______, with the corporate power and authority to conduct its business, to execute and deliver this Agreement, and to perform the obligations contemplated herein.

(b) This Agreement has been duly and validly authorized, executed and delivered by the Placement Agent and constitutes the valid, binding and enforceable agreement of the Placement Agent, except to the extent that (i) such enforcement may be subject to the effect of bankruptcy, insolvency, reorganization, moratorium, fraudulent conveyance and other similar laws relating to or affecting the rights of creditors generally and general principles of equity (regardless of whether such enforcement is considered in a proceeding in equity or at law), and (ii) the indemnification provisions of this Agreement may be held to violate public policy (under either federal or state law) in the context of the offer or sale of securities.

(c) The Placement Agent's execution and delivery of this Agreement, and the performance of its obligations hereunder, will not result in a breach or violation of any of the terms and provisions of, or constitute a default under, its certificate of incorporation or bylaws, any agreement or instrument to which it is a party or by which it is bound, or any judgment, decree, order or, to its knowledge, any statute, rule or regulation applicable to the Placement Agent.

(d) As of the date of the Placement Memorandum, the information contained in the Placement Memorandum relating to the Placement Agent, if any, does not include any untrue statement of a material fact or omit to state a material fact necessary in order to make the statements therein, in light of the circumstances under which they were made, not misleading.

(e) The Placement Agent is (i) a broker-dealer duly registered pursuant to the provisions of the Exchange Act, (ii) a member in good standing of the NASD, and (iii) duly registered as a broker-dealer under the applicable statutes and regulations of each state in which the Units will be offered and sold, except such states in which the Placement Agent is exempt from registration or such registration is not otherwise required. The Placement Agent will maintain all of its registrations, as well as those of each individual who participates in the offer or sale of the Units as the Placement Agent's agent or registered representative, in good standing throughout the term of the Offering, and the Placement Agent will comply with all statutes and other requirements of law applicable to it with respect to its brokerage activities within those jurisdictions. To the extent required by applicable law, any individual who participates in the offer or sale of the Units as the Placement Agent's agent or registered representative will be duly registered as a registered representative or principal of the Placement Agent pursuant to the provisions of the NASD rules.

(f) Neither Placement Agent nor any of its directors or officers nor any beneficial owner of 10% or more of any class of its equity securities, nor any of their respective affiliates (nor any other person serving in a similar capacity):

(i) has been convicted within ten years prior to the date hereof of any crime or offense involving the purchase or sale of any security, involving the making of a false statement with the Commission, or arising out of such person's conduct as an underwriter, broker, dealer, municipal securities dealer or investment adviser;

(ii) is subject to any order, judgment or decree of any court of competent jurisdiction temporarily or preliminarily enjoining or restraining, or is subject to any order, judgment, or decree of any court of competent jurisdiction, entered within five years prior to the date hereof, permanently enjoining or restraining such person from engaging in or continuing any conduct or practice in connection with the purchase or sale of any security, involving the making of a false filing with the Commission or arising out of the conduct of the business of an underwriter, broker, dealer, municipal securities dealer or investment adviser;

(iii) is subject to an order of the Commission entered pursuant to section 15(b), 15B(a), or 15B(c) of the Exchange Act, or is subject to an order of the Commission entered pursuant to section 203(e) or (f) of the Investment Advisers Act of 1940;

(iv) is suspended or expelled from membership in, or suspended or barred from association with a member of, an exchange registered as a national securities exchange pursuant to section 6 of the Exchange Act, an association registered as a national securities association under section 15A of the Exchange Act, or a Canadian securities exchange or association for any act or omission constituting conduct inconsistent with just and equitable principles of trade;

(v) is subject to a United States Postal Service false representation order entered within five years prior to the date hereof; or is subject to a restraining order or preliminary injunction entered under section 3007 of title 39, United States Code, with respect to any conduct alleged to constitute postal fraud;

(vi) has been or has been named as an underwriter of any securities covered by any registration statement which is the subject of any pending proceeding or examination under section 8 of the Act, or is the subject of any refusal order or stop order entered thereunder within five years prior to the date hereof;

(vii) has taken or failed to take any other act or is subject to any other order or proceeding that would make unavailable any limited offering exemption from registration or qualification requirements of federal or state securities laws;

(viii) has filed a registration statement that is the subject of a currently effective stop order entered pursuant to any state's securities law within five years prior to the date hereof;

(ix) has been convicted within five years prior to the date hereof of any felony or misdemeanor in connection with the offer, purchase or sale of any security or any felony involving fraud or deceit, including but not limited to forgery, embezzlement, obtaining money under false pretenses, larceny or conspiracy to defraud;

(x) is currently subject to any state administrative enforcement order or judgment entered by that state's securities administrator within five years prior to the date hereof or is subject to any state's administrative enforcement order or judgment in which fraud or deceit, including but not limited to making untrue statements of material facts and omitting to state material facts, was found and the order or judgment was entered within five years prior to the date hereof;

(xi) is subject to any state's administrative enforcement order or judgment that prohibits, denies or revokes the use of any exemption from registration in connection with the offer, purchase or sale of securities; or

(xii) is currently subject to any order, judgment or decree of any court of competent jurisdiction temporarily or preliminarily restraining or enjoining, or is subject to any order, judgment or decree of any court of competent jurisdiction permanently restraining or enjoining, such party from engaging in or continuing any conduct or practice in connection with the purchase or sale of any security or involving the making of any false filing with the state entered within five years prior to the date hereof.

3. Sale of the Units by the Placement Agent. The Company and the Placement Agent hereby agree as follows:

(a) The Offering will be made within the United States solely to Investors to whom the Placement Agent has furnished copies of the Offering Materials and in reliance upon the exemption from registration under section 4(2) of the Act and the provisions of Regulation D, and as permitted in the jurisdictions in which the Units are to be offered. The Placement Agent shall make reasonable inquiry to determine whether an Investor is purchasing for its own account or if it is purchasing for the account of others. In the case of any purchaser acting on behalf of one or more third parties, the Placement Agent shall make reasonable inquiry to determine that each such third party is an Investor.

(b) The Company hereby appoints the Placement Agent as its exclusive selling agent to solicit prospective purchasers of the Units and as such to effect sales of the Units, on a best efforts basis, for the Company during the period commencing with the date of the Placement Memorandum and ending on the Final Closing Date (as defined below). The Company may not terminate the Placement Agent's agency hereunder unless (i) the Placement Agent fails to perform its obligations hereunder in all material respects, (ii) the Placement Agent materially breaches any of its representations and warranties contained herein, or (iii) the Placement Agent's performance of its obligations hereunder constitutes gross negligence or willful misconduct. Subject to the terms and conditions and upon the basis of the representations and warranties herein set forth, the Placement Agent accepts such appointment and agrees to use its best efforts to find prospective purchasers for the Units in accordance with the terms and conditions of this Agreement.

(c) Each person desiring to purchase Units will be required to complete and execute the Subscription Documents. Each Subscriber will deliver payment by check payable to the order of "_____ Bank Escrow Agent for The.com, Inc." or by wire transfer, in the amount of the aggregate purchase price of the Units subscribed for. Each Subscriber will return to the Placement Agent such Subscription Documents together with such a check (or wire transfer) and any other documents that may be required under state securities laws or by the Company.

Neither the Placement Agent nor any investment advisor is permitted to sign any Subscription Agreement for any Investor. The Placement Agent will ascertain that each Subscription Documents submitted by a Subscriber has been completed and executed by such Subscriber, and Placement Agent will then forward such Subscription Documents, such other documents and a copy of such check to the Company and shall forward such check and a copy of such Subscription Documents and other documents to _______ Bank (the "**Escrow Agent**").

(d) In the case of on-site supervisory review, such checks must be transmitted to the Escrow Agent by the end of the next business day following receipt by the Placement Agent and, in the case of off-site supervisory review, checks must be transmitted to the Placement Agent's final review office ("**Final Review Office**") by noon of the next business day following receipt by the Placement Agent; such checks must be further transmitted to the Escrow Agent by the end of the next business day following receipt by the Final Review Office, all in compliance with the Commission's interpretive letter dated October 16, 1984. Transmittal of the Subscription Documents to the Company will be effected in accordance with the same timetable.

(e) Upon receipt of a Subscriber's Subscription Documents, the Company will determine promptly whether it wishes to accept the proposed purchaser as a holder of Units in the Company, it being understood that the Company reserves the right to reject the tender of any Subscription Agreement before the end of the second business day following the Company's receipt of the Subscription Agreement, and to reject all tenders after the maximum number of Units has been sold; provided, however, that any acceptance by the Company is subject to the fulfillment of all of the terms and conditions relating to the Offering contained in this Agreement and the Offering Materials, and that any failure by the Company to expressly reject a tender of a Subscription Agreement shall not be deemed to constitute an acceptance thereof. Should the Company determine to reject the tender, it will promptly notify the Escrow Agent and the Placement Agent of such determination. The Placement Agent will notify the Subscriber of such determination, and the Escrow Agent will issue and mail (or wire transfer) to the Subscriber, a check in an amount equal to the tendered purchase price of the Units by noon of the business day following the day that the Company indicates to the Escrow Agent that the tender has been rejected. As soon after the Minimum Offering Date (as defined below) as is practicable, the Company will issue to each Subscriber purchasing Units (individually, a "**Purchaser**" and collectively, the "**Purchasers**") a notification signed on behalf of the Company showing the total number of Units sold, and evidencing such Purchaser's interest in the Units.

(f) All payments received and accepted from Purchasers, except as hereinafter provided, will be deposited in an escrow account (the "**Escrow Account**") with the Escrow Agent. However, mere deposit of a check or receipt of a wire transfer will not constitute acceptance by the Company of a Subscription Agreement. Such funds may be temporarily invested only in investments permissible under Rule 15c2-4 of the Securities and Exchange Commission (the "**Commission**"). Prior to the Minimum Offering Date, the Company will have no right to obtain any funds from the Escrow Agent. The right of the Company to receive funds on the Minimum Offering Date is subject to fulfillment of the conditions specified in Section 8 hereof. Funds for Units purchased by Investors on or before the Minimum Offering Date will be made available to the Company on the Minimum Offering Date. After the Minimum Offering Date, the Escrow Agent has a continuing duty to deposit checks of Investors whose subscriptions have been accepted by the Company and to return checks to Subscribers whose subscriptions have been rejected, comply with the other terms of this Agreement, and make available to the Company, in immediately available funds, the additional funds deposited by such Investors (to the extent the escrowed funds have been collected) which are received after attainment of the Minimum Offering Amount (as hereinafter defined).

(g) Prior to the Final Closing Date or termination of the Offering, the Company shall from time to time amend the Placement Memorandum in order to update the information contained therein as follows, and the Placement Agent shall cooperate with the Company in connection with any amendments thereto. The Company, with the cooperation of the Placement Agent, shall update the Placement Memorandum as required by Section 6(b) hereof, at any time when the Placement Agent may deliver the Placement Memorandum to any Investor. In such event, the Company promptly will notify the Placement Agent by telephone, promptly confirmed in writing by telecopy, to suspend solicitation of offers to purchase Units, and, if so notified by the Company, the Placement Agent shall forthwith suspend such solicitation and cease using the Placement Memorandum until such time as the Company advises that solicitation may be resumed. If, in connection therewith, the Company shall, with the cooperation of the Placement Agent, decide to amend or supplement the Placement Memorandum, the Company (i) will advise the Placement Agent promptly by telephone (with confirmation in writing by telecopy), (ii) will prepare an amendment or supplement to the Placement Memorandum that will correct such untrue statement or omission or will make such other change as may be necessary, and (iii) will supply such amended or supplemented Placement Memorandum to the Placement Agent. If such amendment or supplement is satisfactory in all respects to the Placement Agent, the Placement Agent will resume the solicitation of offers to purchase Units.

4. Closing Dates and Minimum Offering Date.

(a) The Company may hold an "**Initial Closing**" of the Offering at any time after subscriptions for the minimum 10 Units have been accepted by the Company and all the conditions to the right of the Company to obtain funds as set forth in this Agreement, including Section 8 hereof, have been satisfied. At the Initial Closing (i) the Company and the Placement Agent shall jointly notify the Escrow Agent to release the funds from the Escrow Account; and (ii) the Company will issue the securities to the Subscribers; and (iii) counsel for the Company shall deliver its opinion to the Placement Agent as provided by Section 8 hereof; and (iv) all accepted subscription amounts will be delivered to the Company. The Company may hold any number of additional "**Interim Closings**" from time to time after the Initial Closing. The Initial Closing and each Interim Closing may be referred to herein as a "**Closing.**"

(b) "**Final Closing Date**" as used herein will mean the earlier of (a) the date on which all of the Units offered are sold or (b) ____ __, 2000 unless the Offering is extended for an additional 60 days by the Company and the Placement Agent in their discretion, in which case, the Final Closing Date shall mean the date that is 60 days after such date.

(c) "**Minimum Offering Date**" as used herein will mean the date, not later than _____ __, 2000, unless the Offering is extended for an additional 60 days as provided above, on which the Company will have received and accepted subscriptions and payments for an aggregate of at least 10 Units ($1,000,000) and such payments have been deposited with and collected by the Escrow Agent (the "**Minimum Offering Amount**"). In the event that subscriptions and payments for at least 10 Units have not been received and accepted by the Company and deposited with and collected by the Escrow Agent on or prior to the Minimum Offering Date, this Agreement will terminate and the Company will have no further obligation or liability hereunder to the Placement Agent except as provided in Section 5(a) below. In the event of such termination, all purchase payments deposited with the Escrow Agent will be returned to the Subscribers and no selling commissions (as hereinafter described) will be payable.

(d) As soon as is practicable after the Minimum Offering Date, the Company will mail or otherwise furnish to the Placement Agent written notification that subscriptions and payments for an aggregate of at least 10 Units ($1,000,000) have been received and accepted by the Company and deposited with and collected by the Escrow Agent.

5. Compensation.

(a) For the services of the Placement Agent in soliciting and obtaining Purchasers of the Units, the Company agrees to pay the Placement Agent (i) a selling commission equal to four percent of the aggregate proceeds received from the sale of the Units (the "**Selling Commission**") and (ii) an amount equal to two percent of the aggregate proceeds received from the sale of the Units as a nonaccountable expense allowance (the "**Expense Allowance**"). In the event that the Offering is terminated for any reason by the Company prior to the completion of the Offering, the Company agrees to pay all accountable fees, costs and disbursements incurred and/or due and payable by Placement Agent and its legal counsel up to an amount which shall not exceed $75,000. In the event Placement Agent without cause terminates the Offering, each party shall bear its own expenses relating to the Offering.

(b) On the Final Closing Date, the Company will sell to the Placement Agent or its designees at an aggregate price of one cent ($0.01) (the "**Warrant Price**") a warrant ("**Agent Warrant**") entitling the Placement Agent to purchase such number of shares of Common Stock as is equal to ten percent of the aggregate number of shares of Preferred Stock sold in the Offering (*e.g.*, 10,000 shares if 10 Units are sold and 100,000 shares if 100 Units are sold). The Agent Warrant is exercisable at any time after the Initial Closing of the Offering and shall expire, if not exercised, three years from the date of the Initial Closing (the "**Warrant Exercise Term**"). The Agent Warrant shall provide the holder with a right to purchase each share of Common Stock at an exercise price equal to $8.00, which exercise price shall be payable by giving the Placement Agent the option to pay the exercise price either (i) by reducing the number of shares issuable upon exercise by such number of shares as the fair market value of which is equal to the exercise price for the number of shares to be exercised or (ii) by paying cash.

(c) The Company agrees and undertakes to enter into, on or before the Final Closing Date, an amendment to the Rights Agreement, which shall be dated as of the date of the Initial Closing, between the

Company and the Purchasers and certain other investors to provide that the Placement Agent will be treated pari passu with the Purchasers of Units and the holders of the Company's Series A Convertible Preferred Stock and Series B Convertible Preferred Stock and that the "**Registrable Securities**" as defined in the Rights Agreement shall include the shares of Common Stock issuable to the Placement Agent upon exercise of the Agent Warrant.

(d) The Selling Commissions and the Expense Allowance will be paid at the time of each Closing of the sale of the Units as follows: (i) with respect to the Initial Closing, the Company will pay the Selling Commissions and the Expense Allowance payable with respect to the Units sold on or before the date of the Initial Closing; and (ii) with respect to an Interim Closing, the Company will pay the Selling Commissions and the Expense Allowance payable with respect to Units sold during the period commencing with the first business day following the previous Closing and ending on the date of such Interim Closing.

(e) The Placement Agent will not be entitled to a Selling Commission with respect to any tendered Subscription Agreement that is rejected by the Company.

6. Further Agreements of the Company.

(a) The Company covenants and agrees that it will pay or cause to be paid (i) all expenses, if any, in connection with the soliciting and obtaining of Purchasers of the Units including reasonable travel expenses in connection with investor presentations, (ii) all expenses and fees in connection with the preparation, printing, filing, delivery and shipping of the Placement Memorandum (including this Agreement and all other exhibits to the Placement Memorandum and any amendments or supplements thereto, and the Blue Sky Memorandum); and (iii) all filing fees required to be paid in connection with the offer and sale of the Units under the securities or Blue Sky laws of the states and other jurisdictions designated in the Blue Sky Memorandum.

(b) If at any time when a Placement Memorandum relating to the Units is required to be delivered under the Act, any event will have occurred as a result of which, in the opinion of counsel for the Company, the Placement Memorandum includes an untrue statement of a material fact or omits to state a material fact required to be stated therein or necessary to make the statements therein, in light of the circumstances under which they were made, not misleading, or if it is necessary at any time to amend the Placement Memorandum to comply with the Act, the Company promptly will prepare an appropriate supplement or amendment thereto, and will deliver to the Placement Agent such number of copies thereof as the Placement Agent may reasonably request.

(c) For three years from the Final Closing Date, the Company will furnish directly to or cause to be furnished to the Placement Agent:

(i) On or prior to the date on which the same shall be sent to shareholders, each communication required to be delivered or otherwise furnished to the holders of Units, including any annual or interim financial statements or other reports of the Company;

(ii) Promptly after receipt thereof, a copy of any notice or communication mailed, telecopied or otherwise delivered to the Company pursuant to any of the agreements relating to any material matter regarding the sale of Units;

(iii) Within 30 days following the end of each quarter, an unaudited balance sheet, income statement and statement of cash flows prepared as of the end of such quarter; provided that the Placement Agent may at any time notify the Company that copies of any or all of such communications need no longer be sent to it.

(d) The Company will furnish to the Placement Agent promptly, as soon as the same shall be filed, copies of all filings by the Company on Form D for the Offering.

(e) For three years from the Final Closing Date, neither the Company nor any affiliate will utilize the names of subscribers for Units obtained by the Placement Agent or any other names of persons obtained from the Placement Agent in connection with this Offering for the purpose of solicitation, or contact such persons in connection with any other offering or other security, unless such person was originally introduced to the Placement Agent by the Company or an affiliate of the Company. Should the names of such persons be utilized contrary to the foregoing, the Company shall pay to the Placement Agent an amount equal to nine percent of the amount invested by such persons in such other offering. This amount shall be due and payable upon the date such person's proceeds are invested.

(f) The Company will cause a Blue Sky Memorandum to be prepared by its counsel relating to the securities or "blue sky" laws of the states designated by the Placement Agent, indicating whether or not the offering of the Units may be made in such states (assuming compliance with the terms of the Blue Sky Memorandum and this Agreement) and advising whether the appropriate Blue Sky action, if any, was taken in each of such jurisdictions so as to permit the offering by the Placement Agent of the Units to the persons resident in each jurisdiction indicated in such Blue Sky Memorandum. In addition, subsequent to delivery of the initial Blue Sky Memorandum, the Company will orally advise the Placement Agent, as information becomes available, of the status of clearance in such jurisdictions originally designated by the Placement Agent and in each additional jurisdiction subsequently designated by the Placement Agent and deliver to the Placement Agent, as promptly as possible, supplements to the Blue Sky Memorandum prepared by its counsel containing written confirmation of clearance status in such jurisdictions and additional jurisdictions. The initial Blue Sky Memorandum, together with any supplements thereto, is hereinafter referred to as the "Blue Sky Memorandum." The Company will provide the Placement Agent with copies of all correspondence relating to "Blue Sky" filings with the state securities commissions, and copies of any permits received from the state securities commissions, for the Offering.

(g) The Company agrees that it will furnish or make available to the Placement Agent or the Placement Agent's counsel any and all documentation reasonably requested in connection with the Placement Agent's due diligence efforts regarding information in the Placement Memorandum.

(h) The Company will not take, and will cause its affiliates not to take, any action in connection with the Offering that would cause the Offering not to comply with Section 4(2) of the Act and Regulation D promulgated thereunder.

(i) The Company will not sell Units to any person if the Company has reason to believe that material information supplied or representations or warranties made by that person are not fully accurate and unless immediately prior to making such sale the Company reasonably believes that such person is an "accredited investor" within the meaning of Section 501(a) of Regulation D.

(j) The Company shall exercise reasonable care to ensure that the Subscribers are not underwriters within the meaning of Section 2(11) of the Act, shall take all actions required by Rule 502(d) of Regulation D and shall place a legend on each certificate which is provided to the

Purchasers stating that the Preferred Shares have not been registered under the Act and, where applicable, state securities laws, and setting forth or referring to the restrictions on transferability and sale of the Preferred Shares.

(k) The Company shall make available to each Investor and any individual advising such Investor the opportunity to ask questions and receive answers concerning the Company and the terms and conditions of the Offering, and to obtain any additional information, to the extent that such information is in the possession of the Company or can be acquired by it without unreasonable effort or expense, necessary to verify the accuracy of the information contained in the Placement Memorandum.

(l) The Company will duly and timely file (i) with the Commission all required reports on Form D with respect to the sale of the Units and (ii) all reports required to be filed under applicable state securities laws and regulations and by the regulatory agencies charged with enforcement thereof.

(m) The Company will notify the Placement Agent immediately upon the Company's receipt of notice of the issuance by the Commission or any state securities administrator of any stop order suspending the effectiveness of any qualification of the Units for sale or enjoining the sale of the Units or of the initiation of any proceeding for that purpose. The Company will make every reasonable effort to prevent the issuance of any stop order and, if any stop order shall be issued, to obtain the lifting of the stop order at the earliest possible time.

(n) The Company covenants that it will furnish to the Placement Agent for its prior approval (as applicable), the form of each notice to be furnished by the Company to the Escrow Agent under the terms of the escrow agreement entered into among the Company, the Escrow Agent and the Placement Agent relating to the Escrow Account.

(o) Except with the Placement Agent's prior consent, no proceeds of the Offering shall be used to pay any debt for borrowed funds, or any debts or obligations owed to any officer, director or shareholder of the Company, or to any of their affiliates. In addition, the proceeds of the Offering shall not be used to repay any presently existing debt for borrowed funds.

(p) For a period of two years after the date of this Agreement, if the Company decides to retain the services of an investment banking firm, the Company will notify the Placement Agent about any Business Transaction (as hereinafter defined) and will consider the Placement Agent's proposal to act as the Company's agent for the Business Transaction. A "**Business Transaction**" means any merger involving the Company or any of its subsidiaries, the acquisition by the Company or any of its subsidiaries of any entity or all or substantially all of the assets thereof, and the acquisition of all or substantially all of the capital stock or assets of the Company or any of its subsidiaries by another entity. The Company agrees to pay the Placement Agent compensation calculated in accordance with the Lehman formula if the Placement Agent introduces an acquisition or merger candidate to the Company and the acquisition or merger is consummated.

(q) Subject to the Minimum Offering Amount being raised by the Placement Agent, the Company and the Placement Agent understand and agree that for a period of three years commencing on the date of the Initial Closing, (i) the Placement Agent may act, in the Company's sole discretion, as the managing underwriter in connection with an initial public offering of the Common Stock (the "**IPO**"), and (ii) if the Placement Agent does not act as the managing underwriter, the Placement Agent shall act as either the co-managing underwriter or an underwriter for the IPO depending upon the mutual agreement of the Placement Agent and the Company.

(r) The Company will enter into the Rights Agreement on and as of the date of the Initial Closing.

7. Further Agreements of the Placement Agent.

(a) The Placement Agent hereby represents that it is currently, and will remain throughout the Offering Period, a member in good standing of the NASD. The Placement Agent agrees that it will not allow commissions to be paid to any other broker-dealer, including foreign broker-dealers registered pursuant to the Exchange Act.

(b) The Placement Agent agrees that it will accept subscriptions only from Investors who have received a copy of the Offering Materials, who have fully completed and executed the appropriate Subscription Documents, and whom the Placement Agent has reasonable grounds to believe, on the basis of information obtained from the Investor and any other information known by the Placement Agent, that the investor is an "accredited investor" as such term is defined in Regulation D of the Rules and Regulations promulgated under the Act. The Placement Agent will not give any information or make any representation in connection with the offering of the Units other than those contained in the Placement Memorandum furnished by the Company. The Placement Agent agrees not to publish, circulate or use any other advertisement or solicitation material without the prior written approval of the Company or otherwise conduct the offering in a manner that would be deemed to be a public offering or violate any Federal or State securities laws applicable to the Offering.

(c) The Placement Agent agrees that if and when the Company supplies it with copies of any supplement to the Placement Memorandum, the Placement Agent will affix such copies of such supplement to copies of the Placement Memorandum already in the Placement Agent's possession, and that thereafter the Placement Agent will only distribute Placement Memoranda containing such supplement and that the Placement Agent will accept subscriptions only from Investors who have received a copy of the Placement Memorandum containing such supplement. The Placement Agent further agrees to comply with all instructions from the Company concerning the destruction of out-dated Placement Memoranda and the use of supplemented or amended Placement Memoranda.

(d) The Placement Agent agrees to solicit Subscribers only in the states and other jurisdictions in which the Blue Sky Memorandum indicates that such solicitation can be made in accordance with any limitations described therein and in the states and jurisdictions in which the Placement Agent is licensed or qualified to make offers and sales of the Units. The Placement Agent agrees not to make offers and sales to residents of foreign countries.

8. **Conditions to the Right of the Company to Obtain Funds and to the Placement Agent's Performance.** The right of the Company to obtain funds from the Escrow Agent on the date of each Closing is, and the obligations of the Placement Agent as provided herein shall be, subject to the accuracy, as of the date hereof and the date of each Closing (as if made on and as of such date), of the representations and warranties of the Company herein, to the performance by the Company of its obligations hereunder, to the accuracy of the statements of the Company made pursuant to the provisions hereof, and to the following further conditions, except that clause (b) below need be satisfied only on the date of the Initial Closing:

(a) No stop order suspending the effectiveness of any qualification of the Units for sale or enjoining the sale of the Units or of the initiation of any proceeding for that purpose or any amendment or supplement thereto will have been issued prior to the date of such Closing and will be in effect at that date, and no proceedings for the issuance of such order will be pending or threatened at that date.

(b) There will have been furnished to the Placement Agent an opinion of counsel for the Company, dated as of the date of the Initial Closing, subject to such assumptions as such counsel will deem necessary to render such opinion, substantially to the effect that:

(i) the Company is a corporation duly organized under the laws of the State of _______ and is validly existing as a corporation under such laws;

(ii) the Sale of the Units and the issuance of the Securities (and the Common Stock issuable upon conversion of the Preferred Shares and upon exercise of the Warrants) has been duly authorized (and to the extent necessary reserved) by all necessary corporate action on the part of the Company. When subscriptions for the Units have been accepted by the Company and payment in full has been received, the Securities (and the Common Stock issued upon conversion of the Preferred Shares and upon exercise of the Warrants and payment therefore in accordance with the terms of the Warrants) will be duly authorized, validly issued, fully paid and nonassessable;

(iii) this Agreement has been duly and validly authorized, executed and delivered, by and on behalf of the Company and constitutes the valid and binding agreement, enforceable in accordance with its terms, of the Company subject to any applicable bankruptcy, insolvency, reorganization or other laws affecting the enforcement of creditors' rights, and to principles of a court of equity with respect to equitable remedies and defenses, from time to time in effect, and except as the indemnity provisions contained herein may be unenforceable for reasons of public policy under court decisions or regulations of the Commission;

(iv) the terms and provisions of any agreements to which the Company or any of the Company's subsidiaries is a party which are exhibits to the Placement Memorandum or are referred to therein, substantially conform in all material respects to the descriptions thereof contained in the Placement Memorandum;

(v) to the best of the counsel's knowledge, information and belief, after making reasonable inquiry, the consummation of the transactions contemplated herein do not conflict with or result in a breach of any of the terms, provisions or conditions of any agreement or instrument to which the Company or any of its subsidiaries is a party or by which the Company or any of its subsidiaries may be bound, or violate any order, rule or regulation applicable to the Company or any court or governmental body or administrative agency having jurisdiction over the Company;

(vi) to the best of the counsel's knowledge, information and belief, after making reasonable inquiry, there is no litigation or governmental proceeding pending, threatened against or involving the property or business of the Company, which would materially and adversely affect the value of the assets or the operation of the business of the Company and its subsidiaries, taken as a whole;

(vii) the offer and sale of the Units, the Securities and the Common Stock issuable upon conversion of the Preferred Shares and upon exercise of the Warrants is exempt from registration under Section 5 of the Act pursuant to the exemption set forth under Section 4(2) of the Act and Rule 506 of Regulation D thereunder;

(viii) based on such counsel's review and participation in discussions in the course of the preparation of the Placement Memorandum concerning the contents thereof, and without having independently verified or assumed the responsibility for the accuracy, completeness or fairness of the statements made in the Placement Memorandum, no facts have come to the attention of such counsel which lead it to believe that the Placement Memorandum (except as to the financial statements, prior performance information and financial projections (if any) contained therein, as to which such counsel need not express any opinion) at the date thereof or at the date of such opinion contained any untrue statement of a material fact or omitted to state a material fact required to be stated therein or necessary to make the statements therein, in light of the circumstances under which they were made not misleading.

(c) The Placement Agent shall have received a certificate, dated as of the date of such Closing, of an authorized executive officer of the Company to the effect that: (i) the representations and warranties of the Company herein are true and correct in all material respects as of the date of such Closing, as if made on and as of such date, and (ii) the Company has complied with all the agreements and satisfied all of the conditions herein contained to be performed or satisfied by it at or prior to the date of such Closing.

Upon receipt by the Company of such certificates and documents, the Company will direct the Escrow Agent in writing to release to the

Company the funds in the Escrow Account relating to the Units to be sold at such Closing.

If any of the conditions specified in this Section 8 will not have been fulfilled when and as required by this Agreement to be fulfilled, this Agreement and all of the Placement Agent's obligations hereunder may be canceled at, or at any time prior to, the Final Closing Date by the Placement Agent. Any such cancellation will be without liability on the Placement Agent's part. Notice of such cancellation will be given to the Company at the address specified in Section 12 hereof, in writing, or by telecopy or telephone confirmed in writing.

9. Indemnification.

(a) Subject to the provisions of paragraphs (b) through (d) of this Section 9, the Company agrees to indemnify and hold harmless the Placement Agent and each person who controls the Placement Agent within the meaning of the Act (collectively, the "Placement Agent Indemnified Parties ") against any losses, claims, damages or liabilities, joint or several, to which such Placement Agent Indemnified Party may become subject under the Act or otherwise, insofar as such losses, claims, damages or liabilities (or actions in respect thereof) arise out of or are based upon (i) any untrue statement or alleged untrue statement of a material fact contained (A) in the Placement Memorandum or any amendment or supplement thereof or thereto, as applicable, or (B) in any Blue Sky application or other document executed by the Company specifically for that purpose or based upon written information furnished by the Company and filed in any state or other jurisdiction in order to qualify any or all of the Units under the securities laws thereof (any such application, document or information being hereinafter called a "Blue Sky Application"), or (ii) the omission or alleged omission to state in the Placement Memorandum or any amendment or supplement thereof or thereto, as applicable, or in any Blue Sky Application a material fact required to be stated therein or necessary to make the statements therein, in light of the circumstances under which they were made, not misleading; and will reimburse the Placement Agent Indemnified Parties for any legal or other expenses reasonably incurred by such Placement Agent Indemnified Party in connection with investigating or defending any such claim, liability or action; provided, however, that the Company will not be liable in any such case to the extent that any such loss, claim, damage or liability arises out of or is based upon an untrue statement or alleged untrue statement or omission or alleged omission made in reliance upon and in conformity with written information furnished to the Company by the Placement Agent specifically for use with reference to the Placement Agent in the preparation of the Placement Memorandum or any such Blue Sky Application or any such amendments or supplements thereto. This indemnity agreement will be in addition to any liability that the Company may otherwise have.

(b) The Placement Agent agrees to indemnify and hold harmless the Company and each person who controls the Company within the meaning of the Act (collectively, the "Company Indemnified Parties"), against any losses, claims, damages or liabilities to which such respective Company Indemnified Party may become subject under the Act or otherwise insofar as such losses, claims, damages or liabilities (or actions in respect thereof) arise out of or are based upon: (i) any untrue statement or alleged untrue statement of a material fact contained (A) in the Placement Memorandum or any amendment or supplement thereof or thereto, as applicable, or (B) in any Blue Sky Application; or (ii) the omission or alleged omission to state in the Placement Memorandum or any amendment or supplement thereof or thereto, as applicable, or in any Blue Sky Application a material fact required to be stated therein or necessary to make the statements therein in light of the circumstances under which they were made not misleading; in each case to the extent, but only to the extent, that such untrue statement or alleged untrue statement or omission or alleged omission was made in reliance upon and conformity with written information furnished to the Company by the Placement Agent specifically for use with reference to the Placement Agent in the preparation of the Placement Memorandum or any such amendments thereof or supplements thereto or any such Blue Sky Application or any such amendments thereof or supplements thereto; and will reimburse such Company Indemnified Party for any legal or other expenses reasonably incurred by the Company in connection with investigating or defending any such loss, claim, damage, liability or action. This indemnity agreement will be in addition to any liability that the Placement Agent may otherwise have.

(c) Promptly after receipt by an indemnified party under this Section 9 of notice of the commencement of any action, such indemnified party will, if a claim in respect thereof is to be made against any indemnifying party under this Section 9, notify in writing the indemnifying party of the commencement thereof; provided, however, that the omission to so notify the indemnifying party will not relieve such indemnifying party from any liability under this Section 9, except to the extent that such failure to notify materially prejudices the indemnifying party's ability to defend the particular claim for which indemnification is then being sought and, provided further, that the indemnifying party shall not be relieved from any other liability that it may have to any indemnified party. In no event shall the indemnifying party be liable for the fees and expenses of more than one counsel for all indemnified parties in connection with any one action or separate but substantially similar or related actions in the same jurisdiction arising out of the same general allegations or circumstances (other than such local counsel as may be employed by counsel to the indemnified parties to render legal advice with respect to the laws of, or legal services in, states or jurisdictions other than those states and jurisdictions in which counsel to the indemnified parties is admitted to practice law). In case any such action is brought against any indemnified party, and it notifies an indemnifying party of the commencement thereof, the indemnifying party will be entitled to participate therein, and, to the extent that it may wish, jointly with any other indemnifying party, similarly notified, to assume the defense thereof, the indemnifying party will not be liable to such indemnified party under this Section 9 for any legal or other expenses subsequently incurred by such indemnified party in connection with the defense thereof other than reasonable costs of investigation. Any such indemnifying party will not be liable to any such indemnified party on account of any settlement of any claim or action effected without the consent of such indemnifying party, which consent shall not be unreasonably withheld.

10. Effective Date. Provided that at least one counterpart of this Agreement will then have been executed and delivered, this Agreement will become effective on the effective date of the Placement Memorandum or upon release by the Company of telecopies, correspondence or other notification to the Placement Agent indicating the effectiveness of the Placement Memorandum, whichever will first occur.

11. Survival of Indemnities, Warranties and Representations. The respective indemnity agreements of the Company and Placement Agent contained in Section 9 hereof, and the respective representations and warranties of the Company and Placement Agent set forth herein, will remain operative and in full force and effect, regardless of any termination or cancellation of this Agreement or any investigation made by or on behalf of the Company or Placement Agent, or any controlling person referred to in Section 9, and will survive the delivery of and payment for the Units, and any successor of the Placement Agent or the Company or of any such controlling person or any legal representative of any such controlling person, as the case may be, will be entitled to the benefit of the respective indemnity agreements.

12. Notices. Except as is otherwise provided in this Agreement, (a) whenever notice is required by the provisions of this Agreement or otherwise to be given to the Company, such notice will be in writing addressed to the Company at __________, attention: ________; and (b) whenever notice is required by the provisions of this Agreement or otherwise to be given to Placement Agent, such notice will be in writing addressed to the Placement Agent at __________________, Attention: _________. Any notice referred to herein may be given in writing or by telecopy or telephone and if by telecopy or telephone will be immediately confirmed in writing. Notice (unless actual) will be effective upon mailing or telecopy transmission, as the case may be.

13. Person's Entitled to Benefit of Agreement. This Agreement is made solely for the benefit of Placement Agent, the Company and the controlling persons referred to in Section 9 hereof, and their respective successors and assigns, and no other person will acquire or have any right by virtue of this Agreement, and the term "successors and assigns," as used in this Agreement, will not include any Purchaser.

14. Governing Law. This Agreement is to be governed by and construed in accordance with the laws of the State of _________, without regard to principles of conflicts of law.

15. Further Conditions. Until the Final Closing Date, this Agreement may be terminated by the Placement Agent at its option by giving notice to the Company, if (a) the Company shall have become a party to any litigation which, in the opinion of counsel to the Placement Agent, could have a material adverse effect on the value of the assets or operation of the business of the Company, (b) there shall have been, since the respective dates as of which information is in the Placement Memorandum, any material adverse change in the condition, financial or otherwise, of the Company, which change in the Placement Agent's reasonable judgment shall render it inadvisable to proceed with the delivery of the Units, (c) there shall have been any important change in market levels, major catastrophe, substantial change in national, international or world affairs, national calamity, postal strike, act of God or other event or occurrence which, in the Placement Agent's reasonable judgment, will materially disrupt the financial markets of the United States, or (d) a general banking moratorium shall have been declared by federal or state authorities.

16. Counterparts. This Agreement may be executed simultaneously in two or more counterparts, any one of which need not contain the signatures of more than one party, but all such counterparts taken together shall constitute one and the same Agreement.

17. Entire Agreement. This Agreement sets forth the entire agreement of the Placement Agent and the Company with respect to the subject matter hereof.

18. Headings. The descriptive headings in this Agreement have been inserted for convenience only and do not constitute a part of this Agreement.

IN WITNESS whereof, the parties have signed this Agreement as of this _____ day of _____, 2000.

THE.COM, INC.

By: ______________________________

Name: ____________________________

Title: ____________________________

THE.PLACEMENT AGENT, INC.

By: ____,
President and Chief Executive Officer

APPENDIX I • PRIVATE PLACEMENT MEMORANDUM

THE.COM, INC.

Minimum Offering: 10 Units
Maximum Offering: 100 Units

Each Unit Consists of 10,000 Shares of Series F Convertible Preferred Stock and a Warrant to Purchase 1,000 Shares of Common Stock
Minimum Investment: $100,000 (One Unit)
Purchase Price: $100,000 per Unit

THIS OFFER IS LIMITED TO ACCREDITED INVESTORS. SEE "INVESTOR SUITABILITY STANDARDS."

The.com Inc. ("The.com, Inc." or the "Company") is an electronic commerce company that is a provider of products and services for selling merchandise, such as software and other digital content, over the Internet and through online services.

The.com, Inc. is offering for sale a minimum of 10 Units and a maximum of 100 Units (the "Offering"). Each Unit consists of 10,000 shares of Series F Convertible Preferred Stock, par value $0.01 per share ("Series F Preferred" or the "Shares"), and a warrant (the "Warrant") to purchase 1,000 shares of Common Stock, par value $0.01 per share (the "Common Stock"), at a price of $100,000 per Unit or $10.00 per share of Common Stock (the "Offering Price"). The Series F Preferred may be voluntarily converted by holders thereof at any time and will automatically convert into shares of the Company's Common Stock at a one share-to-one share conversion ratio (subject to adjustment) upon the completion of an initial public offering of Common Stock. The Warrant is exercisable at any time between one and three years after the Initial Closing (as defined below) at an exercise price (the "Exercise Price") of $10.00 per share of Common Stock. There is no assurance that the Company will be able to consummate an initial public offering. See "Description of Capital Stock—Series F Preferred."

The Placement Agent, Inc. is acting as the exclusive placement agent ("Placement Agent") to offer and sell the Units on a "best efforts" basis. The Placement Agent will receive commissions and fees described in the table below with respect to the Units. The Units are being offered solely to a limited number of "accredited investors" as defined in Regulation D of the Securities Act of 1933, as amended (the "Securities Act"). Neither the Units nor the underlying Series F Preferred and the Warrants have been registered under the Securities Act or under the securities laws of any state. The Units are being sold pursuant to an exemption from registration under Section 4(2) of the Securities Act and Rule 506 of Regulation D thereunder and comparable exemptions under state securities laws.

The.com, Inc. may hold an initial closing of the Offering at any time after subscriptions for the minimum 10 Units have been accepted ("Initial Closing"). The.com, Inc. may hold any number of additional interim closings after the Initial Closing (each an "Interim Closing" or a "Closing"). Bridge financing of $5,000,000 plus accrued interest of approximately $100,000 as of ______ (the "Bridge Notes") may be exchanged at the option of each holder of the Bridge Notes for Units at the Offering Price at the Initial Closing or at a subsequent Closing. See "Recent Developments – Bridge Financing." Any Units issued in exchange for the Bridge Notes will be counted in determining whether the minimum 10 Units have been accepted. The Offering is expected to expire 90 days from the date of this Offering Memorandum, subject to an extension for 60 days without notice to Investors at the option of the Company and the Placement Agent. Pending each Closing, prospective investors' payments for Units will be deposited in a segregated escrow account with ________ Bank, _____, _____, as escrow agent ("Escrow Agent"). Funds will be promptly refunded, without interest, if sales are not consummated. See "Plan of Placement" and "Subscription Procedures."

THESE SECURITIES HAVE NOT BEEN APPROVED OR DISAPPROVED BY THE SECURITIES AND EXCHANGE
COMMISSION OR ANY STATE SECURITIES COMMISSION NOR HAS THE SECURITIES AND EXCHANGE COMMISSION OR ANY STATE SECURITIES COMMISSION PASSED UPON THE ACCURACY OR ADEQUACY OF THIS MEMORANDUM. ANY REPRESENTATION TO THE CONTRARY IS A CRIMINAL OFFENSE

	Subscription Price	Placement Agent Commissions[1]	Proceeds to Company[2]
Per Unit	$100,000	$7,000	$93,000
Total Minimum[3]– 10 Units	$1,000,000	$70,000	$930,000
Total Maximum[3][4] 100 Units	$10,000,000	$700,000	$9,300,000

(1) The Placement Agent will receive commissions of 7.0% of the Offering Price for each Unit sold by the Placement Agent. Excluded from this table is a non-accountable expense allowance of 3.0% of the Offering Price for each Unit sold that will also be paid to the Placement Agent. The Placement Agent will also receive a warrant to purchase a number of shares of Common Stock equal to 10% of the aggregate number of shares of Common Stock into which the shares of Series F Preferred sold in this Offering are convertible as of the final Closing at an exercise price of $5.00 per share (the "Agent Warrant"). See "Plan of Placement."

(2) Before deducting the non-accountable expense allowance of 3.0% of the Offering Price of the Units sold that is payable to the Placement Agent and other expenses related to the Offering (other than commissions payable to the Placement Agent) that are payable by the Company and are estimated to be $100,000. See "Use of Proceeds."

(3) Includes any Units issued in exchange for the Bridge Notes. See "Recent Developments."

(4) The Company reserves the right to sell up to 50 additional Units on the same terms as set forth herein in the event this Offering is oversubscribed. If all of such additional Units were sold, the Subscription Price, Placement Agent Commissions and Proceeds to Company would be $15,000,000, $1,050,000 and $13,950,000, respectively. See "Plan of Placement."

THE PURCHASE OF THE UNITS ENTAILS A HIGH DEGREE OF RISK. THE.COM, INC. HAS A LIMITED HISTORY OF OPERATIONS AND IS SUBJECT TO THE SUBSTANTIAL RISKS INHERENT IN A NEW BUSINESS ENTERPRISE. THERE IS NO MARKET FOR THE COMPANY'S SERIES F PREFERRED STOCK, WARRANTS OR COMMON STOCK. NO INVESTMENT IN THE UNITS SHOULD BE MADE BY ANY PERSON FINANCIALLY ABLE TO LOSE THE ENTIRE AMOUNT OF THEIR INVESTMENT. SEE "RISK FACTORS."

The date of this Offering Memorandum is ______ __, 2000

THE INFORMATION CONTAINED IN THIS CONFIDENTIAL PRIVATE PLACEMENT MEMORANDUM ("MEMORANDUM") IS CONFIDENTIAL, PROPRIETARY TO THE.COM, INC., AND PROVIDED TO PROSPECTIVE INVESTORS IN THE COMPANY SOLELY FOR SUCH INVESTORS' CONFIDENTIAL USE IN EVALUATING THE OFFERING OF UNITS. THIS MEMORANDUM IS FURNISHED ON THE EXPRESS UNDERSTANDING THAT, WITHOUT THE PRIOR WRITTEN PERMISSION OF THE COMPANY, SUCH PROSPECTIVE INVESTORS WILL NOT RELEASE, COPY, DISCUSS OR USE THIS MEMORANDUM OR THE INFORMATION CONTAINED HEREIN FOR ANY PURPOSE OTHER THAN EVALUATING A POTENTIAL INVESTMENT IN THE UNITS.

THIS MEMORANDUM WAS PREPARED FROM INFORMATION PROVIDED BY THE COMPANY. THE PLACEMENT AGENT HAS NOT INDEPENDENTLY VERIFIED EITHER THE INFORMATION CONTAINED IN THIS MEMORANDUM OR OTHERWISE MADE AVAILABLE TO IT IN CONNECTION WITH ANY INVESTIGATION OF THE COMPANY. THEREFORE, THE PLACEMENT AGENT MAKES NO REPRESENTATIONS OR WARRANTIES AS TO THE ACCURACY OR COMPLETENESS OF SUCH INFORMATION. FURTHERMORE, BECAUSE THIS MEMORANDUM REFLECTS THE COMPANY'S CURRENT KNOWLEDGE AND INFORMATION, NOTHING CONTAINED IN THIS MEMORANDUM CONSTITUTES, OR SHOULD BE RELIED ON AS, A PROMISE OR REPRESENTATION AS TO THE COMPANY'S FUTURE PERFORMANCE.

NO INVESTOR MAY BORROW FUNDS THROUGH A MARGIN LOAN OR OTHERWISE FROM THE PLACEMENT AGENT OR ITS AFFILIATES OR ANY SELECTED DEALER PARTICIPATING IN THE OFFERING OF THE UNITS IN ORDER TO PURCHASE OR CARRY THE UNITS.

THIS OFFER MAY BE WITHDRAWN AT ANY TIME BEFORE THE INITIAL CLOSING OR ANY SUBSEQUENT CLOSING AND IS SPECIFICALLY MADE SUBJECT TO THE TERMS DESCRIBED IN THIS MEMORANDUM. THE COMPANY AND THE PLACEMENT AGENT EACH RESERVE THE RIGHT TO REJECT ANY SUBSCRIPTION, IN WHOLE OR IN PART, FOR ANY REASON WHATSOEVER OR TO ALLOT TO ANY PROSPECTIVE INVESTOR LESS THAN THE NUMBER OF UNITS SUBSCRIBED FOR BY SUCH PROSPECTIVE

INVESTOR. REJECTED SUBSCRIPTIONS WILL BE PROMPTLY RETURNED TO THE SUBSCRIBER WITH THE AMOUNT OF THE REJECTED SUBSCRIPTION FUNDS. PRIOR TO CLOSING, ALL SUBSCRIPTION FUNDS WILL BE DEPOSITED IN AN ESCROW ACCOUNT WITH __________ BANK, AS ESCROW AGENT.

THIS MEMORANDUM DESCRIBES THE COMPANY, ITS BUSINESS PLAN, ITS FINANCIAL CONDITION, AND THIS OFFERING. PROSPECTIVE INVESTORS SHOULD CAREFULLY EVALUATE THE "RISK FACTORS" DESCRIBED IN THIS MEMORANDUM. PRIOR TO THE COMPLETION OF THE OFFERING, THE COMPANY WILL GIVE PROSPECTIVE INVESTORS THE OPPORTUNITY TO ASK QUESTIONS OF AND TO RECEIVE ANSWERS FROM THE COMPANY ABOUT THE TERMS AND CONDITIONS OF THE OFFERING, THE COMPANY OR ANY OTHER RELEVANT MATTERS, AND TO OBTAIN ANY ADDITIONAL INFORMATION TO THE EXTENT THE COMPANY POSSESSES SUCH INFORMATION OR CAN ACQUIRE IT WITHOUT UNREASONABLE EFFORT OR EXPENSE.

THIS INVESTMENT INVOLVES A HIGH DEGREE OF RISK. NO TRADING MARKET FOR THE SERIES F PREFERRED STOCK, WARRANTS OR COMMON STOCK OF THE COMPANY (THE "SECURITIES") CURRENTLY EXISTS, AND IT IS ANTICIPATED THAT NO PUBLIC MARKET FOR THE SECURITIES WILL DEVELOP AND THAT THE SECURITIES WILL BE TRANSFERABLE ONLY UNDER CERTAIN LIMITED CIRCUMSTANCES. OFFEREES SHOULD THOROUGHLY CONSIDER THE INFORMATION SET FORTH IN THIS MEMORANDUM, INCLUDING, IN PARTICULAR, THE RISK FACTORS CONCERNING THE COMPANY AND ITS BUSINESS. THE PURCHASE OF THE SECURITIES OFFERED HEREBY IS SUITABLE ONLY FOR, AND MAY BE MADE ONLY BY, ACCREDITED INVESTORS WHO HAVE NO NEED FOR LIQUIDITY OF THEIR INVESTMENT AND UNDERSTAND AND CAN AFFORD THE HIGH FINANCIAL AND OTHER RISKS OF INVESTMENT IN THE SECURITIES.

THE SECURITIES OFFERED HEREBY ARE SUBJECT TO RESTRICTIONS ON TRANSFERABILITY AND RESALE AND MAY NOT BE TRANSFERRED OR RESOLD EXCEPT AS PERMITTED UNDER THE SECURITIES ACT AND APPLICABLE STATE SECURITIES LAWS, PURSUANT TO REGISTRATION OR EXEMPTION THEREFROM. INVESTORS SHOULD BE AWARE THAT THEY WILL BE REQUIRED

TO BEAR THE FINANCIAL RISK OF THIS INVESTMENT FOR AN INDEFINITE PERIOD OF TIME.

THIS MEMORANDUM CONSTITUTES AN OFFER ONLY TO THE OFFEREE WHOSE NAME APPEARS IN THE APPROPRIATE SPACE ON THE COVER PAGE HEREOF AND TO WHOM THIS OFFERING MEMORANDUM IS INITIALLY DISTRIBUTED BY THE OFFEROR. THIS MEMORANDUM DOES NOT CONSTITUTE AN OFFER TO SELL OR A SOLICITATION OF AN OFFER TO BUY IN ANY JURISDICTION WHERE, OR TO ANY PERSON TO WHOM, IT IS UNLAWFUL TO MAKE SUCH OFFER OR SOLICITATION IN SUCH JURISDICTION. EXCEPT AS OTHERWISE INDICATED, THIS MEMORANDUM SPEAKS AS OF THE DATE HEREOF. NEITHER THE DELIVERY OF THIS MEMORANDUM NOR ANY SALE MADE HEREUNDER SHALL, UNDER ANY CIRCUMSTANCES, CREATE ANY IMPLICATION THAT THERE HAS BEEN NO CHANGE IN THE AFFAIRS OF THE COMPANY AFTER THE DATE HEREOF OR THAT THE INFORMATION CONTAINED HEREIN IS CORRECT AT ANY TIME SUBSEQUENT TO ITS DATE.

EACH PROSPECTIVE PURCHASER SHOULD CONSULT ITS OWN ATTORNEY, ACCOUNTANT, AND BUSINESS ADVISOR AS TO LEGAL, TAX, AND RELATED MATTERS CONCERNING THIS OFFER. PROSPECTIVE INVESTORS ARE URGED TO REQUEST ANY ADDITIONAL INFORMATION THEY MAY CONSIDER NECESSARY IN MAKING AN INFORMED INVESTMENT DECISION.

THIS MEMORANDUM CONTAINS SUMMARIES BELIEVED TO BE ACCURATE CONCERNING CERTAIN DOCUMENTS, BUT REFERENCE IS HEREBY MADE TO THE ACTUAL DOCUMENTS (COPIES OF WHICH WILL BE MADE AVAILABLE TO PROSPECTIVE INVESTORS UPON REQUEST) FOR COMPLETE INFORMATION CONCERNING THE RIGHTS AND OBLIGATIONS OF THE PARTIES THERETO, AND ALL SUCH SUMMARIES ARE QUALIFIED IN THEIR ENTIRETY BY THIS REFERENCE.

THE COMPANY RESERVES THE RIGHT TO REJECT ANY SUBSCRIPTION, IN WHOLE OR IN PART, OR TO ALLOT LESS THAN THE NUMBER OR AMOUNT OF UNITS TO WHICH ANY PROSPECTIVE PURCHASER HAS SUBSCRIBED. EACH PROSPECTIVE PURCHASER, BY ACCEPTING DELIVERY OF THIS MEMORANDUM, AGREES (I) TO THE FOREGOING, (II) TO MAKE NO

PHOTOCOPIES OF THE MEMORANDUM AND RELATED DOCUMENTS AND (III) IF THE PROSPECTIVE PURCHASER DOES NOT SUBSCRIBE FOR THE SECURITIES OR THE OFFERING IS TERMINATED, TO RETURN THIS MEMORANDUM AND ALL RELATED DOCUMENTS TO:

THE PLACEMENT AGENT, INC.

ALL INQUIRIES CONCERNING THIS MEMORANDUM AND THE OFFERING SHOULD BE DIRECTED TO ____________ AT THE.COM, INC., ____________, (__) ___-____.

TABLE OF CONTENTS*

* Page number references within this document refer to the original agreement and have not been altered for publication of *Financing Start-Ups*.

This Confidential Private Placement Memorandum contains certain forward-looking statements that involve substantial risks and uncertainties. When used herein the words "anticipate," "believe," "estimate," and "expect" and similar expressions as they relate to the Company or its management are intended to identify such forward-looking statements. The Company's actual results, performance, and achievement could differ materially from the results, performance, or achievements expressed in, or implied by, these forward-looking statements. Factors that could cause or contribute to such differences include those discussed in "Risk Factors."

HTTP://WWW.__________

INFORMATION CONTAINED IN THE COMPANY'S WEB SITE IS NOT A PART OF THIS MEMORANDUM.

The.com™ is a registered trademark of the Company. The.com, Inc. and the The.com, Inc. logo and other names of The.com, Inc. and/or The.com, Inc. products, including The.com, are trademarks and service marks of the Company. All other trademarks, service marks and trade names referred to in this Memorandum are the property of their respective owners.

SUMMARY

The following summary is qualified in its entirety by detailed information appearing elsewhere in this Memorandum. Unless the context requires, the "Company" refers collectively to The.com, Inc. and its wholly owned subsidiaries. Unless otherwise indicated, the information in this Memorandum assumes that the over-allotment option described under "Plan of Placement" has not been exercised.

The Company

The.com, Inc. (the "Company") has established a leadership position in the electronic commerce ("e-commerce") technology and services area of the Internet. The Company is investing in the The.com, Commerce Network, its core technology platform, in an effort to make its e-Commerce products and services among the most widely used means for transacting commerce over the Internet. The The.com, Commerce Network consists of the The.com, technology and merchant services.

The Company is leveraging its strengths in the software and computer-related products sector to move into the broader e-Commerce marketplace. To accelerate the Company's growth in the non-computer sector of e-Commerce, the Company recently acquired Internet shopping aggregation companies. These acquisitions have formed the basis for the Company's Commerce Network, which is an Internet commerce hub that offers shoppers items for sale from a variety of manufacturers. Through the use of the Company's e-Commerce infrastructure and the establishment of its relationships with its premier online customers, the Company intends to provide buyers and sellers with a superior shopping experience. The Company will offer its e-Commerce services to its existing catalog clients as they move to online retailing.

E-Commerce has reached a critical mass and is expected to continue growing dramatically. For instance, Forrester Research expects online retail sales to grow by more than 250%, or to $17 billion by 2001 from an estimated $4.8 billion today. Many factors are driving the expansion of the e-Commerce market, including business needs, technology advancement, government and industry regulation and competitive pressures. As e-Commerce expands, many traditional businesses are finding that new smaller competitors are entering their marketplace. The Company intends to remain a leader in this emerging market by using the Company's Commerce Network to secure its position. Specifically, the Company believes that its success will depend largely on its ability to (i) establish its e-Commerce technology as an industry standard, (ii) substantially increase the number of merchants participating in the The.com, Commerce Network, (iii) provide its customers with outstanding value and a superior shopping experience, and (iv) achieve sufficient sales volume to realize economies of scale. Accordingly, the Company intends to invest heavily in technology, marketing (including customer acquisition and retention), sales, operating infrastructure and development.

The Company expects to generate revenues through various sources that primarily include licensing, merchandising, product sales, service fees and processing/transaction fees. The Company's revenues and revenue growth will, in part, depend on the willingness of more merchants and consumers to adopt e-Commerce as an acceptable method for selling and buying goods and services.

As a pioneer in the e-Commerce business, the Company has over 100 experienced e-Commerce professionals on staff. In addition, the Company has a seasoned executive team with nearly 100 years of combined experience in the Internet, software, computer systems, and directing marketing businesses.

SUMMARY OF THE OFFERING

Issuer:	The.com, Inc., a ______ corporation
Offering Price:	$100,000 per Unit or $5.00 per share of Series F Preferred. Minimum investment is $100,000 (one Unit), which requirement the Company in its sole discretion may waive.
Payment:	The purchase price for the Units is payable in U.S. dollars upon delivery of the Subscription Agreement.
Securities Offered:	The Offering consists of a minimum of 10 Units and a maximum of 100 Units. Each Unit consists of 10,000 shares of Series F Preferred at an Offering Price of $5.00 per share and a Warrant to buy 1,000

shares of Common Stock at the Exercise Price of $5.00 per share. The Warrant is exercisable at any time between one and three years after the Initial Closing. If the maximum 100 Units are sold, the Company will issue to purchasers of the Units 1,000,000 shares of Series F Preferred and Warrants to purchase 100,000 shares of Common Stock, which, in the aggregate, equals approximately 10% of the Company's outstanding stock (assuming (i) the Company does not issue any shares of capital stock after the date hereof except pursuant to this offering, (ii) the conversion of all shares of the Series A Convertible Preferred Stock ("Series A Preferred"), Series B Convertible Preferred Stock ("Series B Preferred"), Series C Convertible Preferred Stock ("Series C Preferred"), Series D Convertible Preferred Stock ("Series D Preferred"), and Series E Convertible Preferred Stock ("Series E Preferred") to shares of Common Stock and (iii) no exercise of stock options and warrants outstanding as of the date hereof). If the minimum 10 Units are sold, the Company will issue 100,000 shares of Series F Preferred and Warrants to purchase 10,000 shares of Common Stock, which represent approximately 1% of the Company's outstanding stock (applying the same assumptions set forth above). The Company reserves the right to sell up to 50 additional Units on the same terms as set forth herein in the event this Offering is oversubscribed. The Series F Preferred, the Warrants and the shares of Common Stock issuable upon conversion of the Series F Preferred and exercise of the Warrants (collectively, such shares of common stock shall be referred to herein as the "Conversion Shares") are restricted

	securities under the Securities Act and are subject to restrictions on transfer. See "Description of Securities," "Capitalization" and "Risk Factors—Risks Related to This Offering—No Public Market; Units and Underlying Securities Not Marketable or Transferable."
Eligible Investors:	Only investors who are "accredited investors" within the meaning of Rule 501 of Regulation D under the Securities Act are eligible to invest in the Units.
Closings:	The Company may hold an Initial Closing of the Offering at any time after subscriptions for the minimum 10 Units have been accepted. The Company may hold any number of additional Interim Closings from time to time after the Initial Closing. The Offering is expected to expire 90 days from the date of this Offering Memorandum, subject to an extension for 60 days at the option of the Company and the Placement Agent without notice to investors. Pending each Closing, prospective investors' payments accompanying their respective Subscription Agreements will be deposited in a segregated escrow account with the Escrow Agent. See "Plan of Placement" and "Subscription Procedures."
Use of Proceeds:	The net proceeds to be received by, the Company from the Offering, after deducting the Placement Agents fees and commissions and other expenses of this Offering payable by the Company, are estimated to be between approximately $930,000 (if the minimum Units are sold) to $9,300,000 (if the maximum Units are sold). The Company expects to use the net proceeds of the Offering to repay the Bridge Notes and for its working capital needs. See "Use of Pro-

ceeds," "Recent Developments," and "Management's Discussion and Analysis of Financial Condition and Results of Operations-Liquidity and Capital Resources."

Description of Series F to a Preferred Stock: Holders of shares of the Series F Preferred will be entitled liquidation preference equal to $5.00 per share prior to any liquidating distributions to the holders of Common Stock and *pari passu* with the other outstanding series of the Company's preferred stock The Series F Preferred will contain customary antidilution adjustments in the case of stock splits, dividends or recapitalizations. Holders of the Series F Preferred will have one vote for each Share and will vote together with the other series of Preferred Stock and the Common Stock as a single class, except to the extent that separate class voting is required by the ________ Business Corporation Act ("BCA"). Each share of Series F Preferred may be voluntarily converted at any time, and will automatically convert upon the completion of an initial public offering, into one share of Common Stock. There is no assurance that the Company will be able to consummate an initial public offering. The Series F Preferred and the Common Stock received upon conversion are "restricted securities" for purposes of the Securities Act and the rules and regulations thereunder and subject to transfer and resale limitations. See "Description of Capital Stock—Series F Preferred Stock."

Description of Warrants: The Warrant included in each Unit entitles the holder to purchase 1,000 shares of Common Stock at an exercise price of $5.00 per share. If the maximum 100 Units are sold, a total of 100,000 shares of Common Stock will be issuable upon exercise of the Warrants (10,000 shares of Common Stock if the minimum 10 Units are sold). The Warrants will contain customary antidilution adjustments in the event of stock splits, dividends, and recapitalizations. The Warrants are exercisable at any time between one and three years after the Initial Closing. Warrants not exercised within three years after the Initial Closing will expire. The Warrants do not confer upon the holder any voting rights or any other rights as a Company shareholder. The Warrants and the Common Stock received upon Warrant exercise are "restricted securities" for purposes of the Securities Act and the rules and regulations thereunder and are subject to transfer and resale limitations. See "Description of Capital Stock."

Registration Rights: Holders of Series A Preferred, Series B Preferred, Series C Preferred, Series D Preferred, Series E Preferred and Series F Preferred (collectively, the Series A Preferred, the Series B Preferred, the Series C Preferred, the Series D Preferred, the Series E Preferred and the Series F Preferred are referred to herein as the "Series Preferred Stock") have "demand" and "piggyback" registration rights. On the earlier of (i) ______ __, 200_ or (ii) nine months after the Company's initial public offering, if requested to do so by owners of 50% of the shares of Common Stock underlying the Preferred Stock and certain other shares of Common Stock as specified in the Second Amended Registration Rights Agreement, and if (a) the public offering price is at least $5.00 per share of Common Stock and (b) the aggregate proceeds of the registered offering are at least $4,000,000 (before expenses), the Company is required to file a registration statement on Form S-1. Thereafter, if the Company is eligible to use Form

S-2 or Form S-3, for three years after the Company's initial public offering, registration rights are available, provided that selling shareholders would be registering at least $750,000 of Common Stock, and it has been one year since the last registration. "Piggyback" registration rights also permit holders of Series Preferred Stock, subject to certain limitations, to sell their underlying shares of Common Stock at any time in connection with any registration statement initiated by the Company. Registration rights relating to an underwritten public offering are subject to an "underwriters cutback" and any demand registration on Form S-1 may be deferred by the Company for a limited time and under limited circumstances; for example, for 180 days if registration would be seriously detrimental to the Company or for 180 days if the Company is already in registration. Holders of the Common Stock issuable upon conversion of the Series F Preferred and upon exercise of the Warrants will be subject to the same registration rights on a *pari passu* basis with holders of the Series A Preferred, Series B Preferred, Series C Preferred, Series D Preferred and Series E Preferred, any warrants relating to such Series Preferred Stock, and the warrants issued to the Placement Agent and holders of certain other shares of Common Stock. In addition, as a condition to their receipt of registration rights, investors in this Offering will agree to refrain from selling Common Stock for up to 180 days after an underwritten public offering of Common Stock is completed (i.e., the date on which a registration statement relating thereto becomes effective), if requested by the managing underwriters of such public offering. See "Description of Capital Stock — Registration Rights."

Resale Restrictions: The Series F Preferred, the Warrants and Conversion Shares will be restricted securities under the Securities Act and applicable state securities laws and, therefore, may only be transferred pursuant to the registration requirements of federal and state securities laws or pursuant to an exemption from such registration requirements. The certificates representing the Series F Preferred, the Warrants and Conversion Shares will bear a restrictive legend setting forth these resale restrictions. Holders will be required to furnish a legal opinion satisfactory to the Company before offering, reselling, pledging, or transferring such securities except pursuant to an effective registration statement under the Securities Act. See "Risk Factors—Risks Related to This Offering—No Public Market; Series F Preferred Units and Underlying Securities Not Marketable or Transferable."

Information about the Company

The Company's principal office is located at ______________. The Company's Web site is located at http://www.________. **Information contained in the Company's Web site is not a part of this Memorandum.**

RECENT DEVELOPMENTS

Third-Quarter Results of Operation

In the quarter ending September 30, _____, the Company's net revenues were $_____, which represents an increase of $_____, or ___%, from net revenues of $________ in the quarter ending June 30, ____. This increase in net revenues was primarily attributable to (1) increases in software and hardware product sales, (2) growth in merchandising revenues and (3) revenues __________. Gross profit increased to $_____ in the quarter ending September 30, ____, from $_____ in the quarter ending June 30, ____. The Company's loss from operations for the quarter ending September 30, ____, of $_______was a slight increase from the loss from operations of $______ in the quarter ending June 30, ____.

Acquisitions

On _______, the Company completed its acquisition of ______ which was doing business as _________ a California-based Internet retailer of consumer products, through the merger of a wholly owned subsidiary of the Company with and into _____ (the "Merger"). _____ was founded in ____by _______, who is now the Company's Executive Vice President for International Projects. In connection with the Merger, the Company issued ______ shares of Common Stock (the "Merger Shares"), valued for purposes of the Merger at $5.00 per share, and assumed $______ of debt by assuming an outstanding promissory note for such principal amount, for a total purchase price of $_________. In ______, the note holder converted the $_____ note plus accrued interest into _____ shares of Common Stock of The.com, Inc. (valued at $6.00 per share).

The Company has recently had discussions with other companies who expressed an interest in an acquisition of or strategic relationship involving, the Company's business. Although the Company continues to have discussions with these companies and may have discussions and meetings with other parties, there can be no assurance that the Company will sell all or any part of its business or will enter into any type of strategic relationship with any other party regarding its business.

Bridge Financing

In _________, the Company engaged The Placement Agent, Inc. to act as the placement agent for a bridge financing (the "Second Bridge Financing"). In the Second Bridge Financing, the Company issued promissory notes in the aggregate principal amount of $________ (the "Bridge Note"). The interest rate on the Bridge Notes is __% per annum. Each purchaser of the Bridge Notes also received a warrant to purchase _____ shares of the Company's common stock at $____ per share for each $100,000 of Bridge Notes that were purchased. The Bridge Notes mature at the earlier of (1) one year from the date the Bridge Notes were issued or (2) immediately after the Company has accepted subscriptions for at least $3,000,000 from the sale of its equity securities.

RISK FACTORS

An investment in the Company involves a high degree of rink. In addition, this Memorandum contains forward-looking statements that involve risks and uncertainties Discussions containing such forward-looking statements may be found under the captions "Summary," "Risk Factors," "Management's Discussion and Analysis of Financial Condition and Results of Operations," "Business," and elsewhere in this Memorandum generally. The Company's actual results could differ materially from those anticipated in these forward-looking statements as a result of many factors, including those set forth in the following risk factors. Accordingly, prospective investors should consider carefully the following risk factors, in addition to the other information concerning the Company and its business contained in this Memorandum, before purchasing the Units.

Risks Related to the Company

Limited Operating History, Accumulated Deficit and Anticipated Future Losses. The Company was incorporated in the State of _____ under the name _____, in _____ and operated initially as a computer training and services company. In _____, the Company refocused its business on e-Commerce technology and distribution. The Company changed its name to The.com, Inc. in _____. Revenues during ____ were insignificant. Accordingly, the Company has a very limited operating history on which an evaluation of the Company and its prospects can be based. The Company has incurred losses of $_________ since its inception through _____, and expects to continue to incur quarterly and annual operating losses for the foreseeable future. For these and other reasons, there can be no assurance that the Company will ever achieve profitability or, if profitability is ever achieved, that it can be sustained. See "Unpredictability of Future Revenues; Potential Fluctuation in Operating Results" and "Management's Discussion and Analysis of Financial Condition and Results of Operations—Overview."

Unpredictability of Future Revenues; Potential Fluctuation in Operating Results. As a result of the Company's limited operating history and the emerging nature of the markets in which it competes, future revenues are uncertain. The Company expects to experience significant fluctuations in its future operating results due to a variety of factors, including, without limitation, the rate at which consumers adopt online shopping, the average sale price and gross margins of products sold online, the rate at which merchants adopt the

Company's technology and services and competitive pressures within the marketplace. Because many of these factors are outside the Company's control, it is difficult to predict their effect on the Company's results of operations for any given period. The Company has a limited amount of historical financial data on which to base its planned operating expenses, which are derived, in part, on expectations regarding future revenues. To the extent that the Company is unsuccessful in increasing its revenues, the Company may be unable to quickly adjust spending to compensate for any unexpected revenue shortfall. As a result, any material decline in demand for the Company's products and services and corresponding decrease in revenues may have an immediate adverse effect on the Company.

Uncertainty of Additional Financing; Immediate and Substantial Dilution. The Company will require additional capital in order to fund its operations, as well as to fund future growth, develop new or enhanced services or products, respond to competitive pressures, and make acquisitions. There can be no assurance that additional financing will be available on terms favorable to the Company or on any terms. If adequate funds are unavailable, the Company may be unable to fund its operations or any expansion, take advantage of acquisition opportunities, develop or enhance services or products, or respond to competitive pressures. Such inability could have an immediate material adverse effect on the Company's business, operating results and financial condition. Because the Company expects to raise additional funds through the issuance of convertible debt or equity securities, shareholders of the Company likely will experience additional dilution. Such securities also may have rights, preferences, or privileges more favorable than the Series F Preferred being issued in connection herewith.

Competition. The market for Internet-based e-Commerce software and services is extremely competitive and the Company expects that such competition will intensify. Certain competitors have significantly greater financial, technical and marketing resources than the Company, and there can be no assurance that the Company will be able to compete successfully. To remain competitive, the Company must respond quickly to (i) changing customer demands and expectations, (ii) new products and enhancements of its competitors, and (iii) advances in Internet-based technologies in general. The Company's failure to remain competitive in any of these respects may have a material adverse effect on the Company.

Dependence on Skilled Personnel. Competition is intense for the skilled technical personnel required by the Company for its business, and there can be no assurance that the Company will successfully attract and retain the personnel it needs to successfully develop new and enhanced products or otherwise compete in the industry. The failure by the Company to attract and retain such personnel may have a material adverse effect on its business.

Uncertain Market Acceptance. The sale and use of the Company's existing products depends not only on the performance and functionality of these products but also on the desire of merchants to sell their products over the Internet. Because of the rapidly evolving nature of the Internet market, whether the company's existing products have the features, technological and performance characteristics, and pricing necessary to achieve widespread customer acceptance is uncertain. Lack of customer acceptance of the Company's products will have an adverse effect on the Company.

Dependence upon Rapid New Product Development. The Company's success depends, in part, upon its ability to rapidly develop new products and services that effectively respond to evolving customer needs. The market for the Company's products is characterized by rapidly changing technology, evolving Industry standards and customer requirements, intense competition, and frequent introductions of new products and services. There is no assurance that the Company will successfully identify new product opportunities and develop and bring new products and services to market in a timely manner. In addition to technical delays, the Company may experience substantial cost overruns in completing development of its software. The Company's inability to rapidly develop and introduce new products and services may have a material adverse effect on the Company.

Technology Development Risks. The Company has limited experience delivering complex Internet products or providing complex Internet service systems. The Company's technology and merchant services are based on the integration of several complex components, the successful integration of which will determine the performance and scalability of the network. The Company needs to maintain an adequate testing and technical support infrastructure to ensure the successful adoption and rollout of products and services to customers. The Company's business also depends on its ability to manage its online systems, which entails maintaining redundant communications lines, creating and managing a call center, and managing order processing and warehousing systems. The Company has limited experience in each of these areas. Failing in any of these areas could lead to significant system downtime and adversely affect the Company's business, financial condition and results of operations.

System Failure Risks. Substantially all of the Company's computer and communications hardware is located at leased facilities in ___________. The Company's systems and operations are vulnerable to damage or interruption from fire, flood, power loss, telecommunications failure, break-ins, earthquake and similar events. Because the Company presently does not have fully redundant systems or a formal disaster recovery plan, there is no assurance that a system failure would not have a material adverse effect on the Company's business, financial condition and results of operations. The Company's servers are vulnerable to computer viruses, physical or electronic break-ins and similar disruptions, which may lead to interruptions, delays, loss of data or inability to fill customer orders. The occurrence of any of the foregoing events could have a material adverse effect on the Company's business, financial condition and results of operations. See "Business—Proprietary Technology."

Management of Growth, Acquisition Risks. The Company will need to increase its sales, achieve widespread distribution of its products among customers, form successful marketing alliances with other Internet providers, and design and implement an effective planning and growth management process. Rapid growth will place a significant strain on the Company's managerial, technical, operational, and financial resources. There is no assurance that the Company's systems, procedures, or controls will be adequate to support the Company's current or future operations. The Company's future operating results also will depend on its ability to expand its sales and marketing organizations, implement and manage new distribution channels to penetrate different and broader markets, including the market for Intranet software products, and expand its support organization accordingly. There is no assurance that management will be able to manage expansion effectively and, at the same time, exploit fully the market for the Company's products and services. If the Company fails to manage its growth effectively, its business, financial condition and results of operations may be materially adversely affected. See "Dependence on Key Personnel" and "Risk of Capacity Constraints; Reliance on Internally Developed Systems; System Development Risks."

Cost of Building Brand Awareness. The Company's initiatives regarding ______will require the Company to build significant brand awareness of _____ on the Internet sufficient to attract consumers to visit its merchants. This will entail significant investment in marketing programs, such as entering into advertising/exclusive provider contracts with Internet portal sites. These investments will not guarantee that an adequate number of shoppers will visit _______ for the Company to break even, which in turn could have a material adverse effect on the Company.

Reliance on Internally Developed Systems, System Development Risks. The efficient and uninterrupted operation of its computer and communications hardware systems and Web sites, transaction-processing systems and network infrastructure is critical to the Company's reputation and ability to attract and retain customers. Any system interruption of the Company's Web sites may adversely affect the Company's ability to conduct business. The Company's Web sites are complex and require considerable technical expertise to maintain. Personnel with technological expertise in this area are in great demand, and there can be no assurance that the Company can attract, train or retain such personnel. In addition, many of the software systems used to support the Company's Web sites, including its e-Commerce operations, were developed internally. These systems will need to be enhanced over time or replaced with superior commercial products, both of which may involve considerable expense.

Online Commerce Security Risks. Online commerce and communications require the ability to securely transmit sensitive information over public networks. The Company relies on encryption and authentication technology licensed from third parties to secure and authenticate sensitive information, such as customer credit card numbers. There is no assurance that such technology will be compromised or breached. Any compromise of the Company's security measures may have a material adverse effect on the Company. A person circumventing the Company's security measures could misappropriate proprietary information or interrupt the Company's operations. The Company likely will need to expend significant capital and other resources to protect against security breaches. In addition, there can be no assurance that credit card companies will not restrict online credit card transactions in the future, which restrictions may have a material adverse effect on the Company.

Risks Associated with International Expansion. As the Company expands its business outside of the United States, the Company will be subject to the risks of doing business abroad. These risks include unexpected changes in regulatory requirements, export and import restrictions, tariffs and other trade barriers, difficulties in staffing and managing foreign operations, longer payment cycles, problems collecting accounts receivable, potential adverse tax consequences, exchange rate fluctuations, increased risks of piracy, limits on the Company's ability to enforce its intellectual property rights, discontinuity of network infrastructures, limits on repatriation of funds and political risks that may limit or disrupt international sales.

Sales and Other Tax Risks. Except for sales made in the state of ________, the Company currently does not collect sales or similar taxes with respect to the sale of products, license of technology, or provision of services into states other than states in which the Company has offices. There is no assurance that one or more states or foreign countries would not seek to impose sales or other tax obligations on companies that engage in online commerce within their jurisdictions. In the event these jurisdictions imposed sales taxes, there would be an increased cost to purchase the Company's product, and the expense of collecting and remitting such taxes may have a material adverse effect on the Company's business.

Absence of Dividends. The Company has never declared or paid cash dividends on its capital stock and does not anticipate paying any cash dividends in the foreseeable future. See "Description of Capital Stock—Dividend Policy."

Dependence on Key Personnel. The Company is substantially dependent upon the services of its executive officers and key employees. The loss of the services of any of its executive officers or other key employees may have a material adverse effect on the Company. The Company's future success also depends on its ability to hire and retain other highly qualified technological and managerial personnel. An inability to attract and retain experienced personnel may have an adverse effect on the Company.

Risks of Infringement. The Company's ability to be successful depends, in part on its ability to protect its proprietary technology. The Company relies on patent, copyright trademark and trade secret laws, employee and third-party non-disclosure agreements, and other methods to protect its proprietary rights. Despite any precautions taken by the Company to guard against disclosure or misappropriation of its proprietary technology, it may be possible to copy or otherwise use the Company's products or technology without authorization or to develop similar technology independently. The Company currently has _____ patents pending in the United States Patent Office covering different aspects of the Company's product architecture and technology. There can be no assurance that any pending or future patent applications will be granted, that any existing or future patents will not be challenged, invalidated or circumvented, or that the rights granted thereunder will provide competitive advantages to the Company. Similarly, there is no assurance that agreements with employees, consultants and others will prevent disclosure of confidential information, that the Company will have adequate remedies available to it if information is disclosed, or that the Company's trade secrets will not otherwise be disclosed or independently developed by competitors. There is no assurance that the Company's efforts to protect its rights under the patent, copyright, trademark and trade secret laws will be effective.

Risk of Absorption of Acquisitions. The Company has successfully completed several acquisitions and will contemplate additional acquisitions in the future as part of its business strategy. The purpose of the acquisitions is to achieve synergy in terms of management skills and economies of scale of operations and obtain access to new technology, markets and customers. If the Company does not successfully absorb an acquisition, financial resources may be squandered, significantly hampering the Company's ability to execute its business plan in other significant ways.

Liability for Information Retrieved from the Internet. Because material may be downloaded from Web sites hosted by the Company and subsequently distributed to others, there is a potential that claims will be made against the Company for negligence, copyright or trademark infringement or other theories based on the nature and content of such material. Although the Company carries general liability insurance, such insurance may not cover claims of this type or may be inadequate to cover all costs incurred in defense of potential claims or to indemnify the Company for all liability that may be imposed. Any costs or judgments or settlements that are not covered by insurance or are in excess of insurance coverage could have a material adverse effect on the Company.

Recent and Continuing Publicity. The Company has received, and may continue to receive, a high degree of media coverage that is not directly attributed to statements by the Company's executive officers and employees. Neither the Company nor the Placement Agent has confirmed, endorsed or adopted these third-party statements for utilization by, or distribution to, prospective purchasers in this Offering.

Risk Related to the Industry Generally

Utilization of Advanced Encryption Technology. The Company's Electronic Software Distribution ("ESD") products extensively utilize advanced encryption technologies. The regulation of such advanced encryption technologies could significantly hamper the Company's ability to expand internationally.

Risk of Intellectual Property Litigation. In its product development efforts, the Company attempts to avoid infringing or violating any known patent or other proprietary rights of third parties. However, this is difficult to achieve in a rapidly evolving technological environment in which numerous unpublished patent applications may be pending with regard to similar technologies at any point in time. The computer software market is characterized by frequent and substantial intellectual property litigation, which often is expensive, diverts resources, and creates uncertainties. If the Company were to discover that its products violate proprietary rights of third parties, there can be no assurance that the Company would be able to obtain licenses and permits that would enable it to continue offering such products without reengineering. There is also no assurance that any such licenses or permits would be available on commercially reasonable terms or that litigation could be avoided or settled without substantial expense. The Company's failure to avoid violations of the proprietary rights of third parties may have a material adverse effect on the Company.

Uncertainties of the Internet as a Commercial Marketplace. The market for the Company's products and services has only recently begun to develop and is evolving rapidly. The development of a market for the Company's products depends upon the increased use of the Internet for commerce. Although the Internet has experienced substantial growth in the number of users and amount of traffic, there can be no assurance that its technological infrastructure will be able to support the demands placed on it by continued growth. It is difficult to predict to what extent the Internet will prove to be a viable commercial marketplace. Critical issues regarding the Internet including reliability, cost, ease of use and quality of service, remain unresolved and may impact the degree to which business is conducted over the Internet. Delays in the development or adoption of new technological standards and protocols, or increased governmental regulation, could also affect the degree to which the Internet is accepted as a commercial marketplace. If the infrastructure or complementary services necessary to make the Internet a viable commercial marketplace are not developed, the Company's business, operating results or financial conditions will be adversely affected.

Uncertainties Regarding Government Regulation. Currently, the Company is not subject to direct regulation by any government agency, other than regulations applicable to businesses generally. Today, few laws or regulations directly govern access to or commerce on the Internet. However, due to the increasing popularity and use of the Internet, it is possible that additional laws and regulations will be adopted, covering issues such as user privacy, pricing, characteristics, encryption and quality of products and services. The adoption of any such laws or regulations may decrease the growth of the Internet, which might materially adversely affect the Company. Moreover, the applicability to the Internet of existing laws governing issues such as property ownership, libel and personal privacy is uncertain. Further, the Company's current or future products may become subject to United States export controls, including controls on encryption technology. The imposition of such export controls, either in their current form or as may be subsequently enacted, may delay the introduction of new products or limit the Company's ability to distribute products outside the United States or electronically. While the Company intends to guard against unlawful exportation, the global nature of the Internet makes it virtually impossible to effectively control the distribution of the Company's products. In addition, various countries may regulate the import of certain technology and may adopt laws that could limit the Company's ability to distribute products in those countries. Any such export or import restrictions, new legislation or regulation, or government enforcement of existing regulations could have a material adverse impact on the Company's business, operating results or financial condition.

Year 2000 Compliance. Many currently installed computer systems and software products are coded to accept only two digit entries in the date code field. These date code fields will need to accept four digit entries to distinguish 21st century dates from 20th century dates. Consequently, computer systems and or software was upgraded to comply with such "Year 2000" requirements. There can be no assurance that the Company's systems are Year 2000-compliant. For example, the Company utilizes third-party equipment and software that may or may not be Year 2000-compliant. Failure of the Company's systems or such third-party equipment or software to operate properly with regard to the Year 2000 problem could require the Company to incur unanticipated expenses to remedy any problems, which could have a material adverse effect on the Company's business, financial condition and results of operations. The Company currently is unable to predict the extent to which Year 2000 compliance issues will affect its vendors' systems (insofar as they relate to the Company's business) or the extent to which the Company would be vulnerable to failure of a major vendor's systems to operate property with respect to the Year 2000 problem. A Year 2000 conversion that is incompatible with the Company's systems could have a material adverse effect on the Company's business, financial condition and results of operations. In addition, because most of the purchases from the Company's Network are paid for using credit cards over the Internet, the Company's operations may be materially adversely affected to the extent its customers are unable to use their credit cards or access the Internet due to Year 2000 problems that are not remedied by their credit card vendors or by the organizations responsible for maintaining and providing access to the Internet.

Risks Related to This Offering

No Public Market; Units and Underlying Securities Not Marketable or Transferable. There is no public market for the Company's securities, including the Units and the underlying Series F Preferred, Warrants, Common Stock and Conversion Shares, and no such market is expected to develop for such securities or the Common Stock in the foreseeable future. The Offering Price for the Units has been determined by negotiation between the Company and the Placement Agent. The sale of the Units is being made without registration under state and federal securities laws in reliance upon the "private offering" exemption of Section 4(2) and Rule 506 of Regulation D under the Securities Act and available exemptions under applicable state securities laws. The Series F Preferred, Warrants and Conversion Shares will be "restricted securities" under the Securities Act and the rules and regulations thereunder and cannot be resold or otherwise transferred unless they are registered under the Securities Act and any applicable state securities laws or are transferred in a transaction exempt from such registration. Consequently, each investor's ability to control the timing of the liquidation of his or her investment in the Company will be restricted. Investors should be prepared to hold their Series F Preferred, Warrants and Conversion Shares indefinitely. There can be no assurance that an initial public offering will be consummated or that an active public market for any of the Company's securities will ever develop or be sustained.

Dilution. The Offering Price per Conversion Share (assuming the Series F Preferred is converted into Common Stock) is substantially higher than the net book value per share of outstanding Common Stock prior to the Offering. Accordingly, purchasers in this Offering will suffer an immediate and substantial dilution of approximately $____ in the net book value per share from the Offering Price. Additional dilution may occur upon exercise of outstanding options and warrants granted by the Company. If additional funds are raised through an initial public offering or other issuance of equity securities, the percentage ownership of the shareholders of the Company will be reduced and shareholders may experience additional dilution. See "Dilution."

Effects of Certain Provisions of the Articles of Incorporation, Bylaws and the _______ Business Corporation Act. Certain provisions of the Company's Articles of Incorporation (the "Articles") and of the ________ Business Corporation Act ("BCA) could delay or hinder a merger, tender offer or proxy contest involving the Company. The Board of Directors has the authority to issue up to 20,000,000 shares of preferred stock, including the 1,000,000 shares of Series F Preferred if the maximum number of Units is sold (100,000 shares if the minimum number of Units is sold), and to determine the price, rights, preferences, privileges and restrictions, including voting rights, of those shares without any further vote or action by the shareholders.

Size of Minimum Offering. As described under "Risks Related to the Company—Uncertainty of Additional Financing; Immediate and Substantial Dilution," the Company requires and is expected to require additional capital in order to fund its operations. The Company expects that raising the minimum offering amount in this Offering would provide it with adequate funds for not more than four months of operations. Failure to raise substantially more than the minimum offering amount in this Offering will require the Company to find additional sources of financing shortly after conclusion of this Offering. Failure to locate such additional financing would require the Company to modify or delay its business plans significantly or jeopardize the Company's ability to continue its operators. There can be no assurance that, if needed, such additional financing can be obtained on terms acceptable to the Company or that such terms may not be more favorable to investors in such additional financing than the terms of this Offering. See "Dilution."

No Preemptive Rights. Investors in this Offering will not become a party to the Company's existing Shareholders Agreement. Therefore, purchasers of the Units will not have any preemptive rights with respect to future issuances of securities by the Company. The Series A Preferred, Series B Preferred, Series C Preferred holders and certain Common Shareholders, who are parties to the Shareholders Agreement have preemptive rights that allow them to purchase new securities issued by the Company, on a pro rata basis and on the same terms that new securities are offered to new investors. These preemptive rights do not apply to certain issuances of securities of the Company and terminate upon consummation of a public offering of the Company's Common Stock in which the aggregate net proceeds to the Company is at least $15,000,000 and the public offering price per share equals or exceeds three times the then-current conversion price of the Series B Preferred Stock if the public offering occurs before January 1, ____ (or four times the then-current conversion price if the public offering occurs after January 1, ____). The current Series B Preferred conversion price is $____ per share.

DILUTION

The net book value of the Company at ______ was approximately $______ or $___ per outstanding share, and after giving effect to the sale by the Company of the maximum 100 Units at a price of $100,000 per Unit or $5.00 per share and assuming only a nominal value is attributable to the Warrants and the receipt of the estimated net proceeds therefrom and assuming the conversion of Series F Preferred into Common Stock, the pro forma net book value of the Company at ________, would have been approximately $________ or $____ per share of Common Stock. This amount represents an immediate increase in net book value of $___ per share of Common Stock to existing shareholders and an immediate dilution of $___ to $___ per share of Common Stock to new investors purchasing Units in this Offering. Computations of net book value per share use Common Stock on an as-converted basis, assuming the conversion of all outstanding Preferred Shares into Common Stock. The following table illustrates this per-share dilution:

Offering Price per share of Series F Preferred[1]		5.00
Net book value per share of Common Stock before Offering[2]	$	
Increase in net book value per share of Common Stock attributable to purchase of Series F Preferred by new shareholders, assuming all shares are converted into Common Stock	$	
Pro forma net book value per share of Common Stock after Offering	$	
Dilution in net book value per share of Series F Preferred to investors in this Offering (assuming conversion into Common Stock)[3]	$	

(1) Before deduction of Placement Agent commissions and fees and offering expenses.

(2) "Net book value" per share represents net worth of the Company (total assets less total liabilities) divided by the number of shares of Common Stock outstanding on an as-converted basis (assuming conversion of Series A Preferred, Series B Preferred, Series C Preferred, Series D Preferred and Series E Preferred).

(3) "Dilution" is the difference between the purchase price paid by a new investor for a share of Series F Preferred (assuming conversion into Common Stock) in this Offering and the net book value per share after the Offering (assuming conversion of all outstanding shares of preferred stock into Common Stock).

The foregoing table assumes no exercise of stock options or warrants outstanding as of ______. As of _______, there were options to purchase approximately _____ shares of common stock at a weighted average exercise price of $___ and warrants to purchase _____ shares of common stock at a weighted average exercise price of $___.

CAPITALIZATION

The following table sets forth the capitalization of the Company at ______, and as adjusted to give effect to the receipt of $________ and $______ of net proceeds from the sale of the minimum and the maximum Units, respectively. The table should be read in conjunction with the financial statements attached hereto as Exhibit A,

"Management's Discussion and Analysis of Financial Condition and Results of Operations" and "Selected Financial and Operating Data" included elsewhere in this Memorandum.

	_____ __, 200_		
	Actual	**As Adjusted**	
		Minimum	**Maximum**
Short- and long-term debt			
Bank line of Credit	$	$	$
Capital leases			
Total short- and long-term debt			
Shareholders' equity:			
Preferred Stock, par value $0.01 per share; 20,000,000 shares authorized:			
Series A preferred stock, _____ shares issued			
Series B redeemable, convertible preferred stock, _____ shares issued			
Series C redeemable, convertible preferred stock, ______ shares issued			
Series D convertible preferred stock, ______ shares issued.			
Series E convertible preferred stock, ______ shares issued.			
Series F convertible preferred stock[(1)]			
Common Stock, $0.01 par value, _____ shares authorized; ______ shares issued;[(2)] _______ shares as adjusted			
Accumulated deficit	()	()	()
Total shareholders' equity			
Total capitalization	$	$	$

---

(1) Includes _______ shares of Series F Preferred issued in the Offering if the maximum Units are sold and _______ shares if the minimum Units are sold.

(2) Does not include shares of Common Stock issuable upon the exercise of the outstanding warrants and stock options and the Warrants that will be issued to the purchasers of the Units and the Agent Warrant that will be issued to the Placement Agent. See "Dilution."

USE OF PROCEEDS

The net proceeds to be received by the Company from the Offering, after deducting the Placement Agent's fees and commissions and other expenses of this Offering payable by the Company, are estimated to be between approximately $________ (if the minimum Units are sold) to $________ (if the maximum Units are sold). The Company expects to use the net proceeds of the Offering for the following principal activities:

	Assuming Minimum Proceeds	Assuming Maximum Proceeds
Repayment of Bridge Notes[1]	$0	$
Working Capital	________	________
Total	$	$ 0

(1) To the extent holders of the Bridge Notes exchange the Bridge Notes for Units at the Offering Price at a closing: (a) such an exchange will be counted toward the minimum 10 Units; (b) the actual cash proceeds received by the Company from the sale of the Units will be adjusted accordingly; and (c) the amount to be allocated to working capital will remain unchanged.

The Company also may use a portion of the proceeds to acquire or invest in businesses, products or technologies that expand, complement or are otherwise related to the Company's current business and products. The Company currently has no written agreements or commitments with respect to any material acquisition or investment that has not been completed and described herein. There can be no assurance that any additional acquisitions will be consummated and, if consummated, what the final terms of such acquisitions will be. Pending use of the net proceeds from this Offering as described above, the Company intends to invest such proceeds in short-term, interest-bearing securities. See "Risk Factors — Risks Related to This Offering — Size of Minimum Offering."

SELECTED FINANCIAL AND OPERATING DATA

The following selected financial data for the periods indicated below should be read in conjunction with the Financial Statements of the Company and the related notes included in Exhibit A and "Management's Discussion and Analysis of Financial Condition and Results of Operations" included elsewhere herein. The statement of operations data set forth below for the quarters ended December 31, ____, March 31, ____ and June 30, ____, and the balance sheet data as of June 30, ____ are unaudited but include all adjustments management deems necessary. The historical results are not necessarily indicative of results that may be expected for any other interim period or for the year ending December 31, ____. All dollar values presented below have been rounded to the nearest hundred dollars. See "Recent Developments."

Historical Financial Data for The.com, Inc.

	Quarters Ended		
	December 31, ____	March 31, ____	June 30, ____
Net revenues	$	$	$
Percent growth (in net revenues from the previous quarter)		%	%
Gross profit			
Loss from operations	( )	( )	( )
In-process research and development			(5,602,200)
Net income (loss)	$( )	$( )	$( )

Balance Sheet Data:	June 30,
Working capital	$
Total assets	
Long-term obligations	
Shareholders' equity	

Historical Financial Data for Subsidiary, Inc.

	Quarters Ended		
	December 31, ____	March 31, ____	June 30, ____
Net revenues	$	$	$
Percent growth (in net revenues from the previous quarter)		(%)	(%)
Gross profit			
Net income (loss)	$,000	$(,000)	$,000

MANAGEMENT'S DISCUSSION AND ANALYSIS OF FINANCIAL CONDITION AND RESULTS OF OPERATIONS

All statements, trend analysis and other information contained in this Memorandum relative to markets for the Company's products and trends in net sales, gross margin and anticipated expense levels, as well as other statements including words such as "anticipate," "believe," "plan," "estimate," "expect" and "intend" and other similar expressions, constitute forward-looking statements. These forward-looking statements are subject to business and economic risks, and the Company's actual results of operations may differ materially from those contained in the forward-looking statements. For a more detailed discussion of these and other business risks, see "Risk Factors."

Overview

The Company has established a leadership position in developing, using and providing e-Commerce technology and services. The Company was incorporated in _______ and from its date of incorporation through the fourth quarter of ____, The.com, Inc. provided its clients with software training and other similar services. In the fourth quarter of ____, the Company began to refocus its business and commenced development of e-Commerce solutions for online merchants and online consumers. The.com, Inc.'s core business is the development of technology and services to assist companies to sell products and services online. The Company has more than ___ merchants that use the Company's technology and services to sell products online. In addition, the Company has a premier Internet site, _______, through which the Company sells software and other computer-related products over the Internet.

The Company recently completed acquisitions of _____, an Internet shopping aggregation company, and _______, a catalog/direct-marketing services company, to facilitate the expansion of the Company's product offerings beyond computer hardware and software products and to provide additional services to the Company's customers in marketing and selling products online. On _______, the Company completed its acquisition of ______, which was doing business as _______, ("______"), a California-based Internet retailer of consumer products, through the merger of a wholly owned subsidiary of the Company with and into _____ (the "Merger"). _____ was founded in ______ by _____, who is now the Company's Executive Vice President for International Projects. In connection the Merger, the Company issued ______ shares of

Common Stock (the "Merger Shares"), valued for purposes of the Merger at $___ per share, and assumed $____ of debt by assuming an outstanding promissory note for such principal amount, for a total purchase price of $______. In _____, the note holder converted the $____note plus accrued interest into _____ shares of Common Stock of The.com, Inc. (valued at $____ per share).

On _________, the Company acquired _______("_______"), a California-based catalog direct marketing services company, in a merger through which Media Assets, merged with and into the Company. The merger consideration consisted of ________ shares of Common Stock of the Company (priced at $____ per share), $________ in cash, and a promissory note in the principal amount of $______ payable in eight equal quarterly installments. In the months of July, August and September ____, Media Assets generated more than $_____ per month in revenue and generated more than $______ in net income for the three months ended September 30, ____. _____ assets formed the basis for the Company's _____ Division.

The Company currently derives its revenues primarily from (1) licensing revenues from merchants that use the Company's technology and services, (2) sales of computer software and hardware products, including Electronic Software Distribution ("ESD") through the Company's proprietary ESD technology, (3) transaction fees from the sales of products by merchants that use the Company's technology or participate in the The.com, Inc. Network, and (4) merchandising fees. With the completion of the Company's recent acquisitions, the Company will have additional sources of revenues, including fees from providing creative and marketing services and position or placement fees from merchants who select a prominent position in the The.com, Inc. Network.

Revenues from the sale of computer products are currently recognized upon either delivery through ESD or shipment of physical product to the end user. The amount payable to the distributor or software publisher is reported as cost of sales. Licensing revenues are generally recognized on a straight-line basis over the term of the licensing contact, which is usually one year. Transaction fees are recognized upon the completion of the transaction. Merchandising fees are generally recognized over the average term of the merchandising program.

The Company has a limited operating history upon which investors may evaluate its business and prospects. Since inception, the Company has incurred significant losses, and as of ______, had an accumulated deficit of approximately $___ million. The Company intends to expend significant financial and management resources on the development of additional services, sales and marketing, technology and operations to support larger-scale operations and greater product and service offerings. As a result, the Company expects to incur additional losses and continued negative cash flow from operations for the foreseeable future. There can be no assurance that the Company's revenues will increase or even continue at their current level or that the Company will achieve or maintain profitability or generate cash from operations in future periods. The Company's prospects must be considered in light of the risks, expenses and difficulties frequently encountered by companies in their early stage of development, particularly companies in new and rapidly evolving markets such as electronic commerce. To address these risks, the Company must, among other things, maintain existing and develop new relationships with merchants, including traditional and online retailers, implement and successfully execute its business and marketing strategy, continue to develop and upgrade its technology and transaction-processing systems, provide superior customer service and order fulfillment, respond to competitive developments, and attract, retain and motivate qualified personnel. There can be no assurance that the Company will be successful in addressing such risks, and the failure to do so would have a material adverse effect on the Company's business, financial condition and results of operations. The Company's current and future expense levels are based largely on its planned operations and estimates of future sales. Revenues and operating results generally depend on many factors, including but not limited to, the volume and timing of orders received, which are difficult to forecast. The Company may be unable to adjust spending in a timely manner to compensate for any unexpected revenue shortfall. Accordingly, any significant shortfall in revenues would have an immediate adverse effect on the Company's business, financial condition and results of operations. In view of the rapidly evolving nature of the Company's business and its limited operating history, the Company is unable to accurately forecast its revenues and believes that period-to-period comparisons of its operating results are not necessarily meaningful and should not be relied upon as an indication of future performance.

Quarterly Results of Operations

The Company has received an audit of its financial statements for each of the years ended December 31, ____, ____ and ____. The following table sets forth certain unaudited quarterly statement-of-operations data for the quarters ending December 31, ____, March 31, ____, and June 30, ____, respectively. In the opinion of management, this information has been prepared substantially on the same basis as the audited financial statements appearing elsewhere in this Memorandum, and all necessary adjustments, consisting only of normal recurring adjustments, have been included in the amounts stated below to present fairly the unaudited quarterly results. The quarterly data should be read in conjunction with the audited financial statements of the Company and the notes thereto appearing elsewhere in this Memorandum. The operating results for any quarter are not necessarily indicative of the operating results for any future period.

Statements of Operations
(unaudited)

	Quarters Ended		
	December 31, ____	March 31, ____	June 30, ____
Net revenues	$	$	$
Cost of revenues			
Gross profit			
Operating expenses:			
Research and development			
Selling, general, and administrative			
In-process research and development	0	0	
Total operating expenses			
Loss from operations	( )	( )	( )
Interest income (expense), net	( )		
Net loss	$ 0	$ 0	$ 0

Quarters ended June 30, ____, compared to March 31, ____

Acquisitions. On ____, the Company acquired ______., which were wholly owned subsidiaries of ________. The acquisition consideration consisted of _____ in cash and _____ shares of the Company's Common Stock (valued at $5.00 per share), with a total value of approximately

$______. The Company believes that the acquisitions will enable it to expand its product and service offerings and establish an international presence. ______ and _________ service assist the Company in providing a complete set of e-Commerce tools, including, but not limited to, front-end store development back-end services (e.g., credit card processing services), and transaction processing services.

Net Revenues. Net revenues increased from $______ in the quarter ended March 31, ____, to $______ in the quarter ended June 30, ____, an increase of ____%. Net revenues increased due to the growth in the licensing of The.com, Inc. online stores and growth in the sales of computer products through the online computer store network. These increases were due to the acquisition of new customers through various marketing programs as well as an increasing number of repeat customers.

Revenues by transaction source for the quarters ended June 30, ____, and March 31, ____, were:

	Quarters Ended		
	March 31, ____	June 30, ____(1)	Percent Change
Revenue Source			
Store licensing revenues	$	$	%
Computer product sales			%
Technology licensing and consulting	______	______	%
Total net revenues	$______	$______	%

(1) Subsequent to June 30, ____, the Company expanded its revenue sources to include merchandising. Merchandising fees were approximately $_____ in September. In addition, transaction fees from merchants, which are included in the above table under computer product sales, have become more significant since June 30th and is currently viewed by the Company to be a source of revenues that is now separate from product sales.

Gross Profit. The gross profit margin increased to % for the quarter ended June 30, ____, from % for the quarter ended March 31, ____. This increase in gross profit margin is primarily a result of (i) the sale of more higher-gross-margin computer products and (ii) the economies of scale achieved from the increased volume of transactions. Cost of revenues primarily reflects the cost of computer products sold through the The.com, Inc. online store network.

Research and Development Expenses. Research and development expenses consist principally of payroll and related expenses for technology development, network operations personnel and consultants, and systems and telecommunications infrastructure. Research and development expenses were $______ for the quarter ended June 30, ____, compared with $______ for the quarter ended March 31, ____. Research and development expenses were primarily attributable to staffing and associated costs related to enhancing the features, content and functionality of the Company's software including network transaction-processing systems, as well as increased investments in systems and telecommunications infrastructure. To date, all research and development costs have been expensed as incurred. The Company believes that continued investment in research and development is critical to attaining its strategic objectives and, as a result, expects research and development expenses to increase significantly in absolute dollars.

Selling, General and Administrative Expenses. Selling, general and administrative expenses consist of payroll and related expenses for executive, accounting and administrative personnel, recruiting, professional fees and other general corporate expenses. Selling, general and administrative expenses were $______ for the quarter ended June 30, ____, compared with $_____ for the quarter ended March 31, ____. The increased level of general and administrative expenses was primarily due to increased salaries and related expenses associated with the hiring of additional personnel and marketing expenses. General and administrative expenses also were higher in the second quarter due to moving, restructuring, public relations, and other expenses, which are nonrecurring, associated with the acquisition of ______ and ______ from ________ (the "Acquisition"). The costs of leasing and operating the new office to be used by personnel acquired as part of the Acquisition are included in selling, general and administrative expenses. The Company expects general and administrative expenses to increase slightly as the Company incurs additional costs related to the growth of its business. The number of employees increased to approximately ___ at June 30, ____, from approximately ___ at March 31, ____. The increase in employees was primarily due to the Acquisition.

In-process Research and Development. The in-process research and development expense during the second quarter resulted from the Acquisition. The Company recorded a nonrecurring charge of $___ million related to the estimated in-process research and development component of the assets acquired.

Interest Income, Net. Interest income, net consists of earnings on short-term investments net of interest expense on capital leases and bank credit lines. Interest income, net was $____for the three months ended June 30, ____, compared with $____ for the quarter ended March 31, ____.

Income Taxes. As of June 30, ____, the Company had approximately $____ million of net operating loss carryforwards for federal income tax purposes, which expire between ____ and ____. The Company's ability to utilize its net operating loss carryforwards may be limited due to changes in control as defined by the Internal Revenue Code. The Company has provided a full valuation allowance on the deferred tax asset, consisting primarily of net operating loss carryforwards, because of uncertainty regarding its realizability.

Quarters ended March 30, ____, and December 31, ____

Net Revenues. Net revenues increased to $____ for the quarter ended March 31, ____, compared to $____ for the quarter ended December 31, ____, an increase of ____%. Net revenues increased due to the growth in the licensing of The.com, Inc. online stores, as well as the growth in the sales of computer products through the online stores. Through March 31, ____, The.com, Inc. had licensed ____ stores compared to ____ stores through December 31, ____.

The Company continued to provide technology licensing and consulting services to third parties during the first quarter. However, revenue from consulting decreased as the company focused on the expansion of its online store network. The Company's consulting services have ceased so that the Company can primarily focus on becoming a leader in providing e-Commerce services.

Revenues by transaction source for the quarters ended March 31, ____ and December 31, ____ were:

	Quarters Ended		
	December 31, ____	March 31, ____	Percent Change
Revenue Source			
Store licensing revenues	$	$	%
Computer product sales			%

	Quarters Ended		
	December 31, ____	March 31, ____	Percent Change
Technology licensing and consulting	______	______	%
Total net revenues	$______	$______	%

Research and Development Expenses. Research and development expenses consist primarily of payroll and related expenses for technology development, consultants, systems and telecommunications infrastructure, as well as the amortization expense for acquired technology. All research and development costs have been expensed as incurred. Continued investment in research and development is critical to the Company's attainment of its strategic objectives, and the Company expects research and development costs to continue to increase. In the fourth quarter of ____, there were nonrecurring research and development expenses that resulted in these expenses being higher in the fourth quarter of ____ compared to the first quarter of ____.

Selling, General and Administrative Expenses. Selling, General and Administrative expenses consist of payroll and related expenses for executive, accounting and administrative personnel, recruiting, professional fees and other general corporate expenses. Selling, General and Administrative expenses increased to $____ for the quarter ended March 31, ____, compared to $____ for the quarter ended December 31, ____, an increase of ____%. The increase in Selling, General and Administrative expenses is primarily due to increased salaries and related expenses associated with the hiring of additional personnel, increased marketing expenses associated with increasing traffic at the company's online store network, and increases in depreciation and professional fees. The number of employees increased to approximately ____ at March 31, ____, from approximately ____ at December 31, ____.

Liquidity and Capital Resources

Since inception, the Company has financed its operations primarily through issuance of Common Stock and Preferred Stock, the net proceeds of which totaled $____ through June 30, ____.

Net cash used in operating activities was $____ in ____ and $____ in the six months ended June 30, ____. Cash used in operating activities in ____ was attributable to a net loss of $____ partially offset by an increase in accounts payable. For the six months ended June ____, cash used in operating activities resulted from a net loss of $____ that was partially offset by a $____ charge for in-process research and development related to the Acquisition and increases in accounts payable. Net cash used in investing activities of $____ and $____ for ____ and the six months ended June 30, ____, respectively, was primarily attributable to purchases of equipment and software licenses in ____ and purchases of equipment and the cash portion of the Acquisition in the six months ended June 30,____.

Cash flows provided by financing activities of $____ in ____ consisted primarily of proceeds from notes payable and sales of preferred stock. Cash flows of $____ from financing activities in the six months ended June 30, ____, consisted primarily of net proceeds of $____ from the issuance of Preferred Stock and Common Stock partially offset by the repayment of $____ of convertible subordinated notes.

As of June 30, ____, the Company had $____ of cash and equivalents. As of that date, the Company's principal commitments consisted of obligations outstanding under operating leases. Although the Company has no material commitments for capital expenditures, it anticipates a substantial increase in its capital expenditures and lease commitments consistent with growth in operations, infrastructure and personnel. The Company expects a significant portion of these capital expenditures to be financed with secured lines of credit

The Company believes that additional capital will be required to fund future development, deployment and commercialization of its products and services. There can be no assurance that additional funds will be available at commercially reasonable terms or at all. Management is evaluating strategies to raise additional capital necessary to meet operating requirements.

BUSINESS

Overview

The Company has established a leadership position in the electronic commerce ("e-Commerce") technology and services area of the Internet. The Company is investing in the The.com, Inc. Network, its core technology platform, in an effort to make its e-Commerce products and services among the most widely used means for transacting commerce over the Internet. The The.com, Inc. Network consists of the The.com, Inc. technology and merchant services. The modular design of the The.com, Inc. Network allows a merchant to choose only the particular products and services that it needs and is expected to increase merchant participation in the The.com, Inc. Network.

Much of the technology underlying the The.com, Inc. Network originally was developed to support the Company's first e-Commerce site. It receives thousands of visitors each day and is among the leading sites for selling software and other computer-related products over the Internet. The.com, Inc.'s Network has over ____ affiliated merchant stores selling over ____ products through the use of the Company's technology.

The Company, by acquiring ____ and ____ in ____, has expanded its e-Commerce infrastructure to provide additional back-end services. The Company's back-end services currently include fraud protection, fulfillment and payment processing services. Such technology and services, which comprise the Company's technology and merchant services, offers buyers and sellers a secure means transact e-Commerce on the Internet. The Company entered into a strategic relationship with ____ ("____") through an exclusive marketing agreement pursuant to which the Company's technology will be integrated with ____'s set-up and configuration products. ____'s products are used by over ____ software developers and over ____ of the top ____ software companies, as recognized by Software Publishers Association to install software on consumer and business desktops. The first implementation of this strategic relationship was demonstrated with the release of ______.

The Company is leveraging its strengths in the software and computer-related products sector to move into the broader e-Commerce marketplace. To accelerate the Company's growth in the non-computer sector of e-Commerce, the Company recently acquired ____, an Internet shopping aggregation company, and ____, a catalog direct-marketing services company whose existing clients include ____. These acquisitions have formed the basis for the Company's Network, which is an Internet commerce hub that offers shoppers items for sale from a variety of manufacturers, and the Company's ____ Division, respectively. Through the use of the Company's e-Commerce infrastructure and the establishment of its relationships with its premier online customers, the Company intends to provide buyers and sellers with a superior shopping experience. The Company will offer its e-Commerce services to its existing catalog clients as they move to online retailing.

E-Commerce has reached a critical mass and is expected to continue growing dramatically. For instance, Forrester Research expects online retail sales to grow by more than 250%, or to $17 billion by 2001 from an estimated $4.8 billion today. Many factors are driving the expansion of the e-Commerce market, including business needs, technology advancement, government and industry regulation and competitive pressures. As e-Commerce expands, many traditional businesses are finding that new smaller competitors are entering their marketplace. The Company intends to remain a leader in this emerging market by using the The.com, Inc. Network to secure its position. Specifically, the Company believes that its success will depend largely on its ability to (i) establish its e-Commerce technology as an industry standard, (ii) substantially increase the number of merchants participating in the The.com, Inc. Network, (iii) provide its customers with outstanding value and a superior shopping experience, and (iv) achieve sufficient sales volume to realize economies of scale. Accordingly, the Company intends to invest heavily in technology, marketing (including customer acquisition and retention), sales, operating infrastructure and development.

The Company expects to generate revenues through various sources that primarily include licensing, merchandising, product sales, service fees and processing/transaction fees. The Company's revenues and revenue growth will, in part, depend on the willingness of more merchants and consumers to adopt e-Commerce as an acceptable method for selling and buying goods and services.

As a pioneer in the e-Commerce business, the Company has over ____ experienced e-Commerce professionals on staff. In addition, the Company has a seasoned executive team with nearly ____ years of combined experience in the Internet, software, computer systems, and directing marketing businesses.

Industry Background

The Internet is revolutionizing the way commerce is conducted. The audience of potential Internet customers in the United States alone now exceeds 60 million people and is growing at a rate of close to 10 million users per quarter, according to data cited in a 1998 report by the U.S. Department of Commerce. Shopping has become one of the most popular activities on the Internet, and the number of people who shop and buy products on the Internet is growing rapidly. Industry reports indicate that more than 10 million households in the U.S. and Canada have purchased at least one product or service over the Internet and project that the number of households worldwide that shop online will double by the end of 1998. Forrester Research expects online retail sales to grow to $17 billion in 2001 from an estimated $4.8 billion in 1998.

To take advantage of this market opportunity, merchants want to build storefronts on the Internet and other commercial online networks. There are several reasons why merchants are pursuing e-Commerce. First, e-Commerce enables merchants, such as traditional retailers and catalog companies, to reach new customers who were previously unreachable due to cost constraints. For example, ActivMedia reports that, for the average online merchant, 60% of online sales are generated from new customers. Second, the cost of processing transactions electronically is substantially less than more traditional methods and this results in lower costs and higher profit margins for such merchants. As the number of online merchants grows to meet the demand created by consumers adopting online shopping, the Company intends to provide to merchants, on an out-source basis, technology and services enabling such merchants to capture higher levels of market share.

Most companies do not have the core competence to undertake what the early Internet pioneers did, which was to build these systems themselves. Businesses are being driven to adopt e-Commerce strategies to lower costs and increase operating efficiencies. Such Companies need a more cost-effective approach to establishing an e-Commerce presence. Consequently, an opportunity exists for software vendors to supply these companies with the tools, packaged applications and infrastructure needed to engage in e-Commerce. E-Commerce companies range from retailers to out-source providers and from infrastructure providers to new media. BT Alex Brown estimated that the market for Internet software and services could approach $7 billion by 2001. This estimate is comprised of $1.4 billion in business-to-business software and $5.5 billion in business-to-consumer software for Internet e-Commerce applications.

Traditional retailers and merchants have been carefully evaluating the financial rewards gained by Internet retailers such as Amazon.com and Yahoo!. Their success has put pressure on companies to pursue the Internet e-Commerce opportunity. Accordingly, this has created an increased demand for e-Commerce services from companies such as Cisco Systems, Open Market, and The.com, Inc.

Strategy

The Company intends, through the continued development or acquisition of e-Commerce technology and marketing services, to be a dominant provider of e-Commerce solutions for online merchants and to incorporate its proprietary technology and online marketing expertise into its products and services. The Company's strategy includes the efficient integration of products and services to ensure that solutions meet merchant partners' mission-critical requirements. The Company's business strategy includes the following key elements:

Provide an End-to-End Solution on a Turnkey Basis. The Company's strategy is to provide a complete e-Commerce solution to its customers. Although the Company recognizes that not all merchants will adopt the full range of the Company's e-Commerce products and services, the Company believes that the modular nature of its products and services will, nevertheless, attract merchants at all stages in the adoption of e-Commerce technologies. Below is a summary description of the e-Commerce supply chain. It describes the critical components connecting buyers and sellers (merchants) online and the Company's role in such chain.

The Company believes that as merchants move from one end of the chain to another, such merchants will continue to adopt the Company's products and services to satisfy their e-Commerce requirements.

To establish and maintain a leading position as an e-Commerce solution provider, the Company has determined that it must provide not only technology and services but also marketing and distribution services. This combination is expected to attract not only top-tier merchant partners, but also a significant share of the merchants establishing an online presence over the next three to five years.

Promote Migration from Basic Package to Comprehensive Solution. The modular design of the Company's e-Commerce solutions allows a merchant to implement only that portion of the The.com, Inc. Network suite of product services that meets its immediate needs. Once established as an e-Commerce solution provider to the merchant, the Company will seek to upgrade that merchant to a more comprehensive e-Commerce solution. For example, several software publishers have expressed interest in the Company's full suite of e-Commerce tools as a direct result of a relationship established from providing digital licensing and processing technology.

Promote Membership in the The.com, Inc. Network. A key element of the Company's strategy is to promote the rapid growth of the number of merchants actively participating in the The.com, Inc. Network. Consequently, the Company must convince merchants and customers of the benefits associated with a well-developed The.com, Inc. Network. These benefits include (a) a uniform shopping experience for customers, (b) enabling merchants to leverage technology enhancements across the The.com, Inc. Network and (c) providing merchants with additional marketing services to attract shoppers. The Company believes that these benefits will enable it to provide a uniform, high-quality, secured shopping experience for merchants and their customers.

Target Traditional Manufacturers, Retailers and Catalogers. The Company has learned that many traditional manufacturers, retailers and catalog companies are keenly interested in automated online retail services. The Company believes that its recent acquisition of a direct marketing catalog company will enable it to assist traditional retailers, manufacturers and catalog companies with limited or no online order processing capabilities to utilize e-Commerce technologies.

Offer Merchants Distribution and Marketing Services. The Company's Network will be the hub for the marketing and distribution services that the Company will offer merchants. The Company will initiate a number of merchandising and customer acquisition programs that will augment the ability of new online merchants to increase sales. Merchants can choose to pay for a prominent placement with the service or they can choose to be part of a large directory. These alternatives allow merchants to participate in e-Commerce at levels commensurate with their commitment to selling products over the Internet. The Company will also offer automated means to allow merchants to build their own online stores that will operate on the The.com, Inc. Network.

Utilize Joint Ventures, Acquisitions and Strategic Marketing Agreements to Increase Market Share. The Company also expects to enter into joint ventures, make acquisitions and enter into strategic marketing arrangements in order to increase its base of merchants for the The.com, Inc. Network. The Company's recent acquisition of ____, and ____ has given the Company access to thousands of merchants and a number of premier catalogers and retailers. A key goal for the Company in connection with any acquisition is to acquire companies with personnel who have highly developed skills. Thus far, the Company's acquisitions have achieved this goal by giving the Company access to individuals who have extensive experience with growth companies that provide services to merchants. For instance, _____ increased its revenues from $____ per month three years ago to over $____ per month in each of November, December and January prior to the Acquisition.

In February ____, the Company entered into an agreement with ____, the leader in installation and configuration programs, under which ____ will market the Company's products and services to ____'s installed base of over 100,000 software developers. If ____ and its customers utilize the Company's technology and services, the Company could develop a leading position in this market. See "Marketing and Promotion."

Expand to International Markets. The Company currently derives essentially all of its revenues from sales to North American merchants and consumers. The Company believes that there is significant opportunity to expand the market for its products and services outside North America. The Company intends, through partnerships, joint ventures or internal expansion, to market its products and services in Europe and Asia.

Products and Services

The.com, Inc. Network

Through the The.com, Inc. Network, the Company offers an integrated set of products comprising a comprehensive e-Commerce solution. The Company's products and merchant services are part of the The.com, Inc. Network. The The.com, Inc. Network is composed of three units: the ____Network, Technology, Merchant Services and the ____ Division. The Company's technology and merchant services include the following:

The.com, Inc. Network

The.com, Inc. network consists of ____, ____ and the ____work. ____ is expected to be a premier destination site on the Internet for shoppers to purchase a broad selection of specialty and unique products. ____ is a premier Internet shopping portal that offers consumers a broad range of products from thousands of retailers, manufacturers, traditional merchants, service companies and mail order firms. The Network consists of over ____ online computer stores that gives manufacturers and software publishers' exposure to hundreds of thousands of potential customers each month. The Company has invested in a number of agreements with high-traffic sites, such as Yahoo! and PC World, to direct shoppers to the Network.

____

In ____, the Company plans to launch ____ as a destination site on the Internet for shoppers to purchase a broad array of products. It will be a ready-made direct marketing sales channel for retailers and manufacturers to sell through to acquire new customers and additional revenue. It will be designed to be an easy, fast, convenient and secure site for purchasing gifts, unique and specialty items and apparel. The Company is making a significant investment to enable it to provide high-level customer service for the site. The site also will serve as a showcase for The.com, Inc.'s technology, demonstrating how it can be used by merchants to increase sales from their sites.

____

____ is an Internet shopping portal that offers merchants a variety of services for growing their business. These services include:

Listing Directory

This is a low-cost directory service in which merchants are listed by product category. Shoppers searching for a particular category of products can locate Internet merchants who carry those products. The Company will market additional TCN services to the merchants listed in the directory. These merchants will also be one of the primary sources for leads for transaction-oriented services that the Company is contemplating and other The.com, Inc.'s products and merchant services. These merchants have the opportunity to upgrade to additional CommerceTrust products and services.

Anchor Tenants

Anchor tenants are ____'s premier merchants and, as such, they are positioned in the most visible areas of the hub and have the greatest prominence within these areas. These merchants typically have products that have broad appeal among shoppers. These merchants will generally pay The.com, Inc. a fee for their positions in the hub and/or a fee for the number of shoppers that make a purchase.

General Tenants

General tenants will have less prominent placement than anchor tenants but will be prominently displayed on ____. They will receive a significant amount of visibility to shoppers through buttons and "banners" on the site. These merchants will pay The.com, Inc. a fee for their positions in the hub and/or the number of merchants delivered to them.

____ Network

The Company currently offers the ____ product suite, which is targeted at the computer products segment. The products and services in this area include:

____

This is one of the leading Web sites for purchasing software and computer-related products. It offers over ____ software products at competitive prices. The site receives over ____ unique visitors per month. Much of the technology created for ____ has been utilized broadly across the The.com, Inc. Network.

Business Stores

These are stores that have a broad selection of software titles that merchants who are already attracting traffic to their sites use as an additional revenue source to leverage their existing traffic. The Company provides hosting, merchandising and customer service and out-sourced services to these merchants.

Personal Stores

Consumers can participate in the Network by establishing a personal store which offers software titles at competitive prices. Participants in the Company's Personal Store program receive in the form of a sales commission a percentage of the transaction revenues associated with these stores. They can have their friends, business associates and family members purchase software from their stores.

The.com, Inc. Technology and Merchant Services

The.com, Inc.'s technology and merchant services offer a comprehensive suite of e-Commerce services. The Company believes that a secure, cost-effective and complete solution for conducting commerce on the Internet – without having to deal with the complexities that go along with it – is what mainstream companies are looking for as they move to the Internet. The.com, Inc. offers merchants the opportunity to get a full turnkey solution through its eStore or allows merchants who already have a presence on the Internet to purchase the modules that will optimize the success of their sites. The.com, Inc.'s technology and merchant services include the following:

eStore

The.com, Inc.'s eStore is designed for merchants who are looking for more than just an online catalog. eStore is a dynamic, robust Web store platform, which, unlike competing Web store solutions, contains a complete suite of e-Commerce services as described below. eStore Merchants do not have to combine and coordinate multiple technologies and service providers in order to establish an online presence. Using the eStore software platform, a merchant can set up a feature-rich, online store stocked with its own products in several days, and all at a fraction of what the merchant would have to pay to develop a similar system itself.

The.com, Inc. eStore includes the following features:

- Compelling, professional store templates offering an intuitive, user-friendly look and feel;
- Sufficient capacity to display all of a merchants product descriptions, images and pricing information;
- Flexible merchandising options for cross selling, upselling and feature items;
- **eCart**: for order processing for flexible, one-step ordering convenience;
- **ePayment**: for real-time payment processing and fraud prevention;
- **eReport**: for real-time order tracking and reporting;

- **eContainer**: for flexible order fulfillment for the electronic download of electronic merchandise; and
- **eDesign**: for a broad range of creative services for developing or enhancing the Company's client's Web presence.

eCart

eCart provides shoppers with an intuitive, one-step order form. In addition, eCart will be Electronic Data Interchange ("EDI") compliant and integrate seamlessly with inventory tracking, back-order management and returns systems. Merchants can use eCart for any number of items on their current Web stores. In addition, shoppers can load their carts with any number of physical goods, software products or other items available on the Web store they are visiting and have their orders processed in one easy step. Each order is formatted and dynamically routed to the correct fulfillment center – whether to a merchant's warehouse or to a distributor.

ePayment

ePayment offers an effective, secure online payment processing system that not only incorporates technology for protecting credit card numbers that are transmitted over the Internet, but also prevents the use of stolen credit card numbers from being used to make purchases. The ePayment system uses AVS ("Address Verification System"), payment-support technology, cutting-edge cryptography, on-the-fly scoring and Secure Socket Layer ("SSL") and other security technologies to keep fraud rates low.

ePayment fraud protection and processing services include:

- Real-time processing of credit card orders and corporate purchase orders; ePayment processes Visa, MasterCard, American Express, Diners Club, Carte Blanche, and Discover cards; and
- Automated tax calculation for most jurisdictions in the U.S. and Canada.

eReport

The Company provides electronic reporting services that allow merchants to track sales in real time and to develop promotional and merchandising programs. eReport is a password-protected Web site offering a broad array of sales tracking and reporting services.

eContainer

eContainer technology provides an efficient and secure method of distributing and selling software and other digital content online. This technology gives software publishers and other digital content providers the option of offering products for secure online buying or only for secure trial purposes using the Company's technology which allows end users to download a product and try the full-featured product prior to purchase. The Company will also offer a variety of services for fulfillment of orders for physical goods.

The eContainer will be a key component of a campaign aimed at over ____ software publishers, which will be launched with ____, a leading provider of set-up and configuration technology to software publishers. The Company's eContainer technology will be exclusively bundled with several ____ offerings.

eDesign

The Company has a staff of direct marketing professionals and experienced Web developers that can help clients design creative materials and web sites and also assists in the implementation of e-Commerce services. This is a key component of the overall turnkey e-Commerce solution that the Company can provide.

The.com, Inc. ____ Division

This division was formed in September ____, through the acquisition of ____. This division offers consumer and business-to-business catalog and retail clients creative, marketing and production services. This division already has a well-known brand, which the Company intends to continue, and a strong reputation in the direct marketing industry. The division services a range of customers from startups to multi-billion dollar corporations in both the consumer and business-to-business categories. Current clients include. The Company intends to market its e-Commerce services to these existing clients of the Company's ____ Division.

Marketing and Promotion

The Company's marketing objective is to achieve broad market penetration in e-Commerce out-sourced services and distribution. The.com, Inc.'s general marketing strategy is designed to widely distribute its technology, increase customer loyalty, maximize the opportunity for repeat purchases, strengthen its brand names, and develop incremental revenue opportunities.

The Company intends to create value for its customers by applying its innovative technology in both the delivery of cost-effective programs and services and in the development of creative and flexible merchandising. For instance, the Company is building shopper loyalty through programs similar to the airline industry's "frequent flyer" programs. The Company believes that its ability to create a cost-effective method for merchants to adopt online retailing, coupled with its ability to offer merchants additional avenues for acquiring shoppers, will provide a compelling reason for merchants to use its services. The Company believes that by creating technology that offers shoppers a compelling and personalized shopping experience, the Company will increase the number of visitors that make a purchase, encourage repeat visits and purchases, and extend customer retention which will in turn ensure the success of its merchants.

The Company currently employs a variety of traditional and online marketing programs and business development and promotional activities to achieve its goals, including the following:

Public Relations. As a result of the Company's public relations activities, as well as unsolicited invitations, the Company has been featured in articles in a variety of newspapers and magazines including Web Week, Computer Reseller News, Wired News, Cnet PC Week, and ____.

Advertising. The Company advertises through the traditional print media as well as online media. This advertising is intended to create awareness of the Company and its key brands as well as to increase sales.

Trade Shows. The Company participates in several industry trade shows throughout the year. The Company also intends to sponsor strategic shows.

Direct Mail. The Company intends to deploy direct mail programs to increase awareness among merchants of its products and services and to generate additional sales.

Joint Marketing Programs. The Company also continues to establish partnerships with high-profile companies that have existing relationships with merchants in a particular industry. For instance, the Company has entered into an exclusive arrangement with ____ to have its technology integrated with ____'s product line. ____ has a dominant position in the software set-up tools and utilities market. Over ____ software developers and over ____ of the top ____ software publishers, as listed by the Software Publishers Association, use these products for installing and configuring their products on consumer and business desktops. In June ____, the Company was selected by Microsoft to preview this technology with the launch of ____ – the first Microsoft product sold only over the Internet The Company expects to rollout the first jointly developed product with ____ early in the first quarter of ____.

Additionally, the Company intends to develop merchant and consumer marketing programs. These marketing programs may be in the form of co-op online and traditional marketing programs, including print ads, direct mail and Internet advertising. These programs will be designed to generate consumer interest in The.com, Inc.'s Network and product lines.

Research and Development

To keep pace with technological developments in the marketplace and address the increasingly sophisticated needs of its customers, the Company intends to expand its existing product offerings and introduce new products and services for Internet-based e-Commerce. The Company expects to receive from its customers and merchants significant product feedback that will be channeled into product development and innovation. While the Company expects that certain new products will be developed internally, the Company may, based on timing and cost considerations, expand its product offerings through acquisitions. In addition, the Company has relied on and intends to continue to rely on external relationships and development resources for development of certain products and components thereof.

Competition

The market for Internet-based products and services is new, intensely competitive, rapidly evolving and subject to rapid technological change. The Company expects competition to increase in the future. The Company competes with Value America, Cybershopper, Cybersource, $hopping.com, Release Software, Digital River, Cyberian Outpost and Amazon.com, and other companies. Most of the Company's current and potential competitors have longer operating histories, larger installed customer bases and greater financial, technical, and marketing resources than those of the Company. Such competition could materially adversely affect the Company's business, operating results or financial condition.

Competitive factors in the Internet-based software and services market include core technology, breadth of product features, product quality, marketing and distribution resources, customer service and support and price. The market and competition are still new and rapidly evolving, and there can be no assurance that the Company will be able to compete successfully in this market See "Risk Factors—Risks Related to the Company—Competition."

Customer Service

The Company's ability to establish and maintain long-term relationships with its customers and encourage repeat visits and purchases depends, in part, on the strength of its customer support and service operations. Furthermore, the Company values frequent communication with and feedback from its customers to continually improve its products and services.

The Company offers the following types of services:

Customer Support. Telephone representatives take orders, respond to questions about the ordering process and answer inquiries concerning the status of orders, shipments and payments. Customer support also is available by e-mail.

Technical Support. Technicians are available during office hours to resolve technical issues facing customers including site functionality and product configuration problems. Technicians also are available by e-mail.

Proprietary Technology

The Company generally relies on trademark, copyright, patent and trade secret laws and employee and third-party non-disclosure agreements to protect b proprietary rights. The Company currently has ____ patent applications pending in the United States relating to the Company's product architecture and technology. Although the Company believes that the pending applications relate to patentable inventions, there can be no assurance that any patents will be granted or that any patent relied upon by the Company in the future will not be challenged, invalidated or circumvented or that the rights granted thereunder or under licensing agreements will provide competitive advantages to the Company. The Company believes that due to the rapid pace of technological innovation for Internet products, the Company's ability to establish and maintain a position of technological leadership in e-Commerce depends more on the skills of its development personnel than the legal protection afforded its existing technology. See "Risk Factors—Risks Related to the Company—Risks of Infringement."

The Company's success depends in part, upon its proprietary software technology. There can be no assurance that its standard intellectual property confidentiality and assignment agreement with employees, consultants and others who participate in the development of its software will not be breached, that the Company will have adequate remedies for any breach, or that the Company's trade secrets will not otherwise become known to or independently developed by competitors. Furthermore, there can be no assurance that the Company's efforts to protect its proprietary technology will prevent others from developing and designing products or technology similar to or competitive with those of the Company.

The Company's success depends in part, on its continued ability to license and use third-party technology that is integral to the functionality of the Company's products. An inability to continue to procure or use such technology likely would have a material adverse effect on the Company's business, operating results or financial condition.

Employees

At ____, the Company had approximately ____ full-time employees and ____ part-time employees, based at the Company's executive offices in ____ and ____. None of the Company's employees is subject to a collective bargaining agreement, and the Company believes that its relations with its employees generally are good.

Facilities

The Company's executive offices are located in ____, in an office building in which, as of ____, the Company leases an aggregate of ____ square feet at a current monthly rental of $____. The office space is leased under two separate lease agreements, which expire on March 31, ____ and June 30, ____, respectively. The Company has an option to extend one of the leases, covering approximately ____% of the floor space, for an additional five years. The Company anticipates subleasing its existing office space in ____ and moving to another office building in ____ during that same period. The Company will pay approximately $____ per month during the initial term of the lease (such amount increasing incrementally thereafter) and that the aggregate amount of space leased in the new facility will be approximately ____ square feet. The Company also has recently opened new office space in ____ as a result of acquisitions.

The Company does not own any real estate.

Legal Proceedings

From time to time the Company expects to be subject to legal proceedings and claims in the ordinary course of its business, including claims of alleged infringement by the Company and its licensees of third-party trademarks and other intellectual property rights by the Company and its licensees. Such claims, even if not meritorious, could result in the expenditure of significant financial and managerial resources. The Company is not aware of any legal proceedings or claims that it believes will have, individually or in the aggregate, a material adverse effect on its business, financial condition or results of operations. See "Risk Factors—Risks Related to the Company—Risks Associated with International Expansion" and—"Risks of Infringement"; "Risk Factors—Risks Related to the Industry Generally—Risk of Intellectual Property Litigation and —Uncertainties Regarding Government Regulation"; and "Notes to Consolidated Financial Statements—Licensing and Development Agreements," attached hereto as Exhibit A.

MANAGEMENT

Executive Officers, Directors and Key Employees

The following table sets forth the name, age as of ____, and position with the Company of each senior management executive and director of the Company.

Name	Age	Position
....		Chairman, President and Chief Executive Officer
....		Executive Vice President
....		Executive Vice President, Chief Financial Officer and General Counsel
....		Executive Vice President and Chief Technology Officer
....		Executive Vice President, International Projects
....		Executive Vice President, Corporate Development
....		Executive Vice President, Direct Marketing Division
....		Senior Vice President Marketing and Business Development
....		Vice President Finance and Operations
....		Vice President Computer Commerce Business Unit
....		Vice President Business Development
....		Corporate Director
....		Corporate Director
....		Corporate Director
....		Corporate Director
....		Corporate Director

Chairman, President, and Chief Executive Officer

Executive Vice President

Executive Vice President, Chief Financial Officer and General Counsel

Executive Vice President and Chief Technology Officer

Executive Vice President, International Projects

Executive Vice President, Corporate Development

Executive Vice President, Direct Marketing Division

Senior Vice President, Marketing and Business Development

Vice President, Finance and Operations

Vice President, Commerce Network

Vice President, Business Development

Corporate Director

Corporate Director

Corporate Director

Corporate Director

Corporate Director

Composition of the Board

There is a voting agreement entered into among the Company and certain of its principal shareholders to ensure that at least a majority of the Company's Directors will remain independent directors until the date on which the Company completes an initial public offering or upon the occurrence of other specified events.

Board Committees

The Audit Committee is responsible for reviewing with management the financial controls, accounting, audit and reporting activities of the Company. The Audit Committee also reviews the qualifications of the Company's independent auditors, makes recommendations to the

Board of Directors regarding the selection of independent auditors, reviews the scope, fees and results of any audit and reviews non-audit services provided by the independent auditors. The members of the Audit Committee are _____, ______ and ______. A majority of the members of the Audit Committee are independent directors.

The Compensation Committee is responsible for the administration of all salary and incentive compensation plans for the executive officers of the Company, including bonuses for the year ending December 31, ____, and subsequent years. The members of the Compensation Committee are _____, ____ and _____. A majority of the members of the Compensation Committee are not employees of the Company.

Executive Compensation

The following table sets forth the compensation paid to or accrued for the Chief Executive Officer and each of the four highest paid executive officers whose annual salary will exceed $100,000 for ____ (collectively, the "Named Executive Officers").

Summary Compensation Table[1]

	Annual Compensation	Long-Term Compensation Awards
	Salary	Number of Shares of Common Stock Underlying Options
	$	
	$	
	$	
(2)	$	
(2)	$[3]	

(1) Salary shown is current annual salary.
(2) Excludes performance-based stock options.
(3) Excludes $20,000 signing bonus.

Option Grants

The following table sets forth information concerning grants of options under the Company's ____ Combined Incentive and Nonqualified Stock

Option Plan and other stock option grants during the first three quarters of ____ to the Named Executive Officers. None of the vested options listed in the table below was exercised as of the date of this Memorandum. All of the options referenced on the table below expire in ____.

Individual Grants	
Number of Securities Underlying Options Granted(1)	Exercise Price Per Share
	$
	$
	$
	$
	$
	$

Number of Securities Underlying Unexercised Options at September 30, ____	
Exercisable	Unexercisable
0	
0	*
0	*

* Excludes performance-based stock options

Director Compensation

Outside directors of the Company do not receive cash compensation from the Company for their service as directors or members of committees of the Board of Directors, but are reimbursed for their reasonable expenses incurred in attending Board of Directors meetings. The Company has granted an option to purchase up to ____ shares of Common Stock at an exercise price of $____ per share to ____, ____ and ____, each of whom were elected to the Board of Directors in ____.

Benefit Plans

___ Combined Incentive and Nonqualified Stock Option Plan

The Company's ____ Combined Incentive and Nonqualified Stock Option Plan ("the ____ Plan") was adopted by the Board of Directors, and approved by the Company's shareholders, in ____. The ____ Plan provides for the grant of qualified or nonqualified options to purchase up to an aggregate of ____ shares of Common Stock to employees, officers, directors, consultants and independent contractors of the Company. As of ____, options to purchase ____ shares were outstanding under the ____ Plan, with exercise prices ranging from $____ to $____ per share, options to purchase ____ shares were available for grant and no options to purchase had been exercised.

The ____ Plan is administered by the Compensation Committee of the Board of Directors, which has the authority to grant options and to specify the terms and conditions of each option so granted, including the number of shares covered by the option, the type of option, the exercise price and the vesting provisions.

Other Stock Option Grants

In ____and during the nine months ended ____, the Compensation Committee of the Board of Directors granted options to purchase shares of Common Stock to certain management employees through direct grant rather than under the ____ Plan. As of ____, ____ options had been granted to various management-level employees, with exercise prices ranging from $____ to $____ per share, and no options to purchase had been exercised.

401(k) Plan

The Company maintains a 401(k) plan that covers all employees who satisfy certain eligibility requirements. Under the plan, employees may make pretax elective contributions of up to ____% of their compensation, subject to the maximum limits on contributions prescribed by law. The 401(k) plan currently has no employer matching provisions on employee contributions.

Employment Agreements

The Company has entered into written employment agreements with ____ of its executive officers: ____.

The agreement with ____ became effective ____. The agreement defines ____'s duties as President and CEO and requires that substantially all of his working time, attention and efforts be devoted to Company business. The agreement sets his annual compensation as set forth in the Summary Compensation Table and footnotes one and two set forth thereunder. The term of the employment agreement expires ____ years from the effective date. In the event the Company terminates ____ or ____ resigns, ____ shall continue to receive his salary for ____ months following his termination under such circumstances. Under this employment agreement ____ received options to acquire ____ shares of Common Stock at $____ per share.

The agreement with ____ became effective ____. The agreement defines ____ duties with the Company and requires that substantially all of his working time, attention and efforts be devoted to Company business. His annual compensation is set forth in the Summary Compensation Table. The term of the agreement expires ____ years from the effective date and is automatically renewed for successive one-year terms unless either party gives notice 90 days prior to the expiration of the term.

The agreement with ____ became effective ____. The agreement defines ____'s duties as Executive Vice President of The.com, Inc. and President of the ____ division of The.com, Inc. and requires that substantially all of his business time, attention and energies be devoted to the performance of his duties under this employment agreement. The agreement sets his annual compensation at $____. The term of the agreement expires on ____. Under this employment agreement ____ received options to acquire ____ shares of The.com, Inc. Common Stock at an exercise price of $____ per share.

The agreement with ____ became effective ____. The agreement defines ____'s duties as Executive Vice President of International Projects and requires that substantially all of his business time, attention and energies be devoted to the performance of his duties under this employment agreement. The agreement sets his annual compensation at $____, and he is eligible for annual bonuses upon attainment of certain discretionary performance goals. The term of the agreement expires on ____, and is automatically renewable for one-year periods unless terminated in accordance with the terms of the agreement. Under this employment agreement, Mr. Kwon received options to acquire ____ shares of Common Stock at $2.00 per share. The options vest in semi-annual increments that decrease over three years.

The agreement with ____ became effective ____. The agreement defines ____'s duties with The.com, Inc. The agreement sets his annual compensation at $____ with a $____ signing bonus, of which $____ was paid upon joining The.com, Inc. and the other $____ will be paid at the end of his first year of employment. In addition, ____ is entitled to receive up to $____ annually upon the achievement of certain revenue and gross profit performance goals. The term of employment is of indefinite duration, with termination provisions included in the agreement. Under this employment agreement, ____ received options to acquire ____ shares of Common Stock with an exercise price of $____ per share with a three year vesting period.

PRINCIPAL SHAREHOLDERS

The following table sets forth, as of June 30, ____, and as adjusted for the sale of ____ shares of Series F Preferred offered hereby, assuming the maximum number of Units is sold and the conversion of all Series F Preferred to Common Stock (giving effect to conversion of the Series A Preferred, Series B Preferred, Series C Preferred, Series D Preferred and Series E Preferred Stock into Common Stock), certain information with respect to the Company's Common Stock owned of record or beneficially by (i) each director and executive officer of the Company; (ii) each person who owns beneficially more than five percent of the Company's outstanding capital stock; and (iii) all directors and executive officers as a group.

Beneficial Owner	Number of Shares Before Offering[1]	Percent of Ownership Before Offering	Percent of Ownership After Maximum Offering[2]
		%	%
		%	%
		%	%
		%	%
		%	%
		*	*
		*	*
		%	%
		*	*
		*	%
		*	*
All Directors and Executive Officers as a group (5 persons)		%	%

*denotes less than 1% ownership

(1) Number of shares before offering does not include shares of Common Stock that principal shareholders could purchase upon exercise of their warrants and stock options.

(2) Calculations do not include the exercise of warrants or options.

CERTAIN TRANSACTIONS

This section details transactions involving more than $50,000, other than employment contracts, that have been entered into since January 1, ____ between the Company and any executive officer, director, or 10% shareholder of the Company.

DESCRIPTION OF CAPITAL STOCK

The Company's authorized capital stock consists of ____ shares of Common Stock, $0.01 par value per share and ____ shares of

Preferred Stock, $0.01 par value per share. The following description of the capital stock of the Company and certain provisions of the Company's Articles is a summary and is qualified by reference to the Articles, a copy of which is attached hereto as Exhibit C. The descriptions of the Common Stock and Preferred Stock reflect changes to the Company's capital structure that will occur upon effectiveness of the designation by the board of the terms governing the Series F Preferred, such designation to be filed with the Secretary of State of the State of ____ prior to the Initial Closing. As of the date hereof, there are approximately ____ holders of record of Common Stock and approximately ____ holders of record of Series Preferred Stock.

Common Stock

The Company has issued and outstanding ____ shares of Common Stock. Each share of Common Stock entities the holder thereof to one vote on all matters submitted to a vote of the shareholders. Because the holders of Common Stock do not have cumulative voting rights, holders of more than 50% of the outstanding shares can elect all of the directors of the Company and holders of the remaining shares by themselves cannot elect any directors. See "Risk Factors—Risks Related to this Offering—Effects of Certain Provisions of the Articles of Incorporation, Bylaws and ____ Business Corporation Act." The Common Stock is not subject to redemption, future calls, or assessments by the Company. Holders of Common Stock do not have preemptive rights or rights to convert their Common Stock into other securities. In the event of a liquidation, dissolution or winding up of the Company, holders of the Common Stock along with holders of the Series A Preferred, Series B Preferred, Series C Preferred, Series D Preferred, Series E Preferred, and Series F Preferred (on an as-converted basis to Common Stock) have the right to a ratable portion of the assets remaining after payment of liabilities and liquidation preferences to the holders of preferred stock.

Dividend Policy

The Company has never paid dividends on any of its capital stock. The Company intends to retain any future earnings to fund operations and the continued development of its business and, thus, does not expect to pay any cash dividends on the series Preferred, including the Series F Preferred or Common Stock in the foreseeable future.

Preferred Stock

As of the Initial Closing, the Company will have ____ shares of preferred stock authorized, of which ____ shares are designated as Series A Preferred, ____shares are designated as Series B Preferred, ____ are designated as Series C Preferred, ____ shares are designated as Series D Preferred, ____ shares are designated as Series E Preferred and ____ shares will be designated as Series F Preferred.

Series A Preferred

The Company has issued and outstanding ____ shares of Series A Preferred Stock. Each share of Series A Preferred Stock may be converted into one share (subject to adjustment for stock splits, stock dividends and recapitalizations) of Common Stock at any time. The Series A Preferred shall automatically convert into Common Stock upon the occurrence of an underwritten public offering of the Company's Common Stock resulting in proceeds to the Company of at least $15,000,000 with a per-share public offering price of at least $____ (subject to adjustment) if the public offering occurs before ____, or a per-share public offering price of at least $____ (subject to adjustment) if the public offering occurs thereafter ("Qualified Public Offering"). The Series A Preferred has one vote for each share of Common Stock into which the Series A Preferred may be converted. Holders of Series A Preferred are entitled to vote on all matters submitted to a vote of the holders of the Common Stock and, generally vote together with the holders of Common Stock and other series of Preferred Stock as one class. The Series A Preferred has a liquidation preference of $____ per share plus any accrued dividends through the date of liquidation.

Series B Preferred

The Company has issued and outstanding ____ shares of Series B Preferred. Each share of Series B preferred may be converted into one share (subject to adjustment for stock splits, stock dividends and recapitalizations) of Common Stock at any time. The Series B Preferred shall automatically convert into Common Stock upon the occurrence of a Qualified Public Offering (as defined above). The Series B Preferred has one vote for each share of Common Stock into which the Series B Preferred may be converted. Holders of Series B Preferred are entitled to vote on all matters submitted to a vote of the holders of the Common Stock and generally vote together with the holders of

Common Stock and other series of Preferred Stock as one class. The Series B Preferred Stock has a liquidation preference of $____ per share plus any accrued dividends through the date of liquidation.

Series C Preferred

The Company has issued and outstanding ____ shares of Series C Preferred. Each share of Series C Preferred may be converted into one share (subject to adjustment for stock splits, stock dividends and recapitalizations) of Common Stock at any time. The Series C Preferred shall automatically convert into Common Stock upon the occurrence of a Qualified Public Offering (as defined above). The Series C Preferred has one vote for each share of Common Stock into which the Series C Preferred may be converted. Holders of Series C Preferred are entitled to vote on all matters submitted to a vote of the holders of the Common Stock and generally vote together with the holders of Common Stock and other series of Preferred Stock as one class. The Series C Preferred has a liquidation preference of $____ per share plus any accrued dividends through the date of liquidation.

Series D Preferred

The Company has issued and outstanding ____ shares of Series D Preferred. Each share of Series D Preferred may be converted into one share (subject to adjustment for stock splits, stock dividends and recapitalizations), of Common Stock at any time. The Series D Preferred shall automatically convert into shares of Common Stock upon the occurrence of a Qualified Public Offering (as defined above). The Series D Preferred has one vote for each share of Common Stock into which the Series D Preferred Stock may be converted. Holders of the Series D Preferred Stock are entitled to vote on all matters submitted to a vote of the holders of the Common Stock and generally vote together with the holders of Common Stock and other series of Preferred Stock as one class. The Company's Series D Preferred Stock has a per-share liquidation preference of $____ per share, plus any accrued dividends through the date of liquidation.

Series E Preferred

The Company has issued and outstanding ____ shares of Series E Preferred. Each share of Series E Preferred may be converted into one share (subject to adjustment for stock splits, stock dividends and recapitalizations) of Common Stock at any time. The Series E Preferred shall automatically convert into Common Stock upon the occurrence of a Qualified Public Offering (as defined above). The Series E Preferred has one vote for each share of Common Stock into which the Series E Preferred may be converted. Holders of Series E Preferred are entitled to vote on all matters submitted to a vote of the holders of the Common Stock and generally vote together with the holders of Common Stock and other series of Preferred Stock as one class. The Series E Preferred has a liquidation preference of $____ per share plus any accrued dividends through the date of liquidation.

Series F Preferred

Each share of Series F Preferred may be converted into one share (subject to adjustment for stock splits, stock dividends and recapitalizations) of Common Stock at any time. The Series F Preferred shall automatically convert into Common Stock upon the occurrence of a Qualified Public Offering (as defined above). The Series F Preferred has one vote for each share of Common Stock into which the Series F Preferred may be converted. Holders of Series F Preferred are entitled to vote on all matters submitted to a vote of the holders of the Common Stock and generally vote together with the holders of Common Stock and other series of Preferred Stock as one class. The Series F Preferred has a liquidation of $____ per share plus any accrued dividends through the date of liquidation preference

Future Series of Preferred Stock

The Company's Certificate of Incorporation authorizes the issuance, upon resolution of the Board of Directors and without further shareholder approval, of up to a total of ____ shares of Preferred Stock, of which ____ shares have been issued and are outstanding, including the ____ shares of Series F Preferred, $.01 par value, included in the Units offered hereby. The terms of all classes or series of Preferred Stock, including dividend rights, conversion prices, voting rights, redemption prices and similar matters, will be determined by the Board of Directors. Further series of Preferred Stock could have voting, dividend and other rights, preferences and privileges superior to those of the Common Stock or the Series F Preferred, except that in the event of a liquidation by the Company, the holders of the Series F Preferred shall have a preference in liquidation of $____ that will be at least *pari passu* to any other series of Preferred Stock of the Company and will be superior to the Common Stock, unless otherwise agreed by holders of at least 50% of the issued and outstanding Series F Preferred. See "Risk Factors—Risks Related to this Offering—Effects of Certain Provisions of the Articles of Incorporation, Bylaws and the Washington Business Corporations Act."

Outstanding Warrants

Warrants — Series C Preferred Stock

The Company has issued and these are outstanding warrants to purchase an aggregate of ____ shares of Series C Preferred Stock (the "Series C Warrants"). The Series C Warrants are at an exercise price of $____ per share. The Series C Warrants expire in ____, subject to earlier termination in the event of a public offering of the Company's Common Stock.

Warrants — Common Stock

The Company has previously issued and there are outstanding warrants to purchase an aggregate of ____ shares of Common Stock (the "Common Warrants"). Of this total, ____ Common Warrants are exercisable at an exercise price of $____ per share of Common Stock and ____ Common Stock Warrants are exercisable by the Placement Agent at $____ per share. The Common Warrants expire in ____. In addition, the Company has issued to The Placement Agent, Inc. warrants to purchase (a) ____ shares of Common Stock at an exercise price of $____ per share and (b) ____ shares of Common Stock at $____ per share. In connection with this Offering, the Placement Agent is entitled to receive the Agent Warrant entitling the Placement Agent to purchase ____ shares of Common Stock at $____ per share if the maximum number of Units is sold and ____ shares of Common Stock if the minimum number of Units is sold.

Warrants to be Issued in this Offering

If the maximum number of Units is sold, the Company will issue to the purchasers of the Units Warrants to purchase an aggregate of ____ shares of Common Stock, which represents approximately ____% of the Common Stock outstanding, (less than ____% if the minimum number of Units is sold). Each Warrant entitles the holder to purchase up to ____ shares of Common Stock from the Company at the Exercise Price of $____ per share. The number of shares of Common Stock issuable upon exercise of the Warrants and the Exercise Price will be adjusted in the event of Stock splits, stock dividends or recapitalizations. The Warrants are exercisable at any time between one and three years after the Initial Closing. Warrants not exercised by that time will expire. The Warrants do not confer upon the holder any voting rights, preemptive rights or any other rights as a Company stockholder. The shares of Common Stock issuable upon exercise of the Warrants are subject to the same registration rights granted by the Company to, the holders of the Series A Preferred, Series B Preferred, Series C Preferred, Series D Preferred, Series E Preferred, and Series F Preferred and the Placement Agent with respect to the warrants to purchase Common Stock that it holds on a *pari passu* basis. See "Registration Rights."

Certain Provisions of the Company's Articles of Incorporation and Bylaws

Certain provisions of the Company's Articles and Bylaws summarized below may have an anti-takeover effect and may delay, defer or prevent a tender offer or takeover attempt that a shareholder might consider to be in his or her best interest, including attempts that might result in a premium over the market price for the shares held by shareholders.

The Company's Bylaws provide that the directors of the Company can be removed from office with or without cause at a special meeting of the shareholders expressly called for that purpose. Vacancies on the Board of Directors may generally be filled only by the affirmative vote of a majority of the remaining directors.

In addition, the Company's Bylaws provide that special meetings of the Company's shareholders generally can be called only by the President, by the Board of Directors, or by the Chairman of Board of Directors or by holders of stock representing at least 25% of the votes entitled to be cast on each issue to be considered at the meeting.

The existence of undesignated Preferred Stock enables the Board of Directors to render more difficult or to discourage an attempt to obtain control of the Company by means of a tender offer, proxy contest, merger or otherwise, thereby protecting the continuity of the Company's management. See "Risk Factors—Risks Related to this Offering—Effects of Certain Provisions of the Articles of Incorporation, Bylaws and the ____ Business Corporation Act."

Limitation of Liability and Indemnification

The Company's Articles contain certain provisions permitted under the BCA limiting the liability of directors. These provisions eliminate a director's personal liability for monetary damages resulting from conduct as a director, except in certain circumstances involving certain wrongful acts, such as: (i) for acts or omissions that involve intentional misconduct or a knowing violation of law, (ii) for conduct violating Section ____ of the BCA (relating to improper distributions to shareholders); or (iii) for any transaction from which the director derives an improper personal benefit. These provisions do not limit or eliminate the rights of the Company or any shareholder to seek non-monetary relief, such as an injunction or rescission, in the event of a breach of a director's fiduciary duty. These provisions will not alter a director's liability under the federal securities laws. The Company's Articles and Bylaws also contain provisions indemnifying the directors of the Company to the fullest extent permitted by the BCA. In addition, the Company's Bylaws permit the Board of Directors to indemnify the Company's officers, employees and agents to the fullest extent permitted by BCA. The Company believes that these provisions will assist the Company in attracting and retaining qualified individuals to serve as directors and officers.

The Company also maintains insurance on behalf of its directors and officers for certain liabilities arising out of their actions in such capacities.

Registration Rights

The following description of the registration rights of the shareholders of the Company is a summary and is qualified by reference to the Second Amended and Restated Registration Rights Agreement (the "Registration Rights Agreement"), a copy of which is attached hereto as Exhibit C. Pursuant to the Company's Registration Rights Agreement executed in connection with this Offering, at any time after the earlier of (i) ____ or (ii) ____ months after the effective date of the first registration statement filed by the Company covering a public offering of its securities, the holders owning 50% or more of the Registrable Common (as defined therein) (which includes all shares of Common Stock issuable upon conversion of the Series A Preferred, Series B Preferred, Series C Preferred, Series D Preferred, Series E Preferred and Series F Preferred and shares of Common

Stock owned by ____ and the holders of the Series Preferred Stock) can request that the Company file a registration statement with the Securities and Exchange Commission covering such shares of Common Stock as well as the shares of Common Stock underlying the Series Preferred Stock, provided, however, that the public offering price is at least $____ per share of Common Stock and the gross proceeds of the offering are expected to be at least $____.

The holders of Series A Preferred, Series B Preferred, Series C Preferred, Series D Preferred, Series E Preferred also have piggyback registration rights with respect the shares of Common Stock underlying the Series Preferred and Series F Preferred subject to a reduction in the number of such shares that can be registered upon the request of the managing underwriters in an underwritten public offering (i.e., customary underwriting "cutback" provisions).

The holders of the Series F Preferred will be treated as Investors (along with the holders of the Series A Preferred, Series B Preferred, Series C Preferred, Series D Preferred and Series E Preferred and the Placement Agent with respect to Agent Warrants and certain holders of the Common Stock) and will become parties to the Registration Rights Agreement with the same registration rights described above and will be subject to certain underwriter's "holdback" obligations as provided in the Registration Rights Agreement. See "Summary of the Offering – Registration Rights."

INVESTOR SUITABILITY STANDARDS

An investment in the Units involves substantial risks and possible loss by investors of their entire investment. The Units will be offered and sold only to prospective accredited investors who: (a) represent among other things, that they are acquiring Units for their own account(s), for investment only and not with a view toward the resale or distribution thereof, that they are aware that the Units have not been registered under the Securities Act or under applicable state securities laws, and their transfer rights are restricted by the Securities Act and applicable laws, and that there is no market for the Units or any of the Company's securities; and (b) are investors meeting the suitability standards hereinafter set forth.

The Company and the Placement Agent will require as a general investor suitability standard that each investor represent in writing that (1) he is a natural person who has a net worth or joint net worth with his spouse exceeding $1,000,000 (excluding the investors home, home furnishings, and automobiles) at the time of his purchase; or (2) he is a natural person who had an individual income in excess of $200,000 in each of the two preceding years prior to the purchase of the Units and has a reasonable expectation of reaching the same income level in the current year or, if purchasing jointly with his spouse, that such joint purchasers had a joint income of $300,000 in each of those years and have a reasonable expectation of reaching the same income level in the current year, or (3) he is a director or executive officer of the Company; or (4) it is either (a) a bank as defined in Section 3(a)(2) of the Securities Act or a savings and loan association or other institution as defined in Section 3(a)(5)(A) of the Securities Act whether acting in its individual or fiduciary capacity, (b) a broker or dealer register pursuant to Section 15 of the Securities Exchange Act of 1934, as amended (the "Exchange Act"), (c) an insurance company as defined in Section 2(13) of the Securities Act, (d) an investment company registered under the Investment Company Act of 1940, as amended ("the Investment Company Act"), or a business development company as defined in Section 2(a)(48) of the Investment Company Act, (e) a Small Business Investment Company licensed by the United States Small Business Administration under Section 301(c) or (d) of the Small Business Investment Act of 1958, as amended, (f) a plan established and maintained by a state, its political subdivisions, or any agency or instrumentality of a state or its political subdivisions, for the benefit of its employees, if such plan has total assets in excess of $5,000,000, or (g) an employee benefit plan within the meaning of the Employee Retirement Income Security Act of 1974, as amended ("ERISA") if the investment decision is made by a plan fiduciary, as defined in Section 3(21) of ERISA, which plan fiduciary is a bank, a savings and loan association, an insurance company or a registered investment advisor, or if the employee benefit plan has total assets in excess of $5,000,000 or, if a self-directed plan, for which investment decisions are made solely by persons that otherwise meet these suitability standards; or (5) it is a private business development company as defined in Section 202(a)(22) of the investment Advisors Act of 1940, as amended; or (6) it is an organization described in Section 501(c)(3) of the internal Revenue Code of 1986, as amended, a corporation, a Massachusetts or similar business trust, or a partnership, not formed for the specific purpose of acquiring the Units, with total assets in excess of $5,000,000; or (7) it is a trust, with total assets in excess of $5,000,000, not formed for the specific Purpose of acquiring the Units, whose Purchase is directed by a sophisticated person who has such knowledge and experience in financial and business matters such that he is capable of evaluating the merits and risks of the prospective investment or (8) it is a corporation, partnership, or other entity and each and every equity owner of such entity certifies that such equity owner meets the qualifications set forth in either (1), (2), (3), (4), (5), (6) or (7) above. As used, in this Memorandum, the term "net worth" means the excess total assets over total liabilities. In determining income, an investor should add to his adjusted gross income any amounts attributable to tax-exempt income received, losses claimed as a limited partner in any limited partnership, deductions claimed for depletion, contributions to an IRA or Keogh retirement plan, alimony payments and any amount by which income from long-term capital gains has been reduced in arriving at adjusted gross income.

The satisfaction of such minimum standards by a prospective investor does not necessarily mean that the Units are a suitable investment for such prospective investor. Certain states require investors to meet higher suitability standards, which are set forth in the Subscription Agreement. The Company and the Placement Agent may make or cause to be made such further inquiry and obtain such additional information as they deem appropriate with regard to the suitability of prospective investors. The Company and the Placement Agent reserve the right to modify the suitability standards with respect to certain investors, in order to comply with any applicable state and local laws, rules, regulations or otherwise.

THE SUITABILITY STANDARDS DISCUSSED ABOVE REPRESENT MINIMUM SUITABILITY STANDARDS FOR THE PROSPECTIVE INVESTORS. EACH PROSPECTIVE INVESTOR SHOULD DETERMINE WHETHER THIS INVESTMENT IS APPROPRIATE FOR SUCH INVESTOR.

PLAN OF PLACEMENT

The Units offered hereby are being offered and sold only to "accredited investors" (as such term is defined by Regulation D promulgated under the Securities Act) on a "best efforts" basis exclusively through the Placement Agent. Accordingly, each subscriber for Units will be required to represent in his or her Subscription Agreement that he or she is an accredited investor. See "Investor Suitability Standards." Furthermore, residents of certain states will be required to meet additional suitability standards established by those states as provided in the Subscription Agreement.

The Units are offered at $100,000 per Unit with a minimum investment of $100,000 (one Unit), which requirement may be waived by the Company in its sole discretion. Additional Units may be purchased in one-unit increments, which requirement may be waived by the Company in its sole discretion. The Offering is expected to expire on or about 90 days from the date of the Offering Memorandum, except that it may be extended for 60 days by the Company and the Placement Agent without any notice to investors. The Company may hold an Initial Closing of the Offering at any time after subscriptions for 10 Units have been accepted by the Company. The Company may hold additional closings after the Initial Closing. The maximum number of Units subject to this Offering is 100 Units; provided, however, the Company reserves the right to sell up to 50 additional Units on the same terms as provided herein if this Offering is oversubscribed.

No public market exists for the Units or the underlying Warrants, Series F Preferred and Conversion Shares, and there can be no assurance that an initial public offering will be completed by the Company or that a public market for the Common Stock will develop in the future. The Units , the Series F Preferred, the Warrants, and the Conversion Shares are restricted securities under the Securities Act. The price to investors of the Units has been determined by negotiations between the Company and the Placement Agent. See "Risk Factors—Risks Related to this Offering—No Public Market; Units and Underlying Securities Not Marketable or Transferable."

ARRANGEMENTS WITH THE PLACEMENT AGENTS

The Company has retained the Placement Agent to offer the Units privately on a best efforts basis. The Placement Agent will receive selling commissions equal to 7.0% of the Offering Price for each Unit sold by the Placement Agent in this Offering. The Placement Agent will also receive a non-accountable expense allowance equal to 3.0% of the Offering Price for each Unit sold. All other expenses, except attorney fees for the Placement Agent incurred in the Offering will be paid by the Company.

The Company has agreed to sell to the Placement Agent upon closing of this Offering the Agent Warrant entitling the Placement Agent to purchase from the Company a number of shares of Common Stock equal to 10% of the aggregate number of shares of Common Stock into which the shares of Series F preferred sold in this Offering are convertible as of the date of the Final Closing. The Exercise Price for each share purchased upon exercise of the Agent Warrant is equal to $____. The Agent Warrant will be exercisable between one and three years after the Initial Closing. The Company has granted the Placement Agent demand and piggyback registration rights with respect to the Common Stock issuable upon exercise of such warrants, subject to underwriter cutback, market conditions and other customary restrictions.

The Company will notify the Placement Agent about any business transaction involving a merger or acquisition of or by the Company or any of its subsidiaries if the Company decides to retain an investment banking firm in such business transaction at any time up to two years from the date of this Offering Memorandum, and the Company agrees to consider the Placement Agent's proposal to act as the Company's agent for such business transaction. In addition, the Placement Agent may act as an underwriter in an initial public offering of the Company's Common Stock for a period of up to three years from the date of the Initial Closing as set forth in the Placement Agent Agreement.

In addition, the Company has agreed to indemnity the Placement Agent against certain liabilities, including liabilities under the Securities Act. Insofar as indemnification for liabilities arising under the Securities Act is permitted, the Company has been informed that in the opinion of the Securities and Exchange Commission such indemnification is against public policy as expressed in the Securities Act and is therefore unenforceable.

The Placement Agent also has acted as the placement agent for the Company in connection with (i) the Company's Series D Preferred financing (the "Series D Financing") pursuant to which the Company completed the sale in ____ of ____ units, consisting of an aggregate ____ shares of Series D Preferred with a per share purchase price of $____ and warrants to purchase an aggregate of ____ shares of Common Stock at an exercise price of $____ per share, (ii) the Company's Series E preferred Financing (the "Series E Financing") pursuant to which the Company completed the sale in ____ of units, consisting of an aggregate of ____ shares of Series E Preferred with a per share purchase price of $____ and warrants to purchase an aggregate of ____ shares of Common Stock at an exercise price of

$____ per share, (iii) the Company's first bridge financing (the "First Bridge Financing") in which the Company issued promissory notes in the aggregate principal amount of $____ bearing an initial interest rate of __% per annum and (iv) the Second Bridge Financing. For its services, the Placement Agent received commissions and other fees totaling approximately $____ for the Series D Financing, Series E Financing, the First Bridge Financing and the Second Bridge Financing. The Placement Agent also received warrants to purchase an aggregate of ____ shares of Common Stock at an exercise price of $____ for the Series D and Series E Financings, and a warrant to purchase an aggregate of ____ shares of Common Stock at an exercise price of $____ for the First Bridge Financing.

SUBSCRIPTION PROCEDURES

To subscribe for Units, the Subscription Agreement, the applicable signature page and the applicable Investor Questionnaire accompanying this Memorandum must be properly completed, executed and delivered to The Placement Agent, Inc., ____, accompanied by a check payable to or wire transfer payment to "____ Bank, Escrow Agent for The.com, Inc." in the amount of $100,000 for each Unit subscribed. Delivery of a Bridge Note previously issued by The.com, Inc. may also be used as payment for the Units. A subscriber desiring to deliver the purchase price for the Units in the form of wire transfer must contact The Placement Agent, Inc. at (___) ___-____ to obtain wiring instructions. The minimum subscription is one Unit, which requirement may be waived by the Company in its sole discretion. Additional Units may be purchased in one-unit increments, which requirement may be waived by the Company in its sole discretion.

All subscription funds will be held in an escrow account maintained by the Company with the Escrow Agent, ____ Bank, until the earlier of the closing for such subscription occurs, the rejection of the subscription or the termination of the Offering. The Company will be entitled to all interest earned on subscription funds to defray costs incurred in connection with the Offering.

Subject to applicable state securities laws, subscriptions delivered to the Placement Agent are not subject to revocation by prospective investors, but may be rejected by the Company, in whole or in part, in its sole discretion, in which event the subscription funds and execution copies of the Subscription Agreement submitted will be returned (by mail) to such subscribers without interest or deduction. As soon as possible after the receipt and acceptance by the Company of subscriptions and collection of the funds paid therefor, the Company will issue certificates for the shares of Series F Preferred and the Warrants underlying the Units subscribed for by all subscribers whose subscriptions have been received and accepted together with their Subscription Agreements countersigned by the Company, and the funds representing such subscription will be released from the escrow account to the Company.

CERTAIN LEGAL MATTERS

The validity of the issuance of the Units offered hereby is being reviewed for the Company by ____. Certain legal matters will be reviewed for the Placement Agent by ____.

INDEPENDENT AUDITORS

The financial statements of the Company at December 31, ____, December 31, ____ and December 31, ____ and for each of the periods ended on such dates, appearing in the Memorandum, have been audited by ____, independent auditors, as stated in their report appearing herein. In August ____, the Company changed auditors from ____ to ____. There were no disagreements with the former auditors.

ADDITIONAL INFORMATION

All prospective investors and their representatives will be provided access to, and are invited to review on a confidential basis, all materials made available with respect to The.com,, the Offering or any other matters set forth in this Offering Memorandum that are not subject to a confidentiality agreement.

The Company will answer inquiries from prospective investors and their representatives relating to The.com, Inc. the Offering, and the sale of Units and will afford prospective investors and their representatives the opportunity to obtain any additional information (to the extent that The.com, Inc. possesses such information or can acquire it without unreasonable effort or expense) necessary to verify the accuracy of the information in this Offering Memorandum. All inquiries should be directed to ____ at (___) ___-____.

APPENDIX J • PRIVATE PLACEMENT PURCHASE AGREEMENT

THE.COM, INC.

COMMON STOCK

PURCHASE AGREEMENT

_______________, 2000

TABLE OF CONTENTS*

Page

* Page number references within this document refer to the original agreement and have not been altered for publication of *Financing Start-Ups*.

COMMON STOCK PURCHASE AGREEMENT

THIS COMMON STOCK PURCHASE AGREEMENT (the "Agreement") is made as of ________________________, by and among The.com, Inc., a ________ corporation (the "Company"), and the investors set forth on Schedule A attached hereto, each of whom is referred to hereinafter as an "Investor" and all of whom together may be referred to hereinafter as the "Investors."

THE PARTIES HEREBY AGREE AS FOLLOWS:

1. Purchase and Sale of Stock.

1.1 Sale and Issuance of Common Stock.

(a) On or prior to the Closing, the Company shall have authorized the sale and issuance to the Investors of up to 1,000,000 shares of Common Stock (as defined below). The Common Stock shall have the rights, preferences, privileges and restrictions set forth herein and in the Investor's Rights Agreement in the form attached hereto as Exhibit A (the "Investor's Rights Agreement").

(b) Subject to the terms and conditions of this Agreement, each Investor agrees to purchase at the Closing and the Company agrees to sell and issue to such Investor at the Closing for a price of fifty cents ($0.50) per share that number of shares of the Company's Common Stock (collectively, the "Shares") set forth opposite such Investor's name on Schedule A attached hereto.

1.2 Initial Closing. The initial closing and delivery of the shares of Common Stock to be issued and sold under this Agreement (the "Initial Closing") will be held at the offices of ____________ at 10 a.m. on ________ __, 2000, or at such other time and place as the Company, in its sole discretion, determines (the "Initial Closing Date"). At the Initial Closing, subject to the terms and conditions hereof, the Company shall deliver to the Investor a certificate representing the Common Stock purchased against payment of the purchase price therefor by check, wire transfer, cancellation of indebtedness or any combination of the foregoing.

1.3 Subsequent Closings. The Company shall have the right to sell and issue additional Common Stock not sold at the Initial Closing to one or more investors on the terms and conditions set forth herein at one or more subsequent closings (each a "Subsequent Closing"). Upon payment of the purchase price of the Shares and execution of a signature page counterpart to this Agreement, and without need of any consent of any other Investor or for an amendment hereto except to add such investor's name to Schedule A to this Agreement, any such investor shall become a party to this Agreement, and shall be deemed an "Investor" for purposes of this Agreement as of the date of the applicable Subsequent Closing (the "Subsequent Closing Date"). The Initial Closing and each Subsequent Closing shall each be deemed a "Closing," and the Initial Closing Date and each Subsequent Closing Date shall each be deemed a "Closing Date" under this Agreement.

2. Representations and Warranties of the Company. The Company, hereby represents and warrants to each Investor that, except as set forth on a Schedule of Exceptions (the "Schedule of Exceptions") furnished to the Investors, which exceptions shall be deemed to be representations and warranties as if made hereunder:

2.1 Organization, Good Standing and Qualification. The Company is a corporation duly organized, validly existing and in good standing under the laws of the State of __________ and has all requisite corporate power and authority to carry on its business as now conducted and as proposed to be conducted in its Business Plan dated _______ __, 2000, heretofore furnished to each Investor by the Company (the "Plan"). The Company is duly qualified to transact business and is in good standing in each jurisdiction in which the failure to so qualify would have a material adverse effect on its business or properties.

2.2 Capitalization and Voting Rights.

(a) The authorized capital of the Company consists, or will consist at the time of the Closing, of 100,000,000 shares of Common Stock, par value $0.01 per share (the "Common Stock"), of which 10,000,000 shares will be issued and outstanding at the time of the Closing. At the time of the Closing, the Company will have authority to issue 25,000,000 shares of Preferred Stock, par value $0.01 per share, of which none will be issued and outstanding at the time of the Closing.

(b) At the time of the Closing, the outstanding shares of Common Stock will all be duly and validly authorized and issued, fully paid and non-assessable and issued in accordance with the registration or qualification provisions of the Securities Act of 1933, as amended (the "Act"), and any relevant state securities laws, or pursuant to valid exemptions therefrom.

Except for rights provided in the Investor Rights Agreement and the options and warrants listed in the Schedule of Exceptions, there are no outstanding options, warrants, rights (including conversion or preemptive rights) or agreements for the purchase or acquisition from the Company of any shares of its capital stock. The Company has reserved 2,500,000 shares of its Common Stock for purchase upon exercise of options granted and to be granted in the future to directors, officers, employees, consultants and advisors under the Company's stock option plan, stock incentive plan or other similar plans. Except for the Investor's Rights Agreement, the Company is not a party or subject to any agreement or understanding, and, to the best of the Company's knowledge, there is no agreement or understanding between any persons and/or entities, which affects or relates to the voting or giving of written consents with respect to any security or by a director of the Company. Following the transactions contemplated hereby, except as set forth in the Schedule of Exceptions and except as set forth in the Investor's Rights Agreement, there will be no preemptive or similar rights to purchase or otherwise acquire shares of capital stock of the Company pursuant to any provision of law, the Articles of Incorporation or the Bylaws of the Company or any agreement to which the Company is a party, or otherwise.

2.3 Subsidiaries. The Company does not presently own or control, directly or indirectly, any interest in any other corporation, association, or other business entity.

2.4 Authorization. All corporate action on the part of the Company, its officers, directors and stockholders necessary for the authorization, execution and delivery of this Agreement and the Investor's Rights Agreement (collectively, the "Ancillary Agreement"), the performance of all obligations of the Company hereunder and thereunder, and the authorization, issuance (or reservation for issuance), sale and delivery of the Common Stock being sold hereunder has been taken or will be taken prior to the Closing, and this Agreement and the Ancillary Agreement constitute, or will, upon execution thereof by the parties thereto, constitute, valid and legally binding obligations of the Company, enforceable in accordance with their respective terms, except (i) as limited by applicable bankruptcy, insolvency, reorganization, moratorium, and other laws of general application affecting enforcement of creditors' rights generally, (ii) as limited by laws and principles relating to the availability of specific performance, injunctive relief, or other equitable remedies, and (iii) to the extent the indemnification provisions contained in the Investor's Rights Agreement may be limited by applicable federal or state securities laws.

2.5 Valid Issuance of Common Stock. The Shares, upon issuance in accordance with the terms of this Agreement, will be duly and validly issued, fully paid, and non-assessable and will be free of restrictions on transfer other than restrictions on transfer under this Agreement and the Investor's Rights Agreement and under applicable state and federal securities laws.

2.6 Governmental Consents. Subject in part to the truth and accuracy of each Investor's representations set forth in Section 3 below, no consent, approval, order or authorization of, or registration, qualification, designation, declaration or filing with, any federal, state or local governmental authority on the part of the Company is required in connection with the consummation of the transactions contemplated by this Agreement, except for the filings pursuant to Regulation D under the Act and any filings required under any applicable state securities laws in connection with the issuance and sale of the Common Stock pursuant to this Agreement, which filings may be properly made after the Closing.

2.7 Offering. Subject in part to the truth and accuracy of the Investor's representations set forth in Section 3 of this Agreement, the offer, sale and issuance of the Common Stock as contemplated by this Agreement are exempt from the registration requirements of any applicable state and federal securities laws, and neither the Company nor any authorized agent acting on its behalf will take any action hereafter that would cause the loss of such exemption.

2.8 Litigation. There is no action, suit, proceeding or known investigation pending or, to the Company's knowledge, currently threatened against the Company that questions the validity of this Agreement or the Ancillary Agreement, or the right of the Company to enter into such agreements, or to consummate the transactions contemplated hereby or thereby, or that might result, either individually or in the aggregate, in any material adverse changes in the assets, condition, affairs or prospects of the Company, financially or otherwise, or any change in the current equity ownership of the Company, nor is the Company aware that there is any basis for theforegoing. The foregoing includes, without limitation, actions, suits, proceedings or investigations pending or threatened (or any basis therefor known to the Company) involving the prior employment of any of the Company's employees, their use in connection with the Company's business of any information or techniques allegedly proprietary to any of their former employers, or their obligations under any agreements with prior employers. The Company is not a party or subject to the provisions of any order, writ, injunction, judgment or decree of any court or government agency or instrumentality. There is no action, suit, proceeding or investigation by the Company currently pending or that the Company intends to initiate.

2.9 Proprietary Information. Each employee and officer of the Company, and each consultant who has had access to confidential or proprietary information of the Company, has executed a Proprietary Information and Inventions Agreement. The Company is not aware that any of its employees, officers or consultants are in violation thereof, and the Company will use its best efforts to prevent any such violation.

2.10 Intellectual Property. To the best of its knowledge (but without having conducted any special investigation or patent search) the Company owns or possesses, has access to, or can become licensed on reasonable terms under, all patents, inventions, trademarks, trade names, copyrights, licenses, information, proprietary rights, and processes necessary for the lawful conduct of its business as now conducted and as proposed to be conducted, without any infringement of or conflict with the rights of others.

2.11 Compliance with Other Instruments. The Company is not in violation or default of any provision of its Articles of Incorporation or Bylaws, or of any material instrument, judgment, order, writ, decree or contract to which it is a party or by which it is bound. The Company has complied in all material respects with all federal, state, local or foreign statutes, rules and regulations and orders applicable to the Company, except where the failure to comply would not have a material adverse effect on the business, properties or financial condition of the Company. The execution, delivery and performance of this Agreement and the Ancillary Agreement, and the consummation of the transactions contemplated hereby and thereby will not result in any such violation or be in conflict with or constitute, with or without the passage of time and giving of notice, either a default under any such material provision, instrument, judgment, order, writ, decree or contract or an event that results in the creation of any material lien, charge or encumbrance upon any assets of the Company or the suspension, revocation, impairment, forfeiture, or non-renewal of any material permit, license, authorization, or approval applicable to the Company, its business or operations or any of its assets or properties.

2.12 Agreements; Action.

(a) Except for agreements explicitly contemplated hereby and the Ancillary Agreement, there are no agreements, understandings or proposed transactions between the Company and any of its officers, directors, affiliates, or any affiliate thereof.

(b) There are no agreements, understandings, instruments, contracts, proposed transactions, judgments, orders, writs or decrees to which the Company is a party or by which it is bound that may involve (i) obligations (contingent or otherwise) of, or payments to the Company in excess of, $50,000, or (ii) the license of any patent, copyright, trade secret or other proprietary right to or from the Company, (other than the license of the Company's or generally available shrinkwrap software and products in the ordinary course of business), or (iii) provisions restricting or affecting the development, manufacture or distribution of the Company's products or services, or (iv) indemnification by the Company with respect to infringements of proprietary rights. The Company is not a party to any written or oral (a) contract with any labor union; (b) contract for the future purchase of fixed assets or for the future purchase of materials, supplies or equipment in excess of normal operating requirements, in excess of $50,000 per annum for all such contracts; (c) contract for the employment of any officer, employee or other person or any contract with any person on a consulting basis, except as set forth on the Schedule of Exceptions, (d) agreement or indenture relating to the borrowing of money; (e) lease or agreement under which the Company is lessee of or holds or operates any property, real or personal, owned by any other party, in excess of $50,000 per annum for all such contracts; (f) lease or agreement under which the Company is lessor of or permits any third party to hold or operate any property, real or personal, owned or controlled by the Company, in excess of $50,000 per annum for all such contracts; (g) contract, agreement or commitment under which the Company is obligated to pay any broker's fees, finder's fees or any such similar fees, to any third party other than for the hiring of employees; or (h) other contract, agreement, arrangement or understanding which is material to the business of the Company. The Company is not a party to any term sheet, memorandum or letter of understanding which could lead to any such contract, agreement, arrangement, understanding or commitment.

(c) The Company has not (i) declared or paid any dividends or authorized or made any distribution upon or with respect to any class or series of its capital stock, (ii) incurred any indebtedness for money borrowed or any other liabilities individually in excess of $50,000 or, in the case of indebtedness and/or liabilities individually less than $50,000, in excess of $50,000 in the aggregate, (iii) made any loans or advances to any person, other than ordinary advances for travel expenses, or (iv) sold, exchanged or otherwise disposed of any of its assets or rights, other than the sale of its inventory in the ordinary course of business.

(d) For the purposes of subsections (b) and (c) above, all indebtedness, liabilities, agreements, understandings, instruments, contracts and proposed transactions involving the same person or entity (including persons or entities the Company has reason to believe are affiliated therewith) shall be aggregated for the purpose of meeting the individual minimum dollar amounts of such subsections.

(e) The Company is not a party to and is not bound by any contract, agreement or instrument, or subject to any restriction under its Restated Certificate of Incorporation or Bylaws that adversely affects its business as now conducted or as proposed to be conducted, its properties or its financial condition.

(f) The Company has not engaged in the past three months in any discussion (i) with any representative of any corporation or corporations regarding the consolidation or merger of the Company with or into any such corporation or corporations, (ii) with any corporation, partnership, association or other business entity or any individual regarding the sale, conveyance or disposition of all or substantially all of the assets of the Company or a transaction or series of related transactions in which more than 50% of the voting power of the Company is disposed of, or (iii) regarding any other form of acquisition, liquidation, dissolution or winding up of the Company.

2.13 Material Liabilities. The Company has no material liability or obligation, absolute or contingent (individually or in the aggregate), except (i) obligations and liabilities incurred after the date of incorporation in the ordinary course of business that are not individually or in the aggregate material and (ii) obligations under contracts made in the ordinary course of business that would not be required to be reflected in financial statements prepared in accordance with generally accepted accounting principles.

2.14 Title to Property and Assets. Except (a) for liens for current taxes not yet delinquent, (b) for liens imposed by law and incurred in the ordinary course of business for obligations not yet due to carriers, warehousemen, laborers, materialmen, and the like, (c) for liens in respect of pledges or deposits under workers' compensation laws or similar legislation, or (d) for minor defects in title, none of which, individually or in the aggregate, materially interferes with the use of such property, the Company owns its property free and clear of all mortgages; liens, loans, and encumbrances. With respect to the property it leases, the Company is in compliance with such leases and, to the best of its knowledge, holds a valid leasehold interest free of any liens, claims, and encumbrances, subject to clauses (a)-(d) above.

2.15 Disclosure. The Company has fully provided each Investor with all the information that the Investor has requested for deciding whether to purchase the Common Stock and all information that the Company believes is reasonably necessary to enable the Investor to make such decision. Neither this Agreement, the Investor's Rights Agreement, nor any other statements or certificates made or delivered in connection herewith or therewith contains any untrue statement of a material fact or omits to state a material fact necessary to make the statements herein or therein not misleading.

2.16 Related Party Transactions. No employee, officer, or director of the Company or member of his or her immediate family is indebted to the Company, nor is the Company indebted (or committed to make loans or extend or guarantee credit) to any of them. To the best of the Company's knowledge, none of such persons has any direct or indirect ownership interest in any firm or corporation with which the Company is affiliated or with which the Company has a business relationship, or any firm or corporation that competes with the Company, except that employees, officers, or directors of the Company and members of their immediate families may own stock in publicly traded companies that may compete with the Company. To the best of the Company's knowledge, no member of the immediate family of any officer or director of the Company is directly or indirectly interested in any material contract with the Company.

2.17 Permits. The Company has all franchises, permits, licenses, and any similar authority necessary for the conduct of its business as now being conducted by it, the lack of which could materially and adversely affect the business, properties, prospects, or financial condition of the Company, and the Company believes it can obtain, without undue burden or expense, any similar authority for the conduct of its business as planned to be conducted. The Company is not in default in any material respect under any of such franchises, permits, licenses, or other similar authority.

2.18 Environmental and Safety Laws. To the best of its knowledge, the Company has complied with all applicable statutes, laws and regulations relating to the environment or occupational health and safety, and to the best of its knowledge, no material expenditures are or will be required in order to comply with any such existing statute, law or regulation.

2.19 Registration Rights; Lock-Ups. Except as provided in the Investor's Rights Agreement, the Company has not granted or agreed to grant any registration rights, including piggyback rights, to any person or entity.

2.20 Employee Benefit Plans. The Company does not have any Employee Benefit Plans as defined in the Employee Retirement Income Security Act of 1974.

2.21 Taxes. The Company has accurately prepared and timely filed all United States income tax returns and all state and municipal tax returns that are required to be filed by it and has paid or made provisions for the payment of all taxes that have become due pursuant to such returns. The Internal Revenue Service has not audited the United States income tax returns of the Company. No deficiency assessment or proposed adjustment of the Company's United States income tax or state or municipal taxes is pending and the Company has no knowledge of any proposed liability for any tax to be imposed upon its properties or assets for which there is not an adequate reserve.

2.22 Labor Agreements and Actions; Employee Compensation. The Company is not bound by or subject to (and none of its assets or properties is bound by or subject to) any written or oral, express or implied, contract, commitment or arrangement with any labor union, and no labor union has requested or, to the best of the Company's knowledge, has sought to represent any of the employees, representatives or agents of the Company. There is no strike or other labor dispute involving the Company pending, or to the best of the Company's knowledge, threatened, that could have a material adverse effect on the assets, properties, financial condition, operating results, or business of the Company (as such business is presently conducted and as it is proposed to be conducted), nor is the Company aware of any labor organization activity involving its employees. The Company is not aware that any officer or key employee, or that any group of key employees, intends to terminate their employment with the Company, nor does the Company have a present intention to terminate the employment of any of the foregoing. Except as set forth on the Schedule of Exceptions, the employment of each officer and employee of the Company is terminable at the will of the Company. To the best of its knowledge, the Company has complied in all material respects with all applicable state and federal equal employment opportunity and other laws related to employment. Except as set forth on the Schedule of Exceptions, the Company is not a party to or bound by any currently effective employment contract, deferred compensation agreement, bonus plan, incentive plan, profit sharing plan, retirement agreement, or other employee compensation agreement.

2.23 Section 83(b) Elections. To the best of the Company's knowledge, all individuals who have purchased unvested shares of the Company's Common Stock have timely filed or will timely file elections under Section 83(b) of the Code and any analogous provisions of applicable state tax laws.

2.24 Real Property Holding Company. The Company is not a United States real property holding corporation within the meaning of Section 897 of the Code.

2.25 Brokers. The Company has no contract, arrangement or understanding with any broker, finder or similar agent with respect to the transactions contemplated by this Agreement.

2.26 Year 2000. The Company's proprietary software, and to the best of the Company's knowledge, all software supplied by or licensed from any party other than the Company, was capable of recording, storing, processing, calculating and displaying calendar dates falling before, on and after January 1, 2000, without loss of functionality or data integrity, except where the failure to do so could not reasonably be expected to have a material adverse affect on the assets, properties, financial condition, operating results or business of the Company.

2.27 Offerees. The Company has not, either directly or through any agent, broker or finder, offered any securities exercisable for or convertible into Common Stock or any security or securities similar to any thereof, for sale to, or solicited any offers to buy any securities exercisable for or convertible into Common Stock, or any such similar security or securities from, or otherwise approached or negotiated in respect thereof with, any person or entity other than the Investors, other "accredited investors" (as that term is defined in Regulation D promulgated under the Act) who have not invested under this Agreement and employees, directors and consultants of the Company, except for offers, solicitations or other actions that would not, under applicable law, be integrated with the sale of the Common Stock hereunder.

2.28 Returns and Complaints. The Company has received no customer complaints concerning its products and/or services, other than complaints that taken together do not constitute a material adverse effect on the Company's business or prospects.

2.29 Plan. The Plan has been delivered to each Investor and has been prepared in good faith by the Company. The Plan does not contain any untrue statement of a material fact or omit to state a material fact necessary to make the statements made therein not misleading, except that with respect to projections contained in the Plan, the Company represents only that such projections were prepared in good faith and that the Company reasonably believes there is a reasonable basis for such projections.

3. Representations and Warranties of the Investors. Each Investor hereby represents and warrants to the Company that:

3.1 Authorization. Such Investor has full power and authority to enter into this Agreement and the Ancillary Agreements, and each such Agreement constitutes its valid and legally binding obligation, enforceable in accordance with its terms except (i) as limited by applicable bankruptcy, insolvency, reorganization, moratorium, and other laws of general application affecting enforcement of creditors' rights generally, (ii) as limited by laws relating to the availability of specific performance, injunctive relief, or other equitable remedies, and (iii) to the extent the indemnification provisions contained in the Investor's Rights Agreement may be limited by applicable federal or state securities laws.

3.2 Purchase Entirely for Own Account. This Agreement is made with such Investor in reliance upon such Investor's representation to the Company, which by such Investor's execution of this Agreement such Investor hereby confirms, that the Common Stock to be received by such Investor (the "Securities"), will be acquired for investment for such Investor's own account, not as a nominee or agent, and not with a view to the resale or distribution of any part thereof, and that such Investor has no present intention of selling, granting any participation in, or otherwise distributing the same. By executing this Agreement, such Investor further represents that such Investor does not have any contract, undertaking, agreement or arrangement with any person to sell, transfer or grant participations to such person or to any third person, with respect to any of the Securities. In particular, such Investor acknowledges that the Company is entering into this Agreement, and will not be registering or qualifying the offer or sale of the Securities under the Act or applicable state securities laws, in reliance upon the truth and accuracy of such Investor's representations and warranties in this Section 3.

3.3 Disclosure of Information. Such Investor believes that he or it has received all the information he or it considers necessary or appropriate for deciding whether to purchase the Securities. Such Investor further represents that he or it has had an opportunity to ask questions and receive answers from the Company regarding the terms and conditions of the offering of the Securities and the business, properties, prospects and financial condition of the Company. The foregoing, however, does not limit or modify the representations and warranties of the Company in Section 2 of this Agreement or the right of each Investor to rely thereon.

3.4 Investment Experience. Such Investor is an investor in securities of companies in the development stage and acknowledges that it is able to fend for itself, can bear the economic risk of its investment, and has such knowledge and experience in financial or business matters that it is capable of evaluating the merits and risks of the investment in the Securities. Such Investor also represents it has not been organized for the purpose of acquiring the Securities.

3.5 Accredited Investor. Such Investor is an "accredited investor" within the meaning of Securities and Exchange Commission ("SEC") Rule 501 of Regulation D, as presently in effect. Such Investor has the financial ability (i) to bear the economic risk of an investment of the Securities, (ii) to hold the Securities for an indefinite period of time and (iii) currently to afford a complete loss of the investment in the Securities without experiencing any undue financial difficulties. Such Investor's commitment to all speculative investments (including the investment in the Securities) is reasonable in relation to his or its net worth and annual income.

3.6 Restricted Securities. Such Investor understands that the Securities it is purchasing are characterized as "restricted securities" under the federal securities laws inasmuch as they are being acquired from the Company in a transaction not involving a public offering and that under such laws and applicable regulations such securities may be resold without registration under the Act, only in certain limited circumstances. In this connection, such Investor represents that it is familiar with SEC Rule 144, as presently in effect, and understands the resale limitations imposed thereby and by the Act.

3.7 Further Limitations on Disposition. Without in any way limiting the representations set forth above, such Investor further agrees not to make any disposition of all or any portion of the Securities unless and until the transferee has agreed in writing for the benefit of the Company to be bound by this Section 3 and the Investor's Rights Agreement provided and to the extent this Section and such agreements are then applicable, and:

(a) There is then in effect a Registration Statement under the Act covering such proposed disposition and such disposition is made in accordance with such Registration Statement; or

(b) (i) Such Investor shall have notified the Company of the proposed disposition and shall have furnished the Company with a detailed statement of the circumstances surrounding the proposed disposition, and (ii) if reasonably requested by the Company, such Investor shall have furnished the Company with an opinion of counsel, reasonably satisfactory to the Company, that such disposition will not require registration of such shares under the Act. It is agreed that the Company will not require opinions of counsel for transactions made pursuant to Rule 144 except in unusual circumstances.

(c) Notwithstanding the provisions of Paragraphs (a) and (b) above, no such registration statement or opinion of counsel shall be necessary for a transfer by the Investor that is a partnership to a partner of such partnership or a retired partner of such partnership who retires after the date hereof, or to the estate of any such partner or retired partner or the transfer by gift, will or intestate succession of any partner to his or her spouse or to the siblings, lineal descendants or ancestors of such partner or his or her spouse, if the transferee agrees in writing to be subject to the terms hereof to the same extent as if he or she were an original investor hereunder.

3.8 Legends. It is understood that the certificates evidencing the Securities may bear one or all of the following legends:

(a) THE SHARES EVIDENCED BY THIS CERTIFICATE HAVE NOT BEEN REGISTERED UNDER THE SECURITIES ACT OF 1933, AS AMENDED, AND HAVE BEEN TAKEN BY THE ISSUEE FOR INVESTMENT PURPOSES. SAID SHARES MAY NOT BE SOLD OR TRANSFERRED UNLESS (A) THEY HAVE BEEN REGISTERED UNDER SAID ACT, OR (B) THE TRANSFER AGENT (OR THE COMPANY IF THEN ACTING AS ITS OWN TRANSFER AGENT) IS PRESENTED WITH EITHER A WRITTEN OPINION OF COUNSEL SATISFACTORY TO THE COMPANY OR A "NO-ACTION" OR INTERPRETIVE LETTER FROM THE SECURITIES AND EXCHANGE COMMISSION TO THE EFFECT THAT SUCH REGISTRATION IS NOT REQUIRED UNDER THE CIRCUMSTANCES OF SUCH SALE OR TRANSFER.

(b) Any legend required by the laws of any other jurisdiction in which the Securities are sold pursuant to this Agreement.

3.9 Risk Factors. Such Investor has carefully read the Plan and acknowledges that the risks inherent in an investment in the Company include, among other things, that (i) a start-up venture such as the Company, with no significant financial or operating history, is inherently risky and speculative, (ii) the projections for the Company set forth in the Plan, as with the projections for any start-up venture, are inherently uncertain and unreliable, and should not be used as a substantial basis for determining to purchase the Securities, (iii) to succeed, the Company will need to attract additional capital and additional personnel, and there can be no assurances that the Company will be able to attract same, (iv) an investment in the Securities is a speculative investment which involves a high degree of risk of loss by such Investor of his or its entire investment therein and (v) there are substantial restrictions on the transferability of, and there will be no public market for, the Securities, and accordingly, it may not be possible for such Investor to liquidate his or its investment in the Securities in case of emergency.

4. Conditions of Investor's Obligations at Closing. The obligations of the Investor under subsection 1.1 of this Agreement are subject to the fulfillment on or before the Closing of each of the following conditions by the Company, any of which may be waived by the Investor:

4.1 Representations and Warranties. The representations and warranties of the Company contained in Section 2 shall be true on and as of the Closing with the same effect as though such representations and warranties had been made on and as of the date of the Closing.

4.2 Performance. The Company shall have performed and complied with all agreements, obligations and conditions contained in this Agreement that are required to be performed or complied with by it on, or before the Closing.

4.3 Compliance Certificate. The President of the Company shall deliver to the Investor at the Closing a certificate stating that the conditions specified in Sections 4.1 and 4.2 have been fulfilled.

4.4 Qualifications. All authorizations, approvals, or permits, if any, of any governmental authority or regulatory body of the United States or of any state that are required in connection with the lawful issuance and sale of the Securities pursuant to this Agreement shall be duly obtained and effective as of the Closing.

4.5 Proceedings and Documents. All corporate and other proceedings in connection with the transactions contemplated at the Closing and all documents incident thereto shall be reasonably satisfactory in form and substance to the Investors, and they shall have received all such counterpart original and certified or other copies of such documents as they may reasonably request.

4.6 Investor's Rights Agreement. The Company and the Investor shall have entered into the Investor's Rights Agreement in the form attached hereto as Exhibit A.

4.7 Due Diligence and No Material Adverse Change. The Company shall have provided the Investor access to such information as the Investor has reasonably requested in connection with its due diligence review and the Investor shall have concluded its due diligence review of the Company to its complete satisfaction and shall be reasonably satisfied that there has been no material adverse change in the business, operations, financial condition or prospects of the Company.

5. Conditions of the Company's Obligations at Closing. The obligations of the Company to each Investor under this Agreement are subject to the fulfillment on or before the Closing of each of the following conditions by each Investor:

5.1 Representations and Warranties. The representations and warranties of the Investor contained in Section 3 shall be true on and as of the Closing with the same effect as though such representations and warranties had been made on and as of the Closing.

5.2 Payment of Purchase Price. Each Investor shall have delivered the purchase price as provided in Section 1.2.

5.3 Investor's Rights Agreement. Each Investor shall have executed and delivered to the Company the Investor's Rights Agreement.

5.4 Qualifications. All authorizations, approvals, or permits, if any, of any governmental authority or regulatory body of the United States or of any state that are required in connection with the lawful issuance and sale of the Securities pursuant to this Agreement shall be duly obtained and effective as of the Closing.

6. Miscellaneous.

6.1 Survival of Warranties. The warranties, representations and covenants of the Company and the Investor contained in or made pursuant to this Agreement shall survive the execution and delivery of this Agreement and the Closing and shall in no way be affected by any investigation of the subject matter thereof made by or on behalf of the Investors or the Company, provided that such representations and warranties need only be accurate as of the execution of this Agreement and the Closing.

6.2 Successors and Assigns. Except as otherwise provided herein, the terms and conditions of this Agreement shall inure to the benefit of and be binding upon the respective successors and assigns of the parties (including transferees of Common Stock). Nothing in this Agreement, express or implied, is intended to confer upon any party other than the parties hereto or their respective successors and assigns any rights, remedies, obligations, or liabilities under or by reason of this Agreement, except as expressly provided in this Agreement.

6.3 Governing Law. This Agreement shall be governed by and construed under the laws of the State of __________ without regard to the conflicts of law principles of such State.

6.4 Counterparts. This Agreement may be executed in two or more counterparts, each of which shall be deemed an original, but all of which together shall constitute one and the same instrument.

6.5 Titles and Subtitles. The titles and subtitles used in this Agreement are used for convenience only and are not to be considered in construing or interpreting this Agreement.

6.6 Finder's Fee. Each party represents that it neither is nor will be obligated for any finders' fee or commission in connection with this transaction. Each Investor agrees to indemnify and to hold harmless the Company from any liability for any commission or compensation in the nature of a finders' fee (and the costs and expenses of defending against such liability or asserted liability) for which such Investor or any of its officers, partners, employees, or representatives is responsible. The Company agrees to indemnify and hold harmless the Investors from any liability for any commission or compensation in the nature of a finders' fee (and the costs and expenses of defending against such liability or asserted liability) for which the Company or any of its officers, employees or representatives is responsible.

6.7 Expenses. Irrespective of whether or not the Closing is effected, each party shall pay its own costs and expenses that it incurs with respect to the negotiation, execution, delivery and performance of this Agreement. If any action at law or in equity is necessary to enforce or interpret the terms of this Agreement, the Ancillary Agreements or the Amended and Restated Certificate, the prevailing party shall be entitled to reasonable attorney's fees, costs and necessary disbursements in addition to any other relief to which such party may be entitled.

6.8 Amendments and Waivers. Any term of this Agreement may be amended and the observance of any term of this Agreement may be waived (either generally or in a particular instance and either retroactively or prospectively), only with the written consent of the Company and the holders of a majority of the Common Stock sold under this Agreement. Any amendment or waiver effected in accordance with this paragraph shall be binding upon each holder of any securities purchased under this Agreement at the time outstanding, each future holder of all such securities, and the Company.

6.9 Severability. If one or more provisions of this Agreement are held to be unenforceable under applicable law, such provision shall be excluded from this Agreement and the balance of the Agreement shall be interpreted as if such provision was so excluded and shall be enforceable in accordance with its terms.

6.10 Notices. Unless otherwise provided, any notice required or permitted under this Agreement shall be given in writing and shall be deemed effectively given upon personal delivery to the party to be notified or five business days after deposit with the United States Postal Service by certified mail, postage prepaid and addressed to the party to be notified at the address indicated for such party on the signature page below or on Schedule A, as the case may be, or at such other address as such party may designate by ten days' advance written notice to the other parties.

6.11 Aggregation of Stock. All shares of Common Stock held or acquired by affiliated entities or persons shall be aggregated together for the purpose of determining the availability of any rights under this Agreement.

6.12 Entire Agreement. This Agreement and the documents referred to herein constitute the entire agreement among the parties with respect to the subject matter hereof and no party shall be liable or bound to any other party in any manner by any warranties, representations, or covenants with respect to such subject matter except as specifically set forth herein or therein.

6.13 Confidentiality. Each of the Investors will treat and hold as such all of the information, data or know-how, whether disclosed orally or in writing or by any other means, relating either to the business affairs of any of the parties or their parent or subsidiary companies or to the business of the Company, and which is, in all cases, of a confidential nature ("Confidential Information"), refrain from using any of the Confidential Information except in connection with this Agreement, and deliver promptly to the disclosing party or destroy, at the request and option of the disclosing party, all tangible embodiments (and all copies) of the Confidential Information which are in his or its possession. In the event that any of the receiving party is requested or required (by oral question or request for information or documents in any legal proceeding, interrogatory, subpoena, civil investigative demand, or similar process) to disclose any Confidential Information, that receiving party will notify the disclosing party promptly of the request or requirement so that the disclosing party may seek an appropriate protective order or waive compliance with the provisions of this Section 6.13. If, in the absence of a protective order or the receipt of a waiver hereunder, any of the receiving party is, on the advice of counsel, compelled to disclose any Confidential Information to any tribunal or else stand liable for contempt, that receiving party may disclose the Confidential Information to the tribunal; provided, however, that the disclosing party shall use his or its reasonable best efforts to obtain, at the reasonable request of the disclosing party, an order or other assurance that confidential treatment will be accorded to such portion of the Confidential Information required to be disclosed as the disclosing party shall designate.

6.14 Termination. Each Investor will cease to have any rights or obligations hereunder (save in respect of any antecedent breach) on the completion by the Investor of a transfer of Common Stock of the Company such that the Investor no longer holds any of the Common Stock in the capital of the Company and such person shall cease to be a holder of Common Stock of the Company.

6.15 Exculpation among Investors. Each Investor acknowledges that it is not relying upon any person, firm or corporation, other than the Company and its officers and directors, in making its investment or decision to invest in the Company. Each Investor agrees that no Investor nor the respective controlling persons, officers, directors, partners, agents, or employees of any Investor shall be liable to any other Investor for any action heretofore or hereafter taken or omitted to be taken by any of them in connection with the purchase of the Common Stock.

IN WITNESS WHEREOF, the parties have executed this Agreement as of the date first above written.

The.com, Inc.

By: ______________________________

Title: ____________________________

Address: __________________________

____

____

____

By: ______________________________

Title: ____________________________

Address: __________________________

____

____

SCHEDULE A

THE.COM, INC.
Common Stock
Investors, Purchase Price and Shares
Initial Closing

Investor	Number of Shares	Total Purchase Price ($)
TOTAL		

Schedule of Exceptions

<u>Section</u>

2.2 The Company intends to issue 10,000 shares of Common Stock each to ____, ____ and ____ for a total of 30,000 shares in consideration for advisory and consulting services.

2.2 The Company has granted options for 1,000,000 shares to employees under its Stock Option Plan.

2.12 The Company has an agreement with ______ whereby it will pay an initial fee of $10,000 and $5,000 monthly thereafter to ______ for _____.

2.16 Shareholder A possesses a minor stock interest in _________. He owns less than a one percent interest in _________ and is not an officer, director, employee, or current advisor of that company.

Exhibit A

Investors' Rights Agreement

APPENDIX K • INVESTORS' RIGHTS AGREEMENT

THE.COM, INC.

INVESTORS' RIGHTS AGREEMENT

________________, 2000

TABLE OF CONTENTS*

Page

* Page number references within this document refer to the original agreement and have not been altered for publication of *Financing Start-Ups*.

INVESTORS' RIGHTS AGREEMENT

THIS INVESTORS' RIGHTS AGREEMENT (this "Agreement") is made and entered into as of ________________ by and among The.com, Inc., a ________ corporation (the "Company"), and the persons identified on the signature page hereof (the "Investors").

Recitals

WHEREAS, the Company and the Investors are parties to the Common Stock Purchase Agreement, dated ________________ (the "Agreement");

WHEREAS, in order to induce the Investors to invest funds in the Company pursuant to the Common Stock Purchase Agreement, the Investors and the Company hereby agree to enter into this Investor's Rights Agreement;

NOW, THEREFORE, in consideration of the mutual promises and covenants set forth herein, all parties hereto agree as follows:

SECTION 1

Restrictions on Transferability of Securities; Registration Rights

1.1 Certain Definitions. As used in this Agreement, the following terms shall have the following respective meanings:

(a) ***"Commission"*** shall mean the Securities and Exchange Commission or any other federal agency at the time administering the Securities Act.

(b) ***"Common Stock"*** shall mean the shares of the Common Stock, par value $0.01 per share, of the Company.

(c) ***"Exchange Act"*** shall mean the Securities Exchange Act of 1934, as amended, or any similar successor federal statute and the rules and regulations thereunder, all as the same shall be in effect from time to time.

(d) ***"Holder"*** shall mean any Investor who holds Registrable Securities and any holder of Registrable Securities to whom the registration rights conferred by this Agreement have been transferred in compliance with Section 1.11 .

(e) ***"Initiating Holder"*** shall mean any Holder or Holders who in the aggregate hold not less than 40% of the outstanding Registrable Securities. For the purposes of such calculation, any and all shares held by Shareholder A, who shall be a party to this Agreement, shall not be considered.

(f) ***"Other Stockholder"*** shall mean persons other than Holders who, by virtue of agreements with the Company, are entitled to include their securities in certain registrations.

(g) ***"Restricted Securities"*** shall mean the securities of the Company required to bear or bearing a legend stating that the shares have not been registered under the Securities Act.

(h) ***"Registrable Securities"*** shall mean (i) shares of Common Stock issued as set forth in Exhibit A and (ii) any Common Stock issued as a dividend or other distribution with respect to or in exchange for or in replacement of the shares referenced in (i) above, provided, however, that Registrable Securities shall not include any shares of Common Stock that have been sold to the public pursuant to a registration statement or Rule 144 or sold in a private transaction in which the transferor's rights pursuant to this Agreement have not been assigned.

(i) The terms ***"register," "registered"*** and ***"registration"*** shall refer to a registration effected by preparing and filing a registration statement in compliance with the Securities Act and applicable rules and regulations thereunder, and the declaration or ordering of the effectiveness of such registration statement by the Commission.

(j) ***"Registration Expenses"*** shall mean all expenses incurred in effecting any registration pursuant to this Agreement, including, without limitation, all registration, qualification and filing fees, printing expenses, escrow fees, fees and disbursements of counsel for the Company, blue sky fees and expenses, expenses of any regular or special audits incident to or required by any such registration, but shall not include Selling Expenses or, except as expressly set forth in Section 1.4 of this Agreement, fees and disbursements of counsel for the Holders (and excluding the compensation of regular employees of the Company, which shall be paid in any event by the Company).

(k) ***"Rule 144"*** shall mean Rule 144 as promulgated by the Commission under the Securities Act, as such Rule may be amended from time to time, or any similar successor rule that may be promulgated by the Commission.

(l) ***"Rule 145"*** shall mean Rule 145 as promulgated by the Commission under the Securities Act, as such Rule may be amended from time to time, or any similar successor rule that may be promulgated by the Commission.

(m) ***"Securities Act"*** shall mean the Securities Act of 1933, as amended, or any similar successor federal statute and the rules and regulations thereunder, all as the same shall be in effect from time to time, corresponding to such act.

(n) ***"Selling Expenses"*** shall mean all underwriting discounts and selling commissions applicable to the sale of Registrable Securities and all fees and disbursements of counsel for any Holder except as set forth in Section 1.4 of this Agreement.

(o) ***"Shares"*** shall mean the Company's Common Stock, par value $0.01 per share.

1.2 Requested Registration.

(a) Request for Registration. If the Company shall receive from Initiating Holders 12 months after the effective date of the first registration statement filed by the Company covering an underwritten offering of any of its securities to the general public (an "initial public offering"), a written request specifying that it is made pursuant to this Section 1.2 and requesting that the Company effect any registration with respect to all or a part of the Registrable Securities having a reasonably anticipated aggregate offering price, net of underwriting discounts and commissions, that exceeds $5,000,000, the Company will:

(i) promptly give written notice of the proposed registration to all other Holders; and

(ii) as soon as practicable, use its diligent best efforts to effect such registration (including, without limitation, filing post-effective amendments, appropriate qualifications under applicable blue sky or other state securities laws and appropriate compliance with the Securities Act) as would permit or facilitate the sale and distribution of all or such portion of such Registrable Securities as are specified in such request, together with all or such portion of the Registrable Securities of any Holder or Holders joining in such request as are specified in a written request received by the Company within 20 days after such written notice from the Company described in clause (i) above is effective.

The Company shall not be obligated to effect, or to take any action to effect, any such registration pursuant to this Section 1.2:

(A) In any particular jurisdiction in which the Company would be required to execute a general consent to service of process in effecting such registration, qualification or compliance, unless the Company is already subject to service in such jurisdiction and except as may be required by the Securities Act;

(B) After the Company has effected one such registration pursuant to this Section 1.2(a) and each such registration has been declared or ordered effective by the Commission;

(C) During the period starting with the date 60 days prior to the Company's good faith estimate of the date of filing of, and ending on a date 180 days after the effective date of, a registration pursuant to Section 1.3, provided that the Company is actively employing in good faith all reasonable efforts to cause such registration statement to become effective;

(b) Subject to the foregoing clauses (A) through (C), the Company shall prepare and file a registration statement covering the Registrable Securities so requested to be registered as soon as practicable after receipt of the request or requests of the Initiating Holders; provided, however, that if (i) in the good faith judgment of the Board of Directors of the Company, such registration would be seriously detrimental to the Company and the Board of Directors of the Company concludes, as a result, that it is essential to defer the filing of such registration statement at such time, and (ii) the Company shall furnish to such Holders a certificate signed by the president or chief executive officer of the Company stating that in the good faith judgment of the Board of Directors of the Company, it would be seriously detrimental to the Company for such registration statement to be filed in the near future and that it is, therefore, essential to defer the filing of such registration statement, then the Company shall have the right to defer such filing for the period during which such registration would be seriously detrimental, provided, that the Company may not defer the filing for a period of more than 180 days after receipt of the request of the Initiating Holders, and, provided further, that (except as provided in clause (C) above) the Company shall not defer its obligation in this manner more than once in any 12-month period.

The registration statement filed pursuant to the request of the Initiating Holders may, subject to the provisions of this Section 1.2(b) and Section 1.12, include other securities of the Company and may include securities of the Company being sold for the account of the Company.

(c) Underwriting. If the Initiating Holders intend to distribute the Registrable Securities covered by their request by means of an underwriting, they shall so advise the Company as a part of their request made pursuant to this Section 1.2 and the Company shall include such information in the written notice referred to in Section 1.2(a)(i) above. In such event, the right of any Holder to registration pursuant to this Section 1.2 shall be conditioned upon such Holder's participation in such underwriting and the inclusion of such Holder's Registrable Securities in the underwriting (unless otherwise mutually agreed by a majority in interest of the Initiating Holders and such Holder with respect to such participation and inclusion) to the extent provided herein. A Holder may elect to include in such underwriting all or a part of the Registrable Securities he holds.

(d) Procedure. If the Company shall request inclusion in any registration pursuant to this Section 1.2 of securities being sold for its own account, or if persons other than Holders shall request inclusion of their securities in any registration pursuant to this Section 1.2, the Initiating Holders shall, on behalf of all Holders, offer to include such securities in the underwriting and may condition such offer on their acceptance of the further applicable provisions of this Section 1. If the Initiating Holders intend to distribute the Registrable Securities covered by their request pursuant to this Section 1.2 by means of an underwriting, the Company shall (together with all Holders and other persons proposing to distribute their securities through such underwriting) enter into an underwriting agreement in customary form with the representative of the underwriter or underwriters selected for such underwriting by a majority in interest of the Initiating Holders, which underwriter(s) are reasonably acceptable to the Company. Notwithstanding any other provision of this Section 1.2, if the representative of the underwriters advises the Initiating Holders in writing that marketing factors require a limitation on the number of shares to be underwritten, the number of shares to be included in the underwriting or registration shall be allocated as set forth in Section 1.12. If the person who has requested inclusion in such registration as provided above does not agree to the terms of any such underwriting, such person shall be excluded therefrom by written notice from the Company, the underwriter or the Initiating Holders. The securities so excluded shall also be withdrawn from registration. Any Registrable Securities or other securities excluded shall also be withdrawn from such registration. If shares are so withdrawn from the registration and if the number of shares to be included in such registration was previously reduced as a result of marketing factors pursuant to this Section 1.2(d), then the Company shall offer to all Holders who have retained rights to include securities in the registration the right to include additional securities in the registration in an aggregate amount equal to the number of shares withdrawn, with such shares to be allocated among such Holders requesting additional inclusion in accordance with Section 1.12.

1.3 Company Registration.

(a) If the Company shall determine to register any of its securities either for its own account or the account of a security holder or holders exercising their respective demand registration rights (other than pursuant to Section 1.2), other than a registration relating solely to employee benefit plans, or a registration relating solely to a Commission Rule 145 transaction, or a registration on any registration form which does not permit secondary sales, the Company will:

(i) promptly give to each Holder written notice thereof, and

(ii) use its best efforts to include in such registration (and any related qualification under blue sky laws or other compliance), except as set forth in Section 1.3(b), and in any underwriting involved therein, all the Registrable Securities specified in a written request or requests, made by any Holder within 20 days after the written notice from the Company described in clause (i) above is effective. Such written request may specify all or a part of a Holder's Registrable Securities.

(b) Underwriting. If the registration of which the Company gives notice is for a registered public offering involving an underwriting, the Company shall so advise the Holders as a part of the written notice given pursuant to Section 1.3(a)(i). In such event the right of any Holder to registration pursuant to this Section 1.3 shall be conditioned upon such Holder's participation in such underwriting and the inclusion of such Holder's Registrable Securities in the underwriting to the extent provided herein. All Holders proposing to distribute their securities through such underwriting shall (together with the Company and the holders of other securities of the Company distributing their securities through such underwriting) enter into an underwriting agreement in customary form with the representative of the underwriter or underwriters selected by the Company.

Notwithstanding any other provision of this Section 1.3, if the representative of the underwriters advises the Company in writing that marketing factors require a limitation on the number of shares to be underwritten, the representative may (subject to the limitations set forth below) exclude all Registrable Securities from, or limit the number of Registrable Securities to be included in, the registration and underwriting. The Company shall so advise all Holders of securities requesting registration, and the number of shares of securities that are entitled to be included in the registration and underwriting shall be allocated first to the Company for securities being sold for its own account and thereafter as set forth in Section 1.12. If any person does not agree to the terms of any such underwriting, he shall be excluded therefrom by written notice from the Company or the underwriter. Any Registrable Securities or other securities excluded or withdrawn from such underwriting shall be withdrawn from such registration.

If shares are so withdrawn from the registration or if the number of shares of Registrable Securities to be included in such registration was previously reduced as a result of marketing factors, the Company shall then offer to all persons who have retained the right to include securities in the registration the right to include additional securities in the registration in an aggregate amount equal to the number of shares so withdrawn, with such shares to be allocated among the persons requesting additional inclusion in accordance with Section 1.12.

1.4 Expenses of Registration. All Registration Expenses, together with reasonable fees of one counsel for the selling Holders, incurred in connection with all registrations pursuant to Section 1.3, up to two registrations per year pursuant to Section 1.5 and one registration pursuant to Section 1.2, shall be borne by the Company; provided, however, that if the Holders bear the Registration Expenses for any registration proceeding begun pursuant to Section 1.2 and subsequently withdrawn by the Holders registering shares therein, such registration proceeding shall not be counted as a requested registration pursuant to Section 1.2. In the event that such withdrawal is based upon material adverse information relating to the Company that is materially different from the information known or available (upon request from the Company or otherwise) to the Holders requesting registration at the time of their request for registration under Section 1.2, such registration shall not be treated as a counted registration for purposes of Section 1.2 even though the Holders do not bear the Registration Expenses for such registration. All Selling Expenses relating to securities registered shall be borne by the Holders of such securities pro rata on the basis of the number of shares of securities so registered on their behalf.

1.5 Registration on Form S-3.

(a) After its initial public offering as described in Section 1.2(a), the Company shall use its best efforts to qualify for registration on Form S-3 or any comparable or successor form or forms. After the Company has qualified for the use of Form S-3, in addition to the rights contained in the foregoing provisions of this Section 1, the Holders of Registrable Securities shall have the right to request registrations on Form S-3 (such requests shall be in writing and shall state the number of shares of Registrable Securities to be disposed of and the intended methods of disposition of such shares by such Holder or Holders); provided, however, that the Company shall not be obligated to effect any such registration if (i) the Holders, together with the holders of any other securities of the Company entitled to inclusion in such registration, propose to sell Registrable Securities and such other securities (if any) on Form S-3 at an aggregate price to the public of less than $1,000,000, or (ii) in a given 12-month period, after the Company has effected two such registrations pursuant to this Section 1.5 in any such period.

(b) If a request complying with the requirements of Section 1.5(a) is delivered to the Company, the provisions of Sections 1.2(a)(i) and (ii) (other than § 1.2(a)(ii)(B)) and Section 1.2(b) shall apply to such registration. The provisions of Sections 1.2(c) and 1.2(d) shall apply to all registrations pursuant to this Section 1.5.

1.6 Registration Procedure. In the case of each registration effected by the Company pursuant to this Section 1, the Company will keep each Holder advised in writing as to the initiation of each registration and as to the completion thereof. At its expense, the Company will use its best efforts to:

(a) Keep such registration effective for a period of 120 days or until the Holder or Holders have completed the distribution described in the registration statement relating thereto, whichever first occurs; provided, however that (i) such 120-day period shall be extended for a period of time equal to the period the Holder refrains from selling any securities included in such registration at the request of an underwriter of Common Stock (or other securities) of the Company; and (ii) in the case of any registration of Registrable Securities on Form S-3 which are intended to be offered on a continuous or delayed basis, such 120-day period shall be extended, if necessary, to keep the registration statement effective until all such Registrable Securities are sold; provided that Rule 415, or any successor rule under the Securities Act, permits an offering on a continuous or delayed basis, and provided further that applicable rules under the Securities Act governing the obligation to file a post-effective amendment permit, in lieu of filing a post-effective amendment which (i) includes any prospectus required by Section 10(a)(3) of the Securities Act or (ii) reflects facts or events representing a material or fundamental change in the information set forth in the registration statement, the incorporation by reference of information required to be included in (i) and (ii) above to be contained in periodic reports filed pursuant to Section 13 or 15(d) of the Exchange Act in the registration statement;

(b) Prepare and file with the Commission such amendments and supplements to such registration statement and the prospectus used in connection with such registration statement as may be necessary to comply with the provisions of the Securities Act with respect to the disposition of all securities covered by such registration statement;

(c) Furnish such number of prospectuses and other documents incident thereto, including a preliminary prospectus and any amendment of or supplement to the prospectus, as a Holder from time to time may reasonably request;

(d) Notify each seller of Registrable Securities covered by such registration statement at any time when a prospectus relating thereto is required to be delivered under the Securities Act of the happening of any event as a result of which the prospectus included in such registration statement, as then in effect, includes an untrue statement of a material fact or omits to state a material fact required to be stated therein or necessary to make the statements therein not misleading or incomplete in the light of the circumstances then existing, and at the request of any such seller, prepare and furnish to such seller a reasonable number of copies of a supplement to or an amendment of such prospectus as may be necessary so that, as thereafter delivered to the purchasers of such shares, such prospectus shall not include an untrue statement of a material fact or omit to state a material fact required to be stated therein or necessary to make the statements therein not misleading or incomplete in the light of the circumstances then existing;

(e) Cause all such Registrable Securities registered pursuant hereunder to be listed on each securities exchange on which similar securities issued by the Company are then listed;

(f) Provide a transfer agent and registrar for all Registrable Securities registered pursuant hereunder and a CUSIP number for all such Registrable Securities, in each case not later than the effective date of such registration;

(g) Otherwise use its best efforts to comply with all applicable rules and regulations of the Commission, and make available to its security holders, as soon as reasonably practicable, an earnings statement covering the period of at least 12 months, but not more than 18 months, beginning with the first month after the effective date of the Registration Statement, which earnings statement shall satisfy the provisions of Section 11(a) of the Securities Act;

(h) In connection with any underwritten offering pursuant to a registration statement filed pursuant to Section 1.2, the Company will enter into an underwriting agreement reasonably necessary to effect the offer and sale of Common Stock; provided, however, that such underwriting agreement contains customary underwriting provisions, and provided further that if the underwriter so requests, the underwriting agreement will contain customary contribution provision; and

(i) Furnish, at the request of a majority in interest of Holders participating in the registration, on the date that such Registered Securities are delivered to the underwriters for sale, or if such securities are not being sold through underwriters, on the date that the registration statement with respect to such securities becomes effective, (i) an opinion dated as of such date, of the counsel representing the Company for purposes of such registration, in a form and substance as is customarily provided to underwriters in an underwritten public offering and reasonably satisfactory to a majority in interest of Holders requesting registration, addressed to the underwriters, if any, and Holders, and (ii) a letter dated as of such date from the independent public accountants of the Company in form and substance as is customarily provided to underwriters in an underwritten public offering and reasonably satisfactory to a majority in interest of the Holders, addressed to the underwriters, if any, and, if permitted, by applicable accounting standards, the Holders requesting registration.

1.7 Indemnification.

(a) To the extent permitted by law, the Company will indemnify each Holder, each of its officers, directors and partners, legal counsel and accountants and each person controlling such Holder within the meaning of Section 15 of the Securities Act, with respect to which registration, qualification or compliance has been effected pursuant to this Section 1, and each underwriter for such Holder, if any, and each person who controls within the meaning of Section 15 of the Securities Act any underwriter, against all expenses, claims, losses, damages and liabilities (or actions, proceedings or settlements in respect thereof) arising out of or based on any untrue statement (or alleged untrue statement) of a material fact contained in any prospectus, preliminary or final, offering circular or other document (including any related registration statement, notification or the like) incident to any such registration, qualification or compliance, or based on any omission (or alleged omission) to state therein a material fact required to be stated therein or necessary to make the statements therein not misleading, or any violation by the Company of the Securities Act, the Exchange Act, any state securities laws or any rule or regulation thereunder applicable to the Company and relating to action or inaction required of the Company in connection with any such registration, qualification or compliance, and will reimburse each such Holder, each of its officers, directors, partners, legal counsel and accountants and each person controlling such Holder, each such underwriter and each person who controls any such underwriter, for any legal and any other expenses reasonably incurred in connection with investigating and defending or settling any such claim, loss, damage, liability or action; provided, however, that the Company will not be liable in any such case to the extent that any such claim, loss, damage, liability or expense arises out of or is based on any untrue statement or omission based upon written information furnished to the Company by such Holder, or its agents, underwriter or persons who control such Holder, and stated to be specifically for use therein. It is agreed that the indemnity agreement contained in this Section1.7(a) shall not apply to amounts paid in settlement of any such loss, claim, damage, liability or action if such settlement is effected without the consent of the Company (which consent has not been unreasonably withheld).

(b) Each Holder will, if Registrable Securities held by him are included in the securities as to which such registration, qualification or compliance is being effected, indemnify the Company, each of its directors, officers, partners, legal counsel and accountants and each underwriter, if any, of the Company's securities covered by such a registration statement, each person who controls the Company or such underwriter within the meaning of Section 15 of the Securities Act, each other such Holder and Other Stockholder and each of their officers, directors and partners, and each person controlling such Holder or Other Stockholder, against all expenses, claims, losses, damages and liabilities (or actions, proceedings or settlements in respect thereof) arising out of or based on any untrue statement (or alleged untrue statement) of a material fact contained in any such registration statement, prospectus, preliminary or final, offering circular or other document, or any omission (or alleged omission) to state therein a material fact required to be stated therein or necessary to make the statements therein not misleading, and will reimburse the Company and such Holders, Other Stockholders, directors, officers, partners, legal counsel and accountants, persons, underwriters or control persons for any legal or any other expenses reasonably incurred in connection with investigating or defending any such claim, loss, damage, liability or action, in each case to the extent, but only to the extent, that such untrue statement (or alleged untrue statement) or omission (or alleged omission) is made in such registration statement, prospectus, offering circular or other document in reliance upon and in conformity with written information furnished to the Company by such Holder its agents, underwriter or persons who control such Holder and stated to be specifically for use in connection with such registration; provided, however, that the obligations of such Holder hereunder shall not apply to amounts paid in settlement of any such claims, losses, damages or liabilities (or actions in respect thereof) if such settlement is effected without the consent of such Holder (which consent shall not be unreasonably withheld) and provided further that in no event shall any indemnity under this Section 1.7(b) exceed the net proceeds from the offering received by such Holder.

(c) Each party entitled to indemnification under this Section 1.7 (the "Indemnified Party") shall give notice to the party required to provide indemnification (the "Indemnifying Party") promptly after such Indemnified Party has actual knowledge of any claim as to which indemnity may be sought, and shall permit the Indemnifying Party to assume the defense of any such claim or any litigation resulting therefrom; provided, however, that counsel for the Indemnifying Party, who shall conduct the defense of such claim or any litigation resulting therefrom, shall be approved by the Indemnified Party (whose approval shall not unreasonably be withheld), and the Indemnified Party may participate in such defense at such party's expense, and provided further that the failure of any Indemnified Party to give notice as provided herein shall not relieve the Indemnifying Party of its obligations under this Section 1.7 to the extent such failure is not prejudicial. No Indemnifying Party, in the defense of any such claim or litigation, shall, except with the consent of each Indemnified Party, consent to entry of any judgment or enter into any settlement which does not include as an unconditional term thereof the giving by the claimant or plaintiff to such Indemnified Party of a release from all liability in respect to such claim or litigation. Each Indemnified Party shall furnish such information regarding itself or the claim in question as an Indemnifying Party may reasonably request in writing and as shall be reasonably required in connection with defense of such claim and litigation resulting therefrom.

(d) If the indemnification provided for in this Section 1.7 is held by a court of competent jurisdiction to be unavailable to an Indemnified Party with respect to any loss, liability, claim, damage or expense referred to therein, then the Indemnifying Party, in lieu of indemnifying such Indemnified Party hereunder, shall contribute to the amount paid or payable by such Indemnified Party as a result of such loss, liability, claim, damage or expense in such proportion as is appropriate to reflect the relative fault of the Indemnifying Party on the one hand and of the Indemnified Party on the other in connection with the statements or omissions which resulted in such loss, liability, claim, damage or expense as well as any other relevant equitable considerations. The relative fault of the Indemnifying Party and of the Indemnified Party shall be determined by reference to, among other things, whether the untrue or alleged untrue statement of a material fact or the omission to state a material fact relates to information supplied by the Indemnifying Party or by the Indemnified Party and the parties' relative intent, knowledge, access to information and opportunity to correct or prevent such statement or omission provided that in no event shall any contribution by a Holder hereunder exceed the net proceeds from the offering received by such Holder.

(e) Notwithstanding the foregoing, to the extent that the provisions on indemnification and contribution contained in the underwriting agreement entered into in connection with the underwritten public offering are in conflict with the foregoing provisions, the provisions in the underwriting agreement shall control.

(f) The obligations of the Company and the Holders under this Section 1.7 shall survive completion of any offering of Registrable Securities and the termination of this Agreement.

1.8 Information by Holder. Each Holder of Registrable Securities shall furnish to the Company such information regarding such Holder and the distribution proposed by such Holder as the Company or its underwriters may reasonably request in writing and as shall be reasonably required in connection with any registration, qualification or compliance referred to in this Section 1.

1.9 Rule 144 Reporting. With a view to making available the benefits of certain rules and regulations of the Commission that may permit the sale of the Restricted Securities to the public without registration, the Company agrees to use its best efforts to:

(a) Make and keep public information available as those terms are understood and defined in Rule 144 under the Securities Act at all times following the effective date of the first registration under the Securities Act filed by the Company for an offering of its securities to the general public;

(b) File with the Commission in a timely manner all reports and other documents required of the Company under the Securities Act and the Exchange Act at any time after it has become subject to such reporting requirements;

(c) So long as a Holder owns any Restricted Securities, furnish to the Holder forthwith upon written request a written statement by the Company as to its compliance with the reporting requirements of Rule 144 (at any time from and after 90 days following the effective date of the first registration statement filed by the Company for an offering of its securities to the general public), and of the Securities Act and the Exchange Act (at any time after it has become subject to such reporting requirements), a copy of the most recent annual or quarterly report of the Company, and such other reports and documents so filed as a Holder may reasonably request in availing itself of any rule or regulation of the Commission allowing a Holder to sell any such securities without registration.

1.10 Transfer or Assignment of Registration Rights. The rights to cause the Company to register securities granted to a Holder by the Company under Sections 1.2, 1.3 and 1.5 may be transferred or assigned by a Holder only to a transferee or assignee who holds or will hold, subsequent to such transfer not less than 50,000 shares of Registrable Securities (as presently constituted and subject to subsequent adjustments for stock splits, stock dividends, reverse stock splits and the like), or to a transferee or assignee who holds or will hold, subsequent to such transfer not less than 50,000 shares of Registrable Securities (as presently constituted and subject to subsequent adjustments for stock splits, stock dividends, reverse stock splits and the like) that (i) is a subsidiary, parent, shareholder, general partner, limited partner or retired partner of Holder, or (ii) is a Holder's family member (or a family member of a Holder's spouse) or trust for the benefit of such person or persons; and provided that the Company is given written notice at the time of or within a reasonable time after said transfer or assignment, stating the name and address of said transferee or assignee and identifying the securities with respect to which such registration rights are being transferred or assigned, and provided further that the transferee or assignee of such rights agrees in writing to assume the obligations of such Holder under this Section 1.

1.11 "Market Stand-Off" Agreement. If requested by the Company and an underwriter of Common Stock (or other securities) of the Company, an Investor shall not sell or otherwise transfer or dispose of any Common Stock (or other securities) of the Company held by such an Investor (other than those included in the registration) during the 180 day period following the effective date of a registration statement of the Company filed under the Securities Act in connection with an initial public offering; provided, however, that:

(a) all Holders and officers and directors of the Company enter into similar agreements; and

(b) such agreements shall provide that any discretionary waiver or termination of the restrictions of such agreements by the representatives of the underwriters shall apply to all persons subject to such agreements pro rata based on the number of shares held.

The obligations described in this Section 1.11 shall not apply to a registration relating solely to employee benefit plans on Form S-1 or Form S-8 or similar forms which may be promulgated in the future, or a registration relating solely to a Commission Rule 145 transaction on Form S-4 or similar forms which may be promulgated in the future. In order to enforce the foregoing covenant, the Company may impose stop-transfer instructions with respect to the shares (or other securities) subject to the foregoing restriction until the end of said 180 day period.

1.12 Allocation of Registration Opportunities. In any circumstance in which all of the Registrable Securities and other shares of Common Stock of the Company (including shares of Common Stock issued or issuable upon conversion of shares of any currently unissued series of Preferred Stock of the Company) with registration rights (the "Other Shares") requested to be included in a registration on behalf of the Holders or other selling shareholders cannot be so included as a result of limitations of the aggregate number of shares of Registrable Securities and Other Shares which may be so included, the number of shares of Registrable Securities and Other Shares which may be included shall be allocated first to the Holders pro rata based on the number of shares of Registrable Securities held by each, and second to holders of Other Shares (including Holders) pro rata based on the number of shares of Other Shares held by each (on an as converted basis); provided, however, that, if any Holder does not request inclusion of the maximum number of shares of Registrable Securities allocated to him pursuant to the above-described procedure, the remaining portion of his allocation shall be reallocated first among those requesting Holders with respect to their shares of Registrable Securities and second among holders of Other Shares (including Holders) and this procedure shall be repeated until all of the shares of Registrable Securities and Other Shares that may be included in the registration on behalf of the Holders and other selling shareholders have been so allocated. The Company shall not limit the number of Registrable Securities to be included in a registration pursuant to this Agreement (i) in order to include shares held by shareholders with no registration rights or to include stock issued prior to the date of this Agreement, other than to the Holders, or any other shares of stock issued to employees, officers, directors or consultants pursuant to the Company's equity incentive plans, or (ii) with respect to registrations under Sections 1.2 and 1.5, in order to include in such registration securities registered for the Company's own account.

1.13 Restriction on Subsequent Registration Rights. After the date of this Agreement, the Company shall not, without prior written consent of the Holders of a majority of the Registrable Securities, enter into any agreement with any holder or prospective holder of any securities of the Company that would grant such Holder registration rights senior to those granted to the Holders hereunder.

1.14 Delay of Registration. No Holder shall have any right to take any action to restrain, enjoin or otherwise delay any registration as the result of any controversy that might arise with respect to the interpretation or implementation of this Section 1.

1.15 Termination of Registration Rights. The right of any Holder to request registration or inclusion in any registration pursuant to this Section 1 shall terminate on the third anniversary of the closing of the Company's sale of its Common Stock in an underwritten public offering under the Act at a per share public offering price of at least $1.00 (as appropriately adjusted for stock splits, recapitalizations, combinations and the like) for an aggregate public offering price of not less than $10,000,000; provided, however, that, with respect to any Holder of less than two percent of the Company's outstanding stock, the right of any such Holder to request registration or inclusion in any registration pursuant to this Section 1 shall terminate at such earlier time as any such Holder shall be able to sell all shares of Registrable Securities held or entitled to be held upon conversion by such Holder under Rule 144 during any 90-day period.

1.16 Limitations on Disposition. Each Investor agrees not to make any disposition of any Shares or Registrable Securities unless and until the transferee has agreed in writing for the benefit of the Company to be bound by this Section 1.16 provided and to the extent this Section is then applicable, and:

(a) there is then in effect a registration statement under the Securities Act covering such proposed disposition and such disposition is made in accordance with such registration statement; or

(b) (i) such Investor shall have notified the Company of the proposed disposition and shall have furnished the Company with a detailed statement of the circumstances surrounding the proposed disposition, and (ii) if reasonably requested by the Company, such Investor shall have furnished the Company with an opinion of counsel, reasonably satisfactory to the Company that such disposition will not require registration of such shares under the Securities Act; provided, however, that the Company will not require opinions of counsel for transactions made pursuant to Rule 144 except in unusual circumstances.

Notwithstanding the foregoing, no such registration statement or opinion of counsel shall be necessary for a transfer which complies with all applicable federal and state securities laws by an Investor (i) that is a partnership to its partners or former partners in accordance with their partnership interests, (ii) that is a corporation to its shareholders in accordance with their equity interests therein or (iii) to family members of an Investor or a trust for the benefit of an individual Investor or family member thereof, provided in each case that the transferee agrees to be bound by this Section 1.16.

SECTION 2

Rights of First Refusal

2.1 Rights of First Refusal. The Company hereby grants to each Investor, as long as the Investor holds at least 50,000 shares of Registrable Securities (as appropriately adjusted for stock splits, recapitalizations, combinations and the like), the right of first refusal to purchase, pro rata, a portion of any New Securities (as defined in Section 2.1(a)) that the Company, from time to time, may propose to sell and issue. Each Investor's pro rata share of the New Securities will be the ratio of (i) the number of shares of Common Stock issued and held, and issuable upon the conversion of the Shares then held, by such Investor as of the date of the Rights Notice (as defined below) to (ii) the total number of shares of Common Stock issued and held, and issuable upon the conversion of the Shares then held by all shareholders of the Company as of such date plus the total number of shares of Common Stock issuable upon exercise of all then-outstanding options, warrants and rights issued by the Company. This right of first refusal will be subject to the following provisions:

(a) "New Securities" will mean any shares of Common Stock or Preferred Stock of any kind of the Company, whether now or hereafter authorized; rights, options, or warrants to purchase said Common Stock or Preferred Stock and securities carrying any such right, option or warrant; and securities of any type whatsoever that are, or may become, convertible into said Common Stock or Preferred Stock; provided, however, that "New Securities" will not include: (i) shares of Common Stock reserved for issuance to officers, directors, employees and consultants of the Company directly or pursuant to a stock option plan or restricted stock plan or similar equity incentive plan or agreement approved by the Board of Directors of the Company; (ii) Common Stock or Preferred Stock of any series issued or issuable pursuant to the exercise of warrants, options or other rights granted in connection with any equipment lease, banking, technology license, vendor or customer relationship or similar non-equity financing transaction approved by the Board of Directors in accordance with reasonable and customary business practices; (iii) shares issued or issuable upon conversion of any series of Preferred Stock; (iv) securities issued in connection with the acquisition of another corporation by the Company by merger, consolidation, purchase of substantially all of the assets, or other reorganization as a result of which the Company owns more than 50% of the voting power of such corporation; and (v) shares of the Company's Common Stock or Preferred Stock issued in connection with any stock split, stock dividend, recapitalization, reclassification or similar event.

(b) If the Company proposes to issue New Securities, it will give each Investor that holds at least 50,000 shares of Registrable Securities (as appropriately adjusted for stock splits, recapitalizations, combinations and the like) written notice (the "Rights Notice") of the Company's intention to do so, describing the New Securities, the price, and the general terms upon which the Company proposes to issue them. Each such Investor will have seven days from the date of delivery of the Rights Notice to agree to purchase its pro rata share of such New Securities for the price and upon the general terms specified in the Rights Notice by giving written notice to the Company setting forth the quantity of New Securities to be purchased.

(c) If any Investor fails to exercise in full its rights of first refusal hereunder, the Company will have 90 days after the date of delivery of the Rights Notice to sell the New Securities that were not purchased by the Investor, at a price and upon general terms no more favorable to the purchasers thereof than the price and general terms specified in the Rights Notice. If the Company does not sell the New Securities within said 90 day period as provided in the preceding sentence, the Company will not thereafter issue or sell any of such New Securities without complying with the provisions of Section 2.1(b) above.

(d) Termination. The rights of first refusal granted in this Section 2 shall not apply to, and shall terminate upon the earlier of (i) the closing of the Company's sale of its Common Stock in an underwritten public offering with an aggregate public offering price of $10,000,000 or more, or (ii) a sale of all or substantially all of the assets of the Company or a merger or consolidation of the Company with or into any other corporation or corporations in which the shareholders of the Company immediately prior to such event retain less than a 50% interest in the surviving entity.

(e) Transfer of Right. The rights of first refusal of each Holder under this Section 2.1 may be transferred to the same parties subject to the same restrictions as any transfer of registration rights pursuant to Section 1.10.

SECTION 3

Covenants of the Company

The Company hereby covenants and agrees, so long as any Holder owns any Registrable Shares as follows:

3.1 Basic Financial Information. The Company will furnish the following reports to each Holder (so long as such Holder owns any Registrable Shares):

(a) As soon as practicable after the end of each fiscal year of the Company, and in any event within 90 days thereafter, a consolidated balance sheet of the Company and its subsidiaries, if any, as at the end of such fiscal year, and consolidated statements of income and sources and applications of funds of the Company and its subsidiaries, if any, for such year, prepared in accordance with generally accepted accounting principles consistently applied, setting forth in each case in comparative form the figures for the previous fiscal year, all in reasonable detail, and audited in each case by independent public accountants of national standing selected by the Company, and a Company prepared comparison to the Company's operating plan for such year.

(b) As soon as practicable after the end of the first, second and third quarterly accounting periods in each fiscal year of the Company, and in any event within 45 days thereafter, an unaudited consolidated balance sheet of the Company and its subsidiaries, if any, as of the end of each such quarterly period, and unaudited consolidated statements of income and statements of cash flows of the Company and its subsidiaries, if any, for such period and for the current fiscal year to date, prepared in accordance with generally accepted accounting principles consistently applied and setting forth in comparative form the figures for the corresponding periods of the previous fiscal year and to the Company's operating plan then in effect and approved by its Board of Directors, subject to changes resulting from normal year-end audit adjustments, all in reasonable detail and certified by the principal financial or accounting officer of the Company, except that such balance sheet need not contain the notes or the end-of-period adjustments required by generally accepted accounting principles.

(c) From the date the Company becomes subject to the reporting requirements of the Exchange Act, and in lieu of the financial information required pursuant to Sections 3.1(a) and (b), copies of its annual reports on Form 10-K and its quarterly reports on Form 10-Q respectively.

3.2 Additional Information and Rights.

(a) The Company will permit any Investor, so long as such Investor (or its representative) owns at least 50,000 Shares, or such number of shares of Common Stock issued upon conversion of 50,000 or more Shares, or any combination thereof (as presently constituted and subject to subsequent adjustment for stock splits, stock dividends, reverse stock splits, recapitalizations and the like) (a "Significant Holder") (or a representative of any Significant Holder), at such Investor's expense, to visit and inspect any of the properties of the Company, including its books of account and other records (and make copies thereof and take extracts therefrom), and to discuss its affairs, finances and accounts with the Company's officers and its independent public accountants, all at such reasonable times during normal business hours as any such person may reasonably request. Notwithstanding the foregoing, the Company shall not be obligated to permit any Significant Holder to visit and inspect the Company's properties more than once in any three-month period.

(b) The provisions of Section 3.1 and this Section 3.2 shall not be in limitation of any rights which any Holder or Significant Holder may have with respect to the books and records of the Company and its subsidiaries, or to inspect their properties or discuss their affairs, finances and accounts, under the laws of the jurisdictions in which they are incorporated.

3.3 Termination of Covenants. The covenants set forth in this Section 3 shall terminate and be of no further force and effect after the time of effectiveness of the Company's first firm commitment underwritten public offering registered under the Securities Act.

3.4 Prompt Payment of Taxes, Etc. The Company will promptly pay and discharge, or cause to be paid and discharged, when due and payable, all lawful taxes, assessments and governmental charges or levies imposed upon the income, profits, property or business of the Company or any subsidiary; provided, however, that any such tax, assessment, charge or levy need not be paid if the validity thereof shall currently be contested in good faith by appropriate proceedings and if the Company shall have set aside on its books adequate reserves with respect thereto, and provided further, that the Company will pay all such taxes, assessments, charges or levies forthwith upon the commencement of proceedings to foreclose any lien which may have attached as security therefor. The Company will promptly pay or cause to be paid when due, or in conformance with customary trade terms or otherwise in accordance with policies related thereto adopted by the Company's Board of Directors, all other indebtedness incident to operations of the Company.

3.5 Maintenance of Properties and Lease. The Company will keep its properties and those of its subsidiaries in good repair, working order and condition, reasonable wear and tear excepted, and from time to time make all needful and proper repairs, renewals, replacements, additions and improvements thereto; and the Company and its subsidiaries will at all times comply with each material provision of all leases to which any of them is a party or under which any of them occupies property if the breach of such provision might have a material and adverse effect on the condition, financial or otherwise, or operations of the Company.

3.6 Accounts and Records. The Company will keep true records and books of account in which full, true and correct entries will be made of all dealings or transactions in relation to its business and affairs in accordance with generally accepted accounting principles applied on a consistent basis.

3.7 Compliance with Requirements of Governmental Authorities. The Company and all its subsidiaries shall duly observe and conform to all valid requirements of governmental authorities relating to the conduct of their businesses or to their properties or assets.

3.8 Maintenance of Corporate Existence, Etc. The Company shall maintain in full force and effect its corporate existence, rights and franchises and all licenses and other rights in or to use patents, processes, trademarks, trade names or copyrights owned or possessed by it or any subsidiary and deemed by the Company to be necessary to the conduct of their business.

3.9 Proprietary Information and Inventions Agreements. The Company will cause each person now or hereafter employed by it or any subsidiary with access to confidential information to enter into a proprietary information and inventions agreement substantially in the form approved by the Board of Directors.

3.10 Qualified Small Business. The Company will use reasonable efforts to comply with the reporting and record keeping requirements of Section 1202 of the Internal Revenue Code of 1986, as amended, and any regulations promulgated thereunder.

SECTION 4

Miscellaneous

4.1 Governing Law. This Agreement shall be governed in all respects by the laws of the State of _______, as if entered into by and between _______ residents exclusively for performance entirely within _________.

4.2 Successors and Assigns. Except as otherwise expressly provided herein, the provisions hereof shall inure to the benefit of, and be binding upon, the successors, assigns, heirs, executors and administrators of the parties hereto.

4.3 Entire Agreements Amendment; Waiver. This Agreement (including the Exhibits hereto) constitutes the full and entire understanding and agreement between the parties with regard to the subjects hereof and thereof. Neither this Agreement nor any term hereof may be amended, waived, discharged or terminated, except by a written instrument signed by the Company and the Holders of at least 50% of the Registrable Share. Any such amendment, waiver, discharge or termination shall be binding on all the Holders of Registrable Securities, but in no event shall the obligation of any Holder of Registrable Securities hereunder be materially increased, except upon the written consent of such Holder of Registrable Securities.

4.4 Notices, Etc. All notices and other communications required or permitted hereunder shall be in writing and shall be mailed by United States first-class mail, postage prepaid, or delivered personally addressed by hand or special courier (a) if to a Holder, as indicated on the list of Holders attached hereto as Exhibit A, or at such other address as such Investor or permitted assignee shall have furnished to the Company in writing, or (b) if to the Company, at The.com, Inc., ______________, attention: Chief Executive Officer, or at such other address as the Company shall have furnished to each Holder in writing. All such notices and other written communications shall be effective (i) if mailed, five days after mailing and (ii) if delivered, upon delivery.

4.5 Delays or Omissions. No delay or omission to exercise any right, power or remedy accruing to any Holder, upon any breach or default of the Company under this Agreement shall impair any such right, power or remedy of such Holder nor shall it be construed to be a waiver of any such breach or default, or an acquiescence therein, or of or in any similar breach or default thereafter occurring; nor shall any waiver of any single breach or default be deemed a waiver of any other breach or default theretofore or thereafter occurring. Any waiver, permit, consent or approval of any kind or character on the part of any Holder of any breach or default under this Agreement or any waiver on the part of any Holder of any provisions or conditions of this Agreement must be made in writing and shall be effective only to the extent specifically set forth in such writing. All remedies, either under this Agreement or by law or otherwise afforded to any Holder, shall be cumulative and not alternative.

4.6 Rights; Separability. Unless otherwise expressly provided herein, a Holder's rights hereunder are several rights, not rights jointly held with any of the other Holders. In case any provision of this Agreement shall be invalid, illegal or unenforceable, the validity, legality and enforceability of the remaining provisions shall not in any way be affected or impaired thereby.

4.7 Information Confidential. Each Holder acknowledges that the information received by it pursuant hereto is confidential and for its use only on behalf of the Company, and it will not use such confidential information in violation of the Exchange Act or reproduce, disclose or disseminate such information to any other person (other than its partners, parent, subsidiaries, employees or agents having a need to know the contents of such information, and its attorneys), except in connection with the exercise of rights under this Agreement, unless the Company or some other party other than the Holder has made such information available to the public generally, or such Holder is required to disclose such information by a governmental body (or order thereof) or pursuant to any law, statute, rule or regulation.

4.8 Titles and Subtitles. The titles of the paragraphs and subparagraphs of this Agreement are for convenience of reference only and are not to be considered in construing this Agreement.

4.9 Counterparts. This Agreement may be executed in any number of counterparts, each of which shall be an original, but all of which together shall constitute one instrument.

4.10 Expenses. If any action at law or in equity is necessary to enforce or interpret the terms of this Agreement, the prevailing party shall be entitled to reasonable attorneys' fees, costs and necessary disbursements in addition to any other relief to which such party may be entitled.

4.11 Aggregation of Stock. All shares of Registrable Securities held or acquired by affiliated entities or persons shall be aggregated together for the purpose of determining the availability of any rights under this Agreement.

4.12 Legend on Share Certificates. Each certificate representing any Shares or Registrable Securities shall be endorsed by the Company with a legend reading substantially as follows:

> "The shares evidenced hereby are subject to an Investor's Rights Agreement, dated ____________________, by and among the Issuer and the Investors (as defined therein) (the

"Agreement") (a copy of which may be obtained upon written request from the Issuer), and by accepting any interest in such shares the person accepting such interest shall be deemed to agree to and shall become bound by all the provisions of the Agreement."

IN WITNESS WHEREOF, the parties have executed this Agreement as of the date and year, first above written.

Company: Shareholders:

The.com, Inc.

By: ______________________ By: ______________________

______________________ Its: ______________________

______________________ Address: ______________________

____

____

____

EXHIBIT A

Subscriber	Number of Shares

APPENDIX L • RIGHT OF FIRST REFUSAL AND CO-SALE AGREEMENT

This Agreement is made and entered into as of ____________ __, 20__ by and among __________________, a ____________ corporation (the "Company"), those investors in the Company listed on Exhibit A attached hereto (the "Investors"), and those founders of the Company listed on Exhibit B attached hereto (the "Founders").

RECITALS

A. Each Founder currently owns that number of shares of the Company's Common Stock ("the Common Stock") and/or owns an option to purchase that number of shares of the Company's Common Stock as shown beside such Founder's name on Exhibit B attached hereto.

B. Each Investor is purchasing from the Company shares of the Company's Series A Preferred Stock ("Series A Stock") pursuant to that certain Series A Preferred Stock Purchase Agreement by and among the Company and the Investors dated as of _________ ___, ______ (the "Series A Purchase Agreement").

C. To induce the Investors to purchase such shares of Series A Stock from the Company and to enter into the Series A Purchase Agreement, each Founder has agreed to grant the Investors certain rights of first refusal and rights of co-sale with respect to the shares of the Company's Common Stock currently owned by such Founder and/or issuable upon exercise of stock options held by such Founder as set forth in Exhibit B attached hereto and any Common Stock or other Stock (as defined below) of the Company hereafter owned or acquired by such Founder, all on the terms and conditions set forth in this Agreement.

NOW, THEREFORE, in consideration of the foregoing recitals and the mutual promises herein contained, and for other consideration, the receipt and adequacy of which is hereby acknowledged, the parties hereto agree as follows:

1. **CERTAIN DEFINITIONS**. For purposes of this Agreement, the following terms have the following meanings:

1.1 "Excluded Stock" means ten percent (10%) of the shares of the Stock held by a Founder on the date of this Agreement.

1.2 "IPO" means the first sale of the Company's Common Stock to the general public pursuant to a registration statement under the Securities Act of 1933, as amended, in which the gross proceeds to the Company (without reduction for underwriter's discounts and commissions or expenses of the sale) equals or exceeds $15,000,000 at a price greater than $2.857 per share of Common Stock (such price to be proportionally adjusted to reflect stock splits, stock dividends, recapitalizations and the like).

1.3 "Offered Stock" means all Stock proposed to be Transferred by a Founder other than Excluded Stock.

1.4 "Stock" means and includes all shares of Common Stock issued and outstanding at the relevant time plus (a) all shares of Common Stock that may be issued upon exercise of any options, warrants and other rights of any kind that are then exercisable, and (b) all shares of Common Stock that may be issued upon conversion of (i) any convertible securities, other than shares of Preferred Stock, then outstanding, which are by their terms then convertible into or exchangeable for Common Stock or (ii) any such convertible securities issuable upon exercise of outstanding options, warrants or other rights that are then exercisable.

1.5 "Transfer" and "Transferred" mean and include any sale, assignment, encumbrance, hypothecation, pledge, conveyance in trust, gift, transfer by bequest, devise or descent, or other transfer or disposition of any kind, including but not limited to transfers to receivers, levying creditors, trustees or receivers in bankruptcy proceedings or general assignees for the benefit of creditors, whether voluntary or by operation of law, directly or indirectly, except for:

(a) any bona fide pledge if the pledgee executes a counterpart copy of this Agreement and becomes bound thereby as if such pledgee were a Founder;

(b) any transfers of Stock by gift during a Founder's lifetime or on a Founder's death by will or intestacy to such Founder's "immediate family" (as defined below) or to a trust for the benefit of Founder or Founder's immediate family, provided that each transferee or other recipient executes a counterpart copy of this Agreement and becomes bound thereby as a Founder. For purposes of this Agreement, the term "immediate family" means Founder's spouse, lineal descendant (whether natural or adopted) or antecedent, brother or sister, or the spouse of any of the foregoing.

(c) any transfer of Stock by a Founder made: (i) pursuant to a statutory merger or statutory consolidation of the Company with or into another corporation or corporations; (ii) pursuant to the winding up and dissolution of the Company; or (iii) at, and pursuant to, the IPO.

2. **NOTICE OF PROPOSED TRANSFER**. Before any Founder may effect any Transfer of any Stock other than Excluded Stock, such Founder (the "Selling Founder") must give at the same time to the Company and the Investors a written notice signed by the Selling Founder (the "Selling Founder's Notice") stating (a) the Selling Founder's bona fide intention to transfer such Offered Stock; (b) the number of shares of Offered Stock proposed to be transferred to each proposed purchaser or other transferee ("Proposed Transferee"); (c) the name, address and relationship, if any, to the Selling Founder of each Proposed Transferee; and (d) the bona fide cash price or, in reasonable detail, other consideration, per share for which the Selling Founder proposes to transfer such Offered Stock to each Proposed Transferee (the "Offered Price"). Upon the request of the Company or any Investor, the Founder will promptly furnish to the Company and to the Investors such other information as may be reasonably requested to establish that the offer and Proposed Transferee(s) are bona fide.

3. **RIGHT OF FIRST REFUSAL**.

3.1 Company's Right of First Refusal. Pursuant to certain Founder's Stock Purchase Agreements executed (or to be executed upon the issuance of Stock) to the Founders, the Company and its assignees have a right of first refusal (the "Company's Right of First Refusal") to purchase all of the Offered Stock, if the Company gives written notice of the exercise of such right to the Selling Founder within thirty (30) days (the "Company's Refusal Period") after the date of the Selling Founder's Notice to the Company. If the Company does not intend to exercise the Company's Right of First Refusal in full or if the Company is not lawfully able to repurchase the Offered Stock, the Company will send written notice thereof (the "Company's Expiration Notice") to the Selling Founder and to the Investors at least fifteen (15) days before the expiration of the Company's Refusal

Period. The Company's Expiration Notice will specify the Offered Stock subject to the Investors' Right of First Refusal described below.

3.2 Investors' Right of First Refusal. If the Company does not exercise its right of first refusal in full, the Investors will have a right of first refusal (the "Investors' Right of First Refusal") to purchase all of the Offered Stock not purchased by the Company. The Investors' Right of First Refusal may be exercised as follows:

(a) Each Investor desiring to purchase any or all of the Offered Stock must, within the fifteen (15) day period commencing on the date of the Company's Expiration Notice (the "Investor Refusal Period"), give written notice to the Selling Founder and to the Company of such Investor's election to purchase Offered Stock, and the number of shares and type of Offered Stock that such Investor desires to purchase. No Investor will have a right to purchase any of the Offered Stock unless the Investors, in the aggregate, exercise their collective Investors' Rights of First Refusal within the Investor Refusal Period to purchase all of the Offered Stock not purchased by the Company.

If the total number of shares specified in the elections of Investors exceeds the number of shares of Offered Stock available for purchase, then (unless the Investors agree otherwise in writing) each Investor electing to purchase will have the right to purchase that number of shares of Offered Stock that is obtained by multiplying the number of shares of Offered Stock available for purchase by a fraction (i) the numerator of which will be the number of shares of Stock then held by such Investor, and (ii) the denominator of which will be the sum of the total number of shares of Stock then held by all Investors electing to purchase the Offered Stock.

(b) Within ten (10) days after expiration of the Investor Refusal Period, the Company will give written notice (the "Investors' Expiration Notice") to the Selling Founder and the Investors specifying either (i) that all of the Offered Stock was subscribed by the Company or Investors exercising their respective Rights of First Refusal or (ii) that all of the Offered Stock is available for purchase by the Investors pursuant to the Right of Co-Sale (as defined below), in which case the Investors' Expiration Notice will specify each Investor's pro rata share of the Offered Stock available for purchase pursuant to such Right of Co-Sale.

3.3 Purchase Price. The purchase price for the Offered Stock to be purchased by the Company or by an Investor exercising its respective Right of First Refusal under this Agreement will be the Offered Price (subject, in the case of the Company, to any rights the Company may have under any Restricted Stock Purchase Agreement to purchase all or some of such Offered Stock at a lower price), and will be payable as set forth in Section 3.4 hereof. If the Offered Price includes consideration other than cash, the cash equivalent value of the non-cash consideration will be determined by the Board of Directors of the Company in good faith, which determination will be binding upon the Company, the Investors and the Selling Founder absent fraud or error.

3.4 Payment. Payment of the purchase price for Offered Stock purchased by the Company or by an Investor exercising its respective Right of First Refusal will be made within ten (10) days after the date of the Investors' Expiration Notice. Payment of the purchase price will made, at the option of the Company or, as the case may be, by an Investor, (a) in cash (by check), (b) by cancellation of all or a portion of any outstanding indebtedness of the Selling Founder to the Company or such Investor, as the case may be, or (c) by any combination of the foregoing.

3.5 Rights of Founder. Upon the date that payment is made for the Offered Stock purchased by the Company and/or the Investors pursuant to their respective Rights of First Refusal hereunder, the Selling Founder will have no further rights as a holder of such Offered Stock and the Selling Founder will forthwith cause all certificate(s) evidencing such Offered Stock to be surrendered to the Company for cancellation, and, as to purchase by Investor(s), for transfer to the purchasing Investor(s).

3.6 Selling Founder's Right to Transfer. If the Investors have not elected pursuant to their Investors' Right of First Refusal to purchase all of the Offered Stock not purchased by the Company, then, subject to the Right of Co-Sale, the Selling Founder may transfer that portion of the Offered Stock permitted to be sold by the Selling Founder to any person named as a Proposed Transferee in the Selling Founder's Notice, at the Offered Price or at a higher price, provided that such transfer (a) is consummated within one hundred twenty (120) days after the date of the Selling Founder's Notice and (b) is in accordance with the terms and conditions of this

Agreement. If the Offered Stock is transferred in accordance with the terms and conditions of this Agreement, then the transferee(s) of the Offered Stock will (other than as provided as to certain transferees required to become parties hereto as provided in Section 1.4 hereof) thereafter hold such Offered Stock free of the Investors' Right of First Refusal, the Right of Co-Sale and all other restrictions imposed by this Agreement; provided that nothing herein will release any such transferee from any obligations or restrictions that may be imposed on such transferee under any Restricted Stock Purchase Agreement. If the Offered Stock is not so transferred during such one hundred twenty (120) day period, then the Selling Founder will not transfer any of such Offered Stock without complying again in full with the provisions of this Agreement.

4. RIGHT OF CO-SALE.

4.1 Right of Co-Sale. Whether or not the Company and Investors have waived or failed to timely exercise their Rights of First Refusal to purchase all of the Offered Stock, each Investor will have the right to participate in the sale of any Offered Stock (the "Remaining-Offered Stock") in the manner set forth herein (the "Right of Co-Sale"). Pursuant to this Section 4, each Investor may transfer to the Proposed Transferee(s) identified in the Selling Founder's Notice (or to the Company or Investors in the event they exercise their right to buy) such Investor's pro rata share of the Remaining Offered Stock (other than any Excluded Stock), by giving written notice to the Selling Founder within ten (10) days after the date of the Investors' Expiration Notice; specifying the number of shares and type of Stock that such Investor desires to transfer to each Proposed Transferee by exercising the Right of Co-Sale. For purposes of this Agreement, an Investor's "pro rata share" will be defined as a fraction, the numerator of which is the number of shares of Stock then owned by such Investor, and the denominator of which is the number of shares of Stock then owned by all Investors having a Right of Co-Sale hereunder plus the number of shares of Stock held by the Selling Founder who proposes the Transfer.

4.2 Consummation of Co-Sale. Each Investor, in exercising the Right of Co-Sale, may effect such Investor's participation in such Transfer by delivering to the Selling Founder at the closing of the transfer of Offered Stock to such transferee (the "Closing") one or more certificates, properly endorsed for Transfer, representing such

Stock to be transferred by such Investor. At the Closing, such certificates or other instruments will be transferred and delivered to the Proposed Transferee(s) set forth in the Selling Founders Notice in consummation of the Transfer of the Offered Stock pursuant to the terms and conditions specified in the Selling Founder's Notice, and the Founder will remit, or will cause to be remitted, to Investor within seven (7) days after such Closing that portion of the proceeds of the Transfer to which Investor is entitled by reason of such Investor's participation in such transfer pursuant to the Right of Co-Sale.

5. **MULTIPLE SERIES, CLASSES OR TYPES OF STOCK**. If the Remaining Offered Stock consists of more than one series or class or type of Stock, each Investor has the right to purchase or transfer hereunder, as the case may be, such Investor's pro rata share of each such series, class or type of Stock; provided, however, that as to the Right of Co-Sale, (a) if such Investor does not hold any of such series, class, or type of Stock, and the Proposed Transferee is not willing, at the Closing, to purchase some other series, class or type of Stock from such Investor as part of such Investor's pro rata share, or (b) if the Proposed Transferee is unwilling to purchase any Stock from such Investor at the Closing (each such circumstance being referred to herein as an "Incomplete Co-Sale"), then such Investor will have the put right (the "Put Right") set forth in Section 6.2 hereof.

6. **REFUSAL TO TRANSFER: PUT RIGHT**.

6.1 Refusal to Transfer. Any attempt by any Selling Founder to transfer any Stock in violation of any provision of this Agreement will be void. The Company will not (a) transfer on its books any Stock that has been sold, gifted or otherwise transferred in violation of this Agreement, or (b) treat as owner of such Stock, or accord the right to vote to or pay dividends to any purchaser, donee or other transferee to whom such Stock may have been so transferred.

6.2 Put Right. If a Selling Founder transfers any Stock in contravention of an Investor's Right of Co-Sale under this Agreement (a "Prohibited Transfer"), or if an Incomplete Co-Sale occurs and the provisions of Section 5 hereof apply, the relevant Investor may require such Selling Founder to purchase from such Investor, for cash or such other consideration as the Selling Founder received in the Prohibited Transfer or Incomplete Co-Sale, that number of shares of Stock (of the same class, series or type as transferred in the Prohibited Transfer or Incomplete Co-Sale, if such Investor then owns Stock of such class, series or type, and otherwise of Common Stock) having a purchase price equal to the aggregate purchase price such Investor would have received in the Closing of such Prohibited Transfer or Incomplete Co-Sale if such Investor had exercised and been able to consummate such Investor's Right of Co-Sale with respect thereto (the Investor's "Put Right"). An Investor may exercise such Investor's Put Right by delivery of written notice to the Selling Founder and the Company (a "Put Notice") within ten (10) days after such Investor becomes aware of the Prohibited Transfer or Incomplete Co-Sale. The closing of such sale to the Selling Founder under such Investor's Put Right will occur within seven (7) days after the date of such Investor's Put Notice.

7. **RESTRICTIVE LEGEND AND STOP-TRANSFER ORDERS**.

7.1 Legend. Each Founder understands and agrees that the Company will cause the legend set forth below, or a legend substantially equivalent thereto, to be placed upon any certificate(s) or other documents or instruments evidencing ownership of Stock by the Founder:

> THE SHARES REPRESENTED BY THIS CERTIFICATE ARE SUBJECT TO CERTAIN RIGHTS OF FIRST REFUSAL AND RIGHTS OF CO-SALE AS SET FORTH IN A RIGHT OF FIRST REFUSAL AND CO-SALE AGREEMENT ENTERED INTO BY THE HOLDER OF THESE SHARES, THE COMPANY AND CERTAIN FOUNDERS OF THE COMPANY. A COPY OF SUCH AGREEMENT IS ON FILE AT THE PRINCIPAL OFFICE OF THE COMPANY. SUCH RIGHTS OF FIRST REFUSAL AND RIGHTS OF CO-SALE ARE BINDING ON TRANSFEREES OF THESE SHARES.

7.2 Stop Transfer Instructions. Each Founder agrees, to ensure compliance with the restrictions referred to herein, that the Company may issue appropriate "stop transfer" certificates or instructions and that, if the Company transfers its own securities, it may make appropriate notations to the same effect in its records.

8. **ESCROW**. As security for the faithful performance of this Agreement, each Founder agrees to immediately deliver all certificate(s) evidencing such Founder's Stock (whether now owned or hereafter acquired by each Founder), together with a stock power for each certificate in the form of Exhibit C attached hereto, or such comparable instrument as the Company reasonably may request, executed by such Founder and his or her spouse (with the date and number of shares of Stock left blank), to the President of the Company or the President's designee (the "Escrow Holder"), who is hereby appointed to hold such certificate(s) and stock power(s) in escrow and to take all such actions and to effectuate all such transfers and/or releases of such Stock as are in accordance with this Agreement. Upon marriage or remarriage of a Founder, so long as he or she still holds Stock, such Founder will deliver to the Escrow Holder a new stock power, or comparable instrument, executed by such Founder and his or her new spouse. Each party hereto agrees that the Escrow Holder: (a) is an intended third party beneficiary of this Section 8, (b) will not be liable to any party to this Agreement (or to any other party) for any actions or omissions except for willful misconduct in violation of this Agreement and (c) may rely upon any letter, notice or other document executed by any signature purported to be genuine and may rely on advice of counsel and obey any order of any court with respect to the transactions contemplated herein. The Stock will be released from escrow hereunder as necessary to effect the Right of First Refusal and Right of Co-Sale and upon termination of both the Right of First Refusal and Right of Co-Sale.

9. **TERMINATION AND WAIVER.**

9.1 Termination. The Investor's Right of First Refusal and Right of Co-Sale will terminate upon the earliest to occur of the following: (a) immediately prior to the closing of the IPO; or (b) the date on which this Agreement is terminated by a writing executed by the Company and holders of a majority of the voting power of the Stock then held by all Investors.

9.2 Waiver. The application of the Right of First Refusal and/or Right of Co-Sale of an Investor as to any proposed Transfer by a Selling Founder of any Stock may be waived in advance of or after such transfer by the written agreement of the Investors holding a majority of the voting power of the Stock then held by all Investors, in which case such waiver will be binding as to all Investors.

The Company and the Investors will have the absolute right to exercise or refrain from exercising any right or rights that each such party may have by reason of this Agreement, including without limitation the right to purchase or participate in the sale of Offered Stock. Neither the Company nor any Investor will incur any liability to any other party hereto with respect to exercising or refraining from exercising any such right or rights. Any waiver by a party of its rights hereunder will be effective only if evidenced by a written instrument executed by such party or its authorized representative.

10. **MISCELLANEOUS PROVISIONS**.

10.1 Notices. Any notice required or permitted to be given to a party pursuant to the provisions of this Agreement will be in writing and will be effective and deemed given to such party under this Agreement on the earliest of the following: (a) the date of personal delivery; (b) one (1) business day after transmission by facsimile or telecopier, addressed to the other party at its facsimile number or telecopier address, with confirmation of transmission; (c) one (1) business day after deposit with a return receipt express courier for United States deliveries, or three (3) business days after such deposit for deliveries outside of the United States; or (d) three (3) business days after deposit in the United States mail by registered or certified mail (return receipt requested) for United States deliveries. All notices not delivered personally or by facsimile will be sent with postage and/or other charges prepaid and properly addressed to the party to be notified at the address set forth below such party's signature on this Agreement or on Exhibit A hereto, or at such other address as such other party may designate by ten (10) days advance written notice to the other parties hereto. All notices for delivery outside the United States will be sent by facsimile or by express courier. Any notice given hereunder to more than one person will be deemed to have been given, for purposes of counting time periods hereunder, on the date effectively given to the last party required to be given such notice. Notices to the Company will be marked "Attention: President."

10.2 Assignment. Inclusion Within Certain Definitions. The rights granted to the Investor pursuant to this Agreement may be assigned by an Investor upon sale or transfer by such Investor of at least 2,000,000 shares of Series A Stock and/or shares of Common Shares issued upon conversion thereof (as adjusted to reflect stock splits, stock dividends, recapitalizations and the like), provided that any transferee shall agree to become subject to the obligations of the transferring party hereunder. Such rights may not be assigned to a transferee which the Company reasonably believes is a competitor or intends to become a competitor of the Company. Notwithstanding the foregoing, any Investor may transfer rights granted pursuant to this Agreement to a transferee if such transferee is an affiliate (as such term is defined in Rule 405 promulgated under the Securities Act) of such Investor. Any permitted transferee of a Investor who is required to become a party hereto will be considered a "Investor" for purposes of this Agreement without the need for any consent, approval or signature of any party hereto. Any permitted transferee of a Founder who is required to become a party hereto will be considered a "Founder" for purposes of this Agreement without the need for any consent, approval or signature of any party hereto.

10.3 Severability. If any provision of this Agreement is held to be invalid, illegal or unenforceable in any respect, such provision will be enforced to the maximum extent possible and such invalidity, illegality or unenforceability will not affect any other provision of this Agreement, and this Agreement will be construed as if such invalid, illegal or unenforceable provision had (to the extent not enforceable) never been contained herein.

10.4 Amendment. This Agreement may be amended only by a written instrument executed by the Company, Investors holding at least fifty percent (50%) of the Stock then held by all Investors and Founders holding at least a majority of the Stock then held by all Founders, provided, that any amendment that treats any Founder in a materially adverse manner that is different from any other Founder shall require the separate approval of such Founder. If an Investor sells or transfers some or all of such Investor's Stock, then any transferee of such Investor shall be entitled to all rights under this Agreement as such Investor would have if Investor owned the Stock so transferred.

10.5 Governing Law. This Agreement will be governed by and construed in accordance with the internal laws of the State of _______________, excluding that body of law pertaining to conflict of laws.

10.6 Obligation of Company; Binding Nature of Exercise. The Company agrees to use its best efforts to enforce the terms of this Agreement, to inform each Investor of any breach hereof (to the extent the Company has knowledge thereof) and to assist each Investor in the exercise of such Investor's rights and performance of such Investor's obligations hereunder.

10.7 Counterparts. This Agreement may be executed in any number of counterparts, each of which when so executed and delivered will be deemed an original, and all such counterparts together will constitute one and the same instrument.

10.8 Entire Agreement. This Agreement, including all Exhibits hereto, each of which is incorporated herein by reference, constitutes the entire agreement of the parties with respect to the specific subject matter hereof and supersedes in their entirety all other agreements or understandings between or among the parties hereto with respect to such specific subject matter.

10.9 Conflict. In the event of any conflict between the terms of this Agreement and the Company's Articles of Incorporation or its Bylaws, the terms of the Company's Articles of Incorporation or its Bylaws, as the case may be, will control. In the event of any conflict between the terms of this Agreement and any other agreement to which an Investor is a party or by which the Selling Founder is bound, the terms of this Agreement will control, except insofar as this Agreement provides otherwise with respect to any Restricted Stock Purchase Agreement. In the event of any conflict between the Company's books and records and this Agreement or any notice delivered hereunder, the Company's books and records will control absent fraud or error.

10.10 Calculation; Binding Effect of Company Notices. All calculations of an Investor's pro rata share will be made by the Company as of the date of the Company's notice in which such pro rata share appears. The pro rata share of an Investor as shown on any notice required hereunder to be delivered by the Company will be binding upon the parties hereto absent fraud or error.

10.11 Headings. The captions and headings of this Agreement are included for ease of reference only and will be disregarded in interpreting or construing this Agreement. Unless otherwise stated, all references herein to Sections and Exhibits will refer to Sections of and Exhibits to this Agreement.

10.12 Continuity of Other Restrictions. Any Stock not purchased by the Company or an Investor under its respective Right of First Refusal hereunder will continue to be subject to all other restrictions, including rights of first refusal, imposed upon such Stock by law, including any restrictions imposed under the Company's Articles of Incorporation or Bylaws, or by agreement.

IN WITNESS WHEREOF, the parties have executed this Agreement as of the day and year first above written.

____

By: ______________________________

FOUNDERS: ________________________

INVESTORS: ________________________

By: ______________________________

Name: ____________________________

Its: _______________________________

EXHIBIT A

THE INVESTORS

Name and Address of Purchaser	No. of Shares of Preferred	Aggregate Purchase Price
____________________		$
TOTAL		$

EXHIBIT B

THE FOUNDERS

Name and Address of Founder	No. of Shares of Common Stock
TOTAL	

EXHIBIT C

STOCK POWER

APPENDIX M • AMENDED AND RESTATED ARTICLES OF INCORPORATION

Amended and Restated Articles of Incorporation of ________________, Inc.

The undersigned, ________ and ______________, hereby certify that:

1. They are the President and Secretary, respectively, of __________, Inc., a __________ corporation (the "Corporation").

2. The Amended and Restated Articles of Incorporation of the Corporation have been approved by the Corporation's Board of Directors.

3. The Amended and Restated Article of Incorporation of the Corporation have been approved by the required vote of the Corporation's shareholders in accordance with Section ___ of the Corporations Code of ___________. The Corporation has one class of voting stock. Each share is entitled to one vote. The total number of outstanding shares entitled to vote with respect to the foregoing amendment is __________. The amendment was approved by the required vote of the shareholders, in that ___________ shares or over 50 percent of the outstanding vote was obtained.

4. The Articles of Incorporation of this Corporation are amended and restated, in accordance with Section ___ of the Corporations Code of ______, in their entirety to read as follows:

I.

The name of this Corporation is ________, Inc.

II.

The purpose of this Corporation is to engage in any lawful act or activity for which a corporation may be organized under the Corporation Law of ________ other than the banking business, the trust company business, or the practice of a profession permitted to be incorporated by the _____________ Corporations Code.

III.

(a) The Corporation is authorized to issue two classes of shares to be designated respectively Common Stock ("Common Stock") and Preferred Stock ("Preferred Stock"). The total number of shares of Common Stock this Corporation shall have authority to issue is Fifty Million (50,000,000) shares and the total number of shares of Preferred Stock this Corporation shall have the authority to issue is Twenty Million (20,000,000). The Preferred Stock may be issued from time to time in one or more series. The first series of Preferred Stock shall be designated Series A Preferred Stock ("Series A Preferred") and shall consist of Four Million Eight Hundred Sixty-One Thousand Two Hundred Eighty Six (4,861,286) shares. The board of directors of the Corporation (the "Board") is hereby authorized within the limitations and restrictions stated in these Articles of Incorporation, to (i) determine or alter the rights, preferences, privileges and restrictions granted to or imposed upon any wholly unissued series of preferred stock other than the Series A Preferred, the number constituting any such series and the designation thereof, or any of them; and (ii) increase or decrease the number of shares of that series, but not below the number of any series then outstanding.

(b) The Corporation shall from time to time in accordance with the laws of the State of ______________ increase the authorized amount of its Common Stock if at any time the number of shares of Common Stock remaining unissued and available for issuance shall not be sufficient to permit conversion of the Series A Preferred.

(c) The issuance of any non-voting equity securities is prohibited.

(d) The relative rights, preferences, and restrictions granted to or imposed on the respective classes of the shares of capital stock or the holders thereof are as follows:

1. <u>**Dividends**</u>. The holders of the Series A Preferred shall be entitled to receive dividends at the rate of $0.0514 per share per annum (as adjusted for any stock dividends, combinations or splits with respect to such shares), payable out of funds legally available therefor. Such dividends shall be non-cumulative and shall be payable only when and as declared by the Board; provided, however, that if the Series A Preferred has not been automatically converted into

Common Stock pursuant to Section 3(b) below by the date which is two (2) years after the first share of Series A Preferred is issued, such dividends shall begin to accumulate from that date (the "Accumulation Date"). If in any year, or years, following the Accumulation Date dividends on the outstanding Series A Preferred at the rate specified are not paid or set apart for the purpose, the amount of the deficiency shall be fully paid or declared and set apart for payment, without interest, before any distribution, by way of dividend or otherwise, is declared, paid, or set apart for shares of Common Stock. The holders of Series A Preferred shall have a dividend preference and no dividends shall be declared and paid with respect to the Common Stock at a rate per share greater than the rate per share at which dividends are paid on the outstanding Series A Preferred.

2. **Liquidation Rights**. In the event of any liquidation, dissolution, or winding up of the Corporation, either voluntary or involuntary (the "Liquidation Event"), distributions to the shareholders of the Corporation shall be made in the following manner:

(a) Liquidation Preference. The holders of the Series A Preferred shall be entitled to receive, prior and in preference to any distribution of any assets of the Corporation to the holders of the Common Stock by reason of their ownership thereof, an amount per share equal to the Liquidation Preference Amount (as defined below), plus any prior declared or accumulated but unpaid dividends on such share of the Series A Preferred. As used herein, the Liquidation Preference Amount shall be (i) $1.028, if the Liquidation Event shall occur on or before the Accumulation Date, or (ii) $1.285, if the Liquidation Event shall occur after the Accumulation Date. The Liquidation Preference Amount set forth in the previous sentence shall be appropriately adjusted for any stock dividends, combinations or splits with respect to such shares. If upon the occurrence of a Liquidation Event, the assets and funds thus distributed among the holders of the Series A Preferred shall be insufficient to permit the payment to such holders of the full aforesaid preferential amount, then the entire assets and funds of the Corporation legally available for distribution shall be distributed among the holders of the Series A Preferred in proportion to the shares of Series A Preferred then held by them.

(b) Distribution of Remaining Assets. After payment to the holders of the Series A Preferred of the amount set forth in Section 2(a) above, the entire remaining assets and funds of the Corporation legally available for distribution, if any, shall be distributed among the holders of the Common Stock and the Series A Preferred in proportion to the shares of Common Stock then held by them and the shares of Common Stock which they then have the right to acquire upon conversion of the shares of Series A Preferred then held by them.

(c) Deemed Liquidation. For purposes of this Section 2, a liquidation, dissolution or winding up of the Corporation shall be deemed to occur if the Corporation shall sell, convey, or otherwise dispose of or encumber all or substantially all of its property or business or merge into or consolidate with any other corporation (other than a wholly-owned subsidiary corporation) or effect any other transaction or series of related transactions in which more than fifty percent (50%) of the voting power of the Corporation is disposed of, provided that this Section 2(c) shall not apply to a merger effected exclusively for the purpose of changing the domicile of the Corporation. For purposes of this section in determining a "change of control", unrelated offerings or issuances shall not be cumulative. Notwithstanding the above, if the Series A Preferred consents to such transaction, then such consolidation, merger or sale of assets shall not be treated as a liquidation, dissolution or winding up.

(d) Valuation of Consideration. In the event of a deemed liquidation as described in Section 2(c) above, if the consideration received by the Corporation is other than cash, its value will be deemed its fair market value. Any securities shall be valued as follows:

(A) Securities not subject to investment letter or other similar restrictions on free marketability: (1) If traded on a securities exchange, Nasdaq or actively over the counter, the value shall be the higher of the closing price of the securities on such exchange on the day of the execution of the agreement setting forth the terms of the liquidation or the closing of such transaction; and (2) If there is no active public market, the value shall be the fair market value thereof, as mutually determined by the Board and approved by the holders of at least a majority of the then outstanding shares of Series A Preferred.

(B) The method of valuation of securities subject to investment letter or other restrictions on free marketability (other than restrictions arising solely by virtue of a shareholder's status as an affiliate or former affiliate) shall be to make an appropriate discount from the market value determined as above in Section 2(d)(A) to reflect the approximate fair market value thereof, as mutually determined by the Corporation and approved by the holders of at least a majority of the then outstanding shares of Series A Preferred.

(e) Notice of Transaction. The Corporation shall give each holder of record of Series A Preferred written notice of such impending transaction not later than ten (10) days prior to the shareholders' meeting called to approve such transaction, or ten (10) days prior to the closing of such transaction, whichever is earlier, and shall also notify such holders in writing of the final approval of such transaction. The first of such notices shall describe the material terms and conditions of the impending transaction and the provisions of this Section 2, and the Corporation shall thereafter give such holders prompt notice of any material changes. The transaction shall in no event take place sooner than ten (10) days after the Corporation has given the first notice provided for herein or sooner than ten (10) days after the Corporation has given notice of any material changes provided for herein; provided, however, that such periods may be shortened upon the written consent of the holders of Series A Preferred that are entitled to such notice rights or similar notice rights and that represent at least a majority of the then outstanding shares of Series A Preferred.

(f) Effect of Noncompliance. In the event that the Corporation fails to comply with the requirements of this Section 2, the Corporation shall forthwith either cause the closing of the transaction to be postponed until such requirements have been complied with, or cancel such transaction, in which event the rights, preferences and privileges of the holders of the Series A Preferred shall revert to and be the same as such rights, preferences and privileges existing immediately prior to the date of the first notice referred to in Section 2(e) hereof.

3. **Conversion**. The holders of the Series A Preferred shall have conversion rights as follows (the "Conversion Rights"):

(a) Right to Convert. Each share of Series A Preferred shall be convertible, at the option of the holder thereof, at any time after the date of issuance of such shares, at the principal office of the Corporation or any transfer agent for the Corporation, into such number of fully paid and nonassessable shares of Common Stock as is determined by dividing $1.028 by the Conversion Price applicable to such share, determined as hereafter provided, in effect on the earlier of the date the certificate is surrendered for conversion or the occurrence of the event causing the conversion. The initial Conversion Price per share shall be $1.028 for shares of Series A Preferred. Such initial Conversion Price shall be subject to adjustment as set forth in Section 3(d) below.

(b) Automatic Conversion. Each share of the Series A Preferred shall automatically be converted into shares of Common Stock at the Conversion Price at the time in effect for such share immediately upon the earlier of (i) the closing of a firm commitment underwritten public offering pursuant to an effective registration statement under the Securities Act of 1933, as amended, covering the offer and sale of Common Stock for the account of the Corporation to the public at a per share price not less than $5.14 per share (appropriately adjusted for any stock split, dividend, combination or other recapitalization), with gross proceeds to the Company of more than $10,000,000, (ii) the date specified by written consent or agreement of the holders of a majority of the then outstanding shares of Series A Preferred, or (iii) the date that at least a majority of the originally issued shares of Series A Preferred have been converted into shares of Common Stock.

(c) Mechanics of Conversion. Except as set forth in Section 3(b), before any holder of Series A Preferred shall be entitled to convert the same into shares of Common Stock and to receive certificates therefor, the holder shall surrender the certificate or certificates therefor, duly endorsed, at the office of the Corporation or of any transfer agent for the Series A Preferred, and shall give written notice to the Corporation at such office that the holder elects to convert the same. The Corporation shall, as soon as practicable after such delivery, issue and deliver at such office to such holder of Series A Preferred, a certificate or certificates for the number of shares of Common Stock to which the holder shall be entitled as the result of a conversion into shares of Common Stock. Such conversion shall be deemed to have been made immediately prior to the close of business on the earlier of the date of such surrender of the shares of such Series A Preferred to be converted or the event causing conversion, and the person or persons entitled to receive the shares of Common Stock issuable upon conversion shall be treated for all purposes as the record holder or holders of such shares of Common Stock as of such date. If the conversion is in connection with an underwritten offering of securities registered pursuant to the Securities Act the conversion may, at the option of any holder tendering such Series A Preferred for conversion, be conditioned upon the closing with the underwriters of the sale of securities pursuant to such offering, in which event the person(s) entitled to receive Common Stock upon conversion of such Series A Preferred shall not be deemed to have converted such Series A Preferred until immediately prior to the closing of such sale of securities.

(d) Conversion Price Adjustments of Preferred Stock for Certain Dilutive Issuances, Splits and Combinations. The Conversion Price of the Series A Preferred shall be subject to adjustment from time to time as follows:

(i) Issuance of Additional Stock below Purchase Price. If the Corporation shall issue, after the date upon which any shares of Series A Preferred were first issued (the "Purchase Date"), any Additional Stock (as defined below) for a consideration per share less than the Conversion Price for the Series A Preferred in effect immediately prior to the issuance of such Additional Stock, the Conversion Price for the Series A Preferred in effect immediately prior to each such issuance shall unless otherwise provided automatically be adjusted as set forth in this Section 3(d).

(ii) Adjustment Formula. Whenever the Conversion Price is adjusted pursuant to this Section 3(d), the new Conversion Price shall be the number determined by multiplying number of shares of Common Stock Outstanding ("CSO") prior to the issuance by the original conversion price ("OCP"); plus the number of additional shares ("AS") issued times the price for the additional shares ("ASP"); and dividing such number by the number of shares of Common Stock Outstanding plus the number of additional shares as set forth below.

$$\frac{(CSO)(OCP) + (AS)(ASP)}{CSO + AS} = \text{New Conversion Price}$$

(A) Definition of "Additional Stock". For purposes of this Section 3(d), "Additional Stock" shall mean any shares of Common Stock issued by the Corporation after the Purchase Date, including Common Stock issued as a result of the conversion of preferred stock or the exercise of options, warrants, or other rights, other than (1) Common Stock issued pursuant to a transaction described in Section 3(d)(ii) hereof, (2) Shares of Common Stock issuable or issued to employees, consultants or directors of the Corporation directly or pursuant to a stock option plan or restricted stock plan approved by the Board, (3) Capital stock, or options or warrants to purchase capital stock, issued to financial institutions or lessors in connection with commercial credit arrangements, equipment financings or similar transactions, the terms of which are unanimously approved by the Board of Directors of the Corporation, (4) Capital stock or warrants or options to purchase capital stock issued in connection with bona fide acquisitions, mergers or similar transactions, the terms of which are unanimously approved by the Board of Directors of the Corporation, (5) Shares of Common Stock issued or issuable upon conversion of the Series A Preferred, and (6) Shares of Common Stock issued or issuable in a public offering prior to or in connection with which all outstanding shares of Series A Preferred will be converted to Common Stock.

(B) <u>No Fractional Adjustments</u>. No adjustment of the Conversion Price for the Series A Preferred shall be made in an amount less than one cent per share, provided that any adjustments which are not required to be made by reason of this sentence shall be carried forward and shall be either taken into account in any subsequent adjustment made prior to three years from the date of the event giving rise to the adjustment being carried forward, or shall be made at the end of three years from the date of the event giving rise to the adjustment being carried forward.

(C) <u>Determination of Consideration</u>. In the case of the issuance of Common Stock for cash, the consideration shall be deemed to be the amount of cash paid therefor before deducting any reasonable discounts, commissions or other expenses allowed, paid or incurred by the Corporation for any underwriting or otherwise in connection with the issuance and sale thereof. In the case of the issuance of the Common Stock for a consideration in whole or in part other than cash, the consideration other than cash shall be deemed to be the fair value thereof as determined by the Board of Directors irrespective of any accounting treatment.

(D) <u>No Increased Conversion Price</u>. Notwithstanding any other provisions of this Section 3(d), except as set forth below, no adjustment of the Conversion Price pursuant to this Section 3(d) shall have the effect of increasing the Conversion Price above the Conversion Price in effect immediately prior to such adjustment.

(1) Stock Splits and Dividends. In the event the Corporation should at any time, or from time to time, after the Purchase Date fix a record date for the effectuation of a split or subdivision of the outstanding shares of Common Stock or the determination of holders of Common Stock entitled to receive a dividend or other distribution payable in additional shares of Common Stock or other securities or rights convertible into, or entitling the holder thereof to receive directly or indirectly, additional shares of Common Stock (hereinafter referred to as "Common Stock Equivalents") without payment of any consideration by such holder for the additional shares of Common Stock or the Common Stock Equivalents (including the additional shares of Common Stock issuable upon conversion or exercise thereof), then, as of such record date (or the date of such dividend distribution, split or subdivision if no record date is fixed), the Conversion Price of the Series A Preferred shall be appropriately decreased so that the number of shares of Common Stock issuable on conversion of each share of such Series A Preferred shall be increased in proportion to such increase of the aggregate of shares of Common Stock outstanding and those issuable with respect to such Common Stock Equivalents with the number of shares issuable with respect to Common Stock Equivalents determined from time to time in the manner provided for deemed issuances in Section 3(d)(i)(A).

(2) Reverse Stock Splits. If the number of shares of Common Stock outstanding at any time after the Purchase Date is decreased by a combination of the outstanding shares of Common Stock, then, following the record date of such combination, the Conversion Price for the Series A Preferred shall be appropriately increased so that the number of shares of Common Stock issuable on conversion of each share of such Series A Preferred shall be decreased in proportion to such decrease in outstanding shares.

(E) Deemed Issuances of Additional Stock. In the case of the issuance (on or after the date hereof) of options to purchase or rights to subscribe for Common Stock, securities by their terms convertible into or exchangeable for Common Stock or options to purchase or rights to subscribe for such convertible or exchangeable securities all or any of which constitute Additional Stock, the following provisions shall apply for all purposes of this Section 3(d):

(1) The aggregate maximum number of shares of Common Stock deliverable upon exercise (assuming the satisfaction of any conditions to exercisability, including without limitation, the passage of time, but without taking into account potential antidilution adjustments) of such options to purchase or rights to subscribe for Common Stock shall be deemed to have been issued at the time such options or rights were issued and for a consideration equal to the consideration (determined in the manner provided in Section 3(d) if any, received by the Corporation upon the issuance of such options or rights plus the minimum exercise price provided in such options or rights (without taking into account potential antidilution adjustments) for the Common Stock covered thereby.

(2) The aggregate maximum number of shares of Common Stock deliverable upon conversion of or in exchange (assuming the satisfaction of any conditions to convertibility or exchangeability, including, without limitation, the passage of time, but without taking into account potential antidilution adjustments) for any such convertible or exchangeable securities or upon the exercise of options to purchase or rights to subscribe for such convertible or exchangeable securities and subsequent conversion or exchange thereof shall be deemed to have been issued at the time such securities were issued or such options or rights were issued and for a consideration equal to the consideration, if any, received by the Corporation for any such securities and related options or rights (excluding any cash received on account of accrued interest or accrued dividends), plus the minimum additional consideration, if any, to be received by the Corporation (without taking into account potential antidilution adjustments) upon the conversion or exchange of such securities or the exercise of any related options or rights (the consideration in each case to be determined in the manner provided in Sections 3(d)(i)(E)).

(3) In the event of any change in the number of shares of Common Stock deliverable or in the consideration payable to the Corporation upon exercise of such options or rights or upon conversion of or in exchange for such convertible or exchangeable securities, including, but not limited to, a change resulting from the antidilution provisions thereof, the Conversion Price of the Series A Preferred, to the extent in any way affected by or computed using such options, rights or securities, shall be recomputed to reflect such change, but no further adjustment shall be made for the actual issuance of Common Stock or any payment of

such consideration upon the exercise of any such options or rights or the conversion or exchange of such securities.

(4) Upon the expiration of any such options or rights, the termination of any such rights to convert or exchange or the expiration of any options or rights related to such convertible or exchangeable securities, the Conversion Price of the Series A Preferred, to the extent in any way affected by or computed using such options, rights or securities or options or rights related to such securities, shall be recomputed to reflect the issuance of only the number of shares of Common Stock (and convertible or exchangeable securities which remain in effect) actually issued upon the exercise of such options or rights, upon the conversion or exchange of such securities or upon the exercise of the options or rights related to such securities.

(5) The number of shares of Common Stock deemed issued and the consideration deemed paid therefor pursuant to Sections 3(d)(i)(E)(1) and 3(d)(i)(E)(2) shall be appropriately adjusted to reflect any change, termination or expiration of the type described in either Section 3(d)(i)(E)(3) or 3(d)(i)(E)(4).

(e) Other Distributions. In the event the Corporation shall declare a distribution payable in securities of other persons, evidences of indebtedness issued by the Corporation or other persons, assets (excluding cash dividends) or options or rights not referred to in Section 3(d)(ii), then, in each such case for the purpose of this Section 3(e), the holders of Series A Preferred shall be entitled to a proportionate share of any such distribution as though they were the holders of the number of shares of Common Stock of the Corporation into which their shares of Series A Preferred are convertible as of the record date fixed for the determination of the holders of Common Stock of the Corporation entitled to receive such distribution.

(f) Recapitalizations. If at any time or from time to time there shall be a recapitalization of the Common Stock (other than a subdivision, combination or merger or sale of assets transaction provided for elsewhere in this Section 3 or Section 2) provision shall be made so that the holders of the Series A Preferred shall thereafter be entitled to receive upon conversion of such Series A Preferred the number of shares of stock or other securities or property of the Corporation or otherwise, to which a holder of Common Stock deliverable upon conversion would have been entitled on such recapitalization. In any such case, appropriate adjustment shall be made in the application of the provisions of this Section 3 with respect to the rights of the holders of the Series A Preferred after the recapitalization to the end that the provisions of this Section 4 (including adjustment of the Conversion Price then in effect and the number of shares purchasable upon conversion of the Series A Preferred) shall be applicable after that event and be as nearly equivalent as practicable.

(g) No Impairment. The Corporation will not, by amendment of its Articles of Incorporation or through any reorganization, recapitalization, transfer of assets, consolidation, merger, dissolution, issue or sale of securities or any other voluntary action, avoid or seek to avoid the observance or performance of any of the terms to be observed or performed hereunder by the Corporation, but will at all times in good faith assist in the carrying out of all the provisions of this Section 4 and in the taking of all such action as may be necessary or appropriate in order to protect the Conversion Rights of the holders of the Series A Preferred against impairment.

(h) No Fractional Shares and Certificate as to Adjustments.

(i) No fractional shares shall be issued upon the conversion of any share or shares of the Series A Preferred, and the number of shares of Common Stock to be issued shall be rounded to the nearest whole share. The number of shares issuable upon such conversion shall be determined on the basis of the total number of shares of Series A Preferred the holder is at the time converting into Common Stock and the number of shares of Common Stock issuable upon such aggregate conversion.

(ii) Upon the occurrence of each adjustment or readjustment of the Conversion Price of the Series A Preferred pursuant to this Section 3, the Corporation, at its expense, shall promptly compute such adjustment or readjustment in accordance with the terms hereof and prepare and furnish to each holder of the Series A Preferred a certificate setting forth such adjustment or readjustment and showing in detail the facts upon which such adjustment or readjustment is based. The Corporation shall, upon the written request at any time of any holder of Series A Preferred, furnish or cause to be furnished to such holder a like certificate setting forth (A) such adjustment and readjustment, (B) the Conversion Price for the Series A Preferred at the time in effect, and (C) the number of shares of Common Stock and the amount, if any, of other property which at the time would be received upon the conversion of a share of the Series A Preferred.

(i) Notices of Record Date. In the event of any taking by the Corporation of a record of the holders of any class of securities for the purpose of determining the holders thereof who are entitled to receive any dividend (other than a cash dividend) or other distribution, any right to subscribe for, purchase or otherwise acquire any shares of stock of any class or any other securities or property, or to receive any other right, the Corporation shall mail to each holder of Series A Preferred, at least ten (10) days prior to the date specified therein, a notice specifying the date on which any such record is to be taken for the purpose of such dividend, distribution or right, and the amount and character of such dividend, distribution or right.

(j) Reservation of Stock Issuable Upon Conversion. The Corporation shall at all times reserve and keep available out of its authorized but unissued shares of Common Stock, solely for the purpose of effecting the conversion of the shares of the Series A Preferred, such number of its shares of Common Stock as shall from time to time be sufficient to effect the conversion of all outstanding shares of such Series A Preferred; and if at any time the number of authorized but unissued shares of Common Stock shall not be sufficient to effect the conversion of all then outstanding shares of the Series A Preferred, in addition to such other remedies as shall be available to the holder of such Series A Preferred, the Corporation will take such corporate action as may, in the opinion of its counsel, be necessary to increase its authorized but unissued shares of Common Stock to such number of shares as shall be sufficient for such purposes, including, without limitation, engaging in best efforts to obtain the requisite shareholder approval of any necessary amendment to the Corporation's Articles of Incorporation.

4. **Voting Rights.**

(a) General. The holder of each share of Series A Preferred shall have the right to one vote for each share of Common Stock into which the Series A Preferred could then be converted, and with respect to such vote, such holder shall have full voting rights and powers equal to the voting rights and powers of the holders of Common Stock (except as otherwise expressly provided herein or as required by law, voting together with the Common Stock as a single class), and shall be entitled, notwithstanding any provision hereof, to notice of any shareholders' meeting in accordance with the by-laws of the Corporation. Fractional votes shall not, however, be permitted and any fractional voting rights resulting from the above formula (after aggregating all shares into which shares of Series A Preferred held by each holder could be converted) shall be rounded to the nearest whole number (with one-half being rounded upward). Each holder of Common Stock shall be entitled to one vote for each share of Common Stock held.

(b) Directors. The Board shall consist of five (5) members. The holders of Series A Preferred, as a class, shall be entitled to elect one (1) member of the Board, and the holders of Common Stock, as a class, shall be entitled to elect the remaining members of the Board.

(c) Protective Provisions. The Corporation shall not, without the prior written consent of the holders of a majority of the outstanding Series A Preferred, voting together as a single class: (i) adversely alter or change the rights, preferences or privileges of the Series A Preferred, (ii) engage in any transaction described in Section 2(c) hereof, (iii) authorize or issue, or obligate itself to issue, any other equity security, including any other security convertible into or exercisable for any equity security, having a preference over, or being on a parity with, the Series A Preferred with respect to voting, dividends, conversion or upon liquidation, (iv) increase or decrease the total number of authorized shares of the Series A Preferred or Common Stock, (v) effect any reclassification, recapitalization or other change with respect to any outstanding shares of stock which results in the issuance of shares of stock having a preference over, or being on a parity with, the Series A Preferred with respect to voting, dividends, conversion or upon liquidation, (v) pay any dividends on, or purchase, redeem or otherwise acquire (or pay into or set aside for a sinking fund for such purpose), any of the Common Stock (other than dividends payable solely in shares of Common Stock), provided, however, that this restriction shall not apply to the repurchase of shares of Common Stock from directors, officers, consultants or employees of the Corporation or any subsidiary pursuant to agreements approved by the Board under which the Corporation has the option to repurchase such shares upon the occurrence of certain events, such as the termination of employment, (vi) license any technology of the Corporation in such a manner as to have the same economic effect as a sale or disposition of all or substantially all of the assets of the Corporation; or (vii) effect any change in the authorized size of the Board. In addition, the Corporation shall not, without the approval of at least eighty-five percent (85%) of the authorized number of members of the Board, increase the number of shares of Common Stock issuable to employees, consultants or directors of the Corporation directly or pursuant to a stock option plan or restricted stock plan above 2,657,874 (as adjusted for any stock dividends, combinations or splits with respect to such shares), inclusive of shares of Common Stock reserved for issuance on the date that the first share of Series A Preferred is issued.

5. **Redemption**. The Series A Preferred is not redeemable.

6. **No Reissuance of Preferred Stock.** No shares of Series A Preferred acquired by the Corporation by reason of redemption, purchase, conversion or otherwise shall be reissued, and all such shares shall be canceled, retired and eliminated from the shares which the Corporation shall be authorized to issue.

7. **Consent for Certain Repurchase of Common Stock Deemed to be Distributions.** Each holder of Series A Preferred shall be deemed to have consented, for purposes of Sections ___, ___ and ___ of the ____________ Corporations Code, to distributions made by the Corporation in connection with any repurchase of shares of Common Stock issued to or held by employees or consultants upon termination of their employment or services or pursuant to agreements providing for the right of such repurchase between the Corporation and such persons.

IV.

The liability of the directors of the Corporation for monetary damages shall be eliminated to the fullest extent permissible under ______________ law.

V.

The corporation is authorized to provide indemnification of agents (as defined in Section 317 of the ____________ Corporation Law) for breach of duty to the corporation and its stockholders through bylaw provisions or through agreements with the agents, or both, in excess of the indemnification otherwise permitted by the ____________ Corporation Law, subject to the limits on such excess indemnification set forth in Section ___ of the ____________ Corporation Law.

IN WITNESS WHEREOF, the undersigned have executed these Amended and Restated Articles of Incorporation this ___ day of ________________.

______________________, President

______________________, Secretary

The undersigned further declare under penalty of perjury under the laws of the State of ____________ that the matters set forth in the foregoing certificate are true and correct of his own knowledge. Executed at ____________, ____________ this ___ day of __________.

____

____

GLOSSARY

acceleration. Action by the SEC declaring a registration statement effective without requiring the applicant to wait the normal 20 days after filing the final amendment.

all-hands meeting. Meeting of all persons involved in preparing a registration statement. This usually means management, company's counsel, underwriter, underwriter's counsel, and independent accountant.

all-or-nothing underwriting. *See* **underwriting agreement.**

best-efforts agreement. *See* **underwriting agreement.**

blue-sky laws. State laws regulating the offering and sale of securities within that state.

bring-up prospectus. *See* **prospectus.**

capitalization table. Tabular form comparing a company's capital structure before the offering and after the proposed sale of the securities—assuming all of the securities or specified portions of the securities are sold. Also called *cap table.*

cheap stock. Common stock sold before a company's first public offering at a price significantly less than the eventual public offering price. It is usually sold to company insiders.

closing date. The date on which the underwriter or escrow agent releases cash received from subscribers and the company issues stock certificates to the underwriter for delivery to subscribers.

comfort letter. Letter from the underwriters' independent accountants intended to give underwriters "comfort" about the transaction and helping them establish that they performed a reasonable investigation of financial and accounting data.

comment letter. Letter from the SEC to the company commenting on a registration statement, proxy statement, or 1934 Act periodic filing.

conformed copy. Copy of a registration statement or other document with typed or printed signatures rather than manual signatures.

consent. Written document signed by an independent accountant, engineer, or other expert, which is filed with a registration statement and confirms that the expert consented to the use of its comments and name in the registration statement.

dilution. Effect that a new issue has on ownership percentage of existing owners, measured by the amount that the offering price exceeds the company's tangible net book value per share.

due diligence. Investigation by those filing a registration statement confirming the accuracy and completion of the disclosures.

effective date. The date securities are permitted to be sold after complying with applicable securities laws.

escrow account. Account under control of a third party in which funds received from subscribers are deposited.

executed copy. Copy of a registration statement or other document with manual signatures. Also called *signed copy.*

experts. Independent accountants, engineers, and others who are experts in a particular field.

final prospectus. *See* **prospectus.**

firm commitment. *See* **underwriting agreement.**

incorporation by reference. Reference to materials previously filed with the SEC, rather than repeating them in their entirety.

intrastate offering. Offering of securities within one state, which is exempt from SEC registration.

letter of intent. Nonbinding letter from the underwriter to the company describing its intent to proceed with an offering and the general terms of underwriting.

letter stock. Unregistered, and therefore restricted, stock. Name is derived from letter normally received from a purchaser stating it is buying for investment only, not for resale (also referred to as *letter security*).

listing application. Application by an issuer to have its securities listed on a national securities exchange. Generally contains information similar to that in a registration statement.

market maker. Securities broker that holds itself out as ready to buy and sell a company's stock.

no-action letter. Letter requested from the SEC staff by an issuer indicating the SEC will not object to action proposed by the issuer (e.g., a particular accounting treatment).

offering circular. Document substantially similar to a prospectus and used for offerings exempt from registration.

over allotment option. Option granted to an underwriter to purchase an issuer's shares beyond what it underwrites. Also called *green shoe.*

posteffective amendment. Amendment to a registration statement filed after the effective date.

preliminary prospectus. *See* **prospectus.**

pricing amendment. Last amendment to a registration statement, used to describe offering price and related data.

private placement. Offering exempt from the registration provisions of the 1933 Act.

prospectus. Formal written offer to sell securities that describes the issuer and securities being sold.

- **bring-up prospectus.** Under the 1933 Act, a prospectus used more than nine months after the effective date must not contain information more than 16 months old. If it does, an updated or bring-up prospectus must be used. Also called *nine-month prospectus* or *Section 10(a)(3) prospectus*.

- **final prospectus.** Offering document that must be circulated to all prospective purchasers, which discloses material facts about the company's operations, its financial status, and details of the offering. A preliminary prospectus precedes it.

- **preliminary prospectus.** Offering document under the registration statement that has not become effective. Also called *red herring.*

proxy statement. Statement submitted to stockholders in connection with solicitation of their vote on a proposed transaction or action. Preliminary proxy materials are submitted to the SEC for prior review. The final proxy statement mailed to the stockholders is called the *definitive proxy.*

quiet period. Period under SEC rule restricting publicity about a company and its offering prior to the effective date.

red herring. *See* **preliminary prospectus.**

releases. Public announcements by the SEC containing important information. Most important are Financial Reporting releases, 1933 Act releases, and 1934 Act releases.

secondary offering. Offering by selling stockholder who retains the proceeds.

shelf registration. Offering approved by the SEC, which will not be immediately issued after effective date, but will be delayed or extended.

stop orders. Order issued by the SEC suspending effectiveness of the registration statement.

tender offer. Offer made to stockholders by a third party wishing to purchase their shares.

tombstone ad. Newspaper advertisement or other statement describing closing of a security offering.

underwriting agreement. Agreement of an underwriter, usually a brokerage firm, to purchase entire block of securities being offered to the public.

- **all-or-nothing underwriting.** Form of best-efforts underwriting under which proceeds of a sale are placed in escrow until minimum level is reached. If proceeds do not reach the minimum, underwriting is canceled and funds returned to the buyers. In some instances, the specified minimum volume is less than the total amount being offered; this is called a *mini/maxi underwriting.*

- **best-efforts underwriting.** Agreement of the underwriter to work diligently to sell shares to third parties, without being obligated to purchase unsold shares.

- **firm commitment underwriting.** Agreement where the underwriter agrees to purchase the entire block of securities to be offered to the public.

underwriting discount. Commission received by the underwriter for its services.

unit. Combination of two securities sold for one price, usually consisting of common stock and warrants, or common stock and debt.

window. Time during which the stock market may be receptive to an offering.

INDEX

References are to sections.

C

J

K

L

M

N

O

P

T

U

V

W

Y

Z

PANEL PUBLISHERS SOFTWARE LICENSE AGREEMENT

READ THE TERMS AND CONDITIONS OF THIS LICENSE AGREEMENT CAREFULLY BEFORE INSTALLING THE SOFTWARE (THE "PROGRAM") TO ACCOMPANY *2003 FINANCING START-UPS* (THE "BOOK"). THE PROGRAM IS COPYRIGHTED AND LICENSED (NOT SOLD). BY INSTALLING THE PROGRAM, YOU ARE ACCEPTING AND AGREEING TO THE TERMS OF THIS LICENSE AGREEMENT. IF YOU ARE NOT WILLING TO BE BOUND BY THE TERMS OF THIS LICENSE AGREEMENT, YOU SHOULD PROMPTLY RETURN THE PACKAGE IN RESELLABLE CONDITION AND YOU WILL RECEIVE A REFUND OF YOUR MONEY. THIS LICENSE AGREEMENT REPRESENTS THE ENTIRE AGREEMENT CONCERNING THE PROGRAM BETWEEN YOU AND PANEL PUBLISHERS (REFERRED TO AS "LICENSOR"), AND IT SUPERSEDES ANY PRIOR PROPOSAL, REPRESENTATION, OR UNDERSTANDING BETWEEN THE PARTIES.

1. License Grant. Licensor hereby grants to you, and you accept, a nonexclusive license to use the Program CD-ROM and the computer programs contained therein in machine-readable, object code form only (collectively referred to as the "Software"), and the accompanying User Documentation, only as authorized in this License Agreement. The Software may be used only on a single computer owned, leased, or otherwise controlled by you; or in the event of the inoperability of that computer, on a backup computer selected by you. Neither concurrent use on two or more computers nor use in a local area network or other network is permitted without separate authorization and the possible payment of other license fees. You agree that you will not assign, sublease, transfer, pledge, lease, rent, or share your rights under the License Agreement. You agree that you may not reverse engineer, decompile disassemble, or otherwise adapt, modify, or translate the Software.

Upon loading the Software into your computer, you may retain the Program CD-ROM for backup purposes. In addition, you may make one copy of the Software on a set of diskettes (or other storage medium) for the purpose of backup in the event the Program Diskettes are damaged or destroyed. You may make one copy of any additional User Documentation (such as the README.TXT file or the "About the Computer Disc" section of the Book) for backup purposes. Any such copies of the Software or the User Documentation shall include Licensor's copyright and other proprietary notices. Except as authorized under this paragraph, no copies of the program or any portions thereof may be made by you or any person under your authority or control.

2. Licensor's Rights. You acknowledge and agree that the Software and the User Documentation are proprietary products of Licensor protected under U.S. copyright law. You further acknowledge and agree that all right, title, and interest in and to the Program, including associated intellectual property rights, are and shall remain with Licensor. This License Agreement does not convey to you an interest in or to the Program, including associated intellectual property rights, which are and shall remain with Licensor. This License Agreement does not convey to you an interest in or to the Program, but only a limited right of use revocable in accordance with the terms of the License Agreement.

3. License Fees. The license fees paid by you are paid in consideration of the licenses granted under this License Agreement.

4. Term. This License Agreement is effective upon your installing this software and shall continue until terminated. You may terminate this License Agreement at any time by returning the Program and all copies thereof and extracts therefrom to Licensor. Licensor may terminate this License Agreement upon the breach by you of any term hereof. Upon such termination by Licensor, you agree to return to Licensor the Program and all copies and portions thereof.

5. Limited Warranty. Licensor warrants, for our benefit alone, for a period of 90 days from the date of commencement of this License Agreement (referred to as the "Warranty Period") that the Program CD-ROM in which the Software is contained is free from defects in material and workmanship. If during the Warranty Period, a defect appears in the Program diskettes, you may return the Program to Licensor for either replacement or, at Licensor's option, refund of amounts paid by you under this License Agreement. You agree that the foregoing constitutes your sole and exclusive remedy for breach by Licensor of any warranties made under this Agreement. EXCEPT FOR THE WARRANTIES SET FORTH ABOVE, THE PROGRAM, AND THE SOFTWARE CONTAINED THEREIN, ARE LICENSED "AS IS," AND LICENSOR DISCLAIMS ANY AND ALL OTHER WARRANTIES, WHETHER EXPRESS OR IMPLIED, INCLUDING, WITHOUT LIMITATION, ANY IMPLIED WARRANTIES OF MERCHANTABILITY OR FITNESS FOR A PARTICULAR PURPOSE.

6. Limitation of Liability. Licensor's cumulative liability to you or any other party for any loss or damages resulting from any claims, demands, or actions arising out of or relating to this Agreement shall not exceed the license fee paid to Licensor for the use of the Program. IN NO EVENT SHALL LICENSOR BE LIABLE FOR ANY INDIRECT, INCIDENTAL, CONSEQUENTIAL, SPECIAL, OR EXEMPLARY DAMAGES (INCLUDING, BUT NOT LIMITED TO, LOSS OF DATA, BUSINESS INTERRUPTION, OR LOST PROFITS) EVEN IF LICENSOR HAS BEEN ADVISED OF THE POSSIBILITY OF SUCH DAMAGES.

7. Miscellaneous. This License Agreement shall be construed and governed in accordance with the laws of the State of New York. Should any term of this License Agreement be declared void or unenforceable by any court of competent jurisdiction, such declaration shall have no effect on the remaining terms hereof. The failure of either party to enforce any rights granted hereunder or to take action against the other party in the event of any breach hereunder shall not be deemed a waiver by that party as to subsequent enforcement of rights or subsequent actions in the event of future breaches.